CRITICAL THINKING AND COMMUNICATION

The Use of Reason in Argument

EDWARD S. INCH

California State University, Sacramento

KRISTEN H. TUDOR

California State University, Sacramento

PEARSON

Boston   Columbus   Indianapolis   New York   San Francisco   Upper Saddle River
Amsterdam   Cape Town   Dubai   London   Madrid   Milan   Munich   Paris   Montréal   Toronto
Delhi   Mexico City   São Paulo   Sydney   Hong Kong   Seoul   Singapore   Taipei   Tokyo

Editor in Chief: Ashley Dodge
Senior Acquisitions Editor: Melissa Mashburn
Editorial Assistant: Courtney Turcotte
Director of Marketing: Brandy Dawson
Executive Marketing Manager: Kelly May
Marketing Coordinator: Theresa Rotondo
Managing Editor: Denise Forlow
Program Manager: Maggie Brobeck
Senior Operations Supervisor: Mary Fischer
Operations Specialist: Mary Ann Gloriande
Manager, Central Design: Jayne Conte

Cover Designer: Suzanne Duda
Cover Image: wongwean/shutterstock
Director of Digital Media: Brian Hyland
Digital Media Editor: Learning Mate Solutions, Ltd.
Digital Media Project Manager: Tina Gagliostro
Full-Service Project Management and Composition: Integra Software Services Pvt. Ltd.
Printer/Binder: RRD/Harrisonburg
Cover Printer: RRD/Harrisonburg
Text Font: 10/12, Janson Text

Credits and acknowledgments borrowed from other sources and reproduced, with permission, in this textbook appear on appropriate page within text.

Library of Congress Cataloging-in-Publication Data
Inch, Edward S.
  Critical thinking and communication : the use of reason in argument/Edward S. Inch,
California State University Sacramento, Kristen Tudor, California State
University Sacramento.—Seventh Edition.
    pages cm
  ISBN-13: 978-0-205-92577-3
  ISBN-10: 0-205-92577-4
  1. Reasoning—Textbooks. 2. Critical thinking—Textbooks. 3. Interpersonal
communication—Textbooks. I. Title.
  BC177.I53 2014
  168—dc23
                                                    2013023538

9

PEARSON

ISBN 10: 0-205-92577-4
ISBN 13: 978-0-205-92577-3

TO OUR MOTHERS

CONTENTS

CHAPTER 6
Reasoning   161

SECTION III   DEVELOPING AND ARGUING EXTENDED CASES   192

CHAPTER 7
Approaching Propositions   193

CHAPTER 8
Case Construction   222

CHAPTER 9
Refutation   256

SECTION IV   COMMUNICATING ARGUMENTS   282

CHAPTER 10
Persuasion   283

CHAPTER 11
Responsibility   315

APPENDIX A

APPENDIX B

APPENDIX C

APPENDIX D

PREFACE

The Seventh Edition of *Critical Thinking and Communication* reflects many current developments in the teaching and learning of argumentation. During the past five years, the field of argumentation has continued to adapt to the needs and interests of an increasingly diverse society and interconnected world. This edition highlights the importance of culturally sensitive and co-orientational forms of argument. Although we have continued to focus on a rhetorical perspective on argument, we do so in the context of building communities of advocates who accept culturally diverse worldviews and practices. More and more, the traditional tools of argumentation are used to build connections, unite people, and build peace.

NEW TO THIS EDITION

We incorporated these themes into this edition by revising and updating with the following features:

- Redesigned chapters in cultural and collaborative argumentation consider how students can adapt arguments to better align with hearers from diverse audiences. Focusing on understanding cultural needs and expectations, the text guides students through ways of designing and framing arguments that are appropriate to specific argument situations and expectations.
- New chapters and approaches for building and refuting extended argument cases develop a "co-orientational" approach. Using the "co-orientational" model, we explore strategies for conversational argumentation focusing on critical listening, analysis, and refutation.
- This edition integrates opportunities to "Apply the Theory" in each chapter. We integrate process-based exercises with chapter discussions to provide students with opportunities to practice argumentation skills and critical thinking processes as they read the theories.
- New chapters in persuasion and responsibility explore how students can design messages, enhance credibility, and present arguments ethically. These are the final two chapters in the text and serve to focus student argument skills into a framework that stresses the audience and ethical requirements when an advocate seeks to change argument recipients.
- New and revised argument case studies provide contemporary and "real" examples of how arguments and argumentation are used in fields ranging from law to politics to public protest. Each chapter begins with a case study that is integrated into the theoretical discussion in a way that explores how everyday arguments can be understood and critically analyzed.

■ New models, diagrams, and process illustrations were developed to better describe the flow and connections of theory to practice. These models provide a strong connection between the discussions in the text and ways of graphically understanding how argumentation theory can be applied.

TEXT STRUCTURE

The book is divided into four sections. The first section, Developing a Conceptual Framework for Argument, focuses on a conceptual framework for argument. Chapter 1 examines the relationship between argument and critical thought and explores how argumentation can improve the ability to examine complex issues. The chapter introduces two significant theoretical constructs that are used throughout the rest of the book: argument spheres and fields. Argument spheres are central to our understanding of how argument situations and contexts develop and can be used to adapt and analyze arguments. Argument fields provide us with a way of understanding the guiding rules and norms that can be used to shape arguments as well as criticize them. The second chapter introduces a co-orientational model of argument. It is developed along with traditional arguer-based models including formal logic and the Toulmin Model. Chapter 3 concludes the section with an exploration of how values and culture shape argument contexts. As the world becomes more interconnected, there is a greater need to develop cultural appreciation and sensitivity toward other approaches to argument. These concepts are explored along with the important role values and value systems play in how we understand and interact with arguments and cultures. It provides readers with approaches for understanding how to argue in value-rich and culturally diverse situations.

Section II, Parts, parses the argumentation model developed in the first section to examine how claims and propositions, evidence, and reasoning work together to form arguments. The chapters in this section consider the nature and function of each component, provide approaches for using these components to construct arguments, and then offer tests to ensure that each part is effectively designed. Chapter 4 looks at how claims and propositions can be developed, understood, and criticized. It introduces types of claims—fact, value, and policy—as well as a consideration of how they function in different argument spheres. The fifth chapter considers evidence and how claims are grounded. It provides readers with tools for understanding and analyzing evidence quality as well as how to identify improper evidence use. Chapter 6 surveys different approaches for reasoning and provides readers with tools for understanding, analyzing, and evaluating the quality of reasoning. Argument analysis and evaluation, themes developed in this section, are later used in Chapters 10 and 11 to help readers understand quality and ethical discourse.

The focus of Section III, Developing and Arguing Extended Cases, is how advocates can move from creating individual arguments to extended, well-developed argument cases. Chapter 7 considers the process and principles associated with analyzing and approaching propositions. It explores the unique questions associated with each type of proposition and introduces concepts related to proving propositions such as "presumption," "burden of proof," and creating "*prima facie*" cases. Chapter 8, then, develops these concepts further by examining how extended cases can be designed and argued. The stock issues associated with each proposition type are discussed, as are strategies for designing extended cases. Chapter 9 looks at the other side of the proposition and surveys methods of refutation. Analytic strategies are developed for each type of proposition and provide advocates with tools for disproving extended cases as well as the assumptions of the propositional arena.

The final section, Communicating Arguments, is about how arguers move from the work of creating arguments and cases to the process of presenting them. Chapter 10 discusses persuasion and how the argument context serves as a rhetorical situation in which arguers and recipients share an environment. We introduce the "narrative paradigm" as well as persuasive strategies to help advocates and recipients interact effectively. The final chapter, Responsibility, takes on the issues of what constitutes "good" argument. What is ethical or not? What is appropriate for the argument context? The first part of the chapter considers language choices then discusses how argument fallacies can be destructive forces. The final section, then, works with the reader to develop a personal code of ethics.

We have provided many study tools in this book—lists of key concepts, answers to selected exercises in Appendix A, chapter summaries, and exercises that require students to apply chapter concepts. Appendix B contains a glossary of all the major concepts developed in the text along with references to their location. Appendix C is devoted to Research Strategies and is intended to provide resources for students who want to learn about debate and, perhaps, try attending a debate tournament. Appendix D, Intercollegiate Debate, is designed as a starting point for finding strong evidence to support arguments. Both Appendixes C and D can be accessed online at www.pearsonhighered.com. The book's study aids should enable students to review for exams, do further reading, and have handy references when reading text material. We have used a variety of examples from law, education, ethics, business, and other fields to illustrate the argument concepts introduced.

This text is available in a variety of formats—digital and print. To learn more about Pearson programs, pricing options, and customization, visit www.pearsonhighered.com.

ACKNOWLEDGMENTS

This textbook has been a part of my life for a long time and it is the result of many people who worked very hard to make it a success. The most important of these is Barbara Warnick of the University of Pittsburg. Her voice and ideas remain strong throughout the book. Her abilities as a co-author, theorist, and focused colleague shaped the evolution of this textbook over many years and editions. My new co-author, Kristen Tutor of California State University-Sacramento, has done a wonderful job of introducing new ideas and approaches for applying argument theories. And, our research assistant, Nickolas Vincent Fletcher from Sacramento State, has worked many painstaking hours to support this project.

Finally, we would like to conclude by thanking individuals who have helped us with the development of this textbook of many years. We would especially like to thank Susan L. Kline of The Ohio State University and Joseph W. Wenzel of the University of Illinois, whose assistance on the First and Second Editions of the book was extensive. We would also like to acknowledge the reviewers for the Third Edition, whose comments and suggestions were excellent: Beth M. Waggenspack, Virginia Tech University; Susan L. Kline, The Ohio State University; Jim Vickrey, Troy State University; Ronald O. Wastyn, James Madison University; Dale Herbeck, Boston College; Steven Schwarze, The University of Iowa; and Mark A. Pollock, Loyola University, Chicago. We would like to acknowledge the assistance of Solveig Robinson, Pacific Lutheran University, and Amanda Feller, Pacific Lutheran University, on the Fourth Edition. We would also like to thank the reviewers of the Fourth Edition: Raymie McKerrow, University of Ohio, and Chris Miller, California State University–Sacramento. We would also like to thank the reviewers of the Fifth Edition: James David Paterson, Imperial Valley College, and Dr. Thomas Preston Jr., University of Texas–Brownville, and all those who helped so much in its development, including Chipo Chikara, Stephanie Christopher, Nigel Barron, Minerva Rios, and Leah Sprain. We are very appreciative of the work Danielle Endres contributed to the Fifth Edition and the expertise she brought to the project. In the Sixth Edition, we want to thank Katie Picket for the work she did helping edit the text and researching some of the case studies. We would also like to acknowledge the reviewers for the Sixth Edition: Martin Mehl, California Polytechnic State University; R. Blaine Davis, California State University–Sacramento; Jason Kemnitz, South Dakota State University; Joshua Butcher, Texas A&M University; Catherine L. Langford, Texas Tech University; Mark Porrovecchio, Oregon State University. We would like to thank the reviewers of the Seventh Edition: Danielle Walker, Cerritos College; David Worth, Rice University; Catherine Egley Waggoner, Wittenberg University; Nicki Michalski, Lamar University.

SECTION I

DEVELOPING A CONCEPTUAL FRAMEWORK FOR ARGUMENT

CHAPTERS

1. ARGUMENT AND CRITICAL THOUGHT
2. CO-ORIENTATIONAL ARGUMENT
3. VALUES AND CULTURE

CHAPTER ONE

ARGUMENT
AND CRITICAL THOUGHT

KEY CONCEPTS

Box 1.1 "Do Beauty Contests Harm Women?" illustrates how arguments can develop over disagreements about an issue. Each day, we are faced with many issues—some small and others more significant. The need for argument arises from our desire to persuade or convince others of a point of view or course of action. When we perceive that something should be done or that others fail to understand our views, we may choose to advocate for our ideas and beliefs—we make arguments to inspire change. When we advocate for significant change or

■ ■ ■ ■ ■

BOX 1.1
DO BEAUTY CONTESTS HARM WOMEN?

Each year, more than 2 billion people worldwide participate in and watch beauty contests. In fact, beyond the many local and regional contests, there are more than fifty world beauty pageants held annually.[1] Although Miss America, among other pageants, has experienced declining audiences over the last thirty years, some pageants, such as Miss World, continue to attract global attention and viewers. Additionally, youth pageants and television programs such as *Toddlers and Tiaras* attract large audiences. Yet, despite their popularity, questions persist about whether they harm girls and women. The following discussion between two students addresses some of these concerns:[2]

Kaidren: Beauty contests undermine women as people. They promote an ideal of female beauty that is unrealistic, and very very few women can achieve it. Yet, this ideal pressures all women to conform to it. This is harmful because it encourages women to diet excessively, contributes to eating disorders, and encourages risky cosmetic surgery. But the "beauty myth" is so powerful that women willingly risk their health and even their lives to achieve what these contests promote.

Ramona: Wait a minute. This argument makes it sound as though women are easily brainwashed and can't figure out fact from fiction. There is nothing wrong with watching and admiring people who are fit, well proportioned, and healthy—in fact, these kinds of messages are especially important when you consider the obesity epidemic. We should strive for fitness. Anyway, both women and men enjoy beauty pageants; more women watch them than men. Women freely choose to enter them. No one is required to participate or watch—people get to make choices. Pageants haven't been forced on anyone and they don't force anyone to make bad choices.

Kaidren: You are missing the point. Healthy lifestyles are important and we should be teaching about how to be healthy. But that is not what beauty pageants do. They single out women as different from men. Women are judged on appearance rather than any other quality. And, achieving the ideal often requires poor health habits such as extreme dieting. Judging women—not men—on their looks subjugates women because it establishes an ideal feminine form that does not include intellect or any other ability. These contests set a standard of femininity that focuses almost exclusively on outward appearance at any cost.

Ramona: What is wrong with judging people on physical appearance? We judge people on particular attributes all the time. We evaluate professors on their ability to teach, irrespective of other abilities. We judge athletes on physical abilities without any concern for their intellect or emotional balance. We judge medical doctors on their skill and not on whether they are nice people. We evaluate people all the time based on physical, mental, or emotional attributes that are appropriate for the situation. Every competition, of every kind, values certain qualities over others and that's OK. Why would we exclude giving women recognition for outward appearance any more than we would exclude awarding a prize for best tattoo or the ability to lift weights?

(continued)

BOX 1.1   CONTINUED

Consider the issues that emerged in this discussion. Both Kaidren and Ramona made arguments for and against pageants. As you read through the arguments again, consider the following questions:

1. Which arguer did a better job—Kaidren or Ramona? Why? Is it because her arguments support a position you already agree with? Or is it because she helped you understand something new and different that convinced you?
2. If you were Kaidren, what would your next argument be if this conversation continued? How do you think Ramona would respond?
3. Do you think these are good arguments? Are any issues or ideas missing? If you had been in the conversation, what would you have added?
4. Did you find any arguments that were not very good? What made them weak? How would you have strengthened them?

---

understanding of complex ideas, we may create many arguments and link them together to support our ideas and positions.

Often, people assume that to argue is bad—that when we have an argument with someone we are having a problem with them. This view is limited. Arguments happen at national and global levels over water rights, poverty, and health care to list just a few. But argumentation and advocacy are also regular features of our daily lives. We argue about which movie to see with our friends, what school we want to attend, or where to go on vacation. We advocate when we negotiate over how much to pay for a car or a house. We create arguments when we try to persuade people to think or behave differently.

Argumentation can be used for either good or bad, depending on the choices made by the advocates. This book focuses on how to positively use the skills of argumentation to (1) help others understand differing points of view, (2) explore ideas and alternatives, and (3) convince others of a need to change or act. Consider, for instance, the exchange between students in Box 1.1. This conversation presented a series of arguments that illustrate how discussion and arguing can work productively in each of these three ways. The students used arguments to help define the issues for discussion, clarify perceptions, and advocate for different points of view. Throughout the conversation, they engaged in the processes that will be the focus of this book: critical thinking and argumentation.

CRITICAL THOUGHT

Many theorists have explored critical thinking and the role it plays in education, our understanding of the world, and our understanding of ourselves.[3] Done well, critical thinking helps us consider issues and problems systematically and rigorously. It is fundamental to our ability to learn and make sense of the world around us. Some, for instance, have described *critical thinking as the process whereby ordinary people apply the scientific method to the ordinary world.*[4] Critical thought requires the ability to analyze and evaluate conclusions based on a coherent understanding of relevant issues. Theorist Joanne Kurfiss offered the following definition for critical thinking:

> an investigation whose purpose is to explore a situation, phenomenon, question, or problem to arrive at a hypothesis or conclusion about it that integrates all available information and that therefore can be convincingly justified.[5]

Often, when confronted with a challenge or problem, people want to leap to a solution or find a quick resolution. Critical thinking asks us to pause. People who think critically about issues will not settle for apparent or obvious solutions. They will suspend judgment while seeking out relevant opinions, facts, and reasons that promote good decision-making.

Cycle of Critical Thought

Critical thought is a complex process and, if done well, it can help us examine and explore intricate ideas to better understand both the issues at hand and the consequences of acting—or not acting. As this book will explore, the world is systemically connected and decisions about acting in one area will have effects in other areas. For instance, we know that exposure to ultraviolet rays can cause skin cancer. Yet, as noted by the Skin Cancer Foundation, "most people don't apply enough" sunscreen and should use products with a Sun Protection Factor (SPF) rating of 30 or higher.[6] Concern over skin cancer and skin damage, over time, has led to more people deciding to reduce their exposure to sunlight and, when in the sun, use high SPF sunscreen for protection. This action makes sense given the risks associated with UV rays. However, an important and seldom discussed side effect of this decision is that many people, particularly children, do not get enough vitamin D.

Normally, sunlight causes the body to produce vitamin D, which is necessary for bone growth and strength. Without enough UV exposure, people have to take steps to ensure a sufficient intake of this vitamin. The point here is that the world is interconnected and decisions often have consequences and implications beyond the immediate decision. A process of systematic critical thinking can help us uncover connections, evaluate options, and inform actions.

Although there are many ways to understand critical thinking, it can generally be considered as a cycle that moves through four interrelated steps: (1) Assess, (2) Explore, (3) Evaluate, and (4) Integrate. These are illustrated in Figure 1.1, "Cycle of Critical Thought."[7] Our ability to move through each of these steps effectively helps ensure quality decision-making. And, although each step may appear relatively simple, they are actually complex. Each step asks us to consider a series of issues and questions so that we can fully explore a given subject. The following text provides greater detail about how we move through the critical thinking cycle and these four steps.

Step 1. Assess. When we assess, we work to clearly identify the problem or issue and then discover the relevant information. Specifically, assessment includes the following questions:

- What is the need? People reason and argue because a need arises. The need for argument can be anything from "Should I do my homework or go out with my friends?" to "Should marijuana be legalized?" In the case of beauty pageants, the students chose a topic for a classroom presentation: "Do beauty contests harm women?" They could

FIGURE 1.1   Cycle of Critical Thought

have spoken on any of a number of possible topics related to pageants. They might have argued, "What should be done about beauty pageants?" Or, they could have asked, "What topic will get us the best grade on this assignment?" The need for argument is simply the impetus for critical thought and discussion. In Chapter 2, when we discuss argument situations, we will talk about the need as the "exigence" for argument. The need helps us frame the conversation so that we know what is included and what is excluded from discussion. Why are we talking about this issue? What are we trying to figure out?

- What is the purpose? Purpose represents the goal of the discussion. It can be as simple as understanding more about beauty pageants or as complicated as statistical analyses of how pageants and the "beauty myth" affect a group's identity and feelings of adequacy. The purpose of inquiry and argument does not need to focus on a particular course of action or what decision should be reached, but it does need to identify the goal of the inquiry: What do we hope to achieve? Why are we having this conversation? In Box 1.1, the purpose of the conversation was to reach an understanding about the potential harms related to beauty contests. We need to emphasize here the importance of understanding the purpose of arguing about a subject. Are we trying to create understanding? Change beliefs? Motivate someone to action? And, even more significantly, do all the people engaged in the argument share the same purpose? If not, discussing and assessing the goals of those involved becomes a primary task. In Chapter 5, we will discuss how propositions frame discussions and debates. They serve to define what is talked about and for what purpose.

- What information is needed? Answering questions and moving a conversation toward an outcome requires appropriate information. With beauty contests, the students needed to clearly understand what pageants are, how they work, and what their effects are. The students also needed to figure out if beauty contests are different from other kinds of events and contests in which people are judged for their appearance or a particular ability. Information can take many forms including statistical data, reports from eyewitnesses, individual observations, or any number of other sources of material that can help a person answer the question. Chapter 6, which focuses on evidence in argument, considers how information can be found and used. Information provides substance for thought. It is the material we draw upon to develop ideas and synthesize new thoughts.

Step 2. Explore. Exploration examines the interpretations and connections that occur within the issues, research, and other parts of the discussion. It includes an exploration of assumptions, biases, and the multiple points of view that affect how we understand and approach issues and ideas. Specifically, this step includes:

■ What are the dominant concepts involved? *Concepts are the theories, definitions, rules, and laws that govern how we think and act.* We know we should wear our seat belts—there are laws as well as theories of accident survival that tell us this. We know that we have a theory of fairness and equality. We have laws that protect minority rights while allowing majority rule. And we know that it is wrong to objectify or subjugate people. These concepts provide support for decisions we make about child beauty pageants or other controversial subjects. Concepts are constructs of the human mind.[8] They represent a framework within which we think and act. People once believed that the sun revolved around the earth and argued strongly against those who challenged that belief, such as Galileo, who in turn argued based on observations and the evidence they collected. Concepts can be slow to change and replacements may be difficult to accept because beliefs are deeply imbedded in our understanding of the world and controversial subjects.

■ What assumptions shape the issues? *Assumptions are the presuppositions and viewpoints we take for granted.* We assume, for instance, that people try to be fair. We assume that we don't want to subjugate people. And we also assume that people will watch beauty pageants, which in turn will sell advertisers' products and services. This is one of the reasons contests such as Miss America and Miss World were started. It is important to understand our assumptions because they represent a "baseline," or starting point, for thought, and if they are flawed or misunderstood, the reasoning that stems from them can also be flawed. Often, assumptions are problematic because they are part of our ways of thinking and are often unknown and unexplored by us. We assume the world is round. We assume that most people will obey laws. And, we act on these assumptions even if they are incorrect. Revealing, testing, and challenging our assumptions helps us understand our own choices and make clearer, better arguments. The challenge, of course, is in identifying them in the first place.

■ What points of view are involved? People reason and think from different points of view. That is why, for instance, two people can see the same movie and have vastly different opinions about its quality. Or why some people support and others oppose beauty pageants. Our points of view come from our individual backgrounds, thoughts, experiences, and attitudes. They help us frame issues and integrate them into our thinking. The students, talking about beauty pageants, illustrate this point. Two educated people, with similar backgrounds, interpreted and understood the issues of beauty contests differently. Whenever we work with other people, we encounter different points of view. Part of critical thought involves a process of interpreting and understanding other views as well as our own.

Step 3. Evaluate. This step examines the quality of information and connections among possible solutions and considers how factors such as bias and points of view affect potential outcomes. Based on this synthesis and integration, approaches for addressing issues emerge and are evaluated until a preferred approach is found. This step includes:

- What can we interpret and infer from our exploration? When we think, we blend new information and ideas into our existing points of view, concepts, and assumptions. From this combination of questioning, examining, researching, and understanding, we reason toward a conclusion. We interpret information and infer from it to reach our conclusions. With beauty pageants, for instance, based on what the students knew, their research, and their conversations, they interpreted their data and inferred conclusions from it. The process of interpretation and inference is one of making sense of data and reasoning from it toward a goal.

- What implications or consequences can we see? Our reasoning and thinking carry with them implications and consequences. If we act on the conclusions we draw, what will happen? If we change our beliefs and attitudes, what effect will that have on future decisions we might make? Even though we often consider in-class presentations as simply another assignment, they have the potential to change attitudes and actions in classroom audiences. If the two students convince a group of students to act—or not to act—to boycott or support beauty pageants, there will be consequences. Critical thought is not a self-contained entity. It carries with it potential outcomes from the process.

Step 4. Integrate. The final step in the critical thinking process involves selecting the preferred alternative, monitoring its effectiveness, and developing strategies for continued understanding and evaluation of how well the solution solves the problem and the conditions that caused it. This step, then, leads back to the first steps of assessing, exploring, evaluating, and integrating potential issues and problems. This final part of the cycle is important. Whatever solutions advocates chose, they have consequences that will raise issues that need to be assessed, explored, evaluated, and integrated. This is how the critical thinking cycle supports our decision-making over many issues and long periods of time. Box 1.2, "Apply the Theory," is designed to help guide you through this process and apply the cycle of critical thought.

Using critical thinking skills effectively helps us understand alternatives and make reasonable decisions. However, when we fail to work through the cycle and consider alternatives, we can make mistakes. Skipping steps or failing to examine our assumptions can yield poor outcomes. Some barriers to critical thought are described in Box 1.3, "Barriers to Effective Critical Thinking."

Critical Thinking as a Skill

The critical thinking cycle we just explored is a powerful tool. It helps us define and focus on a need, identify ways of thinking about the need, and then design approaches for addressing

■ ■ ■ ■ ■

BOX 1.2
APPLY THE THEORY: THINKING CRITICALLY

Consider the topic introduced in Box 1.1 and the implications for youth beauty pageants as well as television programs such as *Toddlers and Tiaras*. Then, think through the parts of the critical thinking cycle and answer the following questions:

Step 1. Assess

1. Is there a need to discuss this subject? What is the need? In a single sentence, describe it.
2. What is the purpose of discussing this subject? Write your purpose in a sentence. What is the goal you seek? Awareness? Action?
3. What information can you find to support your purpose? Using any Internet search engine, identify and paraphrase three sources that support your purpose.

Step 2. Explore

1. Identify and write down three concepts that support and three concepts that don't support youth beauty pageants.
2. For each concept, write down at least one assumption that supports the concept.
3. Brainstorm and write down the different points of view shaping the discussion. Identify points of view that are different than your own.

Step 3. Evaluate and Interpret

1. Based on what you have read and what you have brainstormed, write down three conclusions you can reach.
2. Think about the implications of each conclusion you reached. Next, write down what you think would occur if you acted on them.
3. What are the implications, both good and bad, of banning all beauty pageants?

Step 4. Integrate.

Each step you have completed has led you to a point where you can make a choice. Considering the choices you have developed, which do you think is best? Why? The answer to this question, why one choice is better than another, informs how we engage and understand argument.

the need. This is why critical thinking is such a vital skill; it helps prevent people from making bad decisions and helps them solve problems. It allows us to consider actions and consequences in rational and systematic ways. This ability has applications far beyond classroom applications and homework assignments. Richard W. Paul and Gerald M. Nosich, noted critical thinking theorists, observed:

> The kind of "work" increasingly required in industry and business is "intellectual," that is, it requires workers to define goals and purposes clearly, seek out and organize relevant data, conceptualize those data, consider alternative perspectives, adjust thinking to context, question assumptions, modify thinking in light of the continual flood of new information, and reason to legitimate conclusions. Furthermore, the intellectual work required must increasingly be coordinated with, and must profit from the critique of, fellow workers.[9]

■ ■ ■ ■ ■

BOX 1.3
BARRIERS TO EFFECTIVE CRITICAL THINKING

The ability to think critically is an important skill. However, most of us have developed habits and thinking skills that inhibit our ability to effectively engage issues and problems creatively.[10] These include:

1. *The "Right Answer" Assumption*. Most issues and problems have many possible answers. Yet, much of our education has taught us to look for the one correct answer. Focusing on finding a single right answer can obscure alternatives and we may miss opportunities. Instead, look for several "correct" approaches or answers and then evaluate which is best.

2. *Confirmation Bias*. People tend to associate with others who are similar to them. We tend to read books we like and listen to concerts featuring bands we like or go to movies we think we will enjoy. Generally, these habits are not harmful until they influence our ability to think critically. When we only read research that supports own assumptions, when we only read news stories that validate our political beliefs, we are confirming what we already know but failing to explore all sides of an issue. When researching a subject, it is important to ask yourself what someone taking the opposite side might read, research, or argue. Understanding other points of view is central to effective critical thinking.

3. *Accepting Authority without Question*. One of the reasons we explore and research issues is because we seek out experts who have more background and knowledge than we do. We assume that because they have written books and articles, given public lectures, and traveled "talk show" circuits, they are irrefutable authorities in their field. But this is not always the case. Sometimes experts are wrong. For instance, Walter Lippmann, American intellectual, writer, and commentator, once made the point that "Among the really difficult problems of the world, the Arab-Israeli conflict is one of the simplest and most manageable."[11] Seek out more than one expert and understand the credentials and qualifications of those you use.

4. *Rules and Logic Must be Followed*. Rules and logic are important and they are part of critical thinking. Rules allow us to live and work together and they are discussed later in this chapter when we talk about spheres and fields. However, rules and logic can impose restrictions on how we think because they tell us what is acceptable and what is not acceptable. An alternative is to assume there are no rules and use analogies to try to see relationships and connections among things that we might not otherwise perceive. Sometimes creative and imaginative approaches can be best. Discovering alternative ways of seeing issues can help open new approaches and ideas.

5. *Being Practical Is Best*. Sometimes people make a decision because they believe it is practical. They might say, "We need to buy a used laptop computer because that is what we can afford." This approach presumes a conclusion because of an assumed constraint without considering alternatives. While issues of practicality ultimately may prevail, try imagining approaches irrespective of practical constraints. Consider what "should" be done as opposed to the feasibility of what "could" be done.

6. *Avoiding Ambiguity*. Ambiguity can be frightening because it introduces uncertainty and risk about decisions. Most people prefer certainty and strive for a clear, predictable understanding of events and actions. If we don't know for sure what will happen, we may decide not to try. However, the gray areas imposed by ambiguity are where creativity and

(continued)

BOX 1.3   CONTINUED

innovative thinking exist. When you find ambiguity, try imagining the many possible outcomes associated with the issues or actions that are in the gray area.

7. *Being Wrong Is Bad.* Much of our upbringing and education imposes an assumption that being wrong is bad. Wrong answers result in bad grades. Wrong behavior results in punishment. As a consequence, people grow to fear being wrong and work hard to avoid it even though that approach may stifle creativity and inhibit finding alternatives. The challenge about being wrong is a tendency to deny or move away from the decision. Or sometimes we simply decide to do nothing out of fear of being wrong. Instead, work to understand why a decision was wrong and what other alternatives existed that might have improved the outcome.

Paul and Nosich go on to comment that supervisors and employers value workers who can reason well and express themselves clearly.

Yet, as much as we claim to prize the value of critical thought and inquiry, we are generally not very good at it. Critical thinking theorists Richard Paul, Linda Elder, and Ted Bartell, for instance, examined thirty-eight public universities and twenty-eight private universities to determine the level and quality of critical thinking instruction. They found that although 89 percent of teachers claimed critical thinking was a primary component of their instruction, only 19 percent could provide a clear explanation of what they taught that was critical, and only 9 percent were actually teaching critical thought.[12] Richard Arum and Josipa Roksa in their book *Academically Adrift: Limited Learning on College Campuses* made the point that forty-five percent or more of college students do not achieve statistically significant gains in their critical thinking and complex reasoning skills by the time they graduate from a university with an undergraduate degree.[13]

Most of us recognize the importance of critical thought even if it is not always taught effectively.[14] And, as important as it is, critical thinking is not an easy skill to develop or use. It requires time, discipline, and practice. As we think, develop ideas, and argue it is important to actively approach our questions with an intentional, critical lens. We should:

- Refine generalizations and avoid oversimplification.
- Generate and assess solutions to problems.
- Compare perspectives, interpretations, and theories.
- Read critically and seek out information that disagrees with our own perspectives.
- Listen critically, seriously considering views with which we disagree.[15]

ARGUMENTATION AND ARGUMENT

Argumentation engages us in the cycle of critical thought. *Argumentation is the process of making arguments intended to justify beliefs, attitudes, and values so as to influence others.* We see argumentation in media ads for products, campaign ads for candidates, newspaper editorials, Internet sites on public issues, business meetings where proposals are made, and in many other places. Argumentation occurs everywhere, and we deal with it as readers, listeners, writers, and speakers on a daily basis. In fact, argumentation is perhaps one of the most important skills we can develop. As participants in a world community and members of democratic communities, argumentation is the means by which we engage in discussion about our present and our future. It is the process by which we exercise democratic rights and self-determination.

Hugh Heclo, a professor of public affairs at George Mason University, took the position that American politics has been transformed in recent decades to become hypersensitive to public opinions and anxieties. Unprecedented access to information from homes using smartphones and tablets as well as the ability to disseminate opinions freely through the Internet and other media have made the individual voice and opinion more powerful than ever.[16] We have the ability to access the world's information in an unprecedented way.

The importance of his observation should not be underestimated. We live in a time where the role of argument, arguers, and recipients has tremendous potential power to shape our world. Technology has allowed ideas and arguments to spread across the world quickly and powerfully. The death of Neda Agha-Soltan provides a clear and tragic illustration of this point. In 2009, following an angrily contested presidential election in Iran, Neda was shot during one of the demonstrations. The event, captured on a mobile phone and uploaded to the Internet, was arguably, as *Time Magazine* put it, "the most witnessed death in human history."[17] Neda, which is the Persian word for "voice," became a symbol for the opposition and stark evidence for arguments about the political and personal outrage of a community. The video was broadcast around the world and millions saw and heard a message of violence, protest, and the struggle to have a voice. To participate globally, we need to fundamentally understand how arguments are made and, just as importantly, how they are refuted.

Process

Argumentation is significant for the development and maintenance of a healthy society. It can occur only when people are interested in hearing or reading what others have to say and in seriously considering others' proposals. When parties engage in argumentation, they agree to certain conventions and tacit principles. Communication theorist Susan Shimanoff made the point that for people to communicate they must "agree on such matters as how to take turns at speaking, how to be polite or how to insult, to greet, and so forth. If every symbol user manipulated symbols at random, the result would be chaos rather than communication."[18]

Advocates agree to rules for conducting the discussion, they make contributions as required, and they seek the approval of the other parties involved.[19] They agree to what is acceptable and not acceptable for the context, how long to speak, how to take turns, and what the process for decision-making is. If people refuse even to listen to the other party, argumentation cannot occur. One of the most common sets of rules for governing debates is "Roberts Rules of Order," which is described in Box 1.4, "Robert's Rules of Order."

Advocates begin by using the critical thinking cycle to generate arguments about the topic being discussed. Argumentation is the process of selecting arguments from that set and connecting them in ways that allow arguers to construct a compelling case for positions or to address needs. For instance, lawyers study all the arguments available in a case, they examine past cases and precedents, they select the best among those, and then connect the arguments together to make a case for the prosecution or defense in courts of law. Legislators study many arguments and then may select a series of arguments to support broad-based policies or

■ ■ ■ ■ ■
BOX 1.4
ROBERT'S RULES OF ORDER

For argumentation to occur, participants need to agree on a set of rules or procedures to govern the process. In personal conversations, these rules are often implicit and understood. They include turn taking, no interrupting, and not shouting. In more formal contexts such as government proceedings or community hearings, the rules tend to be more explicit and clearly developed.

The most widely used rules for debating are *Robert's Rules of Order Newly Revised*.[20] These rules describe when someone can speak, for how long, and about what. They are designed to keep arguers on task and focused on the questions being discussed. The rules are extensive and are designed to ensure that all relevant voices are heard, the process for giving voice is fair and complete, and the outcomes will support both critical thought and critical evaluation of ideas.[21]

political change. Businesses may consider many possible arguments for a product or service, group the best individual arguments together, and advocate for their products and services in marketing and public relations campaigns. A model of the process of argumentation can be found in Figure 1.2, "Model of Argumentation Process." In this figure, arguers use the four steps of the critical thinking cycle to develop issues into potential arguments (Steps 1 and 2). Some of those arguments will be more or less significant than others (Step 3). By carefully selecting the best arguments to support the arguer's overall completion, the process of argumentation seeks to integrate many ideas and issues into a single, overall conclusion or position (Step 4).

Speeches, essays, group discussions, legislation, and political campaigns are all platforms where argumentation can take place. Argumentation is composed of individual arguments. *An argument is a set of statements in which a claim is made, support is offered for it, and there is an attempt to influence someone in a context of disagreement.*

It is important to understand argument in this sense—a claim, plus support for it in the form of reasoning and evidence—as distinguished from interpersonal arguments or

Individual Arguments

Overall Conclusion

FIGURE 1.2 "Model of Argumentation Process"

Arguer *generates* multiple, potential arguments

Arguer *selects* a set of arguments that best reach the conclusion disputes.[22] In this latter sense, "argument" is a kind of (usually unpleasant) interpersonal exchange, as when we say, "John and Mary were having an argument." Sometimes described as "quarrels" or "squabbles," these kinds of arguments usually involve two or more persons engaged in extended overt disagreement with each other.

That is not the sort of argument with which this book is concerned. Arguments of the kind described here occur when we say something like, "John made an argument in support of his proposal for the new marketing plan." This view considers whether an argument is sound and effective; it emphasizes argument as a reasoning process and considers arguments as units rather than as interactive processes.

Arguments are only one kind of communication. When we greet someone ("Hello, how are you?"), issue commands ("Shut the door"), vent our emotions ("I hate it when you do that!"), make promises ("I'll return your book tomorrow"), and so forth, we do not produce arguments. To clarify the differences between arguments and other forms of communication, we will describe the important features of argument according to our definition.

Characteristics

First, to be considered an argument, an arguer, generally, should make a claim. *A claim is an expressed opinion or a conclusion that the arguer wants accepted.* In the beauty pageant discussion, some claims were:

> Beauty contests undermine women as people.
>
> There is nothing wrong with watching and admiring people who are fit, well proportioned, and healthy.
>
> Judging women on their looks subjugates them.

Claims take on different forms in various contexts; they function as claims in relation to the support offered for them. As we will show in Chapter 5, claims in a given individual argument may themselves function as forms of support for the main claim, or thesis statement, of an extended argument. Examples of main claims include in criminal law the charge brought against the defendant by the prosecution; in the legislature the briefer version of a proposed bill or piece of legislation; and in medicine the diagnosis and recommended treatment regimen. In argumentation and debate, these main claims are often called *propositions* or *resolutions.*

When someone makes a claim, he or she is expected to offer support for it in the form of reasons and information. If we issue a command or make a promise ("I will pick you up at 10"), we commit ourselves by making the statement, and no further proof is necessary.[23] Likewise, pure description ("The setting sun was reflected in a rosy haze"), small talk ("Things are so-so, could be better"), and other neutral statements generally do not make claims—they do not advance statements on which there is disagreement.

Sometimes, we can decide whether a statement is a claim only by considering its context. Arguers often leave their evidence, reasoning, or claim unstated. Do the following examples contain claims?

> When guns are outlawed, only outlaws will have guns.
>
> Coors Light, 'cause coffee's nasty after football.
>
> Every time I'm nice to him, he ignores me.

If we know that the first statement is a bumper sticker displayed by an opponent of gun control, we can conclude that it is a claim. Spelled out, it would say, "making guns illegal means that only those who circumvent the law will have guns." Knowing that the second statement occurred in a beer ad would indicate that the claim is "[Buy] Coors Light" and that the remainder is a good reason for doing so. It is ambiguous whether the third statement is a claim or not. Knowing more about the person's relationship to her friend would help us to determine whether it is a claim. Some claims can be recognized as claims only when we know about the speaker's intention, the claim's relation to the other statements made along with it, or the situational context in which a claim is made.

The second characteristic of an argument is that support is offered for the claim. Claims are supported both by the evidence and reasoning or inferences that connect the evidence to the claim. Evidence comes in many forms, but it always functions as the foundation for argument or the grounds on which arguments are based. When we make an argument, we move from statements we believe our receivers will accept (evidence) to statements that are in dispute (claims). *Evidence consists of facts or conditions that are objectively observable, beliefs or statements generally accepted as true by the recipients, or conclusions previously established.*

Evidence does not consist only of objectively observable facts. From a rhetorical point of view (i.e., that arguers seek acceptance for their claims from audiences), it makes sense to regard any proposition, or belief accepted by everyone in the audience, as a starting point for argument. There are many statements ("A person is innocent until proven guilty" or "One ought to keep one's promises") that are not facts but that could function as evidence in relation to a claim because the hearers would accept them as reasonable assumptions. The nature of evidence and how it functions in an argument will be discussed more fully in Chapter 5.

In the beauty contest discussion at the beginning of this chapter, statements viewed as evidence by the speakers and accepted by others count as evidence. Examples of such statements include:

We have an obesity epidemic.

Both women and men enjoy beauty pageants.

We evaluate teachers, athletes, and professionals on particular attributes.

To be counted as evidence, statements should be accepted and viewed as relevant and true by the parties in a dispute or audiences to whom arguments are addressed. (If only one party—the arguer—accepts a statement, then it is a claim, not evidence.) So, for instance, when Kaidren says that "the 'beauty myth' is so powerful that women willingly risk their health and even their lives," Ramona does not accept that as true and, therefore, it does not function as evidence; rather it functions as a claim. If, however, Kaidren provided credible support from research, expert sources, or other trusted references that was accepted by Ramona, then this statement could be used as evidence. In other words, if people in an argument agree to the statement, it is evidence.

The arguer who begins by establishing claims based on statements that are not accepted will not get far. For statements to function as evidence and provide reliable grounds for claims, they must be acceptable to the recipients. For instance, if Kaidren could show specific examples of how pageants have been harmful or present credible support for how they have eroded women's rights, then Ramona's statements about their positive attributes would not be able to function as evidence because they would be in dispute. The process of argumentation begins with testing assumptions about what is true for the parties involved and then building—argument by argument—until a conclusion is reached.

Claims are also supported by the link that the arguer makes between the evidence and the claim. The part of the argument containing reasoning is frequently called the inference. Reasoning can take various forms. Those that occur most frequently will be described in Chapter 6, and you will become experienced at identifying them. *Reasoning constructs a rational link between the evidence and the claim and authorizes the step we make when we draw a conclusion.* Reasoning answers the question, "How did you get from the evidence to the claim?"[24] It consists of general principles that explain how the evidence and the claim are connected.

The study of argument is made all the more interesting because arguers often do not explicitly state their inferences. They provide evidence and make claims, but often one can only guess how the link between the two was made. For example, if we study the evidence presented by the pageant discussants along with their claims, we will find that some of their inferences, all unstated, were functioning in the argument:

Women imitate beauty behavior seen in pageants and, as a result, engage in unhealthy practices in an attempt to achieve an idealized view of beauty.

Because both women and men enjoy pageants, women choose the consequences as opposed to having someone else impose a standard for beauty on them.

Judging people based on their physical beauty is the same thing as judging athletes and doctors on their skills.

Inferences usually make explicit a link, which enables the arguer to connect evidence with claims and thus construct an argument.

The third and last characteristic of arguments is that they are attempts to influence someone in a context where people disagree with one another. The phrase "attempts to influence" is important because the arguer may or may not succeed. The recipient of the argument is free not to agree with the expressed opinion of the arguer. The person to whom the argument is addressed may accept the claim, reject it, or continue to express doubts about it.

To say that arguments are "attempts to influence" means that there must be a recipient, or "arguee," to whom the argument is addressed that is capable of responding to it. Arguees must be open-minded and able to change their beliefs or actions because of the argument. Furthermore, in choosing argument instead of command or coercion, arguers recognize that the process of argument is reciprocal—that initiative and control pass back and forth as arguers state their viewpoints and as recipients weigh their support and decide whether to accept the argument or not.[25]

This reciprocal nature is especially important because sometimes recipients may decide to accept or reject an argument because of the relationships they have with the arguer or because the arguer fails to address important values or issues even if the argument is logical and well constructed.

While listening to arguments, recipients retain the option of challenging, questioning, criticizing, or countering the expressed opinions of the arguer. The influence that arguments aim to bring about assumes many forms. Arguers may want recipients to become concerned about an issue on which they are ambivalent or neutral, to shift favorable to unfavorable attitudes or vice versa, or to change behavior.

Arguments are attempts to influence *someone*. An argument may be addressed to oneself, to another person, to a small group, to an audience, or to multiple audiences. Arguments occur in writing, in conversation, in public speeches, and in all forms of communication. Argument is a complex phenomenon that occurs in numerous forms and media of communication and that is addressed to many different kinds of audiences.

Finally, to say that argument occurs only when there is disagreement or the potential for disagreement means that the topic addressed must be controversial, capable of inciting opposing opinions from the parties involved. For example, consider the following dialogue:

John: Should we go to a movie tonight?

Mary: Fine, what would you like to see?

John: How about *Skyfall*?

Mary: OK, do you want to go to the 7 o'clock showing?

John: Sure.

There is no argument here because there is no opposition. If Mary had rejected the whole idea of going to the movies, or if she had proposed another film and given reasons for preferring it, argumentation would have occurred. But as long as parties to a discussion agree with the opinions expressed, they will not produce arguments. Box 1.5, "Apply the Theory," provides you with an opportunity to work with argument characteristics.

- - - - -

BOX 1.5
APPLY THE THEORY: PROVE THIS IS AN ARGUMENT

As discussed in this section, arguments consist of three interrelated parts. First, arguments must make a claim. The claim expresses what the arguer wants the recipient to do or think. Second, arguments must have support. Support takes two forms: evidence and reasoning. And, finally, arguments must attempt to influence someone. Non-controversial statements are not arguments—they are simply descriptions. Using these defining requirements, is the following an argument?

Entertainment producers for television and film should be prohibited from depicting tobacco use in any form. It shouldn't be too hard to see why. We know how dangerous tobacco use is. That has been known for decades. We also know that smoking in adults has declined in recent years—but it has risen in teens and young adults. Cigarette advertisements are already largely prohibited or restricted but because of gaps in legislation, tobacco companies have simply shifted their methods to using product placement in films and on TV. If you just look at what is being produced, cigarettes can be seen everywhere. And they are seen most often in programs intended for teens. It's interesting that the American Lung Associate found that PG-13 movies have more tobacco use than R-rated movies that are intended for adults.[26] This should be stopped; we should protect young people from these "hidden" ads for smoking.

ARGUMENT CONTEXTS

Arguments occur in response to a question or need for inquiry. They develop among arguers, recipients, and larger communities. This section focuses on argument contexts. It will look at why members from different groups and situations interpret arguments differently and how arguers can use their knowledge of contexts to craft better arguments. In the case developed in Box 1.6, "Coffee Is Hot," Liebeck and her advocates and McDonald's and its advocates were not alone exchanging claims and evidence. Public opinion was involved. Congress became involved. Doctors and lawyers were involved. Each group that was party to the argument had its own background, assumptions, and standards for evaluating the quality and validity of the arguments produced. The types of arguments created by various advocates depended on the contexts for which they were used.

When most people hear of this case, they conclude that Liebeck represents another person who "beat the system." Coffee is hot—that is not McDonald's fault. If people are burned, that is their own fault. We live in a litigious society where examples such as this illustrate the need to change the legal system. Sherman Joyce, president of the American Tort Reform Association, argued that Liebeck's case pointed out "a lot of the problems with the system…It demonstrates that the system needs reform."[30] At the same time, Robert H. Scott, the trial judge in the case, wanted to send McDonald's a stern warning. He said that it "was appropriate to punish and deter" McDonald's given its history of burns.[31] And members of Congress moved quickly to pass legislation to reduce the amount of damages a plaintiff could collect.

Liebeck's case illustrates how a common set of facts—what happened to Stella Liebeck—can be examined, reviewed, and debated among different groups of people who arrive at very different conclusions. Members of the legal community thought that punitive damages would deter McDonald's from unsafe and unnecessary practices. Political lobbyists used the case to illustrate the need for reform and argued that the punitive award was an abuse. Politicians looked for ways to act on the perceived abuses and wrote legislation to minimize any future abuses.

Cases such as this are not all that uncommon. For instance, when two teenagers from the Bronx sued McDonald's for making them obese, many responded that it was preposterous to hold a fast-food chain accountable for individual choice. Critics claimed that the girls were to blame for their own ignorance and lack of willpower. And, some said, if anyone were to blame, it should be their parents for failure to exercise reasonable control as well as family genetics.[32]

Although this case was dismissed, arguments about the unhealthy consequences of fast food continue to make their way into the public sphere. When New York City's mayor, Michael Bloomberg, promoted legislation limiting the size of sugary beverages sold in the city's restaurants, sports venues, movie theatres, and street carts to 16 ounces, critics began calling him "Nanny Bloomberg" and called for personal responsibility and not government regulation.[33] These are examples of how arguments about personal issues and responsibilities can move into the realm of public debate. Newspaper articles, books, and even an award-winning documentary film, *Super Size Me*, made the very technical arguments of science, medicine, court cases, and the role of government part of the public debate about health.

Manufacturers of fast food and snack food began to listen to arguments generated in public contexts. Kraft Foods, producer of Oreo cookies, announced that it would reduce the

■ ■ ■ ■ ■
BOX 1.6
COFFEE IS HOT

The following story has become something of an urban legend—the story of the woman who spilled hot coffee in her lap and sued McDonald's because she was burned. Her judgment was for $2.9 million dollars. Many people have heard of the case, and most think the verdict is an indication of the decline of justice in the United States and how lawyers are beginning to make it impossible for a business to manufacture anything without being sued. "Of course coffee is hot. If you spill it on yourself, you will get burned," people will say. Because of this case, most places that serve coffee to go with plastic lids will have accompanying warnings that "Coffee is Hot."

Although most people are probably aware of the case, they are probably not aware of what happened. The account most people have heard does not tell the full story. In an effort to clarify the issues and present a more complete accounting of events, filmmaker Susan Saladoff, released her documentary *Hot Coffee* at the Sundance Film Festival in 2011.[27] It explored the case, the way in which arguments were made, and how they were interpreted. Some of the details surrounding Stella Liebeck, McDonald's, and hot coffee follow:

Stella Liebeck's life changed dramatically on February 27, 1992. She was an active and energetic 79-year-old woman who had just retired from a long career as a department store cashier making $5,000 per year.

That morning she did not have time for breakfast at her daughter's house. Her son, Jim, was catching an early flight out of Albuquerque, New Mexico, and to get him to the airport on time, she and her grandson, Chris, had to leave at dawn. Chris drove his *Ford Probe* and after dropping Jim off, Stella and he went to a McDonald's restaurant drive-through to buy breakfast.[28]

Chris pulled the car into a parking space so Stella could add cream and sugar to her coffee. She had a difficult time getting the top off of the cup. "I took the cup and tried to get the top off," she later testified. She looked for a place to put the cup down, but the dashboard was slanted and there was no cup-holder in the *Probe*. She described what happened next: "Both hands were busy. I couldn't hold it so I put it between my knees and tried to get the top off that way." With a strong tug the top came off and scalding coffee poured all over her lap. She screamed and tried desperately to get her sweatpants off as the 185-degree-Fahrenheit coffee burned. By the time she and Chris reached the emergency room, Stella had suffered second- and third-degree burns across her buttocks, her thighs, and her labia. All she remembered was the pain.

Although the jury initially awarded her $2.9 million for pain, suffering, and injuries, a judge later cut the amount to $640,000. Yet her case became one of the leading examples supporting tort reform in Congress—an attempt to diminish runaway damage claims in lawsuits. Was her case unjust? Was her case another example of lawyers trying to get all they can out of the system? The answer may not be as clear as it at first seems.

Liebeck spent seven days in the hospital and then three more weeks recuperating at home. During that time her movement was limited and she was in constant pain from the burns. She was again hospitalized for skin grafts over the affected areas of her body and, while practically immobilized and in pain from the grafts, her body weight dropped from 20 to 83 pounds.

Initially she was not interested in suing. In a letter she wrote to McDonald's, she asked that they turn down the temperature of the coffee and requested $2,000—the amount of her out-of-pocket expenses. McDonald's offered her $800. Upon further investigation, Liebeck discovered that McDonald's had been sued in the past for keeping its coffee too hot and that McDonald's had received more than 700 burn complaints over 10 years. In fact, beverages over 135 degrees Fahrenheit are considered too hot for human consumption. Yet, the company continued to sell coffee at the same 185-degree-Fahrenheit burning temperature.[29]

size of its portions in single-serving packages. McDonald's ended the super size meal option and reduced the size of some of its servings. Frito-Lay decided to reduce or eliminate trans fats from their foods because of possible health risks associated with them.[34]

People from different associations and groups often see different things in the world around them. That is because all of us use our assumptions, beliefs, and experiences to help frame our experiences. We talk of many different subjects and have our own rules of discourse. Lawyers, for instance, have very strict rules for what can serve as evidence for an argument. In science, certain types of evidence and reasoning are considered superior to others. For instance, scientists tend to look for cause and effect and tend not to reason from analogy or personal feelings. For them, claims or hypotheses should be proven objectively.

Advocates do not present their arguments in a vacuum. They draw arguments from their knowledge, background, and research in a particular topic and adapt their arguments to an audience's need and interest in that topic. From an arguer's assessment of the connection between an audience and a message, arguments are formed. When scientists write about their research in academic journals, they approach their audience differently than if they were discussing the same research to a national audience on a late-night television program. When arguing before their peers, physicists or astronomers tend to employ technical proofs and reasons because the audience is expert in the field. In front of public audiences of nonexperts, the same scientists tend to employ different forms of evidence and reasoning so that a general audience can understand the claims.

Arguments develop in an environment of advocacy that we refer to as argument context. *Argument contexts grow out of the confluence of arguer, question or need, and audience.* Just as the physical environment influences how plants or animals will grow, argument contexts influence how arguments are developed and communicated. This confluence, or relationship, among arguer, need, and recipients that creates arguments' contexts can be described and understood through two related concepts: argument fields and argument spheres.

Fields

When we discussed the cycle of critical thinking earlier, we noted how important it is for advocates to explore and understand issues and subjects. Part of that process involved seeking out relevant authorities that could frame and inform argument development. Argument fields focus on the context for expertise. An attorney can speak effectively about the law and Liebeck's legal standing. A doctor could talk about the severity of her burns. However, it is unlikely that the physician would be able to effectively negotiate a legal settlement. Lawyers and doctors are from different argument fields. *Argument fields are sociological contexts for arguments and are marked by patterns of communication that participants in argumentative disputes can recognize.*[35]

Fields provide arguers with a context for exploring and interpreting subjects, as well as a framework for interpreting, creating, and evaluating arguments. Argument fields provide field members with an understanding of the rules and conventions governing the development of arguments as well as their interpretation. Perhaps argumentation theorist Joseph Wenzel put it best when he said to think of fields as representing "some sort of universe of discourse."[36] Different professions—such as law, education, medicine, or politics—have a language and set of rules for argument that govern how arguments are made and judged.

These rules may be external to the arguers in the sphere, and they provide a basis by which the arguments can be developed and evaluated.

The very fact that an argument takes place in a law court, a corporate boardroom, a medical care setting, or an art class may influence the procedures that are used and the standards that are applied to make arguments and judgments about arguments. Argument fields define the rules for engagement and resolution. In other words, they determine what kind of evidence and support will be considered appropriate for a claim. This is why attorneys, medical doctors, filmmakers, and Congress could all reach different conclusions about whether Liebeck "scammed" the system or was a victim of corporate excess. Each used different standards and assumptions to frame their opinions. Some fields are highly defined with rigid rules, whereas other fields are loosely defined with norms for arguing.

In *The Uses of Argument* and subsequent works, philosopher Stephen Toulmin emphasized the importance of argument fields in understanding and interpreting argument.[37] The arenas in which arguments are developed influence the forms of argument, the bases on which inferences are made, and the means for deciding disputes. These fields are both social and communicative phenomena. In other words, people, through interaction, make fields for argument; they act as the source for the conventions and criteria used in conducting arguments, and they are an important feature of argumentation.[38]

Characteristics

Argument fields include such examples as law, ethics, medicine, science, and aesthetics. Furthermore, each of these fields has subfields (e.g., the subfields of law include tort law, family law, criminal law) that function as fields for increasingly specific arguments. Describing what fields exist at any given moment can be difficult because we are constantly surrounded by and involved in many different fields. Nevertheless, the field in which arguments are produced affects the nature of the argument; as the field changes, so does the way the argument is constructed. Robert Rowland made the point that it "seems obvious that arguments vary by field."[39]

Although they can be complex and difficult to isolate, generally fields share five common characteristics:

- They are a human creation.[40] This means that fields develop over time through social interaction. People create them, shape them, and change them.
- People with shared goals develop them.[41] People sustain interaction and develop fields when they share objectives and purposes. In science, for example, the purpose is to identify the laws of nature; in ethics, the purpose is to distinguish what is good and morally right from what is not; and in medicine, the purpose is to promote health by preventing and curing illness.
- They develop specialized language and rules.[42] When people converse to achieve their objectives, there are certain rules of conduct as well as language that facilitate their objectives. We may call such specialized language *jargon*, but for the members of a field, the language carries unique meanings.
- People may belong to many fields.[43] Humans share many different objectives and adhere to many different sets of rules. There are, for instance, attorneys to abide by

the rules of the legal profession who also teach and follow those rules. They may also belong to a political party and follow the ideology of the organization. Any single person may belong to and practice the standards of many different fields. We can be members of as many fields as serve our interests or objectives.

■ Fields survive only as long as they serve the common purpose of their members and as long as they can adapt to changing objectives.[44] When a field no longer serves its members and cannot adapt to meet their needs, it will disappear.

These five dimensions can describe any field. For example, if we look at the field of law, we would say first that law is a human creation. Lawyers were not needed until human beings began developing rules and laws for governance and discovered a need to have a group of people interpret and apply the rules. Second, the legal field consists of people with shared goals. Lawyers and judges work to apply the law in civil and criminal matters to punish wrongdoers and seek justice. Third, members of the legal field develop their own specialized language to describe activities and directions in their field. They talk about writs (any legal documents used for court action), habeas corpus (a type of document used to release someone from unlawful imprisonment because of lack of due process), praecipe (writs that command a defendant to do the thing required or show just reason why he or she cannot), and estoppel (a document that prevents someone from acting in contradictory ways to the detriment of another party), among many other terms. A field develops a unique language that unites and binds its members and gives them a language within a language (in this case a legal language within English) that identifies them as members of a community or field. Fourth, members of the legal fields may also belong to many other fields. For instance, many politicians are either practicing or former attorneys and judges. Some lawyers move into education and teach at law schools. Finally, lawyers need to be able to adapt to changing conditions and times for the field to survive. As new laws are passed, members of the legal community need to remain current so that the correct rules and precedents are applied to their cases. As laws become more complex, attorneys often find themselves in specialized areas within the field. They may, for instance, specialize in laws pertaining to intellectual property or the preservation of the environment, among many other areas. Failure to adapt to changing rules and laws can lead to individual members of the field being disbarred or to the dissolution of the field itself. Box 1.7, "Apply the Theory," guides you through a process of understanding how fields work.

BOX 1.7
APPLY THE THEORY: WHAT IS YOUR FIELD?

As this section pointed out, we all belong to many fields. And, as we discussed, fields can be defined along five dimensions: human creation, specialized language and rules, membership in multiple fields, and common purpose. Using these categories:

1. Can you demonstrate that "higher education" is a field?
2. Identify an example that illustrates how the field of higher education "fits" in each category.

Standards

Argument fields are important for arguers and critics alike because they provide us with a means of understanding and interpreting arguments. When we evaluate arguments to determine whether they are true or false, good or bad, valid or invalid, we apply two sets of tests: field-dependent standards and field-invariant standards.[45] *Field-dependent standards are the rules, norms, and prescriptions guiding the production of arguments in a particular field.* These are the standards that the particular field identifies as appropriate for evaluating arguments. Therefore, legal standards pertaining to hearsay evidence applied to legal arguments would constitute field-dependent standards. Most arguments in the technical sphere rely on field-dependent standards.

Field-invariant standards apply generally, regardless of the field of argument. Regardless of the field in which an argument is presented, there are certain standards that apply regardless of the particular contexts. For instance, an advocate should not attempt to deceive recipients. Arguers should not seek to undermine or diminish other advocates. Arguments should be presented that have all the required parts of an argument: claim, evidence, reasoning, and an attempt to influence.

The notion of an argument field is valuable because understanding fields helps arguers understand many of the rules and conventions for judging between competing claims in a controversy. They define the assumptions used by advocates in the situation. Depending on which standards from which fields are applied to arguments, the results can be very different. This is why it is important for advocates to be aware of the fields from which they argue and to learn as much about the field for argument as the subject of argument.

Spheres

The concept of argument spheres provides us with a way of understanding argument situations by considering the elements of arguer, recipient, and message. *Argument spheres are social constructs that guide how arguments are produced and evaluated.* Thomas B. Farrell and G. Thomas Goodnight, in their discussion of argument spheres, suggest that argument contexts can be described as belonging to one of three types—personal, technical, and public.[46] This sounds very similar to the discussion about fields with an important difference. While fields focus on the expertise of the members, argument spheres are broader and consider how the relationship among arguer, recipient, and situation intersect.

Personal sphere arguments are made and evaluated by people who are engaged in a personal relationship. Technical sphere arguments are made among people who are experts in their respective fields. Public sphere arguments are arguments made to general audiences that are evaluated using standards created by the general audiences. They are intended to be understood and evaluated using the general tools and abilities of larger, public audiences. Of the three spheres, the technical sphere is the one most rigidly defined by fields.

Figure 1.3, "The Three Argument Spheres," illustrates the connections among the three types. It is important to note that the three spheres can overlap. That is because sometimes technical arguments become personal and that personal arguments may become public. And, as we have discussed with Liebeck's case, some technical arguments can become public. All three spheres interact with one another.

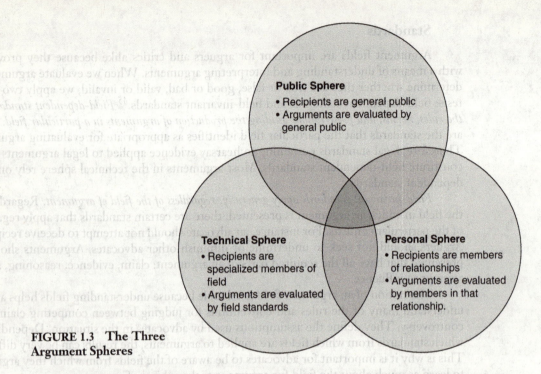

Public Sphere
- Recipients are general public
- Arguments are evaluated by general public

Technical Sphere
- Recipients are specialized members of field
- Arguments are evaluated by field standards

Personal Sphere
- Recipients are members of relationships
- Arguments are evaluated by members in that relationship.

FIGURE 1.3   The Three Argument Spheres

The variables of arguer, audience, and message are influenced by the sphere in which the arguments take place. Whereas some audiences, such as a legal judge, require precise reasoning from specific kinds of evidence, other audiences may be moved more personally by their passions and feelings toward issues such as gun control or abortion and may apply very different standards to judge the value of the argument. The context for the argument informs the advocate of the rules, conventions, and constraints that should govern the development of the arguments.

Liebeck's case provides some important clues as to how argument contexts function. Liebeck's experience defined a central set of issues around which arguments for and against tort reform were debated. Although tort reform had been an issue for several years, her case provided an opportunity to bring the debate into the open. Further, it showed a clash between two powerful communities of people: lawyers and politicians. Many members of the legal profession saw this as an example of how well the justice system works in America. A single, elderly woman can beat a giant corporation when the corporation does something wrong. The political community, however, saw this case as another abuse of legal power.

Technical

The technical sphere contains arguments that adhere to rules that are more formalized and rigorous and tend to be generated by particular groups of people, such as doctors or lawyers. Arguments in this sphere might include the arguments made in academic papers and essays, legal arguments, scientific arguments, and religious arguments. They tend to be specialized and focused toward a particular audience in a particular field. Field-based, technical arguments tend to influence arguments in the other spheres because when we research a subject and evaluate the quality of evidence we locate, we tend to rely on authority and expert opinions, which are grounded in the technical sphere.

Perhaps our most common exposure to technical argument is in the workplace, where people develop a language and set of rules that are unique to their own profession and interests. Professionals in any given field, from law, to medicine, to construction and manufacturing, share an understanding of what is a reasonable or unreasonable argument. Consequently, arguments that are coherent and well argued by the members of that field may be meaningless to other recipients who are not members of that field.

This is what happened in Liebeck's case. Once attorneys became involved, the arguments shifted from the personal experience of being burned and in pain to the legal implications of damage and liability. The arguments moved toward a focus on law and legal precedent, and different rules for arguing applied to the more specialized arguers and recipients. The language of the arguments changed, as did rules of evidence, reasoning, and presentation of argument. Unlike personal arguments, the community of people that uses the standards of the community evaluates these arguments. Arguments in this sphere are most often judged using field-dependent standards.

Personal

The personal sphere contains the relatively informal arguments among people in typically casual settings. Personal arguments are those among friends and family governed by the inter-personal rules for arguments generated in the relationship. Typically, personal arguments do not pay careful attention to evidence, reasoning, or well-framed claims. The rules and procedures for personal arguments are determined by the relationship and not by external forces.[47] For instance, when Liebeck and her daughter discussed how to arrange for in-home care while she recovered from her burns, the arguments were personal and based on a private understanding of the relationship and its needs. Personal sphere arguments are best under-stood by the participants because of the nature of their relationship with one another. And, therefore, personal sphere arguments are evaluated using the standards set by the members of the relationship and field-invariant standards.

Public

The public sphere contains arguments that are intended for public or general audiences. These arguments are evaluated by publicly understood and accepted standards for criticism and analysis. Public arguments include the kinds of arguments politicians might make or that a public relations officer for a corporation might present. Editorials in newspapers typi-cally are written for the public sphere. Whereas the public sphere has relatively formalized rules for appropriateness (e.g., one cannot make slanderous comments about another), the rules are understood and used by a broader public than those of the technical sphere, which focuses on a particular community of people. Most often, then, they are evaluated through field-invariant standards.

The concept of the public sphere, as opposed to either the technical or personal spheres, has a dual meaning. First, the term *public* suggests that it is open and available for inspection by others. Second, public matters are those that affect a community of individuals;

they are issues of common concern that are the subject of much public discourse. Politics is an example of public discourse, as is consumer product safety and foreign trade agreements.

The public sphere is also a blend of issues related to personal, technical, and public concerns. Individual values are often debated in the public arena; for example, we experience arguments over the need for gun control or the legalization of certain controlled substances. These might typically be seen as personal arguments about personal choices, yet these arguments find their way into the public arena as a means to create a social agenda and to promote certain values. Similarly, technical arguments become the substance for extended public debates. The causes of cancer or AIDS that are systematically studied and researched by scientists become the subject of public debates about policies and programs to remedy the diseases.

The public sphere provides an important venue for arguers. It offers them opportunities to extend knowledge and to focus on the plights or successes of others. People working in technical spheres may highlight issues for the public sphere by creating "events" that elevate issues to a public level. John W. Delicath and Kevin Michael Deluca offered an example of this when they wrote of the possibilities to create "image events" (staged protests designed for media dissemination) to bring environmental issues, which are largely technical, into the public sphere.[48] Former U.S. presidential candidate and environmentalist Al Gore attempted a similar strategy with his documentary *An Inconvenient Truth*, which was intended to create public discourse over technical arguments.

This is important, because once issues reach the public sphere they can be heard by a mass audience. David Zarefsky noted that the public sphere "represents the ideal of full and equal participation and deliberation by those with interests in a decision. It shuttles between unbridled individualism and unchecked collectivism, between rampant self-interest and totalitarian rule, between freedom and social order."[49] No matter how one considers it, the public sphere is a significant domain for arguments that have the potential to affect a culture, its institutions, or its people. Zarefsky's challenge to all arguers is to find ways to enhance occasions for deliberation—to seek venues for making arguments that have the potential to transform and change culture and society by blending arguments from the personal, the technical, and the public.[50]

The Liebeck case is a good example of how public argumentation works. In the beginning, Stella Liebeck talked with her daughter and McDonald's on a personal or private level, asking that the hospital bills be covered. When she was unsuccessful, she sought the technical advice of professionals who pursued the case in the technical sphere of law. Following her award for damages, politicians created a series of public arguments to inspire tort reform and attempt to impose controls on a legal system that seemed to have gone out of control. The same event generated arguments in all three spheres and moved from the personal to the technical to the public. Box 1.8, "Apply the Theory," develops how spheres can be used to understand the differences in everyday arguments.

USING ARGUMENT CONTEXTS

The preceding discussion of argument fields and spheres developed the idea that arguments are constrained by the norms or rules for appropriate argument as established by the field and sphere. In other words, arguments in the personal sphere are shaped by standards for

---

BOX 1.8
APPLY THE THEORY: SPHERES OF EDUCATION

Consider your current school or organization. Can you describe how arguments around campus "fit" within the three spheres? For example, many college campuses struggle with issues related to plagiarism. The technical sphere arguments tend to focus legalistically on what rules are in the student code of conduct or some similar document. Public sphere arguments discuss the larger, moral issues of copying someone else's work. And, personal sphere arguments tend to be highly relational and look at whether it is acceptable for one friend to copy the work of another. Think of your institution and:

1. Identify five technical sphere arguments in your institution. Where can you find them? What do they look like?
2. Using these five arguments as a guide, what examples of public sphere arguments can you find looking in your school newspaper, website, public presentations, or other public settings?
3. What personal arguments have you had about these issues? What form did they take?
4. How are arguments developed in each sphere different? How are they the same?

---

evaluation that the participants decide to use. Technical arguments, however, are shaped and evaluated by external field-based criteria generated by the members of the technical sphere. And public arguments are evaluated by standards appropriate for judging common arguments targeted at the general populace.

Using Fields to Interpret Contexts

Toulmin, among others, concluded that arguments are judged according to the standards of the field for which they are produced.[51] This occurs in the technical sphere. Different standards are applied in the field of law than in the field of politics. And standards used in either of these fields are different from those in medicine or education. But, these standards influence public and personal sphere arguments as well.

For example, consider the debate that has surrounded President John F. Kennedy's assassination for decades. The FBI and prosecutor's office (legal field) in 1963 believed there was sufficient evidence to indict Lee Harvey Oswald for the murder. Witnesses saw him rush by with a panicked expression. He fit the general description of a man who left the schoolbook depository building, and when he was arrested Oswald yelled, "Well, it is all over now," and tried to shoot one of the arresting officers.[52] The legal field has rules for evidence and is swayed particularly by physical evidence (the rifle, Oswald's fingerprints) and eyewitness testimony (what he said before the shooting, his behavior after the shooting). In the legal field, these were enough for an indictment.

Yet the scientific community did not think Oswald could have acted alone. An 8-mm home movie of the assassination recorded by Abraham Zapruder showed precisely when the shots were fired and showed which bullets hit the president. Rifle experts timed the lapse between the shots and then tested the rifle allegedly used to assassinate Kennedy. The rifle, they concluded, required a minimum of 2.3 seconds between shots to operate the bolt and re-aim. Because Oswald shot three times—and assuming the first bullet was in the chamber—the total time required by Oswald if he acted alone was a minimum of 4.5 seconds; yet Zapruder's film shows that 4.8 seconds were necessary, which made it possible but not very likely that Oswald could have reloaded, aimed, and fired in the time allowed. Furthermore, the second bullet fired has been dubbed by conspiracy theorists as the "magic bullet." What made this bullet appear magical is that it appeared to strike Kennedy and then change direction and hit Governor John Connally. Because bullets travel in straight lines, and because few thought that one bullet could do as much damage as this one appeared to have done, the scientific community was unconvinced of the single assassin theory.[53]

In 1964, the Warren Commission (political field) was convened, and in 1978 the House Select Committee on Assassination was created. Both groups were charged with investigating and reaching a conclusion regarding who assassinated Kennedy. Their conclusions were that one man had the time to aim and fire and that even the "magic bullet" could have passed through both President Kennedy and Governor Connally. There was no second gunman, the two panels found, and there was no one other than Oswald who could have committed the crime.[54]

Personal sphere arguments often concluded that an extensive conspiracy must have been involved. Public arguments swayed back and forth around which field was most likely correct. A few years ago, a British television company produced a public sphere argument when it attempted to stage the trial of Lee Harvey Oswald, which never actually took place. The program's producers flew all the remaining, living participants to London for the mock trial. Defending Oswald was Gerry Spence, who was a highly successful defense attorney and known for defending high-profile clients such as Karen Silkwood and Imelda Marcos. Vincent Bugliosi, the prosecutor in the Charles Manson case, prosecuted Oswald. The jury was drawn from a pool of Dallas voters, and the judge was also drawn from Texas. The witnesses in the case were either eyewitnesses at the time, the recorded testimony of eyewitnesses, or experts who had testified in either the Warren or House Select Committee hearings. At the conclusion of the trial, the jury concluded that Oswald was the assassin and returned a unanimous verdict of "guilty."[55]

It is interesting that for several decades, more than two hundred books, a dozen documentary films, and a Hollywood feature film have been dedicated to this one event in history. Although there are many explanations for the continued interest in Kennedy's assassination, one reason is that members of different fields and arguments in different spheres continue to offer conflicting opinions and support them with different forms of evidence and reasoning. In the field of medicine, pathologists have suggested that the bullet's path is inconsistent with the lone assassin theory. Yet, legal and political fields seem to have enough evidence to conclude Oswald's guilt. And members of the scientific community argue that one person did not have time to fire all of the shots. Conflicts among fields are brought about by different rules of what constitutes acceptable reasoning or evidence and can lead to confusion among different audiences.

Using Spheres to Interpret Contexts

Understanding the role played by spheres is important in understanding how to produce and receive arguments. Arguments need to be adapted to the appropriate sphere for which they are intended. Arguments are shaped, understood, and judged differently depending on the sphere in which they operate. Notice, for example, how arguments changed as Liebeck's case was placed into different spheres as well as the role different fields played in the interpretation of arguments. Initially Liebeck had no intention of suing McDonald's. She wrote them a letter asking them to reimburse her for out-of-pocket medical expenses (about $2,000) and to reduce the temperature of their coffee. This was a personal argument. It was governed by the rules created by the relationship between McDonald's and Liebeck.

McDonald's offered $800, which was not an acceptable amount. At that point, Liebeck turned to a professional who might help her persuade McDonald's to pay for her treatment. The professional was a member of the legal field who worked to focus the arguments at a technical level toward a judge and jury. The professional argued that the coffee was a defective product and that it was unsafe according to the law. The jury awarded Liebeck $2.9 million on the strength of technical arguments. The verdict and the award were based on the rules established in the legal profession. These were highly formalized rules developed and understood by a highly specialized community.

The media then carried the story to the public, which heard that a person was awarded almost $3 million for burning herself with hot coffee. The standards for judging the argument at a public level were very different, and the award seemed unreasonable because commonly held public standards and beliefs are that coffee is hot. This is why pro–tort reform protesters later carried signs saying, "She spilled it on herself." To the public, the trial and award did not make sense.

Certain arguments have an appeal beyond the sphere in which they were produced. In such cases, arguments may be criticized and evaluated by multiple sets of standards as different communities attempt to understand and evaluate them. An interesting example of an argument that was adapted to both the technical and public spheres is the one presented in Rachel Carson's book *Silent Spring*.[56] This book was written initially for a technical audience about the dangers of a pesticide, DDT, in the environment. Carson warned that DDT was destroying the integrity of robins' eggs and posed a serious long-term threat to the ecosystem. Her argument was heard beyond the technical community to which it was addressed; the book soon found its way to bookstore shelves, and her arguments became the basis for public legislation to ban the pesticide in the United States. Similarly, technical works such as dissertations or academic papers may occasionally attract a general reader when they put forth ideas that appeal to different communities.

Arguments do not reside in a given sphere forever. For any subject of argument, the sphere can become larger or smaller as time progresses. Arguments may move from public discussion to technical to personal discussion and back again. Argument contexts change over time, depending on the audiences and the salient or important issues that affect them. Carson's book today would receive less attention than it did in 1970 because the public sphere for that argument is very small; DDT has already been banned, and the time for the argument has passed. Similarly, the arguments in the book would exist in a relatively small technical sphere because the claims in the book have already been accepted. Other arguments, however, may find that their opportunities within any given sphere are large as interest increases.

Groups of people interested in similar topics and issues may be able to identify and facilitate argument transitions among spheres. These groups, which Archon Fung of the John F. Kennedy School of Government at Harvard University referred to as "mini-publics," act as an educational forum, a participatory and advisory group, or a problem-solving entity.[57] Mini-publics work in the overlap between spheres. In any case, the idea is that small groups of people can help transition ideas from technical and often hidden arenas to public spheres that attain national or global attention. Skilled arguers have this capacity.

An interesting study conducted by sociologist Gianpaolo Baiocchi examined this idea when he wrote about how small publics—groups of people with similar interests—can work together to create an impetus for change in a larger, broader public discussion. His study focused on participatory governance in Brazil, and his conclusion demonstrated an important link between the technical and public spheres. People may band together to fight poverty or injustice for their own neighborhood and community. They may also attain a sufficient critical mass to then take those issues to the larger, policy-making sphere.[58]

SUMMARY

This book focuses on critical thinking and argumentation. Critical thinking, a vital skill in today's society, enables a person to investigate a situation, problem, question, or phenomenon to arrive at a viable hypothesis or conclusion. It includes such skills as clearly stating a question for discussion, clarifying the meaning of terms, developing and applying evaluative criteria, and evaluating the credibility of sources. Once you have gathered information on a topic and analyzed it using these processes, you must communicate your reasoning to others.

This process is called argumentation, which involves making arguments intended to justify beliefs, attitudes, and values so as to influence others. Argumentation is the second focus of this book. It involves constructing cases for or against a proposal. Argumentation occurs in law court cases, governmental legislation, marketing campaigns, and business proposals. Such extended cases are made up of individual arguments. An argument is a set of statements in which a claim is made, support is offered for it, and there is an attempt to influence someone in a context of disagreement. A person making a claim is expected to offer further support by using evidence and reasoning. Evidence consists of facts or conditions that are objectively observable, beliefs or statements generally accepted as true by the recipients, or conclusions previously established. Reasoning is frequently expressed in the form of inferences, constructs a rational link between the evidence and the claim, and authorizes the step we make when we draw a conclusion.

Arguments are produced for particular contexts, and they are generally evaluated with respect to their time and place. These contexts influence the way arguments are created, understood, and evaluated. Contexts are an important part of the argument's development because they shape the way arguers attempt to influence recipients. Generally, argument contexts are the intersection of two concepts: argument fields and argument spheres. These two concepts help us understand how to produce and evaluate arguments.

Argument fields help provide a context for making and interpreting arguments. Fields are specialized contexts that determine the rules for acceptable evidence, the types of issues to be considered, the rules or procedures for conducting arguments, the requirements for proving a case, and even the specialized language in which arguments are expressed. Examples of such fields are law, medicine, and science. Fields are important in judging between competing claims because they provide the basic principles in which many forms of reasoning are based. Some standards for judging arguments are field dependent and arise from the particular context in which the argument is made. Other standards are field invariant and apply to all arguments regardless of their contexts.

Argument spheres are the specific contexts in which people argue. Recipients understand arguments and coordinate them through their own frames of reference through the use of argument spheres. Generally, argument spheres are of three types: personal, technical, and public. When people argue in personal spheres, the arguments are relatively informal and casual. Arguments in the technical sphere are governed by rigorous and specialized rules, which serve to specify the types of acceptable evidence and reasoning. Public-sphere arguments are arguments that are produced and evaluated in a public arena. They are intended for public audiences and are criticized using public standards. Depending on the sphere the arguer operates in, arguments are adapted and criticized using the rules or conditions of the given sphere.

EXERCISES

(Please note: Throughout the book, exercise items marked with an asterisk have answers provided in Appendix A.)

Exercise 1: Identifying Arguments. Can you distinguish a statement that is an argument from one that is not? Remember that an argument

    A. Puts forth a claim
    B. Offers support for it
    C. Makes an attempt to influence someone

Now, consider the following statement:

    If it rains tomorrow, I'm going home.

This is not an argument because the speaker offers neither a claim nor support for it. Rather, she merely states her intention, which does not depend on the other person's acceptance. Furthermore, the speaker does not explicitly try to influence anyone else but merely states what she herself intends to do. Consider the following statements, decide whether or not they are arguments, and explain the reasons for your decision. Remember that statements of one's emotional state or pure descriptions are not generally viewed as arguments.

  *1. There is a plethora of credible scenarios for achieving human-level intelligence in a machine. We will be able to evolve and train a system combining massively parallel neural nets with other paradigms to understand language and model knowledge, including the ability to read and understand written documents...We can then have our computers read all of the world's literature—books, magazines, scientific journals, and other available material. Ultimately, the machines will gather knowledge on their own by venturing into the physical world, drawing from the full spectrum of media and information services, and sharing knowledge with each other (which machines can do far more easily than their human creators).

        Ray Kurzweil, *The Age of Spiritual Machines: When Computers Exceed Human Intelligence* (New York: Viking, 1999), 3.

  2. Fred: Why are you leaving so early for the meeting?
        Gale: Sue asked me to pick her up on the way. Are you going to watch that movie at 8 o'clock?
        Fred: Yeah. It lasts until 10 and then I thought I'd go to bed early.
        Gale: Fine. I'll see you in the morning.

3. Today's students are no longer the people our educational system was designed to teach… today's students *think and process information fundamentally differently* from their predecessors. These differences go far further and deeper than most educators suspect or realize. "Different kinds of experiences lead to different brain structures," says Dr. Bruce D. Perry of Baylor College of Medicine…It is very likely that *our students' brains have physically changed*—and are different from ours—as a result of how they grew up. But whether or not this is *literally* true, we can say with certainty that their *thinking patterns* have changed.

Marc Prensky, "Digital Natives, Digital Immigrants," *On the Horizon* 9 (October 2001).

4. I try to remember when this rivalry between my daughter and me first began. I can't. It sometimes seems that we have always been this way with each other, that we have never gotten along any better or differently. I would like to make my daughter less miserable if I can, to help her be happier and much more pleased with herself, I don't know how.

Joseph Heller, *Something Happened* (New York: Ballantine Books, 1974), 179.

*5. As a linguist, Mr. McWhorer (a professor of linguistics at the University of California at Berkeley and a senior fellow at the Manhattan Institute, a policy research group in New York City) knows that grammatical rules are arbitrary and that in casual conversation people have never abided by them. Rather, he argues, the fault lies with the collapse of the distinction between the written and the oral. Where formal, well-honed English was once de rigueur in public life, he argues, it has all but disappeared, supplanted by the indifferent cadences of speech and ultimately impairing our ability to think.

Emily Eakin, "Going at the Changes in, Ya Know, English," *New York Times* (November 15, 2003), www.nytimes.com

6. Charles: I think students care more about politics and the issues of higher education than at any time in the past.

Fred: You are wrong. Students have terrible voting turnout, they don't read newspapers or engage in any kind of conversation about the major issues of the day. The more I teach college students, the more I begin to think they are just not engaged.

Charles: Maybe their political expression is not in the classroom. I walk around campus and I hear their conversations. I watch protests and look at how students argue with one another. I think it is possible that we have failed in education. Students are learning on their own because we haven't designed a curriculum to inform and inspire. Students are active; I just don't think we see it all the time.

7. I don't think anyone would disagree that animals are different from human beings. But, does that give us the right to abuse them? To subject them to painful experiments so that we can wear pretty cosmetics? We use animals to make our lives easier. Sometimes we use them as fashion accessories. Sometimes we use them to test new medical treatments and drugs. If it is true that human beings are the most evolved beings on the planet, doesn't that mean we have that much more responsibility to ensure that all living beings are cared for?

8. John: Should we figure out salary raises on a 3 percent cost of living increase plus bonuses if people performed exceptionally?

Judy: That will work as long as we have enough in the budget to cover it. How much is available to us?

John: Well, we have a reserve fund to cover any excesses. I think we should start out with what the staff ought to receive and concern ourselves with what's available later on.

Judy: That sounds fine to me, as long as we have some excess.

9. Newspapers, my friend, are a thing of the past. People no longer read in a linear fashion—they pick and choose. They jump around. The old style is gone, replaced with e-readers. People want to consume information differently than in the past. The digital video recorder (DVR) gave us the ability to watch what we wanted when we wanted. The e-reader is the same thing. We pick our articles, we pick what we are interested in reading. There was a time, when people would sit and read an entire newspaper. Not now. We want headlines and, if something sparks our interest, we might read more. It's a new world. The consumer has become their own editor—what is relevant and what is not. I think that's good.

*10. Chevelle: I am truly worried about student debt. Too many young people are saddled with huge and seemingly insurmountable debt just to finish their bachelor's degrees. It seems as though our educational system has put so much pressure on students to get a degree and then hasn't provided them with enough resources to complete the degree.

Amy: But that's the deal, right? Degrees benefit students. Why should the government pick up the costs? We know that a college education will help students get jobs, earn a good living, and be successful. College graduates earn much more than other people. Why shouldn't they pay for their own success? That just seems right, doesn't it?

Chevelle: But if we go that route, only students with resources and wealthy families will ever get a college education. What about all those who don't have the money? It seems to me that you are saying we should go ahead and let wealth and privilege determine success. If we provide access for all of our students, then we can help all of our society be better off. Education is a public good, not just a private good. When we recognize that and provide qualified students with access, we will all be better off.

Exercise 2: Developing Critical Thinking. The United States is suffering from an overweight and obesity epidemic and it is not alone. The World Health Organization (WHO) has reported that more than 1.4 billion adults, age 20 and older, worldwide are overweight and more than 500 million of these people are obese (http://www.who.int/mediacentre/factsheets/fs311/en/). Health care systems in many countries are being overwhelmed by weight-related illnesses. What should be done? Using the critical thinking cycle discussed in this chapter, how would you approach answering this question?

1. *Question at issue:* What is the need that has arisen?

2. *Purpose:* What is your goal with this inquiry?

3. *Information:* What information do you need to reach a reasonable conclusion?

4. *Concepts:* What laws, rules, and principles guide your inquiry as you look for an answer?

5. *Assumptions:* What are our presuppositions? Do any need to be questioned?

6. *Points of View:* What perspectives come into play here? Are individuals responsible? Should the sale of sugary items be restricted?

7. *Interpretations and Inferences:* What conclusions can you reach given the material you have found? How did you arrive at your conclusions?

8. *Implications and Consequences:* What would be likely to happen if your solutions were adopted? What would critics say or do? What would supporters say or do?

Exercise 3: Fields. We have discussed the role of argument fields in

- Providing grounds for decisions
- Implying requirements for what audiences expect from argument
- Implying rules arguers will follow in argumentation

One example of a field in which argument occurs is medicine. Based on what you know about argument fields, how would you answer the following questions?

- What kinds of grounds do medical doctors use in their research papers, public presentations, or the diagnosis of a disease?
- What constitutes acceptable evidence for medical arguments?
- In what spheres do medical doctors operate?
- What are the audience expectations of this field?
- What are some conventions or rules followed by doctors?

Exercise 4: *Personal Fields.* What argument fields are you associated with? Using the description of fields presented in the text, how would you characterize these fields?

NOTES

1. A list of pageants and their links can be found at "World Beauty Pageants Information," at http://www.allsrilanka.com/directory/tools/women/beauty_pageants.htm (accessed May 10, 2012). Some specific information about the purpose and goals of pageants can be found at Miss America, "Participate and Earn Scholarships," at http://missamerica.org/scholarships/purpose.aspx (accessed May 10, 2012).

2. A valuable resource for reading and reviewing contemporary topics that are used in competitive academic debate can be found at *Debatabase* at http://idebate.org. This conversation was drawn from classroom debates and from *Debatabase*, "Are beauty contests harmful?" http://idebate.org/debatabase/debates/culture/house-would-ban-beauty-contests (accessed May 10, 2012). See also Colleen Ballerino Cohen, Richard Wilk, Beverly Stoeltje (eds.), *Beauty Queens on the Global Stage: Gender, Contests, and Power* (New York: Routledge, 1996); Sarah Banet-Weiser, *The Most Beautiful Girl in the World: Beauty Pageants and National Identity* (Berkeley and Los Angeles, Calif.: University of California Press, 1999); and Naomi Wolf, *The Beauty Myth* (New York: HarperCollins, 2002).

3. Critical thinking is an important subject that has been studied and developed extensively by a variety of theorists. Some good sources for background information include: Jason Braithwaite, "Critical Thinking, Logic and Reason: A Practical Guide for Students and Academics," 2006, at http://www.scribd.com/doc/11568291/Critical-Thinking (accessed May 10, 2012); "Critical Thinking Definition, Instruction, and Assessment: A Rigorous Approach," at http://www.criticalthinking.net (accessed May 10, 2012); and good video can be found at "Critical Thinking," at http://www.youtube.com/watch?v=6OLPL5p0fMg (accessed May 10, 2012).

4. Steven D. Schafersman, "An Introduction to Critical Thinking," January 1991, http://www.freeinquiry.com/critical-thinking.html (accessed June 30, 2008).

5. Joanne Kurfiss, *Critical Thinking: Theory, Research, Practice, and Possibilities* (Washington, D.C.: Association for the Study of Higher Education, 1975), 2. There are many definitions used for critical thinking that get at similar themes. A good source for these is "The Critical Thinking Community," which can be found at http://www.critical-thinking.org.

6. Elizabeth K. Hale, MD, "Ask the Expert: How Much Sunscreen Should I Be Using On My Face and Body?" at http://www.skincancer.org/skin-cancer-information/ask-the-experts/how-much-sunscreen-should-i-be-using-on-my-face-and-body (accessed May 2, 2012).

7. Much has been written about critical thinking as a process for systematically evaluating issues and their inter-relationships. This section and Figure 1.1 are adapted from Richard Paul and Linda Elder, *The Nature and Functions of Critical and Creative Thinking* (Dillon Beach, Calif.: The Foundation for Critical Thinking, 2004); Joan Trabandt, "Critical Thinking in Online Discussions," 2002, at http://www.nvcc.edu/home/jtrabandt/discussion/default.html (accessed June 30, 2008); Peter A. Facione, "Critical Thinking: What It Is and Why It Counts," 2007, at http://www.insightassessment.com/pdf_files/what&why98.pdf (accessed July 1, 2008). There are also many resources available through Paul and Elder at the Foundation for Critical Thinking (www.criticalthinking.org).

8. Paul and Elder, 25–26.

9. Richard W. Paul and Gerald M. Nosich, "A Model for the National Assessment of Higher Order Thinking," in *Critical Thinking: What Every Person Needs to Survive in a Rapidly Changing World*, A. J. A. Binker, ed. (Santa Rosa, Calif.: Foundation for Critical Thinking, 1992), 87–88.

10. W. R. Minto, "Barriers to Critical Thinking: Challenges and Opportunities," April 30, 2012, at http://www.effectivethinking.org/2012/04/barriers-to-critical-thinking (accessed June 18, 2012); Brian Clark, "Do You Recognize These 10 Mental Blocks to Creative Thinking?"

at http://www.copyblogger.com/mental-blocks-creative-thinking (accessed July 1, 2008); and Gene Pinder, "Eight Barriers to Critical Thinking" at http://ezinearticles.com/?Eight-Barriers-to-Critical-Thinking&id=716694 (accessed June 18, 2012).

11. Mohammed El-Nawawy, The Israeli-Egyptian Peace Process in the Reporting of Western Journalists (Greenwood: Westport, CT, 2002), 1. An interesting essay on this subject can be found at Douglas Buchanan, "The Experts are Always Wrong," *The Gates of Horn*, at http://www.gatesofhorn.com/content/experts-are-always-wrong (accessed June 18, 2012).

12. Dr. Richard Paul, Dr. Linda Elder, and Dr. Ted Bartell, "Study of 38 Public Universities and 28 Private Universities to Determine Faculty Emphasis on Critical Thinking in Instruction," at www.criticalthinking.org/pages/study-of-38-public-universities-and-28-private-universities-to-determine-faculty-emphasis-on-critical-thinking-in-instruction/558 (accessed June 8, 2004).

13. Richard Arum and Josipa Roksa, *Academically Adrift: Limited Learning on College Campuses*, Kindle Ed. (Chicago, Ill.: University of Chicago Press, 2011), 828.

14. Several studies have been conducted that make this point. See Sara Rimer, "Study: Many College Students not Learning to Think Critically" *Hechinger Report*, January 18, 2011, at http://www.mcclatchydc.com/2011/01/18/106949/study-many-college-students-not.html#_jmp0_ (accessed May 16, 2012).

15. Paul and Nosich, 101; see also, James H. McMillan, "Enhancing College Students' Critical Thinking: A Review of Studies," *Research in Higher Education* 26 (1987): 3–29.

16. Hugh Heclo, "Hyperdemocracy," *The Wilson Quarterly* 23 (1999): 62.

17. Krista Mahr, "Neda Agha-Soltan," *Time Specials* at http://www.time.com/time/specials/packages/article/0,28804,1945379_1944701_1944705,00.html (accessed May 16, 2012).

18. Susan B. Shimanoff, *Communication Rules: Theory and Research* (Beverly Hills, Calif.: Sage), 31–32.

19. H. P. Grice, "Logic and Conversation," in *Syntax and Semantics: Vol 3. Speech Acts*, Peter Cole and Jerry L. Morgan, eds. (New York: Academic Press, 1975), 45.

20. National Association of Parliamentarians, "Parliamentary Procedure," at http://parliamentarians.org/procedure.php (accessed May 16, 2012).

21. "A good place to start is "Roberts Rules of Order Online," at www.rulesonline.com (accessed May 16, 2012) and www.parlipro.org (accessed May 16, 2012) for tutorials and explanations.

22. Daniel J. O'Keefe, "Two Concepts of Argument," *Journal of the American Forensic Association* 13 (1977): 121–128; and "The Concepts of Argument and Arguing," in *Advances in Argumentation Theory and Research*, J. Robert Cox and Charles Arthur Willard, eds. (Carbondale, Ill.: Southern Illinois University Press, 1982), 3–23.

23. Frans H. van Eemeren, Rob Grootendorst, and Francisca Snoeck Henkemans, *Fundamentals of Argumentation Theory* (Mahwah, N.J.: Erlbaum, 1996), 2–4.

24. Stephen Toulmin, *The Uses of Argument* (Cambridge: Cambridge University Press, 1958), 98.

25. Douglas Ehninger, "Argument as Method: Its Nature, Its Limitations, and Its Uses," *Speech Monographs* 37 (1970): 102–103.

26. http://www.lung.org/stop-smoking/about-smoking/facts-figures/children-teens-and-tobacco.html (accessed July 5, 2012).

27. Susan Saladoff, *Hot Coffee*, at http://www.hotcoffeethemovie.com/default.asp?pg=press (accessed June 2, 2012).

28. A good description of the facts of the case can be found in Beth Taylor, McDonald's Hot Coffee Case Facts" January 31, 2011 at http://suite101.com/article/mcdonalds-hot-coffee-case-facts-a340620 (accessed June 1, 2012).

29. Further descriptions of the case and litigation can be found at Matthew Tozer, Esq., "The McTruth about the infamous McDonald's Coffee Burn Case," *California Legal News Report Index*, 2007, at http://www.legal-news-california.tozerlaw.com/mcdonalds_coffee_case.html (accessed June 2, 2012); and from Aric Press, Jenny Carrol, and Steven Waldman, "Are Lawyers Burning America?" *Newsweek* (March 20, 1995): 32–35.

30. Aric Press, Jenny Carroll, and Steven Waldman, "Are Lawyers Burning America?" *Newsweek* (March 20, 1995): 32–35.

31. Press, Carroll, and Waldman, 35.

32. McDonald's Corp. and Kraft Foods Inc., "'Big Food' Gets the Obesity Message," *New York Times*, July 10, 2003: A22.

33. Michael Janati, Bloomberg Ratchets up War on Obesity: Proposes Ban on Soda," *Washington Times*, June 2, 2012, at http://communities.washingtontimes.com/neighborhood/life-line-healthful-habits-made-simple/2012/jun/2/bloomberg-ratchets-war-obesity-proposes-ban-soda/ (accessed June 2, 2012).

34. The Wall Street Journal, "Obesity Suit Against McDonald's Is Dismissed by Federal Judge," Shirley Leung, *Wall Street Journal* (September 5, 2003): B4.

35. A discussion of fields, definitions, and function can be found in: Robert C. Rowland, "The Influence of Purpose on Fields of Argument," *Journal of the American Forensics Association* 18 (1982): 229–245; David Zarefsky, "'Reasonableness' in Public Policy Argument: Fields as Institutions," *Dimensions of Argument: Proceedings of the Second Summer Conference on Argumentation*, George Ziegelmueller and Jack Rhodes, eds. (Annandale, Va.:

Speech Communication Association, 1981): 89; Thomas A. Hollihan and Kevin T. Baaske, *Arguments and Arguing: The Products and Process of Human Decision Making* (New York: St. Martin's Press, 1994): 35.

36. Joseph Wenzel, "On Fields of Argument as Prepositional Systems," *Journal of the American Forensic Association* 18 (1982): 204.

37. Stephen Toulmin, *The Uses of Argument* (Cambridge: Cambridge University Press, 1958), 13–15. Further information can be found in Charles A. Willard, "Argument Fields and Theories of Logical Types," *Journal of the American Forensic Association* 17 (1981): 129–145.

38. Charles Kneupper, "Argument Fields: Some Social Constructivist Observations," in *Dimensions of Argument: Proceedings of the Second Summer Conference on Argumentation*, George Ziegelmueller and Jack Rhodes, eds. (Annandale, Va.: Speech Communication Association/ American Forensic Association, 1981), 80–87.

39. Rowland, "The Influence of Purpose on Fields of Argument," 228.

40. Willard, "Argument Fields," in *Dimensions of Argument*, 21–42.

41. Willard, 41.

42. R. Rowland, "Argument Fields," in *Dimensions of Argument*, 56–79; and "The Influence of Purpose on Fields of Argument," 228–245.

43. Rowland, "Argument Fields," 64.

44. Kneupper, 82.

45. Toulmin, 1958, 33.

46. Thomas B. Farrell and G. Thomas Goodnight, "Accidental Rhetoric: The Root Metaphors of Three Mile Island," *Communication Monographs* 48 (1981): 271–300.

47. Very good discussions of the types of spheres and their definitions can be found in Theodore O. Prosise and

Greg R. Miller, "Argument Fields as Arenas of Discursive Struggle," *Argumentation & Advocacy* 32 (Winter 1996): 111–129; and David Zarefsky, "The Decline of Public Debate," *USA Today Magazine* 126 (March 1998): 56–59.

48. John W. Delicath and Kevin Michael Deluca, "Image Events, the Public Sphere, and Argumentative Practice: The Case of Radical Environmental Groups." *Argumentation* (August 2004): 315.

49. Zarefsky, 1998, 56.

50. The loss of the public sphere and the need to reclaim public arenas for discussion were developed in D. Ambrozas, "The University as Public Sphere," *Canadian Journal of Communication* 23 (Winter 1998): 73–89; Gordon R. Mitchell, "Pedagogical Possibilities for Argumentative Agency in Academic Debate," *Argumentation & Advocacy* 35 (Fall 1998): 41–61; Carol Winkler and David M. Cheshier, "Revisioning Argumentation Education for the New Century: Millennial Challenges," *Argumentation & Advocacy* 36 (Winter 2000): 101–105.

51. Toulmin, 1958, 33.

52. Gerald Posner, "It Was Him All Along," *Night & Day* (October 1993): 8.

53. Posner, 12–13.

54. Posner, 12–13.

55. Vincent Bugliosi, *And the Sea Will Tell* (New York: Ivy, 1991), 632–634.

56. Rachel Carson, *Silent Spring* (Boston: Houghton Mifflin, 1994).

57. Archon Fung, "Survey Article: Recipes for Public Spheres: Eight Institutional Design Choices and Their Consequences," *The Journal of Political Philosophy* (2003): 338.

58. Gianpaolo Baiocchi, "Emergent Public Spheres: Talking Politics in Participatory Governance," *American Sociological Review* (February 2003): 52.

CHAPTER TWO

CO-ORIENTATIONAL VIEW OF ARGUMENT

CHAPTER OUTLINE

KEY CONCEPTS

In Chapter 1, we discussed how arguments occur in contexts that are defined by their fields and spheres. This chapter examines how arguments are developed in and around the relationships among arguers and recipients. Box 2.1, "Does a College or University Have the Right or Responsibility to Censor the Arts?" illustrates how sometimes relationships among arguers and recipients can become complex because of multiple needs and multiple goals. The question of whether or not a school or the government has a right or responsibility to censor expression is difficult because of the varied needs and competing values of those involved. Students, for instance, may want to broaden their understanding of controversial and challenging issues through the arts, demonstrations, and discussion. Yet, university administrators or government officials may fear the message because it challenges accepted beliefs and practice or may cause protests and violence.

■ ■ ■ ■ ■

BOX 2.1

DOES A COLLEGE OR UNIVERSITY HAVE THE RIGHT OR RESPONSIBILITY TO CENSOR THE ARTS?

Most countries around the world have grappled with issues related to censorship and what expression should be allowed and what expression should be banned. Sometimes, when artists push at accepted cultural norms to make political or social points clear, they are seen as crossing some threshold of appropriateness. This occurred in 2005 when the Danish newspaper *Jyllands-Posten* published editorial cartoons depicting the Islamic prophet Muhammad in a manner that linked Islam to terrorism. Demonstrations and outbreaks of violence ensued, and many college newspapers debated whether or not to reprint any of the cartoons.[1] In most cases, however, sexual content and its appropriateness for public viewing are primary reasons for censoring art. In 2002, for instance, Attorney General John Ashcroft refused to be photographed in front of two partially nude statues in the Great Hall of the Department of Justice and spent $8,000 on blue drapes to hide them.[2]

On occasion, schools are pressured to remove an art exhibit or stop a controversial performance or production. The pressure may come from the school's administration or from community members who object to the content of the art. High schools, colleges, and universities often struggle with decisions about what artworks can be shown and what should not be open to public view. For example, in 2006, Penn State University student Josh Stulman was informed that the university had cancelled his upcoming art exhibition because it violated the university's policies related to nondiscrimination, harassment, and hate. His exhibition was based primarily on the conflict in the Palestinian territories and raised questions concerning the destruction of Jewish religious shrines, anti-Semitic propaganda, disregard for the treatment of prisoners, and the indoctrination of youth into terrorist acts.[3]

There are many examples across the world that illustrate how groups work to balance the needs for expression with issues related to public decency and safety. Consider the following conversation between two college students, Juli and Steve, as they grapple with when and where colleges and universities have a right to censor artistic expression.[4]

Steve: I can't believe the college is thinking about banning the *Laramie Project*.[5] We are adults and this is a college. We should be able to see and hear what we want, when we want. This play addresses important social issues that should be discussed on our campus. It should not be banned just because it makes some people in the community uncomfortable.

BOX 2.1   CONTINUED

Juli:	Our rights to see this play or have a controversial art exhibition are not more important than someone else's rights—even when it comes to free speech. People have threatened to protest this play and our campus police are worried about violence and vandalism. We have no right to put others at risk and if a protest turns ugly, that's what could happen. If our freedoms potentially hurt others, they should be limited. Ironically, this play makes that point. We limit hate speech—we don't allow people to say what they want because it may have harmful consequences. Artistic work is like any other form of speech; it should have limits if it hurts others. Artistic expression should not be exempted from censorship any more than any other kind of speech.
Steve:	Maybe, but people's rights should not be limited or eliminated unless there is a very very clear and present threat to the safety of others. With art—and with this play—no one has proved a clear danger to our campus or our community. Protests don't hurt anyone—the opposite is true. Protests could highlight the dangers of homophobia and discrimination. And, if this play might offend someone, they don't have to see it. As long as people have a choice to see it or not, there should be no problem and no limitation on expression. My only point here is that all art forms—this play, music, art exhibitions—can have significant and important messages that combat hate, stereotypes, and serve to bring us to a better understanding of one another. Before it is censored, the school, the government, or whoever has a burden to prove there would be some harm.
Juli:	Fair enough. I think, though, that it is important to remember that censorship can be targeted so that some classes of people are protected—like kids. After all, movies have ratings to allow some people to see them while keeping others out. Censorship can be used to protect kids from excessive sex and violence or having to deal with issues in this play. The issue is that not all content is appropriate for everyone. And, in our community, maybe this play is not a wise choice. That should have been taken into consideration.
Steve:	Censorship, even with age ratings or using a community standard, is a problem because it seeks to limit what people can see and think. This is bad. When we allow others to tell us what is OK to see or not, we are giving away our rights to think freely and we are allowing community sensitivity to influence our education and our thoughts. People are not forced to see this play or any other potentially offensive art. They get to choose—and they should make the choice—not the college, not the community, and not the government.

Consider the arguments that emerged in this discussion and think about the following questions:

1. If you were editing a college newspaper and asked to print some potentially offensive editorial cartoons that could be considered as discriminatory or hateful, would you? What if they were a significant story such as the ones published in *Jyllands-Posten*?
2. If you were a college administrator and a major contributor to the college threatened to withdraw significant support for student scholarships unless you cancelled a controversial exhibition, would you? How would you make that decision? What would you tell the students? What would you tell the contributor?
3. What are the conditions under which you would support a ban on an art exhibition? Where is your threshold? In other words, at what point and with what evidence do you make a decision?

The conversation developed in Box 2.1 explores some of these issues. Steve makes the argument that the decision to ban a play or any form of speech should meet a very high threshold that demonstrates an immediate threat. For Steve, especially as a student, controversial and potentially disturbing messages are an important part of education. Juli takes a different point of view. Although she recognizes the need for controversial expression, her perspective is that it should be balanced against the interests of multiple audiences and constituents. In both cases, the advocates build their arguments on a broad base of evidence and use a variety of reasons to support their claims.

If you look at their arguments as simply a collection of parts and if you try only to identify each of the claims, reasons, and pieces of evidence that compose the total series of arguments, it would be easy to miss how the complete arguments are structured or the connections among the smaller, individual arguments. And, you would miss how the argument might affect an audience. When we seek to persuade people by advocating for a position, we make use of individual arguments that, when combined, make an overall persuasive case intended to affect the recipients.

A co-orientational approach to argument presumes that the relationship between arguer and recipient is as important as the content of the argument. Arguments may be strong and well substantiated, but if the hearer does not trust the arguer or suspects that the arguments are poorly constructed, then even the best arguments will fail. This chapter explores traditional perspectives of argumentation, examines arguer-based approaches toward the construction of arguments, and, finally, turns to a co-orientational approach toward the design of arguments.

PERSPECTIVES

Argumentation is a complex process with many dimensions and for centuries scholars have differed on how it should be described and explained. Some hold the view that arguers have an obligation to determine the truth through the use of true premises (evidence) and sound reasoning.[6] Others, however, argue that the "truth" frequently cannot be decisively determined and that argumentation should be studied as a means of influence in the social and political marketplace.[7] Still others, noting the tension between rational and non-rational factors of influence, have concluded that "a central focus of argumentation is on discovering and applying the general standards for determining what is true or reasonable."[8]

Joseph W. Wenzel summarized the various perspectives on argument and concluded that they could be put into three categories—logical, dialectical, and rhetorical.[9] These are not three different kinds of arguments; rather, they are three different ways of looking at argumentation. The logical perspective asks, "Is the argument sound?" The dialectical perspective asks, "Has the discussion been handled so as to achieve a candid and critical examination of all aspects of the issue in question?" And, the rhetorical perspective asks, "Has the arguer constructed the argument so as to successfully influence a particular audience?"

Figure 2.1, "Argument Perspectives," illustrates how perspectives influence interpretations and points of view. Each perspective emphasizes a different set of functions and features of argumentation, which, in turn, may lead to different conclusions. All three perspectives are useful because they help us understand different point of view about a subject. The significance

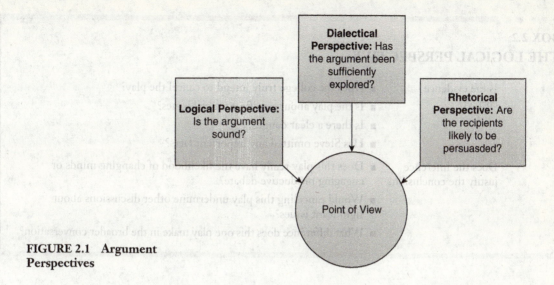

FIGURE 2.1   Argument Perspectives

of any one perspective at any time depends on the arguer's purpose and the situation in which the argument is made. Perspectives might best be understood if we examine the argument developed in Box 2.1 at the beginning of the chapter from each of the three perspectives.

In the discussion, Steve presents the following evidence to ground his arguments: (1) The college is considering a ban on speech and (2) the Laramie Project is about significant social issues. He then makes the inference that because censorship inhibits free thought, it should only be tolerated if a significant and immediate harm can be proven. And, as he points out, censorship is almost always bad and especially in this case because the college had not proved any imminent harm.

Logical Perspective

If we use a logical approach with this example, we will view it as a set of statements made up of premises and a claim or conclusion. *The logical perspective emphasizes the accuracy of the premises and the correctness of the inferences linking premises and evidence to the claims they support.* An argument favorably evaluated from the logical perspective will be based on correct evidence and will use reasoning that is sound according to the standards of logic. Box 2.2, "The Logical Perspective," illustrates how we can analyze the argument using this perspective.

The logical perspective views argumentation as a collection of arguments addressed to an audience of rational individuals well informed on the topic of the dispute.[10] It removes arguments from their situational contexts and considers them primarily as statements connected by logical inferences. The inferences are identified, classified, analyzed, and critiqued by comparing their structure and adequacy with prescriptions from logical theory. Using the logical perspective, the question is whether or not Steve identified strong evidence and then reasoned effectively to draw his conclusions. If he did, then the argument is sound. Advocacy from a logical perspective, then, focuses on how well the argument is grounded in truth and reasoned in a rational manner.

■ ■ ■ ■ ■

BOX 2.2
THE LOGICAL PERSPECTIVE

Is the evidence correct?	■ Does the college truly intend to cancel the play? ■ Is the play about significant social issues? ■ Is there a clear danger? ■ Has Steve omitted any important facts?
Does the inference justify the conclusion?	■ Does this play really have the likelihood of changing minds or engaging productive debate? ■ Would canceling this play undermine other discussions about significant issues? ■ What difference does this one play make in the broader conversation?

Dialectical Perspective

Viewing the example from the dialectical perspective leads us to consider this argument as one move in an ongoing process of inquiry about censorship, the arts, and the importance of free speech. By refraining from deciding on a position or course of action until all aspects of the question have been thoroughly explored, a dialectical approach to argumentation searches for significant issues, identifies alternatives, generates standards or criteria for selection, and uses them to test proposals. *The dialectical perspective focuses on and enhances a candid, critical, and comprehensive examination of all positions relevant to the topic.* It makes a concerted effort to discover what is true by seeking out as many points of view as possible.

In the *Laramie Project* controversy, Steve articulated the free speech position on the issue. Juli took a more moderate approach and argued that there are cases where a university might have reasonable cause to restrict speech. A dialectical perspective would also seek out viewpoints from university administrators, campus police, and people opposed to the message in the plays—among many other potential voices. Box 2.3, "The Dialectical Perspective," considers the kinds of questions this perspective raises. The dialectical perspective developed here follows a pattern of inquiry very similar to the cycle of critical thought developed in Chapter 1.

Argumentation viewed from a dialectical perspective focuses primarily on the process of reaching the best, most true conclusion. The assumption is that the best conclusion will be accepted if all relevant points of view and issues have been carefully considered and discussed. Advocacy, from this perspective, focuses on the discovery of as many issues as possible related to the subject.

Rhetorical Perspective

Viewing the example from a rhetorical perspective means that we see it as addressed to an audience in a particular social and political context. In other words, this perspective considers the relevant argument spheres and fields. In the *rhetorical perspective, arguments*

■ ■ ■ ■ ■

BOX 2.3

THE DIALECTICAL PERSPECTIVE

How do we assess the issues?	■ What are the immediate concerns?
	■ Have threats been made?
	■ Has a decision been made? If not, how much time before a decision will be made?
	■ What message does this play send about the university? Its arts programs?
What are the primary issues and assumptions?	■ What are the worst-case fears people have about the play? What are those grounded in?
	■ What has been the experience at other venues for the play?
	■ Why does limiting expression in this case affect free-speech overall?
	■ Does this play undermine or support the university's mission and identity?
What are the most important considerations?	■ What are the most central and core issues involved in this discussion?
	■ Does free speech outweigh public safety?
	■ Will the free exchange of ideas be affected by this case?

are viewed as appeals to an audience, and we must take account of the circumstances in which the argument was made and the strategies used to influence its audience. Box 2.4, "The Rhetorical Perspective," considers how the argument between Steve and Juli might be understood using the rhetorical perspective.

■ ■ ■ ■ ■

BOX 2.4

THE RHETORICAL PERSPECTIVE

How do we understand the arguments?	■ Will the recipients see Steve and Juli as trustworthy? Knowledgeable?
	■ Who will they most likely believe most? Why?
	■ What strategies do Steve and Juli use to sway the recipients to their respective points of view?
	■ How are the arguments structured? How is evidence used?
	■ Are there other arguments that might have been used?
How do we understand the audience?	■ Are Steve and Juli aware of the interests and values of the recipients?
	■ What sphere are the recipients most likely placed in? What field?
	■ Which arguments best "fit" the sphere and field?
	■ Do any arguments violate field rules or guidelines?

The rhetorical perspective on argument is important because of its emphasis on arguments as forms of communication. By taking account of the circumstances in which the argument was produced (sphere and field), the arguer's intent, and the beliefs and values of those to whom arguments are addressed, the rhetorical perspective enables one to interpret and evaluate the content of the arguments themselves. Advocacy from this perspective focuses on how well the arguer is able to address the recipient's needs and interests in a way that persuades them to accept the arguments.

HOW PERSPECTIVES ARE USED

Understanding that any argument can be viewed from any of these three perspectives is important. Each perspective has a different emphasis and serves a different purpose. The logical perspective focuses on the structure of an argument and on its logical soundness when removed from a context. (This is the perspective of many courses in formal and informal logic.) The dialectical perspective uses the process of argumentation as a means to contribute to thorough, reasoned, and careful deliberation about an issue. The rhetorical perspective emphasizes the argument's effectiveness in persuading its audience. Box 2.5, "Apply the Theory," works to develop how each of these perspectives affects our understanding of arguments.

BOX 2.5

APPLY THE THEORY: PERSPECTIVES

Using the three perspectives, analyze Juli's and Steve's arguments. Can you identify how perspectives affect how the argument might be viewed? Assume that Juli and Steve present their arguments in two different public forums. The first is in front of the student body at their school. The second is to the school's board of trustees.

1. Using the logical perspective.
   a. Identify Steve's best argument and Juli's best argument.
   b. Are these arguments true and valid? Would both sets of recipients agree with this?
   c. Based on this perspective, which advocate did the better job?
2. Using the dialectical perspective.
   a. Did the arguers explore the topic sufficiently? Did they identify issues you would have addressed?
   b. Are there issues that the groups of recipients would have wanted to be discussed?
   c. Following their exchange, do you think recipients would leave thinking they had a good, dialectical exchange?
3. Using the rhetorical perspective.
   a. Did the arguers present arguments that were likely to persuade their recipients? How would these arguments affect the two different groups?
   b. What arguments are mostly likely to be persuasive? Why?

Understanding argument perspectives is important because at different times the use of one perspective makes more sense than use of another. For instance, in Chapter 6 when we discuss reasoning, we focus on the logical perspective. In Chapters 7, 8, and 9 when we discuss the construction and refutation of argumentative cases, we emphasize the dialectical perspective and its usefulness in discovering vital questions on a given topic. In Chapter 10 we are particularly concerned with the kinds of questions raised by a rhetorical perspective, which is concerned with the arguer's relationship to other parties and how arguments can be persuasive.

ARGUER-BASED ARGUMENTS

Much of the study of argument has centered on the use of arguer-based models that emphasize the logical or dialectical perspectives. These approaches consider how advocates develop and produce arguments and they focus on finding and presenting sound evidence and strong reasoning. The assumption behind an arguer-based approach is that careful research, strong argument construction, and skillful presentation should sway an audience to accept the claims presented. This also means that arguments can be understood, analyzed, and refuted independent of their context and their audiences.

The arguer-based approach has its roots in the field of formal logic. During the first half of the twentieth century, most students studied logic in a philosophy course, where they concentrated on the forms and application of formal and symbolic logic.[11] Logic in these courses was considered to be a formal science, a type of theoretical study free from any immediate practical application. Such study reduced arguments to their basic elements and expressed the relationship among the parts in a standardized form for the purposes of comparison and analysis. There are times when using an arguer-based approach is appropriate. In fact, Chapters 7 and 8 are designed around how arguments are constructed and linked together. The problem with this approach, however, arises when arguers use it and ignore the relationship between arguer and recipient.

Formal Logic

Formal logic is defined by its form—that is the root of the word "formal." And, although many ancient civilizations such as Babylon, China, and India employed elaborate systems of reasoning and logic, the most sophisticated and enduring understanding of logic is generally recognized as coming from ancient Greece and the work of theorists such as Aristotle.[12] In formal logic, arguments are reduced to their basic elements and expressed in standardized forms for purposes of building, comparing, and analyzing arguments and advocacy.[13] *Formal logic is the study of how conclusions are reached using structured statements.* The structured statements are the premises or grounds for arguments that—provided they are true and valid—lead recipients to a conclusion. Generally, when we speak of formal logic and the use of structured, formal statements, we are talking about the syllogism. Syllogisms work deductively from broadly stated premises to specific conclusions. *Deductive reasoning is the process of moving from general statements to specific conclusions.*

Over many centuries, theorists and philosophers have used and modified the theories and study of formal logic. In the seventeenth century, for instance, Sir Francis Bacon argued that the Aristotelian view of the syllogism was fallible and illogical and he offered alternatives that stressed inductive forms of reasoning.[14] *Inductive reasoning is a process of moving from particular examples, observations, or instances to general conclusions.* By the nineteenth century, logicians had begun to modify the syllogism further to include new types such as hypothetical and disjunctive forms that will be discussed shortly.

A complete discussion of the reasoning forms of formal logic would be quite lengthy and beyond the purpose or scope of this book. However, extensive explanations of this topic are available in other sources for those interested in studying the applications of syllogistic reasoning in everyday argument.[15] This discussion is intended as an introduction to formal logic, which can provide a useful theoretic background to informal logic that will be developed in Chapter 6.

Syllogism

Aristotle's model of the syllogism is the original foundational unit of logic study. He focused on deductive reasoning using a categorical form that will be discussed shortly. Generally, a *syllogism is made up of three statements, includes three terms associated in pairs with each other through the statements, and draws a conclusion from a major and minor premise.* Syllogisms can be portrayed with a simple, mathematic elegance as illustrated in Figure 2.2, "Syllogisms."

In this illustration, there are three statements (major premise, minor premise, and conclusion) and three terms (A—middle term, B—major term, and C—minor term). The major term, B, is the predicate term for the conclusion. The middle term, A, occurs in both premises but not in the conclusion. The minor term, C, functions as the subject of the conclusion. Notice how each term is used exactly twice and, provided that the premises are true and valid, the conclusion is also true and valid. Box 2.6, "Truth and Validity," discusses this concept.

Major Premise

• A (middle term) = B (major term)

Minor Premise

• C (minor term) = A (middle term)

Conclusion

• Therefore, C (minor term) = B (major term)

FIGURE 2.2   Syllogisms

■ ■ ■ ■ ■

BOX 2.6

TRUTH AND VALIDITY

The terms truth and validity are important when trying to understand arguments. When we discuss refutation in Chapter 9, one of the strategies we will talk about has to do with whether the evidence (premises for arguments) is true. *Truth represents the degree to which the premises for an argument align with verifiable facts and reality.* If we are using a logical perspective, the premises should be externally verifiable. However, a rhetorical perspective would allow for perceptions held by the recipients to be considered "truths."

Similarly, "validity" has to do with how well the premises connect the evidence to the conclusion. In other words, *validity is the degree to which the evidence supports the claim.* If an arguer presents evidence but then fails to clearly and coherently connect the evidence to the claim, the argument is invalid.

Essentially, Aristotelian syllogisms work by means of classification or categorization. For instance, consider the examples of whales developed in Figure 2.3, "Understanding Syllogisms." Notice how three terms (mammal, warm-blooded being, and whale) occur twice in each statement and are used only two times each in the argument. If the statements made in the major and minor premises are true and if the form of the syllogism is correct, the conclusion necessarily follows. The categories in this example were "mammals" and "warm-blooded." If it is true that all mammals are warm-blooded and that all whales are mammals, then it always follows that every whale is warm-blooded. One could not reach the conclusion "Therefore, all whales are fish" given the terms and premises. That would be invalid. By identifying the "middle term"—mammal—with the other two terms, one can reliably connect the remaining terms together in a necessary relationship.

Major Premise

• A (middle term) = B (major term)
• All mammals (middle term) are warm-blooded beings (major term)

Minor Premise

• C (minor term) = A (middle term)
• Whales (minor term) are mammals (middle term)

Conclusion

• Therefore, C (minor term) = B (major term)
• Therefore, whales (minor term) are warm-blooded beings (major term)

FIGURE 2.3   Understanding Syllogisms

Syllogisms		
Categorical	Disjunctive	Hypothetical
• All A are B	• Either A or B	• If A then B
• C is an A	• Not B	• A will not happen
• Therefore, C is a B	• Therefore, A	• Therefore, B will happen

FIGURE 2.4   Types of Syllogisms

Although this example is straightforward—all whales are warm-blooded—it depends on the certainty of the premises. If the premises were only probably true or if there is doubt whether they are always true, the conclusion, too, would be probable. Consider the following:

Major Premise:	Disney mostly makes great movies.
Minor Premise:	Disney made *John Carter*.
Conclusion:	Therefore, *John Carter* is a great movie.

While the "greatness" of *John Carter* may be debatable (given it is considered to be one of the worst box office flops of all time), because there are exceptions to the major premise—Disney makes *mostly* great movies—the conclusion is also only probably true.

Because most premises have exceptions or are only probably true, the conclusions are also only probably true. Generally, there are three forms of the syllogism that are used by arguers seeking to draw probable although not necessary conclusions from premises. The three forms are categorical, disjunctive, and hypothetical. Figure 2.4, "Types of Syllogisms," provides a comparison.

Categorical Syllogism

The first type of syllogism providing a form of argument that can be used in practical reasoning is the categorical syllogism. *The categorical syllogism is a logical argument that draws a necessary conclusion from two premises stated as simple propositions containing categorical terms that designate classes.* The categorical syllogism works from a principle of classification, that is, by putting objects or people into groups and assigning characteristics to them, a conclusion can be drawn. Here are some examples of categorical syllogisms:

Major Premise:	All tests are biased (category = tests).
Minor Premise:	The SAT is a test (SAT = member of category).
Conclusion:	Therefore, the SAT is biased.
Major Premise:	No gravesites should be robbed (category = gravesites)
Minor Premise:	The *Titanic* is a gravesite (Titanic = member of category)
Conclusion:	Therefore, the *Titanic* should not be robbed.

For arguments of this type to be sound, two conditions must be met. First, the initial statement must be true. That is, the predicate of the statement must apply to all the persons or things named in the subject. Second, the instance named in the second or minor premise must fall within the class with which it is associated. As long as the categories are true and accurately described—that the SAT is really a test and that the *Titanic* is really a gravesite—then the conclusion is also likely to be true.

Disjunctive Syllogism

A second form of syllogism that provides a basis for argument is the disjunctive syllogism. Unlike the categorical syllogism in which we make a judgment about something based on its membership or inclusion in a class, a disjunctive syllogism uses a process of exclusion or elimination. *Disjunctive syllogisms set forth two or more alternatives in the major premise, deny all but one in the minor premise, and affirm the only remaining alternative in the conclusion.* We can state this form of reasoning symbolically as follows:

Major Premise:	Either A or B.
Minor Premise:	Not A.
Conclusion:	Therefore, B.

For example:

Major Premise:	Dr. Burnett said I would receive either an "A" or a "B" for the semester depending on how well I did on the final.
Minor Premise:	I failed the final.
Conclusion:	Therefore, I will receive a "B."
Major Premise:	Next year I will study away in either China or Australia.
Minor Premise:	I don't think I should study in China because I don't speak the language.
Conclusion:	Therefore, I will study in Australia.

Disjunctive syllogisms present two or more alternatives. One by one, each alternative is eliminated until the option that remains is selected in the conclusion. For this type of argument to be sound, two conditions must be met. First, all possible alternatives must be identified. If they are not, an unnoticed alternative that is not considered may turn out to be the best. During gasoline shortages in the late 1970s, many people claimed that we must either ration gas or entirely deplete our oil reserves. As it turned out, the increased price of oil led to many energy-saving measures that made rationing unnecessary. In the first part of the twenty-first century, people were again faced with the question—drill for oil in environmentally sensitive areas or face economic collapse. But these arguments fall short because they do not consider other energy resources, conservation, or new alternatives.

Second, any proposed choices must be separate and distinct. Otherwise, they cannot be eliminated one by one. For example, suppose we assume that we could go to either the mountains or the seashore on vacation and that we made a choice based on that belief. In some areas of the country, however, mountains and seashore are within a day's drive of each other, and both can be included in a single vacation, so use of disjunctive reasoning to choose between them might lead to a poor conclusion.

Hypothetical Syllogism

A third type of syllogism is known as the hypothetical syllogism. *Hypothetical syllogisms are arguments that do not involve a direct comparison; rather they contain a conditional major premise that is either affirmed or denied in the minor premise. The conclusion is what remains.* They take this form:

Major Premise:	If A then B.
Minor Premise:	A will occur.
Conclusion:	Therefore, B will happen.

An example of a hypothetical syllogism, then, looks like this:

Major Premise:	If I oversleep, I will be late for work.
Minor Premise:	I overslept.
Conclusion:	Therefore, I will be late for work.
Major Premise:	If college tuition continues to rise, fewer students will be able to attend college.
Minor Premise:	Tuition is continuing to rise.
Conclusion:	Fewer students will be able to attend college.

Typically, we use this kind of argument to express causality or predict what might happen in the future. For instance:

Major Premise:	If I smoke, I will suffer negative health consequences.
Minor Premise:	I choose to smoke.
Conclusion:	Therefore, I will suffer from negative health consequences.

As with other forms of syllogisms, the hypothetical syllogism is only as strong as its premises.

Enthymeme

Syllogisms are a relatively neat mathematical structure. While they are used for analyzing and criticizing arguments, everyday discourse does not often conform to their rigid structure—most arguers are less precise and they tend to omit a premise or even the conclusion because they assume the recipients already know them. This means that the argument form is probably not as obvious or clear as in a formal syllogism.

These types of arguments are called enthymemes, and they depend on the recipients' ability to supply the missing statement. In his *Rhetoric*, Aristotle described a *rhetorical* form of the syllogism to be used in speeches and public discourse.[16] *An enthymeme is a rhetorical syllogism that calls upon the audience's existing beliefs for one or both of its premises.* Aristotle said that in most forms of public speaking, one would not want explicitly to state all of one's premises, for that would belabor the point and bore the audience. To see how an enthymeme works, consider the following example:

Mario is an Italian, so he is probably Roman Catholic.

Sacramento State is a public university so tuition is probably inexpensive.

■ ■ ■ ■ ■

BOX 2.7

APPLY THE THEORY: CREATING SYLLOGISMS

Using the case study presented at the beginning of the chapter, write one of each type of syllogism.

	CATEGORICAL	DISJUNCTIVE	HYPOTHETICAL
Major Premise			
Minor Premise			
Conclusion			

In each of your syllogisms, circle the "middle term" and ensure it appears only twice in two different premises. Then underline the "major term" and check that it occurs only twice and in a premise and the conclusion. Finally, underline the "minor term" and see if it occurs only twice in the minor premise and conclusion. When you have finished, convert each of your examples to an enthymeme.

In the first example, the major premise, "Most Italians are Roman Catholic," is implied because the arguer believes that most recipients already know and accept this as a fact. Similarly, the second example implies the major premise that "Public universities have low tuition costs." Box 2.7, "Apply the Theory," explores how syllogisms are developed and presented.

Toulmin Model

Formal logic dominated the study of argumentation for centuries. It treated reasoning forms as if they had the consistency and rigor of mathematical equations, and as if the relationship between terms and premises was as simple and unequivocal as in algebra and geometry. However, it should be apparent from the preceding discussion that human beings do not argue, reason, or communicate with such precision—and even if they did, people might disagree with conclusions even if, logically, they should be accepted. Emotion, deeply held beliefs, and personal assumptions, values and needs can all play significant roles in how arguments are understood and accepted.

Formal logic and the syllogism are not adequate for studying and learning the forms of reasoning employed by people in daily arguments using imprecise language and evidence. Although formal logic can help us critically understand how a particular argument functions, it is not very useful for studying and learning the forms of practical argument.

In the 1950s and 1960s, a number of scholars in philosophy and other fields began to criticize formal logic and to propose alternatives for the study of argument. For example, Stephen Toulmin, in his book *The Uses of Argument*, criticized formal logic for its rigid structure and inadequate description of how people actually argue.[17] He noted that everyday arguments could never be held to be as universally valid as the reasoning forms in a syllogism.

Because formal logical relations depend on the use of symbols ("A," "B," and "C"), they strip arguments of their everyday meanings, ambiguities, and equivocations. Therefore, they could mislead students by assuming that the use of terms is always clear and never varies. Toulmin also said that statements in "real" arguments have more functions than three (major premise, minor premise, conclusion), and he presented a model of argument to show some of these other functions. As Toulmin observed, substantive everyday claims are usually viewed as *probably* true rather than as *certainly* and *always* true, as implied by formal logic.

Toulmin wrote that an argument is like an organism.[18] Its individual parts each have a different function in relation to the claim. If an argument "works" (i.e., is acceptable to the recipients in the audience), it is because all its parts perform their functions and work together to form an organic whole. Toulmin's model of argument identifies how each statement in an argument functions in relation to the claim and does justice to all the things an argument ought to do in order to be cogent. If important parts of the argument are implied or omitted, the Toulmin Model directs an arguer or critic to determine what they are and to supply them.

Parts of the Model

Toulmin's model contains six parts that are defined primarily by their function in an argument. These six parts are shown in Figure 2.5, "Toulmin's Model of Argument."

Each of these parts can be described as follows:

1. *Data.* The term *data* is synonymous with the term evidence as defined in Chapter 1 as *facts or conditions that are objectively observable beliefs or premises accepted as true by the audience, or conclusions previously established.*

2. *Claim.* Toulmin's concept of claim is the same as defined in Chapter 1. Claims consist of the expressed opinion or conclusion that the arguer wants accepted.

3. *Warrant. The warrant expresses the reasoning used to link the data to the claim.* According to Toulmin, if the data answer the question, "What information do you have to go on to reach your conclusions?" then the warrant answers the question, "How did you get there from that data?"[19] Warrants may take the form of rules, principles, or conventions. They may also be explicit statements of reasoning such as will be discussed in Chapter 6. It is important to remember that the warrant expresses the reasoning that enables us to connect the data to the claim.

FIGURE 2.5 Toulmin's Model of Argument

4. *Backing. The backing consists of further facts or reasoning used to support or legitimate the principle contained in the warrant.* Backing often consists of accepted principles or facts arising from the field in which the argument takes place. For example, the field of medicine universally accepts the principle that treatment regimens should be based on what has proved effective in prior clinical practice. Backing supports the warrant in very much the same way that data support the claim.

5. *Qualifier. The qualifier is a colloquial adverb or adverbial phrase that modifies the claim and indicates the rational strength the arguer attributes to it.*[20] In other words, how certain is the arguer of the claim? When arguers make claims, they attribute greater or lesser degrees of strength to them. Some warrants authorize an unequivocal acceptance of the claim, whereas others may have much weaker force. The person making the diagnosis on the head wound in the following example recommends a certain treatment "strongly." Other qualifiers frequently used to modify claims are "probably," "certainly," and "possibly." When they occur in arguments, qualifiers fulfill an important function because they indicate the degree of certainty that arguers feel regarding their claims.

6. *Reservation.* Sometimes there are expectations of limitations that invalidate or diminish the application of the warrant. Toulmin includes these in his model as the reservation. *The reservation states the circumstances or conditions that undermine the argument.* It is the exception to the rule expressed in the warrant. In the example below, the arguer says that penicillin is recommended unless the patient is allergic to it. An allergic reaction, then, is a condition that would invalidate the recommendation to administer antibiotics. In the Toulmin Model, the qualifier and reservation are linked because, to the extent that circumstances or conditions restricting the claim exist, the strength of the claim is limited.

Toulmin recommended that the six parts of the model should be set out to show their interrelationships. Beyond the minimum three parts (claim, warrant, data) of the model, when the additional three parts are added to the diagram, we can see more clearly how they function in the argument. The backing undergirds or supports the warrant. The qualifier modifies the claim by showing the strength the arguer attributes to it. And the qualifier is related to any reservations that express exceptions to the claim by stating conditions that undermine the force of the argument.

Using the Model

Of these six parts, three are the most important: claim, data, and warrant. As with the enthymeme, an arguer may omit parts that recipients are likely to supply. However, when we diagram and analyze arguments, minimally the three of these parts must be expressed. Consider the following example:

Twelve hours ago, the patient fell from a motorcycle and had a severe blow to the head accompanied by a deep scalp wound. He is pale, dizzy, and lethargic and has a low fever. The treatment strongly recommended includes flushing and stitching up the wound, administering antibiotics, and bed rest. Clinical experience has shown that without such treatment, infection will set in within approximately 48 hours. Penicillin is most effective unless the patient is allergic to it.

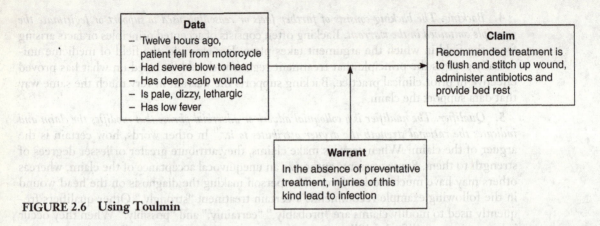

Data
- Twelve hours ago, patient fell from motorcycle
- Had severe blow to head
- Has deep scalp wound
- Is pale, dizzy, lethargic
- Has low fever

Claim
Recommended treatment is to flush and stitch up wound, administer antibiotics and provide bed rest

Warrant
In the absence of preventative treatment, injuries of this kind lead to infection

FIGURE 2.6   Using Toulmin

What functions as data or evidence in this argument? Clearly, the circumstances of the accident and that patient's symptoms are readily knowable or observable facts. The claim—the conclusion or end point of the argument—is the specific recommended treatment. The warrant, or reasoning connection linking the data to the claim, is a causal prediction about what will happen to the patient if measures to prevent infection are not used. This prediction is based on a background and understanding of medicine and is based on prior experience with patients in similar conditions and circumstances.

The Toulmin Model is set out in a spatial pattern that is intended to show how the statements in the argument are linked to each other—what supports what and what leads to what. This arrangement indicates that the data lead to the claim and that the step made from one to the other is supported by the warrant. The data, warrant, and claim of the specific argument we've been considering would therefore be diagrammed as in Figure 2.6, "Using Toulmin."

The figure shows how the Toulmin Model is useful in identifying each statement's function in the argument. It indicates that the data serve as the argument's grounds and starting point; the claim as its end point; and the warrant as its rational support. This illustration focuses on the three primary parts of the Toulmin Model that are required minimums.

Applying all six parts of the model to the example we have just discussed yields the diagram in Figure 2.7, "Toulmin Model Using Six Parts." The elegance and usefulness of the model become clear when we see how the functions of the various statements in the arguments are revealed through the model. As we have observed, the diagram reveals that the existence of previous clinical experience backs up the prediction made in the warrant. Furthermore, we can see that penicillin is recommended "strongly" but not "absolutely." The recommendation is tempered by the reservation "unless the patient is allergic to penicillin" and is thus functionally connected to the qualifier because it limits its strength.

This argument from the field of medicine was relatively straightforward and easily comprehended. To test the capacity and usefulness of the Toulmin Model, let us consider this more complex argument from the field of law:

FIGURE 2.7   Toulmin Model Using Six Parts

On the thirteenth day of August, 1880, George R. Falls made his last will and testament in which he gave small legacies to his two daughters, Mrs. Smith and Mrs. Phillips, the plaintiffs in this case, and the remainder to his grandson, John E. Falls. The testator, at the date of his will, owned a farm and considerable personal property. He was a widower and thereafter, in June 1902, he was married to Mrs. Jones. At the date of the will, and subsequently to the death of the testator, his grandson lived with him as a member of his family.

At the time of his grandfather's death, John was 16 years old. John knew of the provisions made in his favor in the will. To prevent his grandfather from revoking such provisions, which his grandfather had manifested some intention to do, and to obtain speedy possession of his grandfather's property, John murdered his grandfather by poisoning him. John now claims the property, and the sole question for our determination is, can he have it?

It is quite true that statutes regulating the making, proof, and effect of wills and the devolution of property, if literally construed, and if their force and effect can in no way and no circumstances be controlled or modified, give this property to the murderer. It was the intention of the lawmakers that the donees in a will should have the property given to them. But it never could have been their intention that a donee who murdered the testator to make the will operative should have any benefit under it. It is a familiar canon of construction that a thing which is within the intention of the makers of a statute is as much within the statute as if it were within the letter; and a thing which is within the letter of the statute is not within the statute unless it be within the intention of the makers.[21]

FIGURE 2.8 Implied Claim

The judge stated the *data* in this argument before he stated his decision. Briefly, they include the following: The deceased left small legacies to two daughters and the remainder of his estate to his grandson; he remarried; he was considering changing his will; his grandson poisoned him; the grandson now claims the estate. The *claim*, or end point, of this argument, does not seem to be explicitly stated but clearly would take the form of the judge's decision in the case. Because the entire passage justifies denial of the property to the donee, we can safely assume that the implied claim is "The donee in this case shall not have the property that has been willed to him." In the Toulmin Model, if the claim is not explicitly stated, it is represented with dashed lines around the claim, as in Figure 2.8, "Implied Claim."

In seeking out the warrant linking the data and claim in this argument, we must discover the reasoning that would link the data and the claim together. In this particular argument, the warrant is explicitly stated in the judge's opinion: "It never could have been [the lawmakers'] intention that a donee who murdered a testator to make the will operative should have any benefit under it." The judge believes this to be a statement of principle inherent in the American legal tradition, and, if there is a precedent for it, he can thereby justify his decision that the property will be denied to the murderer. It is important to note that this warrant arises from the principle that legal statutes should be applied in ways congruent with the intentions of the lawmakers who proposed and approved them.

Only one remaining part of the Toulmin Model is expressly stated in this argument. It is the *backing*; the principle that undergirds the warrant is expressly stated in the decision ("A thing which is within the letter of the statute is not within the statute unless it be within the intention of the makers"). The judge alludes to this as a "familiar canon of construction," which would be common knowledge among legal professionals. Because of its status as knowledge, this statement can function as support for the warrant. The finished diagram—which contains four of the Toulmin Model's six parts—is shown in Figure 2.9, "Adding Warrant and Backing."

The Toulmin Model is a powerful tool that offers a method for analyzing and criticizing arguments. Analysts can examine passages for each component of an argument, assess their strength, and offer a critique of what worked, what did not work, and what might have been improved in a given argument. Box 2.8, "Apply the Theory," works through this process.

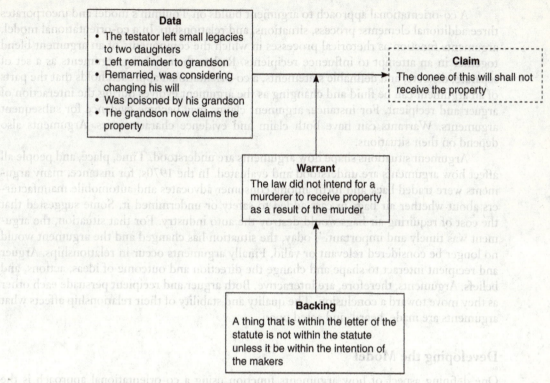

Data
• The testator left small legacies to two daughters
• Left remainder to grandson
• Remarried, was considering changing his will
• Was poisoned by his grandson
• The grandson now claims the property

Claim
The donee of this will shall not receive the property

Warrant
The law did not intend for a murderer to receive property as a result of the murder

Backing
A thing that is within the letter of the statute is not within the statute unless it be within the intention of the makers

FIGURE 2.9   Adding Warrant and Backing

BOX 2.8
APPLY THE THEORY: WORKING WITH THE TOULMIN MODEL

Analyze either Juli's or Steve's arguments developed in Box 2.1, using the Toulmin Model:

1. Identify the claims, warrants, and data.
2. Can you find examples of backing, qualifiers, or reservations?
3. Draw the finished diagram using Figure 2.7 as a template.
4. Does your finished diagram show any strengths or weaknesses?

A CO-ORIENTATIONAL APPROACH

As useful as the Toulmin Model is, it has two important limitations. First, it focuses on a static view of argument. It considers that each part of the argument—claim, warrant, data, backing, reservation, and qualifier—can be expressed in a statement with a defined function. And, second, it focuses on the producer of the argument more than on the recipient.

A co-orientational approach to argument builds on Toulmin's model and incorporates three additional elements: process, situations, and relationship. In a co-orientational model, arguments function as rhetorical processes in which the components of an argument blend together in an attempt to influence recipients. Rather than viewing arguments as a set of separate, discrete, and definable statements, a co-orientational approach holds that the parts of an argument can be fluid and changing as the argument evolves during the interaction of arguer and recipient. For instance, argument claims may become evidence for subsequent arguments. Warrants can have both claim and evidence characteristics. Arguments also depend on their situations.

Argument situations shape how arguments are understood. Time, place, and people all affect how arguments are understood and evaluated. In the 1970s, for instance, many arguments were traded back and forth among consumer advocates and automobile manufacturers about whether air bags in cars added to safety or undermined it. Some suggested that the cost of requiring air bags would destroy the auto industry. For that situation, the argument was timely and important. Today, the situation has changed and the argument would no longer be considered relevant or valid. Finally arguments occur in relationships. Arguer and recipient interact to shape and change the direction and outcome of ideas, actions, and beliefs. Arguments, therefore, are interactive. Both arguer and recipient persuade each other as they move toward a conclusion. The quality and stability of their relationship affects what arguments are made, heard, and acted upon.

Developing the Model

One defining aspect of how arguments function using a co-orientational approach is the level of agreement that separates an argument's starting point (or premise) from its claims, and whether the amount of agreement between arguer and recipient regarding the claims allows statements to be accepted without further support or evidence.

There is almost universal agreement that free speech is an important, essential element for democratic societies. Without freedom of expression, freedom of thought is compromised, and once that happens, critical thinking and decision-making are significantly undermined or curtailed. Almost all recipients can readily accept this as evidence. But the question of whether a college or the government has the right or responsibility to regulate or limit any form of free speech is much more controversial—some argue that the First Amendment to the U.S. Constitution guarantees the right to say anything or behave in any way a speaker chooses. And, even those who recognize that limits must be placed on free speech are uncertain where to draw the line. Should pornography be banned? When and under what conditions? Should speakers be allowed to use "hate speech" to get their message across? If not, under what conditions should restrictions be made? Should the neo-Nazi party be allowed to parade in Jewish communities and on public streets? Should a newspaper print editorial cartoons that might offend members of a religion? Should a college stage a play that might prompt violent demonstrations? Where are the limits?

These are all difficult questions, and they depend on a complex relationship among the speakers, recipients, community, and cultural standards. Many assumptions that underpin each of these questions are too controversial to be accepted as evidence and are themselves argument claims that need to be proved. The Co-Orientational Model of

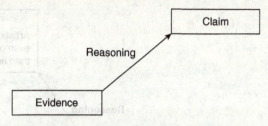

FIGURE 2.10   Co-Orientational Model

argument considers the complex nature of these questions and relationships involved in any given argument context. The connection between evidence and claim is represented in Figure 2.10, "Co-Orientational Model." In this figure, evidence functions to ground the claim, and reasoning is used to connect the two parts of the argument. It is important to note that reasoning in this model is a process and not static. It represents the arguer's attempt to influence recipients by developing connections between evidence and claim.

The discussion in Box 2.1 provides a good illustration of how the Co-Orientational Model works. Both Juli and Steve develop different arguments as they move through a discussion of whether or not it is appropriate to ban a play. Consider, for example, Juli's argument in which she suggested there are occasions when limiting speech or art is justified:

> Our rights to see this play or have a controversial art exhibition are not more important than someone else's rights—even when it comes to free speech. People have threatened to protest this play, and our campus police are worried about violence and vandalism. We have no right to put others at risk, and if a protest turns ugly, that's what could happen. If our freedoms potentially hurt others, they should be limited. Ironically, this play makes that point. We limit hate speech—we don't allow people to say what they want because it may have harmful consequences.
> Artistic work is like any other form of speech; it should have limits if it hurts others. Artistic expression should not be exempted from censorship any more than any other kind of speech.

Figure 2.11, "Using the Co-Orientational Model," shows how Juli moved from her evidence (facts about censorship and free speech) to her claim that there are times when censorship of artistic expression is justified. This diagram provides an easy way to see how the parts of the argument function in relation to each other within a co-orientational framework and how they work together as a whole.

Level of Dispute

Arguments occur where there are disagreements about issues within a topic. If, for instance, everyone agreed that the *Laramie Project* should be banned from campus, there would be no need for Juli's arguments. Arguments occur only when people disagree with one another. This separation—what the arguer and recipient agree to and what are the points of disagreement—describes an imaginary line that separates the statements of belief and value with which recipients agree from those with which they disagree. In other words, for any issue

FIGURE 2.11   Using the Co-Orientational Model

we can think of, there is a line that separates what we are willing to accept from what we are unwilling to accept initially.

For instance, we might discuss the relative strengths and weaknesses of President Franklin D. Roosevelt and his four-term presidency. Even if you were a staunch political conservative and truly believed Roosevelt almost destroyed American freedoms through a strong centralized government, there is some aspect of Roosevelt's presidency you would accept. You might not agree with the arguer who says Roosevelt was the best president, but you would probably accept that he was president. You would also probably accept that he was elected to four terms and that under Roosevelt many government programs for economic reform were passed. Although you might not accept the value of such programs, you would probably agree with the facts of his administration (the Works Progress Administration was established; the United States entered World War II). The point to be made here is that for any issue you can think of, there is a level of agreement about certain facts.

The level of dispute is an imaginary line that separates what is accepted by the recipient from what is not accepted. Arguments that occur below the line are already accepted by the hearers, and those that occur above it are not accepted. The term *line* may be a little misleading here. We are not suggesting that all issues have clearly demarcated lines that all recipients of argument acknowledge. Such a position would fail to recognize that people do not have their minds made up on all issues. Rather, we can think of this line or level of dispute as a "fuzzy" or relatively abstract area in which people neither accept nor reject arguments immediately. Therefore, the level of dispute is the lowest common level of proof that recipients are willing to accept.

Figure 2.12, "Level of Dispute," helps illustrate the role played by the level of dispute. Evidence in this model falls below the level of dispute because if evidence were disputed

FIGURE 2.12
Level of Dispute

and fell above the line, then the evidence itself would need to be proved and anchored to the audience's accepted knowledge. In other words, the evidence would become the subject or claim of an argument. The key is simply that arguments seek to move the audience from positions already accepted or agreed upon to new and different positions. An advocate, then, seeks to use acceptable evidence to reason with recipients to accept a new claim. Similarly, the claim must always fall above the level of dispute. Otherwise, the argument is already accepted and is considered evidence.

The level of dispute exists and is drawn in the minds and perceptions of argument recipients. An arguer's objective is to adapt the evidence, reasoning, and claims to the recipient's understanding of the subject being argued. Although this may appear to be a relatively straightforward task, it can become more complex as the number of listeners increases. Someone with a great deal of experience in one area may have a relatively high level of dispute. Someone with little knowledge of the area will have a relatively low level of dispute. When these two people are in the same audience, the arguer has the difficult task of adapting to the different levels of dispute of the different individuals. Often the result is arguments directed toward the lowest common denominator that everyone in the audience can agree with and understand. Although the lowest-common-denominator approach may appeal to some, it is just as likely to bore the other recipients.

The arguer chooses and adapts the level of dispute to the audience. This is a choice unique for each situation and audience. If arguers receive feedback from the recipients indicating confusion or disagreement, they may decide to raise or lower the level while arguing. For a critic examining the argument, understanding the level of dispute is important because its location implies the type of recipients assumed by the arguer and offers a better understanding of the argument context.

Role of Reasoning

Reasoning connects the evidence and the claim. It serves as both a logical and persuasive bridge between the two ends of an argument. By means of the inferences made, reasoning acts to draw a strong relationship between that which is known and accepted by the recipients and that which is unknown or unaccepted by the recipients. Juli makes the argument that potentially offensive artistic expression could be equated with hate speech or other kinds of messages that can lead to violence or threaten community interests. If it causes vandalism or violence, or if it diminishes the rights of others in the community, artistic expression should be limited. Therefore, because everyone has rights and because no one group has the right to assert its own free-speech interests ahead of others', certain kinds of expression such as a controversial play could be censored.

In the Co-Orientational Model, reasoning is important because it is a process that draws recipients from the known and accepted evidence toward the disputed claim. As a process, reasoning plays the significant role of connecting the arguer with the recipient over a set of issues and ideas. Arguers choose which lines of reasoning best accomplish this task. In this case, Juli's position is one that many recipients might initially reject without much discussion or thought. Most people believe that free speech is important and banning anything—especially art—carries with it a high burden to prove it is harmful. Juli's reasoning, though, provided an approach for Steve to understand her perspective. By comparing staging the *Laramie Project* to other instances where most recipients would accept regulated speech, she offered reasoning that connected the evidence to the claim. This is not to say, however, that Juli is correct or that recipients will unquestioningly accept her argument. But it provides a good illustration of how reasoning works to link the parts of the argument together and raise the level of dispute.

Argument Chains

Once an argument is proved, what happens to the level of dispute? If Steve accepts Juli's claim, what happens next? Logically, if the claim is proved and those to whom it is addressed accept it as a valid conclusion, then the level of dispute rises such that the claim now falls below the line, as illustrated in Figure 2.13, "Proved Claim." This means that an advocate can now use the proved claim as evidence for another argument.

The process of linking proven claims to unproven claims is called chaining, and it is shown in Figure 2.14, "Argument Chain." *An argument chain uses a proved argument as evidence for an unproved claim.* For example, Juli responds to Steve's comments and builds new arguments grounded in her original statements while accounting for Steve's reservations:

> Fair Enough. I think, though, that it is important to remember that censorship can be targeted so that some classes of people are protected—like kids. After all, movies have ratings to allow some people to see them while keeping others out. Censorship can be used to protect kids from excessive sex and violence or having to deal with issues in this play. The issue is that not all content is appropriate for everyone. And, in our community, maybe this play is not a wise choice. That should have been taken into consideration.

FIGURE 2.13
Proved Claim

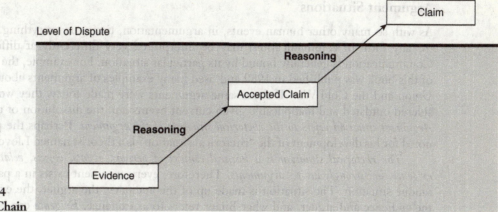

FIGURE 2.14
Argument Chain

In this argument, Juli links her new reasoning and claims to her original statements by adding that censorship could be adapted to particular situations and for specific audiences. That way, she suggests, community standards can be addressed as well as the interests of individual audiences such as children. She modified her argument to address issues raised by Steve and introduced evidence and reasoning to build on her original claim and reach a conclusion that the censorship could be targeted to specific types of expression.

The concept of chained arguments holds many important implications for building *macro arguments*, or extended argumentative cases, which will be developed more fully in Chapters 7, 8, and 9. In an extended case, the arguer's central thesis or claim in a macro argument may lie far above the level of dispute, and many preliminary claims may have to be established before the central claim is adequately supported. If the arguer begins with facts and premises accepted by everyone to whom the argument is addressed and builds arguments one step at a time, the level of dispute can be raised in increments until the central claim is proved. Box 2.9, "Apply the Theory: Diagramming with the Co-Orientational Model," provides an opportunity to use this model.

BOX 2.9

APPLY THE THEORY: DIAGRAMMING WITH THE CO-ORIENTATIONAL MODEL

Take a look at the claims made by Steve in Box 2.1. If his main or primary claim is that "Censorship is always unwarranted," can you:

1. Identify the claims, reasoning, and evidence that help him reach that conclusion.
2. Diagram an argument chain that proves his final claim.
3. Are there any "gaps" in the chain that need to be addressed?

Argument Situations

As with so many other human events, in argumentation, timing is everything. Arguments (or any form of communication) may be interpreted very differently at different times. Communication is generally bound by its particular situation. For example, the first edition of this book was published in 1989 and used many examples of arguments about the Soviet Union and the Cold War. If these same arguments were made today, they would be considered outdated and inapplicable given current events and the dissolution of the U.S.S.R. *Argument situation refers to the rhetorical situation of the argument.* Perhaps the person most noted for his development of the "rhetorical situation" is a theorist named Lloyd F. Bitzer.[22]

The rhetorical situation is a natural context of persons, events, objects, relations, and an exigence that strongly invites arguments. Therefore, every argument exists in a particular and unique situation. The situation is made up of the audience, the arguer, the experiences of the audience and arguer, and what Bitzer refers to as exigence. *Exigence* can be defined as *"an imperfection marked by urgency; it is a defect, an obstacle, something waiting to be done, a thing that is other than it should be."*[23] In other words, arguments are not developed randomly but are instead called into existence by some exigence—there is some cause or reason for us to argue. When Martin Luther King Jr. delivered his "I Have a Dream" speech, he presented it to a particular audience at a particular time. He was responding to decades of discrimination, and he was urging action on a pending comprehensive civil rights bill. His audience comprised more than 250,000 people who had come to Washington, D.C., to protest for civil rights. It was the largest demonstration ever held in the United States to that time, and the situation required a cornerstone address. King's address met the exigence of the situation.

Not all exigencies, however, require such important arguments. Presenting an argument in class to fulfill the requirements of an assignment may address the exigence of the assignment, but it also addresses an exigence in a larger sense. *An exigence is also a contemporary problem or issue that needs to be addressed.* This is why classroom assignments address significant or important issues as opposed to trivial ones. The exigence is like a question waiting for an answer. The point is simply that particular situations call for particular arguments, and speakers who are able to identify and understand the requirements of the rhetorical situation may be able to develop arguments that fit the needs of the argument context.

Over time, argument situations change. Issues that might have been relevant and important at one time in the personal sphere may develop and move into a technical or public sphere. Some arguments drop out of all three spheres over time as arguments are accepted, rejected, or become irrelevant. Box 2.10, "How Situations Change with Time," provides some examples of how time changes the kinds of issues that people discuss. As argument contexts change, the people involved in them change, different participants become engaged in the issues discussed. For instance, in 1981 when Bill Gates claimed, "640K ought to be enough for anybody," his audience was a relatively small group of people in a relatively technical field. As computers and discussions about them entered the public sphere, more people became involved in arguments over the technology.

Generally, argument situations have four characteristics. First, the situation invites arguments. Our arguments are in response to some problem, proposition, or other issue that is important for our recipients. Without a problem or issue that needs to be considered, there is little reason for argument. King's "I Have a Dream" speech was designed in response to a problem of racial inequality. It was adapted to a particular audience at a particular time

■ ■ ■ ■ ■

BOX 2.10

HOW SITUATIONS CHANGE WITH TIME

Timing makes a great deal of difference in when and where arguments are made. Consider the following claims:

- "Computers in the future may weigh no more than 1.5 tons."—*Popular Mechanics*, 1949
- "I think there is a world market for maybe five computers."—Thomas Watson, chair of IBM, 1949
- "There is no reason anyone would want a computer in their home."—Ken Olson, president of Digital Equipment Corporation, 1977
- "Who the hell wants to hear actors talk?"—H. M. Warner, Warner Brothers, 1927
- "Stocks have reached what looks like a permanently high plateau."—Irving Fisher, Professor of Economics, Yale University, 1929
- "Everything that can be invented has been invented."—Charles H. Duell, Commissioner, U.S. Office of Patents, 1899
- "640K ought to be enough for anybody."—Bill Gates, 1981

and place. If the United States were truly integrated—if King's "dream" had already been fulfilled and equal rights were enjoyed by all—there would have been no need for the speech, and it is unlikely that King would have presented it.

Second, arguments must be fitting to the situation. Even though arguers may be able to identify a problem, not just any argument will fit. If King, for instance, had written a speech about the need for more space exploration or better pay for migrant farm workers, the speech would not have fit the situation because the audience and occasion would not have been appropriate for the subject. Similarly, if an advocate makes an argument that is not relevant to the recipients or that does not address the important issues of a dispute, then the argument does not fit.

Third, situations prescribe the criteria for a fitting response. If we agree that a response must fit the situation, the requirements for the fit should be clear: the context for the argument, the issues involved, and that the participants understand the demands of the situation. Those demands—the needs of the situation—represent criteria for evaluating how well an argument fits. This means that if King's speech fit the situation, then the criteria for judging the fit must be identifiable such that King could have understood them and adapted the speech to them. King knew that he was expected to offer a message of hope to those engaged in the struggle for civil rights, acknowledge the sacrifices many had made, call for redress of discrimination against persons of color, and emphasize the importance of nonviolent protest. He did all this so admirably and his speech so fit the occasion that it has come to be regarded as one of the most masterful speeches of the twentieth century.

Fourth, argumentative situations are impermanent. This means that just as situations arise and invite argument, they also dissolve or become unimportant. Just as some questions go unanswered, so do situations. Situations, then, are temporary and, if unanswered, will dissipate and lose their significance. Had King chosen not to speak during the demonstration, his opportunity for argument would have been lost, and "I Have a Dream" might have been nothing more than a manuscript somewhere. Even if he had spoken a day later, the situation would have dissipated as the demonstration broke up and people went home.

Argument Relationships

Because arguments evolve through the interaction among arguers and recipients, the connection or relationship among the participants is important. Every message involves a content (the set of issues being discussed) and a relationship (what is the connection among the participants).[24] Earlier we discussed the content of arguments and examined how all of the pieces are put together to move people toward a claim. This section examines the relationships among argument participants.

Argument relationships are the interdependent connections that exist between arguers and recipients. In other words, we create arguments with people who we believe can affect the outcome or change their own beliefs or behaviors—we do not tend to create arguments for people who cannot shape or enact the claims. Therefore, an attorney will make an argument to a judge because the judge has the power to make a decision. The same arguments would be irrelevant at the attorney's home because the recipients there would have no ability to act on the claim. In Box 2.1, Steve argued that the college should not be allowed to ban the production of the *Laramie Project*. Even though Juli probably cannot change whatever decision the college makes, Steve's arguments may affect her own behavior or beliefs, which, in turn, may affect the way she talks and thinks about issues related to censorship.

Steve's argument is that controversial productions on a college campus should be allowed because of their potential positive influence on discussions and decisions at the college. He and Juli are interdependent with respect to this argument. Their developing conversation and series of arguments affect the other's point of view. If you examine the sequence of arguments, you will notice that Steve begins with a broad statement about censorship that, through his interaction with Juli, becomes more refined and focused. The arguments develop in a way that shapes and focuses the thinking of each arguer.

In any argument, the participants evaluate how to manage the content of the dispute as well as their relationships. If the relationship is very important and the content is less important, an arguer may choose to be less forceful and direct than if the content of the argument was very important. In the discussion between Juli and Steve, for instance, the content was important, but both protected the relationship. Both arguers listened to and incorporated elements of the other's ideas into their own arguments. If their focus was on content over relationship, we would probably not see as much agreement or movement toward a common understanding. Some arguments, while important, focus on enhancing the relationship. For instance, what to have for dinner or what movie to see are arguments in which the relationship is considerably more important than the particular content. Other arguments, particularly those with a fast-approaching deadline or in which the content is so important that there needs to be a decision, may undermine the relationship in favor of specific action. Arguments about safety, security, or life-and-death decisions all carry a significant weight based on their content that may override the relationship.

How arguers treat the connection of relationship and content can be referred to as a style. *An argument style is the orientation arguers choose to use to balance content and relationship needs in an argument situation.* In other words, people make a choice when they argue: Is having the claim accepted more or less important than the relationship with the recipients? Although there is almost infinite variation on this balance, argument styles can generally be classified in five types: competitor, facilitator, escapist, negotiator, and accommodator.[25] These are illustrated in Figure 2.15, "Argument Styles," and are defined as follows:

- *Competitor.* Arguers using this style seek to win over another person or group. *A competing style prizes the content far more than the relationship, and it seeks to demonstrate that a particular set of arguments is superior to alternatives.* This style is often seen in courts of law where one attorney seeks to win by discrediting or undermining the arguments of another attorney. Generally, competing styles view arguments as winning or losing and that the success of one advocate necessarily means a loss by the other.

- *Facilitator. A facilitative style seeks to find ways in which all of the participants to an argument can succeed mutually.* This style values both strong content and strong relationships. When arguers use a facilitative style, they approach argument situations with the belief that other parties have equally important arguments and ideas that need to be discussed and understood. People using this style see argument as an opportunity to explore ideas and develop strong relationships. This approach is used in mediation settings and in problem-solving groups. A facilitative style looks to argumentative outcomes that allow all parties to succeed.

- *Escapist.* Arguers may use this style to withdraw and avoid becoming involved in an argument. *An escapist style is used when neither the content nor the relationship are considered very important because it means that issues needing resolution are ignored or abandoned.* When this style is used, arguers allow the argument situation to pass and the issues to go unaddressed.

- *Negotiator. A negotiating style is used when content goals and relationship goals are both moderately important.* When this approach is used, arguers are willing to compromise both

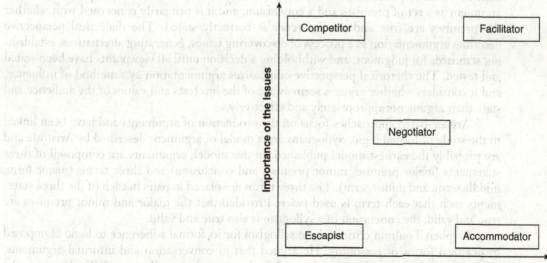

FIGURE 2.15 Argument Styles

content and relationship such that all of the involved parties will give something up but also receive something of value. The goal is to find a middle ground among the positions advocated. Examples of this approach can be found in most negotiation settings, such as in sales or between management and unions about pay and benefits.

■ *Accommodator. Arguers use an accommodating style when the importance of the relationship is much greater than the importance of the content.* In such cases, arguers will tend to back down against other viewpoints in an effort to maintain a strong relationship. When people accommodate, they elect not to be involved in argument but rather strive for harmony in the relationship. Examples can be found in many situations, but often politicians will back down on a particular argument in favor of preserving a strong relationship for a future argument when the relationship may be needed.

Each style discussed here has advantages and disadvantages associated with it. Generally, we hope that argument allows for facilitative or collaborative decision-making in which multiple ideas are examined in a spirit that embraces the importance of argument as a vehicle for developing both understanding and relationship. However, different situations often call for other styles.

SUMMARY

This chapter focused on developing a co-orientational approach to argument. A co-orientational approach presumes a significant relationship between arguer and recipient. Further, the particular context and situation in which arguments occur shape the way people view and understand arguments. We began with a discussion of argument perspectives, examined arguer-based models, and concluded with the development of a co-orientational model for argument.

Argumentation can be viewed from three different but complementary perspectives, each of which emphasizes different aspects of argument. The logical perspective views an argument as a set of premises and a conclusion, and it is primarily concerned with whether the premises are true and the inference is correctly stated. The dialectical perspective describes argumentation as a process of discovering issues, generating alternatives, establishing standards for judgment, and withholding a decision until all viewpoints have been stated and tested. The rhetorical perspective emphasizes argumentation as a method of influence, and it considers whether arguers seem aware of the interests and values of the audience and state their arguments appropriately and effectively.

Arguer-based approaches focus on the production of arguments and have been linked to the study of formal logic. Syllogisms are a model of argument described by Aristotle and are probably the earliest model published. In this model, arguments are composed of three statements (major premise, minor premise, and conclusion) and three terms (major term, middle term, and minor term). The three terms are placed in pairs in each of the three statements such that each term is used twice. Provided that the major and minor premises are true and valid, the conclusion of a syllogism is also true and valid.

Stephen Toulmin criticized the syllogism for its formal adherence to logic as opposed to practical forms of reasoning. He argued that in conversation and informal arguments, syllogisms did not provide a useful model for how people actually argued. Toulmin's model includes three parts that are explicitly or implicitly present in every argument (data, warrant, and claim) and three parts that are included in many arguments (reservation, qualifier, and backing). These parts work together and describe how advocates adapt their arguments to different situations and contexts.

The chapter concluded with the development of a co-orientational approach. Using this approach, arguments are designed with an audience in mind and for a particular situation. In this model, arguments are based on statements accepted by the recipients and for which no further support is needed. Because these statements provoke no disagreement, they fall below the level of dispute. When they are successively used to support new claims, the level of dispute rises, and the formerly contested claim becomes a premise for a new argument. When a proven argument is used as evidence for an unproven claim, the result is an argument chain. The concept of a level of dispute is useful because it illustrates how the extent of the recipient's agreement with the arguer's claims may vary as the argument is being made.

Arguments are produced for particular situations and are judged by their time and place. These situations influence the way arguments are created, understood, and evaluated. Situations are an important part of an argument's development because they shape the relationship among arguers and recipients.

Argument situations change over time. Arguments that would have been appropriate for a given audience at a given time may not be appropriate years later or even days later. Arguments change as people, issues, and knowledge about the world change. Argument situations refer to the rhetorical situation of the argument. Bitzer contended that a rhetorical situation arises from the context of person, events, objects, relations, and exigence, which together call for an argument to be produced. Argument situations have four characteristics. First, they ask for an argument to be offered. Just as a question invites an answer, an argument situation invites an argument. Second, the argument must be a fitting answer to the situation. The answer offered should be relevant to the question asked. Third, the standards for judging a fitting response should be embodied in the situation. The arguer should know how to adapt the arguments to the situation. And fourth, argument situations are temporary. Situations arise, they exist, and, if left unanswered, they disappear.

Finally, argument relationship describes the interdependent connection among arguers and recipients. Every argument carries both content and relationship components. When arguments are made, arguers choose how to balance these two variables and typically use one of five styles: accommodator, competitor, escapist, facilitator, and negotiator.

EXERCISES

Exercise 1: Using Models. Using the arguments developed in Box 2.1, diagram any of the arguments using Toulmin's model. Include claims, data, warrant, backing, qualifiers, and reservations. Take the same argument and use the Co-Orientational Model to diagram it. Identify the claim, evidence, reasoning, and level of dispute.

1. What similarities and differences did you find?

2. Which model offers you a better way to understand the argument?

3. Use the critical thinking process discussed in Chapter 1: What issues would you expect Juli and Steve to address? Do they address them? How does this affect the quality of the arguments?

Exercise 2: Diagrams. Diagram each of the following arguments using both the Toulmin Model and the Co-Orientational Model of argument. Then, based on what you know, criticize each argument. What makes it strong? What makes it weak? For example:

> Capital punishment for murderers is widely supported by the general population. A Harris Poll in 1975 reported 59 percent of the public was in favor of capital punishment, and that proportion reportedly was increasing. Another poll in 1978 asked the question, "Are you in favor of the death penalty for persons convicted of murder?" The results showed 66 percent of the populace in favor of the death penalty.

Criticism

These polls are very outdated. Perhaps public opinion has shifted since the 1970s. Besides, just because the public supports something does not mean that it should be favored.

Arguments for Analysis and Criticism

*1. It is the chemical firms that release the most troubling types of molecules into the environment. In Baton Rouge, according to company data, an Exxon chemical plant was leaking 560,000 pounds of benzene yearly, while just south of there, according to a survey by the Sierra Club, eighteen plants in and around St. Gabriel and Geismar dumped about 400 billion pounds of toxic chemicals into the air during the first nine months of 1986.

Michael H. Brown, "The Toxic Cloud," *Greenpeace Magazine* (October–December 1987): 17.

2. But it was when Abbado had the orchestra to himself in the Tchaikovsky *Marche Slave* that the real magic showed. This hackneyed piece was treated with respect, and Abbado built it steadily to one final climax rather than playing each eruption as a show-stopping event.

[The following two arguments are excerpted from a group discussion on the right to die. Assume that all the participants are working together to construct *one* argument and are pursuing a shared thought line.]

3. Anne: Technology has affected every single part of this issue. We can prolong life or not depending on what tools we choose to use.

   Carrie: Yes, technology is a big one.

   Anne: I don't really feel that technology is just the mechanical aspect. It's chemical, biological, physical, everything. The advances in technology have gone so far that it can prolong life, yeah, but when you get in the position of an irreversibly comatose-type state, it's out of step with what people are. You know, should a person's life be prolonged just to vegetate? Are they prolonging ill health, or are they prolonging life? Technology has reached the outer limits where it's gone beyond what human beings are.

   Carrie: It's gone beyond the purpose for which medical technology was originally intended. Its goal was to enhance human life, whereas now it just prolongs death, dying, and pain.

4. Steve: The Hippocratic Oath, which states doctors must do everything within their power to keep the patient alive, is also a problem.

   Carrie: But the idea of the Hippocratic Oath is a problem. It says, "So far as power and discernment shall be mine, I will carry out the regimen for the benefit of the sick and will keep them from harm and wrong." Now the doctors or the law,...someone should explain the Hippocratic Oath to everyone, what exactly those words mean.

   Anne: But it's an archaic document. I mean, it talks about Greek gods ....

Leigh: It's so ambiguous. It doesn't have to do with today's society.

Steve: It's been outgrown by technology.

5. Is it not the great defect of our education today…that although we often succeed in teaching our pupils "subjects," we fail lamentably on the whole in teaching them how to think: they learn everything except the art of learning. It is as though we had taught a child mechanically and by rule of thumb to play "The Harmonious Blacksmith" upon the piano, but had never taught him the scale or how to read music; so that, having memorized "The Harmonious Blacksmith," he still had not the faintest notion how to proceed from that to tackle "The Last Rose of Summer."

Dorothy L. Sayers, "The Lost Tools of Learning," *National Review* (January 19, 1979): 91.

6. The Internet is probably the most powerful invention in the history of humankind. Yet, it is arguably the most dangerous. Never before have so many people been able to disseminate information, ideas, and suggestions into the public discourse. That is the power of the tool. The ability for any person to reach an audience of millions upon millions is far beyond the power Gutenberg must have felt upon inventing the printing press. But the danger lies in the quality of information. When the channels for distributing information are limited, reviews take place. Editors edit. Sources are verified and cited. With the Internet there is no such precaution or protection. Remember the case of the University of California Los Angeles student who ranted against international students talking on their mobile phones in the library. She could have done many things to find a quiet place to study—but her decision to post a mean and vicious rant on *YouTube* meant that millions saw her. The video had been replicated so many times; she could not take it down. In the end, she left school, people were angry. The Internet is powerful and it is dangerous.

7. Combined with this drive to provide public funding for religious and other private schools has been an unprecedented tsunami of assaults on the public schools serving 90 percent of our K-12 students. These assaults involve wholesale slashing of public school budgets, layoffs of teachers and other school personnel, increases of class sizes, elimination of instructional and other programs, intense propaganda campaigns against teachers and teacher unions, and attacks on the very idea of religiously-neutral, democratic public education. Together, this two-front war on religious freedom and public education constitutes nothing short of a major national crisis.

Edd Doerr, "The Great School Voucher Fraud," *Americans for Religious Liberty*, July 2012, http://www.arlinc.org/articles.html (accessed July 29, 2012).

8. The reality is that many economies around the world—and certainly the US economy—are dependent on workforces composed of many illegal aliens. This has been a significant issue in the United States and many other industrialized nations that offer relatively safe, high paying jobs to people willing to work hard to support their families and improve their quality of life. It is time for the US, as well as the rest of the world, to implement programs of amnesty to allow millions of undocumented people to stay and continue to work—legally. There have been laws passed in many U.S. states that threaten deportation and imprisonment if an illegal alien is caught. These laws have disrupted families and fines levied against employers have made it difficult for even long-term, dependable workers to get a job. These are jobs that most legal residents have thumbed their noses at. It is time to share wealth and opportunity and it is time to take away the fear that many people live under on a daily basis.

9. When Fidel Castro came to power in Cuba in 1959, the United States was gravely concerned about having a communist government just 90 miles off its shores. Moreover, Castro's close ties with the Soviet Union threatened U.S. security, especially if the Soviets decided to deploy nuclear weapons in Cuba. Following a disastrous attempt to overthrow Castro with the failed Bay of Pigs invasion and reaching the edge of nuclear war with the Cuban Missile Crisis, the

United States instituted a near total ban on trade of any kind with Cuba. These sanctions are no long acceptable and should be lifted. They were not successful in removing Castro from power; rather, they have severely hurt the Cuban people economically and have limited their access to basic human necessities—food, clothing, shelter, and medicine. There is simply no reason to continue these sanctions and certainly there is no danger from Cuba's government. The Cold War is over; it is time to make peace.

10. It is getting ridiculous. Apple, for instance, has a patent on "slide-to-unlock" a phone, which is distinguished from a "tap" which is a "zero-length swipe." Apple sues Samsung because Samsung's phone is rectangular with curved corners. That design is patented. Then Samsung sues back because the radio frequency control systems in the iPhone might infringe on Samsung patents. These are just two examples of hundreds upon hundreds of intellectual property (IP) lawsuits that cost consumers billions and slow down technological innovation. It is time to end intellectual property rights as we know them. IPs cover many things ranging from music to literature and art to inventions, symbols, and names. They are everywhere. And whomever holds the patents on intellectual property rights can charge royalties to anyone who wants to use them even if they are so vague and abstract it is not clear, exactly, what is being covered (is it a swipe or a tap?). These rights give individuals and companies near monopolies over the production of new technologies and materials. They even give companies the right to control what pharmaceuticals can be produced and prescribed. This kind of power is dangerous. It limits our economy and our lives. It allows markets and innovation to be controlled by a few people with a profit motives. It really is time to change the patent system.

Exercise 3: Steroids. Following is the text of a speech presented by Representative Cliff Stearns in the *Congressional Record.* After reading the entire speech, apply the concepts in this chapter by accomplishing the following objectives:

1. Locate all the claims, reasoning, and evidence in the speech. Draw a line under each one and label it.

2. Apply the standards for the logical, dialectical, and rhetorical perspective.

   a. For the logical perspective, consider whether the evidence offered by the author appears to be accurate, whether his reasoning seems sound, and whether there are links established between his premises and conclusions.

   b. For the dialectical perspective, consider whether all aspects of the questions are thoroughly explored, whether all issues are considered, and whether standards for judgment are provided. Does this article contribute to public discussion about drug use in athletics?

   c. For the rhetorical perspective, consider whether this article adapted to the author's audience and whether it addresses the circumstances and contexts relevant to the topic in our society.

3. How does Stearns try to create a relationship with his audience? What techniques does he use? Do you think they are effective?

4. What critical conclusions can you reach about the argument? Does it seem reasonable? How might Stearns have improved it?

STEROIDS IN SPORTS

I'm a big sports fan. I have had the opportunity to play sports in high school and in an industrial league. I played it in the Boys Club back in 90-pound football. And I think, like most of us, we understand that the vast majority of stars today were a testament to true hard work. Their performances, victories, records, and careers seemed to capture the straightforwardness of honesty, hard work, and integrity that is based upon the heart of sports today, at least in the past, the ideal that sports allow success based upon merit, whether it be on the court, the field, or the track.

Unfortunately…the scourge of steroids and performance-enhancing drugs is not simply a footnote in the history of sports in America. Steroid use goes much deeper, to the basic integrity of sports and all of athletics. At the most fundamental level, steroid use is just plain cheating. And it is illegal.

Furthermore, steroid use involves significant health risks for all athletes who use them. Studies suggest that use of steroids can lead to stunted growth in adolescents, increased risk of heart and liver disease, as well as cancer and hormonal problems for both men and women. And that is why these and other factors demand that our elite athletic organizations, both professional and amateur, establish uniform, world-class drug-testing standards that are consistent and robust, just as our criminal laws are today.

However, the most worrisome development is that steroids are not only infiltrating their professional and elite amateur leagues, they are finding their way into middle schools and high school sports programs. In fact, according to the most recent Monitoring for the Future survey, funded by the National Institute on Drug Abuse, 3.5 percent of high school seniors have used steroids, with similar percentages for grades 8 through 10. These are alarming numbers that represent just a part of the susceptible youth population that is out there. These estimates suggest that the high school steroid problem is just as great, if not greater, than it is in the professional leagues.

As any parent knows, high school is a trying time for many kids, let alone student athletes. These exceptional kids now face yet another hazard all the way to adulthood that is trying to claim the safe haven of sports as its next growth market. We must take an aggressive stand against this plague before these pressures lead young student athletes to use steroids, its destructive effects on honesty and fair play and ultimately, their very health and well-being….

Richard Pound, the founder and chair of the World Anti-Doping Agency, says, "Do we want our children to be forced to become drug addicts in order to be successful in sports? Like it or not, sports stars are heroes and idols to our kids. Our kids copy their heroes' behavior. That's why we have to encourage the stars to be good role models both on and off the field." Congress must continue to look into the use of illegal steroid and performance-enhancing drug use.

Professional leagues have an obligation to be the gold standard with regard to education, detection, and sanctions for the illicit use of steroids and other performance-enhancing drugs. The recent scandals in baseball, the Olympics, professional wrestling, and in other professional amateur sports have served to highlight the significance of the steroids problem.

Now, sometimes I'm asked back in the district why I care about drugs in sports. Shouldn't the athletes perhaps do whatever they want? They are only hurting themselves, is the reply. The use of steroids and performance-enhancing drugs by athletes today goes beyond just the integrity of the sport. By using illegal drugs, athletes are, in effect, telling our children that the only way to be successful and compete at the highest level is to cheat. That is not the message I want our children to hear.

Representative Cliff Stearns, *Congressional Record* (February 26, 2008): H1033–H1034.

NOTES

1. This event has been the subject of much debate. More background can be found in AFP, "Danish book about Muhammad cartoon controversy to go ahead despite threats," *New York Post*, September 29, 2010, http://www.nypost.com/p/news/international/danish_book_about_ muhammad_cartoon_9EU68NwfmSaTSvK3hAiqiP (accessed May 29, 2012); Kevin Sullivan, "Muslims' Fury Rages Unabated Over Cartoons," *The Washington Post*, February 11, 2006, http://www.washingtonpost.com/wp-dyn/content/article/2006/02/10/AR2006021001822.

html (accessed May 29, 2012); Craig Whitlock, "Bin Laden Threatens Europe Over Muhammad Cartoons," *The Washington Post*, March 20, 2008, http://www.washingtonpost.com/wp-dyn/content/article/2008/03/19/AR2008031902603.html (accessed May 29, 2012).

2. More information can be found in "Justice Department covers partially nude statues," *USA Today*, January 29, 2002, http://www.usatoday.com/news/nation/2002/01/29/statues.htm (accessed April 16, 2008).

3. Adapted from Jessica Remitz, *The Daily Collegian Online*, April 21, 2006, http://www.collegian.psu.edu/archive/2006/04/04-21-06tdc/04-21-06dnews-13.asp (accessed April 15, 2008).

4. For more information about the arts and arts censorship, see PBS, "Culture Shock: Are the arts dangerous?" 2000, http://www.pbs.org/wgbh/cultureshock/ (accessed April 16, 2008); and Steven C. Dubin, *Arresting Images: Impolitic Arts and Uncivil Actions* (New York: Routledge, 1992).

5. The Laramie Project is a controversial play written by Moisés Kaufman and members of the Tectonic Theatre project about the 1998 murder of Matthew Shepard. His death is widely believed to be the result of a hate crime motivated by homophobia. The play draws out many themes—religious, political, social—that some find challenging and it has often been protested and in some cases shut down over fears of violence.

6. Frans H. van Eemeren, Rob Grootendorst, and Francisca Shoeck Henkemans, *Fundamentals of Argumentation Theory: A Handbook of Historical Backgrounds and Contemporary Developments* (Mahwah N.J.: Erlbaum, 1996), 33–37.

7. Ray Lynn Anderson and C. David Mortenson, "Logic and Marketplace Argumentation," *Quarterly Journal of Speech* 53 (April 1967): 143–151.

8. George Ziegelmueller, Jack Kay, and Charles A. Dause, *Argumentation: Inquiry and Advocacy* (Englewood Cliffs: Prentice-Hall, 1990), 3.

9. Joseph W. Wenzel, "Three Perspectives on Argument," in *Perspectives on Argumentation*, Robert Trapp and Janice Schuetz, eds. (Prospect Heights, Ill.: Waveland Press, 1990), 9–26.

10. Chaim Perelman and Lucie Olbrechts-Tyteca, *The New Rhetoric: A Treatise on Argumentation*, trans. J. Wilkinson and P. Weaver (Notre Dame, Ind.: University of Notre Dame Press, 1969), 34.

11. We include here only a brief history of logic in the twentieth century. The origins of formal logic go back to Aristotle's *Prior Analytics* and *Posterior Analytics*, and early accounts of practical reasoning appear in Aristotle's *Topics*, *Rhetoric*, and *Sophistical Refutations*, all written in the fourth century B.C. Historical background for the study of reasoning can be found in Frans H. van Eemeren, 33–37.

12. For more information on this subject, consider Aristotle's, *Prior Analytics*, trans. Robin Smith (Indianapolis:

Hackett, 1989); and Harry J. Gensler, *Introduction to Logic* (New York: Routledge, 2002).

13. A good primer that describes formal logic and explains how it is used can be found at University of California, Davis, on its Web site "Logic Primer." It is located at http://tellerprimer.ucdavis.edu (accessed April 22, 2008).

14. Francis Bacon, *The Great Instauration*, 1620, http://www.constitution.org/bacon/instauration.htm (accessed April 22, 2008).

15. For excellent accounts of traditional syllogistic logic, see *The Encyclopedia of Philosophy*, s.v. "Logic, Traditional"; Edward P. J. Corbett and Robert J. Connors, *Classical Rhetoric for the Modern Student*, 4th ed. (New York: Oxford University Press, 1999), 38–59; Irving M. Copi and Carl Cohen, *Introduction to Logic*, 12th ed. (New York: Pearson Education, 2005); and James D. Carney and Richard K. Scheer, *Fundamentals of Logic*, 2nd ed. (New York: Macmillan, 1974). For a book that applies syllogistic forms and criteria to practical argument, see Gerald M. Nosich, *Reasons and Arguments* (Belmont, Calif.: Wadsworth, 1982).

16. Aristotle, *Rhetoric*, trans. W. Rhys Roberts, ed. Jenny Bak (Mineola, N.Y.: Dover Publications, 2004), 1357a and 1395b.

17. Stephen Toulmin, *The Uses of Argument* (Cambridge: Cambridge University Press, 1969), 94–210.

18. Toulmin, 94.

19. Toulmin, 98.

20. Stephen Toulmin, Richard Rieke, and Allan Janik, *An Introduction to Reasoning*, 2nd ed. (New York: Macmillan, 1984), 86.

21. Adapted from *Riggs vs. Palmer*, 115 N.Y. 506 (1889), 22 N.E. 188.

22. Lloyd F. Bitzer, "The Rhetorical Situation," *Philosophy and Rhetoric* 1 (1968): 1–5.

23. Bitzer, 4.

24. Paul Wattzlawick, Janet Helmick Beavin, and Don D. Jackson, *Pragmatics of Human Communication: A Study of Interactional Patterns, Pathologies, and Paradoxes* (New York: Norton, 1967).

25. There are many resources that have discussed how these styles work in different environments and situations. See Robert R. Blake and Jane S. Mouton, *The New Managerial Grid* (Houston: Gulf Publishing, 1994); William W. Wilmot and Joyce L. Hocker, *Interpersonal Conflict*, 5th ed. (Boston: McGraw-Hill, 1998); H. Markman, S. Stanley, and L. L. Blumberg, "Communicating Clearly and Safely: The Speaker-Listener Technique," *Making Connections: Readings in Relational Communication* (Los Angeles: Roxbury Publishing, 1996); and Merrell E. Dean, "Managerial Styles," *Air University Review*, March-April, 1976, http://www.airpower.maxwell.af.mil/airchronicles/aureview/1976/mar-apr/dean.html (accessed June 30, 2012).

VALUES AND CULTURE

CHAPTER OUTLINE

KEY CONCEPTS

Human societies are complex. They develop over generations of experience, symbols, histories, and structures that give us meaning and frameworks for understanding our surroundings. Just as people and their experiences are different from one another, so are our communities different as well. Each has its own identity, its own story, and its own values. These features guide what people believe, what is important to them, and how they behave. Argumentation often takes place among people who may or may not share common sets of experiences, values, or even approaches for creating or understanding arguments. Lack of common approaches for understanding and interpreting arguments may lead to misunderstanding and even violence.

The long-running debate over whaling is the subject of Box 3.1, "Should Whales be Hunted for Food?" This case provides us with a good example of how different cultural

■ ■ ■ ■ ■

BOX 3.1

"SHOULD WHALES BE HUNTED FOR FOOD?"

Human beings have hunted whales for thousands of years, but with the tools of the industrial revolution of the nineteenth century, whaling became an important and profitable industry. The growth of cities and mechanization increased demand for lighting and lubrication oils that could be produced from whale blubber. Whale meat, bones, and other parts of the animal were used to feed people and make a wide array of other goods including corset stays, combs, art, and even buggy whips. But the oil was the most important product and made the industry profitable.[1]

By the start of the twentieth century and the shift to petroleum-based products, the whaling industry began to decline. However, as new and more efficient hunting technologies were introduced, whaling became profitable again. Better tracking, hunting, and processing capabilities led to international alarm in the 1960s and 1970s as whale numbers plummeted and many whale species approached extinction. Globally, people began calling for a halt to whaling, and in 1982 the International Whaling Commission (IWC) passed a ban that took effect in 1986.[2] Most, but not all, whaling countries and cultures chose to abide by the ban, and within a few years the whale populations began to rebound.[3]

Both Norway and Japan continued whaling and have been the subject of much international criticism.[4] Some other groups such as the Native American Makah tribe in the northwest United States continue limited whale hunting and claim it is an essential part of its culture. The Makah make the point that "the conduct of a whale hunt requires rituals and ceremonies which are deeply spiritual. They are the subject and inspiration of Makah songs, dances, designs, and basketry."[5] Without whaling, leaders say, a significant part of the tribe's identity is lost.[6]

As the whale population has increased in recent years, Japan and Norway have called for lifting the ban to allow for regulated hunting. The IWC and most Western nations support continuing the ban. Whaling has been a regular conversation topic among many nature and conservation groups that look for ways to accommodate multiple interests while preserving the species. Some organizations, such as Greenpeace, have engaged in nonviolent protests and rallies to persuade whalers to stop. Another organization, Sea Shepherd, has used more forceful and direct action to prevent whaling. Consider the following discussion as the question of whale hunting is examined:

Chelsea: I know it's not politically correct, but there is no good reason we shouldn't be allowed to hunt whales for food—especially when people around the world are starving. Whales should be treated just like any other animal. I'm not saying that we hunt them to extinction, but they could be a good resource for food, oil, and many other products. As long as their numbers are healthy, why not?

Alex: That is the kind of thinking that took most whale species to the edge of extinction. There is no good reason to hunt whales. We don't need their oil; we don't need

BOX 3.1   CONTINUED

	their bones for art or clothes. And, we certainly don't need their meat for food—especially if it means we destroy an important and unique animal.
Chelsea:	But whales are no longer near extinction. The whaling ban worked and their numbers are increasing. I'm not saying it should be a free-for-all; whaling should be regulated and managed appropriately. My point is, though, that the IWC ban worked, whales are out of danger. It is time to lift the ban and allow hunting to resume.
Alex:	Check your evidence: There is very little factual material about how many whales are left. The numbers are certainly not as high as pro–whale hunters suggest. When the IWC ban went into effect, whales were nearing extinction. If we don't learn from our history, we could kill off important species—and for no good reason.
	Besides, even if you are right and there are many whales out there, we still should not kill them. Whales are special. They are intelligent, they are social, and they have language. We should not butcher intelligent and aware beings. It is morally wrong to hunt and kill species that appear to have so many social and intellectual traits in common with us.
Chelsea:	There is no good measure of whale intelligence. Most research has been done on dolphins, and it is highly controversial. People outside Western countries do not hold this view—that whales are somehow uniquely special and deserve special consideration—widely. They are not in need of special protection any more than other animals. Who are we to tell other cultures what is right or wrong? If Norway or the Makah want to hunt whales, what gives us the right to say we know better?
Alex:	Even if you are right, whale-hunting techniques are cruel and involve animals suffering a slow death. When a nursing mother is killed, the calf dies too, further depleting the population. If whaling is expanded, more inexperienced hunters with limited skills and technology will increase the suffering of these animals.
Chelsea:	You are talking about people who hunt whales in a traditional way. Whale hunting is an important aspect of some people's cultural heritage. For the Faroese islanders of the North Atlantic, the Makah in the USA, and the Bequia people of St. Vincent in the Grenadines, their cultures are deeply affected through whaling. For them, hunting a few whales each year is important for their economy and their cultural identity. Who are we to take that from them?

Consider the arguments that emerged in this discussion and consider the following questions

1. As you read the exchange, do you notice any of your own biases emerging? Where do they come from? Are they cultural? Are they based on your own values?
2. What arguments were compelling for you? What arguments didn't work? What do you base your assessment on?
3. Does one culture or one cultural perspective have the right to judge other cultures? For instance, is it appropriate for Western nations to pass judgment about the practices of non-Western societies? Why?
4. If a ban on whaling undermines the cultural identity of a people, does the international community have the right to impose the ban? What basis would you use to make that decision?

perspectives affect arguments. Some cultures have chosen to hunt whales even though whale hunting has been banned by international agreement. Protestors such as Greenpeace have used nonviolent methods to stop hunters, but other organizations such as Sea Sheppard have admitted to sinking whaling vessels and destroying property.[7] Whereas Sea Sheppard characterizes Greenpeace as "ocean posers," Greenpeace claims that Sea Sheppard is nothing more than a group of pirates. In any case, Greenpeace employs a set of values and nonviolent practices that differ greatly from those of the more aggressive and forceful Sea Sheppard. Both organizations oppose whale hunting but at the same time hold different sets of values that shape their behavior.

This chapter focuses on the important role played by culture and values in argumentation. These two elements shape how arguments are made, interpreted, and evaluated. The significance of these in argument situations discussed in Chapter 2 was emphasized by Joseph Wenzel, who wrote, "In the course of social life, we pass through innumerable contexts in which arguing may occur. All of these are framed by the general matrix of our sociocultural system as well as the special features of each occasion."[8] This sociocultural system incorporates values and assumptions that play an important role in making arguments and judging argument practices.

CULTURE AND ARGUMENTATION

An American woman who was spending a year studying in Greece went to the post office to pick up a package that had been mailed to her from home in the United States. The package was addressed to her in care of the Greek friend with whom she was staying. The postal clerk told the woman that he could not release the package to her because it was addressed to her friend and not to her. Her friend was out of town and, because she needed her package immediately, she began to try to persuade the clerk to give it to her. She pointed to her own name on the package label; she showed the clerk her passport to assure him of her identity; she reasoned with him, arguing that the package had her name on it and therefore must be hers. Regardless of what she said, the clerk continued to maintain that he could not give her the package because it was not addressed to her. Finally, he announced that it was his break and slammed the parcel pickup window shut, leaving her to storm out of the post office in disgust.[9]

Here we see a case of cross-cultural miscommunication that could be attributed to many causes. Perhaps the clerk felt that the woman was aggressive and insulting; perhaps he did not like Americans; or perhaps the woman did not speak Greek well enough to make her point. It's possible, however, that she used the wrong persuasive strategy. What else could she have done in this situation? She might have attempted to bribe the clerk, or tell him a story about some other person who lost his job because he denied service to people, or she might have returned to the post office later and refused to leave until she was given her package. The fact is that persuasive strategies and argument practices vary across cultures. By "culture" here, we do not necessarily mean some identifiable ethnic group such as a tribal culture or a national culture. Instead of being dependent on demographic or physical characteristics, a culture arises from shared experience, practices, and values. *Cultures are systems of shared meanings that are expressed through different symbolic forms such as rituals, stories, symbols, and myths that hold a group of people together.*[10]

This definition of culture implies that people who share a common culture enact the same communication patterns when they communicate with one another. In one culture, a person may make a point by telling a story, while in another culture, people may convey their views obliquely through third parties or by implication. Realizing this, many argumentation theorists and scholars believe that the view of argument we presented in Chapter 1—that an argument states a viewpoint in a context of disagreement through claims, evidence, and reasoning—is culture bound. It is true that not all members of every culture make arguments in this way.

For example, Japanese speakers prefer to avoid direct conflict, argument, and making explicit claims for a point of view. When communicating, they consider it a virtue to be able to catch on quickly to another's viewpoint without requiring the other person to openly state his or her position.[11] In a study of African American youth, Patrick McLaurin found that there were "few instances of direct, overt attempts to persuade a peer or significant other to change behavior."[12] McLaurin concluded that the groups he observed "seemed to shun direct, persuasive appeals."[13]

Role of Culture

When people engage in arguments, their background, values, and beliefs provide them with frameworks for interpreting what is being said as well as how to respond to it. This is the role of culture. All of us are members of at least one culture and probably belong to many. Culture can describe membership is a large group of people such as being Norwegian or Namibian. But cultures are much more complex than national boundaries. They can also describe much smaller groups such as memberships in organizations, being Asian American, or being a part of a social organization. In this respect, cultures are composed of many social groups and fields.

Cultures are closely connected to the kinds of arguments and communication patterns they use. Just as argument fields shape how arguments are used and evaluated, the same is true for cultures. And, just as arguments shape fields over time, arguments also have the power to shape cultures. How we express ourselves, how we advocate, and the assumptions we make have the potential to sustain, shape, or alter cultures.[14] This means that the process of argumentation is particularly important when cultures intersect and connect with one another.

We learn about other cultures much the same way as how we learn about argument fields—through a process of observation, discussion, and argument. Whenever we interact cross-culturally or within our own culture, we learn themes about cultural beliefs, values, and norms and we learn rules for interaction. We learn what is important—whether it be money or experiences, freedom or safety, among many others. And, we learn what is not important.

Generally, cultures can be classified as relatively individualistic or relatively collectivist. *Individualistic cultures focus on individual achievement and regard each person as distinct from others.* Individualistic cultures tend to promote individual goals (as opposed to family, organizational, or other social groups) and celebrate individual achievement. Freedom and independence are prized. These cultures highlight accomplishments such as best student, most valuable player, or salesperson of the year. They look at individual accomplishments over group accomplishment and use individuals as the mark of success. Steve Jobs, for instance, was hailed as the person who turned Apple around. Henry Ford was the person who ushered in the modern assembly line with Ford.

Collectivist cultures are different. *Collectivist cultures focus on the success of group affiliations over individual achievement.* Whereas the mark of success for an individualistic culture rests on individual achievement and success, collectivist cultures celebrate success through common effort, engagement with the community, and social stability.[15] Figure 3.1, "Individualistic and Collectivist Cultures," provides some examples of how some cultures can be classified.[16] Ultimately, the question of what defines cultural membership is one of what themes hold groups together and help create an identity.

Different cultures have a tendency to use different approaches to argument. For some cultures, there is an emphasis on selecting words carefully to directly convey meanings and ideas. For other cultures, the focus is more about the argument context than about the words chosen to convey the issues. The idea of argument context is important here because different cultures approach context through their own lenses. Theorist Edward Hall made the point that the context "carries varying proportions of the meaning."[17] In other words, if we were to analyze an argument, how much meaning can we draw from the words on the page or would we need to examine background and situation?

Cultural approaches to argument can be characterized as relatively low-context or relatively high-context. In *low-context situations, arguers have the majority of contextual information available to them in the arguments themselves.* Low-context situations are ones in which the people in the situation incorporate their meanings within the argument. As Hall pointed out, therefore, "the spoken word carries most of the meaning."[18] Advocates say what they intend directly within the argument. Arguers from individualistic cultures generally use low-context advocacy. For instance, courtroom transcripts and legal decisions tend to be very low-context arguments. Many years later, anyone reading the ruling in *Plessy v. Fergusson* should have enough information to understand the arguments and the decision. Similarly, contracts are low-context documents. They specify, exactly, what is expected and what will be done.

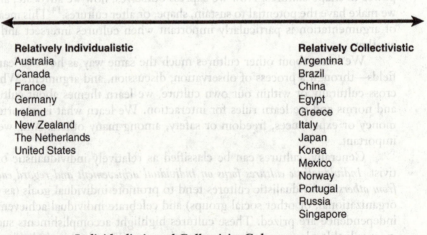

Relatively Individualistic	Relatively Collectivistic
Australia	Argentina
Canada	Brazil
France	China
Germany	Egypt
Ireland	Greece
New Zealand	Italy
The Netherlands	Japan
United States	Korea
	Mexico
	Norway
	Portugal
	Russia
	Singapore

FIGURE 3.1   Individualistic and Collectivist Cultures

Alternatively, *high-context argument situations omit large parts of argument meaning and advocates depend on the recipients' ability to interpret meaning from the situation.* In these cases, rather than using language to convey the majority of meaning, arguers may use facial expression, tone of voice, gestures, and shared understanding of broader issues that gave rise to the situation. High-context environments involve people interpreting the situation and drawing meaning from it. Hall characterized high-context communication as being faster and more efficient than low-context communication because it relies on intuitive understanding among the participants. However, high-context communication can also lead to much misunderstanding if parties misinterpret meanings drawn from situational elements.

High-context arguments are often found in collectivist cultures. Personal and family decisions are often understood because of the argument context that gave rise to them. Arguments in these situations such as whether to adopt, move to a new community, or even run for public office are all examples of high-context situations.

Because different cultures understand the process and expectations of argumentation differently, cultural styles and approaches also vary. Cultural analysts can identify tendencies that use particular reasoning forms, types of evidence, as well as approaches for managing disagreement and conflict. In intercultural settings in which members of different cultures engage in argumentation, the opportunity for misunderstanding is heightened because of potential dissonance among styles, approaches, evaluation standards, values, and symbols used by different groups of people. And, when we evaluate arguments, we draw from cultural values and understandings of what is appropriate and reasonable. Some of these understandings vary considerably across cultures, whereas others remain relatively consistent.

Multicultural Argument

In a multicultural world, what should we do when we seek to influence others who do not share the same assumptions or value systems as us? There are many approaches to answering this question. Some theorists maintain that we should argue about the pros and cons of a question because that is the best way to discover the significant issues and to promote critical thinking. This view is commonly held among Western theorists who embrace Aristotle's view that:

> We must be able to employ persuasion, just as strict reasoning can be employed, on opposite sides of a question not in order that we may in practice employ it in both ways (for we must not make people believe what is wrong), but in order that we may see clearly what the facts are, and that, if another man argues unfairly, we on our part may be able to confute him.[19]

Those who advocate pro–con argument believe that exploring opposing sides of a case through explicit arguments such as those in political debates and law courts is the best way to weigh opposing sides and reach a good decision.[20]

When arguers emphasize confrontation and competition, they run the risk that their arguments and emphasis on pro–con alternatives will alienate people from other cultural perspectives. For example, Deborah Tannen said that an issue is often "not composed of two sides but is a crystal of many sides."[21] She has observed that we often think and speak of argument as being very competitive. For example, we regularly speak of "winning" arguments or "beating" a person's position. This sets up a mutually exclusive win–lose outcome, which fails to promote open-mindeness, good listening, and alternative approaches to problem solving.

Both of these views have merit. Competitive debate and pro–con argumentation can reveal the points at issue and the underlying facts and values in a controversy. On the other hand, splitting a topic or question into two opposing sides dichotomizes the issue and does not align well with the communication values and practices of some cultures. To address this question, we propose an enlarged and inclusive view of argument and advocacy.[22]

When faced with a decision, there are many ways in which parties to a controversy can express their points of view and deliberate about the best outcome. They can begin by identifying the areas where they agree (those that fall below the level of dispute). Rather than immediately dividing the issue into pro and con arguments, disputants can work collaboratively to entertain all aspects of the issue and to include all the criteria that should be applied to decide the best outcome.

In their book *Getting to Yes*, Roger Fisher and William Ury suggested using a "One-Text Procedure" as a way to find common ground, limit the number of issues in dispute, and move toward a constructive agreement.[23] The one-text approach is simply a process whereby the parties in a dispute work to identify and agree upon (down to the way a document is worded) the common facts and assumptions in the discussion. This was the process used by Israel, Egypt, and the United States in meetings at Camp David in 1978 in an attempt to design a framework for lasting peace. Fisher and Ury described the process, "the United States listened to both sides, prepared a draft..., asked for criticism, and improved the draft again and again until the mediators felt they could improve it no further."[24] The one text served to ground peace discussions and, ultimately, President Carter of the United States, President Anwar Sadat of Egypt, and Prime Minister Menachem Begin of Israel signed the peace agreement. Similarly, a project called "A Common Word" has promoted conversations among the world's religious leaders in an attempt to identify "one text" that might help bridge some religious divides. The project has involved discussions and conversations among many global leaders from many beliefs including those representing Christian, Islamic, and Jewish faiths.[25]

By listening carefully to others to identify common ground and showing respect for views that differ from their own, participants in a dispute can discover new perspectives on the topic. It is often the case, as Irwin Mallin and Karrin Vasby Anderson observed, "the best persuaders not only listen to others, but also incorporate their perspectives into a shared solution."[26] This was the point we discussed in Chapter 2 with facilitative argument styles.

Cultural Argument Patterns

In an increasingly complex and interconnected world, we should consider the various approaches and styles in which people from different cultural backgrounds organize and express their beliefs. A recent study of African American, Asian, Asian American, and European American students found, not surprisingly, that students from different backgrounds and cultures had different ways of stating their viewpoints.[27] Generally, four different patterns of argument were apparent in the way members of different cultures and backgrounds interacted. These are described in Box 3.2, "Cultural Patterns," and include the following four types of patterns: deductive, inductive, abductive, and narrative.

BOX 3.2
CULTURAL PATTERNS[28]

Deductive	■ States claim or position explicitly
Pattern	■ Subsequent statements or support are designed to support the initial claim
	■ Disagreement with another position is assumed
	■ The reasoning is usually quasi-logical or casual
Inductive Pattern	■ One speaker has a viewpoint
	■ That speaker uses various examples or statistical generalizations to support that viewpoint
	■ The general claim being supported can be stated at either the beginning or the end
	■ Additional examples, when added, add cogency to the viewpoint
Abductive Pattern	■ Speakers work collaboratively to reach a conclusion
	■ Speakers share reasoning; one person's statement may serve as a premise for the other's claim
	■ Hypothetical cases may be used to test the speakers' reasoning
	■ The conclusion is not stated at the beginning but emerges from the discussion
Narrative Pattern	■ Narratives are used to make a point
	■ Narratives come from the speaker or others' personal experiences
	■ Narratives are mini-stories that describe circumstances and involve other characters and in which the narrator plays a role
	■ The point, if it is explicitly stated at all, is often stated at the end of the story

When arguers made their claims directly and at the beginning of their argument, they used a deductive pattern. An example of this pattern is in Box 3.3, "Deductive Pattern Example." With a deductive pattern, arguers provide explicit and clear claims that are then supported typically using logical or enthymematic reasoning. Arguments of this type are relatively easy to diagram and analyze because they are complete and leave little to individual interpretation.

Inductive patterns, like deductive patterns, are clear, and their claims and support are explicit, but the claim—if stated directly—is typically at the end of the argument. The support, generally examples and generalizations, comes first. Box 3.4, "Inductive Pattern Example," provides an illustration.

Abductive patterns do not generally have an explicit claim. Rather, the claim is emergent. *With abductive patterns, speakers work collectively to reach a common conclusion.* Arguers

■ ■ ■ ■ ■

BOX 3.3

DEDUCTIVE PATTERN EXAMPLE

There is no good reason to hunt whales for food. It makes no sense. This is the kind of thinking that took most whale species to the edge of extinction. It is an expensive source of meat, difficult and dangerous to harvest, and we run the risk to driving these animals to extinction. Before the IWC ban on whaling we almost exterminated most species and with no good reason.

■ ■ ■ ■ ■

BOX 3.4

INDUCTIVE PATTERN EXAMPLE

Joan: Do you think that news coverage should be objective?

John: No, because it is the news media's responsibility to gather information and mobilize public opinion. If their coverage is purely neutral, then they can't do that.

Joan: What do you mean?

John: Well, consider the war in Bosnia. Before the United States became involved, there was a lot of media coverage of people behind barbed wire fences in concentration camps. After we entered the fighting, someone revealed that the whole picture was posed. The people were on the wrong side of the barbed wire fence, which ended 3 feet outside the frame of the picture! But if that picture hadn't been run in the newspapers, we would not have intervened, and there was genocide going on over there.

Joan: But isn't it the news media's responsibility to provide objective reporting?

John: No. It's their responsibility to arouse public interest, to get people involved. If they were really objective, then nothing would happen. No one would know what's going on.

Joan: Doesn't that put an interpretation on the news?

John: Yes, well it *should*. Take the Oklahoma City bombing. Dozens of people, including children and infants, were killed. The media coverage was done in a way as to arouse public outrage, and it should have.

share reasoning and support and develop an outcome together through conversation. This type of argument is generally considered collaborative and is illustrated by the example in Box 3.5, "Abductive Pattern Example."

Finally, *narrative patterns involve stories and reports to express views*. With this pattern, arguers use experiences to describe circumstances that help develop the argument. The claims in such arguments are seldom stated explicitly and, if they are, generally occur at the end of the narrative. An example of narrative and experiential argument can be found in Box 3.6, "Narrative Pattern Example."

BOX 3.5
ABDUCTIVE PATTERN EXAMPLE

Carmella:	What do you think sexual harassment is?
Jerry:	Anything that makes the other person uncomfortable in, I don't know…a sexual way. What is your take on it?
Carmella:	I guess, just anything that makes the other person uncomfortable, you say? Granted, the person doing the so-called harassing may not think it's uncomfortable to them, but just as long as the receiver thinks it's uncomfortable (and it should be told to the harasser) then it's going too far.
Jerry:	Then it's basically up to the receiver to decide what harassment is.
Carmella:	To a certain extent. It can't be every little thing, you know, that could be considered sexual harassment. Some of the things that have been coming up lately, little things, that can be blown really out of proportion, shouldn't be included.
Jerry:	Yes, I think people have definitely gotten carried away. A long time ago, there were things that would not even be considered harassment, but now it's different.

BOX 3.6
NARRATIVE PATTERN EXAMPLE

Elephants are magnificent creatures. They are the largest land animals in existence. They are intelligent; they live in families. Despite their size, often more than 7 tons, they walk almost silently. They are an important part of the ecosystem that supports life in the savannah. Growing up, I was always fascinated with them. I studied them. When I was in university, I was able to travel to Africa and see them in their natural environment. They are amazing.

Yet, they are in danger. Their population has dwindled from almost 10 million a hundred years ago to fewer than 800,000 today. People ask, why should I work so hard to save the elephant from extinction?. Personally, I think the answer is obvious.

The only reason these animals are on the edge of extinction is human greed and ignorance. Poachers kill elephants to harvest ivory and other parts of the animal that can be turned into carvings, jewelry, and medicines. They sell their illegal goods on the black market to people ignorant of the costs to the environment, the elephant, and the world.

I was in Kenya's Tsavo National Park in January 2013. I was there shortly after rangers discovered the remains of an entire family of elephants—twelve in all. Adults and juveniles alike had been poached for their ivory. These animals suffered for no reason other than human greed for economic gain. The brutality was stark against the peaceful backdrop of the park. I think about the scene every day and wonder when we will decide as a world community to protect species that are so vulnerable to our vanity, greed, and ignorance. This needs to stop.

BOX 3.7

APPLY THE THEORY: DESIGNING CULTURAL ARGUMENTS

This section explored how different cultures use different patterns for developing arguments. The case study in Box 3.1 focused on the issue of whaling. Most countries have ended whaling, although Norway and Japan continue. If these countries design arguments for a global audience to defend and justify their practices, what might those arguments look like? Write an argument for each pattern: deductive, inductive, abductive, and narrative. What are the strongest elements of each argument?

These four patterns for expressing a point of view demonstrate that people from different cultures reason and express themselves differently. Researchers who have studied reasoning patterns in international negotiations, for example, have found that European Americans generally favor inductive reasoning in which specific claims are backed by facts, whereas members of other cultures may rely on arguments from tradition or authority.[29] Their findings make it apparent that different cultures use different normative standards to evaluate arguments. Box 3.7, "Apply the Theory," provides a guide for developing arguments from different cultural viewpoints and structures.

Culture provides us with a framework for understanding and interpreting arguments and helps us evaluate their appropriateness. As people become adjusted to a culture, they learn the basic assumptions of that culture so that they can perform their roles and abide by its rules, values, and morality. When we make an argument, our recipients understand our basic cultural assumptions and use them as a framework for evaluating ideas and arguments.

Using culture as a frame for argument practices can be problematic, however, because cultures in a globalized society are becoming increasingly less differentiated. In North America, for example, one finds residents who belong to many cultural groups—European Americans, Latin Americans, Native Americans, African Americans, Asian Americans, and others. Furthermore, many of these residents belong to more than one cultural group. Even within specific cultural groups, there are differences in values and clusters of values. We should therefore be cautious about making any ready generalizations based only on a given cultural group to which people might belong.

Developing Cultural Competence

There is little challenge to the premise that cross-cultural communication competence is increasingly important in a multicultural world. In a world defined by technology and instant access to information and people through the Internet and using a variety of media, it is not surprising that developing competence has become a significant theme in higher education.[30] Developing competence in cross-cultural argumentation has the potential to play a significant role in creating relationships and opportunities for peaceful resolutions to disagreements and open conflict. A particularly important example and model for developing intercultural argument competence can be found in Truth and Reconciliation Commissions. One analyst noted that "throughout the world, truth commissions have been created under the assumption that getting people to understand the past will somehow contribute to reconciliation between those who were enemies under the ancient regime."[31] The point here is simply that effective multicultural argumentation has the potential to shape our world in positive ways.

Developing intercultural competence in argument involves being sensitive to diverse cultural norms and expectations. *Intercultural competence in argument is defined as the ability of an arguer to function in a manner that is perceived to be relatively consistent with the needs, capacities, goals, and expectations of individuals from one cultural environment while satisfying one's own needs, capacities, goals, and expectations.*[32] Intercultural argument competence, then, means that arguers need to have the ability to understand and adapt their arguments to situational requirements of culture.

B. D. Ruben wrote that intercultural communication competence could be divided into seven behavioral characteristics: display of respect, argument interaction posture, orientation to knowledge, empathy, role behavior, interaction management, and tolerance of ambiguity. These are described in Box 3.8, "Intercultural Competence."[33] Taken together, these seven behavioral characteristics provide a template for understanding and adapting to various cultural settings.

BOX 3.8
INTERCULTURAL COMPETENCE

BEHAVIOR	DESCRIPTION
Display of Respect	Ability to argue with respect and positive regard for other people, including understanding behavioral clues such as eye contact, body posture, voice (tone and pitch), and displays of interest.
Argument Interaction Posture	Ability to respond to others in argument situations in descriptive, non-evaluating, and nonjudgmental ways.
Orientation to Knowledge	Being able to recognize that members of different cultures apply differing field-dependent standards for evaluating evidence, reasoning, and claims. Therefore, what constitutes a valid argument may be variable across cultural situations.
Empathy	Ability to put oneself in another's position or context to try to understand their goals and needs.
Role Behaviors	Ability to be functionally flexible in different settings and situations and to know when it is appropriate to act as an advocate or recipient.
Interaction Management	Ability to take turns in discussion and debate and understanding when to initiate or terminate argument interaction based on reasonably accurate assessments of needs and desires of others.
Tolerance of Ambiguity	Ability to react to new and ambiguous situations with little visible distress or discomfort.

VALUES AND VALUE SYSTEMS

Often, our evaluation of arguments as well as our own approach to creating arguments depend on our understanding of what is right and wrong. For instance, is it right to hunt whales to extinction? At the same time, is it right for Western countries to tell people who have a strong cultural connection to whaling that they can no longer practice those traditions? The power of argumentation and its influence on people are considerable. Arguments influenced the International Whaling Commission (IWC) to pass a ban, and arguments are now being used to try to persuade the IWC to reverse it. As individual arguers, we should not take our own arguments for granted but should understand their potential effects. Given the context in which arguments are made, we should be able to evaluate whether our arguments are appropriate, reasonable, and sensitive to cultural expectations. Our assessment of a particular situation requires us to explore more than the issues. We also need to explore the assumptions and values that undergird the issues being discussed.

Values are pervasive both in the life of society and the life of the individual. They help guide our actions and provide a framework against which our decisions are evaluated and understood. *Values can be defined as desirable, transituational goals, varying in importance, that serve as guiding principles in people's lives.*[34] In other words, we each have value systems that we apply in different occasions and contexts to achieve certain personal or social goals. Our individual values as well as our connection with cultural values help us answer questions about whether hunting whales for food is good or bad because of how whaling affect our basic value assumptions.

Terminal and Instrumental Values

A value is a particular kind of belief. Rather than being descriptive or capable of being true or false, a value is prescriptive; it helps us judge whether an action or state of being is desirable or undesirable. Milton Rokeach, who researched American values for three decades, divided values into two main categories: instrumental and terminal. *Instrumental values concern modes of conduct or the means for fulfilling other values. Terminal values concern desirable end states of existence.*[35] We get an education (instrumental value) so that we can find a rewarding career (terminal value). We work hard (instrumental value) so that we can have a comfortable life (terminal value). Examples of instrumental values are educational opportunity, leisure time, and economic prosperity. Instrumental values have a means–end relationship with certain terminal values such as family security, an exciting life, a sense of accomplishment, and self-respect. Rokeach estimated that, whereas an individual possesses a limited number of terminal values—somewhere between one and two dozen—the total number of instrumental values may be several times that number because we use many avenues or instruments to reach our objectives or terminal value states.

Value Systems

Value systems can be described as having three significant characteristics: value content, value structure, and value consensus.[36]

Content

Value content refers to the motivational goals expressed in the value. Specifically, how do values guide and motivate our behaviors? Shalom H. Schwartz and Galit Sagie argued that there are ten distinct motivational value clusters that seem to remain consistent across cultures. Illustrated in Box 3.9, "Value Content," they are self-direction, stimulation, hedonism,

■ ■ ■ ■ ■

BOX 3.9
VALUE CONTENT

VALUE	DEFINITION
Self-Direction	■ *Terminal values:* Independent thought and action (choosing, creating, exploring)
	■ *Instrumental values:* Creative, free, independent, curious, chooses own goals
Stimulation	■ *Terminal values:* A varied, challenging, and exciting life
	■ *Instrumental values:* Daring, novel, exciting
Hedonism	■ *Terminal values:* Pleasure and enjoying life
	■ *Instrumental values:* Sensual gratification, play
Achievement	■ *Terminal values:* Personal success through demonstrating competence according to social standards
	■ *Instrumental values:* Ambition, influence
Power	■ *Terminal values:* Social status and prestige, control or dominance over people and resources
	■ *Instrumental values:* Social power, authority, wealth
Security	■ *Terminal values:* Safety; harmony; and stability of society, relationships, and self
	■ *Instrumental values:* Family security, national security, social order, cleanliness, reciprocation of favors
Conformity	■ *Terminal values:* Restraint of actions, inclinations, and impulses likely to upset or harm others and violate social expectations or norms
	■ *Instrumental values:* Self-discipline, obedience, politeness, honoring parents and elders
Tradition	■ *Terminal values:* Respect for, commitment to, and acceptance of the customs and ideas that traditional culture or religion provide
	■ *Instrumental values:* Accepting one's position in life, humility, devotion, respect for tradition, moderation
Benevolence	■ *Terminal values:* Preservation and enhancement of the welfare of people with whom one is in frequent personal contact
	■ *Instrumental values:* Helpfulness, honesty, forgiveness, loyalty, responsibility
Universalism	■ *Terminal values:* Understanding, appreciation, tolerance, and protection for the welfare of all people and for nature
	■ *Instrumental values:* Broad-mindedness, wisdom, social justice, equality, world peace, a world of beauty, unity with nature, environmental protection

achievement, power, security, conformity, tradition, benevolence, and universalism. Their argument is that we are motivated by power, the drive for achievement, or any of the other values they cluster together. Arguably, whale-hunting cultures are driven by values from this list, including self-direction and tradition. And, Greenpeace or Sea Shepherd may act out of terminal values that include achievement and benevolence. Our actions reflect the values that are important to us, and the decisions we make reinforce their significance in our own mind-set.

Structure and Hierarchy

Value structure refers to the dynamic relations among the values in our individual value system. This means that some values are more important than others, and over time the relative importance of some values may change because the relative importance of values is dynamic. Rokeach made some important distinctions about the nature of types of values. He noted that each person has values organized into a value system. *A value system is an enduring organization of beliefs concerning preferred modes of conduct or end states of existence according to their relative importance.*[37] By this, Rokeach meant that each of us has values that are organized into hierarchies. A value hierarchy *is an ordering of values so that some are ranked more highly than others.* For example, people who want to prohibit logging in our national forests may value environmental preservation over jobs and growth. Or, is hunting whales for food is more important than preserving an intelligent species?

From the 1960s through the 1980s, Rokeach conducted extensive studies of American value systems. Narrowing the list of terminal values to eighteen, he surveyed large samples of the American public to discover how these eighteen terminal values were ordered. These eighteen values are shown in Box 3.10, "Apply the Theory."

Three observations about this ranking of values are particularly noteworthy. First, American values appear to be stable across time. Although some value rankings may change, they do not change much. Concerning this stability, Rokeach and his coauthor noted that "such highly stable findings would seem to suggest that there is little, if any, value change occurring in American society, at least in the thirteen-year period under consideration. Many social scientists would probably interpret such findings as confirming the widely shared view that human values are deep-lying components of collective belief systems and are thus inherently resistant to change."[38]

Second, men and women as well as African Americans in the United States have similar rankings. In contrast to the stereotype that men value achievement and intellectual pursuits, whereas women value love, affiliation, and the family, Rokeach found that these values were similarly ranked. In regard to race, the rank orderings of African Americans and whites were similar, with the exception of the value of equality, which was ranked second by African Americans and twelfth by whites. Furthermore, when Rokeach matched African Americans with the whites in his survey according to education and socioeconomic status, the differences between the two races in value rankings either disappeared or became minimal, again with the exception of the different rankings of equality.[39]

Third, this ranking of terminal values was specific to American culture. Rokeach gathered information on value rankings from Australians, Canadians, and Israelis and found sizable differences among cultures. Israelis ranked national security second, whereas Americans never ranked it higher than tenth. Canadians ranked happiness, mature love, and true friendship much more highly than did Americans.

■ ■ ■ ■ ■

BOX 3.10

APPLY THE THEORY: VALUE HIERARCHY

Consider the rank-order list of American values developed by Rokeach and answer the questions that follow:

1. Family Security
2. World at Peace
3. Freedom
4. Self-Respect
5. Happiness
6. Wisdom
7. Sense of Accomplishment
8. Comfortable Life
9. Salvation
10. True Friendship
11. National Security
12. Equality
13. Inner Harmony
14. Mature Love
15. Exciting Life
16. World of Beauty
17. Pleasure
18. Social Recognition

How would you hierarchically organize this list? Are there any values missing? Which values are important in the "whale hunting" debate?

Seymour Lipset, who has done extensive cross-cultural comparisons between Americans and Canadians, has noted that Americans are more religious, more patriotic, more populist and antielitist, and more socially egalitarian than Canadians and citizens of other developed countries. America is also more "antistatist" (distrustful of centralized government) than all other developed nations and thus is exceptional in the low level of support it provides for its poor in welfare, housing, and medical care. Lipset reports that among the developed nations, the United States has the highest proportion of its people living in poverty.[40] These studies of American values indicate that the orderings and priorities we place on various terminal values are culture-specific. People of different cultures and ethnicities will perceive and respond to value arguments in different ways. They will view as important those values that concern them most directly. The question of which values are ranked most highly by recipients should always influence the design of one's value argumentation.

When our values come into conflict, we rely on our hierarchies to guide us toward appropriate actions. For example, what happens in a case in which parents want a student to major in business and the student wants to major in theater? The values of security (having college paid for) and conformity (honoring parents and obedience) are placed in opposition to the value of self-direction (choosing, creating, and exploring one's own goals). The choice will ultimately be based on the student's assessment of which values are most important and where they fit along a value hierarchy. With the whale hunting, the value of upholding cultural tradition conflicts with environmental and species perseveration.

Consensus

Value consensus is the degree of concurrence among members of a society concerning their values. If all the members of a society hold the ten value clusters in high agreement, then consensus is high. If there is little agreement, consensus is low. Consensus is important because it describes how well individual actions are tolerated or accepted in a given culture. Box 3.11, "Ben & Jerry's

---

BOX 3.11
BEN & JERRY'S ICE CREAM

Ben & Jerry's Ice Cream has a three-part mission that has served as its core identity since it was founded in 1978: (1) a social mission emphasizing improving quality of life in the community; (2) a product mission focusing on high quality, all natural ice creams; and (3) an economic mission recognizing the need for shareholders to make a profit.

These three mission elements have served to define the core values and activities of Ben & Jerry's Ice Cream.[41]

In 2000, the company was purchased for $326 million by Unilever, a large, international conglomerate that owns Dove Soap and Lipton Soup among many other businesses. Unilever, unlike Ben & Jerry's, was not ranked among the most socially responsible companies in the world and many expressed concerns that Unilever's ambition to take the company global would undermine or altogether eclipse Ben & Jerry's socially driven values and mission.

Initially, there seemed to be cause for concern—that Ben & Jerry's would lose its identity. Some analysts warned that Ben & Jerry's, like many other companies before, would begin to conform to the less socially responsible, larger organization of Unilever. Warren Bennis, an expert on corporate culture and transformations, emphasized this point when he noted that most companies become "pretty much the color of the company" that acquires them. And in this case, the color of Unilever is not nearly as socially progressive.[42]

Yet, Ben & Jerry's mission and values seem to have thrived as a part of the larger company. It remains highly ranked as a socially responsible organization because of its use of fair trade ingredients, community engagement though community-base projects, and its corporate philanthropy programs.[43] And, it seems as though Unilever, which owns other ice cream brands including Good Humor, Popsicle, and Breyers, has taken the lead from the smaller company. It pledged to expand the Ben & Jerry's socially progressive mission and its active philanthropic philosophy. One analyst noted that Unilever "seems to have raised the bar for corporate social responsibility."[44]

Unilever began to transform its own mission to incorporate more of the Ben & Jerry's philosophy. It appears, Bennis noted, that the smaller company with its flower-child image and strong socially responsible agenda may well influence the larger company, which may help prove that the socially responsible choice is also the better choice for business. This sentiment was echoed by Unilever executive Jostein Solheim, who said, "The world needs dramatic change to address the social and environmental challenges we a facing. Values led business can play a critical role in driving that positive change."[45]

Ice Cream," provides a case study that serves as a good example of how value consensus works. People and organizations often assume that although social responsibility and philanthropy are positive values that should be part of the corporate mission, these values are often fulfilled at the expense of the "bottom line." The value consensus is that profits come before social programs and that one often benefits at the expense of the other. Ben & Jerry's was founded on the premise that social activism was equally as important as profits and a quality product, and it succeeded in fulfilling both values.

Process of Value Change

Most cultures experience some level of value consensus. They may believe in the importance of individual self-direction and independence. They may focus on the importance of traditions or the environment. For the United States, values of a world at peace, family stability and security, and freedom are all generally accepted and acknowledged core values. Nicholas Rescher observed, "there unquestionably exists (and will continue to exist) a prominent value consensus in America."[46] In our own society and in others, however, certain values are unstable and fluctuate in their importance and in the extent to which people adhere to them.[47] Because these fluctuations affect the hierarchies used in argumentation, advocates should be sensitive to them.

Values change in three ways. One type of value change occurs when a value that was held by a minority becomes more widely disseminated and becomes a majority value. Rescher has labeled this *value redistribution*, which is *a process in which a value becomes more and more widely diffused throughout a society until virtually all its members adhere to it*. During the Vietnam War, anti-war protesters staged marches, rallies, draft card burnings, sit-ins, and other forms of activity against the war. The existence of peace logos, signs, and symbols along with speeches and rallies gradually raised the consciousness of the general population about peace as a value so that it came to be more widely held. Ultimately, American sentiment against the war was a major factor influencing political figures to bring an end to our involvement in Vietnam.

Rescher noted that in the normal course of events, values come to be emphasized or deemphasized; that is, they come to be more or less important to the people who hold them. *In value emphasis, values move upward in a value hierarchy. In value de-emphasis, they move downward.* This increase or decrease in the extent of our adherence to values can be brought about by new information or by changes in our social or economic environment. For example, new information about the causes of cancer, heart attack, and stroke has noticeably changed Americans' awareness of good health in prolonging life. This increased emphasis on good health has changed our attitudes and behavior regarding exercise, smoking, and salt and cholesterol intake. Changes in the economic environment in the early 1990s led to a dramatic decrease in the number of professional jobs available to college graduates. As a result, college students came to value their education in terms of its "marketability" and sought degrees in business, engineering, and computer science in increasing numbers.

Rescher cited value restandardization as a third factor affecting the way in which values are applied within a society. *Value restandardization is a process in which standards used to measure whether a value is being met increase or decrease.* For example, the criteria to measure whether one has an adequate standard of living have changed over the years. In the late 1940s and early

■ ■ ■ ■ ■

BOX 3.12

APPLY THE THEORY: HOW VALUES CHANGE

Using the discussion in Box 3.1, identify the following processes:

1. What values are apparent in the discussion? How would you organize them on each side of the issues in a hierarchy?
2. Value redistribution is a process in which a value becomes more widely diffused. What examples of value redistribution occur in the conversation?
3. Value emphasis is a process that promotes values so that they move up in the value hierarchy. What values seemed to have been emphasized in the whale debate? How would you emphasize values?
4. Value deemphasis means that values move down the value hierarchy. Are there examples of deemphasis in the discussion? How would you approach value deemphasis?
5. Value restandardization involves changing criteria by which we measure something. Can you identify examples of restandardization in the discussion? How would you restandardize the values in the case study?

1950s, costs and inflation were low; most families had only one car; and mortgages were well within the reach of middle-class incomes. Today, in many areas, even modest homes are expensive; cable television and telephones are considered basic utilities; lifestyles often require that most families have two cars; and many other costs have risen. Standards for an adequate income and lifestyle have changed dramatically over the past forty years.

In addition to cultural variations in value rankings, values vary in response to changing social conditions. As time passes, certain values may become more widely diffused in a society, may increase or decrease in importance, or may be restandardized. Value advocates should consider what factors—new information, technological development, or economic fluctuation—might affect the values they are discussing. Also, when incompatible values conflict, advocates should determine what standards audiences are likely to use to choose between them. As we shall see in the remaining sections of this chapter, audience adherence plays a major role in establishing basic premises in a value argument. Box 3.12, "Apply the Theory," uses the whale-hunting controversy developed in Box 3.1 to explore value change.

CULTURE AND VALUES

Culture and values are very closely linked. Within every culture, systems of values operate and assign levels of importance to events and beliefs. Some cultures value possessions and others value people. Some cultures value collectivism and relationships, whereas others value individualism. Some value progress and change, whereas others value tradition. Differences such as these imply that arguers from one culture who seek to influence those from another culture should be aware of how values of their recipients are prioritized. Advocates should not assume that their own values, which may not be shared by the members of their audience, can be used as starting points or premises for arguments.

Cultural differences in values and argument practices can be illustrated by reference to the civil rights movement of the 1960s and 1970s. Many African Americans during that period shared the belief that they were disadvantaged and discriminated against in housing, education, and individual rights. Differing groups formed around differing views about what was to be done about these conditions. Dr. Martin Luther King Jr. and his followers believed in nonviolent protest and resistance to gain equal rights, while Stokely Carmichael and his followers were more militant.

Carmichael preached violence and separatism. He made the point that "institutions that function in this country are clearly racist, and that they're built upon racism...." His message continued that as long as this premise was true, equality remained impossible and that white supremacy would continue. The issue, then, Carmichael argued, was not about integration; it was about the fight against white supremacy.[48]

In his message, Carmichael appealed to audience members who apparently believed that white people could not be trusted, that promises of equality and integration were just a subterfuge, and that nonviolent protest will never succeed in obtaining the things that African Americans want and need to function. He felt that his audience would agree that confrontation and use of aggressive tactics might be the only way to achieve their ends.

Carmichael's statement can be contrasted with that of another African American, Barbara Jordan, who gave the keynote address to the 1976 Democratic National Convention. In her message, Jordan observed how unusual it was for a national political party to offer the stage to an African American, yet, she pointed out, "but tonight here I am." Her keynote address focused on the American Dream, its potential, and the opportunity afforded by democracy to all people in the United States—regardless of race.

She argued that "We are attempting to fulfill our national purpose: to create and sustain a society in which all of us are equal...."[49]

While Carmichael believed that promises of integration and equality were a hoax perpetrated on African Americans by whites, Jordan believed that real equality between the races was possible, that progress had been made toward this goal, and that she (as a keynote speaker at a national convention) was living proof of that. Whereas Carmichael assumed that confrontation and protest were the only means of achieving basic civil rights for African Americans, Jordan felt that equality could best be achieved if all Americans—white and black—worked together for the common good.

The dramatic contrast between the arguments of these two speakers reveals the influence of two subcultures—one militant and the other nonviolent—within the African American culture at that time. This contrast also reveals the important role that values play in making arguments. Values can fulfill multiple functions whenever someone makes an argument. Some of the values used by Carmichael and Jordan include honesty, social justice, equality, and social harmony, and both speakers assumed a certain level of agreement by their audiences that those values were important and that some values were more important than others. Each speaker, then, used agreement on values as a starting point or form of evidence for his or her arguments.

All cultures develop value systems that indicate acceptable modes of conduct, and thus premises, which arguers can use to argue for their claims. When you are talking with a person from a culture different from your own, you should consider whether that person shares your values. If not, you would be well advised to consider what that person *does* consider to be important before you begin making your arguments. Furthermore, not every culture shares Western culture's preference for logical argument and empirical evidence. If you want to influence people from a culture different from your own, you might want to consider using stories or metaphor to communicate your ideas. Although this book focuses on Western modes of argument, we do want to point out that they are not the only ways to effectively present your ideas to others.

SUMMARY

This chapter examined how the concepts of culture and value affect argument situations, arguers, and recipients. The first part focused on cultures and their role in shaping argument interactions. Culture is important to understanding argument practices because values arise from cultural background. This means, then, that culture affects the ways in which we argue. Some cultures, such as the United States and Germany, are individualistic and emphasize individual achievement. These cultures tend to develop low-context arguments that are direct and attempt to convey the majority of meaning through the argument structure. These cultures often emphasize adversarial, two-sided forms of argument, in which there can be a winner and a loser. Other cultures, such as Argentina, China, and Norway, are considered relatively collectivistic and focus on the success of the community. They typically emphasize high-context argument styles and offer multiple points of view and collaborative outcomes.

Four different patterns of argument style are commonly used: deductive (claim followed by proof), inductive (examples followed by general conclusion), narrative (the use of stories to reach a conclusion), and abductive (comparing and contrasting experiences to reach a conclusion). Further, each culture determines the standards by which arguments are understood and evaluated. Arguers should keep in mind that in any argument situation, there are many diverse, cultural values at work, many argument styles and strategies available, and many ways to further sound decision making.

The second part of the chapter examined values and how they shape and influence argumentation. Values are generally organized into value systems. A value system consists of value content, value structure, and value consensus. Value content refers to the clusters of values held as important by a culture. These include self-direction, stimulation, hedonism, achievement, power, security, conformity, tradition, benevolence, and universalism. Value structure describes the hierarchy, or relative importance, we place on values, and value consensus is the relative degree of acceptance values have within a given culture. Understanding value systems is important to value advocates who must gauge arguments to suit the values and attitudes of an audience. Furthermore, when individuals or groups of people disagree about values, it is often because their value systems are ordered differently.

In any society, value hierarchies are subject to fluctuation and change. Values may become more widely held because a persistent minority successfully argues for their importance. Because of new information or changes in the social or economic environment, values may become more or less emphasized. The standards that are applied to determine whether a value has been met may become more or less stringent. Because audience adherence is a vital factor in establishing the basic premises in a value argument, advocates should be aware of factors that may bring about changes in the importance and pervasiveness of values in society.

EXERCISES

Exercise 1: Cultural Arguments. Below are several passages. Each uses one of the four methods for stating a point of view described in Box 3.2. These ways of organizing speech are deductive, inductive, abductive, and narrative. For each passage, identify the pattern used and justify your selection. What is the stated or implied viewpoint of the writer or speaker? How does he or she support it?

1. *I talk with American students every day. Many of them come to college poorly prepared and without focus. They will be asked to take on large debt for degrees they no little or nothing about. They have high ambitions but few goals or strategies for achieving the goals they have. They pursue social interests over academic interests in a culture that diminishes academic achievement. It is not surprising. Students can achieve good grades with relatively little effort. In their book *Academically Adrift*, Richard Arum and Josipa Roska point out that, compared with a generation ago, students read less, write less, perform worse on critical thinking and engagement measures, and spend very little time studying. It is pretty clear to me that we have reached a crisis point when we are preparing our students worse today than yesterday. Our educational system has failed us.

2. The world lives under the threat of nuclear war and I believe it is time that the United States forcefully end nuclear weapons development programs in any nation that does not already have them. The proliferation of nuclear weapons is frightening—especially when enemy states such as Pakistan and India both have nuclear capabilities. Too many countries already possess the technology and are developing delivery mechanisms. North Korea and Iran both represent potential, lethal states that are close to developing the capabilities to wipe out their adversaries with nuclear weapons. With every bomb built, the world faces greater instability. Greater instability risks accidents, misunderstanding, and a serious potential for uncontrolled conflict. This is one technology that would be best un-invented if that were possible—but, of course, it isn't. The best we can do now it to stop its future development.

3. The worst mistake is to execute someone wholly innocent. Now that executions are approaching 100 per year in the United States, the chances rise that at least one will be the wrong guy. Perhaps. But it has pretty clearly not happened in Washington [State]. This state has executed three men, none who claimed he didn't do it. In 1993, it hanged Westley Alan Dodd, who owned up to raping and murdering little boys and said he'd do it again; in 1994, it hanged Charles Campbell, who came back from prison and murdered the witnesses against him; and in 1998, it executed by lethal injection Jeremy Sagastegui, who murdered two women and a three-year-old boy, and who wanted to die.

Bruce Ramsey, "A Difficult Road to Death," *Seattle Times* (April 16, 2000): B9.

4. *The documentary *Reunion—Ten years after the war* is the story of a group of Serbian and Albanian students who originally met right before NATO began bombing Kosovo. The Albanian students talked about the hardships under Serbian rule and how much their lives were shaped by the daily presence of an oppressive government. Freedom and opportunity were aspirations with little hope of coming true. Then NATO began a bombing campaign to remove Milosevic from power and protect the rights of the Kosovo Albanians. Ten years later, the power has shifted and there are very few Serbs left in Kosovo's capital city, Pristina. Most have left to return to Serbia or other, safer places. The Serb students, in the documentary, now sound as the Albanian students did a decade earlier. They lament the loss of freedoms and opportunities. Just in these few stories it was interesting to think about how power and privilege so powerfully affect the right and lives of so many.

5. I am of the opinion that we have lost part of what makes us great. More than 20 percent of the global population lives in absolute poverty. There is serious disease and death from illnesses

that Western medicine has the capability of curing. Children go malnourished while many of us waste more food in a day than they eat in a week. More than a billion people do not have clean water to drink or a shelter to sleep in. What makes people great is the ability to rise above ourselves as individuals and think about how we can help humanity. Albert Einstein once asked that, given we had the ability to feed the world, provide medical attention to all those who need it, and give everyone clean water, why didn't we do that? It is time to ask that again. Why don't we? In short, we should. We should do it now. We should all commit to giving as generously as we can to the charities that work to solve these issues.

6. "Fracking" is a cost-effective way to extract natural gas from the Earth's crust. Natural gas is plentiful; it can help North America to become energy independent. Natural gas is relatively clean. My concern is that environmentalists who overclaim the long-term damage to the stability of the Earth's crust are actively working to undermine new jobs, economic growth, and prosperity because of unproven fears. It is time to move on and put people and jobs first.

7. From a discussion of the Internet's effect on young people:

    Adam: Is the Internet changing the nature of childhood, or are children changing the nature of the Internet? I think both. I grew up with a computer. I've used the computer ever since I was three. When we got an iPad I don't think I have let it out of my sight. I've grown up completely connected to the Net and I definitely wouldn't be the person I am without it. I also change the Internet. I blog, design Web pages, and belong to many online communities—from Facebook to interactive gaming.

    Austin: I think it is a bit of both. Kids are one of the driving forces of the Internet because of our incredible abilities to adapt. If the Internet had come along twenty years down the road, I don't think that I would adapt to it as quickly as I did. Also, the Internet is changing kids in many ways. Penpals are written to through e-mail and Facebook. Homework assignments are passed around through file attachments and with Blackboard or Moodle.

    Adapted from Don Tapscott, *Growing Up Digital: The Rise of the Net Generation* (New York: McGraw-Hill, 2009), 77–78.

8. A picture may well be worth a thousand words, but as historical documents, photographs are subject to the same questions as written documents. Despite initial appearances, photographs are not objective. Photographic images were created for specific purposes and for audiences. No photograph can be accepted as "representative" of a way of life without additional documentation. The many factors that influenced what photographs show include the wishes and capabilities of the photographers, and the responses of [their subjects].

    Victoria Wyatt, *Images from the Inside Passage: An Alaskan Portrait by Winter & Pond* (Seattle: University of Washington Press, 1989).

9. More and more of our communication is not face-to-face, and not with people we know. The proliferation and increasing portability of technology isolate people in a bubble. When I was a child, my family got the first television on our block, and the neighborhood children gathered in our dining room to watch *Howdy Doody*. Before long, every family had its own TV—but each had just one, so, in order to watch it, families came together. Now it is common for families to have more than one television, so adults can watch what they like in one room and the children can watch their choice in another—or maybe each child has a private TV to watch alone.

    Deborah Tannen, *The Argument Culture: Moving from Debate to Dialogue* (New York: Random House, 1998), 240.

10. Since Nixon declared war in 1971, the United States has been engaged in a "War on Drugs." We fight it every day and on almost every street in the United States. We spend billions patrolling boarders looking for drug smugglers, finding dealers, busting users, and incarcerating just about everyone we can locate who is involved in the drug trade. Yet, only about 10 percent of Americans believe we are winning the war. Many more consider it to be a multi-billion dollar

failure. Why? Because as much as we invest in trying to stop drugs from coming into the United States, people who use the drugs are willing to pay more to get their supply—and increased revenue means drug smugglers can develop better and more sophisticated technologies. Planes, boats, and now even submarines are being used to get drugs into the country. Our own addiction has created a demand that will always overwhelm our ability to win the war. We need to take on a different approach. Some say legalize all of it—maybe that is the answer. But whatever approach we take must be taken within the United States to curb demand from illegal sources.

Exercise 2: Flag Burning. What follows is an excerpt from a Supreme Court decision on flag burning (*Texas v. Johnson* 491 U.S. 397 [1989]). In this case, a man named Johnson participated during the 1984 Republican National Convention in Dallas, Texas, in a political demonstration to protest the policies of the Reagan administration and some Dallas-based corporations. After a march through the city streets, Johnson burned an American flag while protesters chanted. He was convicted of desecration of a venerated object in violation of a Texas statute, and the state court of appeals upheld the conviction. However, the Texas court of criminal appeals reversed the ruling, holding that the state could not punish Johnson for burning the flag in this situation because his action was expressive conduct protected by the First Amendment provisions protecting freedom of expression. The decision was appealed to the U.S. Supreme Court, which ruled in favor of Johnson. Following is an excerpt from the majority opinion, which was authored by Justice William Brennan. In regard to his value-based argument, answer the following questions:

1. What values does Justice Brennan affirm in this opinion?
2. What values does Brennan view as opposed to his position?
3. What criteria for evaluation does Brennan apply in the decision?
4. What is your own value position in regard to Brennan's specific argument?

MAJORITY OPINION IN *TEXAS V. JOHNSON*

The State asserts an interest in preserving the flag as a symbol of nationhood and national unity.... Johnson was prosecuted because he knew that his politically charged expression would cause "serious offense." If he had burned the flag as a means of disposing of it because it was dirty or torn, he would not have been convicted of flag desecration under this Texas law: Federal law designates burning as the preferred means of disposing of a flag... The Texas law is thus not aimed at protecting the physical integrity of the flag in all circumstances, but is designed instead to protect it only against impairments that cause serious offense to others... Whether Johnson's treatment of the flag violated Texas law thus depended on the likely communicative impact of his expressive conduct.

Texas argues that its interest [is] in preserving the flag as a symbol of nationhood and national unity... Quoting extensively from the writings of this Court chronicling the flag's historic and symbolic role in our society, the State emphasizes the "special place" reserved for the flag in our Nation... The State's argument is not that it has an interest simply in maintaining the flag as a symbol of, no matter what it symbolizes; indeed, if that were the State's position, it would be difficult to see how that interest is endangered by highly symbolic conduct such as Johnson's. Rather, the State's claim is that it has an interest in preserving the flag as a symbol of and... According to Texas, if one physically treats the flag in a way that would tend to cast doubt on either the idea that nationhood and national unity are the flag's referents or that national unity actually exists, the message conveyed thereby is a harmful one and therefore may be prohibited.

If there is a bedrock principle underlying the First Amendment, it is that the government may not prohibit the expression of an idea simply because society finds the idea itself offensive or disagreeable...

Texas' focus on the precise nature of Johnson's expression, moreover, misses the point of our prior decisions: their enduring lesson, that the government may not prohibit expression simply because it disagrees with its message, is not dependent on the particular mode in which one chooses to express an idea. If we were to hold that a State may forbid flag burning wherever it is likely to endanger the flag's symbolic role, but allow it wherever burning a flag promotes that role—as where, for example, a person ceremoniously burns a dirty flag—we would be saying that when it comes to impairing the flag's physical integrity, the flag itself may be used as a symbol—as a substitute for the written or spoken word… We would be permitting a State to "prescribe what shall be orthodox" by saying that one may burn the flag to convey one's attitude toward it and its referents only if one does not endanger the flag's representation of nationhood and national unity.

We are tempted to say, in fact, that the flag's deservedly cherished place in our community will be strengthened, not weakened, by our holding today. Our decision is a reaffirmation of the principles of freedom and inclusiveness that the flag best reflects, and of the conviction that our toleration of criticism such as Johnson's is a sign and source of our strength. Indeed, one of the proudest images of our flag, the one immortalized in our own national anthem, is of the bombardment it survived at Fort McHenry. It is the Nation's resilience, not its rigidity, that Texas sees reflected in the flag—and it is that resilience that we reassert today.

The way to preserve the flag's special role is not to punish those who feel differently about these matters. It is to persuade them that they are wrong… We can imagine no more appropriate response to burning a flag than waving one's own, no better way to counter a flag burner's message than by saluting the flag that burns, no surer means of preserving the dignity even of the flag that burned than by—as one witness here did—according its remains a respectful burial. We do not consecrate the flag by punishing its desecration, for in doing so we dilute the freedom that this cherished emblem represents.

Exercise 3: Situation Analysis. Read the following three situations and analyze the values that clash:

SITUATION 1

Your parents are paying for your university education. Paying the tuition and housing bills can be a hardship for them, but their hope is that you succeed with your education and complete a degree in business. Although you appreciate their sacrifice and are loyal to them, your passion is to become an actor and attempt to find a career in entertainment. Therefore, you wish to major in theater. Unfortunately, when you shared this wish with your parents, they not only opposed your choice, saying it was "unrealistic" and "very unlikely," but they also told you that if you chose to major in anything but business, they would end their financial support for your education.

SITUATION 2

Your university is a large research institution that conducts studies in cancer and AIDS prevention and treatment. You were attracted to the school in the first place because it has the best premedical program in the state, and your goal is to become a doctor. Although you support finding cures for these diseases, you are also very opposed to the live animal research conducted in university laboratories. You become even more concerned when you discover that part of the required coursework in your biology and premed major will be assisting with some of these research projects and conducting vivisections on the animals. Yet you know that a biology major is the first step toward a medical degree that will help you find cures for people later on.

SITUATION 3

You are a member of a group in a business communication class. Your final project, worth half of your grade, is to conduct an analysis of a local business, write a research paper focusing on marketing strategies and suggestions for improving the business, and present your project to the class at the end of the term. Four of the five members of your group worked hard to produce a quality paper and design a thoughtful presentation. One member, however, rarely showed up at meetings, came unprepared when he did come, and failed to do his fair share. Everyone in the group is angry with him, but no one is willing to confront him or tell the professor about his lack of effort. This is particularly disturbing to the other group members because the final grade for the paper and presentation will be the same for everyone—even the person who didn't work. The presentation is in two days.

Based on each of the situations and your understanding of values, answer the following:

1. Using Rokeach's hierarchy of values, what is the "correct" course of action in each situation?

2. What do you think is the correct course of action for each situation? What values support your conclusions?

3. How would you organize the terminal value hierarchy in a way that is consistent with your own decision-making?

NOTES

1. "Whaling Past to Present," ThinkQuest, at http://library.thinkquest.org/05aug/00504/Sea_pages/historyofwhaling.htm (accessed May 30, 2008).

2. The IWC main Web site provides information about the Commission and offers reports and documents related to whaling. Its addresses are http://www.iwcoffice.org/index.htm and http://ourworld.compuserve.com/homepages/iwcoffice/.

3. More information can be found at "Saving the Whales," at http://www.ypte.org.uk/docs/factsheets/env_facts/saving_the_whales.html (accessed May 30, 2008).

4. Encyclopaedia Britannica's Advocacy for Animals, "Hunting the Whales," June 4, 2007, http://advocacy.britannica.com/blog/advocacy/2007/06/hunting-the-whales/ (accessed May 29, 2008).

5. Makah Whaling Tradition, Makah.com, at http://www.makah.com/whalingtradition.html (accessed April 30, 2008).

6. A discussion of the controversy can be found in Richard Blow, "The Great American Whale Hunt," *Mother Jones*, September/October 1998, at http://www.motherjones.com/news/feature/1998/09/blow.html (accessed May 30, 2008).

7. "Activists Disagree on Whaling Protests," *Sydney Morning Herald*, at http://www.smh.com.au/news/whale-watch/activists-disagree-on-whaling-protests/2008/01/31/1201714116250.html (accessed May 2, 2008).

8. Joseph Wenzel, "On Fields of Argument as Propositional Systems," *Journal of the American Forensic Association* 18 (1982): 204.

9. This example was taken from Barbara Johnstone, "Linguistic Strategies and Cultural Styles for Persuasive Discourse" in *Language, Communication, and Culture: Current Directions*, Stella Ting-Toomey and Felipe Korzenny, eds. (Newbury Park, Calif.: Sage, 1980), 144.

10. Charles Conrad, *Strategic Organizational Communication*, 2nd ed. (Fort Worth: Holt, Rinehart, & Winston, 1989), 4.

11. William B. Gudykunst and Tsukasa Nishida, *Bridging Japanese/North American Differences* (Thousand Oaks, Calif.: Sage, 1994), 30.

12. Patrick McLaurin, "An Examination of the Effect of Culture on Pro-Social Messages Directed at African-American At-risk Youth," *Communication Monographs* 62 (1995): 312.

13. McLaurin, 320.

14. Joseph F. Healey and Eileen T. O'Brien, eds., *Race, Ethnicity, and Gender: Selected Readings*, 2nd ed. (Thousand Oaks, Calif.: Pine Forge Press, 2007); and Fred E. Jandt, *An Introduction to Intercultural Communication: Identities in a Global Community* (Thousand Oaks, Calif.: Sage Publications, 2009).

15. Edward Hall, *Beyond Culture* (New York: Anchor Books, 1989).

16. It is important to note that classifying cultures as being collectivist or individualistic depends on many fluid variables. For instance, a collectivist culture may exhibit many of the traits we discuss generally but become individualistic in how it approaches business or security negotiations. This figure is intended as an illustration of how some cultures have been identified. A more detailed account can be found at James W. Neuliep, *Intercultural Communication: A Contextual Approach* (Los Angeles, Calif.: Sage, 2012), 48–56.

17. Hall.

18. Hall.

19. Aristotle, *Rhetoric*, trans. W. Rhys Roberts, ed. Jenny Bak (Mineola, N.Y.: Dover Publications, 2004), 1355a.

20. Thomas O. Sloane, *On the Contrary: The Protocol of Traditional Rhetoric* (Washington, D.C.: Catholic University of American Press, 1997).

21. Deborah Tannen, *The Culture of Argument: Moving from Debate to Dialogue* (New York: Random House, 1998), 10.

22. We agree with the view stated by David E. Williams and Brian R. McGee in a recent special issue of *Argumentation and Advocacy*, "Revisioning Argumentation Education": "We believe that the traditional argumentation course may overemphasize competition, but we are not convinced that the idea of competitive argument should be banished from the classroom." [See their essay in vol. 36 (Winter 2000): 109.]

23. Roger Fisher and William Ury, in *Getting to Yes*, Kindle, ed. (New York: Penguin, 1991), 1770.

24. Fisher and Ury, 1770.

25. *Official Website of the Common Word*, at http://acommon word.com (accessed July 1, 2012).

26. Irwin Mallin and Karrin Vasby Anderson, "Inviting Constructive Argument," *Argumentation & Advocacy* 36 (2000): 131.

27. Barbara Warnick and Valerie Manusov, "The Organization of Justificatory Discourse in Interaction: A Comparison Within and Across Cultures," *Argumentation* 14 (2000): 381–404.

28. Barbara Warnick and Valerie Manusov, "The Organization of Justificatory Discourse in Interaction: A Comparison within and across Cultures," *Argumentation* 14 (2000): 381–404.

29. E. S. Glenn, D. Wittmeyer, and K. A. Stevenson, "Cultural Styles of Persuasion," *International Journal of Intercultural Relations* 1 (1977): 52–66.

30. Much has been written on the importance of developing intercultural communication competencies. For examples, see Betty Leask, "Bridging the Gap: Internationalizing University Curricula," *Journal of Studies in International Education* 5(2) (2001): 100; Johann Le Roux, "Effective educators are culturally competent communicators," *Intercultural Education* 13(1) (2002): 37–48.

31. James L. Gibson, "Does Truth Lead to Reconciliation? Testing the Causal Assumptions of the South African Truth and Reconciliation Process," *American Journal of Political Science* 48(2) (2004): 201.

32. B. D. Ruben, "Human Communication and Cross-Cultural Effectiveness," in *Intercultural Communication: A Reader*, 3rd ed., L. A. Samovar and R. E. Porter, eds. (Belmont, Calif.: Wadsworth, 1982): 336.

33. Adapted from B. D. Ruben, "Cross-Cultural Communication Competence: Traditions and Issues for the Future," *International Journal of Intercultural Relations* 13(3) (1989); and Ruben, "Human Communication and Cross-Cultural Effectiveness," 331–339.

34. Shalom H. Schwartz and Galit Sagie, "Value Consensus and Importance: A Cross-National Study," *Journal of Cross-Cultural Psychology* 31 (2000): 465–468; see also Bradley R. Agle and Craig B. Caldwell "Understanding Research on Values in Business: A Level of Analysis Framework," *Business & Society* 38 (1999): 326–388; Soyeon Shim and Pitti Shim, "A Personal Value-Based Model of College Students' Attitudes and Expected Choice Behavior Regarding Retailing Careers," *Family & Consumer Sciences Research Journal* 28 (1999), 28–52.

35. Milton Rokeach, *The Nature Human Values* (New York: The Free Press, 1973), 7–8.

36. Schwartz and Sagie, 465–470.

37. Rokeach, 7–8. Another theorist who divided values along these lines is Donald Walhout, who distinguished between social values (political stability, equality, freedom, etc.) and individual values (social participation, friendship, proper self-love). See his *The Good and the Realm of Values* (Notre Dame: University of Notre Dame Press, 1978), 45–46.

38. Milton Rokeach and Sandra J. Ball-Rokeach, "Stability and Change in American Value Priorities," *American Psychologist* 44 (1989): 777.

39. Rokeach, 57–59 and 66–72.

40. Seymour Lipset, *Continental Divide: The Values and Institutions of the United States and Canada* (New York: Routledge, 1990), 37–39.

41. A discussion of the company mission, values, and agenda can be found at http://www.benjerry.com/activism (accessed June 26, 2012).

42. Lauren Coleman-Lochner, "Ben & Jerry's Plans to Stay Cool," *The Record* (April 19, 2000): 1; Carl M. Cannon, *Policy: Charity for Profit* (June 17, 2000); Gary Dessler, "How to Earn Your Employees' Commitment," *The Academy of Management Executives* 13 (May 1999): 58–67.

43. Jo Bilson, "Corporate Social Responsibility at Ben & Jerry's," at http://suite101.com/article/corporate-social-responsibility-at-ben--jerrys-a211754 (accessed on June 26, 2012).

44. Megan Palos, "Unilever Raises the Bar for Corporate Social Responsibility," April 11, 2011, at http://www.business2community.com/trends-news/unilever-raises-the-bar-for-corporate-social-responsibility-023838 (accessed on June 26, 2012).

45. "Division President: Jostein Solheim, Ben & Jerry's Homemade," at http://www.foodprocessing.com/ceo/jostein_solheim.html (accessed on June 26, 2012).

46. Nicholas Rescher, *Introduction to Value Theory* (Englewood Cliffs, N.J.: Prentice-Hall, 1969), 115. See also Rokeach and Ball-Rokeach, 777.

47. The account of value change in this section is drawn from Rescher, 111–118.

48. Stokely Carmichael, "Black Power," in *Black Protest: History, Documents and Analysis*, Joanne Grant, ed. (New York: Fawcett Premier, 1968), 459.

49. Barbara Jordan, "Democratic Convention Keynote Address," in *Contemporary American Speeches*, 7th ed., Richard L. Johannesen, R. R. Allen, and Wil A. Linkugel, eds. (Dubuque, Lowa: Kendall/Hunt, 1992), 371, 373.

SECTION II

PARTS

CHAPTERS

4. CLAIMS

5. EVIDENCE

6. REASONING

CLAIMS

When disputes arise arguers make arguments. As we noted in Chapter 1, arguments consist of claims, evidence, and reasoning. When we parse arguments, we break them up into their components, which allow us to examine, understand, and evaluate each of the parts that compose the argument. Consider the arguments for and against illegal file sharing developed in Box 4.1. As you read the arguments, you can see how the speakers developed each of the parts of the argument. There are claims about legality and ethics; there is evidence about laws and the impact of illegal downloads; and there is reasoning that helps develop the claims and illustrate each speaker's point of view.

BOX 4.1

SHOULD INTERNET ACCESS BE PERMANENTLY DISCONTINUED FOR PEOPLE WHO SHARE FILES ILLEGALLY?

By some estimates, more than 8 million people are logged into file-sharing networks around the world at any one time. With more than 900 million illegal music files available on these networks, along with movies, texts, and images, illegal file sharing is one of the single largest uses of the Internet.[1] College and university students represent some of the most active participants in these networks that share illegally copied and distributed files. In response to calls from recording artists and movie studios, the U.S. Congress has worked to strengthen copyright laws and increase penalties for violators. Higher-education leaders are being asked to move quickly and aggressively to eliminate illegal peer-to-peer (P2P) sharing on their campuses.[2] Senator Lamar Alexander, for instance, demanded that colleges and universities immediately "adopt policies and educational programs on their campuses to help deter and eliminate illicit copyright infringement occurring on, and encourage educational uses of, their computer systems and networks."[3] Despite their efforts, law enforcement and campus officials have found it difficult to control because of the ease of access to the Internet and inexpensive technology.

The core of the controversy is copyright law. Copyright laws state that if a work is going to be used, the original producer must give permission for its use and, generally, the author should be compensated for it. When a song is sold on iTunes, for instance, the original recording artist receives a royalty payment for the sale. When a college or university stages a play, typically, it pays fees to the copyright holder for the use of the script.[4] But technologies that provide easy ways of reproducing and distributing original works have made circumventing copyright simple. Although governments have worked to adapt laws to meet these threats, almost anyone with a computer and access to the Internet has the ability to illegally share files with others. This is why the Internet has been described as the biggest threat to copyright since the invention of the printing press.

In response, recording artists and studios have worked aggressively to stop illegal file sharing, and many copyright violators have been taken to court. Their focus has been individual users and the result has been that hundreds of people, mostly college students, have been prosecuted for sharing files without proper permission or paying royalties. Penalties, when applied, have been severe. Mother of four, Jamie Thomas-Rasset, for instance, was found guilty of pirating twenty-four protected songs and her penalty was $62,500 per song.[5] Comcast, Cablevision, Verizon, AT&T, and Time Warner Cable have all agreed to monitor their networks and alert the Recording Industry Association of America (RIAA) and the Motion Picture Association of America (MPAA) of suspected illegal sharing.[6] If found guilty, subscribers could have their Internet services discontinued. Similar legislation is pending or has been passed in Europe. File sharing has been a widely discussed and debated issue on college campuses; included in the

(continued)

BOX 4.1 CONTINUED

debate is whether or not a college or university should turn over student file-sharing records. Following is a discussion between two students about appropriate sanctions if they are caught pirating protected content:

Cathy: Pirating songs and movies is wrong and unethical. An honest person would never swap music, movies, games, or any other file without paying for them. File sharing has completely destroyed the music industry and that hurts all of us who want to purchase quality music. People no longer buy music; they rip it off. Artists have been hurt; music stores have gone bankrupt. Pretty soon, there will be no new music because artists won't be able to afford to live. Anyone caught pirating protected files on campus should be expelled.

Nick: The fact that people share files without paying for them is the fault of the music industry. Record producers pack albums full of tracks that no one wants and then force you to pay excessive amounts of money for one good song buried in the middle of ten bad songs. Sites like iTunes have made it better, but even so, the music is too expensive. Besides, file sharing gives people more choices and people discover artists they didn't know existed. I am not saying we should rip off artists, but file sharing lets us discover new bands and it gives young artists an opportunity to be heard—and that doesn't happen on commercial radio or television where big labels pay high premiums to get songs played over and over. File sharing gives people a choice and provides a level playing field for new artists. Expelling a student for sharing files is a little extreme, don't you think?

Cathy: Your argument doesn't make any sense. You are saying that new artists will be better off giving their music away so that they can be heard. But if they never make any money, how will they produce the songs in the first place? I understand that MP3 files could help promote new artists, but that is not what people download. I have read that only ten songs in a thousand were from relatively unknown artists. Besides, even if everything you say is true, nothing prevents new artists from putting up content for free. My only point is that sharing should be done with permission. We should not allow stealing, especially when there are legal, low-cost alternatives.

Nick: Copyright laws need serious updating. Sharing is not stealing. Whenever anything is released to the public, it has been shared, and once someone has paid for a book, song, movie, or anything else, why can't they share it with whomever they choose? That's Michael Moore's point. Once you buy one of his documentaries, his view is he wants people to see it. He gets paid and then you can share. Libraries pay for a book once and then allow anyone to check it out. If I buy a DVD, don't I have the right to show it to my friends? I'm allowed to record my favorite song off the radio. What makes sharing MP3s so different? Our copyright laws need to adapt to new technologies.

Cathy: Maybe the laws should change and maybe they are outdated. But that doesn't matter. File sharing is illegal. People who do it without permission are breaking the law. While the Digital Millennium Copyright Act has a fair-use provision for personal purposes, it does not allow those copies to be traded. You and I can rip a CD we bought, but when we give it away to someone else, we have broken the law. There is no difference between sharing the track with someone else and stealing it from the store.

BOX 4.1   CONTINUED

Nick: The law needs to change. File sharing helps artists. When people have a chance to preview tracks, new artists get discovered. No one has demonstrated a negative effect on artists. Musicians were worried when recordable CDs were introduced. The movie industry opposed recordable DVDs. Yet, at the end of the day, music and movie sales went up.[7] With more download opportunities, companies have new markets. Television and movie studios have found new audiences for vintage programs. Copying files has been going on a long time, and I don't see any evidence it has harmed anyone.

Cathy: You are wrong. Illegal file downloads have decreased legal sales, and that is why so many stores are getting out of the music sales business. To make a profit, producers will have to raise prices, and that hurts people who buy music and movies legally. The industry will figure out a way to make a profit, and ultimately illegal downloads will result in increased costs for people who follow the law. The recording industry cannot compete against illegal downloads, and everyone will end up paying the price.

Consider the arguments that emerged in this discussion and answer the following questions

1. Should students be expelled for illegal file sharing? What arguments persuade you that this conclusion is correct?

2. Which advocate was stronger in terms of developing quality arguments? Why do you think so?

3. If sharing protected files is illegal, why do people do it? If you represented a recording studio, what would you do?

4. Take a close look at the claims made by each speaker. Were they strong or weak? What makes a claim strong?

An in-depth understanding of each of these parts both improves our ability to present arguments to recipients and allows for meaningful criticism of their appropriateness and effectiveness. This chapter focuses on developing claims and propositions. As we discussed in Chapter 1, a claim is the end point of an argument; it is "an expressed opinion or a conclusion that the arguer wants accepted." As discussions unfold, arguers make decisions about their positions and create claims to support that position. With the case of illegal file sharing, Cathy's position is simply that illegal activity is bad and should be banned. Her claims all support that larger point of view. Nick, on the other hand, takes a less legal point of view and creates claims that support what is in the best interests of the consumer as well as the producers. As recipients of this discussion or any other set of arguments, we must be able to identify an arguer's claim and distinguish it from the evidence and reasoning used to support it. Doing so enables us to analyze and competently criticize arguments made by others.

NATURE OF CLAIMS

Whenever we argue, we use claims and propositions. Both serve an important function in arguments because they help define and focus the direction of a discussion or debate. At this point, it is useful to distinguish clearly between claims and propositions. Argument claims, as defined in Chapter 1, are the end points of an individual argument. They are supported by reasoning and evidence and focus on a single issue or idea. When we argue, we may develop many different arguments, and each of those arguments has a claim. For instance, when Nick says, "copyright laws need serious updating," he is making an argument. But it is only one of many arguments he makes, and each of those other arguments also has a claim. Taken together, he develops a set of arguments that take a position on the main discussion topic: "Should Internet access be permanently discontinued for people who share files illegally?"

Propositions

Beyond the claims of individual arguments, however, lie propositions. *Propositions are overarching or main claims that serve as the principal claim of an extended argument.* Extended arguments occur whenever a group of individual arguments are collected together to prove a larger point or proposition. Propositions in an extended argument function like the thesis in an essay. This means first that propositions are a type of claim. They are the primary point made by an arguer. Second, propositions focus the field of discussion. They define and limit the issues that are available to arguers in a dispute. For instance, when Nick and Cathy talk about illegal file sharing, the topic area serves as a proposition. It includes some issues—what is legal, what protections exist, whether artists are harmed—and it excludes other issues—should Nick and Cathy go out for pizza? Propositions, by their nature, include some issues and exclude others.

Issues are important to the process of developing arguments, and they were introduced in Chapter 1 as things to consider when engaged in critical thinking and reflection. *Issues are the various points of potential disagreement related to a proposition.* As main claims, propositions set the boundary of acceptable and reasonable issues relevant to a particular topic. In other words, they create a propositional arena that defines what issues are appropriate for discussion. *A propositional arena is the ground for dispute and includes all the issues for controversy within a given proposition.* Propositions are supported by individual arguments that are developed from the issues within the propositional arena. These individual arguments are all related in some way to the proposition and may either support or deny it. Propositions thus provide a framework for understanding the relevance of individual arguments.

Figure 4.1 provides a good illustration of how propositions serve to limit the issues in a discussion. In this figure, potential and relevant issues for debate are contained within the field. These include A, B, C, D, E, F, G, and H. With this model, the file-sharing example could be looked at as a collection of the following issues:

A   Is it legal?
B   Does it harm new artists?
C   Did it destroy record stores?
D   Is it immoral and unethical?
E   Does illegal sharing actually increase legal sales?
F   Does illegal sharing open up new markets?
G   Is the consumer harmed?
H   Will artists and studios go bankrupt?

These issues, among many others, can be found in the propositional arena. Irrelevant issues are excluded by the proposition's boundary. In the figure, these issues are represented as I,

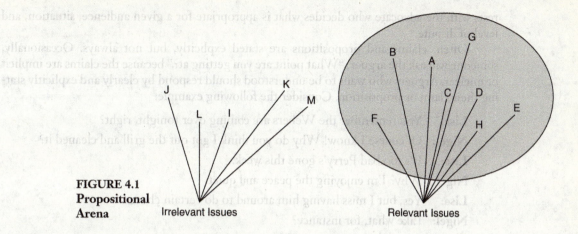

FIGURE 4.1
Propositional
Arena

Irrelevant Issues   Relevant Issues

J, K, L, and M. Examples of irrelevant issues that should be excluded from the discussion might be:

I   Should we go out for pizza?
J   There is no good music being produced anyway.
K   This is a dumb topic for a debate.
L   Should we have tax code reform?
M   What do you want to do tomorrow?

It is important for arguers and recipients to be clear about the meaning of a proposition because it determines what is included and excluded from the discussion. And, if irrelevant issues are allowed to become part of an argument, discussions and debates can be sidetracked to the point that the proposition may not be addressed at all.

This is the role of the parameter. *The parameter is the boundary that defines the propositional area and determines which issues are inside the arena and which are outside.* Parameters are determined by the way advocates define the proposition. For instance, if the term "file sharing" was defined to be all types of files both legal and illegal, the number of issues within the arena would increase significantly. If, on the other hand, the definition of "file sharing" means only songs obtained electronically, then the number of total issues within the arena would drop. This is why language and language abstraction, which we will discuss in Chapter 11, are important.

Using Claims and Propositions

Every proposition contains within its field more issues than an arguer can reasonably address—and it is not important that an arguer address every potential issue. The relevant question is, "What issues must be argued so that the advocate can make the point with the recipients?" In Figure 4.1, for instance, issues A, C, D, and H may be very important, while the others are less so. Arguers select from the available issues and construct extended argument cases focusing on the proposition. Some issues may never be addressed. The choice rests with the advocate who decides what is appropriate for a given audience, situation, and level of dispute.

Often, claims and propositions are stated explicitly, but not always. Occasionally, someone will ask the arguer, "What point are you getting at?" because the claims are implicit or unclear. Arguers who want to be understood should respond by clearly and explicitly stating their claim or proposition. Consider the following example:

Lisa: You remember the Webers are coming over tonight, right?

Nigel: Of course I know! Why do you think I got out the grill and cleaned it?

Lisa: It's too bad Perry's gone this week.

Nigel: Why? I'm enjoying the peace and quiet.

Lisa: Yes, but I miss having him around to do certain chores.

Nigel: Like what, for instance?

Lisa: Like mowing the lawn, for instance.

Nigel: Oh, you want me to mow the lawn, is that it?

Lisa wanted Nigel to mow the lawn for two reasons: They had guests coming over for a cookout, and the regular lawn mower was out of town. But her statements made no sense to Nigel until he discovered that her claim was, "I think you should mow the lawn."[8]

In essays, speeches, and other forms of one-way communication, claims are usually stated at the beginning or at the end of the argument. This placement occurs because arguers like to either state their position and then support it or present evidence or reasoning followed by a conclusion. Where are the claims in the following paragraphs?

For hundreds of years, authors have written about the loyalty and dedication bestowed on owners by their dogs. Dogs teach us about gift giving and generosity. They teach us about relationships and mutual responsibility. In fact, some have argued that dogs are a part of an "anti-economy." They give without requiring payment. They care without stipulation or reservation. These characteristics led Agnes Repplier to comment: Dogs "will love and admire the meanest of us, and feed our colossal vanity with their uncritical homage." If all people modeled their behavior after dogs, we would live in a much happier world.[9]

The labels we use affect how others perceive us and how we see ourselves; they shape how we see others and how we want to be seen by them; they are used by those in power to define the rest even as they struggle to define themselves. They shape who we are.[10]

The beginning sentence in the first paragraph put forward the claim that the remainder of the paragraph supported, and the final sentence in the second paragraph did the same. Someone wanting to identify the central claim in a paragraph can also watch for terms like *therefore, then,* and *so* that show the conclusion is coming.[11]

On the other hand, informally developed arguments—such as arguments developed among friends in a conversation—may not have clearly placed claims. This is because claims often emerge and develop as we argue. We tend not to begin discussions with a claim and then proceed in some strict, rational order.

Propositions often emerge and are formulated over time. Initially, they are tentatively stated and then honed and refined as participants become knowledgeable about vital issues in a dispute. For example, prosecutors study the particulars of a case before bringing charges;

legislators study and revise bills before they are introduced; doctors study a patient's symptoms before issuing a diagnosis; and most of us think and read about social and political problems before we venture to express opinions about them.

Networks of Claims

Long essays, speeches, extended discussions, and lengthy conversations in which efforts to argue and influence are taking place frequently contain a network of related claims that are combined to support a proposition. Figure 4.2 illustrates this.

Figure 4.2 displays a network of claims supporting the proposition "The lack of a clear policy for treating patients in irreversible comas is a problem in our society."[12] These are similar to argument chains introduced in Chapter 2 except that when advocates design extended arguments, the chains become networks of interconnected arguments. With these networks the proposition is supported by a hierarchy of subsidiary claims—principal sub-claims, secondary sub-claims, and sub-sub-claims.

With this example, the principal sub-claims state four major problem areas: lack of a definition of "death," rapid technological advancement, physical liability, and inconsistent procedures for decision-making. Each of these four principal sub-claims is in turn supported by clusters of secondary sub-claims and sub-sub-claims. Taken together, the sub-claims form an argument chain that reaches from the level of dispute to the proposition. The further the proposition is away from the level of dispute, the more layers of sub-claims are necessary to prove the proposition. The more complex and controversial a proposition, the longer the chain of arguments required to support the proposition.

In extended arguments such as the one illustrated in Figure 4.2, argument claims begin with assumptions or factual statements (see the two leftmost columns) that function as evidence because they are accepted by all parties to the discussion. They, therefore, fall below the level of dispute and act as starting points linked together through reasoning and evidence to support further claims. The network of claims as a whole in turn supports a main claim or proposition that possesses certain characteristics arising from its role as a central thesis. Because the proposition functions as it does within the context of an extended argument, it can be identified only within that context.

Fields, Propositions, and Claims

Depending on the field in which they occur, extended arguments supporting a main claim or proposition appear in many forms. In journalistic circles, they may appear as editorials; in criminal law, as cases constructed by the prosecution or defense; in business, as recommendations to management; in religious settings, as sermons and theological discussions; and in academic research, as articles in scholarly journals.

The field of argument determines the form of proposition for an extended argument. In a parliamentary setting, propositions may appear as motions ("I move that we abolish the university's core curriculum in general education"). In argumentative discussions, they may be expressed as an opinion ("MTV is a menace to the morality of today's youth"). In legal cases, they appear as indictments ("The state charges John Smith with reckless driving"). In medicine, they take the form of diagnosis and recommended treatment ("The patient appears to have a uterine fibroid tumor; surgery to remove it is recommended").

Proposition

The lack of a clear policy for treating patients in irreversible comas is a problem in our society.

Principal Sub-Claims

There is no commonly accepted definition of "death."

Technological advances have outstripped society's resources for dealing with the problem.

There is no consistency from state to state or even from hospital to hospital in applying criteria for euthanasia.

Secondary Sub-Claims

Legal definitions rely only on irreparable cessation of cardiac and respiratory activity.

Medical sources want to add brain activity as a criterion.

Moral definitions provide little agreement because of diverse religious views on what is "life."

Heart rate and respiration now can be maintained when no other signs of consciousness or brain function are present.

Technology violates its original function, which was to enhance or help life.

Because of ambiguity in deciding how to treat comatose patients, doctors are subject to liability suits, and charges of manslaughter and even murder.

Doctors experience many difficulties because of uncertainty regarding policy in this area.

Doctors are forced to violate the Hippocratic Oath.

In Kansas, the doctor alone makes the decision. In Massachusetts, the family decides.

Sub-Claims

Particular court opinions have relied on the presence of heartbeat and respiration to determine when death occurs.

The "Harvard Report" recommends including a flat EEG as one criterion for cessation of life.

Prolongation of death, dying, and pain demeans life.

The Hippocratic Oath states: "So far as discernment shall be mine, I will carry out the regimen for the benefit of the sick and will keep them from harm and wrong."

The Hippocratic Oath is subject to many different interpretations.

Sub-Sub-Claims

FIGURE 4.2 Network of Claims

Because a proposition provides the focal point for issues in a dispute, the absence of a clearly formulated statement of the main claim to be argued is problematic. In some situations in which you will argue, the proposition will be formulated by another party to the dispute or by some agent authorized to state it in advance. At other times, however, you yourself will be able to state the proposition to be supported. Such an opportunity might arise in interpersonal argument when no one has clearly formulated the central question to be discussed. You may also need to formulate a proposition for an essay or speech you plan to make. The next section, therefore, discusses the criteria for clear, precise propositions.

FORMULATING PROPOSITIONS

People who engage in argument expect certain things to happen. Their expectations grow out of the conventions, or implicit "rules," for conducting arguments that influence argumentative discussions in our society.[13] Because people expect that arguments are made for specific purposes and are directed toward specific goals, arguers need to formulate their propositions and statements of opinion to meet others' expectations. This section will consider the basic requirements for expressing well-developed propositions and claims. Individual claims and propositions need to be both controversial and clear.

Controversiality

All claims and propositions should be controversial. *If a claim or proposition is controversial, it states a position that is not currently accepted or adhered to by the audience.* As we noted in Chapter 1, argumentative theses are concerned with matters that are controversial. After all, if everyone agrees about an issue, what need is there to argue? In fact, statements that are not controversial probably serve the function of evidence rather than claims. As main claims for extended arguments, propositions also need to be balanced and to challenge the status quo to ensure an overall discussion of the topic that is both fair and provocative. People do not argue about things such as whether the earth is round or whether murder is wrong. Instead, they use their understanding of these accepted claims as evidence to ground other claims. In selecting a topic, advocates should choose something that will be important and controversial to their audience. For example, advocates defending the proposition "Education is beneficial to society" or "Freedom is important in a democracy" might be met with ambivalence or disinterest from their readers or listeners. They might wonder why such a thesis needs to be defended since everyone already agrees with it.

When issues require the recipients to have specialized knowledge or background, the arguer has two responsibilities. First, the arguer should provide the recipients with sufficient information about issues to make them aware of the controversy. And second, the arguer should provide sufficient depth to the issues to develop the recipients' capabilities to make reasoned judgments about the arguers. For example, if the arguer were going to discuss means for resolving conflicts in the Middle East, the arguer would have to provide the recipients with sufficient history and cultural knowledge to be able to make a reasonable interpretation of the arguments.

In deciding on a proposition for discussion or debate, it is wise to canvass newspapers and other current periodicals. What is controversial and the subject of public attention at one time may be of little interest later because the matter has been settled or because other issues seem more pressing. Questions of what to do about the polio epidemic or whether we should have mandatory seat belt laws were very controversial at one time. However, a vaccine was found for polio, and the passage of seat belt laws has successfully reduced the number of highway fatalities. The controversiality of a proposition may depend on what issues are timely and of significant public interest.

Clarity

When people engage in argument, they expect to know the argument's goal and how to determine when the issue has been resolved. Ambiguous, unclear, muddled claims and propositions generally lead to muddled argumentation. *Clarity refers to how well a claim focuses arguments on a particular set of issues.* People need to know where they are starting in order to decide when they have finished. If, through ambiguous wording, the claim allows multiple interpretations or fosters misunderstanding, then it is not clear. Consider Figure 4.3. When a claim is unclear, the issues on or near the edge of the propositional arena are not clearly included or excluded. If a proposition is stated clearly, it is easier to decide which issues are relevant and which are not. But if a proposition is ambiguous, the relevant issues are less apparent, and arguers may find themselves discussing extraneous matters or tangential issues.

Ambiguous Terms

One major source of confusion in stating propositions is the use of ambiguous terms that are interpreted one way by one party to the dispute and another way by the other. Since each party is interpreting the proposition differently, each arguer has a different starting point and is probably going in a direction unanticipated by the other. For example, consider a dispute between two professors discussing the merits of non-graded credit options for students. Both are unaware that there are actually *two* such options at their university. One option, Credit/No Credit, is offered on a class-wide basis in which all students take the class as Credit/No Credit. The second option is Satisfactory/Non-Satisfactory, which can be elected by individual students in courses where other students take the

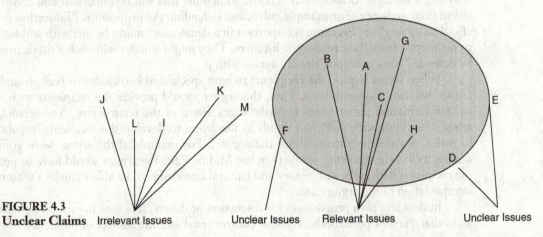

FIGURE 4.3
Unclear Claims   Irrelevant Issues   Unclear Issues   Relevant Issues   Unclear Issues

course for a grade. Professor Jones, who teaches a Credit/No Credit course, is talking with Professor Smith.

Smith: I think the pass/fail grading system is just a way of letting students goof off.

Jones: That's not true! The students in my class work just as hard as they would for a grade!

Smith: Oh, come on! They just use pass/fail grading to make life easier for themselves. It's the easy route to accumulating credits.

Jones: That would only be true if students worked only for grades. Some are motivated more by the subject matter and the pleasure of learning.

Smith: You surely are an idealist. Everyone knows that it's the concrete payoffs that allow students to get ahead that really motivate them.

Jones: All I can speak from is my own experience.

This discussion is not going in a profitable direction, primarily because of the ambiguity of the phrase "pass/fail grading system." For example, if Professor Jones made it clear that he was speaking of the Credit/No Credit designation that is mainly used for activity-based and performance courses (internships, readers' theatre, orchestra, etc.), his statements about motivation and the pleasure of learning might be more readily accepted by Professor Smith. Here are two more examples of ambiguous terms in propositions:

Euthanasia should be allowed when the patient and family consent to it.

Does "euthanasia" in this claim refer to removal of life support systems (passive euthanasia) or to administering drugs or other means to induce death (active euthanasia, or "mercy killing")?

Grades are not an effective means of determining a student's intelligence.

Does "determine" here mean "to obtain knowledge of" or "to bring about as a result"? Both are accepted dictionary definitions, yet they lend very different interpretations to the claim. Examples such as these show the desirability of using precise and exact terms when stating claims.

Double-Barreled Statements

A second source of confusion and lack of clarity in stating claims is the "double-barreled" statement. *Double-barreled claims advance two or more claims simultaneously and, as with ambiguous terms, often lead arguers in separate directions because the relevant issues for each part of the claim are different.* Because double-barreled claims and propositions include issues from two or more propositional arenas, arguers often find it difficult to focus on and define the arena under dispute. If a proposition or claim has different objectives, the arguer should divide it into separate claims—one for each objective. Figure 4.4 illustrates the problems of double-barreled claims. In this diagram, the overlap is where issues are shared. But outside of the part that overlaps, the separate parts of the claim have their own sets of issues. This becomes a problem of clarity. The double-barreled claims encompass issues that support one idea and not the other. The result is that an arguer is faced with confusion regarding which issues are relevant and which issues are not depending on what argument is being made.

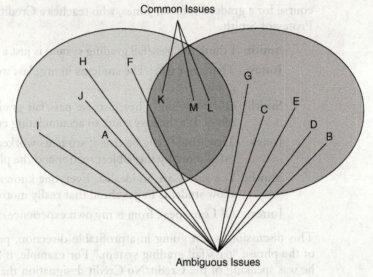

FIGURE 4.4 Double-Barreled Claims

Confusion because of double-barreled claims has occurred in the example of the discussion between Professors Smith and Jones. Smith's claim really is that "opportunistic students exploit the pass/fail grading system." Consequently, Smith and Jones are actually discussing two issues simultaneously—whether non-graded options have an effect on student learning and performance, and whether students are likely to take the "easy way out." If Smith had more clearly stated his claim and if Jones and Smith had agreed on what the main claim was to be, their discussion might have been less diffuse and more profitable. Here are two additional examples of double-barreled claims broken into two separate claims:

Double-barreled claim: The U.S. federal government should cut the income tax rate to stimulate the economy.

Claim 1: The U.S. federal government should cut the income tax rate.

Claim 2: Cutting the income tax rate will stimulate the economy.

Double-barreled claim: If corporations test employees for drugs, they should also test for alcohol, which is the biggest drug of all.

Claim 1: Alcohol is the "biggest" (most frequently used) drug of all.

Claim 2: Drug testing should be combined with alcohol testing by corporations that test for substance abuse.

The desirability of breaking double-barreled claims into separate claims is illustrated by the rules of parliamentary procedure. *Robert's Rules of Order* state that only one proposal or claim can be considered at a time. If someone proposes a motion with a dual idea, the motion should be divided into separate motions that can be debated separately.[14] Dividing related but separate ideas allows participants in a discussion to recognize their starting point and to know when they have reached their goal. Stating individual ideas separately enables arguers to recognize the points on which they agree and the points on which they disagree, thereby conforming to the conventions of argument and promoting productive, orderly discussions.

Balance

A productive, fair discussion of the issues in a dispute can result only when the topic of discussion is stated in a form with which both parties feel comfortable. Recipients can be drawn into a discussion and persuaded by the evidence an arguer offers only when they are convinced that the arguer has a balanced perspective on the topic. *Balance is the requirement that the issues for and against a proposition be included equally in the propositional field.* When the topic is specifically and clearly stated in neutral language, the field is left open for both its proponents and its opponents to discuss it freely. In fact, a neutral, dispassionate statement of the proposition is a convention in many forums of argument. In law, the charges brought against a defendant are stated neutrally and are agreed upon before the trial can begin (Ms. Jones committed libel against Ms. Davis; Mr. Smith is charged with driving while intoxicated). In business management, decision makers usually discuss a specific policy or course of action that has been recommended (Should we acquire the Widget Company as a subsidiary of our operation? Does the preliminary information we have on this product line indicate that it should be heavily promoted?).

When a proposition for discussion is stated in connotative or prejudicial language, however, the deck is stacked against the viewpoint that opposes the proposition because the issues available to the opposing arguers have been limited or tainted by the emotionally loaded language. Furthermore, speakers and writers who state their theses in ways that reveal personal biases cause their audiences to become suspicious. Consider, for example, the following propositions:

Space exploration is the world's biggest money waster.

Stupid and evil recidivists should be put away for life.

Propositions such as these overstate one's case and close off rather than promote open discussion because extraneous language serves to limit the issues available to the arguers. Propositions that avoid connotative language, superlatives, and stereotypes encourage all parties to the dispute to consider all available options and decision proposals. The propositions given above could be rephrased to be more neutral. As a general rule of thumb, the wording of the proposition should be agreeable to all parties of a dispute.

Funds invested in space exploration should be significantly reduced.

Repeat offenders should receive life imprisonment.

It is important to note that this requirement is for propositions and not all claims. When advocates build extended arguments in favor of propositions, the expectation is that other arguers will develop alternatives. Propositions are important and unique because they are the one statement that all advocates should agree with and because they frame the way a conversation develops and how it is focused.

Challenge

One of the characteristics of an argument that we discussed in Chapter 1 is that it is an attempt to influence someone else. *Challenge means that an arguer's claim confronts recipients' existing values, beliefs, or behaviors.* Generally, the arguer who initiates the dispute by stating the initial claim expresses dissatisfaction with a prevailing belief or state of affairs.

The arguer tries to change the other's attitudes or behavior to something different from what the attitudes or behavior would be if no argumentation took place.

A proposition for argument or debate should, therefore, challenge what people already believe or do. This is more than the requirement of being controversial. Whereas controversy refers to how ready a recipient is to agree to or believe in a proposition or claim, challenge focuses on changing the recipient in some way. This convention is based on the principle that there is no reason to defend an already accepted practice or belief unless it is questioned or criticized. Richard Whately, a nineteenth-century educator and clergyman, described this convention and its implications for argument.[15] He observed that in most argumentation there was a presumption and a burden of proof. The presumption favors the position that, because it is already accepted, "preoccupies the ground" in a controversy until some challenge is made against it. The person initiating the dispute therefore has the burden of proof entailed in making such a challenge.

The metaphor of preoccupying ground that Whately uses is carried through in the associations we make when we hear the word *claim*. A land claim is a claim to a parcel of land owned or possessed by someone else. The agency or the institution against which the claim is made enjoys no other advantage than the prerogative to retain the land if the claim is not upheld and accepted.

Therefore, the implication of Whately's concepts is that arguers who advance claims should challenge existing beliefs, policies, and states of affairs. Those who put forward proposals or advocate new ideas assume the *burden of proof*, which *obligates arguers to provide good and sufficient reasons for changing what is already accepted*. Those who defend existing beliefs and practices enjoy the *presumption*, that is, *the predisposition to favor an existing practice or belief until some good reason for changing it is offered*. The following claims do not challenge existing beliefs and practices and thus do not fulfill the burden-of-proof requirement:

School desegregation is desirable.

California should continue to rely on sales and property taxes for revenue.

The legal drinking age in the United States should be twenty-one.

Propositions such as these do not advocate change, and if arguments supporting them were not made, the policies and conditions they advocate would continue anyway. The following propositions, on the other hand, assume a burden of proof for the person who defends them because they challenge beliefs and policies that are presently accepted.

A nationwide system of magnet schools is desirable.

Washington State should implement an income tax.

The U.S. legal drinking age should be set at eighteen.

Because they raise the possibility of innovations and new policies, such propositions challenge the present system. They also fulfill our expectation that attempts at influence be necessary and justified. Box 4.2, "Apply the Theory," guides you through each of these requirements for developing claims.

■ ■ ■ ■ ■

BOX 4.2
APPLY THE THEORY: WRITING CLAIMS

This section focused on the four requirements for writing claims: clarity, challenge, controversiality, and balance. Based on what you have read, write three claims and answer the following questions:

	Claim 1:	Claim 2:	Claim 3:
Is this claim clear? Double-barreled? Ambiguous terms?			
If this were a proposition, is it balanced? How do you know?			
Is this controversial? What, exactly, makes it generally unaccepted by your recipients?			
Does this claim challenge? What does it ask your recipients to do or believe that they do not do now?			

CLASSIFICATION

Generally, claims can be classified using three continua. These are illustrated in Figure 4.5 and include type, expression, and emergence. The concept of a continuum is useful here because it suggests that claims are interconnected—they "fit" into ways of thinking and knowing, they carry assumptions about the types of issues an arguer needs to address, and they help us understand an arguer's goals and direction. Knowing how a claim functions using each continuum in any given argument or situation can help the arguer decide what issues or questions need to be addressed. Some claims are stated expressly and refer to sources or conditions that can be readily checked for verification. Yet, other claims and propositions may not be stated directly and depend on the recipient to consider the supporting material and then draw the conclusion the arguer sought. Advertising often uses this form of argument. Abercrombie

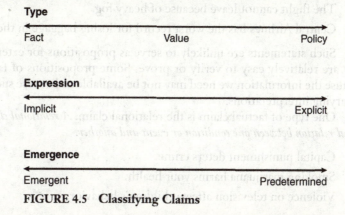

FIGURE 4.5   Classifying Claims

and Fitch ads, for instance, have been criticized for sexual images and no clear message about what the company expects the consumer to purchase. Of course, there is a clear message—it is implicit in the ad, but there is a message.

Sometimes arguers do not know what the proposition is until the end of the argument is reached—claims emerge as the argument develops. Other claims, such as those involving social values or policies, require more complex forms of support. For example, in Figure 4.2, the claim restating the Hippocratic Oath can be verified merely by referring to the text of the oath itself. If the group discussing euthanasia were to question whether "prolongation of death, dying, and pain demeans life," however, it would have to spend some time defining the terms of the claim and generating criteria to decide whether certain practices "demean life." This section will explore each of the three continua of claim classification and examine how these concepts influence the way we argue.

Types of Claims

Many category schemes for classifying claims have been proposed.[16] Some are very complex and suggest dozens of types, whereas others are much simpler and argue that it is impossible to divide claims into subtypes. However, the simplest and most frequently used scheme divides claims into the categories of fact, value, and policy. We will use this scheme here because it includes the major recognized types of claims used as subjects of argument and because the sets of issues each type generates can be distinguished from the sets of issues generated by the other two.[17]

Factual

Factual claims make inferences about past, present, or future conditions or relationships. They are described in Box 4.3. If a statement is about a condition or relationship that is already known and readily apparent to participants in the argumentation, it functions as *evidence*, or, in a network of claims, as a sub-sub-claim used as a starting point for argument. Remember from Chapter 1 that previously established claims could be used as evidence in new arguments that build on them.

Some statements of fact are straightforward and easily established, therefore not disputable. For example:

Mary weighs more than John.

The flight cannot leave because of heavy fog.

Central Airlines has the worst record for losing baggage in the United States.

Such statements are unlikely to serve as propositions for extended arguments because they are relatively easy to verify or prove. Some propositions of fact are difficult to prove because the information we need may not be available or because such information is subject to varying interpretations.

One type of factual claim is the relational claim. *A relational claim attempts to establish a causal relation between one condition or event and another.*

Capital punishment deters crime.

Smoking marijuana harms your health.

Violence on television affects children's behavior.

■ ■ ■ ■ ■

BOX 4.3
FACTUAL CLAIMS

Definition: *Factual claims make inferences about past, present, or future conditions or relationships.*

- Factual claims are relatively easy to prove because the needed information is generally available and clear. Example: Mary weighs more than John.
- Some factual claims require clear definitions and strong supporting material because they include terms that may be ambiguous. Example: Capital punishment deters crime.
- Factual claims are generally one of three types: relational, predictive, and historical.

Definition: *Relational claims attempt to establish a causal relation between one condition or event and another.*

Example: A diet high in fat will harm your health.

Definition: *Predictive claims are based on the assumption that past relationships and conditions will be repeated in the future.*

Example: Every home in the United States and Canada will have an Internet connection by 2020.

Definition: *Claims of historical fact rest on the strength of probable evidence to which we have access.*

Example: There was no evidence of weapons of mass destruction in Iraq.

Researchers have completed many studies on each of these topics, and their results do not agree. Sifting through and comparing information on such topics is worthwhile because the inferences made in the claims are so controversial.

A second type of factual claim that makes an argumentative statement about what will happen is the predictive claim. *A predictive claim is based on the assumption that past relationships and conditions will be repeated in the future.* Because information that might prove such claims is often not available, predictive claims often serve as the subject of argumentation. For example:

A staffed space mission will reach Mars by 2020.

The world economy is headed for a massive depression by 2018.

A severe shortage of teachers will occur by the year 2025.

Such claims are usually supported by descriptions of long-term trends and statistically based projections; they also involve studying causal relationships that may be affected by unanticipated developments and events.

A third type of factual claim is the *claim of historical fact*, which *rests on the strength of probable evidence to which we have access.* Because historical records and artifacts may be damaged, destroyed, or lost as time passes, evidence supporting historical claims may be as unavailable as that supporting predictive claims. Extensive controversy has surrounded the following claims:

The Shroud of Turin was worn by Jesus in the tomb.

Aliens visited ancient human cultures more than 5000 years ago.

Lee Harvey Oswald was the sole assassin of John F. Kennedy.

Supporters of such claims collect and describe as much circumstantial evidence as possible to convince skeptics that their claims are true. Historical claims cannot be positively proven because direct evidence to support them is unavailable.

The three types of factual claims that can serve as the subject of argument, then, are relational claims, predictive claims, and historical claims. Relational claims connect two conditions and infer that one of them has brought about or will bring about another. Predictive claims are grounded in the assumption that past events will be repeated in the future and make a claim about some future occurrence. Historical claims are descriptive and informational and are usually based on a preponderance of evidence that a particular account or interpretation of past events is the correct one. All three deal with matters that are disputable because the information we would need to establish them conclusively is insufficient or unavailable. They describe how or why something has come about or will come about in ways that are controversial and subject to argument.

Value

In Chapter 3 we described values as desirable, transituational goals that serve as guiding principles in people's lives. They represent fundamental positive or negative attitudes toward certain end states of existence or broad modes of conduct.[18] Such fundamental attitudes influence our conceptions of what is desirable or undesirable in a given situation. Joseph W. Wenzel has noted that "values exist in an intersubjective realm of agreements that are the fabric of a community; they exist in the actions and discourse of persons constructing, sustaining, testing, and revising the rules by which we will live and act together."[19] Examples of values expressing fundamental conceptions of desirable end states are equality, salvation, self-fulfillment, and freedom; those regarding models of conduct are courage, honesty, and loyalty.

Value claims, then, assess the worth or merit of an idea, object, or practice according to standards or criteria supplied by the arguer. They are described in Box 4.4. Value claims help shape our choice making and indicate to us what we ought believe and do. When we make value

---

BOX 4.4

VALUE CLAIMS

Definition: *Value claims assess the worth or merit of an idea, object, or practice according to criteria supplied by the arguer.*

- Values are fundamental positive or negative attitudes toward certain end states of existence or broad modes of conduct such as equality (end state) and honesty (mode of conduct).
- Value claims focus on the values held by the participants in a dispute.
- Values govern our choices and indicate what we *ought* to do.

Examples:

Stem-cell research is beneficial to society.

Grading undermines the quality of education.

Censorship of Internet pornography is justified.

claims by assigning a value to an object, practice, or idea, we are actually making recommendations to others. Following are examples of value claims:

Capital punishment is beneficial to society.

Private schools provide better elementary and secondary education than public schools.

Edgar Degas's paintings are ethereally beautiful.

In each of these claims, a value judgment is made. The first deals with social benefit, the second with quality, and the third with aesthetic merit. The claims also involve an object of evaluation that may be an idea, a practice, a person, or a thing. Analysis of value claims must be located within some field or framework that implies the standards or criteria for the value judgment. For example, judging capital punishment according to its social benefits might involve a utilitarian standard whereby we try to determine whether capital punishment provides the greatest good for the greatest number of citizens. Criteria suggested by a utilitarian standard might include the following:

- Does capital punishment actually prevent capital crimes?
- Does implementing capital punishment save more lives than it takes?
- Does capital punishment discriminate against minorities?

Understanding values as discussed in Chapter 3 is important. How we understand values depends on argument situation, the relative importance of the value in a hierarchy, and the degree to which it is important to the hearers.

Policy

Policy claims call for a specific course of action and focus on whether a change in policy or behavior should take place. These are illustrated in Box 4.5. Policy claims frequently deal with complex social, political, or economic problems, but they may also deal with actions on a much

---

BOX 4.5
POLICY CLAIMS

Definition: *Policy claims call for a specific course of action and focus on whether a change in policy or behavior should take place.*

- The claims focus on action and/or policies.
- They frequently deal with complex social, political, and economic problems that rely on an understanding of values and facts.
- Policy claims imply dissatisfaction with the *status quo* or a belief that a change in behavior would be beneficial.

Examples:

Pierce County should legalize prostitution.

California should pass a 1 percent sales tax to fund schools.

We should rent this apartment.

smaller scale. In the conversation between Nigel and Lisa near the beginning of this chapter, Lisa's implication that Nigel should mow the lawn must be considered a policy claim. Other examples of policy claims are the following:

> The Kitsap County government should legalize prostitution.
>
> Sales of handguns to private citizens in the United States should be banned.
>
> You should not smoke cigarettes in public places.

When making policy claims, arguers express either dissatisfaction with present practices or a belief that a change in practices or behavior would be an improvement. Factual claims focus on what exists or is likely to exist. Value claims make a judgment. Policy claims consider facts and values and move to action. In this sense, they are future oriented and focus on what the next steps should be. Box 4.6, "Apply the Theory," will guide you through the process of developing each type of claim.

Interconnection

Having divided propositions and claims into the three types just discussed; we must make one important observation. The three categories are not discrete and unrelated to one another, but are instead interconnected. Factual claims serve as the foundation for both value and policy claims. We are not inclined to make value or policy claims in the absence of fact claims. For example, to argue the value claim "Restricting access to the Internet for children is desirable," we must also understand and accept certain fact-based arguments. These might include the following:

> There are pornographic sites on the Internet that might harm children.
>
> There is language on the Web that is not suitable for children.
>
> There are topics on the Internet that children are not developmentally ready to understand.

Fact claims are the basis for making most of our value and policy claims. They provide arguers with a foundation for the claims that follow.

Similarly, value claims assume the existence of certain facts and serve as the basis for making policy claims. We might make the claim, for instance, that "censoring pornographic material is desirable." This value claim assumes the existence of certain facts (the existence

---

■ ■ ■ ■ ■

BOX 4.6
APPLY THE THEORY: TYPES OF CLAIMS

This section described how each type of claim works within an argument and for what purpose. Based on what you know about factual, value, and policy claims:

1. Write down a controversial subject.
2. Using the same subject, write a factual claim, a value claim, and a policy claim.
3. Do these claims meet the requirements of well-worded claims developed earlier?

of pornographic material) and at the same time provides a justification for a policy action (pornography should be banned). All three types of claims, therefore, are linked together by networks of subsidiary or foundational claims: fact claims supporting value claims, value claims supporting policy claims, and policy claims assuming facts and values.

Such a network could be seen if we were to discuss the policy claim "Sales of handguns to private citizens in the United States should be banned." In this case, we might consider one or all of the following claims:

> The number of handgun deaths and injuries in our country is appalling. (Value claim)
>
> The licensing and regulation of handgun sales is inconsistent from state to state. (Factual claim)
>
> Eliminating handguns will decrease the number of unpremeditated and accidental gun injuries. (Predictive factual claim)
>
> The "right to bear arms" is not as important as the public's right to safety and freedom from harm. (Value claim)

An examination of the network of claims supporting policy propositions will always reveal subsidiary claims of fact and value. Furthermore, a value proposition such as "compulsory national service for all U.S. citizens is desirable" will involve decisions about policy. What is to be done to provide the needed service? Does "compulsory national service" mean a universal draft, required public service, or some other practice?

Arguers need to keep in mind that because different types of claims are interdependent, they are not always easily distinguished from one another. For example, if an arguer claimed that "driving above the speed limit is harmful," the claim seems to come to rest somewhere on the continuum between fact and value. The term *harmful* implies a value. What is meant by harm? How do we evaluate harm? At the same time, we can assume that excessive speed results in a fact of harm.

Between each classification (fact, value, policy) there is a "gray zone" in which claims may hold both fact and value elements or value and policy elements. Furthermore, no claim exists independently. Because certain facts are true, we tend to value things. Because certain values are important, we tend to make policies. Similarly, our policies reflect our values, which in turn reflect our understanding of how the world works (facts). Claims of various types often occur in conjunction with each other and are interdependent. If arguers can identify and distinguish them, however, they will be able to focus on the issues and vital questions that the claims imply.

Expression

Some claims are expressed explicitly, whereas others remain implicit and rely on recipients to reach the conclusion on their own. *Explicit claims are stated clearly and publicly such that both the arguer and recipient are equally aware of their meaning.* In Chapter 3 we discussed how different cultures approach argument. Explicit claims are typically found in Western traditional arguments, whereas implicit claims are more often found in Asian or some African cultures. *Implicit claims are not stated publicly and are understood by the participants engaged in the argument.* These claims rely on the arguers having sufficient contextual knowledge of the argument situation to be able to clearly understand and argue about the topic. Because implicit claims are open to interpretation, they are seen as less confrontational than explicit claims that can polarize an argument.

Consider the following explicit claims:

Schools should expel students who bring any weapon to school—even toy weapons.

The United States should pass an amendment to eliminate the Electoral College.

The drinking age should be reduced to eighteen.

Marijuana should be decriminalized.

Each of these claims is clear and can be understood even if the recipient did not know the history or context that generated the claim. Each one clearly divides the argument field and provides an advocate with a clear propositional arena. Contrast these explicit claims with the following conversation between a married couple:

Kyle: I can't believe you are home late again. This is ridiculous!

Minerva: Work has been really busy this month. I can't help it.

Kyle: Work should not define your life. You are already putting in a sixty-hour week.

Minerva: I'll try to do better, but I need a little patience right now.

It is hard to know exactly what the proposition is in this exchange because unless we know the context that created the exchange, it is difficult to interpret its meaning. The implicit claims could be:

We need to spend more time together.

Because you are not working, I need to work harder to make ends meet.

You are ignoring your family.

Depending on the argument situation, the relationship among arguers, and the culture, claims can be both explicitly stated or implicitly understood. An argument critic trying to examine an argument needs to be aware of how implicit claims function and should be able to examine the larger context to find the underlying assumptions, relationships, and cultural connections.

Emergence

When a court convenes, it examines a proposition. It might consider the guilt of someone, whether legislation was constitutional or not, or if the process was appropriately conducted. In any case, courts decide on propositions that are determined in advance. Examples might include:

John Doe is guilty of murder.

The Broadcast Decency Act is unconstitutional.

An appeal should be granted because the evidence was tainted.

Legislatures and governing assemblies are similar. They meet to discuss whether a particular action should be taken or if a decision should be made. These are all examples of predetermined claims. *Predetermined claims are claims that precede and guide an extended argument.*

In other words, these are claims and propositions that initiate arguments. When a claim is predetermined, the propositional arena, sets of issues, and direction for the arguments are all fairly well defined. The advocates know in advance what the focus of the discussion or exchange will be.

However, in many conversational arguments, claims and propositions emerge from the discussion—they are not predetermined. These types of claims are referred to as emergent claims. *Emergent claims are claims and propositions that develop within an exchange among advocates; they are not agreed to in advance.* In these cases, people focus and develop the propositional arena through the course of the exchange as the conversation unfolds. The arguers might have had an idea about a direction for a discussion, but the specific proposition was not stated or agreed on by the participants in advance. Consider the following exchange between two friends:

Donna: I'm thinking about going to a movie.

Amanda: Me, too. Is there anything good playing now?

Donna: I don't know. I heard that the *I Am Legend* sequel was pretty good. It's playing at the Grand. I also heard that *Rainbow 6* was pretty good.

Amanda: I think I would rather see *Rainbow 6* than *I Am Legend*.

Donna: That works for me. Let's go.

The proposition that emerges from this conversation is "Let's go to see *Rainbow 6*," but it did not exist as a proposition before Donna and Amanda began talking.

When critics examine arguments, the proposition and structure of claims can be deceiving if the analyst fails to consider how propositions and claims function in the complete argument. Is it a fact or value or policy claim? Is it implicit or is it clearly stated? Figure 4.6 illustrates some questions to ask in trying to analyze the claims and arguments. Do the arguers

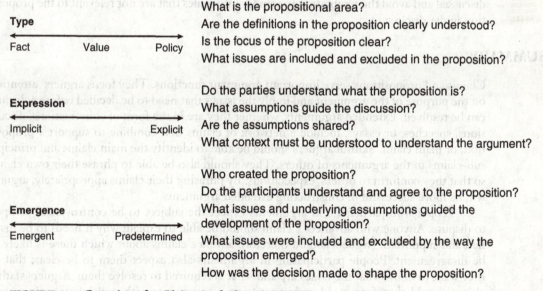

Type

Fact   Value   Policy

What is the propositional area?
Are the definitions in the proposition clearly understood?
Is the focus of the proposition clear?
What issues are included and excluded in the proposition?

Expression

Implicit   Explicit

Do the parties understand what the proposition is?
What assumptions guide the discussion?
Are the assumptions shared?
What context must be understood to understand the argument?

Emergence

Emergent   Predetermined

Who created the proposition?
Do the participants understand and agree to the proposition?
What issues and underlying assumptions guided the development of the proposition?
What issues were included and excluded by the way the proposition emerged?
How was the decision made to shape the proposition?

FIGURE 4.6   Questions for Claim Analysis

FIGURE 4.7 Classifying Claims

really know what the proposition is that they are discussing? One way of examining the role of propositions in any extended argument is simply to chart it. Figure 4.7 provides an example of this for the proposition: "The United States Congress should amend the 1982 Nuclear Waste Policy Act to allow for research of non-geological nuclear waste storage sites." This is a predetermined, expressed policy proposition. If, however, it were an implicit, emergent policy proposition, an analyst would need to consider the assumptions of the advocates, the situation for the exchange, and the issues involved in reaching the conclusions.

Being able to classify claims along these three dimensions is important because we are then able to understand where ambiguity and misunderstanding may emerge. If a proposition is emergent, for instance, advocates may need to pay careful attention to some of the high-context elements of the exchange to draw meaning from the argument situation. If propositions are largely implicit, arguers must be careful to remain focused on the issues discussed and avoid the temptation to wander into issues that are not relevant to the proposition under discussion.

SUMMARY

Claims and propositions serve important argument functions. They focus arguers' attention on the purpose of the argument and imply the issues that need to be decided before a dispute can be resolved. Extended arguments, whether they are in the form of conversations, discussions, speeches, or essays, include a network of claims that combine to support a proposition, or main claim. Skillful arguers should be able to identify the main claims and principal sub-claims in the arguments of others. They should also be able to phrase their own claims so that they conform to others' expectations. By phrasing their claims appropriately, arguers will be more successful in constructing extended arguments.

People who participate in arguments expect the subject to be controversial or open to dispute. Anyone who advances a claim should be able to explain why it needs to be justified and supported. Arguers should therefore advance claims about which there is likely to be disagreement. People participating in arguments also expect them to be clear; that is, they want to know what the issues are and what is required to resolve them. Arguers stating claims should therefore avoid ambiguous terms, statements with multiple meanings, and statements that introduce multiple issues simultaneously. Furthermore, stating claims in a biased or prejudiced way forestalls open discussion of the options to be considered. Claims should therefore be stated objectively, and stereotypes and connotative terms should be avoided. Finally, people expect arguers to take issue with prevailing attitudes and practices. If an arguer attempts to influence someone, he or she must make a claim that would change what would continue to be done or believed had the argument not taken place. In presenting an argument for change, the arguer assumes the burden of proving there is good reason for the change to be made.

Claims can be classified using three continua. The first continuum is type; the second continuum is expression; and the final one is emergence. There are three major types of claims that are made in arguments. Each type of claim calls for a different type of analysis to identify the issues that the claim implies. Claims of fact make inferences about the past, present, or future conditions or relationships. Sometimes factual claims are readily verifiable and agreed on by all parties to the dispute, or come to be agreed on as the argument progresses. At other times, factual claims cannot be conclusively established because the needed information is unavailable, in conflict, or subject to conflicting interpretations. Value claims assess the worth or merit of something according to standards supplied by the arguer. The focus of disputes on value claims is on the fundamental attitudes (values) of participants in the argumentation. Value disputes may involve ethical, aesthetic, or moral judgments. Policy claims call for a course of action or change in the beliefs of others. They usually express dissatisfaction with present practices or a belief that a change in policy or behavior will bring improvement. It is important to remember that claims are not separate and discrete. Rather, each of the three types of claims may often rely on other types of claims for its support.

Depending on the relationship among the arguers and the context for the discussion, claims may be explicit or implicit. Explicit claims are those that are stated publicly and are understood by the arguers. Other claims may be implicit and not stated publicly, but rather they are understood and exist as part of the web of assumptions that underlie the relationship or history of the advocates.

Finally, some claims are predetermined, whereas others are emergent. Predetermined claims and propositions are those that exist and are understood prior to the arguers beginning their discussion. Emergent claims stem from the conversation and are understood as a result of a discussion.

EXERCISES

Exercise 1: Propositions. In this chapter, four criteria were described that enable you to decide whether a proposition is well formulated. They are as follows:

- *Controversiality.* The proposition should state a thesis that is potentially disputable rather than one about which most people would agree.
- *Clarity.* The proposition should be clearly and precisely stated; ambiguous terms and double-barreled claims should be avoided.
- *Balance.* The claim should be stated in objective, neutral language rather than in a way that reveals the personal biases or prejudices of the person making the claim.
- *Challenge.* The proposition should confront an audience's prevailing beliefs, values, or state of affairs.

Using these criteria, criticize the following propositions. Are they well formulated? If not, why not? How could they be reformulated to function more effectively?

1. *Exercise is good for one's health.
2. Pirating music through the Internet is justified.
3. The United Nations is ineffective.
4. Plea bargaining is a good and essential means of case disposal.
5. *Euthanasia is a desirable and necessary medical practice.
6. Suing McDonald's for contributing to obesity is a frivolous lawsuit.
7. The U.S. government should adopt broadcast decency laws.
8. People who are HIV-positive should not be allowed to teach in public schools.
9. The United States should reduce its deficit by cutting wasteful social programs.
10. All schools should adopt school uniforms for their dress code.
11. Schools should become more rigorous.
12. Degenerate and perverted pornographic material should be pulled from every bookstore and magazine stand in America.
13. Good salespeople are effective.
14. *Women should have access to abortion on demand.
15. Legalization of casino gambling has made the rich richer and the poor poorer.
16. Education is good.
17. America's industries need to invest in manufacturing if the United States is to be internationally competitive in the twenty-first century.
18. People who own large cars with big engines are wasteful, stupid, and trying to destroy our environment.
19. Dams are destructive to the environment and should be removed.
20. Parties are a way of life in college.

Exercise 2: Claim Continuum. This chapter discussed a continuum within which three types of claims could be identified: fact, value, and policy. Fact claims make inferences about past, present, or future conditions or relationships; they can be explanatory, predictive, or historical. Value claims judge an idea, object, person, or practice by some value standard or set of criteria. Policy claims advocate a course of action that is not currently followed. Where would you place each of the following criteria on the continuum of claims?

1. *Extraterrestrial beings visited Earth during prehistoric times.
2. Every state should require that all teachers pass a proficiency examination.
3. All nations should destroy their biological weapons.
4. Illegal immigrants generally take jobs U.S. citizens do not want.
5. Discrimination is never justified.
6. Marijuana should be legalized in all fifty states.
7. Mandatory seat belt laws violate our constitutional rights.
8. Polygraph evidence is better than eyewitness testimony in criminal trials.
9. Pornography causes sex crimes.

10. Required automotive emissions tests are an inefficient means of ensuring clean air.

11. The U.S. welfare system has abandoned the poor.

12. The United States should not interfere in the social, political, and economic affairs of other nations.

13. Movies made today in America have more graphic violence and gratuitous sex than they did ten years ago.

14. Higher education in America is the best in the world.

15. Colleges and universities should stress technical and applied subjects over the liberal arts.

Exercise 3: Developing a Case. Select three topics on which you would like to develop an argumentative case. A list of suggested topics is given, but you may choose some other topic area. What is important is that you already know enough about the topic to construct claims related to it. Within each topic area, construct a proposition of fact, a proposition of value, and a proposition of policy. Be sure that the propositions you supply adhere to all the guidelines for working propositions supplied in this chapter and listed in Exercise 1. Here is an example:

Topic area:	Alcohol abuse
Proposition of fact:	Alcohol-related accidents bring about more deaths than any other cause in the United States.
Proposition of value:	Alcohol is a more dangerous substance than marijuana.
Proposition of policy:	The allowable BAC (blood alcohol content) in drivers should be significantly reduced across the nation.

Suggested topics (or select three of your own):

Abortion	Endangered species	Political campaigns
AIDS	Environment	Poverty
Animal rights	Financial aid for students	Religion
Capital punishment	Foreign policy	Restricted driver licenses
Censorship	Gun control	Trade barriers
Consumer protection	Illegal drugs	
Crime	Inner cities	

NOTES

1. Helen Nugent, "File Sharing Takes Up to 95% of Net Use at Aight," *The London Times*, February 12, 2008, http://business.timesonline.co.uk/tol/business/industry_sectors/technology/article3353372.ece (accessed May 3, 2008).

2. Katherine S. Mangan, "College Could Face Lawsuits Over Illegal File-Sharing," *The Chronicle of Higher Education*, October 4, 2002, http://chronicle.com/free/2002/10/2002101401t.htm (accessed May 4, 2008).

3. Steve Tally, "Senate, Industry Target Illegal File Sharing Across Campus Networks," *Purdue News Service*, July 10, 2006, http://news.uns.purdue.edu/html3month/2006/060710.Tally.sharing.html (accessed May 3, 2008).

4. Copyright laws can be complex and they vary by country. There are, however, some good guides. For instance, "Know Your Copy Rights," produced by *the Association of Research Libraries*, can be found at http://www.knowyourcopyrights.org/bm%7Edoc/kycrbrochurebw.pdf (accessed May 3, 2008) and provides guidelines for educational use of protected material. There is also a good guide to peer-to-peer file sharing written by Fred von Lohmann, "Peer-to-Peer File Sharing and Copyright Law: A primer for Developers," February 2003, at http://iptps03.cs.berkeley.edu/final-papers/copyright.pdf (accessed May 2, 2008).

5. "What is a fair penalty for Illegal File-sharing or piracy?" http://www.myce.com/news/what-is-a-fair-penalty-for-illegal-file-sharing-or-piracy-36230/ (accessed July 31, 2012).

6. Erika Morphy, "ISPs Agree to Mete Out Punishment for Illegal File-Sharing," *E-Commerce Times*, July 8, 2011, http://www.ecommercetimes.com/story/72833.html (accessed July 29, 2012).

7. Nick is referencing a study reported on the BBC that suggested illegal downloading can increase legal sales. More information can be found at "Downloading 'myths' challenged," *BBC News Channel*, July 27, 2005, http://news.bbc.co.uk/1/hi/technology/4718249.stm (accessed May 4, 2008).

8. Lisa's original "claim" was actually a veiled request to mow the lawn. When requests are supported by reasons, they function as arguments. Study of such argument forms occurs in Sally Jackson and Scott Jacobs, "Structure of Conversational Argument: Pragmatic Bases for the Enthymeme," *Quarterly Journal of Speech* 66 (1980): 251–265; and Frans H. van Eemeren, Rob Grootendorst, Sally Jackson, and Scott Jacobs, *Reconstructing Argumentative Discourse* (Tuscaloosa: University of Alabama Press, 1993).

9. Adapted from Stephen H. Webb, "It's a Dog's Love," *UTNE Reader* (January/February, 1996): 61.

10. Kevin P. Phillips, "Is the Party Over?" *Seattle Times* (July 20, 1986): A16.

11. More techniques for identifying claims and conclusions on the bases of contextual cues were discussed in Chapter 3.

12. These claims are drawn from a group discussion of the topic "What policy should be enacted in regard to patients in potentially irreversible medical situations?" The discussion occurred at the University of Washington on May 8, 1983. Student participants were Steven McCornack, Ann Hurd, Leigh Chang, Anne Bigelow, Carrie O'Connor, Liza Thomas, and Margo Welshons. This discussion predated a significant Supreme Court decision that ruled that patients have the right to refuse medical treatment and to write living wills precluding extraordinary measures to prevent death.

13. A good deal of work has been done in elaborating the conventions or "rules" of argument. By a rule, we mean "a regularity (formalized…written, understood, or tacitly observed) that defines an activity." See Gary Cronkhite, "Conventional Postulates of Interpersonal Argument," in *Argument in Transition*, David Zarefsky, Malcolm O. Sillars, and Jack Rhodes, eds. (Annandale, Va.: Speech Communication Association/American Forensic Association, 1983), 697. See also Frans van Eemeren and Rob Grootendorst, *Speech Acts in Argumentative Discussions* (Dordrecht, The Netherlands: Foris Publications, 1984).

14. General Henry M. Robert, "Division of a Question," *Robert's Rules of Order Revised*, 1915 version, April 11, 2000, at www.constitution.org/cs_refer.htm (accessed May 5, 2000).

15. Richard Whately, *Elements of Rhetoric*, Douglas Ehninger, ed. (Carbondale, Ill.: Southern Illinois University Press, 1963), 112–113.

16. For example, some authors break down proposition types into fact/value (including descriptive, predictive, or evaluative statements that assert the existence or worth of something) and policy, which advocates a course of action. See George Ziegelmueller, Jack Kay, and Charles Dause, *Argumentation: Inquiry and Advocacy*, 2nd ed. (Englewood Cliffs, N.J.: Prentice Hall, 1990), 14–15. Church and Wilbanks describe another unique category scheme that divides propositions into those of inference, value, and policy, with the category of inference subdivided into trait, relational, historical, and predictive inferences. See Russell T. Church and Charles Wilbanks, *Values and Policies in Controversy* (Scottsdale, Ariz.: Gorsuch Scarisbrick, 1986), 35–42.

17. A fourth type of claim is the claim of definition, or classification. Examples would be "This is an act of burglary" and "By 'euthanasia,' I mean the removal of life support from terminally ill patients." To support claims such as these, the arguer justifies the definition or classification by referring to a source that others find acceptable. The arguer may also have to show that the chosen definition is applicable. Only rarely do definitive claims serve as central theses in argumentation; they more frequently function as subsidiary claims when participants disagree about how to define a term in the main claim or proposition.

18. Daryl J. Bem, *Beliefs, Attitudes and Human Affairs* (Belmont, Calif.: Brooks/Cole, 1970), 16.

19. Joseph W. Wenzel, "Toward a Rationale for Value-Centered Argument," *Journal of the American Forensic Association* 13 (1977): 153.

EVIDENCE

CHAPTER OUTLINE

KEY CONCEPTS

Evidence plays a vital role in argumentation and decision-making. Without it or by misusing it, people make mistakes and reach erroneous conclusions. This is why assessing and exploring are such central parts of the critical thinking cycle we described in Chapter 1. Theorists

Russel R. Windes and Arthur Hastings suggested that the acceptance of conclusions and decisions in the absence of evidence "has resulted in decisions and actions which have led to indescribable human suffering and misery—to wars and material destruction, to political inequities and the suppression of human rights, to economic catastrophes, to unjust persecutions, to mob violence, and to superstition and prejudice."[1] World history has witnessed countless examples of suffering and aggression based on evidence that was faulty, erroneous, or used unethically. Nazi Germany and the extermination of millions of Jewish people is certainly an example. So are the war crimes committed as the former Yugoslavia broke into independent republics. And, according to many analysts, the U.S. invasion of Iraq was based on faulty evidence. In each of these cases, one lesson that became increasingly clear was that if recipients hear something enough times, they will begin to accept it as true.[2]

Not only do we need to be aware of the absence or misuse of evidence in arguments we hear and read, but we also should be mindful of the need to use evidence in arguments we make. In numerous studies of the effects of evidence on persuasiveness, researchers have found that audiences are nearly always more influenced by arguments supported with evidence than those that are not.[3] Particularly in situations in which an arguer is unknown to an audience or does not have an established reputation with them, evidence is vital in establishing the credibility of claims and arguments the arguer makes. Researchers who have studied the effect of evidence on the persuasiveness of arguments have found that speakers unknown to or only moderately respected by an audience will be more successful if they use evidence to support their claims.[4] As recipients, critics, and producers of arguments, then, it is important for us to be aware of the vital role played by evidence.

In Chapter 1, we defined evidence as "facts or conditions objectively observable, beliefs or premises generally accepted as true by the audience, or conclusions previously established." Evidence is what we produce whenever we are asked to prove something or when someone asks us, "How do you know?" or "What have you got to go on?"

Box 5.1 provides a good illustration of how evidence is used in everyday conversational arguments. The advocates in this case are students, and most people would not assume that they are credible sources to talk about a "fat" tax based on their experience or background. They are not scientists or economists. They have not personally conducted any studies of how obesity affects health or how taxes affect consumption. However, throughout their arguments, the speakers ground their claims in statements that are accepted by the other advocate. Those statements serve as evidence. For instance:

Junk-food restaurants are popping up everywhere.

Some hamburgers have more than 1,000 calories.

Overweight and obesity have reached epidemic proportions.

Some cultures hold overweight and obesity in high esteem.

Lack of exercise is a contributing problem.

A study from Great Britain shows that increased taxes on junk food decrease consumption.

During the discussion, the speakers offered evidence to support their claims. In this case, the evidence was relatively informal. The advocates did not provide specific sources for their evidence nor did they reference the qualifications or credentials of any experts who produced the evidence. If challenged, speakers need to provide the source and qualifications for

BOX 5.1
SHOULD THERE BE A "TWINKIE" TAX?

In 1994, Dr. Kelly Brownell of Yale University published an op-ed piece in the *New York Times* that advocated taxing unhealthy foods.[5] The suggestion was met with much ridicule, and opponents quickly dubbed it the "Fat Tax," "Twinkie Tax," and "Snack Tax." Yet, in some circles, it gained attention and support as a means to help alleviate the consequences of overweight and obesity. A tax, some said, in addition to potentially decreasing unhealthy food consumption, might also help pay for nutrition education and physical exercise programs.

Overweight and obesity are a worldwide epidemic. The World Health Organization (WHO) reported that globally there are more than a 1.4 billion overweight adults, with at least 200 million men and 300 million women classified as obese.[6] These numbers are expected to grow and each year at least 2.8 million adults die from complications arising from being overweight and obese.[7] Diet is the primary cause as more people in more countries increase their consumption of energy-dense, nutrient-poor foods that have high levels of sugar and saturated fat. Many rich and poor countries work to manage the problems brought on by overweight and obesity. For instance, the five countries with the most overweight adults are Nauru, Federated States of Micronesia, Cook Island, Niue, and Tonga. Ninety percent or more of their adult population are overweight or obese.[8] The United States ranks as the ninth heaviest country in the world, with 74.1 percent of its adult population classified as overweight.[9] Almost 30 percent of American children under the age of nineteen are overweight or obese, as are nearly 1 in 5 Chinese adults.[10]

The implications for health and health care are significant. Obese and overweight people experience higher frequencies of cardiovascular disease, diabetes, musculoskeletal disorders, as well as some cancers. The Centers for Disease Control, for instance, claimed that for the United States, overweight and obesity cost as much as $92.6 billion annually in 2002, representing approximately 9.1 percent of total U.S. medical expenditures. Half of these costs were paid for by government assistance programs including Medicare and Medicaid, making overweight and obesity a significant taxpayer obligation.[11]

The WHO also offered many approaches that nations could use to reduce junk-food consumption. Among them were age restrictions, education campaigns, and zoning strategies for fast-food restaurants.[12] To pay for some of these efforts, the WHO suggested that nations might use a "fat" tax to promote healthy living, balanced eating, and exercise. Just as alcohol and cigarette taxes have been correlated with a decline in consumption, many argue the same would happen if snack foods were taxed. A study in the *British Medical Journal* found that a "fat" tax, properly developed, could help prevent up to one thousand deaths each year from heart disease in Great Britain.[13]

However, just as many people rallied in support of "fat" taxes, many have been skeptical. Some argue that a "fat" tax would be regressive because it targets the least educated and the least financially able. And, there is a great deal of discussion about the validity of studies linking taxation to positive health outcomes.[14] But even if the tax resulted in decreased junk-food consumption, some claim that governments have no right to interfere with individual liberties and freedom of choice.

(continued)

BOX 5.1 CONTINUED

Consider the following debate in which these issues are developed and pay attention to how evidence is used in support of claims:

Leah: The world needs to get a handle on obesity. Even in my hometown in Colorado, there is a huge increase in the number of junk-food restaurants popping up everywhere—full of people all the time. People like high-calorie, high-fat foods that have no nutritional value. Some fast-food hamburgers have more than 1,000 calories. That's ridiculous. This kind of eating leads to obesity and contributes to a worldwide epidemic. Children model our behavior, and they learn from their parents. Not only are we increasing our own risk of disease, but we are passing it down the generations. There is absolutely no reason to allow this kind of behavior. I really support taxing junk food to get people to stop eating it. A tax makes sense; we use tax policies all the time to help people make good choices. We tax cigarettes and alcohol. We give tax breaks to people who save for retirement. We give tax breaks to companies that decide to go "green." Using our tax policies to save lives is reasonable and important. Besides, being fit and healthy is a desirable personal goal that we should support. People who take care of themselves perform better at work and in their private lives. Because this is a global problem that affects many people, governments are justified in creating incentives and taxes to improve lives.

Kyle: I understand what you are saying about being healthy, but in many parts of the world, being fat represents prosperity and fertility—we shouldn't apply a U.S. standard to other cultures. In many places, larger people are viewed as stable and self-sufficient. Besides, a "fat" tax makes it seem as though being overweight is bad. Everybody is different—a weight chart or some standard of being overweight doesn't take into account genetics or what is healthiest for each individual. What message does that send to kids who struggle with bulimia and anorexia? Doesn't a tax threaten to increase eating disorders? Weight and health issues may not be related to junk food. Eating disorders are often driven by the impression that society demands skinny, and a government policy that taxes junk food may reinforce that perception. We should not assume that being overweight automatically says someone is unhealthy.

Leah: Being overweight or obese causes severe medical problems including high blood pressure, cancer, heart disease, and diabetes. It doesn't matter if fat is attractive or not; people die from it. If a "fat" tax is introduced, junk-food consumption will drop. People will eat healthier—and if they don't, then the tax revenue can help support education, nutritional alternatives, and exercise programs. A recent study in Great Britain showed that a "Twinkie" tax could prevent hundreds of premature deaths each year and cut heart disease by 10 percent. If we tax cigarettes and alcohol to promote health, it seems to me this is the same thing. Why shouldn't we tax unhealthy food? We know it contributes to obesity. It seems to me that we have an opportunity to fix a serious problem.

Kyle: We can make a decision to tax or not tax, but these just gloss over the real problem. Regardless of the decisions we might make about a "fat" tax, the larger health-related issues are caused by socioeconomic factors, exercise, and education. Health is at least as much about exercise as it is about diet, and this is a bigger problem with lifestyle that is not recognized. A "fat" tax makes it sound as though we have solved something when we haven't.

(continued)

BOX 5.1   CONTINUED

Consider the arguments that emerged in this discussion and attempt the following questions:

1. As you read through the case study, how is evidence used? Is it done effectively?
2. What kinds of arguments are most convincing? In those arguments, what evidence was used? Why did you find it believable?
3. If you were researching to find support for each side, where would you look? What kind of evidence would you hope to find?

---

the evidence to be acceptable—failing that, the evidence becomes an issue, above the level of dispute. The argument field, as we discussed in Chapter 1, determines the level of formality as well as the rules for introducing evidence. Conversations among friends are fairly informal. If this argument were occurring in a court of law, the field would require expert witnesses and credible testimony that could be produced in the courtroom. If this argument were occurring in a legislature considering a "fat" tax, statements could be read, experts could be called to testify, and personal experience could support the arguments. In each case, the rules of the field determine how evidence can be introduced and what evidence is credible.

When evidence is used effectively, it can enhance an arguer's credibility even about subjects with which the advocate might have little direct experience or expertise. The students drew up on their research and observations to support their claims and enhance their credibility. Evidence serves to ground the argument and support its believability. The introduction to Box 5.1 also provides evidence from credible sources that is introduced in a more formal, explicit way.

This chapter will discuss the nature and types of evidence, ways to evaluate the quality of evidence, procedures for locating evidence in libraries and resource materials, and guidelines for using evidence to support your arguments. After reading this chapter, you should be able to recognize various types of evidence and evaluate the quality of evidence used in your own and others' arguments.

NATURE OF EVIDENCE

Our definition of evidence from Chapter 1 indicates that evidence is not simply concrete facts or observable behavior. Rather, the defining characteristic of evidence is that it is accepted by the audience and can be used to support statements (claims) that are not accepted. The three ways in which evidence statements can function will be discussed in this section so as to reveal the nature of various forms of evidence.

First, evidence can stem from objectively observable conditions in the world. For most people, this is what evidence is. Evidence is simply what we can see and hear, feel, touch, and smell. For instance, your desk can serve as evidence that is objectively observable; so can the color of the sky or the number of people in your argumentation class. These are things that can be seen or discovered by anyone looking for them.

Second, beliefs or premises generally accepted as true by the audience can function as evidence (as long as they do not clearly disagree with directly observable evidence). This view of evidence can be problematic for some people because it means that evidence is not always concrete. However, the concept of level of dispute introduced in Chapter 2 can provide a useful means for understanding this view of evidence. Evidence can be used as support because it lies below the level of dispute. If evidence fell above the line, then it would become a focal point for argument, instead of support for a claim.

For instance, in Box 5.1, Leah claimed that a study conducted in Great Britain demonstrated that a properly designed tax could save hundreds of people who die prematurely each year in Britain. Her argument is that if a "Twinkie" tax existed, there would be less consumption. With less consumption, there would be less disease. As long as Kyle accepts these statements, they can serve as evidence in the argument. However, if Kyle discovered that the British study was inaccurate or used inappropriate methodologies for collecting its results, then the statements about the research could not be used as evidence. They would become the subject of argument regarding whether taxes can actually improve health.

As long as an argument's recipients find the statements acceptable and reasonable, the statements can function as evidence. If, however, the recipients believe—either correctly or incorrectly—that the statements are flawed or false, then an argument would need further support, and instead of functioning as evidence, the controversial statements become claims. Kyle, therefore, could have challenged the evidence and asked Leah to provide better support from credible sources. Then, Leah would have had to make the claim that the British study was a good study and provide evidence and reasons supporting that claim. But if Kyle does not challenge the statements, they can function as evidence. Provided a statement falls below the level of dispute, it functions as evidence.

Third, conclusions that have been previously established can serve as evidence. In the argument developed in Box 5.1, if Kyle accepts Leah's claims regarding the dangers of fast food, then her argument that we should do something to reduce the consumption of fast food can be based on the accepted claim. Once the first claim that fast food causes illness is accepted, then it can be used as evidence to support the next argument because—once accepted—it falls below the level of dispute. By doing this, Leah is creating an argument chain built on her experience and research, which leads to claims about the dangers of junk food as well as possible approaches for managing the obesity epidemic. At each step, once the claim was proved, she was able to use it as evidence to support the next claim.

A prospective car buyer can provide a useful example of how people might commonly use evidence. There are many publications to help car buyers choose from hundreds of makes and models. One of the most prominent of these is *Consumer Reports*, which tests dozens of automobiles each year. These tests and surveys can provide the prospective buyer with a wealth of evidence: the price of the car and options, predicted reliability, comfort and convenience, ease of service, drivability, and performance. With the information from *Consumer Reports*, John, a prospective car buyer, goes looking for a new car. He drives many makes and models and notes the features in each of the cars he tests. With all of this information, he selects the car he wants and sits down to bargain with the dealer.

The *Consumer Reports* evidence is useful to John in making an argument with the dealer for a better price. He can tell the dealer that he likes the car but the $25,000 price is too high because the consumer magazines claimed that the dealer paid only $17,000 for the car in the first place. He can also claim that the car was not quite as comfortable, reliable, or gas-efficient as he had hoped, and perhaps he should look elsewhere for another car. In each case, John appeals to evidence to support his claims about the car. Suppose, however, that the dealer rejected John's $17,000 figure and asserted that the particular car with its options cost him a good deal more. John's original evidence would then become a claim because it would be disputed and the subject of argument.

This illustration points to the nature of evidence. Evidence is not always concrete nor is it always certain. In fact, evidence can be placed on a continuum from concrete, objectively observable, and certain evidence to evidence that is probably true. For instance, John knew the car existed. He could make an argument for the car's existence and have little difficulty getting people to agree with him. John could use any of the car's physical features as evidence without much fear of contradiction. On the other hand, suppose John argued that *Consumer Reports* conducted a reliability study on the car. Evidence from such a study is not directly experienced by the participants in an argument, and because neither party had a concrete experience with the evidence, there is room for dispute. It could be that no such study was conducted, or that John's interpretation of the study is wrong, or that the study was biased. The results of the study and John's interpretation of them are probable but not certain. Sometimes evidence functions as fact; at other times it functions as opinions or premises accepted by the audience.

TYPES OF EVIDENCE

Evidence can be divided into two broad classifications—fact and opinion as to fact.[15] Facts may be thought of as things people believe to be the case, either because they have experienced them firsthand or because they regard them as the truthfully reported experiences of others. Many times, however, we do not have the expertise to directly observe and interpret events. For example, none of us observed the fall of the Roman Empire. But we have knowledge of the events surrounding the fall as well as historical analyses of why it fell that have been given to us by scholars from multiple disciplines. These people examined the historical records and, based on their expertise, rendered an opinion about the causes and implications of the fall of the empire. This type of evidence, evidence that depends on the expert and credible interpretation of facts, is referred to as opinion as to fact. It is probably worth mentioning here that factual evidence is distinct from factual claims discussed in Chapter 4. Factual claims are controversial statements about history, relationships, or future events. Faculty evidence is not controversial. Evidence is only evidence if it falls below the level of dispute.

Fact Evidence

One way that people come to believe that something is a fact is through the perception of their senses. Another is through common experience. We can talk about the history of the United States and the Civil War. Although none of us have directly experienced the Civil War, it is part of our common heritage. We do not question it because we accept it as a fact, a historical occurrence well substantiated in many sources. Factual evidence can be further divided into three types that vary in the form in which they occur.

Reports and Descriptions

Reports and descriptions are nonnumerical or narrative accounts of some object or occurrence. They often occur in arguments as examples and illustrations and may make a passing reference to something or describe it at some length. Here are two examples of this type of evidence:

Tombstone, Arizona, a Wild-West town known for mock gunfights, plank sidewalks, hitching posts, and Western atmosphere, passed a measure requiring horses to wear diapers or dung bags to help keep the streets clean. People thought it looked pretty silly, but it is having an effect on keeping the streets clean.[16]

Parson pled "not guilty" after his arrest last August. But, he admitted to U.S. District Judge Marsha Pechman, that he had, in fact, downloaded the original Blaster worm, modified it, and then uploaded it to the Internet. Different versions of the Blaster worm crippled computer networks around the world last summer. Parson's version created a denial-of-service attack against Microsoft Windows Update Web site as well as personal computers running the Windows operating system. The US Federal Government estimates his version inundated more than 48,000 computers.[17]

Reports and factual descriptions such as these lend immediacy and vividness to many arguments. They help recipients identify with the characters and relate to the situations described. And they bring home or dramatize situations or conditions that might otherwise seem remote and unimportant.

Statistics

Statistics are facts and figures that have been systematically collected and ordered so as to convey information. Generally, statistics provide a quantitative summary of the characteristics of a population or sample (selectively chosen instances) of a population. Statistics may take the form of averages, numerical comparisons, percentages, totals, or estimates, for example. Following are some examples of statistics:

Dr. Harvey Sugerman, president of the American Society for Bariatric Surgery, has researched instances in which gastric bypass surgeries have gone wrong. He estimated that of the more than 11,000 procedures that will take place in the United States this year, complications might affect as many as 20 percent of the patients. And, of those, he projected that as many as 25 percent will die. His findings have been corroborated by multiple other researchers including some from the Mayo Clinic who also found that up to 16 percent of the surgery patients developed peripheral neuropathy resulting in tingling, numbness, or severe pain.[18]

In the 2000 census, 4 million Americans described themselves as Indian American or Alaska Native. Of these, nearly 70 percent lived in urban areas and 25 percent lived in counties served by health-care agencies that receive federal funding for Indians.[19]

Statistics lend credence to arguments by showing that problems and conditions are not limited to isolated instances but instead affect many people in many different types of situations. Statistics are useful in showing the breadth of a problem, and reports and descriptions are used often to show its depth or human consequence.

Artifacts

Artifacts are physical evidence that helps to prove an argument. An artifact is simply a physical object that a speaker might use to prove a point. For example, exhibits in a trial are artifacts. X-ray films showing the damage caused by smoking are also artifacts. Artifacts may also take the form of demonstrations. Often a trial lawyer will demonstrate how a piece of evidence works in order to make a point. Teachers will have students do an exercise or science experiment to illustrate a concept. These are artifacts that help support claims. Since we are influenced more strongly by what we see and experience than by what we hear or read, artifacts can be a very effective form of factual evidence because they involve the recipients of argument in multidimensional ways.

Opinion as to Fact Evidence

When advocates make arguments that are based on their own firsthand knowledge and understanding of the facts, then they are making arguments grounded in fact-based evidence. However, sometimes the facts surrounding an issue are excessively complex or large, such that an advocate cannot reasonably review all the factual material. In such cases, arguers turn to others who have examined the factual evidence and distilled it into meaningful compilations or opinions.

The second broad type of evidence, then, is opinion as to fact. Opinion evidence is someone's interpretation of the meaning of factual evidence. Whereas facts are based on direct or indirect experience, opinions are judgments about how an event or state of affairs is to be understood, evaluated, or dealt with. In using opinion evidence, the advocate uses the statements of others' judgments and estimations to support his or her own claims. Consider the following opinion statement and the claim it might support:

> A few years ago, at the annual American Psychological Association convention in Toronto, psychologists presented an in-depth analysis of the American Presidents. Opinions from more than 100 experts were sought and the raters designed and completed a battery of standardized tests designed to evaluate each of the Presidents. Several of these tests included more than 100 questions. Their goal was to develop a personality profile of each of the past US Presidents and develop a rating system to help guide voters in future elections. The psychologists looked at many dimensions including their: level of neuroses, openness to the experience of others, intelligence, extroversion, agreeableness, among others. Their conclusions included the following.

> Ronald Reagan was the least neurotic of all the Presidents. Richard Nixon was the most. Thomas Jefferson was the most intelligent and Theodore Roosevelt was second. Warren G. Harding was the least open to the experience of others and he was the least conscientious. Bill Clinton was the second least conscientious. George Washington was rated as the most conscientious. James Madison and Abraham Lincoln were rated among the most agreeable. Theodore and Franklin Roosevelt were among the most extroverted; Bill Clinton was third.[20]

The factual data compiled by the psychologists are extensive and overwhelming. A single arguer researching the same question would take weeks to read through all the material and, assuming the advocate had the appropriate education, she or he might be in a position to use it as factual evidence in support of a claim. However, for most people, the quantity of factual evidence and the expertise required to understand it means that arguers often rely on the opinions of others in developing their own arguments. Using this study as opinion evidence, an arguer might be able to make the following argument:

Claim: George Washington was the best president we have had.

Evidence: Psychologists presented a paper at the American Psychology Association Convention in Toronto that concluded he was the most conscientious of all our presidents, in the upper third in intelligence, open to the opinions of others, and an agreeable president.

Reasoning: These elements, taken together, make Washington the most balanced of all our presidents because he exhibited far above average abilities in each of the areas studied by the psychologists.

Just as arguers can draw on factual evidence in the form of reports, statistics, and artifacts, arguers can also draw on the opinions of others about what reports, statistics, and artifacts mean. In other words, just as there are three types of factual evidence, there are three parallel types of opinion evidence. These include opinion as to reports and descriptions, opinion as to statistics, and opinion as to artifacts. Box 5.2, "Apply the Theory," will help guide you through a process of working with evidence.

BOX 5.2
APPLY THE THEORY: WORKING WITH EVIDENCE

Using the case study developed in Box 5.1, can you identify an example of each type of evidence? In the chart below, write in examples that clearly illustrate the type of evidence used.

Factual Evidence
- Reports and Descriptions
- Statistics
- Artifacts

Opinion Evidence
- Reports and Descriptions
- Statistics
- Artifacts

As you work through your identification of evidence, you probably found some challenges. First, while reports and descriptions are fairly easy to find, as are statistics, artifacts tend to be difficult to introduce into an argument because showing the artifact can be difficult. Rather, we tend to describe artifacts, which, then, become a report or description. And, second, opinion as to fact evidence parallels the same types as factual evidence. This is because someone is interpreting for us the meaning of a report or description, the meaning of statistics, or the meaning of an artifact.

EVALUATING EVIDENCE

Just as a house or any structure is only as strong as the foundation on which it is built, so is an argument only as strong as the evidence used to support it. As arguers and as recipients of argument, we need to be aware of the quality of evidence so that we can judge others' arguments and select strong evidence to support our own arguments.

The remainder of this section will list and describe criteria to be applied to various types of evidence. Applying criteria such as reliability, expertise, objectivity, consistency, recency, and relevance to our own and others' evidence supplies us with a system for judging the quality of support provided for claims. The result can only be to make us better critics and users of argument.

Reliability

One question many audiences ask about a source is whether or not the source is reliable. *A reliable source is one that has proven to be correct many times in the past.* An excellent example of a reliable source is cited by Robert P. Newman and Dale R. Newman in their book on evidence:

[Senator J. William] Fulbright's overall record of prophecy is pretty good. He warned President Truman that unless atomic energy were put under international control, there would be a monstrous arms race and proliferation.... He told Secretary [of State John Foster] Dulles that arms shipments to India and Pakistan would lead to war between the two. He...warned President Kennedy the Bay of Pigs would be a fiasco.[21]

Given Senator Fulbright's accuracy record for predictions, political leaders would have done well to listen to his opinions. People naturally trust sources and other people who have been proven right in the past. Thus we are likely to put our confidence in a Wall Street newsletter that accurately predicts stock market fluctuations or in *Consumer Reports*, whose product assessments have repeatedly proven to be correct.

Expertise

Studies on factors affecting whether a source is believed have indicated that the most important factor is the recipients' perception of the source's competence.[22] *Expertise is the possession of a background of knowledge and information relevant to the subject matter under discussion.* Generally, we determine whether or not someone is an expert in a subject area by examining or considering the nature and extent of his or her experience with the topic. Education and formal training in a subject are one index as to whether a person is qualified. Experience may be gained in other ways, however.

Any given senator would not necessarily be considered an expert on the conduct of Pentagon business, whereas a senator who had chaired the Senate Armed Services Committee for a number of terms would probably be considered an expert on the status of American armed forces. Any person who has published favorably reviewed books or articles on a subject is generally accepted as an expert on that subject. Furthermore, people who hold elective offices in professional organizations, generally, are highly regarded because recipients assumed that their peers respect them.

However, professors, elected officials, and other people who tend to be viewed as credible sources are not necessarily experts on all issues. Expertise in one area does not extend to areas outside the individual's particular area of knowledge. A professor of communication who has written extensively on Internet campaign strategies has the expertise to comment on the Web-based campaign strategies of candidates in an election, but probably does not have the expertise to assess the potential economic benefits of each candidate's tax plan. In the case of the latter, an expert in economics would likely be a better source.

Because of the importance of expertise in establishing the acceptability of evidence with most audiences, it is vital for arguers to fully cite their source's qualifications and experience with the topic. Instead of saying "John Smith concluded that performance-enhancing drugs may cause health risks such as heart disease and high blood pressure," an advocate should say "Dr. John Smith, a professor of sports medicine at the University of Oregon, reported in the May 2003 issue of the *New England Journal of Medicine* after seven years of investigation that..." Unless the source's qualifications and experience with the topic are fully reported to recipients, they will have no way of making any judgment about the source's expertise.

An exception lies with sources whose qualifications are known by or are generally accepted by the audience. If it is generally known and accepted that the president holds certain qualifications and expertise in particular aspects of U.S. policy, you need not state her or his qualifications explicitly. That said, because you can never be sure of the audience's knowledge of certain sources, it is better to fully cite your source's qualifications, even if the audience knows them, than to risk your audience not knowing or accepting your source as credible. Emphasizing the source's credentials can enhance the argument's persuasiveness by showing that evidence is taken from someone whose knowledge and expertise can be trusted.

Objectivity

Recipients feel confident in trusting sources they believe are objective about the topic of the argument. *Objectivity refers to a source's tendency to hold a fair and undistorted view on a question or an issue.* An objective source does not have views strongly colored by a personal emotional investment in one ideological viewpoint on the topic. We can hardly expect a member of the People for the Ethical Treatment of Animals (PETA) to provide a well-balanced discussion of the pros and cons of animal testing in the medical field. Nor can we expect a representative from the Focus on the Family (a conservative organization devoted to preserving family values) to provide a complete and balanced account of the state of family values in the United States. In both of these cases, the sources would not be considered objective because they hold a clear set of views on those issues.

We should not expect all sources to be completely impartial in their analyses of issues. After all, if they did not have a viewpoint to argue, they would not be making a claim of supporting a point of view. We should, however, expect sources to be unbiased. *A bias is an unreasoned distortion of judgment or a prejudice on a topic.* A biased source usually has a personal stake in the outcome of an argument and is thus unlikely to provide a fair account of differing points of view, as the examples of PETA and Focus on the Family demonstrate. This is not to suggest that either PETA or Focus on the Family cannot be used for source material in an argument. Rather, an advocate should look for alternative points of view that can help balance or counter any accusation of bias. If an arguer fails to balance the potential bias of source material, the objectivity of the evidence could be called into question and thereby the evidence would fall above the level of dispute.

Bias can also overwhelm or influence reasoning, choice of supporting material, or design of statistical measures to ensure a certain outcome. For example, if PETA decided to run a poll of public opinion about animal rights, it is possible that the sample would be drawn from those visiting the PETA Web site instead of a random sample and that the questions might be designed to increase the likelihood of answers that support PETA's cause. Biased sources are not objective. Arguers who draw from such sources are likely to discover that their audiences are aware of the biases of such groups and, as such, are suspicious of information taken from them. Nonobjective sources can weaken your argument and hurt your credibility as a speaker. You should always strive to find objective, nonbiased sources for your arguments.

Consistency

Recipients of an argument expect evidence used to be consistent with other information and with itself. Consistency with other information is called external consistency. *External consistency is the agreement of evidence with sources of information other than the source being used.* A piece of evidence that runs counter to what is already believed or known about a topic is not necessarily wrong, but the arguer using it has the burden of proving that the evidence is correct and can be reconciled with other seemingly incompatible facts the audience already believes or accepts. After all, the mainstream of opinion, or even of what is thought to be "knowledge," is not always correct. For example, Galileo argued that the Earth revolved around the sun at a time when most people believed the sun revolved around the Earth. Columbus believed that one could reach Asia by sailing west at a time when most people thought someone attempting such a voyage would fall off the edge of the Earth. However, when evidence fails to agree with other credible facts and sources, it can be detrimental to acceptance of an argument.

Advocates can increase the acceptability and believability of their arguments by using a sufficient amount of evidence from different sources to show that their support is externally consistent. Recipients of arguments can assure themselves that evidence is externally consistent by comparing it with facts they already know or information to which they have access.

Evidence should also be internally consistent. *Internal consistency is the absence of self-contradiction within the information provided by a source.* When political leaders and other public figures contradict themselves, the media and the public take great delight in pointing it out. For instance, in a student presentation about a presidential election, Betty argued that one of the candidates was inconsistent in his policies. She noted that the candidate, as a senator, voted against increased funding for national security in 2000, but that same candidate called for increased national security spending in his 2012 campaign. Betty claimed that this and other similar examples of internal inconsistency were reasons that the candidate would make a poor president.

Few things are more damaging to an arguer's credibility than the appearance of inconsistency or self-contradictions in statements. Although it is cliché to charge politicians with this offense, consistent internal contradictions or broken promises make people wary of politicians. When arguers contradict themselves, they diminish the level of trust and credibility they have with their audiences.

Keep in mind that the appearance of internal inconsistency may reveal that there is more to the story than what is presented. Recall Betty's argument about the inconsistency of a presidential candidate. Betty's classmate Amanda responded to this argument in Betty's presentation by stating that the reason for the inconsistency was that times have changed between 2000 and the time of the election. Amanda argued that terrorist attacks on the country in 2001 might have changed the candidate's mind on an issue. This brings up an important point with regard to internal consistency. People can change their minds over time as new evidence is discovered and as they have new experiences. It is also possible that people change their minds by being persuaded by other arguers.

Recency

As a general rule, arguers should be aware of whether their evidence is sufficiently current on the topic of their argument. The extent to which evidence must be recent varies with the topic of discussion. Advocates examining Internet technologies, cancer research, or international terrorism should rely on the most recent evidence available because our knowledge about such topics changes frequently, perhaps daily. Evidence about the world, objects, people, or anything else that changes needs to be current.

Other topics may be less affected by the comparative recency of evidence. Evidence relating to human rights or capital punishment, for example, may be of more enduring usefulness because conditions and values relating to these topics are less subject to change. Consequently, speakers appealing to values such as "life, liberty, and the pursuit of happiness" are arguing from safe ground because such values are an enduring part of American political life regardless of when the appeal was made.

Relevance

It is not uncommon for an arguer to present something that sounds like evidence and to connect it with a given claim, when in fact, the evidence is unrelated to the claim as made. *Relevance refers to whether the evidence as stated is topically and sufficiently related to the claim as made.* Consider the following example of an ad for pain-relief medication:

> **Evidence:**   Nine out of ten doctors recommend aspirin for headaches.
>
> **Claim:**   Aspirin is a powerful all-purpose medication.

A close examination of these two statements quickly reveals that the claim goes well beyond what is warranted by the evidence. First, the doctors stipulated a specific purpose for aspirin use and did not say it was "all-purpose." Second, the doctors made no statement about the aspirin's potency. So the evidence as stated does not relate to the claim as made.

One might think that irrelevant or unrelated evidence would be obvious, but often it isn't. The evidence is frequently somewhat related but does not directly support the claim because of the way it is worded or qualified. To detect this problem, we should be aware of the way the language and focus of the claim relate to the language and focus of the evidence. The following excerpt from a student presentation illustrates how irrelevant evidence might appear to support a claim when, in fact, it does not.

A 2002 Safe Schools study showed that 36% of all secondary schools paddle children in a typical month. For junior high schools the figure jumps to 61%. Children all across the United States are being legally beaten under our laws.

The arguer uses a very connotative term—"beaten"—in her claim. Is this term, normally associated with child abuse, which is illegal, to be equated with paddling? Furthermore, do the arguer's statistics show that this is happening "all across the country"? The answer to both of these questions is, probably not. The study makes no mention of geographical location, and punishment deemed legal by the courts should not be equated with abuse. Therefore, the claim departs from and exaggerates the evidence given to support it.

Access

When an arguer cites opinion as to fact about a situation or event, recipients should expect the source of that opinion to have been in a position to observe directly the matter in question. *Access depends on whether someone offering an opinion is or has been in a position to observe firsthand the matter being disputed.* A person who has not directly experienced something must rely on reports or summaries provided by others or on impressions based on limited information. But anytime we hear or read something secondhand, certain features and aspects are filtered out by the perspective and viewpoint of the person who reports it to us. The features identified and reported may not at all be the ones we would notice if we had an opportunity to observe the situation ourselves firsthand. The further we move from the original situation as directly observed by eyewitnesses, the greater the possibility for misinterpretation or error.

Consider the following example. Syria's civil war began in March of 2011 and escalated as President Bashar al-Assad fought to retain power and defeat rebels with the strength of his well-trained and well-armed military. By the summer of 2012, reports emerged that the al-Assad regime was preparing to use chemical weapons to stop the rebellion. On August 21, 2012, U.S. president Barack Obama warned the Syrian president that proof of chemical or biological weapons use would constitute crossing a "red line" that would trigger a U.S. response.[23] By 2013, reports from inside Syria claimed that these weapons had been used. U.S. defense secretary Chuck Hagle, in April 2013, announced that there was some evidence that the al-Assad regime had used chemical weapons on a small scale. Because this crossed the "red line" the Obama administration came under increasing pressure to act on behalf of the rebels. However, other sources suggested that rebels had "planted" or "manufactured" this evidence as a means of triggering a U.S. response to support them in a conflict they were losing.[24]

Should the Obama administration have moved to support the rebels quickly because the "red line" had been crossed? For days and weeks following reports of chemical weapon use, this question was a regular part of the headlines. The challenge, though, was that there was no good way to verify information because U.S. intelligence did not have reliable, trustworthy sources with clear access to artifacts and events. Reports, primarily, came from parties with an interest in U.S. involvement. Without the benefit of direct observation of the conditions in Syria during alleged chemical strikes, the United States depended on testimony from people who either had an interest in the outcome or people who had heard about it second- or thirdhand. Box 5.3, "Apply the Theory," will help guide you through a process of evaluating quality evidence.

- - - - - -

BOX 5.3
APPLY THE THEORY: EVALUATING EVIDENCE

This section developed seven tests for assessing the quality of evidence: Reliability, Expertise, Objectivity, Consistency, Recency, Relevance, and Access. Failing these tests does not necessarily mean that the evidence is of poor quality but it may mean that more research and analysis is needed to support its conclusions. Select any evidence developed in Box 5.1 and analyze its quality two ways: (1) assess the strength of evidence using the quality tests developed in the chapter and (2) for each test indicate the relative strength of evidence by rating it from a low of 1 to a high of 5:

CRITERION	RATING	EVALUATION
Is the source reliable? How do you know?		
Is the source an expert? What would make the source credible on this subject?		
Is the source relatively objective? What biases do you think might exist?		
Is the source consistent? Are there any internal contradictions? Is the evidence externally consistent with what is generally believed?		
How recent is the evidence? Have conditions changed or does the date of the evidence matter?		
Is the evidence relevant? Does it directly and clearly support the claim?		
Did the source have sufficient access to the evidence? Did the source have any barriers that might hide part of the evidence from them?		

The goal here is to try and identify the relative strength of the evidence. Most evidence isn't perfect. The key is in understanding where evidence is deficient so that it can be explained or supported with additional evidence.

EVALUATING STATISTICAL EVIDENCE

Statistics can often challenge arguers in several important ways. Most people struggle trying to understand statistics let alone how they were developed or presented. Statistics tend to have an ethos about them that makes us want to trust the number more than a report or description. When arguing, however, and presented with statistics, one should keep in mind the adage "Figures lie and liars figure."

All of the standards we have just described for fact and opinion evidence apply equally well to statistics. Statistics are the end result of a process subject to human bias and human error. Questions on a survey can be loaded; the people surveyed can be subjectively chosen;

comparisons may be made of noncomparable units; and reports of findings can be slanted. Actually, statistics are often no more reliable than other forms of evidence, yet people often think statistics are true. As Newman and Newman laconically observed:

> If you would not believe a man who testifies that he has seen a flying saucer, do not believe him when he claims to have seen fourteen flying saucers each measuring twenty-two feet in diameter and weighing eleven tons.[25]

Gathering, using, and assessing statistics nevertheless present problems and challenges different than in other forms of evidence. This section will alert you to difficulties that frequently arise when arguers use statistics to support their claims. Advocates should take care to avoid these pitfalls in conducting research. Recipients should scrutinize the statistics they hear and read and be alert to some of these practices and mistakes.

Pseudostatistics

Sometimes we hear statistics applied to phenomena and situations in which it is difficult, if not impossible, to imagine how the statistics could have been compiled using good statistical methods. Here are three examples:

> According to *Esquire* magazine, February, 1964, Judy Garland sang "Over the Rainbow" 1,476 times.
>
> Seven out of every ten Americans cheat on their income taxes.
>
> *Mega Foods* has developed a revolutionary line of *Food* Vitamins and *Food* Minerals that are up to sixteen times more effective than the so-called "natural" vitamins and we can prove that with scientific research.

Although the first case appears innocent enough, a closer look invites criticism. Specifically, how does anyone know precisely how many times Garland sang "Over the Rainbow"? Did someone count every time the song was sung in rehearsal, on stage, and in the shower? It is unreasonable to assume that this statistic could be accurate because there is almost no way it could have been collected. Similarly, the second piece of evidence would be difficult to arrive at reasonably. In order to collect the figure seven out of ten, what would a researcher have to do? Ask a group of people which one of them cheats? How would each of the respondents interpret what is meant by "cheat"? Given people's concern about tax audits, how many would honestly say they cheat? And how would "scientific research" determine that a certain brand of vitamins and food supplements is precisely sixteen times more effective than the natural alternative? Would respondents have to feel sixteen times better? Would they need to be sixteen times more resistant to disease? Was the study based on self-reports of people taking the vitamins and supplements, or on some other measure? We don't know.

Comparing Noncomparable Units

In essence, this practice, which emerges most frequently when longitudinal trends are reported, involves comparing dissimilar items while assuming they are the same. For example, due to inflation, the value of the dollar has declined. The 2013 dollar does not have the same value that the 1971-dollar did. This is why salary comparisons and commodity prices are always "adjusted for inflation" when across-time comparisons are made. A similar problem arises when advocates use the federal government's crime statistics. The definition of what constitutes a felony or a misdemeanor varies from one time or location to another. When new types of crimes are included in the class of felonies, the felony rates appear to increase simply because the method of classification has changed.

The Environmental Protection Agency (EPA) has had to address this issue as hybrid and electric cars have become more widely used. The standard measure of efficiency has traditionally been "miles per gallon" (MPG) and cars' MPG numbers have been used to compare cars. In fact, the U.S. federal government has a law that requires car manufacturers to have a fleet average of 27.5 MPG.[26] But how would the Chevrolet Volt or Nissan Leaf fit into this classification? Technically, electric cars can achieve unlimited mileage on a gallon of gas. Comparing electric, hybrid, and gasoline-powered cars does not work well because the units we use (MPG) are noncomparable.

Unrepresentative Samples

A sample is a population or group of people or objects that researchers survey when a study is conducted. Most researchers do not have the time, money, or ability to survey or study every individual in a given state or the country. Consequently, researchers must draw upon a group or sample of people small enough to work with. Conclusions about the sample are then generalized to a broader group. One example is the studies of college students that conclude that seventy percent will graduate after four years and find employment in their chosen field. This statistic was arrived at by surveying a group of students and then generalizing the conclusions to all other students. Certain questions need to be answered before such evidence should be used or accepted. Was the sample representative? Was the sample too small? Was the sample randomly selected?

A representative sample is one that possesses all the characteristics of the larger group from which it is drawn. For example, if the general population of college students on which a study is done is 35 percent college freshmen, 20 percent college sophomores, 10 percent juniors, and 35 percent seniors, then a representative sample is one made up of approximately the same proportion of individuals. In this sense, a representative sample is a group drawn from a larger group that shares most of the larger group's characteristics. As another example, one survey on Web use gathered its data from Internet users who were promised a chance at prizes for answering the survey questions.[27] Critics of the survey argued that this was not a representative sample of Web users but only those who were motivated to compete for prizes. Similarly, surveys that use telephones to gather data may not use mobile phones or phones listed on the national "Do Not Call" list. As a result, significant segments of the population may be excluded.

Poor Methodology

Sound methods for gathering statistical information should guard against redundancy and bias when responses are counted. For example, surveys that count some of the respondents twice or those that count only people who are highly motivated to respond are using poor statistical methods. One example is the compiling of casualty statistics during the Vietnam War. Officers in the various services frequently sought totals of the number of enemy dead after battles. Various platoons were dispersed to conduct body counts, but there was no way to ensure that one platoon would not duplicate another's count. Furthermore, it was difficult to distinguish civilians from soldiers because many Vietnamese soldiers did not wear uniforms. Combat conditions also made counts very difficult to conduct. Nevertheless, casualty totals, however inaccurate, were reported.[28]

PRESENTING EVIDENCE

When we make a decision on the basis of someone else's argument, we generally have certain expectations about the evidence presented to us. We hope it has been fully reported, is of the best possible quality, and is not misrepresented or intentionally distorted. Information that is second rate or distorted does not provide reliable grounds for decision-making. Arguers and recipients of argument should be aware of the ethical obligation to cite accurately the sources used to support arguments. In Chapter 11 we will explore the ethical dimensions of presenting arguments in more detail; however, there are some principles that should be discussed here. This is because there are many ways to interpret and communicate evidence so as to mislead recipients about its nature or quality, and not all involve deliberate falsification. Everyone would agree that adding to or altering a source's words is unethical, but often selectively omitting words or sentences is also ethically questionable.

In Chapter 1, we discussed the role of argument spheres and argument fields. Determining how to use evidence and what rules or standards apply to that evidence is largely contingent on these two variables. The arguments developed in Box 5.1 were between two friends exploring issues related to "fat" taxes. The arguments occurred in a personal sphere where there was an ongoing relationships and knowledge of the other. If, however, those arguments appeared in a technical sphere—a courtroom or legislative assembly—the evidence presented would have been inadequate because it would not have met the minimum field-specific standards for technical arguments in those arenas. And, if the arguments were presented to a public sphere, the audience would have expected much more detailed evidence and source citation. The standards for evaluating arguments depend on their contexts.

The overarching question is, "Does the manner in which an arguer uses evidence give recipients an accurate and faithful picture of the nature and intent of the source?" The central ethical issue is whether or not the recipients had a reasonable and significant choice to decide whether to believe what was presented. Chapter 11 will explore the issues of ethics and reasonable choices in arguments. To clarify the implications of these issues, we will consider some of the practices to be avoided.

Omitting Words

Omitting words to make the evidence more favorable to the arguer's claim is unethical. Quotations from sources should be faithful to the context from which they are taken. If the citer of the source omits qualifying words or phrases or otherwise alters the meaning of the original, the practice is unethical. It is not difficult to completely reverse the meaning of a quotation by leaving part of it out. For example, an arguer once claimed that:

> For a man who is supposed to be a champion of democracy, it is odd that Lincoln said: "You can fool all of the people some of the time." This doesn't show much faith in the judgment of the people.

While this claim uses Lincoln's words, its interpretation was flawed because it does not include the remainder of Lincoln's statement, which was:

> You can fool some of the people all the time and all the people some of the time, but you can't fool all the people all the time.

Omitting statements from quotations to make them support one's point is easy to do, but it is wrong because it misleads and deceives the audience.

Identifying Secondary Sources

When arguers fail to distinguish between primary and secondary sources, they can potentially deceive the recipients. *A primary source is the original source of the evidence.* This means that *the primary source is the source in which the evidence first appeared.* Eyewitness accounts, original documents (letters, diaries, personal notebooks), and transcripts of speeches as originally delivered are examples of primary sources. Primary sources provide the most immediate possible account of what was said by the source at the moment it was uttered.

Secondary sources are those that compile, analyze, or summarize primary sources. Secondary sources often provide an interpretation or a restatement of what was originally said. For example, Thomas Jefferson's own correspondence about events leading to the Declaration of Independence is a primary source; an account of the Revolutionary War period in a history book is a secondary source. An original editorial is a primary source; a reprinting or summary of that editorial is a secondary source.

Arguers should use primary sources whenever possible because they are authentic and there is less possibility for error when they are used. When original or primary evidence is unavailable, arguers may use secondary sources, but they should always report that the information was cited in a secondary source and give credit to the secondary source. Information in a secondary source may have been shortened, changed, or edited. For example, *Reader's Digest* often changes and alters the articles it republishes. It is therefore important for recipients to know that the arguer is not citing the original source.

Qualifying Sources

Advocates should give all relevant information about the source from which the evidence was taken. When sources are cited, arguers should provide complete information about where the evidence was found, and the qualifications of the sources should be given. This includes the name of the author (if available), his or her qualifications or expertise, the date the statement was made, and the publication information. The arguer should provide enough information so that recipients could track down and find the information if they wanted. Fully disclosing source information makes the argument appear more credible and the arguer more trustworthy.

It is important to note that there are differences between oral and written citations. In written arguments, arguers follow reference style guides that provide rules for how to cite sources in essays, term papers, or research projects. Most style guides, such as the Modern Language Association (MLA) or the American Psychological Association (APA) manuals or the *Chicago Manual of Style*, provide guidelines for citing sources in the text of an essay and in a full bibliography at the end of the paper. Generally, arguers should include the qualifications or expertise of a source either in the text of the paper or in the notes attached to the essay. For example, a written source citation should look something like this:

> Dr. James Brilhart, professor of anthropology at the University of California at Berkeley, argued, "there is no such thing as a primitive language" ("Primitive Languages," *Time*, November 26, 1980, p. 25).

A full source citation, in this case including the article title, the magazine in which the article was published, and the full date, should be given in a way that follows the rules of the style guide used.

In the case of oral arguments, recipients generally will not have access to written versions of the full source citations. It is important, therefore, that arguers provide enough of the citation information orally so that the recipients have the opportunity to locate the material if they wish. For example, an oral presentation might cite the source as follows:

> Dr. James Brilhart, professor of anthropology at the University of California at Berkeley, argued in the November 26, 1980, issue of *Time* that "there is no such thing as a primitive language."

Alluding to one's sources vaguely ("according to several articles that have appeared recently") is unacceptable. If an arguer fails to provide a date, for instance, the result could be misleading. What if an arguer decided to leave out the date in the preceding statement about primitive language? A good deal of research has been done on language behavior recently, and, if the recipients thought the comment was current, they would be deceived.

Ethical requirements for using evidence, then, include citing the words of the author so that the citation conforms to his or her intentions and to the context; distinguishing between primary and secondary sources; and providing recipients with complete information about the source's qualifications and where the evidence was found. Omission or addition of words or information to make the evidence appear more favorable to one's claim is unacceptable.

Plagiarism

Engaging in plagiarism not only undermines an arguer's credibility but it is an unethical practice that undermines academic and personal integrity. *Plagiarism is the use of another person's ideas or words without proper attribution.* Different fields, as discussed in Chapter 1, apply different standards for what constitutes plagiarism. Similarly, as described in Box 5.4, "Cultures and Plagiarism," cultures have varying rules related to plagiarism.

In a corporate environment, it is not uncommon to have project proposals drafted that draw on the contributions of many people who may or may not be cited. Personal arguments among friends may not require complete source citations. However, most technical and public sphere arguments rely on credible and accurate attributions of source material. It is important for an advocate to be clear about the sphere and field rules that apply to their arguments.

In the academic field, plagiarism can take several forms, including:

- Failure to include or have available an accurate source citation sufficient to allow recipients to find the information.

■ ■ ■ ■ ■

BOX 5.4
CULTURES AND PLAGIARISM

In American universities, plagiarism tends to be strictly defined and strictly enforced. Penalties range from failing an assignment to failing the course and in some cases a university may suspend or expel a student. These rules of academic conduct often surprise international students who come from cultures where plagiarism is not treated as negatively.

In Chapter 3, we explored high and low context communication and the idea that some cultures can be classified as collectivist and others are more individualistic. International students are often taught that to understand the American view of plagiarism, they need to understand these two cultural values. Individualism requires respect for the individual contributions of others and to take their ideas without attribution is equivalent to theft of property. The individual character of American culture means that individual achievements and contributions to society should be treated distinctly from other contributions and achievements. Similarly, the low-context nature of many Western cultures including the United States means that the message should contain all of the necessary components to fully understand it—this includes source references and appropriate attributions.[29]

These cultural values can pose problems for students who come from collectivist and high-context communication cultures in which students are often taught to depend on classmates for answers. Consider, for example, the case of one international student, Magied Alsqoor from Saudi Arabia and president of the International Students Association at St Cloud State University, who explained,

> I think people in Saudi Arabia are very close to each other and so we grow up helping each other. It's a good thing, but it becomes a problem for Saudis in the U.S. We often get out of an exam and share questions with others and we think it's a common thing because we grow up in a society that tells us to share things and wish the best for your friends. In Saudi Arabia, your accomplishments are not recorded by your name, but by your tribe or family.[30]

- Using another person's ideas without citation.
- Using another person's words without citation.
- Borrowing part or all of another's work without proper citation.
- Using a paper writing service.[31]

Knowingly submitting work that is plagiarized is unethical as we will discuss in Chapter 11. To avoid plagiarism, it is important that arguers cite sources and take steps to avoid it. These steps include:

- When researching, take careful notes that include quotation marks when you use someone else's words and complete citation information.
- When writing or presenting a speech, give citation information every time you use someone else's words or ideas.
- When in doubt, cite your source.

As we have discussed, using evidence from well-qualified sources to support your arguments makes them stronger. Plagiarism is not only unethical, but failure to cite your sources weakens your own credibility.

SUMMARY

It is vital to be aware of the absence or misuse of evidence in arguments we hear and read and to avoid these problems in the arguments we make. As defined in Chapter 1, evidence includes objectively observable facts and conditions, generally accepted beliefs or premises, and previously established conclusions. The purpose of this chapter was to discuss the nature and types of evidence and to provide guidelines for using evidence.

Evidence functions as such because it is accepted by recipients and can be used to support other statements. If participants in an argument dispute a statement, it cannot function as evidence because it is not agreed on. Generally, evidence falls into two broad classifications—fact and opinion as to fact.

Factual evidence comes from our observations and experience. It includes reports and descriptions of events or phenomena, statistics, and artifacts that are actual objects used to support an argument. Factual evidence is expected to mirror physical reality.

Opinion evidence is someone's interpretation of the meaning of factual evidence. When an arguer uses opinion evidence, he or she uses the statement of someone else to support a claim. Opinion evidence from experts is useful when an arguer does not have a great deal of personal experience with the subject of the argument.

We should be aware of the quality of evidence so that we can judge the quality of support for our own and others' arguments. Evidence should come from reliable sources who have been proven correct many times in the past. Sources for evidence should have expertise in the subject matter of the argument, and it is important that audiences be informed of sources' qualifications when evidence is given. Sources should be objective, offering an undistorted and fair view of the question or issue. Evidence should be consistent, both with itself and with evidence from other sources. It should also be recent, particularly on topics in which conditions change over time. Evidence offered to support a claim should be directly relevant to the claim as stated, rather than tangential or irrelevant. People who testify about a situation should have had access to it and an opportunity to observe it firsthand. Otherwise, the evidence is hearsay and less reliable. Finally, arguers who cite the statements of others should be accurate. They should not violate the context or intended meaning behind a quotation by omitting crucial words, making secondary sources seem to be primary, or omitting information about the source's qualifications or where the information was found.

Like other forms of evidence, statistics are often subject to bias and human error as well as errors by the people who use them. There are certain problems unique to the discovery and use of evidence, however. First, we should be aware of pseudostatistics, those that are applied to phenomena and situations in which it is difficult to imagine how they could have been compiled using good statistical methods. Second, we should be cautious about comparing noncomparable units that seem to be of the same class but that are actually different. Third, we should use a representative sample, one that includes all the important characteristics of the group from which it was drawn.

EXERCISES

Exercise 1: Using Evidence. The following passages help illustrate correct and incorrect uses of evidence. For each passage, try to identify the primary weaknesses by applying the following criteria as discussed in this chapter.

Tests of Evidence. Apply each of the following tests to the passages:

Reliability	Evidence should be drawn from sources that have proven to be correct many times in the past.
Expertise	Evidence should be drawn from sources having a background of knowledge in relevant information.
Objectivity	Evidence should be taken from sources who hold a fair and undistorted view on a question or issue.
Consistency	Evidence should agree with other sources and should be consistent with itself.
Recency	Evidence should be based on the most current information available.
Relevance	The facts and evidence presented should be relevant to the claim that is made.
Access	Evidence should be drawn from sources who have observed firsthand the matter being disputed.

Now, here is the evidence to be evaluated.

1. *Mr. Herbert Kause convincingly argued last month that pregnant women should restrict their intake of caffeine. According to studies he conducted over the past six years, he has found strong evidence that supports the conclusion that caffeine is dangerous to unborn children.

2. Recently, at the University of Wisconsin, a study was conducted on listening and study patterns of freshmen students in beginning speech course. This study found that students in this course exhibited a lack of concentration in their studies and note taking. Therefore, we can conclude that college students have poor study skills.

3. In a special advertisement on Zenith Data Systems, Enrico Pesatori, Zenith Data Systems president and chief executive officer, said, "We have taken many major steps over the past eighteen months to respond to our customers' needs for innovative, aggressively priced products, and to adapt to the upheaval in the PC industry. The product lines we have developed will clearly distinguish Zenith Data Systems in the marketplace."

4. But, in actuality, almost 25,000 people are involved in fatal alcohol-related accidents per year. Of these 25,000 people, over 25 percent are under the age of twenty-one. This means we are losing over 6,000 young people per year because of alcohol. There are several reasons a nationwide drinking age should be enforced. Statistics show that raising the age would save over 750 young lives per year nationwide.

5. *We should reinstitute the military draft in this country. After all, we should recall John F. Kennedy's famous words, "Ask not what your country can do for you, ask what you can do for your country." Our country is currently in a military force crisis, and a military draft is something we can do for our country.

6. As the National Rifle Association has argued, if handguns were made illegal, then only those people who abide by the law would be barred from obtaining handguns. The criminals and the smugglers and racketeers would still have them.

7. A nationwide survey of college freshmen by Alexander W. Astin in 1991 revealed that 85.5 percent of those polled agreed that the government is not doing enough to control pollution. Water and air pollution controls should definitely be increased.

8. According to the Environmental Policy Institute and the Health and Energy Institute, "The Food and Drug Administration allowed irradiation of canned bacon in 1963 based on Army research. Five years later the FDA rescinded the approval, saying that the tests had been improperly structured and sloppily conducted."

9. A cosmetics company conducted a study of prospective customers for a new skin lotion. They sent 10,000 questionnaires to these customers, asking them to compare the new product with a variety of other products. Ninety percent of those responding favored the new skin lotion; therefore, the cosmetics company should proceed with production of the new lotion.

10. *Dr. Harvey Brenner concluded a study of unemployment in 1975. He argued that for each 1 percent increase in the unemployment rate, the death rate increases by 36,667 lives. Therefore, the federal government should take immediate action to decrease the levels of unemployment in this country.

11. People like high-calorie, high-fat foods that have no nutritional value. Some fast-food hamburgers have more than 1,000 calories. That's ridiculous. This kind of eating leads to obesity and contributes to a worldwide epidemic. Children model our behavior, and they learn from their parents. Not only are we increasing our risk of disease, but we are passing it down the generations.

12. Cheating in school has reached epidemic proportions. In a study conducted at a large eastern university, researchers discovered that 88.3 percent of the students cheated at some point in their academic careers.

13. In an advertisement signed by Bill Gates, chairman of Microsoft Corporation, and his CEO, Steve Ballmer, the two men early in the year 2000 predicted that appellate courts considering a court order to break up their company "will reaffirm the well-established legal precedent that antitrust law should encourage—not discourage—firms to improve their products rapidly to meet customer needs." Therefore, the antitrust decision against Microsoft should be overturned.

14. On March 3, 2000, the National Rifle Association's Institute for Legislative Action criticized President Bill Clinton's claim that "13 children are killed by guns every day." The NRA pointed out that to reach the "13 children" figure, President Clinton and antigun groups counted anyone under the age of twenty as a child. Since there are relatively few handgun deaths among children under fourteen but a much greater number among young adults age fifteen to nineteen, adding both groups together increases the number of deaths among "children" by 569 percent.

15. The *Cecil Textbook of Medicine* reported in its fifth edition on page 1,031 that "in a series of patients studied post-mortem more than 90 percent complained of shortness of breath."—From the *Journal of Irreproducible Results*, 40(2), (1995): 15.

Exercise 2: *Editorial Analysis.* Find an editorial in a local newspaper or magazine and analyze the evidence in it. When you are done, you should be able to answer the following:

1. What types of evidence did you discover?
2. What were the strengths and weaknesses of the evidence?

Exercise 3: *Evidence Evaluation.* Below are a number of pieces of information that could be relevant as evidence for certain claims in argumentative speeches or essays. To complete this exercise, divide into groups of three or four. Within each group, each individual should decide which *types* of resources (e.g., the Internet, books, periodicals, newspapers) should be examined for the answers to these questions and then inform the other group members of where she or he plans to look. When everyone has had an opportunity to locate the information in question, reconvene your group. Then consider the following questions:

1. Did everyone find the same answer to the question? What was it?
2. If different sources differed in the answer, how can the discrepancy be resolved?
3. How long did it take to find the answers to the questions in the various sources available? (That is, which sources were the easiest to use and the most efficient?)
4. How credible and in-depth is the information provided in the various sources?
5. Based on your experience, develop a "position statement" to share with the class about your group's views on the best strategies and venues for conducting research to locate evidence.

Now here are the questions to answer:

1. What are the demographics (age, income, profession, etc.) of Internet users?
2. What has happened to the hole in the ozone layer?
3. What major instances of terrorism have occurred against U.S. citizens (at home or abroad) during the past twelve months?
4. What is the most effective form of birth control currently available?
5. What bills related to gun control are currently being considered by the U.S. Congress?
6. What are said to be the major causes of domestic violence (spousal and child abuse) in the United States?
7. What are the most promising treatments presently available for AIDS?
8. What are the gun-control laws in four nations, not including the United States?
9. How promising is solar power as a major energy resource?
10. What is the current status of the deforestation of rain forests? Who benefits from clearing the forests?

Exercise 4: Plagiarism. Plagiarism is a serious issue on college and university campuses, especially in an era when information is easily accessible over the Internet. This exercise asks you to analyze plagiarism policies in the following ways:

1. What is the policy at your home institution? How is it organized? What are the sanctions?
2. Find the plagiarism policies of two other colleges or universities—include at least one international institution. How are they similar? How are they different?
3. If you found differences, why do you think they exist?

Exercise 5: Driving with Cell Phones. Read the following persuasive appeal by the National Highway Transportation Safety Administration. The evidence presented in this document provides support for banning mobile telephone use in vehicles. Read the argument and do the following:

1. Identify the types of evidence used.
2. Assess the quality of the evidence.

USING A CELL PHONE WHILE DRIVING IS DANGEROUS

A growing body of research suggests that using a cell phone while driving is a serious safety problem—even if a driver's hands are on the steering wheel....

    With 2,600 highway deaths and 330,000 injuries per year linked to cell phone use, according to a recent Harvard University study, the search for ways to mitigate distracted driving is becoming urgent....

Automakers are loading up vehicles with ever-more sophisticated technologies—such as screen-based navigation systems, dashboard entertainment consoles, and MP3 players—challenging engineers with how to continue the business boom without further compromising safety.

Automakers have made a huge bet that hands-free technology would be the answer. Services such as OnStar from General Motors Corp. let customers make calls over a voice-activated in-car cell phone, talk to an operator to get directions, or even consult with a concierge for shopping or restaurant recommendations....

But the latest research shows people talking on cell phones are distracted even if their hands remain on the steering wheel. The National Highway Traffic Safety Administration (NHTSA) is currently conducting in-depth research at its National Advanced Driving Simulator, run jointly with the University of Iowa. Preliminary research released last month indicates clear trade-offs with hands-free technology. Even though their hands remained on the wheel, study subjects using voice-activated systems take longer to dial—a potentially dangerous distraction....

"The distraction risks associated with cell phone use do not diminish with hands-free devices," said Rae Tyson, spokesman for NHTSA.

To the extent that hands-free technology gives drivers a false sense of security and prods them to engage in longer phone conversations, it may even exacerbate the safety problem, Tyson said....

Despite the safety concerns, customers' desire to stay connected to the outside world is only expected to increase. With some 163 million cell phone subscribers in the United States, NHTSA estimates that 3 percent of U.S. drivers are talking on cell phones at any given time.

A 2003 study by the Harvard Center for Risk Analysis suggested a very real safety problem exists when drivers are paired with cell phones.

The study found an estimated 2,600 deaths a year could be linked to cell phone use. Cell phone use also is connected to approximately 330,000 moderate to critical injuries annually and 1.5 million instances of property damage a year, the study found.

But the Harvard researchers wanted to quantify the potential cost, measured in lost productivity, of banning cell phone use in cars. They concluded that taking cell phones away from drivers would cost $43 billion a year in lost economic activity—about the same economic value of the lost lives and injuries.

"It's like cars themselves," said Joshua Cohen, co-author of the study. "Cars kill 40,000 people a year. That translates into a one in a 100 chance that a child born today will eventually die in a car crash. Yet we still have cars. Why? Because they are very useful...."

Adapted from National Highway Transportation Safety Administration, "An Investigation of the Safety Implications of Wireless Communications in Vehicles," November 1997, www.nhtsa.dot.gov/people/injury/research/wireless (accessed December 1, 2004); and American Automobile Association Web site, "Drive Safer, Talk Later: The AAA *Guide* to Cell Phones and Driving," www.aaawa.com/traffic_safety/cell_phones.html (accessed December 14, 2004).

NOTES

1. Russel R. Windes and Arthur Hastings, *Argumentation and Advocacy* (New York: Random House, 1965), 95.

2. For an account of Nazi propaganda efforts, see Randall L. Bytwerk, *Julius Streicher* (New York: Stein & Day, 1983).

3. John C. Reinard, "The Empirical Study of the Persuasive Effects of Evidence: The Status After Fifty Years of Research," *Human Organization Research* 15 (1988): 3–59; E. James Baesler and Judee K. Burgoon, "The Temporal

Effects of Story and Statistical Evidence on Belief Change," *Communication Research* 21 (1994): 582–602.

4. Reinard, 41–42.

5. A very good discussion of these issues can be found in Paul Fieldhouse, "Taxing Food," *Current Issues: The Inside Story*, http://politiquespubliques.inspq.qc.ca/fichier.php/146/DCTaxingFood.pdf (accessed May 10, 2008).

6. World Health Organization, "Overweight and Obese," March 2013, http://www.who.int/mediacentre/factsheets/fs311/en/index.html (accessed July 3, 2013).

7. World Health Organization, "Global Strategy on Diet, Physical Activity and Health," http://www.who.int/dietphysicalactivity/publications/obesity/en/index.html (accessed July 3, 2013).

8. Lauren Streib, "World's Fattest Countries," *Forbes*, http://www.forbes.com/2007/02/07/worlds-fattest-countries-forbeslife-cx_ls_0208worldfat.html (accessed May 9, 2008).

9. Streib.

10. MSNBC, "Nearly 1 in 5 Chinese Overweight or Obese," http://www.msnbc.msn.com/id/14407969/ (accessed May 9, 2008); and "Overweight and Obesity," *KidsHealth for Parents*, http://www.kidshealth.org/parent/nutrition_fit/nutrition/overweight_obesity.html (accessed May 9, 2008).

11. Centers for Disease Control and Prevention, "Overweight and Obesity: Economic Consequences," http://www.cdc.gov/nccdphp/dnpa/obesity/economic_consequences.htm (accessed May 9, 2008).

12. Center for Consumer Freedom, "WHO Wants a Fat Tax?" http://www.consumerfreedom.com/news_detail.cfm/headline/2336 (accessed May 10, 2008).

13. David Charter and Sam Lister, "Junk food under attack by fat tax," *The Times* (London), February 19, 2004.

14. Gary Becker and Richard Posner, "The Fat Tax—Posner's Comment," *The Becker-Posner Blog*, http://www.becker-posner-blog.com/archives/2006/10/the_fat_taxposn.html (accessed May 10, 2008).

15. A discussion of this division and the types of evidence is presented in George W. Ziegelmueller and Charles A. Dause, *Argumentation: Inquiry and Advocacy* (Englewood Cliffs, N.J.: Prentice-Hall, 1975), 49–82. See also a discussion of the types of evidence in J. Vernon Jensen, *Argumentation: Reasoning in Communication* (New York: Van Nostrand, 1981), 107–137.

16. Mark Shaffer, "Raising a Stink over Horse Diapers," *Tacoma News Tribune* (September 25, 1995): A4.

17. For more information, see also John Cook, "Blaster worm sender bound for prison," *Seattle Post-Intelligencer*, August 12, 2004, http://seattlepi.nwsource.com/business/185885_blaster12.html (accessed December 5, 2004); Laura Sulllivan and Stephen Kiehl, "Youth charted in virus attach," *The Baltimore Sun*, August 30, 2003, at http://articles.baltimoresun.com/2003-08-30/

news/0308300036_1_computer-worm-blaster-worm-blaster-computer (accessed April 24, 2013); Leslie Brooks Suzukama, "Internet Virus Arrest Naps Hopkins Teen," *Free Republic*, August 30, 2003, at http://www.freerepublic.com/focus/f-news/973227/posts (accessed April 25, 2013).

18. Additional information can be found at Linda A. Johnson, "Deaths Raise Fears over Stomach Stapling," *Seattle Post-Intelligencer*, August 11, 2004, at http://seattlepi.nwsource.com/national/apscience_story.asp?category=1500&slug=FIT%20 Stomach%20 Stapling (accessed August 11, 2004); Lisa Lucier, "Gastric bypass and stomach-stapling patients should recognize risk of nerve injury post-surgery," *Medical News Today* (October 15, 2004), http://www.medicalnewstoday.com/releases/14985.php (accessed April 25, 2013).

19. Lornet Turnbull, "Study: Urban Indians Face Health Disparities," *Seattle Times* (March 18, 2004): B1.

20. Shari Roan, "Psychologists Rate Presidents' Personalities," *Tacoma News Tribune* (August 14, 1996): SL13.

21. Robert P. Newman and Dale R. Newman, *Evidence* (New York: Houghton Mifflin, 1969), 95–96.

22. This research is summarized in Robert N. Bostrom, *Persuasion* (Englewood Cliffs, N.J.: Prentice-Hall, 1983), 79–81.

23. CNN Wire Staff, "Obama warns Syria no to cross 'red line,'" *CNN*, August 21, 2012, at http://www.cnn.com/2012/08/20/world/meast/syria-unrest (accessed May 18, 2013).

24. Joe Coscarelli, "Syria May Have Crossed Obama's 'Red Line' With Use of Chemical Weapons," *Daily Intelligencer*, April 25, 2013, at http://nymag.com/daily/intelligencer/2013/04/syria-may-have-crossed-obamas-red-line.html (accessed May 18, 2013).

25. Newman and Newman, 223–224.

26. Hank Green, "Obama calling for 42 MPG fleet average by 2016," Ecogeek.org, at http://www.ecogeek.org/automobiles/2753 (accessed July 31, 2102).

27. Colleen Kehoe, et al. "Results of GVU's Tenth World Wide Web User Survey," *Graphics Visualization and Usability Center*, May 14, 1999, at www.gvu.gatech.edu/user_surveys/survey-1998-10/tenthreport.html (accessed June 21, 2000).

28. Newman and Newman, 211–213.

29. John Gill, "Cultural insight can help tackle plagiarism," *Times Higher Education*, April 24, 2008, http://www.timeshighereducation.co.uk/news/cultural-insight-can-help-tackle-plagiarism/401564.article (accessed July 4, 2013); David L. Di Maria, "Plagiarism from a cross-cultural Perspective," *Al Jamiat* (accessed August 10, 2012).

30. Di Maria.

31. UW Committee on Academic Conduct in the College of Arts and Sciences, *UW's Faculty Resource on Grading*, at http://depts.washington.edu/grading/issue1/honesty.htm (accessed March 29, 2005).

REASONING

CHAPTER OUTLINE

KEY CONCEPTS

This chapter considers the reasoning process used in argument. You may recall from Chapter 1 that reasoning is the rational link between the evidence and the claim in the argument; it authorizes the step arguers make when they connect an argument's evidence to its claim. This is the point of the violent video game discussion in Box 6.1, "Should Violent Video Games be

Banned?" In the discussion, both JP and Spencer had researched and formulated opinions about whether violent games such as *Doom* or *Mortal Kombat* should be sold. Based on the evidence Spencer found, he reasoned that such games posed a significant risk to public safety. JP, on the other hand, found evidence that suggested Spencer's reasoning was flawed. He reasoned that in the absence of conclusive evidence demonstrating a risk, we should not allow government to censor expression or entertainment. Based on their research and consideration of the subject, each advocate reasoned to his conclusions and shared those reasons with the other.

When we reason, we make connections, distinctions, and predictions; we use what is known or familiar (evidence) to reach conclusions about the unknown or unfamiliar (claims). In reasoning, we might break a whole into its component parts, consider the precise ways in which the parts are connected, extrapolate from a situation we can see to some underlying condition, or in some other way think about the world and how it operates.

Within the framework of perspectives on argument we introduced in Chapter 2, a focus on reasoning emphasizes the logical perspective on argument (as opposed to the rhetorical or dialectical perspectives). The logical dimension of argument is primarily concerned with whether the links or connections the arguer makes in reaching a conclusion are sound and make sense to recipients. Good critical thinking involves good reasoning that meets certain tests for the particular kind of reasoning being used. In this chapter, we will describe six forms of reasoning frequently used in everyday discussions and consider the tests for those six types of reasoning.

▪ ▪ ▪ ▪ ▪
━━

BOX 6.1
SHOULD VIOLENT VIDEO GAMES BE BANNED?[1]

On April 20, 1999, two students, Eric Harris and Dylan Klebold, killed twelve students and a teacher. Twenty-three others were wounded before Harris and Klebold killed themselves at Columbine High School in Colorado. With no apparent triggering event or cause behind the massacre, investigators looked for some motivation to explain the assailants' behavior. Some blamed the parents; others blamed the school and cliques of students. Michael Moore's documentary film *Bowling for Columbine* linked the tragedy to a culture of violence in the United States. Other observers noted the teens' obsession with the violent video game *Doom* and argued that it and others of its genre, such as *Mortal Kombat* and *Wofenstein 3D*, lead to violent outbursts among some individuals and might have served as one cause of the Columbine massacre.[2]

There has been an ongoing controversy over violent media almost since the beginning of television. Studies have examined media violence in efforts to demonstrate conclusively that exposure to certain types of stimuli can have harmful and even tragic effects. Although media violence has been studied for years, as of yet there remains division in the scientific field regarding the exact relationship between exposure to violent images and violent outcomes.[3] Looking for clear answers and in response to growing public pressure to regulate or ban violent media content, the U.S. Senate passed a bill in 2006 requiring the Centers for Disease Control and Prevention (CDC) to investigate how electronic media affect children.[4]

The video game industry, in an effort to self-regulate and eliminate the need for government action, established the Entertainment Software Rating Board (ESRB) in 1994. The ESRB moved quickly to pass and implement a global labeling system that has now rated almost 10,000 games along a continuum from "EC" for "early childhood" players through "AO" for "adults

(continued)

BOX 6.1   CONTINUED

only."[5] The European Union is working on a stronger rating system with possible bans for certain violent video games.[6]

Yet, there remains a great deal of controversy over what the research demonstrates. Are violent games the cause of violent behavior? Or, do violent people act out through violent media? Are these games simply a symptom of potential problems? Does a ban or increased regulation increase safety and diminish violent behavior? Consider the discussion between two students, Spencer and JP, and analyze how their argument develops—especially the connections each makes that link claims to evidence.

Spencer: It's time to ban violent video games. I've read about this all year, and it seems to me that there is a very clear link between violent games and violent behaviors. Last week, I read an article by Amanda Schaffer that surveyed existing research, and she is pretty clear about three conclusions it reaches. First, the more children are immersed in violent video games, the more likely they will get into fights and act aggressively. Second, there is longitudinal evidence that shows that, over time, the more children play violent video games the more they become physically and verbally aggressive. And, third, the bulk of experimental studies reach the same conclusions.[7] There are hundreds of studies that support these conclusions, but even if the studies are not absolutely definitive, the preponderance of evidence is clear. One of the best articles I read was by psychologist Craig Anderson, who reviewed the myths and facts in the scientific literature.[8] He shows there are problems with letting children play violent games. Violent video games teach violence, and they teach violence as a way to solve problems. When people are placed in violent role-playing games, they learn and practice how to find aggressive solutions to conflict. We need to ban these games; there is no good reason for them to be sold.

JP: Wait a minute. The research isn't as clear as you might think. Even if you just go online and search using Google or Bing, you find thousands of entries showing all kinds of explanations and conclusions, many of which don't agree. I've read the material that says there is a link between violent media and violent behaviors, but I have also read many studies that show there is no causal relationship. For instance, take a look at a really interesting article by Dmitri Williams and Marko Skoric published in *Communication Monographs*.[9] They concluded that there is no conclusive support showing that violent video games contribute significantly to increased violent behavior in the "real world." And, some people such as Dr. Cheryl Olson have noted in interviews that experimental data are mostly from studies of college students with study designs that *assumed* a link between violent games and violent behavior.[10] It is not surprising, because of the way the study was set up, to find an association between violent games and violent behavior. My only point is that the data are not clear. You and I have played violent video games, we might get frustrated and angry if we lose, but we don't act out beyond the game. Increased aggression inside the game does not necessarily translate to violence outside. I think it is more likely that violent people like violence and choose entertainment that supports their predisposition. Because they are already violent, they watch violent TV shows and movies and they play violent games. In fact, violent video games may actually be beneficial for these people. A recent study by Unsworth, Devilly, and Ward makes the point that perhaps violent video games actually play a cathartic role—which could be a positive outlet for otherwise violent behaviors.[11]

(continued)

BOX 6.1 CONTINUED

Spencer: Even if what you are saying is true, violent video games still pose a significant risk because *some* people may act out on the basis of a game. Several authors have made the point that the interactive nature of video games blurs the lines that separate reality from fantasy, meaning that people who have a violent predisposition may be more likely to act out aggressive fantasies. It seems to me that these games—whether they are the cause of violence or make violence more acceptable—should not be allowed if there is any level of risk associated with them.[12] And, there is a risk that players who are already disturbed may become even further agitated by these games and that they will act out the fantasies.

JP: The evidence is not sufficiently clear to support what you are saying. But even if it were, you cannot ask government to restrict every possible risk. There is no clear, causal connection that shows playing violent games results in aggressive behavior. Government restrictions on the possible risk undermine our rights to free expression, allow government censorship, and place someone in charge of what we do for entertainment. This is a very dangerous path that we should not follow.

QUESTIONS TO CONSIDER

1. How was reasoning used in the preceding discussion? Did you find it effective? Why?
2. Which arguments seemed to have the best reasoning? What made the reasoning persuasive?
3. Which arguments had the weakest reasoning? Why did they appear weak?
4. If you were Spencer and you were going to reply to JP's last comment, what would you say? What reasons would you use?
5. Why do you think some members of the scientific community conclude that violent video games are harmful, but other scientists say they are not? What does this tell you about field theory that was developed in Chapter 1?

ROLE OF THE ADVOCATE

Competent arguers can evaluate their own and others' reasoning, construct good arguments, and identify the unstated assumptions and connections people make in their arguments. They can also analyze other people's arguments to discover strengths and weaknesses. As we noted in Chapter 1, reasoning, along with claims and evidence, is one of the three basic components of any argument. Claims, as you will recall, are the end points of arguments, and evidence is the beginning or grounding for an argument. Reasoning serves as the process that connects evidence with claims.

In moving from what is known and acceptable (the evidence) to what is unknown or controversial (the claim), arguers often state their reasoning in an inference. *An inference states the step one has made in linking the evidence to the claim.* Inferences can be explicit or implicit in an argument. For example, we might explicitly say, "Don't play in the street because a car might hit you." On the other hand, we might simply say, "Don't play in the street. You might get hurt." In this case, the inference, "because a car might hit you," is unstated or implicit. In studying and analyzing the arguments of others and in detecting possible weaknesses in reasoning, it is important to be able to identify the type of reasoning used in the argument, even if the arguer does not state it.

When people argue, they use various inference patterns that they may not always be able to identify and explain. Sometimes you can "flush out" a person's reasoning by way of a challenge ("Wait a minute, how did you reach that conclusion, based on the information you just gave me?"). Often, the unstated inference is the weak point in the person's argument. If you can identify how the arguer connected the claim to the evidence, you will know what type of reasoning was employed. Each kind of reasoning suggests a set of tests or questions that function as standards to evaluate its quality. Knowing what type of reasoning was used and what tests to apply will improve your critical-thinking skills as you become better able to analyze and critique others' arguments.

Knowing the various reasoning forms will not only make you a better argument critic, it will make you a better arguer. Knowing how reasoning functions and the tests and standards for judging it will help you monitor the effectiveness and quality of your own reasoning, which, in turn, is another important critical-thinking skill. Argument theorist Stephen Toulmin observed that a "sound" argument is "one that will stand up to criticism."[13] Each of the inference types discussed in this chapter—quasilogical, analogy, generalization, cause, coexistence, and dissociation—must meet certain standards to be judged as sound.[14] Knowing these types and the applicable tests will enable you to foresee possible weaknesses in your arguments and anticipate objections others might raise to them.

FORMAL LOGIC AND PRACTICAL REASONING

In Chapter 2, we discussed how the Toulmin model helped theorists evolve our way of understanding arguments from the formal construction of the syllogism to the practical and informal understanding of arguments in conversations and everyday interactions. Although many philosophers were at first understandably cool toward Toulmin's approach, teachers and scholars in the fields of speech and English were more enthusiastic about it. They had been teaching students for some time how to construct and critique arguments expressed in everyday language designed for real audiences, and they thought that Toulmin's model for analyzing arguments and his view that arguments were constructed and supported by principles in specific fields were very useful.

At about the same time that Toulmin's book appeared, two European scholars, Chaim Perelman and Lucie Olbrechts-Tyteca, published the English translation of *The New Rhetoric: A Treatise on Argumentation*.[15] Like Toulmin, these two authors argued that sole reliance on formal logic to study practical arguments was inadvisable. Their approach was different from, yet complementary to, Toulmin's.

Unlike Toulmin, who was primarily concerned with a *logical* perspective on argument, Perelman and Olbrechts-Tyteca were interested in a *rhetorical* perspective. They began their work by observing how all sorts of arguers—public speakers, essayists, and even philosophers—constructed their arguments with an audience in mind. Arguers who wanted their arguments to succeed, they said, selected the various elements that make up their arguments with an eye to their audience. They use premises they know their audience agrees with, values they believe recipients hold, examples with which they are familiar, and language they will understand. Perelman and Olbrechts-Tyteca concluded that arguers make use of reasoning forms recognizable to their audiences.[16]

Perelman and Olbrechts-Tyteca worked by studying arguments in use—in speeches, essays, books, and articles. They described the reasoning forms they found in these sources and, after ten years of studying arguments, advocates, and usage, they identified categories of argument forms used in practical argument.[17] In this chapter, we will adopt their category scheme and focus on the six most significant, widely used categories of reasoning—quasilogical, analogy, generalization, causal, coexistential, and dissociation. These are the reasoning forms most frequently used by arguers.[18]

REASONING AS INFERENCE MAKING

Of the six inference types we will discuss in this section, the first five—quasilogical, analogy, generalization, cause, and coexistential—are *associative schemes*; they *bring together elements and evaluate or organize them in terms of one another*. They may bring together the elements in terms of equivalence, comparison, contrast, sequence, or some other connection, but the reasoning works because each part of the argument is viewed in terms of the other. The sixth form is a *dissociative scheme*; it *aims to disengage or disunite elements originally considered as a unity*. Dissociation is unique from the other five types, but equally important.

Before we begin our discussion of the argument types, we want to remind you that some arguments may fall into more than one type. This is because real arguments in daily life do not possess the neatness and clarity of the forms of mathematics and formal logic. An argument might make a causal claim based on a comparison (analogy), or it might use examples to show that a causal relationship exists. This can be a problem when critics attempt to identify arguments by type, as in some of the examples in the exercises at the end of this chapter. In these cases, more than one correct classification of an argument may be possible. What is important is to correctly identify at least one of the reasoning forms occurring in an argument, and not to be too troubled by some overlap among the forms.

Quasilogical Arguments

Quasilogical arguments are labeled "quasi" because they appear similar to the syllogistic structures of formal logic. Their similarity to the formal reasoning of logic or mathematics gives quasilogical arguments a compelling air, and people often find them persuasive because of their simplicity and clarity. *Quasilogical arguments place two or three elements in a relation to one another so as to make the connections between them similar to the connections in formal logic.* It would be fair to say that quasilogical arguments can be reduced to formulas because of their simplicity and clarity.

For example, one could make the argument:

> If the Seattle Mariners can beat the Texas Rangers, and if the Texas Rangers can beat the Oakland Athletics, then it only makes sense that Seattle should be able to beat Oakland.

This is simply stated and formulaic, but the statement is probable and not certain like the statements in formal logic. In the following section, we will emphasize three types of quasilogical arguments that are quite common—transitivity, incompatibility, and reciprocity.

These arguments are rhetorical and co-orientational, which means they are based in the recipients' willingness to accept the probability that the conclusion will come true.

Transitivity

Transitivity arguments are structured like categorical syllogisms discussed in Chapter 2. *They have three terms that are associated with one another through a process of classification, but the relationships among the terms are probable and not certain, as in the syllogism.* Nevertheless, the relationships established among the terms by the arguer are so clear and simple that they seem compelling—just as with formal logic. Consider the following example:

As a student at a private university, Mary is paying high tuition.

This could be reconstructed in the form of a categorical syllogism, as:

Major Premise: All students at private universities pay high tuition.
Minor Premise: Mary is a student at a private university.
Conclusion: So, Mary pays high tuition.

Notice that the middle term (students at private universities) appears in both the major and the minor premises. The middle term functions like an equal sign; it enables the arguer to associate the remaining two terms ("pay high tuition" and "Mary") in the conclusion of the argument.

Transitivity arguments, as with logical arguments developed in Chapter 2, have to meet certain tests to be considered cogent, and these tests generally are related to their form. First, they must contain three and only three terms. If they have four or more terms, they do not have the simple infrastructure of the categorical syllogism and thus cannot be classified as transitivity arguments. Second, their premises must be true. Because the conclusion of a transitivity argument simply combines the substance of the two premises, those premises must be true, or the conclusion will be just as false as the premise with which one starts. Third, all three of the statements must be stated (or restatable) as simple classifications. If the relations are too complex ("is greater than," "leads to," "is comparable to," "represents," and so forth), then the inference is not a simple categorical inference, and the argument is not a transitivity argument. Fourth, the middle term must occur in both of the premises so it can fulfill its "equals" function and make it possible to connect the remaining two terms in the conclusion.

Incompatibility

The next type of quasilogical arguments is incompatibilities. *Incompatibilities are similar to disjunctive syllogisms in that they imply two alternatives between which a choice must be made; that is, one must choose one or the other, not both.* The problematic nature of the incompatibility results because both alternatives are stated at the same time. Because the two alternatives are opposite each other and are being stated simultaneously, their combination is "incompatible" and creates a situation that should be resolved. Here are two examples:

The US needs to make a choice. Currently, it sells China a tremendous amount of coal that is burned to generate electricity to power factories that produce goods that are then shipped to the US. This is good for both economies. But all the coal being burned is causing tremendous environmental damage. If we want to protect the environment, the US should end all coal exports.

The cosmetic business is a multi-billion dollar a year business. From shampoo to hair color to lipsticks, consumers buy these goods and support industries that in turn employ thousands of people. But cosmetic projects are subject to rigorous Food and Drug Administration testing to ensure that they are safe and effective for the purposes they are intended. In order to demonstrate safety, many of these products are tested in lab animals that are subjected to painful and debilitating experiments. How can we use products that have caused so much pain and suffering? We need to stop buying any product that came about because of animal testing.

The first argument sets up a choice between the economy and the environment. Its point is that the two choices cannot coexist—as long as the United States continues to sell coal to China, the environment will be damaged. The second argument presents a similar choice between the welfare of animals and cosmetic testing. To end the suffering of these lab animals, the arguer claims, we need to stop buying those products. In both cases, the arguers are affirming mutually incompatible and conflicting ideas together. Incompatibilities, then, contain two alternatives that are incompatible and show a conceptual conflict or a conflict of interests.

Incompatibilities can be tested in much the same way as disjunctive syllogisms. First, the two terms must indeed be mutually exclusive; if they can be maintained together, then no contradiction exists. Second, they must be viewed as necessarily relevant to each other. If one of the terms can be defined as irrelevant, then the incompatibility can be resolved.

Reciprocity

The third form of quasilogical argument to be considered in this section is argument from reciprocity. *Reciprocal relationships are reflected in the "if-then" nature of the argument* ("if you do something, then you will get something"). Consider the following reciprocal argument:

Major premise: If you expect your teachers to treat you with respect, you should treat them with respect.

Minor premise: You expect your teachers to respect you.

Conclusion: So, you should treat them with respect, too.

Reciprocal relations assert a hypothetical relationship between two situations or conditions and imply a mutual dependence between them: "You should treat your teachers with respect." Reciprocity implies symmetry; the two parts of the argument are related to each other, and their equivalence is emphasized.

Reciprocity is based on our belief that individuals and situations that can be put into the same category should be treated in the same way. It emphasizes the characteristics that make situations or persons equivalent to each other. How can teachers who show disrespect for students, expect respect in return? Students, teachers, and all the members of a university work and learn in the same place; they all likewise deserve respect.

Reciprocity arguments may be stated in various ways:

What is honorable to learn is also honorable to teach.

Do unto others as you would have them do unto you.

If I don't get my exercise today, I'll feel tired tomorrow.

In both cases, what is valid or acceptable in one situation is considered equivalent to what is valid or acceptable in another.

Arguments from reciprocity generally should meet two tests. They should equate two situations, individuals, or phenomena with each other. If more than two are implied, then the argument falls into some other classification. Furthermore, the arguer should use the symmetry between the two to argue that they should be treated reciprocally. Since the claim of reciprocity arguments is that the two elements should be treated together and equivalently, the arguer must highlight the similarity between them.

Quasilogical arguments occur frequently and are commonly used in ordinary speech. People using quasilogical arguments generally attempt to simplify a situation by reducing it to a very limited number of component parts and then set those components into clear and unequivocal relations. The clarity and simplicity of these relations thereby give their arguments the same compelling nature that we find in formal logic and in mathematics. Box 6.2, "Apply the Theory," provides some additional examples of how these reasoning forms function in arguments.

BOX 6.2
APPLY THE THEORY: QUASILOGICAL ARGUMENTS

CHARACTERISTICS

- Sort of logical; resembles formal logic; limited to two or three terms.
- Views two elements as equal to, incompatible with, or dependent on each other.
- Relationship between the elements appears simple and clear.

EXAMPLES

Transitivity:	Bill's friends are my friends, and you're a friend of Bill's, you are a friend of mine.
As syllogism:	Bill's friends are my friends. You are Bill's friend. So, you are my friend.
Incompatibility:	The candidate says he's opposed to nepotism, but he appointed his cousin as director of the White House Travel Office. (Nepotism is hiring or appointing relatives.)
As syllogism:	No opponents of nepotism appoint their relatives. This candidate appointed his relative. So, this candidate is not really opposed to nepotism. (And his words and actions are incompatible.)
Reciprocity:	Meeting our responsibilities means doing a better job.
As syllogism:	If we do a better job, we will meet our responsibilities. We are doing a better job. So, we are meeting our responsibilities.

APPLICATION

Using the case developed in Box 6.1, write a quasilogical argument for each type:

Transitivity

Incompatibility

Reciprocity

Analogy

Like reciprocity, analogy emphasizes the similarity between two elements. *An analogy reasons that because two objects resemble each other in certain known respects, they will also resemble each other in respects that are unknown.* Analogy differs from reciprocity, however, because its purpose is different. A reciprocity argument claims that two situations should be treated alike; an analogy makes an attribution about something that is unknown. Most of our early learning occurs by means of analogy. The child who discovers that the flame of a candle is hot and can burn fingers will avoid other fires in the future. We come to expect that what has happened in the past will happen in the future, that similar situations will have similar outcomes, and that similar objects will exhibit the same characteristics. Such regularities give order and uniformity to our experience and interpretation of the world.

Literal

There are two forms of analogy. The first is the literal analogy and the second is figurative analogy. *A literal analogy compares two objects of the same class that share many characteristics and concludes that a known characteristic that one possesses is shared by the other.* The inference made in a literal analogy can be represented by Figure 6.1, "Structure of Analogies," and it can be stated as follows:

Object X has characteristics A, B, C, and D.

Object Y has characteristics A, B, and C.

Therefore, Object Y will probably possess characteristic D as well.

Characteristic D, while not known to certainly exist, is probably present which, then, is the subject of the advocate's reasoning.

For example, students have expressed a great deal of concern regarding tobacco use on U.S. university campuses. Approximately 30 percent of American university students smoke and use other tobacco products.[19] Smoking rates are often as high or higher at universities

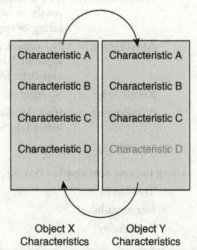

FIGURE 6.1   Structure of Analogies

in other countries. Concerned over health consequences associated with both smoking and secondhand smoke, students on some campuses have approached university administrators asking for campus-wide bans on tobacco. Many of these requests have been successful with more than 648 campuses banning tobacco products.[20] Large state public university systems including Ohio, Oregon, and Maryland have moved to implement tobacco bans.

In 2012, California State University (CSU), Fullerton, became the first of the 23-campus CSU system to ban smoking on university property—even including smoking inside a personal car with the windows rolled all the way up.[21] Fullerton's public affairs office expected complaints and opposition, but did not receive many. Implementation of the ban is moving forward and many of the other California State campuses have implemented or are considering similar bans.

Some concerns were raised that such a ban either would not work or that people would simply shift their smoking to other venues off campus—not solving any problem, just moving it. If people disregarded the rule, some said, enforcement would be nearly impossible. Or, if people moved their tobacco use to places just outside campus then all that would have happened is that the problem was moved but not solved.

When students at Sacramento State approached their administration and faculty senate about a smoking ban, they argued that almost everyone could agree that tobacco use was bad and that a ban made sense. The issue, they argued, was one of how to implement a ban. They reasoned by analogy that California State University, Fullerton, was able to pass a policy and its implementation, so far, had gone smoothly. Because Fullerton, a similar campus with similar student demographics, was able to begin an effective implementation strategy, Sacramento State should be able to as well. Figure 6.2, "Smoking Ban," shows how the analogy worked.

In this analogy, the *evidence* consists of all the statements of similarity among campuses—Fullerton and Sacramento. The *claim* draws the conclusion that implementing a ban (the unknown characteristic) will go smoothly; and the *inference* is that Fullerton's experience should resemble Sacramento's in all relevant ways.

Literal analogies are subject to tests of at least three different kinds. The first has to do with the *quality of the comparison*. To have probative value, literal analogies must compare two

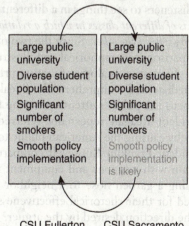

FIGURE 6.2   Smoking Ban   CSU Fullerton   CSU Sacramento

objects that belong to the same class. In the preceding example, Fullerton and Sacramento are clearly in the same class of public, California universities. They share similar size and demographics. These characteristics strengthen the analogy. However, if there were significant differences (if Sacramento's tobacco use was three times Fullerton's rate) and the compared objects are not alike in respects relevant to the conclusion of the analogy, the comparison is undermined. The similarities cited must also be relevant to the comparison and to the claim to which it leads. In the example comparing Sacramento to Fullerton, some aspects (patterns of smoking consumption, cultural differences and similarities, general disposition toward smoking and smokers) are relevant to the claim about whether a smoking ban will work.

The second test for literal analogies has to do with *quantity*; is there a sufficient number of similarities to support the comparison? How many are enough? Obviously, there is no unequivocal answer to this question. The larger the number of relevant similarities, the more probable the conclusion. For example, the analogy could still work effectively if the universities shared only one common characteristic (smoking patterns) but differed significantly with size and demographic characteristics, but it would be stronger if multiple characteristics were shared (smoking patterns, size, and demographic characteristics).

The third test for a literal analogy is related to *opposition*; are there any significant dissimilarities that would undermine the comparison? For example, if Fullerton had already passed a smoking ban and the new action eliminated other types of tobacco, that difference could undermine the comparison because Sacramento was significantly different. Or, if another CSU had attempted to ban tobacco product and had a terrible experience, the comparison would be diminished because another similar university had different results. These examples illustrate the importance of considering possible significant differences when one advances a literal analogy or comparison to prove a claim. For additional examples of how literal analogies work, see Box 6.3, "Apply the Theory."

Figurative

The second type of analogy is the figurative analogy. From a logical point of view, figurative analogies do not have probative value but can be used to illustrate a point or to get listeners to see things in a different light. *The figurative analogy is a comparison between two objects of different classes in which a relation or quality within one is said to be similar to a relation or quality within the other.* Since the two objects in a figurative analogy are not truly similar, the comparison is metaphorical and illustrative rather than concrete and literal.

Figurative analogies function primarily to make what is remote or poorly understood immediate and comprehensible. Speakers and public figures often use figurative analogies to focus the public's attention on the features of a situation that they want to emphasize.[22] President Reagan repeatedly referred to the Strategic Defense Initiative as a "shield," thereby causing the American public to see it as a passive barrier to be used only for defense. President Franklin Roosevelt compared the Lend Lease Act by which we supplied Great Britain with weapons and equipment to fight the Germans in World War II to the act of lending a garden hose to a neighbor to put out a house fire. Figurative analogies can be tested for their rhetorical effectiveness: Do they cause audiences to reshape their attitudes in the direction desired by the arguer? These analogies cannot be tested on logical grounds, however, because they compared items and objects from different classes.

BOX 6.3

APPLY THE THEORY: ANALOGY ARGUMENTS

CHARACTERISTICS

- Assumes two objects, situations, or events are similar.
- One is known; the other is less known.
- Assumes that if the two are similar in ways that are known, they will also be similar in other ways.
- Makes an attribution to a comparatively unknown object, situation, or event.

EXAMPLES

As it becomes easier and easier to obtain images and documents online in the home, it is possible that people will download and copy these somewhat indiscriminately. The advent of the photocopy machine led researchers to become less discriminating and to copy articles of only marginal interest…. In a similar way, online access to full-text documents and digital images may lead people to accumulate items of only marginal interest.[23]

Evidence: Photocopy machine led to indiscriminate copying of articles.

Inference: Online access to full text and images may lead to accumulation of marginal items.

In this fiftieth anniversary of the end of World War II, Germans remain understandably nervous about the staying power of fascism, which was largely a product of the interwar years. How much more cautious, then, should Americans be about assuming that racism and sexism—much older and more pervasive problems—have been defeated by a mere thirty years of legal and social initiatives?[24]

Evidence: Germans are still concerned about fascism fifty years after the Holocaust.

Inference: Americans today cannot assume racism and sexism are no longer problems.

APPLICATION

Using the case study developed in Box 6.1, design an argument from literal analogy.

Generalization and Argument from Example

In a *generalization, one reasons that what is true of certain members of a class will also be true of other members of the same class or of the class as a whole.* As in the analogy, one begins with what is known or familiar (the examples that have been observed) and moves to what is less well known or less familiar. Furthermore, since reasoning is usually on the basis of characteristics that are known, the same type of inference is made in the generalization as is made in the analogy. The generalization, however, involves more than two instances and often makes claims about a whole class of objects.

Generalizations move from some to all members of a class. For example:

Because the rabbits I have seen have short tails; all rabbits must have short tails.

We've had a dry spell during July and August for the last three years, so there must be one every summer.

It is difficult if not impossible for anyone to interact with and have knowledge of an entire class of something. We cannot know all rabbits nor have we experienced all dry spells in late summer months. Instead, we observe samples of the whole. We look at some rabbits and experience some dry summer months. From those observations, we make a conclusion about a larger, unseen, and unexperienced class. For instance, the characteristics (short tails, dry spell) that have been observed are generalized and applied to the class as a whole (rabbits, summer seasons). This sort of inference is illustrated in Figure 6.3, "Structure of Generalizations."

Generalizations assert members of a class possess the relevant characteristics of the entire class. In other words, to be a member of a group, certain characteristics define both the individual and the whole.

Generalizations occur very frequently, and we use them to make conclusions about groups of people or experiences that exist beyond our direct knowledge. We also see professionally produced generalizations in the form of Gallup polls, Nielsen ratings, market surveys, clinical experimentation, and other forms of statistical sampling where the population sampled is considered to represent the general population. Generalizations are also used when an arguer has been able to observe some but not all the members of a class and wishes to make a claim about the class in general. For example, Amanda explains why she monitors her child's television viewing by referring to the programs she has seen:

Amanda: I never let Heather watch Saturday morning cartoons. I try to find something else to occupy her time.

Amy: Why? I surely do appreciate their babysitting potential.

Amanda: Listen; have you ever watched that stuff? Crass commercialism and violence, that's all it is.

Amy: Oh, come on. You're exaggerating.

Amanda: No, I'm not. I watched *She-Ra* and *Hercules* and two other adventure cartoons one morning. Over one-third of the time was devoted to commercials for candy and toys. And I counted thirty-two violent acts in two hours of programming. I can think of better ways for my child to spend her time!

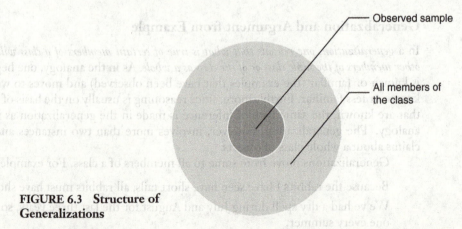

Observed sample

All members of the class

FIGURE 6.3   Structure of Generalizations

In her argument, Amanda makes an inference about the programs she has not watched based on the programs she has watched. Her *evidence* is that one-third of the time was devoted to commercials and that she saw thirty-two violent acts. Her *claim* is that these programs display "crass commercialism and violence." Her *inference* is that *She-Ra*, *Hercules*, and two other programs are typical of all Saturday morning cartoons.

Another form of generalization is reasoning from example. Whereas a generalization will make a general statement based on observation of a number of examples, an argument from example will make a general statement based on observation of just *one* example. *Argument from example seeks acceptance for some general rule or principle by offering a concrete, particular case.* Suppose Amanda had said, "In one of the programs I watched, there were eight fights in twenty minutes. The characters used swords, knives, and their fists to resolve every problem. Every disagreement led to a confrontation, and every confrontation led to a fight. This program shows how continuously violent these cartoons can be." As in the discussion between Amanda and Amy, Amanda is trying to establish a general trend. She does this by describing in detail a single program she has seen. The form of reasoning is illustrated in Figure 6.4, "Structure of Reasoning from Example."

Like the analogy, arguments from generalization and example are subject to tests of *quality*, *quantity*, and *general opposition*. First, the example or examples cited must be *relevant* to the general claim. If the programs Amanda cited were not cartoons, or if they were cartoons intended for older or adult viewers, her generalization would not be relevant to a claim about children's cartoons. Furthermore, the example or examples cited must be *typical* of the class in question. If no other Saturday cartoon has as many as eight acts of violence in a single showing, then the one Amanda watched could not be considered representative of the rest of the cartoons, and her generalization would be open to question.

Second, the criterion of *quantity* (applicable only to the generalization) can be met only when Amanda has cited a sufficient number of examples. There are nearly three dozen children's cartoons aired on commercial networks and cable channels on most Saturday mornings.[25] Are Amanda's four examples enough to support her general claim? The cogency and persuasiveness of her claim will surely depend on the number of examples she can cite. This

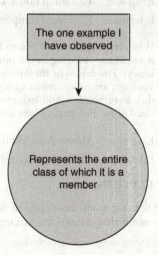

**FIGURE 6.4   Structure of
Reasoning from Example**

raises the question of how many examples are sufficient to support a generalization. There is no clear-cut answer because the requisite number of examples depends on the particular argument and the size of the available sample. There should be enough examples to satisfy the audience and to be weighed against possible counterexamples.

Third, the existence of counterexamples provides the test of *opposition* to both generalization and argument from example. Cartoons such as *Arthur, Dragon Tales*, and *The Magic School Bus* contain very few or no acts of violence and portray characters who cooperate peacefully with one another and have a good time. If Amy listed or described programs such as these, Amanda would have to reconsider whether the characteristics of violence and commercialism really apply to all children's cartoons. For additional examples and practice with generalization and reasoning from example, see Box 6.4, "Apply the Theory."

BOX 6.4

APPLY THE THEORY: GENERALIZATION AND REASONING FROM EXAMPLE

CHARACTERISTICS

- Assumes that what is true of one or some members of a class will also be true of others or of the whole class.
- The evidence is the presentation of specific instances.
- The inference is that these are representative of others.

EXAMPLES

Along with reducing tax rates, we must also aggressively reduce tax rules and regulations. It's estimated that last year alone, American taxpayers spent 1.8 billion hours filling out their tax forms. Businesses spent twice as much time sending the IRS over 1 million reports.[26]

Evidence: 1.8 billion hours, over 1 million business tax forms.

Inference: Represent complicated tax rules and regulations.

When one teaches about Marco Polo, or William of Normandy, or Goethe, or Joan of Arc, one is essentially engaging in the process of transmitting information about a cultural heritage and legacy. The names of the Africans, Ibn Battuta, or King Sundiata of Mali, or Ahmed Baba, or Yenenga, are never spoken in high school classes, and under the current curricular structure, if they were heard, would lack credibility even though they are by world standards certainly the equal of the Europeans I have mentioned in contrast.[27]

Evidence: Marco Polo, William of Normandy, Goethe, Joan of Arc.

Inference: These represent the exclusion of African figures from American classrooms.

APPLICATION

Using the case study developed in Box 6.1, write (1) an argument using generalization and (2) an argument that reasons from example.

Cause

Arguments from cause claim that one condition or event contributes to or brings about another condition or event. Causal arguments are also arguments from succession; one event must happen before the other. Furthermore, the causal event must produce or bring about the effect.

There are two forms of causal argument. The first, and weaker form, is the necessary condition. *A necessary condition is one that must be present for the effect to occur.* To remain alive, people must consume both fluids and food. If either of these two necessary conditions is lacking, death from dehydration or starvation will result. In order to communicate, two people must speak the same language or at least understand the same nonverbal code. Reasoning from necessary condition is a relatively weak form because the effect is not guaranteed by the cause. For example, food does not *cause* life; it is simply *necessary* for life to continue.

The second form of causal argument is the sufficient condition. *A sufficient condition for an event or effect is a circumstance in whose presence the event or effect must occur.* In other words, the presence of a sufficient condition guarantees that the subsequent effect will occur. A broken fan belt on an automobile guarantees that the engine will overheat. If lightning strikes overly dry timber, a fire will result. Furthermore, a number of necessary conditions, taken together, may guarantee an effect. The presence of oxygen, combustible material, and temperatures in a certain range, taken together, constitute a sufficient condition for fire. Some general examples of causal argument are presented in Box 6.5, "Apply the Theory."

Causal influences are complex and frequently difficult to sort out and identify. The preceding examples of causes as necessary and sufficient were supported with examples of physical, natural, or mechanical phenomena in which causal sequences are clear and inevitable. In everyday affairs, however, causal sequences are often embedded in sets of necessary and sufficient conditions that mutually influence one another in complex relationships. Consider the following argument for increased state support of public education:

> We should increase our support for public education in our state. Rather than being a drain on our revenues, such an increase is actually a long-term investment. Increased funding will lead to a small class size, better facilities, and improved materials for use in the classroom. Students will complete their education with better skills than they now have and be more productive contributors to the workforce.
>
> This, and the new industry which an improved educational system will attract to our state, will, in the long run, increase our tax base, which will result in improved revenues for state government.

An arguer advancing such claims would have available data on the effects of increased state support on student–teacher ratios, capital improvements, and educational resources. These would serve as *evidence*. The arguer's *claim* would be, "We should increase our support for public education in our state." The arguer's inferences are a series of causal claims: first, increased funding will lead to improved education; second, better-educated students will become more productive workers; third, increased productivity will improve the tax base and thus increase state revenues in the future. This network of causal claims is represented in Figure 6.5, "System of Causal Influence."

Like the other forms of reasoning, causal argument has tests to gauge its adequacy. The *quality* test deals with whether the cause is a necessary or sufficient condition for the

■ ■ ■ ■ ■

BOX 6.5
APPLY THE THEORY: CAUSAL ARGUMENTS

CHARACTERISTICS

- Asserts that one condition or event brings about another condition or event.
- "Weak" cause: first condition must be present for effect to occur.
- "Strong" cause: first condition guarantees effect will occur.
- Evidence is the physical presence of causes and effects.
- Inference is that one condition or event brings about the other.

EXAMPLES

The new beltways and interstates offered cheap access to farmland on the fringe, and the result was suburban sprawl and disinvestment in existing business districts. People are waking up to the fact that low density, auto dependent sprawl has profound consequences on our quality of life and our individual and collective pocketbooks. The Chicago region grew 4 percent in population and 40 percent in land area from 1970 to 1990.[28]

Cause: Beltways and interstates.

Effect: Suburban sprawl, disinvestment in existing business districts.

Cause: Low density, auto dependent sprawl.

Effect: Consequences for quality of life, pocketbooks.

A great deal of effort has gone into discovering and analyzing the ways in which humans could be exposed to radioactive materials from a [nuclear] waste repository. Dozens of scenarios have been offered. In the one that has received the most attention, waste canisters corrode, and water leaches radioactive elements…out of the spent fuel or vitrified high-level waste, then carries them into groundwater. People would be exposed if they used the water for any of the usual purposes: drinking, washing, or irrigation.[29]

Cause: Stored radioactive materials' leakage into groundwater.

Effect: People exposed to radioactivity.

APPLICATION

Using the arguments developed in Box 6.1, write an argument that uses necessary causal reasoning and one that uses sufficient causal reasoning.

claimed effect. The fact that the necessary (as opposed to sufficient) condition does not *guarantee* the effect suggests weaknesses in the argument. Increased funding for education might be spent hiring more administrators and bureaucrats rather than on items that directly affect students; thus, education might not necessarily be improved. Furthermore, if a desired effect can be attained in the absence of the purported cause, that cause is not necessary. If the schools could be improved by being reorganized, or if teachers could be trained differently without spending more money, then increased funding could not be said to be a necessary cause.

FIGURE 6.5   System of Causal Influence

The test of *quantity* is applied to a causal argument when one considers whether the cause is sufficient to produce the effect. If increased funding alone will not measurably improve the quality of education, then funding improvement alone is not enough. Other measures, such as improvement in teacher training programs and enhanced counseling to prevent student dropouts, may also be needed.

Finally, the test of *opposition* suggests that first, the effect may have been produced by some other cause; second, the effect may be the cumulative result of many causes working together; or third, there may be some other, unanticipated cause working counter to the cause the arguer has cited. For example, increased funding for schools may not lead to improved learning because of other forces in society, such as poverty and drug use, that undermine formal education. Factors such as broken families, child abuse, and racism might cause the failure of education even when large sums of money are spent to improve the schools.

Many times, although two events are related to each other, the relationship is neither necessary nor sufficient. For an argument to meet the tests for causal reasoning, it must be fairly rigorous. Because of the many causes that can contribute to a particular effect, and because of the possibility that alternative causes can intervene and reduce or eliminate the expected effect, reasoning that relies only on linear, one-to-one cause–effect relationships is risky.

A method that has proved useful in discussing the relationships among phenomena is correlation. *A correlation claims that two events or phenomena vary together; an increase or decrease in one is accompanied by an increase or decrease in the other.* For example, if a market analyst observed that improvements in the economy would be bad for bond values (because higher interest rates devalue existing bonds carrying lower rates), the analyst would be correlating economic health, higher interest rates, and bond values with one another. The arguer who wishes to show a causal relationship among phenomena is often well advised to show that a variation in one will probably contribute to a variation in the other—an argument more modest than direct causal argument, but also less risky because it acknowledges the possibility of alternative and counteracting causes.

Coexistential Arguments

An argument from coexistence reasons from something that can be observed (a sign) to a condition or feature that cannot be observed. The sign or indication functions as the evidence; the existence of the condition or the essence it indicates is the claim; and inferring from what we can observe to something we cannot observe constitutes the inference. Coexistential reasoning is illustrated in Figure 6.6, "Structure of Coexistential Argument." As in analogy and generalization arguments, the inference moves from what is known (the sign) to what is unknown or less known (the condition or essence).

We frequently use signs that we can observe to infer conditions we cannot observe directly. A sore throat and runny nose are symptoms or signs of a cold. Buds on vegetation are a sign that spring is on the way. Or, consider the inference in the following conversation, for example:

Jill: You need to put oil in your car before you drive it today.

John: Why? Is the oil low?

Jill: Well, the oil light was on when I came home last night.

In this conversation, Jill's *evidence* is that the oil light came on. Her *claim* is that the oil is low. And her *inference* is that the light is a reliable indicator of the amount of oil in the car.

This example illustrates an important distinction between two forms of argument that are often confused—sign and cause. In a sign argument, the arguer intends to claim that a condition exists; in a causal argument, the arguer intends to explain *why* a condition exists or how it came about. Jill's intent is to claim that the oil is low in the car, not why or how it came to be that way. There could be an oil leak, the engine could be burning oil, or oil could have been consumed through normal wear and tear: If Jill had proposed one of these factors as leading to the low oil, she would have been making a causal argument.

Sometimes the distinction between coexistential and causal reasoning is subtle and depends on how the argument is worded. Consider the following examples:

The merchants downtown are beginning to close early and have installed iron grill-work on their windows. Crime must be becoming a serious problem in the community.

Discrimination has existed in this country for a long time. This is shown by the Civil Rights Act, the Voting Rights Act, and the equal-opportunity laws, all of which would have been unnecessary if discrimination did not exist.

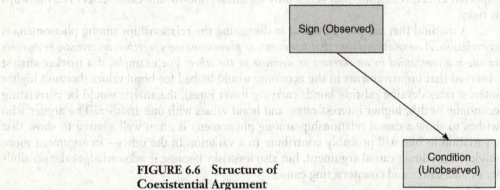

**FIGURE 6.6 Structure of
Coexistential Argument**

Both of these are coexistential arguments that claim an unobserved condition—crime or discrimination—exists. In both of these examples, the arguer's intent was to show that certain underlying conditions existed, *not* to show their cause or how subsequent events came about. They could be viewed as causal arguments if the arguer had claimed that crime had caused the merchants to put up the grillwork or that discrimination brought about antidiscrimination legislation, but these would be claims of a different type from the one in the preceding example.

In coexistential arguments, both the sign and the condition it indicates coexist or occur at the same time. Two varieties of coexistential argument are person/act argument and argument from authority. *Person/act argument reasons from a person's actions to his or her character or essence.* The act is taken as the sign; the person's character is taken as the essence.

> John turned in his last two papers late, hasn't washed his dishes in a week, and has a month's worth of dirty laundry piled up. He must be a procrastinator.

Unlike other forms of coexistential argument, person/act inferences often occur in the other direction; we reason that a person's essence or character will result in certain acts. ("Don't expect John to turn in his paper on time; he's a real procrastinator, and everybody knows it.")

Another variant of coexistential argument is argument from authority. *Argument from authority reasons that statements by someone presumed knowledgeable about a particular issue can be taken as evidence sufficient to justify a claim.* In argument from authority, the actual quote or statement functions as the evidence (sign); the claim is that whatever the quote attests is true (unobserved condition); and the reasoning is that the authority is qualified and accurate on the matter in question. Consider the following example:

> A team of researchers, led by John A. Ruben of Oregon State University, has concluded that birds descended from reptiles, not dinosaurs, as has long been claimed. Their claim is based on observation of the most complete fossil of the reptile *Longisquama* ever found, which has about eight pairs of long appendages resembling feathers.[30]

The presumed feathers on the fossil and the research team's conclusion function as *evidence* in this argument; the *claim* is that birds descended from reptiles; and the *inference* is that the research team is a qualified authority to speak on the subject.

Like many other forms of reasoning, coexistential arguments must meet the tests of quality, quantity, and opposition. Sign, person/act, and authority arguments meet the test of *quality* when the relationship between the indication and the condition it indicates is constant and reciprocal. If the relation is only sporadic or intermittent, then the inference is unreliable. If a car's electrical system is shorting out, its oil light may come on even when the oil level is fine. One might see occasional grillwork on a building in an area because it is used for decoration, not protection. Making person/act ascriptions is usually a little risky because people do not invariably behave the same way all the time. (John might surprise you and actually get his paper written by the due date!) And authorities are often wrong on an issue, however compelling their credentials might be. The quality of authoritative arguments also depends on the quality of the source itself. Is the person cited truly an expert with current firsthand information relevant to the claim? The tests for authoritative opinion evidence, such as expertise, objectivity, consistency, and access, were discussed in Chapter 5.

The test of *quantity* is met when there are enough signs of the condition in question. We could be surer that crime was a problem in an area if there were further indications of it—a greater police presence and a higher incidence of arrests and convictions. We are more confident of claims based on authoritative statements when an arguer can cite multiple authorities with credible credentials on the issue.

Coexistential arguments meet the test of *opposition* when there are no countersigns that work against the arguer's claim. Frequently, the presence of a condition might be disputed because there are as many signs indicating that it does not exist as there are signs indicating that it does. A common example of this is speculation about the health of the economy. In a given fiscal quarter, durable goods orders and housing starts may increase, causing some economists to announce that the country is entering a period of economic growth. Meanwhile, unemployment may rise and productivity decline, causing other experts to point to these as countersigns that indicate economic decline. This same standard may, of course, be applied to arguments from authority; we are more likely to believe authoritative arguments when there are no other equally credible authorities testifying on the side of the issue opposite the one in question. For additional examples and practice with coexistential argument, see Box 6.6, "Apply the Theory."

■ ■ ■ ■ ■

BOX 6.6
APPLY THE THEORY: COEXISTENTIAL ARGUMENTS

CHARACTERISTICS

- Claims that two things coexist.
- Reasons from something that can be observed (a sign) to a condition that cannot be observed.
- What is known is the concrete sign; what is unknown (or claimed) is the condition.
- Could reason from a person's acts to his or her character, or from an authoritative statement to an unobservable condition.

EXAMPLES

One of the central criticisms of the World Trade Organization (WTO) is that it is a fundamentally undemocratic body.... Consider its dispute resolution system: The WTO's dispute panels are its most undemocratic features. These panels are composed of three trade lawyers that are not bound by "conflict of interest" rules. All proceedings are closed to the public and the press. All documents are kept secret. There is no outside review or appeal after a decision has been made.[31]

Signs: Three-member panels, closed proceedings, secret documents, no outside review.

Condition: WTO is undemocratic.

Federal assistance to parochial schools...is a very legitimate issue actually before Congress. I am opposed to it. I believe it is unconstitutional. I've voted against it on the Senate floor this year.[32]

Sign: I voted against it.

Condition: I believe it is unconstitutional; I am opposed to it.

APPLICATION

Using the case study developed in Box 6.1, write two coexistential arguments. First, write one based on person/act and second, write one based on authority.

Dissociation

The last type of inference to consider is dissociation. Unlike arguments from quasilogical, analogy, generalization, example, cause, and coexistence—which bring together or associate ideas—dissociation disengages, or differentiates, between two ideas. Furthermore, arguers using dissociation seek to assign a positive value to one of the ideas and a lesser or negative value to the other. *Dissociation arguments disengage one idea from another and seek a new evaluation of both ideas.* Most dissociations are based on the distinction between appearance and reality, with reality being what is valued. Perhaps one of the most famous speeches using this form of reasoning was "I Have a Dream" by Dr. Martin Luther King Jr.[33] A full text of the speech can be found in several places online (http://www.archives.gov/press/exhibits/dream-speech.pdf). As you read the speech, consider the dissociations where one concept is put in opposition to another. For instance, King says that he dreams his children will live in a nation that judges them "not by the color of their skin" (Concept 1) "but by the content of their character" (Concept 2).[34]

Here the external appearance—the color of one's skin—is dissociated from the internal substance—the content of one's character—and greater value is placed on the second concept. The claims in dissociative arguments are usually implied. Here, King's claim was that people should not be judged by outward appearance BUT by qualities of character. The success of King's argument is based on society's recognition that substance is more important and more to be valued than surface appearances. In a sense, this commonly recognized and accepted distinction functions as the basis or grounds for King's argument.

Dissociations are based on value hierarchies. *A value hierarchy places one value or values above another value or values.* There are many value hierarchies that are recognized and accepted in American society: The objective is valued over the subjective, the end over the means, the unique over what is common, and the permanent over the transitory.[35] Dissociative arguments make use of these hierarchies and especially of the appearance/reality hierarchy to dissociate concepts.

To clarify how value hierarchies are used in dissociative arguments, we will consider two more examples. In the first, a frustrated voter complains:

> I'm tired of all the rhetoric in this presidential campaign. I want to see the candidates engage in some substantive debate on the real issues.

This arguer dissociates "substantive debate" (real) from the candidates' "rhetoric" (appearance). Her use of *substantive* and *real* makes it clear that it is the second idea—engaging on the real issues—that she values. Or, consider another example from a discussion on corporate takeovers.

> I don't see a takeover plan here that's going to be beneficial to the corporation. It's a one-time hit, where we get a spike in the share price, and we cash out a corporation instead of operating it as a viable entity sometime into the future.

The value hierarchy behind this dissociation is the permanent as opposed to the transitory. The "beneficial" plan, the corporation as a "viable entity" (permanent), is dissociated from the "cash out," the "one-time hit" (transitory). For additional examples of dissociation, see Box 6.7, "Apply the Theory."

■ ■ ■ ■ ■

BOX 6.7
APPLY THE THEORY: DISSOCIATION

CHARACTERISTICS

- Disengages two ideas.
- Assigns a positive value to one of the two ideas and a lesser value to the other.
- Can usually be stated in a "not this…but that" form.
- Based on accepted value hierarchies (evidence).
- Links to a less accepted or unrecognized value hierarchy.

EXAMPLES

Ask not what your country can do for you—ask what you can do for your country.[36]

Accepted hierarchy: Altruism over selfishness (not stated explicitly).

Claimed hierarchy: What you can do for your country over what your country can do for you.

Real objectivity does NOT mean the reporter has no opinion. Anyone with a pulse has an opinion. The reporter's JOB is to have an opinion, to aggressively dig up the facts, and apply his or her carefully honed opinion to sort it all out…. Objectivity means the reporter is ultimately alone with the facts, and must make a SUBJECTIVE decision what to write. They must be independent of organized agendas and interest groups, not independent of their own judgment.[37]

Accepted hierarchy: Objectivity over subjectivity.

Claimed hierarchy: A reporter's "objective" (i.e., considered) opinion versus a reporter with a bias who is not objective.

APPLICATION

Using the subject developed in Box 6.1, write a dissociative argument.

The tests for dissociation arguments are much more appropriately applied from the rhetorical rather than the logical perspective. Dissociation arguments rest on hierarchies accepted by the arguer's audience. The *quality* of dissociation depends on the pervasiveness and strength of the value hierarchy used by the arguer. For example, during the 1992 presidential campaign, Vice President Dan Quayle repeatedly appealed to "family values" over other "lifestyle choices." He sought to dissociate family units made up of single parents and homosexual couples from the traditional two-parent family. His argument appealed to those audiences who believed the nuclear family unit should be valued over other kinds of families because the dissociations he sought to make depended on that hierarchy. Dissociation can meet the test of *opposition* when there are no hierarchies more pervasive and more accepted than the one the arguer is using. The segment of the American public that values freedom of choice over the more traditional lifestyle options questioned Quayle's dissociation.

SUMMARY

This chapter defined and described the types of reasoning used in arguments. The reasoning an arguer uses is expressed in an inference statement that links the argument's evidence with its claim. Often, arguers do not expressly state their reasoning in an inference statement. The ability to determine the nature of an unexpressed inference and its workings is an important critical-thinking skill. Therefore, this chapter explains the various reasoning forms and the standards for judging them.

The first form of reasoning is quasilogical, which is based on formal logic and the syllogism. Quasilogical arguments are composed of a limited number of statements (three or less), and state relationships between a limited number of terms (three or less). The simplicity and clarity of quasilogical arguments make them seem compelling and persuasive. This chapter describes three kinds of quasilogical arguments—transitivity, incompatibilities, and reciprocity. Transitivity arguments are based on the categorical syllogism and link terms together through a middle term that functions like an equal sign. Incompatibilities are based on the disjunctive syllogism and state two incompatible alternatives at the same time, thus implying a contradiction. Reciprocity arguments state two mutually dependent alternatives and imply that they should be treated equivalently.

The second reasoning form is analogy. Analogies claim that because two objects resemble each other in certain known respects, they will also resemble each other in respects that are unknown. Literal analogies compare objects in the same class, whereas figurative analogies compare relations or qualities of objects in different classes. The probability or cogency of analogies depends on the number of similarities shared by the compared objects, the relevance of those similarities to the argument's claim, and the number of dissimilarities between the compared objects.

The third form of reasoning includes generalization and reasoning from example. A generalization attributes characteristics shared by certain members of a class to the class as a whole, whereas argument from example reasons from a concrete, particular case to a general tendency, rule, or principle. The strength of reasoning from generalization or example depends on how typical the example or examples are of the class, whether there are counterexamples, and, in the case of generalization, whether there are sufficient examples to represent the class as a whole.

Causal reasoning is the fourth reasoning form. Arguments from cause claim that one condition or event contributes to or brings about another condition or event. Causal relations take two forms: the necessary condition for an effect is one that must be present for the effect to occur, and the sufficient condition is a circumstance whose presence guarantees the effect will occur. The cogency of causal arguments depends on whether the cited cause alone is sufficient to guarantee the effect and whether there are counter causes working against the claimed cause–effect relationship. Furthermore, relations among phenomena are rarely as linear and rigorous as causal reasoning implies. For that reason, arguers wishing to show that variations are related often use correlation rather than causation.

Coexistential arguments are the fifth form of reasoning. An inference based on coexistence reasons from something that can be observed (a sign) to a condition or feature that cannot be observed. Two of the most common types of coexistential arguments are person/act inference and reasoning from authority. In order for coexistential arguments to be cogent, the relation between the sign and the condition it indicates must be reciprocal, the number of signs indicating the condition must be sufficient, and there should be no significant countersigns.

The sixth and last form of reasoning is dissociation. Dissociation distinguishes between ideas rather than bringing them together, as do other forms of reasoning. Dissociative arguments disengage one idea from another and seek a new evaluation of both ideas. Dissociations connect the first idea with what the audience most values (reality) and the other idea with what is less valued (appearance). They thereby break the links between the ideas and cause the dissociated idea to be more valued. The tests for dissociation arguments depend on how strongly the audience actually holds the values relevant to the argument.

EXERCISE

Identifying Reasoning. For each of the following arguments,

    A. Identify what type of argument it is: quasilogical, analogy, generalization or example, cause, coexistential, or dissociation.

    B. Identify the evidence, claim, and inference. (Remember that the inference is often implicit. If it is not explicitly stated, supply it.)

    C. Provide two questions that you might use to test the argument.

Note: It is important to remember that sometimes an argument can fall into more than one classification. For example, an argument might make a causal claim based on a comparison (analogy), or it might use examples to show that a causal relationship exists. Note, too, that you will find some of these arguments quite controversial. They should be interpreted as sympathetically as possible, that is, in line with what the author intended. The three steps described are demonstrated in regard to the following argument:

> But as our Nation has succeeded in setting a course for financial responsibility, students across the country have struggled to do the same. The rising price of higher education puts college out of reach for many promising young people, and it saddles those who do get an education with an unsustainable debt, a debt that causes them to delay buying their first home, put off having children, or give up the goal of starting a business. Today Americans have more than $1 trillion in student loan debt. There is more student loan debt than credit card debt, and the average graduate owes more than $25,000 when they get out of school. I think a college education should free young people to achieve their dreams, not saddle them with crushing debt for the rest of their lives.

Senator Harry Reid, "Student Loans," *Congressional Record*, May 22, 2013, S3202.

A. This is an argument from cause.

B. Evidence: Loan debt is more than $1 trillion. More is owed in student loans than all the credit card debt in the United States. The average graduate owes more than $25,000.

    Claim: College debt is saddling students with crushing debt for the rest of their lives.

    Inference: The rising price of education limits access for some students while resulting in crushing debt for others that prevents them buying a house, having children, or starting a business.

C. Are there other ways to pay for a college education that would not result in this level of debt? How much of this debt is because of student choices—delaying graduation for a second major, changing majors, expensive colleges over public?

*1. The listener should often be shown the conclusion contained in the principle. From this principle, as from the center, light shines on all parts of the work. In much the same way, a painter plans his painting so that light emanates naturally from a single source to each object. The whole work is unified and reduced to a single proposition enlightened in various ways.

François Fénelon, *Letter to the French Academy*, Barbara Warnick, trans. (Lanham, Md.: University Press of America, 1984), 68.

2. Many of the stories depicting sexual harassment as a severe problem spring from "consultants" whose livelihoods depend upon exaggerating its extent.... Susan Webb, president of Pacific Resources Development Group, a Seattle consultant, says she spends 95 percent of her time advising on sexual harassment. Like most consultants, Miss Webb acts as an expert witness in harassment cases, conducts investigations for companies and municipalities, and teaches seminars. She charges clients $1,500 for her thirty-five-minute sexual harassment video program and handbooks.

Gretchen Margenson, "May I Have the Pleasure...," *National Review* (November 18, 1991): 37.

3. It is said by those who have examined the matter closely that the largest number of divorces is now found in communities where the advocates of female suffrage are most numerous, and where the individuality of woman as related to her husband, which such a doctrine inculcates, is increased to the greatest extent. If this be true, it is a strong plea... against granting the petition of the advocates of woman suffrage.

Joseph Emerson Brown, "Against the Woman Suffrage Amendment," in *American Forum*, Ernest J. Wrage and Barnet Baskerville, eds. (Seattle: University of Washington Press, 1960), 341.

4. Any presidential candidate who would take a holiday on a remote Caribbean island with a woman to whom he is not married and with whom he plans to spend a nonworking vacation is the biggest idiot who walked the face of the earth and for that reason alone is unqualified to be President of the United States.

Adapted from a statement by Jeff Greenfield, "Politics, Privacy, and the Press," in *Ethics in America* television series (Corporation for Public Broadcasting, 1989).

*5. If we burn the forests of the Amazon, we are told, our planet's lungs will give out, and we will slowly asphyxiate. Surely we have better, more practical reasons for not burning them than to stave off universal catastrophe. I can easily imagine similar arguments that would have required the interior of North America to remain empty of cities—and yet I don't think this continent is a poorer place now than it was 20,000 years ago.

Thomas Palmer, "The Case for Human Beings," *The Atlantic Monthly* (January, 1992): 88.

6. We observe here today not a victory of party but a celebration of freedom—symbolizing an end, as well as a beginning—signifying renewal, as well as change.

John Fitzgerald Kennedy, "Inaugural Address, 1961," in *Speech Criticism: Methods and Materials*, William A. Linsley, ed. (Dubuque, Iowa: William C. Brown, 1968), 376.

7. Carla Kiiskila, a resident of a section of north Wallingford that seems pretty tranquil until you try to cross the street, wrote to the Engineering Department to complain about the hazards of N. 50th Street at Sunnyside Avenue.... Kiiskila complains that she has several times narrowly escaped being hit and had to run for the curb to get across 50th.

So the Engineering Department's van Gelder came out to examine the intersection. No doubt there's a danger and a problem there, he admits. [One citizen] got the Engineering folks to try crossing at the speed of an 85-year-old, and proved it was impossible. She unwittingly proved her point afterward, when she went to cross back (at normal speed) and very nearly got hit by a speeding car that spun broadside to avoid hitting her.

Eric Scigliano, "How Can a Citizen Cross the Road?" *The Weekly* (August 27–September 2, 1986): 22.

8. 1991 statistics from the Carnegie Foundation for the Advancement of Teaching show that SAT scores are directly proportional to family income. Students from families with incomes under $10,000 score an average of 768 (combined verbal and math scores) out of a possible total of 1,200. Students from families with incomes in the $30,000 to $40,000 range have scores averaging 884. Students from families with incomes over $70,000 have scores averaging 997. Since scholastic aptitude is related to a student's position on the wealth/poverty scale, which has a lot to do with where a family lives (affluent suburb or inner-city slum), alleviating poverty would be one way of improving scholastic aptitude.

Edd Doerr, "Whither Public Education?" *The Humanist* (November/December 1991): 41.

9. Scandal has been part of the American system from the beginning. There were allegations of sexual misconduct during the Washington presidency. The Washington cabinet almost broke up over Hamilton and Jefferson fighting with each other. These are the problems that happen in a democratic government subject to public information.

Adapted from a statement by Rudolph W. Giuliani, "Public Trust, Private Interests," in *Ethics in America* television series (Corporation for Public Broadcasting, 1989).

10. Mass culture is in some senses lonely and individualistic. The reasons for this can be summed up, as usual, in a single word: television. More and more, entertainment is about observing and absorbing, not about participating. It is a matter of millions of atomized individuals, each on a solitary couch, clutching a solitary beer, with the set turned on and the zoom lenses beamed at singers or players or stars.

Lawrence Friedman, *The Horizontal Society* (New Haven, CT: Yale University Press, 1999), 25.

*11. Let us not seek to satisfy our thirst for freedom by drinking from the cup of bitterness and hatred. We must forever conduct our struggle on the high plane of dignity and discipline. We must not allow our creative protest to degenerate into physical violence. Again and again we must rise to the majestic heights of meeting physical force with soul force.

Martin Luther King Jr., "I Have a Dream," in *Speech Criticism*, 381.

12. Video games work just like the operant conditioning used by modern armies to train soldiers.... Whereas soldiers in World War II were taught to shoot (calmly, at stationary targets), soldiers sent to Vietnam were taught to kill—as a conditioned response. They were trained, in full combat garb, to shoot instantly at human-shaped figures that suddenly popped up in front of them. This is very much like the training many children receive playing video games in which lifelike figures pop up and the player has to respond automatically by aiming and pulling a trigger—and gets instant reward if the target is hit.

Deborah Tannen, *The Argument Culture: Moving from Debate to Dialogue* (New York: Random House), 248–249.

13. The awesome power of government needs to be constantly checked by defense lawyers so that mere accusations don't inevitably turn into guilt. As Justice Brandeis said, "In order to promote liberty, we need eternal vigilance."

Adapted from a statement by Jack Litman, "To Defend a Killer," in *Ethics in America* television series (Corporation for Public Broadcasting, 1989).

14. The deficit is a hard problem, but we know that it is not the wallet Washington lacks, it is the will! We know Washington…will find $500 billion to bail out banks and bankers that stole people's money. Think about it; $5 billion would allow us to reach nearly every child eligible for *head start*, and yet, we're told we don't have the resources. But when it comes to S and L's, we are ready to commit 100 times that amount. How does that make sense? Are savings and loans 100 times more important?

Mario Cuomo, "Is Government Working?" in *Contemporary American Speeches*, 7th ed., Richard L. Johannesen, R. R. Allen, and Wil A. Linkugel, eds. (Dubuque, Iowa: Kendall/Hunt, 1992), 320.

15. The [Supreme] Court's description of the place of *Roe [v. Wade]* in the social history of the United States is unrecognizable. Not only did Roe not, as the Court suggests, *resolve* the deeply divisive issue of abortion, it did more than anything else to nourish it by elevating it to the national level where it is infinitely more difficult to resolve.

National politics were not plagued by abortion protests, national abortion lobbying, or abortion marches on Congress, before *Roe v. Wade* was decided. Profound disagreement existed among our citizens over the issue—as it does over other issues, such as the death penalty—but that disagreement was being worked out at the state level.

Justice Scalia, dissenting, *Planned Parenthood v. Casey*, 505 US 995. Supreme Court 1992.

16. A campaign for president or prime minister looks a lot like show business, or the selling of show business, with its live appearances and TV interviews, its spot advertisements on TV, its market research and focus groups. When Bill Clinton campaigned for the American presidency in 1992, there was "little to distinguish" his appearance in San Francisco's Mission District "from a movie premiere," as one author put it.

Lawrence Friedman, *The Horizontal Society* (New Haven, Conn.: Yale University Press, 1999), 35.

17. [T]he first amendment to the Constitution does not protect only nice speech or only attractive speech, or only popular speech. We would not need a Constitution for that purpose. The great thing about the United States of America is that our Constitution protects any crackpot who wants to stand on his soapbox and express any oddball point of view that pops into his mind.

John Danforth, "Against a Constitutional Amendment Banning Flag Burning," in *Contemporary American Speeches*, 2000, 334.

18. Let the skeptics of this peace recall what once existed among these people. There was a time when the traffic of ideas and commerce and pilgrims flowed uninterrupted among the cities of the fertile crescent. In Spain, in the Middle East, Muslims and Jews once worked together to write brilliant chapters in the history of literature and science. All this can come to pass again.

President Bill Clinton, "Statements by Leaders at the Signing of the Middle East Pact," *New York Times* (September 14, 1993, International Edition): A6.

19. For a member of this president's inner circle to admit that the federal government is so massive that it is essentially not practical for the chief executive to hold it accountable or for the president to effectively manage it is simply stunning. It also begs the question, if it is no longer possible for the president of the United States to oversee all the federal agencies assigned to him and hold them accountable, then who is? Is anyone?

Representative Christine Johnson, "Federal Government is too large and has too much control," *Congressional Record*, May 22, 2013, p. H2842.

20. The evidence is clear, cumulative, and robust enough to rule out dismissal or denial. And it has been accumulating for over two decades…. What it points to is this: Information technology,

upon which we are now very dependent, has occasioned an epidemic of chronic, often crippling, workplace injuries and layoffs. It has also failed remarkably to reduce workloads or, in most cases, to boost productivity. As a result, computers have significantly raised the cost of doing business and intensified the pace of work without delivering on many of the benefits presumed, promised, or imagined to have accompanied the information age.

R. Dennis Hayes, "Digital Palsy: RSI and Restructuring Capital," in *Resisting the Virtual Life*, James Brook and Iain A. Boal, eds. (San Francisco, Calif.: City Lights, 1995), 173.

NOTES

1. The topics for this discussion were drawn from The International Debate Education Association, which can be found at http://idebate.org/debatabase/debates/culture/house-would-ban-sale-violent-video-gamescensor-violent-video-games.

2. Sean Swint, "Violent Video Games Linked to Aggressive Behavior," *WebMD*, at http://www.webmd.com/news/20000424/children-violence-video-games (accessed on May 12, 2008).

3. A very clear discussion of current research and the relationship of violent video games to violence can be found in Craig A. Anderson, "Violent Video Games: Myths, Facts, and Unanswered Questions," *APA Online*, 2003, at http://www.apa.org/science/psa/sb-anderson.html (accessed on May 12, 2008).

4. Eric Bangeman, "Senate Bill Mandates CDC Investigation Into Video Game Violence," *Ars Technica*, at http://arstechnica.com/news.ars/post/20060918-7771.html (accessed on May 17, 2008).

5. The video-game rating system is described on the ESRB Web site, which can be found at http://www.esrb.org/ratings/ratings_guide.jsp (accessed May 18, 2008).

6. Tom Samiljan, "Should Violent Video Games be Banned?" *Yahoo! Tech*, at http://tech.yahoo.com/blogs/samiljan/4146 (accessed on May 18, 2008).

7. Amanda Schaffer, "Don't Shoot: Why Video Games Really Are Linked to Violence," *Slate*, at http://www.slate.com/id/2164065/ (accessed on May 18, 2008). See also Craig A. Anderson, Douglas A. Gentile, and Katherine E. Buckley, "Violent Video Game Effects on Children and Adolescents: Theory, Research, and Public Policy" (New York: Oxford University Press, 2006).

8. Anderson.

9. Dmitri Williams and Marko Skoric, "Internet Fantasy Violence: A Test of Aggression in an Online Game," *Communication Monographs* 72 (June 2005): 217–233.

10. "New Book Cuts through Violent Video Game Myths," *Slashdot*, March 7, 2008, at http://interviews.slashdot.org/article.pl?sid=08/03/07/226235 (accessed on May 21, 2008).

11. G. Unsworth, G. J. Devilly, and T. Ward, "The effects of Playing Violent Video Games on Adolescents: Should Parents Be Quaking in Their Books?" *Psychology, Crime and Law* 13 (2007): 383–394.

12. John Borland, "Blurring the Line Between Games and Life," *CNET* New.com, February 28, 2005, at http://ecoustics-cnet.com/Blurring+the+line+between+games+and+life/2100-1024_3-5590956.html (accessed May 21, 2008); and Julie Hilden, "The Attacks on 'Violent' Video Games and 'Torture Porn' Films: Two Different Strategies To Try to Get around First Amendment Protections," *Find Law: Legal News and Commentary*, September 17, 2007, at http://writ.news.findlaw.com/hilden/20070917.html (accessed on May 21, 2008).

13. Stephen Toulmin, *The Uses of Argument* (Cambridge: Cambridge University Press, 1958), 8.

14. Our typology of inferences is taken from Chaim Perelman, *The Realm of Rhetoric*, W. Kluback, trans. (Notre Dame, Ind.: University of Notre Dame Press, 1982), 53–137.

15. Perelman and Olbrechts-Tyteca, *The New Rhetoric: A Treatise on Argumentation*, John Wilkinson and Purcell Weaver, trans. (Notre Dame, Ind.: University of Notre Dame Press, 1969).

16. This point is emphasized in Barbara Warnick and Susan L. Kline, "*The New Rhetoric*'s Argument Schemes: A Rhetorical View of Practical Reasoning," *Argumentation and Advocacy* 29 (1992): 1–15.

17. Perelman explains their method of research in "The New Rhetoric: A Theory of Practical Reasoning," in *The Rhetorical Tradition*, Patricia Bizzell and Bruce Herzberg, eds. (Boston, Mass.: St. Martin's, 2001), 1384–1409.

18. In a study of 622 arguments in five televised panel discussions, Warnick and Kline found that 37 percent of the arguments were quasilogical; 22 percent were causal; 12 percent were coexistential; 5 percent were generalization or example; 6 percent were analogical; and 4 percent were dissociative. In considering these percentages, it is important to note that many arguments were classified into two or more of these categories.

19. Americans for Non-Smokers' Rights, "Colleges and Universities," at http://www.no-smoke.org/goingsmokefree.php?id=447 (accessed on August 29, 2012).

20. Kimberly Railey, "Smoking Bans: Tobacco-Free College Campuses On the Rise in the US," *Christian Science Monitor*, July 25, 2012 at http://www.csmonitor.com/USA/Education/2012/0725/Smoking-bans-Tobacco-free-college-campuses-on-rise-in-US (accessed August 29, 2012).

21. Cal State Fullerton to Become First Smoke-Free CSU Campus, *Los Angeles Times*, May 18, 2012, at http://latimesblogs.latimes.com/lanow/2012/05/smoking-ban.html (accessed August 29, 2012).

22. Perelman and Olbrechts-Tyteca, 385.

23. Howard Besser, "From Internet to Information Superhighway," in *Resisting the Virtual Life*, James Brook and Iain A. Boal, eds. (San Francisco: City Lights, 1995), 9.

24. Mary Steward van Leeuwen, "The Affirmative Action Glass: Half-Full or Half-Empty?" *Books and Culture* (September/October 1995): 15.

25. *TV Times* (supplement to *Seattle Times*), August 26, 2000.

26. Bob Dole, "Weekly Radio Address," July 13, 1996. *Online, CNN Time, Allpolitics*, at http://allpolitics.com/news/9607/13/gop.radio/transcript/shtml (accessed July 15, 1996).

27. Molefi Kete Asanti, "Imperatives of an Afrocentric Curriculum," in *Contemporary American Speeches*, 7th ed., Richard L. Johannesen, R. R. Allen, and Wil A. Linkugel, eds. (Dubuque, Iowa: Kendall/Hunt, 1992), 265.

28. Preston Shiller and Hank Dittmar, "Nation of Highways Paved with Opportunities and High Costs," *Seattle Post-Intelligencer* (July 23, 1996): A9.

29. Chris G. Whipple, "Can Nuclear Waste Be Stored Safely at Yucca Mountain?" *Scientific American* (June 1996): 76.

30. Adapted from "Down with Dino Birds?" *Scientific American* 283 (September, 2000): 32.

31. "The WTO History, Record, and Agenda," *Ruckus* (student newspaper) (October, 1999): 6.

32. John F. Kennedy, "The Responsibility of the Press," in *"Let the Word Go Forth": The Speeches, Statements, and Writings of John F. Kennedy*, Theodore Sorenson, ed. (New York: Delacorte Press, 1988), 126.

33. The full text of the speech can be found at http://www.archives.gov/press/exhibits/dream-speech.pdf (accessed May 18, 2013).

34. The full text of the speech can be found at http://www.archives.gov/press/exhibits/dream-speech.pdf (accessed May 18, 2013). Martin Luther King Jr., "I Have a Dream," in William A. Lindsay, *Speech Criticism: Methods and Materials* (Dubuque, Iowa: William C. Brown, 1968), 382.

35. For a description of hierarchies accepted in Western society, see Gregg B. Walker and Malcolm O. Sillars, "Where is Argument? Perelman's Theory of Values," in *Perspectives on Argumentation*, Robert Trapp and Janice Schuetz, eds. (Prospect Heights, Ill.: Waveland, 1990), 134–150.

36. John F. Kennedy, "Inaugural Address," in *Contemporary American Speeches*, 7th ed., Richard L. Johannesen, R. R. Allen, and Wil A. Linkugel, eds. (Dubuque, Iowa: Kendall/Hunt, 1992), 350.

37. Real People for Real Change PAC, "What's Wrong with the Entertainment and New Media?" 1996, at www.realchange/org/why.htm (accessed July 15, 1996)

SECTION III

DEVELOPING AND ARGUING EXTENDED CASES

CHAPTER SEVEN

APPROACHING PROPOSITIONS

CHAPTER OUTLINE

ARGUING ABOUT FACTS, VALUES, AND POLICIES
Approaching Fact-Based Propositions
Approaching Value-Based Propositions
Value Hierarchies
Principles for Constructing Value Arguments
Approaching Policy-Based Propositions

RELATING FACTS, VALUES AND POLICIES

ISSUE MAPPING

PRINCIPLES OF CASE CONSTRUCTION
Burdens of Proof and Presumption
Prima Facie Cases
Clear Definitions
Understanding Situations

SUMMARY

EXERCISES

KEY CONCEPTS

Consider the discussion in Box 7.1, "Should Parents be Allowed to Select the Sex of Their Children?" The issues developed in this case have been discussed for years, but recent advances in technology have become the subject of much new and intense debate. Most people who have read about and discussed this subject would probably agree with Katie—that the possibilities are frightening and potentially uncontrollable as the ability to manipulate genetics increases. The benefits of sex selection, as Gerald alludes, are that these technologies offer the opportunity to diminish disease, create choice, and balance families.

BOX 7.1

SHOULD PARENTS BE ALLOWED TO SELECT THE SEX OF THEIR CHILDREN?[1]

Is it a boy or a girl? How many times have soon-to-be parents been asked that question? Historically, answers have been vague, but technological advances have made it possible for parents not only to know the sex of their unborn child but to choose it. The development of new techniques such as sperm-sorting, prenatal testing, pregnancy termination, and the implementation of genetically tested embryos ensure babies will be born the chosen sex. With genetic diagnosis, an embryo is created and analyzed in a test tube before being placed in the womb. Sperm-sorting organizes the sperm in a way that makes it more likely to fertilize the egg with the selected chromosome. Sex selection is technologically possible, but should it be done?

There are many possible advantages. Many families want to choose the sex of their child in an effort to balance families as well as to prevent gender-specific diseases from being passed to offspring.[2] Some parents would prefer to raise a girl or a boy. And, new genetic technologies make it possible to sequence nearly the entire genome of a fetus using the saliva of the father and a blood sample from the mother.[3] This means it may soon be possible to do more than simply select a child's sex—parents may soon be able to obtain an entire DNA blueprint months before a child is born.[4] This means parents could screen for possible birth defects and genetic disorders, as well as improve IQ scores, choose height, eye and hair color, and skin color.

However, these advances have potentially negative consequences. In 1979, China announced its one child per family policy, developed in response to fears about rapid population growth and associated socioeconomic consequences.[5] Although the policy successfully limited population growth, more so in urban than in rural areas, it had the significant and serious consequence of creating a gender imbalance. In many cultures, boys are seen as more valuable than girls, and China is no exception. This bias led to a decrease in the numbers of girls born in China and a significant imbalance in the ratio of males to females in communities across the country.[6]

The statistics are disturbing. In 1981, shortly after the policy was adopted, there were 108 boys born for every 100 girls. By 1990 the ratio was 111:100. In 2010 the ratio had risen to 117:100. And in some rural areas of China, the imbalance is as high as 163:100.[7] And the problem does not exist in China alone. Cultural biases assert themselves when technology allows communities to limit the existence of one gender. Using ultrasound scanning for sexual selection is illegal in many places, but that does not stop its use.

More than thirty countries, including Canada and the United Kingdom, have banned sex selection on the grounds that it reinforces gender inequality; however, the United States still has no policy regulating its use.[8] And, according to a 2007 study, 42 percent of surveyed fertility clinics had used sex selection by implanting embryos of the chosen sex in the mother.[9]

Cultural factors represent just one set of issues in the discussion about sex selection. Social, scientific, and ethical issues are also involved. Socially, could gender selection produce a greater amount of gender inequality? Or would the opposite happen? Will scientific progress make birthing a business focusing on the production of genetically perfect babies? Or will we be able to eliminate significant diseases and birth defects from the gene pool? If given the opportunity,

(continued)

BOX 7.1   CONTINUED

would you choose the sex of your child? Consider the following discussion between Gerald and Katie and note how the arguments work together to develop an extended understanding of the issues.

Gerald: The issue doesn't seem that complicated to me. Why shouldn't families be able to use whatever technology is available to choose and establish the kind of family they want to raise? I think choosing the sex of your child allows people to be better parents because they are raising the sex they want and are more comfortable with. Given the choice, I would want to eliminate the possibility of having a child with a gender-specific disease. It's an issue of choice and freedom that we should be able to practice.

Katie: When you look at sex selection in terms of only America, it seems simple. But I think we have a social responsibility as human beings to protect rights. We need to protect the rights of children and women. Looking at the situation, I think the issues of gender inequality and aborted children would become larger and unmanageable, as it is in China. Women could easily become a minority around the world. Why is that right? Why should we allow it? If we are not careful, we will end up institutionalizing a gender bias that subjugates women.

Gerald: I don't think giving women the ability to choose the sex of their child is producing gender inequality at all. It's giving women more control over their bodies and their families. I also think that many women will choose to have girls, thus balancing the effects of cultural values and preferences.

Katie: Maybe, but just the fact that there is a choice between genders, that one is possibly better than the other, illustrates inequality. Our society already has a hard time balancing gender inequalities as it is; I don't think we need another source to combat.

Gerald: I don't think choosing a sex creates inequality at all. I think it's just an individual preference. Most people would choose a girl because they want to raise a girl, not because they think girls are better than boys. That's beside the point. In any case, don't you think it makes sense to develop technologies that help us reduce disease and birth defects?

Katie: Okay, but I think that sex selection might be balanced only if everyone is educated on population and gender percentages. But would that really affect their decision on what child to have? I can see some benefits if we find a way to regulate how technologies are used, but how do we regulate them? We have no control over other countries and what they choose to do. We don't have the right to push our cultural values and laws onto other cultures. And, how far do you push the technology? Do we start genetically engineering all of our children? This seems like a slippery slope that has the potential to end in disaster.

Gerald: Again, I see the uses of these technological advances as ways to prevent disease, mental illness, addiction problems, and other kinds of medical and social issues we face. If obesity ran in my family, I would want to take advantage of an opportunity to limit that gene from being passed to my children. Think of the decrease in obesity after generations that could occur in America?

(continued)

BOX 7.1   CONTINUED

Based on this discussion, consider the following questions:
1. What types of claims, evidence, and reasons were used in this discussion?
2. Did the speakers adequately respond to the issues and arguments presented by the other?
3. Which speaker was more persuasive? Why?
4. How would you have organized this argument?
5. If you were going to present a ten-minute speech on this topic, which side would you choose? How would you outline the presentation?

The discussion between Katie and Gerald is one type of extended discussion that explores several different issues and offers a variety of argument types. Sometimes conversations such as these unfold in an informal and even haphazard way. In more formal situations, though, advocates often have extended periods to present their arguments. Arguers tend to give extended presentations in courts of law, legislative assemblies, and for most public presentations. They speak to other advocates and recipients and then listen to responses.

This chapter focuses on how advocates should approach propositions. In particular, we will examine how to analyze and interpret propositions, use the relationships among claims, and map issues. We will also introduce principles of case construction exemplified in various arguments contexts. In the following chapters we will extend these concepts to focus on constructing and refuting cases. Appendix D, "Intercollegiate Debate" online at www.pearsonhighered.com, offers some practical guidance for using the ideas developed in this chapter and the next two for people interested in participating in a competitive debate tournament.

ARGUING ABOUT FACTS, VALUES, AND POLICIES

Propositions establish arenas for argument as we discussed in Chapter 4. In that chapter, Figure 4.1, "Propositional Arenas," illustrated how we define propositions creates areas for argument that include many potential issues. It is important to recognize that while propositional arenas contain many issues, not all will be developed in an extended argument. The advocate's task is to analyze the arena for the issues most relevant to the situation and develop an extended argument supporting or opposing the proposition.

To develop an overall position on a proposition, advocates must know how to identify the significant and controversial issues within the field of argument. This is the cycle of critical thought that was introduced in Chapter 1. Further, arguers should know how to find the relevant evidence to support their claims through research. They need to be able to articulate their arguments and support them when opposed. Advocates also will need to know how to select from a large number of potential arguments the ones that will be most effective with your audience.

In completing these steps, advocates begin the process of constructing an extended argumentative case. *A case is a set of interconnected arguments supporting or opposing a proposition.*

As we discussed in Chapter 4, a proposition is the "main claim" or "overarching claim" of an extended argument. Examples would be the following:

Sex selection will create a global gender imbalance.

John Doe is guilty of murder in the first degree.

Euthanasia for terminally ill patients is desirable.

The federal government should pass broadcast decency legislation.

Cases favoring such propositions might take the form of a speech in support of some legislation or a case for the defense or prosecution in a criminal trial; or they might develop as part of a conversation among business associates or friends. A network of claims and sub-claims, each supported by further argument, characterizes extended argument cases. Box 7.1 provides a good illustration of many of the issues and claims that an arguer might use to support a proposition. Which of these arguments is developed and presented depends on the proposition and the context for the argument. If the proposition were "Sex selection will create a global gender imbalance," then the propositional arena would include issues pertinent to this primary claim. These issues could include:

Would China's experience be replicated on a global scale?

Is there a global preference for one sex over another?

Can technology assist with the elimination of diseases and birth defects?

What are the moral and ethical implications for gender selection?

Is choice the most important value?

Some of these issues are more significant than others. As arguers construct extended cases, they decide which issues are most important for a particular situation. They assess which arguments are most appropriate and most persuasive based on the sphere as well as the background, experiences, and values held by the recipients.

Approaching Fact-Based Propositions

We make extended arguments about fact-, value-, and policy-based propositions almost daily and, whereas value and policy cases are probably more common in public sphere argument, cases about propositions of fact are common in private sphere arguments as well as certain other fields such as law or history. These fields focus almost exclusively on fact-based propositions such as:

Chris Smith is guilty of theft.

Anne Jones is guilty of reckless driving.

Jack the Ripper was Queen Victoria's nephew.

Each of these propositions addresses factual issues. Lawyers, judges, juries, and historians tend to be concerned with extended fact cases that can prove the probable truth of the proposition. Similarly, members of the medical field will diagnose or predict diseases using factual propositions. They might argue that:

Smoking cigarettes causes emphysema.

Laser eye surgery will correct your nearsightedness.

Taking this prescription will alleviate your symptoms.

A kidney transplant will save a patient's life.

Other fields may use fact propositions for discussion and deliberation. Policy-makers often engage in fact-finding studies to determine whether certain policies work. Scientists use fact propositions (such as hypotheses) to argue about the nature of the world and universe ("There once was life on Mars."). Fact propositions, as discussed in Chapter 4, can be classified in three ways: historical, relational, and predictive. Fact-based cases can be developed using any of these types of fact propositions.

At one time or another, most of us have developed extended cases based on fact propositions. Arguers use these to help establish what was, is, or will be. Consider, for example, the following propositions that might be part of an academic assignment:

America's military buildup during the 1980s caused the collapse of the Soviet Union.

Cutting financial aid means fewer students can attend college.

Life on Earth began with living cells from Mars.

People are inclined to believe that facts and statistics are true. However, as we observed in Chapter 5, there are many "facts" about which people disagree. Chapter 1, for instance, discussed the question of whether John F. Kennedy was killed by a single assassin. Because this assassination actually happened, there is only one "correct" answer to the question of who killed Kennedy. Yet, for years, various government agencies and other interested parties have debated about whether Lee Harvey Oswald acted alone or with someone else—or whether Oswald was even involved.

It is a fact that China has a one child per family policy. It is also a fact that some families choose to ignore the law and that the ratio of boys to girls is increasing rapidly. But there is disagreement about why the ratio is increasing and whether illegal means are used to reduce the number of girls. Virtually all legal arguments focus on questions of fact. Does the U.S. Constitution allow same-sex couples to marry? Was U.S. health care reform constitutional? Does Britain's National Health Service cost more than it saves? Is an accidental shooting an assault in the first degree or the second degree?

Most extended arguments begin with questions about facts—even if the proposition is about values or policies. For instance, we might argue about the environment and our individual carbon footprints. There is disagreement about whether atmospheric pollution leads to global warming and climate change and, if so, to what extent this is a negative consequence of burning fossil fuels. In medicine, there are numerous debates about questions of fact. For example, to what extent do birth control pills and hormones lead to an increase in the rate of cancer among women? How harmful are elevated levels of cholesterol, and what are the most effective ways of lowering cholesterol levels? These are all potentially questions of fact—questions that might serve as the basis for extended arguments with other types of propositions.

Approaching Value-Based Propositions

In Chapter 3 we defined values as positive or negative attitudes toward certain end states of existence or broad modes of conduct. Examples of values are freedom, equality, self-respect, and family security. When we express our values, we express our own conceptions of the worth of objects or ideas. Values, then, regulate our orientations toward the objects and experiences in our lives. Our values help us understand how to behave. If health is an important value, we may choose to exercise. We would not choose to smoke. If wealth is important, we may choose a career path that provides a substantial income even if it is not particularly satisfying at a personal level.

Value-based propositions are often an important part of discussions about facts and whether to accept or reject policy recommendations. Recall from Chapter 3 that values inform our choice making and help us decide what we ought believe and do. Value propositions are commonly argued in the public sphere and often arise in fields such as philosophy, religion, and even education, business, and politics. For example, in policy-making, it is common for value-based arguments to be at the root of disagreements about what policies should be adopted. When deciding whether we should adopt new environmental standards, for example, the following value propositions might be argued:

Environmental protection is desirable.

Protecting the environment is beneficial to society.

The creation of jobs is more important than the protection of the environment.

To support fact and policy claims, arguers may refer to truths and to facts that are verifiable and recognized by the audience. For example, if someone were to claim, "China's One-Child Policy has led to gender imbalance," that person could use studies examining the birth rates of male and female babies before and after the policy was enacted in China. But if the claim was, "banning sex-selection technologies is desirable," a different strategy would be required. Here, the advocate would have to draw upon value hierarchies and relationships among values recognized in society to provide justification for banning all sex selection procedures.

With some argument fields, facts, values and policies are tied closely together. This tends to be the case with reproductive rights and health. Consider, for example, Box 7.2, "Abortion and Crime." While there are many viewpoints and counterarguments that can be made about this example, their analysis caused a great deal of controversy and it provides an illustration of how facts and values inform one another and can intermingle.

These examples illustrate why the research findings of Rokeach and others who have studied American values, which we explored in Chapter 3, are so important to value argument. When people disagree about values, a choice must be made, and one criterion for deciding among competing values is their relative status in the larger society.[10]

Value Hierarchies

Chaim Perelman and Lucie Olbrechts-Tyteca, discussed in Chapter 6, identified particular hierarchies that seem to be widely accepted across Western cultures and therefore are used as a foundation for many value arguments.[11] For example, a person could value family as well as recreation, but family would come first on the value hierarchy, meaning he or she would likely skip a day at an amusement park to be with family for an important event. When we make arguments, we can use these hierarchies to highlight the values our recipients would find most appealing. Which of the hierarchies is appropriate would depend on the situation and recipient. Perelman and Olbrechts-Tyteca identified

▪ ▪ ▪ ▪ ▪

BOX 7.2
ABORTION AND CRIME

Steven D. Levitt and Stephen J. Dubner's book *Freakanomics: A Rogue Economist Explores the Hidden Side of Everything* became the center of controversy and debate over its assessment of the significant decline of crime rates in the United States during the 1990s.[12] The book itself is an attempt to apply economic principles to contemporary problems as a way of understanding everyday issues through different lenses. With chapters titled "What do schoolteachers and sumo wrestlers have in common?" "How is the Ku Klux Klan like a group of real-estate agents?" and "Why do drug dealers still live with their Moms?" the book touched off many debates and rebuttals.

The most discussed chapter, however, was "Where have all the criminals gone?" During the 1990s the United States experienced a significant drop in crime. Levitt and Dubner explored many possible explanations: strong economy resulting in more jobs, more police on the street, stronger laws and more severe punishments, better use of technology and surveillance, among others. They analyzed each explanation to determine what role, if any, it played in crime reduction. Each was dismissed except one—*Roe v. Wade*, which was upheld by the U.S. Supreme Court in 1973 and made abortion legal. They noted that the significant number of abortions in the first year, one in four live births, increased to one in 2.25 live births by 1980, and that a significant population of children who would have been born were not. And, because affluent women had more medical options including abortion prior to *Roe v. Wade*, the population most affected was unmarried, teen mothers, who lived in poverty.

Their conclusion was that "the very factors that drove millions of American women to have an abortion also seemed to predict that their children, had they been born, would have led unhappy and possibly criminal lives."[13] The reason that crime decreased so dramatically, they argued, was simply that these children were never born.

Their conclusions angered many people. Some took it as a justification and defense of abortion. Others argued it unfairly stereotyped poor people and minorities.[14] Some theorists countered that the analysis was too simplistic and did not take enough variables into consideration. Steve Sailer, for instance, made the point that "This fiasco reveals much about what's wrong with public policy discourse in modern America. Fifteen minutes of Googling would have shown book reviewers of *Freakanomics* that the abortion-cut-crime theory hadn't come close to meeting the burden of proof...."[15]

Freakanomic's authors had advanced a factual claim that attempted to explain crime rates. Theorists who commented on how the methodology was flawed and how the authors failed to provide sufficient evidence to prove their claim debated a factual proposition. However, others drew from the factual claim that an implicit value proposition was being argued—namely that security (crime rates) was more important than life (abortion). While the book focuses on factual claims, many readers drew from it support for one value hierarchy over another including debates about the intrinsic worth of individuals, autonomy, life, and security.

Every type of claim is closely tied to and connected with the other types. Values are linked to facts, as are policies. Policies depend on values and facts. They are merged in many ways and should be treated as having common threads that underscore arguments.

Quantity	Quality	Existent	Essence	Person
Most	Unique and Original	Concrete	Central to Identity	Dignity and Autonomy
↑	↑	↑	↑	↑
Least	Common and Regular	Possible	On the Fringe	Subjugation and Humiliation

FIGURE 7.1   Value Hierarchies

the following five value hierarchies that can be used to develop extended value arguments: quantity, quality, existent, essence, and person. These hierarchies are shown in Figure 7.1, Value Hierarchies.

The first value hierarchy is that of quantity—whatever produces the greatest good for the largest number of people at the least cost is to be preferred. The *hierarchy of quantity values more over less and evaluates alternatives based on effects and outcomes, and comes from utilitarianism* ("We should subsidize health-care cooperatives to provide affordable health care for all citizens of the country."). Second is the *hierarchy of quality, which values what is unique, irreplaceable, or original.* Human life is often viewed from this perspective, as are great works of art ("The Sistine Chapel is worth restoring, even at great cost, for the works of Michelangelo cannot be replaced.") Third is the *hierarchy of the existent*, which *values the concrete over the possible* ("You should accept that job offer you have now rather than waiting for another one that might not materialize.") Fourth is the *hierarchy of essence*, which *values what is at the core of a group or class rather than what is on the fringes.* ("Free enterprise is central to what this country is all about, and we should do whatever we can to preserve free enterprise.") The fifth *hierarchy* is that of *the person* and *values the dignity and autonomy of the person over all competing values.*[16] ("Euthanasia allows a person death with dignity, and a dignified death is more important than life for a terminally ill person.") The hierarchies of quantity (more over less), quality (the unique over the common), the existent (the concrete over the merely possible), essence (the central over the peripheral), and the person (individual dignity and autonomy over all else) are commonly accepted throughout society and can be used as a basis for value claims.

Perelman and Olbrechts-Tyteca remind us when speakers want "to establish values or hierarchies or to intensify the adherence they gain," they may "consolidate them by connecting them to other values or hierarchies."[17] In the preceding examples, such things as affordable health care, the restoration of the Sistine Chapel, free enterprise, and euthanasia were said to be preferable because of their association with the values higher in these five pervasive hierarchies. Each of these five hierarchies is common and used frequently in arguments. Box 7.3, "Apply the Theory," will help guide you through a process of working with values.

■ ■ ■ ■ ■

BOX 7.3

APPLY THE THEORY: USING VALUE HIERARCHIES

The case studies in Boxes 7.1 and 7.2 imply values related to sex-selection and abortion. Using the five value hierarchies shown in Figure 7.1, consider the following:

1. Which value hierarchies are being used?
2. Which seem to be the strongest values?
3. What arguments can you make to either strengthen or refute the value claims being made?
4. How could you use value redistribution, value emphasis, and value restandardization with any of these arguments?

Principles for Constructing Value Arguments

The works of Rokeach and Perleman and Olbrecths-Tyteca suggest principles that can be quite useful in approaching arguments about values:

1. Generally, terminal values should be viewed as more significant and important than instrumental values. Terminal values focus on goals and where we want to be. Instrumental values help identify how to achieve terminal values—but the end states tend to be more important.
2. When choosing between competing instrumental values (i.e., choosing the most effective means to an end), arguers should select the value that best meets the particular needs of the argument situation and field.
3. In choosing one value over others, arguers should consider the hierarchies of quantity, quality, the existent, essence, and the person if they are applicable to a particular choice or course of action.
4. Value systems tend to be relatively stable over time as discussed in Chapter 3. These hierarchies can provide useful starting points for understanding how recipients might organize priorities.
5. While stable, values are not entirely fixed. Because values tend to change slowly, arguers should consider the possibilities of value redistribution, value emphasis, and value restandardization as described in Chapter 3.

When a choice must be made between competing values, or when an arguer seeks to defend a particular value hierarchy, these five principles can provide the means for justifying a shift or change in values or for opposing value orderings proposed by other advocates.

Consider the proposition "Environmental protection is more important than the creation of jobs." When approaching this proposition, advocates would need to prove that protecting the environment supports a terminal value such as harmony of the natural world. The instrumental value, which helps to achieve that end, is environmental protection. The advocate might justify the value hierarchy of environment over jobs by first proving a more immediate need for environmental protection. This could be achieved by arguing that job creation will always fluctuate with the economy, but if we lose an endangered species or destroy an ecosystem, it cannot be recovered.

Using the value hierarchies of quality and quantity, the advocate could argue that there will be more positive effects on a larger number of people if we prioritize the environment. The opponent could link the instrumental value of job creation to a terminal value such as family security or stability of society. Though job creation does go up and down, the opponent might try to prove that when the economy is not strong the immediate job creation would stimulate the economy and help all people in society. The arguer could use the value of essence by arguing that free enterprise is the core of our democracy, and environmental protection at the expense of the free market should be avoided. Additionally, the opponent could argue that the value of the person outweighs—that this value is best met by ensuring everyone in society has a job, which promotes individual dignity and autonomy.

Approaching Policy-Based Propositions

The decision to act or not to act involves a process of policy argumentation. For example, consider the following three claims:

The United States should ban the use of sex selection technologies.

The United States should permit the sale of organs.

I should study tonight.

These statements are policy propositions that focus arguments around specific choices and actions. Each asks recipients to behave or cooperate in certain ways and, presumably, if the arguments supporting the claims are sufficient, then recipients will support or pursue particular courses of action.

Policy arguments differ from fact and value arguments in a significant way. Policy arguments are future-bound. If we argue that the United States should ban the use of sex selection technologies or that we should allow organ sales, we promote a future action. Because historical policies and actions cannot be changed through argument, when we make policy proposals we focus on what should be done from this time forward. The future-action nature of policy arguments is fundamentally different from value arguments because fact and value arguments can examine and evaluate whether current and past conditions were true, justified, or reasonable. In value-oriented discussions, we can say:

Banning the use of sex selection technologies is justified.

Allowing the sale of organs is beneficial.

Studying is a good idea.

In fact-orientated discussions we could argue:

The use of sex selection technologies will lead to gender imbalance.

The number of organ transplants will double in the next ten years.

When I have studied in the past, I have received good grades.

As discussed above, fact and value propositions can study what currently is, what should have been in the past, or even what facts and values we would hold as true or reasonable in the future because the focus of such argumentation is definition or evaluation—not action. We can evaluate the past and present to learn, but we cannot act differently in the past. Policy propositions are bound to future actions. For example, China's One-Child policy was implemented to control overpopulation (fact), and we can look to the past to learn that many decided male children were more desirable than female children (value) and that decision led to a gender imbalance in China (fact). With a policy proposition, we will examine what future actions might look like, and what effects these policies might result in.

Another consideration when approaching policy propositions is the idea that extended policy arguments function systematically, which means that as we seek to change one part of a system through our arguments, we change the overall nature of the system. Such changes carry with them both benefits and costs that arguers should understand and consider. It is not always clear how policy arguments affect our lives. We make decisions about how our lives will be conducted, but we may not always be aware of the short- and long-term consequences and benefits of the actions we take. *A systems perspective recognizes that the world is a complex and interconnected set of relationships between and among component parts that compose a whole, and that one change in any part of the system changes the other elements of the system.* This means, then, that a system is a set of parts that are interrelated and form a whole unit.[18] As illustrated in Figure 7.2, "Systemic Response," when systems are pressured to change, the rest of their components react to the pressure and rebalance themselves. This process is known as finding equilibrium or by the Greek term *homeostasis (homeo = same, stasis = point) meaning to find an internal stability or balance.*

Therefore, changes in policies and practices can have widespread effects throughout a system. This is because most systems have many parts, each of which has a particular role and function. Since all the parts of a system are interconnected and affect one another, some consideration must be given to the extent to which a change in one part of the system will affect the others. Furthermore, most systems operate within a larger environment, and that environment can affect or be affected by changes in the system.

Consider the emergence of Massive Open Online Courses, known as MOOCs. Offered by many universities, including elite institutions such as Stanford, Harvard, and MIT, these courses are open to anyone with an Internet connection.[19] Most are free, some offer the option to earn course credit for a fee. Many are taught by top professors, such as Sebastian Thrun, who was a professor at Stanford and a fellow at Google when he offered a MOOC

Resulting in other elements responding to find stability

Part of a system is pressured to change

FIGURE 7.2 Systemic Response

on artificial intelligence. That course had 160,000 students from 190 countries enrolled.[20] After several positive experiences with the courses, Thrun left Stanford to pursue his own education company that will offer MOOCs.[21] These online courses have many interrelated parts, such as faculty who teach them, course designs, teaching resources, available technology, and students. When students in a course have different levels of preparation for higher education, the teacher will likely have to alter the content of the course.

Simplifying course design and lowering admission requirements might increase student access, but it also might decrease the amount students learn. MOOCs might offer a flexible learning environment and open up access to the world's most elite professors and institutions, but they still exclude people who are not technologically literate or lack access to technology. And, the larger environment might be affected if state legislatures cut back on funding for colleges and universities because policy makers view distance learning as a better means of providing continuing education.

What affects one part of the system can be felt throughout the system. Any policy decision carries benefits and costs for the entire system. People act in contexts, and the actions we take affect our contexts. When we take actions in a system, we experience both benefits and costs. The benefits are all the advantages associated with the decision, and the costs are all the associated disadvantages. Online learning, for instance, may provide access to education for millions of students who could not otherwise earn a degree. It helps break down barriers for nontraditional students in terms of both cost and ability to attend classes. There are also costs associated with online learning. Those same students do not receive the benefits of working with other students or one on one with their professors. Their education may not be as rich as it might have been if they were on campus. The quality of the relationships among faculty and students may not be as good, and resources devoted toward distance learning may take away from other educational programs for on-campus students.

When we evaluate whether we should engage in a particular action, we evaluate the likelihood of the benefits as well as the likelihood of the costs throughout the system. Presumably, most people act when the net benefits are perceived to be greater than the net costs or disadvantages associated with an action.

RELATING FACTS, VALUES AND POLICIES

As we discussed in Chapter 4, fact, value, and policy propositions are not separate and discrete entities. Rather, their characteristics blend with one another along a continuum of claims that ranges from facts to policies. Figure 7.3, "Continuum of Claims," illustrates this concept. Claims are related, and each implies the others. For instance, policy claims are based on underlying values and the existence of certain facts. If, for instance, sex-selection technology will cause global gender imbalance (predictive fact claim), then it makes sense to decide whether family, community, or national choice is more important than creating gender numerical inequity (value claim). If we find that sex selection might lead to an unwanted and unjustifiable gender inequity, then we may advocate banning the technologies and procedures that allow it (policy claim). The policy claim would not have been made or supported unless there were facts and values to back it up.

| Fact-based propositions | Value-based propositions | Policy-based propositions |

FIGURE 7.3
Continuum of Claims

We make decisions about what course of action to take based on our assessment of potential benefits and costs. This means that policy decisions depend on our being able to make a factual assessment that some outcomes are likely and that those outcomes have value. A policy advocate, then, might engage in the following process to evaluate the benefits and disadvantages of a policy action, as illustrated in Box 7.4, "Costs and Benefits of Banning Sex Selection Technologies." In this case the potential benefits are evaluated against the potential costs, and the comparison is directly related to our value system and our assessment of the facts. What is likely to happen? What is important? In this case, the factual assessment of the risks associated with genetic engineering and the value assessment of choice are the primary issues.

BOX 7.4

COSTS AND BENEFITS OF BANNING SEX SELECTION TECHNOLOGIES

BENEFITS	COSTS
We avoid a "social time bomb."	Family and community choice will be limited.
Natural determination of sex ratios ensures survival of humankind.	Some families and communities will develop less safe, illegal technologies.
The sexes will be more equal.	Underlying bias is ignored when the only action is to ban technology.
Banning the technology prevents a "slippery slope" of genetic engineering.	We lose opportunities to eradicate some birth defects and genetic diseases.

Every policy decision makes assumptions about values and facts. Deciding whether or not to pursue a policy direction depends on careful analysis of the potential costs and benefits. Cost–benefit analysis asks, "What are the potential outcomes?" And "How important or dangerous are they?" This assessment uses predictive factual claims to determine likelihood, and value claims to determine importance.

Just as policies are grounded in facts and values, facts and values also imply policies. For example, if a patient is terminally ill, in tremendous pain, and with no hope of recovery (fact arguments), then we might decide that this person should have the right to decide if the continued struggle to live was more important than making the choice to die (value argument). If everyone could agree that certain forms of euthanasia were justified and desirable in certain circumstances, then lawmakers would enact legislation making those forms of euthanasia legal (policy argument). The reason that there is so much variation in abortion laws in different states is that there is no fact consensus about when life begins and no value consensus between pro-choice and pro-life factions in various parts of the country.

Although facts, values, and polices are tied to one another, the types of claims and evidence used in policy and fact arguments are different from those in value arguments. In selecting policies, people make decisions about what action to take based on their assessment of the risks involved and the potential benefits. In most cases, they are likely to choose policies that are more beneficial than the alternatives. If people perceive that protecting sex equity has a greater benefit than protecting choice, then sex selection technologies will continue to develop.

ISSUE MAPPING

Argument theorists have often pointed out that familiarity with multiple views on an issue improves one's own arguments as well as one's ability to anticipate and respond to others' views. Josina Makau has observed, "The quality of deliberation on controversial issues depends, in large measure, on the arguers' ability to thoughtfully consider as many alternative perspectives as possible."[22] Many people who first approach a topic think they have their minds made up. As they conduct research on the topic and read the opinions of various authorities, they begin to see that the situation or the solution is not as readily apparent as they first thought. It is possible that in the process of researching for a speech or debate, students will actually shift their opinions to the side opposite to the one they had favored in the beginning!

Research on critical thinking reveals that critical flexibility in our thinking is a good thing. Researchers have found that inexperienced or undisciplined thinkers seek quick closure on a topic, neglect audience attitudes and possible objections, and fail to take into account obvious weaknesses in their own arguments. Experienced thinkers, in contrast, withhold their opinions until they have gathered relevant information, begin by analyzing and interpreting the problem, study the attitudes of their potential audience, and develop a broad range of lines and types of arguments to support a claim.[23]

To assist you in becoming an expert thinker of the latter type, we recommend that you construct an issues map when analyzing a proposition. *An issues map is a synthesis of the context, situation, participants, and issues associated with a proposition.* Issues maps are intended to help advocates explore as completely as possible the issues that define a propositional arena. An issue map is valuable because it allows advocates to consider more than one viewpoint in a context. It helps identify points of agreement, points of difference, and the context and situation for the argument. Box 7.5, "Issues Map," is

■ ■ ■ ■ ■
BOX 7.5
ISSUES MAP

ANALYZING THE PROPOSITION

Proposition
Review the discussion of propositions in Chapter 4. What is the proposition for the current discussion? *Example: Sex selection technologies should be banned.*

Definition
Considering the discussion of propositional arenas in Chapter 4, what does this proposition mean? Define any terms that might be ambiguous. *Example: "Sex selection technologies" refers to methods used to ensure the gender of a fetus. This would include pre-implantation technologies such as sperm-sorting and embryo genetic diagnosis and post-implantation methods such as selective abortion.*

DESCRIBING THE ARGUMENT CONTEXT

Situation
Review the discussion of argument situations developed in Chapter 2. Provide a summary of the propositional arena. What happened? When? *Example: Currently in the United States, the use of sex selection technologies is legal, though in 30 other countries including Canada and the United Kingdom these procedures are illegal. There has been an increase in reports of use of sex selective abortion in the United States, and in May of 2012, the U.S. Congress voted to reject a ban on these procedures. These procedures are used to avoid passing on sex-linked genetic disorders, for family balancing, and for preference of one sex over the other.*

Context
Consider the characteristics of spheres and fields in Chapter 1. What spheres are involved? Has this proposition been grounded mostly in personal, technical, or public arenas? What fields are involved? Are there any field-dependent standards that should apply? *Example: The debate about the use of sex selection technologies straddles all spheres. In the technical sphere, the fields of medicine and science are grappling with how to proceed with research and technology that can eliminate disease but also lead to gender imbalance. The debate in that sphere is about whether or not use of such technologies is ethical, particularly sex selective abortions. Some argue that it is not the role of the physician to ask why a woman is seeking an abortion, whereas others report instances of women being pressured into seeking such procedures due to pressure from families or cultural attitudes about the value of male and female babies. There is additional discussion in the technical sphere about the use of technologies to select other features, such as eye or hair color, and whether this could eventually lead to selecting of other physical and mental characteristics.*

Parties
The parties of an argument are the participants involved. Argument participants are developed in Chapter 2. Who is involved? Can you identify the primary parties who are affected by these issues? Can you identify secondary parties? Are any other groups or entities affected by this proposition? *Example: The debate over this proposition will be in front of a class of college students enrolled in an argumentation course. Some will also be doing in-depth research on this topic, but many may not have had opportunity to hear extended arguments on this issue. The students will have to consider how such a policy would affect them and the nation as a whole.*

(continued)

BOX 7.5   CONTINUED

ASSESSING THE ISSUES INVOLVED

Fact Issues
Based on the discussion in Chapter 4 regarding factual claims, identify the issues focusing on causal relationships, predictions of future events, and historical interpretation. *Example: Can sex selection technologies be used to prevent genetic disease? Will the use of these technologies result in gender imbalance in the United States?*

Value Issues
Based on the discussions in Chapters 4 and 8 regarding value claims, what are the issues that ask for evaluation or judgment? What are the comparisons of worth or importance within the propositional arena? *Example: Is the availability of such technologies desirable? Is freedom of choice more important than gender equality?*

Policy Issues
Using the material from Chapters 4 and 8 about policy propositions, what actions or behaviors have been suggested to resolve the disagreement? What has been tried before? What worked, what didn't, and why? *Example: Should the government ban the use of sex selection technologies? What have been the costs and benefits of banning these technologies in other countries?*

DETERMINING ARGUMENT POTENTIAL

Goal
What would a successful outcome for this proposition be? What are the goals of the involved parties? Can the goals of the involved parties be met? *Example: The goal of the debates is to inform the audience about the costs and benefits related to the use of sex selection technologies. At the conclusion of the debate, recipients should be able to express an informed opinion about whether or not the proposition is true.*

Parties
Can the identified parties achieve the goals? What other parties might need to be involved? *Example: The debaters should be able to provide sufficient information to assist the audience in forming an opinion about the issue. The debaters will need to provide the audience with evidence from credible sources of evidence about the costs and benefits.*

Resources
What resources are needed for the goal to be met? Are those resources available? What additional resources are needed? *Example: The audience will need to be informed about the history and context related to this issue. Arguers will need to fully inform the audience of the costs and benefits related to the proposition.*

Alternatives
Are there other ways of looking at the issues to find alternative approaches and solutions for the issues in the propositional arena? *Example: The debate will feature an advocate presenting arguments for the proposition and an opponent presenting arguments against the proposition. This will allow the audience to hear arguments from various perspectives so that they might reach a decision about the truth of the proposition after carefully considering the two presentations.*

a template using the example of banning sex selection technologies.[24] As you will probably notice, the template draws on the theoretical framework for understanding arguments developed in Chapters 1, 2, and 3. A student preparing for a debate about the use of sex selection technologies, to take place in front of her argumentation class, created this particular map.

The first part of an issues map is the proposition that serves as the focus for discussion. An issues map should ensure that the proposition is clearly understood and that the issues that fall within the propositional arena are discussed. This is where any terms that might be ambiguous or unfamiliar to the audience should be defined. The second part of the map provides a detailed description of the propositional arena. In this section, an arguer identifies the situation, contexts, and parties involved in the arena. This area of the map would describe the situation which invited argument, such as a debate for a class assignment. Audience considerations would be explored here, such as what the audience will expect and what will be appropriate in constructing arguments about the issue. The intention is to describe the scope of the argument and consider how the audience will shape which arguments should be presented, and how they should be presented. In the third section of the map, an arguer describes the issues involved in the proposition. Here the claims, evidence, and reasons developed by the advocate as described in Chapters 4, 5, and 6 are useful. This section of the map divides the research into three categories: issues related to the facts of the proposition, issues related to values, and issues related to policy implications. The goal is to find out what issues are important and what has been considered in the research. Finally, the map examines the argument potential. *Argument potential refers to the opportunity to influence the propositional arena through argument.* It involves questions such as the following: What would be an acceptable outcome for the argument? Are there opportunities for multiple parties to succeed? Are the people involved in the argument empowered to affect a positive change that can meet goals? What resources would be needed? What alternatives have been explored? Again, the consideration here is the particular situation and context in which the arguments are being developed. For example, in a public sphere debate in front of voters about a proposed new policy, the parties involved would be the general public, the advocates for change, and the opponents of change. The goal of the advocate and opponent would be to inform the audience of voters so that they have the resources (in this case, information) to make an educated choice about how to vote.

A well-written and developed issues map provides advocates with a way of understanding and interpreting a propositional arena. There are a couple of important points to keep in mind about using issues maps. First, maps do not take a position on a proposition. They are intended only to explore the issues within the propositional arena. Maps describe, they define, and they help focus arguments. In fact, if an issues map is prepared well, all the parties to an argument should be able to read it and agree with what it says. They may dispute some of the arguments developed in the issues, but they should agree that those are arguments made about the particular subject—not that they are correct, just that they are made. Second, issues maps serve as source material for extended case construction. An issues map may be used to develop a fact, value, or policy case and should also include the opposing arguments and issues. Therefore, when we use a map, we are using it to help shape both our advocacy and counteradvocacy. Box 7.6, "Apply the Theory," focuses on using the template to analyze and assess a proposition.

■ ■ ■ ■ ■

BOX 7.6
APPLY THE THEORY: USING THE TEMPLATE

Using Box 7.5 as a guide, how would you assess the argument potential for the following proposition: "The United States should substantially and immediately cut its carbon emissions." Your assessment should include:

- Analysis of the proposition
    - Is it clear?
    - Do terms need to be defined?

- Description of the argument context
    - What is the situation that gave rise to this argument?
    - What contexts shape this argument (spheres, fields)?
    - What parties are involved?

- Identification of the issues in the propositional arena
    - What are the factual issues?
    - What are the value issues?
    - What are the policy issues?

- Determination of the argument potential
    - What are your goals as an advocate?
    - What goals function for the parties in the dispute?
    - What resources are needed for the goals to be met?
    - Are there acceptable alternatives?

Completing these questions for this and other propositions should provide you with a clear understanding of the dispute and what possible approaches you may have for addressing the issues.

PRINCIPLES OF CASE CONSTRUCTION

The process of decision making occurs in many venues and with many varied participants. Decisions are made in courtrooms, legislatures, boardrooms, and voting booths and among family and friends. They are made as part of a process of ongoing discussion about issues and topics and through the use of argument. Ideally, decisions are reached because the participants are informed about the issues being discussed and are able to advocate ideas and positions about those topics. Argumentation and decision making are the processes we use in our society to reach reasonable consensus about the issues we face. To some extent, the problems and issues that we consider significant change over time. In some years, we may be concerned about the economy, unemployment, inflation, and interest rates, whereas in other years we are more worried about war and world peace. Different issues and concerns emerge each year as the contexts for argument change and evolve.

Issues such as abortion, capital punishment, environmental protection, and crime control are continuing sources of disagreement and debate. If we wish to become seriously involved in discussions of topics such as these, we need to understand how to research and construct an issues map to that helps us survey and become familiar with the issues in the propositional arena. Once we have completed an issues map, the next step is to draw on it to develop an extended argument case. Whether the case is oriented toward facts, values, or policies, there are certain recognized principles exemplified in legal briefs, legislative proposals, speeches, and academic debates that we should use. Before we discuss the specific methods of case construction in the next chapter, therefore, we need to discuss the general principles of case construction.

Burdens of Proof and Presumption

The person advocating change and challenging the existing framework for thinking and acting has the burden of proof and must overcome the presumption in favor of what currently exists or is accepted. As we described in Chapter 4, the burden of proof is the obligation of the arguer advocating change to overcome presumption through argument. If the issues map has been developed well, in most cases it should be clear what changes are being advocated.

Presumption "preoccupies the ground" of the controversy and is assumed to be reasonable until it is successfully challenged by some new belief, value, or action. Recall from Chapter 4 that presumption is the belief that current thinking, attitudes, values, and actions should continue in the absence of good arguments for their change. When approaching extended cases, presumption can be understood using the aphorism "if it ain't broke, don't fix it" (because you may end up making it worse than when you began). Therefore, the function of the burden of proof for the advocate is to prove that the risks inherent in change can be overcome by the benefits of change.

Copernicus, for example, once made the argument that the Earth revolved around the sun. Because his claim was not accepted by the church or majority of scholars at the time, he had the burden to prove his argument. The existing framework of beliefs (that the sun revolved around the Earth) had presumption. Once the church, other scholars, and the rest of the world came to accept (over a period of time) that his argument was correct, then a new reality—that the Earth revolves around the sun—was presumed to be correct, and any new subsequent interpretation of the facts would have the burden of proof.

It is important to note that people are predisposed to favor what they currently believe and what exists.[25] In other words, people are by nature conservative when it comes to making decisions based on argument; they will be persuaded to support a change only if they come to believe it is a good idea. The convention of presumption in argument thus does not imply that the present system of value *should* be favored; it only implies that arguers should recognize the necessity of overcoming this conservative predisposition if they expect to make an effective argument. In the field of law, for instance, the concepts of burden of proof and presumption form the foundation for much legal argument. An accused is presumed innocent unless proven guilty. In the absence of substantial argument that proves beyond a reasonable doubt that a defendant is guilty, to ensure a fair trial we will presume that the person is innocent.

There are times when it is unclear which side of an issue has presumption and which side has the burden of proof, because facts, values, and polices may be inconsistent or not fully determined. For instance, with capital punishment different researchers dispute whether it deters crime. Some argue that people do not commit capital offenses because they fear the death penalty. Others contend that people who commit such crimes are not driven by concern for possible penalties but by their passions or disregard for the law. Studies conflict about whether capital punishment effectively deters crime. Furthermore, public attitudes on capital punishment do not lie clearly on one side or the other of the issue. Many other countries do not have capital punishment and find it inhumane yet others embrace it as a way to eliminate criminals. In the case of a topic such as this, the location of the presumption may be less important, and the convention of argument is that whoever asserts a position has the burden of proof for that argument.[26]

Prima Facie Cases

Whenever an arguer develops an extended case, it is important that the central issues of the propositional arena be addressed. The issue map should provide a good guide toward the discovery of these issues. For example, if the main proposition of a fact-based dispute was that "Watching violence on television causes violence in children," certain issues are likely to come to mind (e.g., What is violence? Are children who watch violence predisposed toward being violent in the first place? Can we demonstrate that increases in violence on television are associated with increases in violence in children?). These issues must be addressed because audiences would expect to hear about them whenever media violence is discussed.

Assume that this topic was a value proposition: "Restricting violence in children's television is desirable." A somewhat different set of issues is suggested. Are these "restrictions" to be total or partial? What standards or criteria should be used to determine whether restrictions are desirable? What values would be fulfilled or furthered by restricting children's programming? How do current social values relate to a restriction on violence in television?

If the topic were a policy proposition, the kinds of issues argued would change again because the audience would expect different types of arguments to prove the proposition. Consider this proposition: "The federal government should ban all violence on television." Not only does this proposition assume prior discussion of relevant facts and values, it suggests an action to address the concerns developed in our assessment of facts and values. In this case, audience members would probably ask, what are the problems associated with violence on television? Are there less restrictive means available to manage the problems? Will this solution actually cure the problem? Do the benefits of this solution outweigh the costs (e.g., potential loss for First Amendment rights and freedoms)?

An advocate who initiates discussion of a topic by proposing a change must present what is called a *prima facie* case. *A* prima facie *case "on its face" presents good and sufficient arguments for adopting the viewpoint or action proposed by an advocate.* Cases are considered *prima facie* when their supporters satisfactorily address all of the major issues a reasonable audience would expect to see addressed. The issues that need to be addressed depend on the proposition and on what the audience knows about it. *Stock issues depend on the type of proposition and are the issues that recipients expect to see addressed in order for the arguer to meet the burden of proof.* By addressing the stock issues, an advocate would be addressing the questions a reasonable audience might want answered before making a decision about the topic at hand. You can think of the stock issues as a framework for constructing your case for a particular issue. For example, on the question of whether research funding should be increased for the investigation of breast cancer, an advocate would probably not need to prove that there is a problem. If the arguer could prove that increased funding of a particular research application would dramatically reduce the incidence of breast cancer, his or her case would be *prima facie*. Therefore, in the absence of opposition or significant questions regarding a proposal, it should be adopted.

Generally, each type of proposition implies its own stock issues. Fact, value, and policy propositions, then, each tend to have a set of issues relevant for that type of proposition. Figure 7.4, "Stock Issues," provides an illustration. To prove a proposition, an advocate should select, minimally, the stock issues appropriate for that proposition. If it is a factual proposition, for instance, those issues are definition, threshold, and application. If, for example, a speaker advocated the policy of raising the gasoline tax to two dollars per gallon, an audience might want to know why—"What is the problem or ill you are trying to remedy?" That is a reasonable question and is one of the policy stock issues. If another arguer wanted to demonstrate that there are times when plagiarizing a research paper is justified, a professor might reasonably be expected to ask, "By using what criteria is that ever appropriate?" This is also a reasonable question for a value proposition, and it questions the standards used to assess the value. The stock issues for each type of proposition are the focus of the next chapter. Box 7.7, "Stock Issues by Proposition," describes the stock issues related to each type of proposition.

Clear Definitions

One of the first issues over which advocates are likely to argue is that of definition of the terms in the proposition. Propositions are designed to establish a propositional arena that includes some issues while excluding others. Clarity, you may recall, is an essential requirement for a well-written proposition because if the language is not clear, then applicable issues are difficult to discern. This is why the issues map is so important in defining the scope of the propositional arena. Advocates need to be able to clearly define the important and potentially controversial terms both in the proposition and related to it. By defining the propositional terms, arguers establish their own views of the basic concepts on which the discussion will develop.

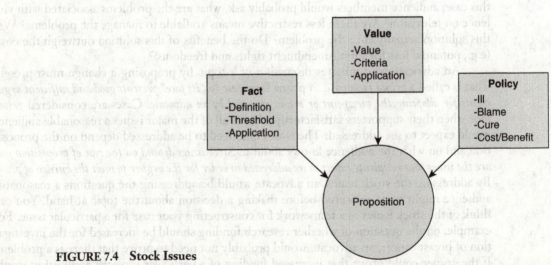

FIGURE 7.4   Stock Issues

▪ ▪ ▪ ▪ ▪

BOX 7.7

STOCK ISSUES BY PROPOSITION

PROPOSITION	STOCK ISSUE	DEFINITION
Fact	Fact Definition	Fact definition consists of arguments that prove historical fact, causal relationships, and predictive facts. *Example: Sex selection will result in gender imbalance.*
	Threshold	The issue of threshold establishes the acceptable limits of definitions. *Example: Gender imbalance exists once the ratio of men to women exceeds 110:100.*
	Application	Application is the argument that the case examined is sufficient proof to verify the definition and its threshold. *Example: Sex selection in China resulted in more than a 118:100 ratio and that would be expected for the rest of the world if we allow these technologies.*
Value	Value	The stock issue of value is subdivided into two sets of issues: value object and value hierarchy. The value object is the central value, or term of the proposition, that will be debated. *Example: Sex imbalance creates inequality.*
		A value hierarchy is the ranking of values favored by each advocate or party in the debate. *Example: Equality is more important than family or community choice.*
	Criteria	Criteria are field- or sphere-dependent standards to be used to decide whether the value object fulfills certain values. *Example: Any practice that causes inequality between sexes should not be supported, researched, or allowed.*
	Application	The stock issue of application uses arguments, applied to the criteria, which demonstrate how the value object is supported or undermined. *Example: Research demonstrates that there is a cultural bias toward male children, meaning that the birth ratio, if people have a choice, will exceed 118:100.*
Policy	Ill	An ill is a current wrong or harm the advocate is trying to resolve. *Example: Sex selection will likely create a "social time bomb."*
	Blame	Blame is the attribution of an ill to causes within the present policy system. *Example: Because there are no current restrictions and people want a choice, they are beginning to use these new technologies.*

(continued)

BOX 7.7   CONTINUED

PROPOSITION	STOCK ISSUE	DEFINITION
	Cure	Cure demonstrates that some course of action can work to solve the ill. *Example*: *Banning sex selection technology will prevent its use.*
	Cost-Benefits	The cost refers to the problems or disadvantages associated with taking a policy action. Benefits are the positive consequences of policy action. *Example*: *Although some will continue to use the technologies illegally, this plan will stop most of the problem.*

Some objects, practices, policies, and other phenomena may be readily understood, whereas others are more complex. If we were considering the topic of euthanasia, for example, arguers supporting the claim that the practice is desirable might provide a definition that includes only passive euthanasia—the withholding or removal of life-sustaining treatment from patients who are dying and have no hope of recovery.[27] Other advocates might disagree and challenge that the definition is insufficiently inclusive. Euthanasia is often said to include measures that bring about death ("mercy killing"). Before the discussion can move forward effectively, both advocates supporting euthanasia and opposing the practice must agree on the meaning of the central terms of the proposition for the outcomes to effectively address the central issues.

There are many methods that can be used to define terms. For example, one may provide actual examples of the value object with which the audience is familiar. (The removal of a feeding tube from the comatose Terry Shaivo is such an example.) The history of the status of the value object in society is another source for definitions. (One could cite a number of court cases and other situations in which euthanasia has occurred.) The term's etymology or derivation is another source. (Euthanasia comes from the Greek *eu* = happy; *thanatos* = death.) The opinions of authorities and experts who have studied the topic may function as a useful source for definitions. Finally, ordinary usage based on dictionary definitions can serve as a basis for definitions.

Arguers should avoid defining terms in ways that are incompatible with the propositions they are advocating. For example, those supporting passive euthanasia because it allows dying patients freedom of choice would not want to stipulate situations in which euthanasia *must* take place. This would deprive patients of freedom of choice by requiring actions mandated by the situation. The characteristics of the proposition that are identified should be compatible with the field of analysis and the issues that are applied within it.

Understanding Situations

The placement of a proposition and argumentation case within the appropriate sphere and field is important because they provide the criteria for evaluating the arguments in the case. The issues map should provide some understanding of the contexts involved in making arguments from a particular propositional arena. Fields such as law, medicine, physics, and economics suggest standards of proof and evidence useful in making evaluations. The priorities, practices, and conventions in certain fields determine what issues are important and how judgments will be made about them. If two fields are applied in evaluating the same issues, the standards and rules drawn from each field may be in conflict. For example, at certain times and in certain jurisdictions, the legal definition for death was "irreparable cessation of spontaneous cardiac and repertory activity," whereas the medical definition was cessation of brain activity as indicated by a flat electroencephalograph. Furthermore, legal decisions are based on the letter of the law and precedent in similar court cases, whereas medical practice is based on medical ethics, which obligate a physician to do nothing to make the patient worse. Clearly, the fields of law and medicine have very different definitions, standards, and procedures for guiding decisions in euthanasia cases.

Arguers should keep their audience's attitudes, values and expectations in mind when they construct cases. If there is a clear presumption in favor of existing policy or in favor of a certain value orientation on a topic, advocates must take that presumption into account as they construct a case. Furthermore, they should be familiar with the major issues related to a topic and make sure they address them. If the case is based on a reasonable proposal and if the relevant claims are supported to the satisfaction of the audience, then the case will be *prima facie*. The general principles of case construction discussed in the next chapter are based on reasonable audience expectations and the conventions of argument. Advocates who carefully take them into account will find that the cases they present will be persuasive and compelling to the audience for which they are intended.

SUMMARY

This chapter focused on how to approach propositions, specifically how to analyze and interpret fact, value, and policy arguments. We began by discussing the nature of extended fact, value, and policy arguments and important concepts related to approaching each. When advocates begin to connect individual arguments in support of a proposition, they are constructing extended argument cases. An extended case develops the issues associated with the proposition in a way that provides clear support for the proposition. Although propositions are classified as fact, value, or policy, advocates should be aware that each type of proposition is related to each other type—they are not exclusive of one another. Rather, policy propositions tend to assume certain facts and values. Similarly, facts exist within our interpretive frameworks of what is valuable or not. And values have implications for policy and tend to assume certain facts.

Extended arguments about fact-based propositions occur in all spheres, and commonly occur in fields such as law, history, and policy-making. There are many facts and statistics upon which people disagree, and most extended arguments begin with questions of fact.

Values govern our choice making, and help us to decide what we ought to do and believe. Value based claims are an important part of discussion about policy making and an important part of discussions about facts. Though they are subjective, many contemporary theorists of argument have successfully provided the means for developing a rational approach to supporting value claims. A value hierarchy is the way we order our values so that some are more important than others. We explored the value hierarchies of quantity, quality, essence, and the person, which have been found by theorists to be widely accepted across Western cultures. We also looked at five considerations for approaching value propositions, which can be used to help justify or oppose a particular value hierarchy.

Extended policy arguments are composed of subsidiary claims supporting a policy proposition and the reasoning and evidence that support them. Policy arguments, unlike other types of argument, ask audiences to make decisions about future actions based on their expectations of what is probable or likely to occur. A systems approach to policy argumentation begins with the assumption that policies are interconnected and that changes in one part of a system have effects in other parts of the system. When we examine the relative merits of any particular policy system, we need to assess not only the policy, but also the extended system of changes it represents and the system it is designed to replace. No action occurs in a vacuum, and advocates as well as listeners need to be aware of the consequences of action or inaction. Understanding systems is important because policy arguments seek to change the complex nature of our social, economic, and political systems.

An issues map isolates and explores the issues within the propositional arena. The propositional arena is the area in which the issues for any given dispute exist. Arguers analyze these issues to determine the scope of the arena, its situation, the types of issues involved, and the potential for argument to affect meaningful change. From their analysis of the issues and their construction of arguments about the proposition, arguers begin the process of developing extended arguments.

Case construction focuses on the process we use to build a *prima facie* extended argument for the proposition. Central to the concept of case construction are four principles. The first principle is burden of proof and presumption. The burden of proof means that advocates have the responsibility to prove that a case and all of its associated risks are warranted beyond the current system. Presumption is the belief that current thinking, attitudes, values, or actions should continue to exist in the absence of compelling arguments to change them.

Second, advocates should construct cases that are *prima facie*. A *prima facie* case is one that meets the burden of proof and overcomes presumption. Generally, *prima facie* cases are composed of arguments that develop all of the stock issues for a proposition. Although the stock issues vary by proposition type, they are defined as the issues the recipients expect to see addressed in order for the arguer to have met the burden of proof. Third, cases should be developed within a clearly defined propositional arena. And, finally, case development should be based on an understanding of the particular argument situation.

EXERCISES

Exercise 1: *Underlying Facts and Values.* Consider the following policy based propositions. Make a list of the fact and value claims that would be a part of the propositional arena for each.

1. The USA Patriot Act should be repealed.
2. *Marijuana should be legalized.
3. *The death penalty should be abolished.

4. The legal drinking age should be lowered to 18.

5. The United States should reinstate the draft.

Exercise 2: Mapping. Based on the propositions above, develop an issues map. For the purpose of this exercise, the issues map need contain only the claims that one might expect an arguer to make. Based on your map, what issues need further investigations?

Exercise 3. The goal of this exercise is to reach a consensus through collaborative debate.

Step. 1. Students select a topic to serve as the proposition. Topics should be accessible to all members of the class. For example:

> The University should eliminate grades.
> The local community should fund a new library.

Step. 2. Together, the students generate all the reasons for and against the proposition.

Step. 3. These reasons are then distributed to members of the class for research purposes.

Step. 4. In-class debate.

First speaker:	Affirmative—in support of the proposition. A student is selected to speak in favor of the proposition. It is his or her responsibility to argue the reasons. Class members may support and offer research materials.
Second speaker:	Negative—in opposition to the proposition. A different student is selected to speak in opposition. It is her or his responsibility to either (1) concede or (2) refute a reason offered by the previous speaker. This speaker may draw on the support and research of the entire class, including the first affirmative speaker.
Third speaker:	Affirmative. Yet another speaker is selected to speak in favor of the proposal. This speaker rephrases those points refuted by the opposition. This speaker must either concede or refute each one. Again, this speaker may draw on the support and research of the entire class, including the first opposition speaker.
Fourth speaker:	Negative. A new speaker is selected to oppose. It is her or his turn to concede or refute the points established by the previous speaker. This person may also use the support of the entire class.

This process continues until all reasons are explored and considered. The goal of the process is for the class to reach consensus. The consensus will be one of three options: maintain the current system or state of affairs, accept the proposition outright, or create a modified plan. In the example of a university eliminating grades, these outcomes might be as follows: keep the current grading system (status quo), eliminate the grading system (affirm the proposition outright), or convert the grading system to pass/fail only (a potential modified plan).

Exercise 4. Read the following three situations and analyze the values that clash:

SITUATION 1

Your parents are paying for your university education. Paying the tuition and housing bills can be a hardship for them, but their hope is that you succeed with your education and complete a degree in business. Although you appreciate their sacrifice and are loyal to them, your passion is to become an actor and attempt to find a career in entertainment. Therefore, you wish to major in theater.

Unfortunately, when you shared this wish with your parents, they not only opposed your choice, saying it was "unrealistic" and "very unlikely," but they also told you that if you chose to major in anything but business, they would end their financial support for your education.

SITUATION 2

Your university is a large research institution that conducts studies in cancer and AIDS prevention and treatment. You were attracted to the school in the first place because it has the best premedical program in the state, and your goal is to become a doctor. Although you support finding cures for these diseases, you are also very opposed to the live animal research conducted in university laboratories. You become even more concerned when you discover that part of the required coursework in your biology and premed major will be assisting with some of these research projects and conducting vivisections on the animals. Yet you know that a biology major is the first step toward a medical degree that will help you find cures for people later on.

Based on each of the situations and your understanding of values, answer the following:

1. What do you think is the "correct" course of action in each situation?

2. What values support your conclusions?

3. How would you organize the terminal value hierarchy in a way that is consistent with your own decision-making?

NOTES

1. Adapted from "Debates: This House Believes that Parents Should be Allowed to Select the Sex of Their Children," *IDEA*, at http://idebate.org/debatabase/debates/philosphical-political-theory/house-believes-parents-should-be-able-choose-sex-their-children (accessed May 23, 2012).

2. Margaret Talbot, "Jack or Jill," *Atlantic.com*, March 2002, http://www.theatlantic.com/past/docs/issues/2002/03/talbot.htm (accessed May 29, 2012).

3. This story was reported in several publications, including, Andrew Pollack, "DNA Blueprint for Fetus Built Using Test of Parents," *The New York Times*, June 6, 2012, http://www.nytimes.com/2012/06/07/health/tests-of-parents-are-used-to-map-genes-of-a-fetus.html?pagewanted=all (accessed June 7, 2012); and Libby Copeland, "The Unanswered Questions of Prenatal Genetic Testing," *Slate Online*, June 7, 2012.

4. Pollack; Copeland.

5. Penny Kane and Ching Y Choi, "China's One Child Family Policy," *British Medical Journal*, October 9, 1999, 319(7215): 992–994.

6. A good explanation can be found in Lesley Stahl, "China: Too Many Men," *60 Minutes*, April 16, 2006, http://www.cbsnews.com/stories/2006/04/13/60minutes/main1496589.shtml (accessed May 29, 2012).

7. Jennifer Hunter, "Are We Headed toward a Lopsided World?" July 23 2011, at http://www.thestar.com/news/insight/article/1029256--are-we-heading-toward-a-lopsided-world (accessed May 29, 2012).

8. Sunita Puri, "I Know It's a Girl and You're Your Help to Get It Out of Me," *Slate Online*, August 2, 2011, http://www.slate.com/articles/double_x/doublex/2011/08/i_know_its_a_girl_and_i_need_your_help_to_get_it_out_of_me.html (accessed May 20, 2012).

9. Puri.

10. For other studies of American values, see Gail M. Inlow, *Values in Transition: A Handbook* (New York: John Wiley, 1972); and Ben J. Wattenberg, *The Good News Is the Bad News Is Wrong* (New York: Simon & Schuster, 1984); Many studies of contemporary American values are available, such as "The 2011 American Values Survey," conducted by the Public Religion Research Institute, at http://publicreligion.org/site/wp-content/uploads/2011/11/PRRI-2011-American-Values-Survey-Web.pdf (accessed May 29, 2012).

11. Chaim Perelman and Lucie Olbrechts-Tyteca, *The New Rhetoric: A Treatise on Argumentation*, trans. John Wilkinson and Purcell Weaver (Notre Dame, Ind.: University of Notre Dame Press, 1969), 83–99. In addition to the hierarchies stated here, these authors noted the

hierarchy of order—that the cause, or that which comes first, should be valued over that which comes later.

12. Steven D. Levitt and Stephen J. Dubner, *Freakonomics: A Rogue Economist Explores the Hidden Side of Everything,*" (HarperCollins e-books: New York, 2006).

13. Levitt and Dubner, 126

14. "*Freakanomics*, Crime and Abortion," September 30, 2005, http://abcnews.go.com/blogs/technology/2005/09/freakonomics_cr/ (accessed August 29, 2012).

15. Steve Sailer, "The *Freakanomics* Fiasco in Perspective," at http://www.isteve.com/Freakonomics_Fiasco.htm (access on September 3, 2012).

16. For further explanation of these hierarchies, see Gregg B. Walker and Malcolm O. Sillars, "Where Is Argument? Perelman's Theory of Values," in *Perspectives on Argumentation*, Robert Trapp and Janice Schuetz, eds. (Prospect Heights, Ill.: Waveland Press, 1990), 143–145.

17. Perelman and Olbrechts-Tyteca, 83.

18. Ludwig Bertalanffy, "General System Theory—A Critical Review," *General Systems* 12 (1962): 1–20.

19. Rhys Blakely, "Google Visionary Revolutionizes Education with a Degree Course for the Cost of Getting Online," *The Times* (London), May 12, 2012; Tamar Lewin, "Instruction for Masses Knocks Down Campus Walls," *The New York Times*, March 12, 2012, http://www.nytimes .com/2012/03/05/education/moocs-large-courses-open-to-all-topple-campus-walls.html (accessed June 28, 2012); Audrey Watters, "Learning from MOOCs," Inside Higher

Ed, March 14, 2012, at http://www.insidehighered.com/blogs/hack-higher-education/learning-moocs (accessed June 28, 2012).

20. Blakely; Lewin; Watters.

21. Blakely; Lewin; Watters.

22. Josina M. Makau, *Reasoning and Communication* (Belmont, Calif.: Wadsworth, 1990), 142.

23. Joanne G. Kurfiss, "Critical Thinking: Theory, Research, Practice, and Possibilities, ASHE-ERIC," *Higher Education Report* No. 2 (Washington, D.C.: Association for the Study of High Education, 1988), 25–34.

24. Adapted from William W. Wilmot and Joyce C. Hocker, *Interpersonal Conflict*, 6th ed. (New York: McGraw-Hill, 2001); and Paul Wehr, *Conflict Regulation* (Nashville, Tenn.: Westview Publishing, 1979).

25. Richard Whately, *Elements of Rhetoric*, Douglas Ehninger, ed. (Carbondale, Ill.: Southern Illinois University Press, 1963), 112–113.

26. For further discussion about burden of proof and presumption in advocacy, see Gary Cronkhite, "The Locus of the Presumption," *Central States Speech Journal* 17 (1966): 276; and Barbara Warnick, "Arguing Value Propositions," *Journal of the American Forensic Association* 18 (1981): 112–115. Permission to draw material from the latter article was granted by the American Forensic Association.

27. Richard Worshop, "Assisted Suicide," *CQ Researcher* 2 (1992): 148.

CHAPTER EIGHT

CASE CONSTRUCTION

CHAPTER OUTLINE

KEY CONCEPTS

Arguments seldom occur in isolation. Usually, when people argue they combine many individual arguments to develop extended exchanges that explore the issues in dispute. As we explored in the previous chapter, they are part of a larger context of discussion and debate. Each chapter in this book provides examples of how these extended arguments develop in conversations, such as the one in Box 8.1, "Should Organs be Sold on the Open Market?" Arguments are almost always part of complex exchanges in which people grapple with issues and ideas and make decisions about facts, values, and policies. Decision-making occurs with varied participants in contexts such as personal discussions and disputes, courtrooms, the workplace, and in political contexts such as the legislature and the voting booth.

■ ■ ■ ■ ■

BOX 8.1
SHOULD ORGANS BE SOLD ON THE OPEN MARKET?[1]

Would you sell a kidney to pay for graduate school? What if selling a lung or skin could help make house payments during economic downturns? Would you be willing to sell an organ of a deceased loved one if it financially helped your family? Most countries have laws prohibiting the sale of organs. The United States outlawed selling organs with the passage of the National Organ Transplant Act in 1984. There are very few places in the world where organs can be sold legally, even though demand has increased steadily for decades.

With surgical advances, improved antirejection drugs, and new diagnostic and tissue-matching techniques, transplant procedures have become much more common and have much better survival rates. More than 2,300 patients receive hearts each year in the United States alone, with about 85 percent surviving for at least a year.[2] And much more than hearts are transplanted. Surgeons have successfully replaced kidneys, lungs, livers, corneas, pancreases, and even faces.[3] In 2011, over 28,000 organ and 46,000 cornea transplant operations were performed in the United States.[4] Success stories continue to multiply, as do the number of operations performed and the survival rates.[5]

Despite increases in successful surgeries, a significant need remains.[6] Each day, about seventy-four people receive a transplant, but more than 110,000 remain on waiting lists.[7] On average, eighteen people die daily waiting for organs to become available.[8]

Globally, organizations have made extensive efforts to promote organ donations. Even so, many potential donors remain reluctant. Their reasons vary from religious to personal to a misunderstanding of how organ donations work. The Mayo Clinic, for instance, has provided a list of myths that seem to make potential donors reluctant.[9] These include:

- If I become a donor, doctors won't work as hard to save my life in an emergency.
- Maybe I am not really dead when they harvest my organs.
- Organ donation is against my religion.
- I am too young to make this decision.
- I am too old; no one would want my organs.
- My family wants an open-casket funeral and that can't happen if I donate my organs.
- I am in poor health, which makes me an unsuitable candidate.

(continued)

BOX 8.1   CONTINUED

- Rich people always seem to move to the front of the line when organs become available; I don't want to support the rich.

- My family will have to pay for the hospital bill and surgery if I donate.

Although education and donation campaigns have worked hard to overcome myths such as these, organ donations lag far behind the need. Because of shortages, there has been growing pressure among many to allow people to sell their organs; the hope is that monetary incentives might overcome attitudes and beliefs based on myths.[10]

Though most of the world prohibits the sale of organs, in Iran the waiting list for kidneys has been completely eliminated since their government began compensating living donors with the equivalent of about $1,200 US dollars and a year of health coverage.[11] Underground markets have developed in many countries, including India, Pakistan, and Israel.[12] The World Health Organization estimated that by 2012 the global black market for kidneys was at 10,000 per year, with a surgery of an illegally donated organ occurring nearly every hour.[13]

Some governments and "entrepreneurs" sell organs under the table, including organs harvested from executed prisoners.[14] Brian Handwerk reported in *National Geographic* that organ recipients can pay as much as $100,000 for illicit organs.[15] The poor and the imprisoned are often targeted as potential donors, and this problem is projected to increase.

With inadequate supplies and a growing underground market, the question of whether to allow legal organ sales has reemerged. Many fear that legally putting a price on organs ultimately gives the rich an advantage, creating unequal distribution of health benefits. Instead of an open market solution, some argue for the elimination of the requirement to obtain consent to procure organs from the deceased.[16]

With inadequate supplies and a growing underground market, the question of whether the sale of human organs should be allowed has reemerged. Below is a discussion between two classmates highlighting many of the arguments in support of allowing compensation for organ donation. As you read the arguments, think about the fact, value, and policy claims that would make up the propositional arena.

Katie:	I wish I had the opportunity to sell my kidney and pay for school. It seems to be a win–win. I can save a life, I don't need the extra kidney, and I can eliminate my college debt.
Jonathon:	I agree. And it's not just college students who could benefit. Why shouldn't the people who donate the organs of their deceased loved ones at least be allowed to have funeral expenses covered?
Katie:	That's a great example of how allowing compensation for organ donation wouldn't just help the rich, but would benefit the most vulnerable people in society. It could give them real choice and help them out. We also need to remind people that there is already a huge underground, illegal market for organs, and many poor people are exploited by brokers who make massive profits by praying on those in need. All our current policies have done is make illegal activity profitable and unsafe. If we could sell our organs, it could be done safely and fairly.
Jonathon:	I have heard that some people object to allowing the sale of organs because they think we should not objectify the human body. But Americans seem to be okay with allowing the sale of blood and sperm, and a woman can get paid a lot to donate her eggs, but you don't hear many people say that's immoral.

BOX 8.1   CONTINUED

Katie: And with the example of blood, sperm, and eggs, we can see that commercial markets have increased the number donors. So far, we seem to have managed these markets well. It seems to me we could do the same thing with organs.

Jonathon: Ultimately, this is about doing something to save human lives. We need to remember how many lives would be saved with more donors. I know I personally wouldn't really think of donating an organ unless I was given money. How else are we going to increase organ donations?

This discussion suggests fact, value, and policy arguments related to the significant issues around organ donation. As you read it, consider the following questions

1. What fact, value, and policy-based propositions might arise from this discussion?
2. What issues seem to be the most important in addressing each type of proposition?
3. Are there other issues or questions you want included in discussion of organ donation?
4. If you were going to design a 10-minute policy presentation in support of allowing compensation for organ donation, how would you organize it?
5. How would you respond to these arguments?

When advocates become seriously involved in the discussion of controversial topics, they use the critical thinking cycle discussed in Chapter 1 to guide research to construct an issues map as we talked about in Chapter 7. These steps allow advocates to develop an understanding of the issues involved in each arena, and then draw on the map to design extended argument cases. This chapter explores methods for developing extended cases that support fact, value, and policy propositions. We will also introduce the issues brief, which draws on the issues map and the stock issues to create an in-depth outline of arguments that support or oppose propositions.

ISSUES BRIEF

In Chapter 7, we discussed how advocates could create issue maps of propositions. An issues map is intended to identify the primary issues that arguers should consider in developing their analysis of a proposition. In particular, we discussed four principles central to constructing cases across fields and contexts: burden of proof, presumption, *prima facie* case, and stock issues. These principles are explored in Box 8.2, "Apply the Theory." In Chapter 1, we referred to these as field-invariant standards as opposed to field-dependent standards because they apply in any argument context.

An issues brief draws on the issues map to provide a detailed and focused outline of arguments used to support and oppose a given proposition. *An issues brief is a synthesis of opposing views on the stock issues of a proposition.* It is important to keep in mind that an issues brief tends to examine two sides of an issue—one supporting the proposition and one opposing it. Of course, on many controversial topics people's attitudes are more complex than that. For example, a person might oppose the death penalty in some cases and yet support

■ ■ ■ ■ ■

BOX 8.2

APPLY THE THEORY: FOUR PRINCIPLES

The following are four field-invariant standards for extended argument cases that are applicable in any argument context:

1. **Burden of proof.**   The advocates for change have the burden of proof, which is the obligation to overcome presumption.
2. **Presumption.**   Presumption is the belief that current facts, attitudes, and policies are sufficient as they are.
3. *Prima facie case.*   Advocates meet the burden of proof by presenting good and sufficient arguments for adopting a new viewpoint or take a new action. These good and sufficient reasons should be acceptable warrants for change on their face.
4. **Stock issues.**   Depending on the type of proposition and what the audience knows about it, arguers will need to select which issues need development and support. The stock issues address the questions that a reasonable audience would want answered in order for the arguer to meet the burden of proof.

Using the case study in Box 8.1 as a guide, how would you answer the following?

1. Where does the burden of proof lie? In other words, does the advocate for banning the sale of organs have the burden or the advocate for prohibiting sale? Why?
2. Where does presumption lie?
3. Before looking into the specific argument, what kinds of arguments would you expect an advocate to make? What questions would you have for an arguer?
4. Imagine the field of arguments that might exist in this propositional arena. Which issues are the most important? If an arguer addressed the issues adequately, would that be a *prima facie* case? What other arguments would an arguer need to present?

it in others. We might favor some statements and positions of a politician and oppose others. Most often people do not take extreme positions on any given issue but instead admit exceptions or recognize the middle ground. The issues map is intended to illuminate these varied points of view. The brief, however, focuses arguments to show specific support and opposition to a proposition.

Actually, the term *brief* is a misnomer because a fully developed brief can be quite long. It involves many issues and options and generally should include evidence and reasoning supporting the outlined claims. Consider the differences between the brief and the map. Whereas the map attempted to outline the issues available for argument within a propositional arena, the issues brief selects the best of those arguments to support or oppose the proposition for a given situation. Not all of the issues developed in the map are used; rather, the issues most appropriate for the situation are selected.

The task of an advocate is to present each of the stock issues as clearly and articulately as possible. Each argument should include the relevant evidence and reasoning in support of the claims such that the audience is able to understand its meaning and relevance to the proposition. The opposition to the proposition needs to do the same, with the exception that the opposition needs only to successfully refute a minimum of one stock issue. The reason is simply that if the opposition to a case can disprove any one of the stock issues, the case is rendered non–*prima facie*, which means it is no longer valid. We will spend more time exploring methods for refuting cases in the next chapter.

The following sections develop an issues brief for each type of proposition we have discussed. Minimally, a brief should explore the stock issues related to the proposition as well as any other important issues that emerged as part the issue mapping.

STOCK ISSUES FOR FACT CASES

When we argue about fact propositions, there are certain stock issues that must be addressed. These, typically, are the issues that emerged from answering the third question in Box 8.2. They are the reasonable questions recipients have about the nature of any given fact proposition, and they should have been identified in the issues map as discussed in Chapter 7. Although many issues can be used to develop fact-based cases, generally we can group them into three categories: issues of fact definition, threshold, and application. Each of the stock issues is illustrated below in Box 8.3, "Stock Issues for Fact-Based Propositions."

BOX 8.3
STOCK ISSUES FOR FACT-BASED PROPOSITIONS

ISSUE	DEFINITION	EXAMPLE
Definition	The stock issue of fact definition consists of statements of historic fact, causal relationships, and predictive facts.	Allowing compensation for organ donation will result in an end to the shortage of most organs.
Threshold	The issue of threshold establishes the acceptable limits of definitions.	Compensation could include monetary payments to individuals or families, health insurance credits, or agreement to pay expenses such as medical, travel, or funeral costs. Organ "brokers" would not be allowed to profit from another person's organs.
Application	Application is the illustration that the case examined is sufficient proof to verify the definition and its threshold.	Thousands of people die each year waiting for organ transplants. Currently, the United States prohibits any type of compensation for donors. Iran allows people to sell their organs on the open market, and that country now has no waiting lists for kidneys, the most commonly needed organ. If we create a similar system here, we can expect the same result.

To illustrate how these issues work, imagine the following conversation between a student, Melanie, and her advisor, Tracy:

Melanie: I took the art course to satisfy the university's art requirement. I don't understand why it doesn't count toward graduation.

Tracy: The university counts only certain art courses. The one you took is a lower division art course and the requirement is that you had to have at least one upper division art course.

Melanie: So what you are telling me is that not all art courses satisfy the art requirement? Only some do? That makes no sense.

Tracy: Sorry, but the course catalog is not always very clear about what counts and what doesn't count. But as you can see here, it does make a distinction about what kinds of courses count for the art requirement.

University course catalogs, along with most contracts or laws, are often rich sources of factual argument. Different parties may read the same documents and come to very different conclusions about what the documents mean. In this case, each of the primary stock issues of fact disputes is present.

Fact Definition

Definition is the first of the stock issues. It is important to distinguish between the two types of definitions presented thus far. In Chapter 4, we discussed definitions of propositions in general, as opposed to definitions of the fact. Before advocates can seek to interpret the meaning of a particular fact or set of circumstances, the nature of the facts must be clearly defined. The fact advocate must clearly define the facts of the case and explain their relevance to the proposition. *The stock issue of fact definition can consist of statements of historical fact, causal relationships, and predictive facts,* as discussed in Chapter 4.

Attorneys and judges in the field of law typically proceed by defining the relevant laws and then determining whether the issues in the case "fit" the legal definitions within those laws. Courts of law examine historical facts in which alleged crimes occurred. From those cases, courts interpret a definition. In the example above about what courses fulfill requirements for graduation, the course catalog needed to clearly define which courses met the art requirement and which courses did not. According to the university catalog, only upper division courses met the requirements and that definition excluded Melanie's course.

Definition is a part of any fact-based argument. If we argue about the existence of life on other planets, we need to define what we mean by *life*. Are we talking about intelligent life or microbes? If we argue that corporal punishment increases discipline and learning in schools, we need to decide if corporal punishment is physical punishment (such as a spanking), emotional punishment (such as humiliation), or some other form of punishment. Without a clear sense of definition, the arguers will not know how to develop the argument case—or even how to prove their issues. The stock issue of fact definition, then, provides a clear end point for the case. In other words, if the advocate can prove that some case meets the requirements of the definition, then the proposition is proven true or correct.

Threshold

The issue of threshold is closely related to the issue of definition. Because much of life and social action is not precise, there are many degrees of behavior and degrees of interpretation. *The issue of threshold establishes the acceptable limits of definitions.* A word or phrase can be defined in many ways. The definition of *life*, for example, has been subject to much debate for decades. Does life start at the moment of conception? Does it start at birth? Does life end when brain activity ends? Or does it end when the heart stops beating?

When we argue about the limits of a definition, we are arguing about its threshold. Although we know that a twenty-year-old, healthy, active college student is alive, we might debate the point at which life begins or ends. Beyond the threshold, we know life exists. The problem for advocates, however, is being able to argue at which point life begins or ends. In the case of the student, the threshold was any upper division art course. The student could take multiple courses in that range, and upper-division courses in addition to the lower-division ones, but the threshold was any one course of upper-division work.

Threshold issues are common in our daily lives and in the workplace. If, for instance, you were planning to buy a new video game, you would encounter the issue of threshold on the side of the game's package. The package might say:
Minimum requirements include:

> 3 gigahertz processor or higher
>
> Microsoft Windows 8
>
> Game Controller
>
> 100 gigabytes of available hard drive space
>
> 4 gigabytes of RAM

These requirements are threshold requirements. If the machine is an Apple iMac running Apple's operating system, the game will not function properly. If any of these minimum threshold requirements is not met, the game will not run. Your machine may far exceed the threshold and be the latest, most up-to-date system, but unless it at least meets the minimum requirements set forth in the threshold, purchasing the game would not be wise.

Similarly, employers use threshold issues in developing want ads. Recently a website ran an ad for the following position:

> Wanted: Public relations consultant. Must have a bachelor's degree in Communication or closely associated area. Must have five years experience in public relations. Knowledge of computers is essential. Must know *Microsoft Office* products. Must be able to travel for work-related projects for periods up to two weeks. Should be good team player and self-starter. Salary competitive.

In this case, the organization is looking for a public relations consultant. For the organization, the threshold for an acceptable candidate centered on the degree earned, experience in the field, knowledge of computers, and travel. Candidates need to meet each of these requirements before they could be considered for the position.

Application

The third stock issue of application focuses on whether the example or phenomenon under consideration meets the requirements of definition and threshold. *Application is the illustration that the case examined is sufficient proof to verify the definition and its threshold.* In other words, application is the argument that some case or phenomenon meets the threshold for the definition. Suppose an applicant for the want ad mentioned earlier submitted a resume that highlighted the following abilities:

- Bachelor's degree in Communication Studies, Sacramento State
- Six years experience in public relations and marketing
- *Microsoft Office* trainer for current employer

This person has submitted an application—an argument that she or he meets the minimum threshold requirement for the position. The application is simply the argument that some instance—the applicant in this case—does or does not meet the requirements set forth in the threshold and definition arguments. Figure 8.1, "Stock Issues Related to Fact," helps make this point. The "application" must be shown by an advocate to be within the "threshold" of the definition to meet or prove the definition. If the application does not meet the threshold requirements, then the proposition is not true.

The student's academic record from the initial example provides another illustration of how an application might be argued. In considering her case, the advisor asks the question, "Did her record meet the requirements of the university?" To answer that question, the advisor could compare her transcript to the threshold to determine whether her performance met the definitional requirements. In other words, the advisor could examine her course, a lower division art course, to see whether it met the threshold requirements. It does not. Suppose, however, that her course had been an upper division art class. In that case, the course clearly would have met the threshold requirement because it was upper division, which in turn would have met the definitional requirement to complete one course of lower-division art. The same process could be used in buying software for a computer. If the computer meets all the threshold requirements to run the software, then the software in question should work.

FIGURE 8.1   Stock Issues Related to Facts

░░░░░

BOX 8.4
APPLY THE THEORY: DEVELOPING A FACT-BASED CASE

Begin with the proposition that "Allowing the sale of organs will substantially decrease voluntary donations." How would you approach developing the stock issues for an extended case?

1. What definitions would you need to develop? Are all the terms of the proposition clear? Does the term *organ* need further clarification? All organs? Human organs?
2. What is the threshold? The proposition uses a potentially ambiguous term, *substantially*. What does that mean—10 percent? More than half? What is the threshold for "substantially decrease"?
3. What examples or "applications" can you find to demonstrate your analysis? Are there other countries that have tried this? Have there been pilot programs? What arguments are available to suggest the truth of the proposition?

Arguers sometimes forget that each of the stock issues represents an argument. Arguments, as we discussed in Chapter 1, require three parts: claim, support for the claim (through evidence and reasoning), and an attempt to influence.

The stock issues related to a proposition help guide advocates about the kinds of arguments they need to make to adequately address the issues, present a *prima facie* case, and meet their burden of proof. Box 8.4, "Apply the Theory," guides you through this process with a fact-based proposition.

STOCK ISSUES FOR VALUE ARGUMENTS

When we argue to change values, we attempt to persuade recipients to redistribute, emphasize/deemphasize, or restandardize some value within their value systems and value hierarchies. These concepts were developed in Chapter 3. This process calls on advocates to find persuasive means to enable audiences to reconceptualize value hierarchies or value systems. To argue for value change successfully, value advocates must address the stock issues for value cases. The stock issues for a value case include values, criteria, and application.[17] These are illustrated in Box 8.5, "Stock Issues for Value-Based Propositions."

As we saw with fact cases earlier, some facts are more difficult to refute than others. It would be difficult to deny, for instance, that there would at least be some increase in organ donation if we allowed donors to receive payment or some other form of compensation. But the question of whether such a system is desirable is much more complex. There are some very important value-based questions raised with regards to the organ donation controversy.

Value

The first of the stock issues in a value argument is "value." This stock issue defines the value and sets the goal or end point for the case arguments. Recall from our discussion of values in Chapter 3 that terminal values are end states of existence, thus the stock issue of value states

■ ■ ■ ■ ■

BOX 8.5

STOCK ISSUES FOR VALUE-BASED PROPOSITIONS

ISSUE	DEFINITION	EXAMPLE
Value	Defines the value and sets the goal or end point for the case arguments.	Allowing compensation for human organ donors is desirable because life is the most important value.
■ Value Object	Arguers must identify two value issues: value object and value hierarchy.	Compensation would allow donors to be given monetary payments or other benefits, such as the cost of funeral expenses, or health care credits.
■ Value Hierarchy	Value object is the central value term of the proposition to be debated. Value hierarchy is the relative importance of the value.	This would allow for the highest possible values to be prioritized: freedom and human life.
Criteria	Field- or sphere-dependent standards to be used to decide whether the value object fulfills certain values. Criteria are the measures, norms, or rules used to judge whatever is being evaluated.	We should minimize the loss of life in any way that respects the freedom of the individual. We value the power of the free market system, and we should allow it to work to save lives by encouraging people to exercise their freedom to profit from the sale of their body parts.
Application	The factual information and experience that can be used to support that the value object meets the criteria.	Many people are dying while waiting for organs. Compensation tends to encourage action, and people should have the freedom to decide whether to sell their body parts, or to receive other types of compensation for saving a life.

the terminal value of the proposition. Clearly identifying which value is most important in the discussion creates a common point of reference for all the participants. If the extended case were about whether censorship should be permitted in school newspapers, advocates might argue that the value of freedom of speech is more important than other competing values. As long as the participants have a clear understanding of the relevant values involved, the discussion or debate can remain focused.

The stock issue of value requires the arguer to identify two concepts: the value object and the value hierarchy. *The value object is an idea, practice, event, policy, or state of affairs that is to be judged by means of evaluation.* In addressing this issue, arguers should establish the value content of the object and define its primary features. In the organ donation example, the value object, the thing being evaluated, was whether allowing compensation for organ donation is desirable. Thus, the arguer would need to define what "compensation for organ donation" means.

The second value issue an arguer needs to address is value hierarchy, the ranking of values favored by advocates or party in an argument. In any extended value case, a certain value hierarchy is implied because, in defending any value orientation, advocates implicitly favor one value or certain values over others. The hierarchy applicable in any evaluation may become explicit only when that evaluation is challenged and contrasted to an alternative hierarchy. Therefore, explicit defense of a particular hierarchy may not be required when the value case is presented initially. However, if no value consensus is reached in the discussion, then the arguers may explicitly discuss value hierarchies and the relative importance of the values being discussed. In Chapter 7 we described four hierarchies that are common in Western cultures: quantity, quality, the existent, and the person. If value hierarchies are brought into the discussion, arguers can select one of these hierarchies and articulate reasons this should be the primary hierarchy most applicable to the situation.

Supporters and opponents of compensation for organ donation might adhere to different value hierarchies. Those advocating for allowing organ donors to be paid would be likely to support the values of life, freedom and the free market, whereas opponents might support equality and fairness or altruism. In defending their respective hierarchies, advocates of each position attempt to intensify their audience's adherence to and appreciation for the values at the top of their hierarchies. In other words, advocates attempt to persuade their listeners to rank values in the same way as they do. In defending a certain hierarchy, value advocates can use the resources provided in Chapters 3 and 7: the distinction between terminal and instrumental values, the needs implied in the situation, Perelman's study of Western hierarchies, Rokeach's value survey, and Rescher's account of value change. In addition, advocates can seek out other studies of American values and value hierarchies.

Criteria

In addition to clarifying the value stock issue, advocates should carefully select the criteria by which they will evaluate the value object. *Criteria are field- or sphere-dependent standards to be used to decide whether the value object fulfills certain values. They are the measures, norms, or rules used to judge whatever is being evaluated.* For example, if we say, "this ice cream is good," we must have in mind certain criteria or standards (creaminess, good taste, natural ingredients) by which we will judge the good ice cream. Here the value would probably be pleasure or enjoyment; if the value object meets or measures up to the standards, it fulfills the value in question; if not, then it must be judged negatively.

The standards that advocates select should be taken from the field or sphere most appropriate to the occasion. Advocates supporting the desirability of allowing financial compensation for organ donation could select individual ethics as their field and argue that the greater good of the individual is its purpose. Within this framework, they could defend the values of human life, free markets, and freedom of choice. The standards these values suggest are that human life should be preserved, and that we should be able to exercise our freedom of choice and ownership of our bodies, before and after death, in the free market to save those lives. If the advocates can establish these three standards, they then need only to prove that financial incentives for organ donation enable those standards to be met in order to establish their case.

Opponents will possibly argue for an alternative sphere and a different set of criteria, but both advocates and opponents of the desirability of compensation for organ donation must validate their criteria through further argument, especially when those standards are questioned or challenged. Three strategies are available for establishing criteria. First, one can link them to more generally accepted and unquestioned standards and argue that because the more general standard is accepted, the audience should also accept the particular standard the advocate is supporting. For example, we allow the sale of blood, sperm, and a woman's eggs; why can we not allow people to be compensated when they give other body parts? Second, the standards can be justified by showing that no other standards take precedence over them. For example, in this country we believe that freedom of choice is more important than life itself. ("Live free or die" was a central motto of the colonial period, and Patrick Henry's "Give me liberty or give me death" is well-known.) In the case of allowing organ donors to be compensated, one could argue that both the values of life and freedom are upheld with such a policy. Third, advocates can show the logical consequences of failing to apply the standards they advocate. Since the current law does not allow for any compensation, the advocate can argue that it actually decreases the number of donors. Thus, if we allow for compensation, there will be an increase in the number of donor and of lives saved.

Figure 8.2, "Stock Issues Related to Values," illustrates these concepts. Once an advocate identifies the value object and value hierarchy, the next step is to identify what standards or criteria can be used to evaluate whether or not a particular example or application comes close to supporting the value. Then, the advocate argues how a particular case or example can filter through the criteria to demonstrate the value is reasonably placed within the hierarchy as is discussed in the next section.

Application

The final stock issue for extended values cases deals with the application of the criteria the advocates established. That is, does the value object meet the standards for fulfilling the values in question? Here is where factual information and experience can be used for evidence. Supporters of allowing financial incentives for organ donation should be able to show that these types of incentives encourage giving and thus save lives. The extent to which the criteria apply and the number of people affected by the criteria are significant here. How many patients are in need of organ transplants? What proportion of these patients are likely to actually get the needed organs if we allow financial incentives for donation? If the proportion is small or there are few people likely to donate organs, the advocates' argument may lack significance.

FIGURE 8.2 Stock Issues Related to Values

Richard Paul and Gerald Nosich note that experienced critical thinkers know how to clarify the values and standards relevant to a situation, compare the values embedded in competing perspectives and interpretations, and question their own framework of thought.[18] Living as we do in a multicultural, diverse society requires us to understand and appreciate value orientations that differ from our own and to respect and incorporate the perspectives of individuals who come from religious and cultural backgrounds and personal experiences dramatically different from our own. Experience in value advocacy can enable many arguers to do this.

Constructing an issues brief will help you to incorporate divergent perspectives into your arguments. Box 8.6, "Value Proposition Issues Brief," features arguments to support

---

BOX 8.6

VALUE PROPOSITION ISSUES BRIEF

Proposition: Allowing compensation for human organ donation is desirable.

Value: How should the value object be defined and understood in a value hierarchy?

Definition: How do we understand the proposition?

Compensation for organ donation shall be defined in the following ways:

   A. Monetary compensation in the form of payment for the organ.

   B. Coverage of funeral expenses for donation of an organ from a deceased loved one.

   C. Desirable is defined as "worth seeking or doing as advantageous, beneficial, or wise."[19]

Hierarchies: What ranking of values should apply to this value object?

Allowing compensation for donation of a human organ preserves and promotes life, freedom, and the power of the free-market.

   A. Freedom is one of the core terminal values, according to Rokeach's value hierarchy.

   B. Allowing compensation for organ donation would provide the greatest good for the greatest number of people.

   C. Allowing compensation for organ donation will increase the number of organ donors. This promotes the value of life by helping to save the lives of the 100,000 on waiting lists in the very near term.

   D. Allowing compensation for organ donation uses the free market, which is central to our country, allowing individuals to exercise their freedom in a way that promotes life saving actions.

Definition: How do we respond to this interpretation?

Merriam-Webster's Collegiate Dictionary includes in its definition of desirable, "advisable."[20] Since there would be negative outcomes related to allowing compensation, it is *inadvisable* to allow.

   A. It would allow for the exploitation of the poor.

   B. It would create a two-tiered system of disseminating organs.

   C. It would assume ownership of body parts, and allow for the commodification of the human body.

Hierarchies: What is a reasonable response to the argument?

Since such policies would be inadvisable and thus not desirable, they do not meet the criteria set up by advocates. Allowing compensation for organ donation would privilege the wealthy and powerful, which violates the values of fairness and equality.

(continued)

BOX 8.6   CONTINUED

Criteria: What standards should be applied to determine whether the value object fulfills the desired values?

To meet the definition of desirable, compensation for organ donation should be limited and controlled. If it is shown to save lives by allowing the free market to increase the number of donors, without incurring additional harms to life or freedom, then it is desirable.

A. Compensation will increase the number of donors.
B. Our priority should be preservation of life.
C. Individuals should be allowed to decide whether they want to profit from their body parts or the parts of the deceased.
   1. We already allow people to be compensated for donating blood, sperm, and eggs.
   2. Current laws on compensation for human organs are overly restrictive and discourage donation.

Allowing compensation for organ donation undermines the value of human life by putting a monetary value on body parts. This will lead to further commodification of the human body, which will ultimately cause exploitation and inequality.

A. While compensating for organs may increase the number of donors, people may feel pressured to end life support for loved ones, or to become living donors due to debt or other situations which could lead to irrational decision making.
B. We should not prioritize saving some lives at the cost of others. The basic value of equality and fairness is violated when those with financial means are able to buy their way to saving their lives, while others might be in a position to risk their lives for financial reasons.

Application: How do the proposed standards apply to the value object?

Allowing compensation for organ donation is desirable.

A. It will save the lives of many of the 100,000 people waiting for organ transplants. Iran, which allows for the legal sale of human organs, has eliminated the waiting list for kidneys.
B. It will put an end to the dangerous illicit market for human organs by dramatically decreasing the need for donors.
C. It rewards people in a tangible way for saving lives, and takes away disincentives such as the risk of lost work time, travel costs, or future medical costs related to being a living donor.

There are many reasons why allowing compensation for organs is, in practice, not desirable.

A. It exploits the most vulnerable in society.
B. It will not be likely to abolish the illicit market for organs, and may in fact encourage the illegal procurement of organs.
C. It takes away any altruistic reason for organ donation.

BOX 8.7

APPLY THE THEORY: ARGUING VALUES

Begin with the proposition "Apple MacBooks are superior to any Windows-based laptop computer." How would you approach developing the stock issues for an extended case?

1. What is the "value object" in the proposition?
2. What value hierarchy "fits" this proposition best?
3. What criteria could be used to make a determination?
4. How does the application (Apple MacBook) work with the criteria to demonstrate the value is supported?

If you were to oppose this extended case, what arguments might you develop? For instance:

1. What other criteria might be used?
2. Can you identify examples where a Windows-based laptop might be better?
3. Was the best hierarchy identified?

There are many ways advocates can approach a proposition. The goal for the arguer is to develop the best narrative that explains through argument the most reasonable interpretation of the proposition.

---

each of the stock issues on the topic of organ donation. In this case, the value object, the subject of evaluation, is compensation for organ donation. When examining this brief, you should realize that each of the arguments is a claim that would need to be supported by evidence, reasoning, and further arguments. What are included are the principal claim (the proposition), and the major subclaims that constitute the case for supporting the proposition.

In this example, advocates for the proposition work to establish through argument how each stock issue can be proven as part of a *prima facie* case. The advocates opposing the proposition provide counterarguments as to why the stock issues have not been proven. Box 8.7, "Apply the Theory," will guide you through the process of building and opposing value-based cases. Concepts related to opposing propositions will be further developed in Chapter 9.

STOCK ISSUES FOR POLICY ARGUMENTS

The value debate described in Box 8.6 suggests a policy action—that human organ sales should be allowed. And, based on a fact and value foundation, the issues developed in Box 8.1, "Should Organs be Sold on the Open Market?" provide a good justification for the policy proposition "The United States should allow the sale of organs." This proposition is based on a factual assessment that current, donated supplies are insufficient and that thousands of people die while waiting on transplant lists. And, it is supported by the value assessment that human life should be preserved.

Although allowing the sale of organs might seem to be a reasonable approach for saving lives, we really have only a probable idea of what the result will be if we change the law.[21] Some experts support organ sales as a means to increase the supply and argue it is the only available near-term solution. Others quickly point out that these organs may not go to the neediest and that there may be undue pressure placed on families and poor people to sell their organs. Ultimately, whatever decision is made about the sale of organs will depend on a careful assessment of the potential benefits and the potential costs.

Policy propositions are simply a prediction of what we believe will occur. Accepting a policy proposition commits a hearer to a future call to action—what should be done. The decision to act, in turn, depends on the listener's assessment of how successful or reasonable the argument *probably* is. In this case, is the prediction that allowing organs to be sold will increase the supply reasonable and probable? Or, could it have tremendous costs to society such as the exploitation of the poor? Box 8.8, "Stock Issues for Policy Propositions," outlines what issues should be discussed when constructing a case for a policy propositions.

BOX 8.8
STOCK ISSUES FOR POLICY PROPOSITIONS

ISSUE	DEFINITION	EXAMPLE
Ill	An ill is a current wrong or harm that needs to be resolved.	There are too few organs to meet the needs of over 100,000 people on waiting lists.
		Thousands die each year because of an inadequate supply of organs.
Blame	Blame is the attribution of an ill to causes within the present policy system.	The National Organ Transplant Act of 1984 prohibits the sale of organs. Many potential donors have strong attitudes against donating organs, ranging from religion and family issues to misunderstanding how donations work.
Cure ■ Plan of Action ■ Plan Effect	Cure represents the ability of a policy action to overcome the ill and blame. It consists of a plan of action and plan effects.	The National Organ Transplant Act should be modified to allow for the regulated sale of organs. By providing a safe, legal means for selling organs, this plan should have the effect of increasing the supply.
Cost-Benefits	The cost refers to the problems or disadvantages associated with taking a policy action. Benefits are the positive consequences of policy action.	A potential cost to this plan is that people may be willing to sacrifice their health to make money from the sale of their organs. Additionally, families may be under increased stress to sell organs of recently deceased loved ones. The potential benefits include saving lives by ensuring a greater supply, and the illicit, unsafe harvesting and sale of organs by organized crime will diminish.

However, even with much less formal and significant policy conversations, the same group of stock issues should be explored by advocates when faced with a policy proposition. Imagine the following exchange between two roommates:

Jessica: I think we should go to Alaska and work in a fish cannery. That might sound like a strange idea, but I've always heard that there is a lot of money to be made, and they are always looking for people to work there.

Nora: Wait a minute! That's an awfully long way from home. Why don't we just find something around here for the summer instead of making such a long trip? I know of two or three fast-food places that are hiring.

Jessica: I'm out of money, and I need to find a good-paying job for the summer. Otherwise I'm just not going to be able to stay in college. Besides, we've decided that we want to work together this summer, right?

Nora: Right. But still, can't we just stay around here? It would be more fun and we know people.

Jessica: We could, but I have a friend who said in her first summer up there she made more than $7,000, and that is much more than we could ever hope to make around here. Besides, it would be fun to get away for a summer.

Nora: Maybe, but I've heard jobs up there are difficult to get.

Jessica: Not unless you know someone, and I do. She said we could get hired without any problem.

This conversation presents an extended policy argument about the proposition "We should work in an Alaskan fish cannery this summer." The friends can either accept or reject it, and through the exchange the stock policy issues are explored.

In reading the discussion, consider the order of the questions and answers. Jessica began with a proposition for going to Alaska to work. It was phrased as a declarative sentence, and Nora did not need to respond. So why did she answer the sentence with a question? Her reason is the same as any listener's reason might be. People often do not accept propositional statements without asking for specific supporting arguments from the speaker. Nora pointed out that they could find jobs nearby, so what made Jessica think they needed to travel to Alaska? In response, Jessica pointed out that few local places were hiring. A correct answer to each question was important: If Jessica had not thought her plan through sufficiently, or if her answers were unsatisfactory, Nora would have rejected her idea because it would not have been *prima facie* (acceptable at first glance).

This conversation is typical of many policy arguments, even very complex arguments about legislation, such as legalizing the sale of human organs. Advocates need to be aware of the stock issues and prove them reasonably before recipients can be expected to take action. As illustrated in Figure 8.3, "Stock Issues Related to Policies," the arguer typically needs to address the issues of "Ill," "Blame," "Cure," and "Cost-Benefits." Unlike fact- and value-based cases, policy cases are a future-orientated process and therefore represented as an arrow with each issue supporting the next. This section develops each of these stock issues in detail, enabling you to identify them and build arguments supporting each type.

**FIGURE 8.3   Stock Issues
Related to Policies**

Ill

When Nora asked Jessica what was wrong with their current plan for summer work, she was asking Jessica to supply an argument proving the stock issue of ill. *An ill is a current wrong or harm the advocate is trying to resolve.* Likewise, if we ask, "What is the problem with policies related to organ donation?" we are also asking for the ill or the harm associated with the current system. In Chapter 2 we discussed the rhetorical situation, which includes the context of persons, events, objects, relations, and an exigence that strongly invites argument. The stock issue of ill describes the exigence, which Lloyd Bitzer defined as "an imperfection marked by urgency; a defect, an obstacle, something waiting to be done, a thing that is other than it should be."[22] Before we legalize organ sales, legislators as well as public audiences will need to be convinced that a problem, or an exigence, exists. People act in the presence of a need—the reason to act. The argument of ill is generally a factual presentation of the exigence for argument.

Before people are persuaded to act, they look for a significant ill or need. Most people do not act without some significant cause. For example, we might drive by litter scattered along a road. Although most of us agree that litter is a problem (an ill), we would probably not stop to pick it up and dispose of it properly; however, if the litter found its way into our front yard, we would be more inclined to do something. It is a question of significance. If the ill is seen as significant for us, we are more likely to act.

Qualitative Significance

The difficult question to answer is whether an arguer is presenting an ill that is significant enough to warrant the type of action proposed. Significance can be either qualitative or quantitative. *Qualitative significance is related to the intensity of the effect; we assess something as significant to the extent that it strengthens or diminishes life or other significant value.* Evaluating qualitative significance usually requires a comparative consideration of values.

An example of a value conflict of this type is shown in controversies about species preservation. To protect fish runs and spawning grounds, some legislators have proposed removal of dams that block fish migration and affect water quality. Those who have opposed dam removal argue that dams are important for irrigation and production of relatively green hydroelectric power. Which is more important: protection of the environment and endangered species or preservation of farms and power sources? The significance of these competing interests is qualitative and value-based; it cannot be easily reduced to quantitative terms.

Quantitative Significance

Quantitative significance is related to the scope of the effects claimed; it asks how many people will be affected how frequently. Quantitative significance is often more easily evaluated than qualitative significance because it simply involves statistical comparison. As long as the evidence available is reliable and accessible, quantitative significance can usually be more easily weighed than qualitative significance. For example, if Jessica argued that going to Alaska for two months would yield $10,000, the quantitative comparison of $10,000 to $3,000 at any other summer job is easier than evaluating the effect of this income on their lifestyles.

Arguing Significance

Most often, when we argue that something is significant, we blend both qualitative and quantitative measures. We do so because issues related to significance involve our understanding of the scope of an ill (how many are affected) and the value of the ill (how important this issue is to us). Is it significant that selling organs helps only one person? How many people constitute a significant ill? How many additional lives will be saved if we make organ sales legal? The answers to these questions are difficult because much depends on the context of the proposed policy. An ill is generally considered significant enough to warrant action if life or the quality of life is threatened. Of course, significance is a relative term, and it depends on how we value life or quality-of-life issues.

For example, preserving a right to free speech or free association has value only to the extent that it helps or hurts people.[23] Or, when we express outrage against animal testing for cosmetics, we argue that it unnecessarily destroys the quality of animal life. But what happens in a case in which animal experimentation is necessary for human survival? In 1992, for example, a baboon liver was transplanted into a human to save that person's life. Is a human life worth more than a baboon's life? These qualitative issues can be difficult questions to answer, but generally they involve the use of a value hierarchy. One of the ways of measuring the significance of an ill is by its impact on living beings.

Blame

We tend to assume that most people in the world are relatively honest and caring and would not intentionally allow an ill to exist. We do not want people to die while waiting for a transplant. But why, then, do we allow people to die when most of us could donate a kidney or sign a donor registration card? Although we may attempt to avoid ills and strive to overcome them, we continue to allow significant ills to exist. We allow thousands to go without needed transplant surgery. We allow people to starve in other parts of the world even while many nations have enough food to feed them. The United States has a tax system that is viewed by many as privileging the wealthy at the expense of the middle class and indigent. Why do we allow such ills to continue?

The stock issue of blame helps explain why people are unable to resolve or diminish ills. Put simply, *blame is the attribution of an ill to causes within the present policy system*. Blame points to the person, people, or agencies responsible for the ill. For the ill to be corrected, the blame must be removed. If the blame for Jessica and Nora's lack of money is lack of jobs, then they must find good summer jobs to provide them with income and to alleviate the ill. If Food and Drug Administration rules are written in a way that encourages animal testing, then they must be rewritten to overcome the ills associated with animal testing. If the legal prohibition for selling organs is the cause of an organ shortage, then we should make sales legal.

Structural Blame

There are two types of blame that act as barriers to resolving ill: structural and attitudinal. *A structural blame is the result of a defect that is an integral part of the nature of the current policy system.*[24] Understanding a structural blame requires understanding a structure. *Structures are the fixed elements or features of a policy system.* Examples of structural elements of policy systems are laws, contracts, treaties, rules, and orders. Taken as a whole, structures reflect the formally accepted rules governing our society and political system. Such structures are "fixed" because they can be removed only by means of formal action taken to replace them with other structures.

In 1896, for instance, the issue of racial discrimination was brought before the Supreme Court, and it ruled in *Plessy v. Ferguson* that separate-but-equal facilities did not discriminate. Consequently, separate white and African American lavatories, schools, and restaurants were seen as fair and just, so long as the facilities were provided equally. In 1954, however, over the issue of equal educational opportunity, the case of *Brown v. Board of Education* was brought before the Supreme Court. This case charged that because of the separate-but-equal rule established in *Plessy*, an ill of educational discrimination existed and African American students were unfairly deprived of educational opportunities. The Supreme Court found for Brown on the grounds that separate was inherently unequal.[25] The Court noted, "We conclude that in the field of public education the doctrine of separate but equal has no place. Separate educational facilities are inherently unequal."[26] The blame for our inability to provide equal educational opportunity was attributed to a fixed structure—the Supreme Court decision in *Plessy v. Ferguson*. To correct the problem of discrimination, the decision had to be overturned—the structure had to be removed.

Attitudinal Blame

A second type of blame is attitudinal. *Attitudinal blame arises from people's beliefs and values, rather than from a law or some other structure of the present system.* Typically, we assume that good people would not allow unnecessary evils to exist. However, if an ill is allowed to exist because of prevailing beliefs or value hierarchies, then an attitudinal blame has been identified. In Box 8.1, the list of myths compiled by the Mayo Clinic provided a good list of attitudes preventing people from donating organs. One concern was that organ donation might be prohibited by religion. Another was the fear that doctors would not expend much effort to save the life of a donor. These, among the other myths, are all attitudes that inhibit actions.

Attitudinal problems may contribute to the continuance of defective structures or failure to adequately support good structures within the system. For example, people smoke even though they know smoking will damage their health and may eventually kill them. The blame does not rest in some law or structure forcing them to smoke; rather, it rests in their attitudes toward smoking. Similarly, although the United States adopted civil rights legislation in 1964, attitudes continue to perpetuate *de facto* segregation in some regions.

Cure

Being able to isolate and attribute blame for a given ill is not particularly useful unless the advocate has some way of resolving the problem. This is the role of cure. Cure is the third stock issue for policy cases and is the one Nora asked for when she said she heard that jobs in Alaska were difficult to get. *Cure demonstrates that some course of action can work to solve the ill.* In other words, if Jessica and Nora go to Alaska, will they find jobs? If we legalize organ sales, will lives be saved? How much of the ill does it cure? How can we change attitudes about donating organs? If it is legal to sell organs, will attitudes still result in too few organs available for transplant? If we mandate desegregation in the schools, do we alleviate discrimination? How much of the ill can the policy action cure?

Plan

Cures consist of two parts: a plan and its effect on the ill. *A plan is the specific program advocated in support of the proposition.* Examples include Jessica's plan to work in Alaska and the government's plan to allow students of many races to attend the same schools to overcome segregation. When advocates specify direct and definite courses of action, they are specifying plans of action.

Plans can be very detailed or very simple. Almost any legislation passed by Congress, from the budget to foreign assistance programs, involves extremely detailed plans that specify almost every action associated with the legislation. These plans can often take many volumes and thousands of pages to describe. On the other hand, Jessica's plan for Nora and her to work in Alaska is very simple and informal. Unlike congressional legislation, her plan is not a law or a contract; it is simply an agreement between two friends to take a particular action to alleviate an ill.

Solvency

Having a plan, however, does not mean it will work. When the U.S. government passed legislation to provide incentives for the production of biofuels based on corn, the hope was that it would alleviate rising fuel prices. The effect was that fuel prices stayed high and the cost of food, particularly corn-based food, rose rapidly. Jessica says working in Alaska will give her enough money to stay in school, but she needs to advance arguments to prove her claim that her plan will work.

This is the role of solvency. *Solvency is the argument that the plan of action can significantly solve or cure the ill.* In other words, what effect does the plan have on the ill? Too often, people assume that if a plan is designed to address an ill, it will automatically work. For example, busing was designed to alleviate the ill of school segregation, but it didn't entirely work. Aside from creating its own myriad problems, the plan in many cases did little to reduce segregated neighborhoods, differences in socioeconomic status, or any of the other variables that contribute to and perpetuate segregation.

Solvency, then, is the argument presented about the relative effectiveness of a plan. If the plan worked a little, is that preferable to nothing? The problem that remained beyond the structure of segregation was the attitude of segregation. Although integration of public schools following *Brown* promoted racial accord in some areas of the United States, in other areas it did not. If the plan cannot overcome prejudiced attitudes, then the ability of the plan to solve the ill is diminished because the social system will seek to undermine it.

Cost-Benefits

Recognizing that policies are adopted within a larger system is an important step in understanding cost. Whenever a system is changed, the entire system changes for both good and bad. Chemotherapy, for instance, can cure cancer and save lives. At the same time, it also can make a person sick and experience significant adverse health consequences. The question is whether the cost of the change outweighs the benefits. *The stock issue of cost refers to the problems or disadvantages associated with taking a policy action.* The assumption is a simple one: For any action we take, we give up or pass by other actions or cause systemic changes that may not be beneficial. Therefore, the issue of cost asks, "What are the negative consequences of this action?"

If Nora and Jessica decide to go to Alaska, their costs might be giving up social activities and friends at home, or they may get homesick. School districts that were forced by *Brown* to bus students to other districts in order to decrease segregation had to spend money on transporting those students instead of on instruction. Students also had to leave their neighborhoods and spend time being bused to schools farther from their homes. If we legalize organ sales, will that put undue pressure on people to sell organs? All of these are consequences or costs of a policy action.

Benefits are the positive consequences of policy action. There are many examples of how enacting a policy will result in positive outcomes.[27] For example, busing can provide greater cultural diversity in the classroom. Students can have an educational opportunity that is superior on average because of a greater mix of teachers, students, and facilities. The worth of the benefits depends on the value structure. How much value do we place on the benefits, and how much value do we place on the cost? If integrating the U.S. educational system is a highly placed value, then the benefits of busing in some areas might outweigh the associated costs.

Cost and benefits are interrelated. When we make decisions, we examine both sides of the system and consider the cost and benefits of competing system alternatives. On the one hand, we look at the cost and benefits associated with the present system. On the other hand, we look at the cost and benefits associated with the proposed system. Whichever system has the greatest net benefits will, presumably, be the system we support. Cost and benefits act as a fulcrum on which policy decisions are weighed. Arguers use this fulcrum to decide which system is most beneficial.

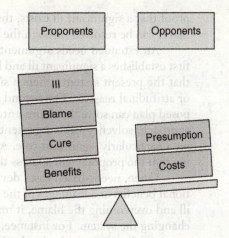

FIGURE 8.4   Cost-Benefit Fulcrum

Figure 8.4, "Cost-Benefit Fulcrum," illustrates this principle. Supporting a policy proposition requires that the net effect of the plan is to outweigh the costs that are incurred through systemic change. Additionally, advocates must overcome the presumption held by the *status quo*. Provided that the arguments in favor of the policy change have greater significance than the arguments opposed to the change, the policy should be adopted. Policy advocates have several options for demonstrating the plan is superior to the existing system. Two of these approaches, "Needs-Analysis" and "Comparative Advantages," are discussed in the following section.

Approaches for Arguing Policies

As observed previously, policy advocacy may occur in many settings—conversations, discussions, debates, editorials, and so on. The advocate may have extended time for speaking and presenting a case, or may have only intermittent speaking times and may have to develop a policy argument in several sections at different times. The situation may have an effect on how the policy argument is developed, structured, and presented. Regardless of situational constraints, policy advocates persuade their audiences that the benefits of their proposal outweigh its cost by showing the consequences of action and inaction through the development of extended arguments. There are two commonly used approaches to developing policy cases: needs-analysis and comparative advantages.

Needs-Analysis Approach

On occasion, an advocate will find a problem that is caused by a defect in the current system that can be resolved. When such is the case, a needs case is appropriate. *A needs-analysis case claims that the ill existing in the current system cannot be corrected within the present system, but can be cured by the advocate's policy proposal.*[28] Needs arguments are very common in persuasive speeches as well as in more extended debates because the format and requirements for the argument are simple and straightforward. All that is required of an advocate is proof that a significant ill exists, that it is caused by some feature of the present system, and that it can be resolved through the proposed plan.

An extended needs argument is developed in two distinct clusters of arguments. The first establishes a significant ill and blame. The ill and blame are developed together to reveal that the present system suffers a significant problem that cannot be resolved for structural or attitudinal reasons. The second cluster presents a plan of action and proves that the proposed plan can solve the ill presented. Because of the importance of the plan of action in this approach, solvency—the arguments supporting the plan's ability to diminish the ill—takes on a particularly significant role. Are there specific and compelling arguments demonstrating that the proposal will address the need?

Often, needs-based cases develop a third cluster of arguments that focus on the additional benefits or advantages of the plan. Although the plan achieves benefits by reducing the ill and overcoming the blame, it may also have additional advantages generated by virtue of changing the system. For instance, busing students will have the effect of curing (at least in part) racially segregated schools. This functions as a benefit. However, there are additional benefits that are not related to the ill or the blame but occur as a natural consequence of changing the system. For instance, beyond integration, students will have the advantage of learning about other cultures and customs and preparing to live and work in a diverse society. These "spin-off" advantages add to the desirability of the plan, although they are not necessarily related to the ill as identified.

The emphasis with the needs-based organizational pattern is how well the plan can cure the ill. The stock issue of cost-benefits is not readily apparent in this format. Although the opposing side might argue about specific costs, the benefits in the case are inherent in the plan's ability to cure the ill. This means that if the case is true, then the benefits will be realized when the plan works and the significance of the ill is diminished and a blame is removed. An outline for this type of case can be found in Box 8.9, "Needs-Analysis Case Developed and Opposed."

Box 8.10, "The United States Should Allow the Sale of Human Organs," illustrates how the policy stock issues can be used to create a basic outline for a needs-based organ donation case. A problem exists (not enough organs) that has a potential solution (allowing the sale of organs on the open market). The important feature of this argument is that the plan must cure the ill and the blame. If the ills cannot be cured, then the plan is irrelevant. While this might seem obvious, advocates often offer plans that only partly solve a problem or only partly overcome the blame. In such cases, the need is only partially satisfied, and the significance of the case is reduced. We will revisit this case in the next chapter to explore the opponent's refutation of the case.

It is important to note in this issues brief that we have outlined only claims. Each of these claims is part of an argument, and the advocates on both sides of the proposition would need to produce supporting arguments, reasons, and evidence to prove their claims are true. Also, there are many other possible arguments in support of the claims. Advocates may choose as many or as few as they perceive are necessary to support the proposition and persuade the recipients. The viability of a needs case rests on the advocate's ability to correctly identify an ill within the present system, to locate the features within the present system that cause the ill, and to remove the deficiencies in the present system through a plan that will work. In other words, the needs analysis

■ ■ ■ ■ ■

BOX 8.9
NEEDS-ANALYSIS CASE DEVELOPED AND OPPOSED

I. There is a need for a new system.
   A. There are significant ills.
   B. The present system is to blame.
II. There is a plan that can solve the problem.
   A. This plan will resolve the ill.
      1. What agent should act?
      2. What mandate should be given to the agent?
   B. This plan will have solve the ill.
III. In addition to solving the ill, the following benefits/advantages will accrue. (optional)
   A. Advantage 1
   B. Advantage 2

I. There is no need for a new system.
   A. The ills are insignificant or do not exist.
   B. The present system is capable of handling any ills should they arise.
II. The plan should not be adopted.
   A. The plan is unneeded or won't work.
      1. This agent is incapable or unqualified to act.
      2. This mandate won't work to cure the ill.
   B. Even if this plan worked, it cannot cure the ill.
III. This plan will receive no benefits.
   A. Benefit 1 won't come true.
      1. The benefit is exaggerated.
      2. The plan of action does not get this benefit.
   B. Benefit 2 won't come true.
IV. The case will accrue many costs.
   A. Cost 1
   B. Cost 2

rests on the premise that the present system has important defects that contribute to a significant ill. The needs approach offers a clear analysis of each stock issue and presents beneficial alternatives for the present policy system. The focus of a needs case is that the current system is unsatisfactory and the best solution is to adopt the advocate's course of action.

Because the needs case seeks to replace the current structure, an arguer should use it when the ill is particularly significant and can clearly be cured through an alternative to the current system. Needs cases must overcome a greater presumption than other types of cases because they present a new system that seeks to replace the old system. Therefore, the evidence and reasoning supporting the cure (that the plan will solve the ill) is particularly important. This means that the role of the opponent is to cast as much doubt on the proposal as possible. Unless the benefits of the plan (through curing the ill as well as additional benefits) are sufficient to overcome the risk inherent in changing systems, the case will probably not be adopted by the audience. We will spend more time discussing refutation of the needs case in the next chapter.

Needs arguments are based on the premise that the current system is a failure because it has been either unwilling or unable to redress a significant ill. On occasion, however, the present system is attempting to address a problem or is addressing a problem in a way that, in the advocate's view, is inappropriate. Such situations may require the use of alternative

▪ ▪ ▪ ▪ ▪ ▪

BOX 8.10

THE UNITED STATES SHOULD ALLOW THE SALE OF HUMAN ORGANS

I. The need for organs far outweighs the supply. (ill)
   A. There are over 100,000 people on the transplant list in the United States.
   B. There are fewer than 30,000 transplant operations in the United States each year because of the lack of donated organs.

II. Current efforts are not adequate to solve the problem. (blame)
   A. Irrational fears related to myths about donating organs keep many people from being donors. (attitudinal)
   B. Current federal laws prohibit the sale of human organs. (structural)

III. Allowing for the regulated sale of organs will eliminate the problem.
   A. The National Organ Transplant Act should be modified to allow for the regulated sale of human organs. (plan)
   B. Allowing compensation for donation will increase the number of donors and close the gap between supply and demand. (solvency)

IV. The advantages to this action are tremendous. (benefits)
   A. We have the potential to save thousands of lives each year.
   B. Because people will be allowed to openly buy and sell organs, the illicit and unsafe market for organ donation will be shut down.
   C. People can make extra money by selling unneeded organs.

I. While there is indeed a gap between supply and demand in the United States, each year the number of donors increases.
   A. The number of registered donors has increased to 94.7 million, a 36 percent increase between 2007 and 2010.[29]

II. Current efforts are adequate to solve the problem.
   A. Many people have religious objections to donation, and these beliefs should be respected.
   B. Current federal laws exist to protect donors and recipients from exploitation.
   C. Current education programs are working to increase the number of donors and should be left alone.

III. The proposed cure will not solve the problem.
   A. If there are so many people who fear or are against donation, then even allowing payment for organs is unlikely to close the gap between supply and demand.
   B. There may be a small increase in kidney donors, but there is still likely to be a shortage of other organs.

IV. The costs associated with the plan outweigh the benefits.
   A. The most vulnerable will potentially be exploited.
   B. The new policy will create a two-tiered system in which the rich will be more likely to receive transplants.
   C. There could be pressure on families to end life-support in order to sell organs while they are still viable.

argument formats. One alternate approach to presenting and supporting policy propositions is the comparative advantages case. Although other approaches are possible, this approach is commonly used and widely adaptable for many different situations. How it is used in policy argument will depend on the nature of the topic being discussed and the situation in which the argument is made.

Comparative-Advantages Approach

Often, there are problems that have no clear-cut or easy solutions. Sometimes, the present system is already attempting to cure the ill, and there is no obvious deficiency in the way the system is dealing with a problem. In such cases, an advocate may want to argue for a new system that is superior to the present system. The case argument that is developed compares the advantages and disadvantages of two competing system alternatives and, hence, is called a comparative advantages case.

The comparative advantages argument develops the position that in comparison with the current system, the proposed system has more benefits. Instead of isolating a problem and offering a cure (as with the needs case) the focus of a comparative advantages argument is to argue that the advocate's proposal is comparatively stronger or more beneficial than the current system.

In a comparative advantages argument, the ways stock issues are developed differs from a needs argument. This is because comparative advantage cases are grounded in a systems approach to propositions. For instance, in a needs argument, the ill was a harm that the current system could not cure. But if the present system has already identified the problem and is trying to cure it, then such an analysis would be redundant because both sides would agree that such an ill exists. For example, there is probably agreement that discrimination exists and that school segregation is bad. The present system is already attempting to solve the problem through mandatory busing and other programs designed to integrate education. An advocate wanting to reduce racial discrimination would probably not have to prove that discrimination is bad because the current system already embraces that view. With a comparative advantages case, however, the advocate would argue that there are more effective ways to reach a goal and address problems than those in the present system. With school busing, then, the advocate might claim that there are better ways to achieve equal educational opportunity than busing. In a comparative advantages case, the ill is interpreted as inadequacies in existing plans and policies. The blame in such an argument rests on the way the current system seeks to cure the ill; the cure is the alternative.

Costs and benefits become especially important arguments in comparative advantage cases. Whereas the needs case proved benefits by alleviating the ill, in a comparative advantages case, the advocate makes the argument that there are many benefits associated with the proposed system and costs associated with the current system. Comparative advantages cases seek to be accepted because they are, on balance, better than the current system. This approach does not attempt to identify a single ill or set of ills or their causes; rather it emphasizes the policy proposed and its effects in comparison to the present system.[30] This means that even if the proposal is not perfect and cannot entirely remove the blame or cure the ill, it is *comparatively* better than the present policy system.

A comparative advantages case fulfills its burden of proof by successfully arguing that the proposed plan is an improvement over the present system and can be favorably compared with other competing systems. To understand how this works, consider a conversation between two college roommates, Creston and Eric.

Creston: I think it is time to move off campus. I hate living in the dorms and I hate eating cafeteria food. In general, I hate living on campus. So many freshmen, so much noise.

Eric: Yes, but living on campus has many benefits. If we move into an apartment, who will cook our meals? Who will clean the bathrooms? Who will we socialize with? It seems to me that what we are doing now is the best alternative.

Creston: You're wrong. Look at it this way—if we move off campus, we will save a lot of money. In fact, I figure that our housing cost will drop by about a third. Besides, the freedom to come and go without worrying about dorm rules and regulations far outweighs any reason to stay in the dorms. Besides, I like the idea of just having time to get away from campus and relax.

Eric: Well, I hadn't thought of it like that. I especially hadn't thought about the cost savings, and I suspect that between you and me, we can cook better than the cafeteria. Let's move!

In this conversation, Creston develops a comparative advantages argument. Both Creston and Eric want a comfortable place to live, they want to save money, and they want freedom. But Creston points out that living off campus will achieve these ends better than living in the dorm. Even though the present policy system, living in dorm rooms, was not bad *per se*, changing policy systems, living off campus, produced more net benefits than net costs.

Consider the issue of nuclear energy in the United States and world. Currently, the United States has nuclear power plants and licenses have been issued to build new plants. Some advocates of nuclear power argue that the U.S. government should do more to encourage the construction of new nuclear plants in an effort to decrease our consumption of other sources of energy, such as fossil fuels. Opponents stress safety issues and problems related to nuclear waste disposal. The case study that opens Chapter 10 outlines many of these issues.

A comparative advantage case on this issue would contrast what is currently being done with what could be done—it compares alternative systems. An advocate would not need to argue that the United States and world have large needs for energy because proponents and opponents alike would agree on that point. Instead, nuclear power advocates would focus their analysis of the ill on deficiencies in the present system. The blame, then, becomes the reason why the present system is unable to remedy its own ill, and the cure is the proof that the alternative will overcome the systemic defects identified in the ill and blame. The policy proposition, "The United States should increase its commitment to nuclear power," is outlined in Box 8.11, "Comparative Advantages Case."

Box 8.12, "Apply the Theory," provides you with an opportunity to use the concepts developed here to design a needs-based and comparative advantages case.

BOX 8.11

COMPARATIVE ADVANTAGES CASE

Proposition: The United States should increase its commitment to nuclear power.

I. *Plan:* The United States should allow the immediate construction of new nuclear power plants.

   A. *Agent: Who should act?* The U.S. Congress should act to ensure new plants are built.

   B. *Mandate: What action should be taken?*

      1. Congress should immediately issue permits for construction to qualified applicants.

      2. Congress should increase loan guarantees to companies constructing new plants.

II. *Benefit 1:* The construction of new nuclear power plants will decrease our dependence on foreign sources of energy.

   A. The scope and effectiveness of the present system is limited *(ill)*. We currently import 58 percent of our oil, much of which comes from countries which have geopolitical problems.

   B. The present system cannot remedy the problem. *(blame)*

      1. The U.S. permit system is slow—it takes years for companies to obtain the proper permits to build.

      2. The financial risks associated with building new plants are too high; companies need loan guarantees to begin building.

   C. With new nuclear power plants, we can decrease imports of foreign oil. *(solvency)*

III. *Benefit 2:* The construction of new nuclear power plants will decrease our dependence on fossil fuels.

   A. Fossil fuels contribute to global warming. *(ill)*

   B. There are not enough nuclear power plants to significantly decrease fossil fuel consumption. *(blame)*

   C. Increasing the number of nuclear power plants will allow us to decrease our reliance on fossil fuels. *(solvency)*

Direct Refutation

I. *Refutation of Benefit I:*

   A. There is no harm to importing foreign oil. (refutes ill)

   B. The United States is currently increasing domestic sources of energy production, including oil and natural gas. (refutes ill)

   C. The permit system is slow to ensure that safety requirements are met. (refutes blame)

   D. Nuclear power plants will take years to come online, which means we won't see any benefit for many years. (refutes solvency)

II. *Refutation of Benefit II:*

   A. We are currently decreasing our consumption of fossil fuels in the United States. Other nations are increasing their dependence while ours decreases. (refutes the ill)

   B. There are many programs in place to decrease global warming in the US. (refutes ill)

   C. While other countries are increasing their use of fossil fuels, there can be no solving the global warming crisis.

      1. Additionally, the time frame for getting the nuclear power plants built is too long—it will be many years before they come online which means there will be no meaningful decrease in fossil fuel consumption in the near-term.

■ ■ ■ ■ ■

BOX 8.12

APPLY THE THEORY: DEVELOPING POLICY CASES

The last section of this chapter considered how policy proposition cases are designed and constructed. The chapter focused on the stock issues for policy debate (Ill, Blame, Cure, and Cost-Benefits) and then suggested two strategic approaches for creating an issues brief. Using Box 7.1, design a needs-based and comparative advantages case using the proposition "Parents should be allowed to select the biological sex of their children." Consider the following questions:

1. Is this better presented as a needs-based or a comparative advantages case? Why?
2. What kinds of issues lend themselves best to each of these formats?

As you worked through writing each type of case, did you notice how the role of solvency changes? With a needs-based case, the plan must solve for the ill and overcome the blame. The plan becomes a stand-alone feature of the policy system. With a comparative advantages case, the plan and, therefore, its solvency are relative to the strengths and weaknesses of the current system.

SUMMARY

This chapter focused on constructing extended cases of fact, value, and policy cases. We began with a discussion of how to develop an issues brief that draws on the issues map developed in the last chapter. The issues brief is a way of examining the arguments for and against a proposition. It provides a way for advocates to learn about and understand contrasting points of view about propositions, which is central to the process of developing critical thought.

Before listeners are likely to accept extended argument cases as *prima facie*, an advocate must adequately prove the stock issues. The stock issues vary by each type of proposition. For fact-based propositions, there are three stock issues—definition, threshold, and application. The stock issue of definition describes the major fact elements of the proposition. It focuses on what the end point of the case will be by offering a clear and concise definition of the terms in the proposition. The stock issue of threshold establishes the limits, or parameters, for the definitions. Threshold is intended to provide a clear way of distinguishing between what is included and excluded by the definitions. Finally, the stock issue of application is the argument that the phenomenon or example under consideration meets the requirements of definition and threshold.

With value-based arguments, advocates must begin by identifying their orientation toward a value object. A value object is an idea, practice, event, policy, or state of affairs that has to be measured in an evaluation. To successfully support a value proposition, the value advocate must address the stock issues of value, criteria, and application. How should the value be defined? What criteria or standards should be applied to determine whether the value object fulfills the desired values? Finally, does the value object in fact meet the standards that have been proposed by the advocate?

With policy propositions, there are four stock issues: ill, blame, cure, and cost-benefits. The ill is a current wrong or harm associated with the present system that the advocate is trying to resolve. The blame is the attribution of the ill to some deficiency in the present system, and blame may be both structural and attitudinal. The cure demonstrates that some course of action can work to solve the ill, and it consists of a plan of action and its effects. The cost is the problems or disadvantages associated with taking an action, and the benefits are the positive consequences of action.

When an advocate constructs an extended policy argument these issues must be addressed. However, depending on situational variables of audience and proposition, the advocate may choose to focus on different aspects of the proposition. We offered two different case construction strategies for arguing in favor of policy propositions discussed in this chapter: needs-based and comparative advantages. A needs-based case maintains that the current system is unsatisfactory and that the best solution is to adopt a new system to replace the defective one. The comparative advantages approach argues that the proposed system can achieve greater advantages than the current system.

Finally, it is important to remember that audiences expect advocates to prove certain sets of issues—we referred to them as stock issues. Failure to prove even one of the stock issues means that the case is not *prima facie*. As we will discuss in the next chapter, if an opponent disproves any of the stock issues, the case fails to meet its minimum burden of proof and should not be accepted.

EXERCISES

Exercise 1: *Identification.* First, identify whether each of the following is a proposition of fact, value, or policy. Next, construct an issues brief for each proposition. For the purpose of this exercise, the issues brief need contain only the claims that one might expect an arguer to make.

*1. Third-party candidates cause diversity in the political process.

2. The welfare system makes people not want to work.

*3. Leif Eriksson discovered America.

4. The Social Security system will be bankrupt in twenty years.

5. Censorship of music with violent lyrics is desirable.

6. Legal physician-assisted suicide is desirable.

7. Increased access to online courses would benefit students.

8. Physician-assisted suicide should be legalized.

*9. The United States should ban the sale of all tobacco products.

10. The United States should abolish the death penalty.

Exercise 2: *Case Outline.* For each of the following policy propositions, outline a needs case or a comparative-advantages case.

1. Proposition: I should buy a new car.

2. Proposition: I should live with my parents until I have established myself in a career.

3. Proposition: The federal government should provide more student financial aid.

*4. Proposition: I should attend a different school.

Exercise 3: Scramble. Below is a set of scrambled claims supporting the proposition "The federal government should legalize the sale, possession, and use of marijuana." Some claims could be used to outline an extended argument using needs analysis, and some could be selected to construct a comparative-advantages case. Organize the scrambled statements to make up a needs-analysis case and a comparative-advantages case. Note that some of the statements will be used in both cases, while some will be used only once.

1. A benefit of regulating marijuana will be to decrease the youth smoking problem.

2. A great deal of money is wasted enforcing present laws; hundreds of millions of dollars are spent, and only 10 percent of marijuana is confiscated.

3. Funds will no longer be spent needlessly enforcing an unenforceable law.

4. The plan will be financed by reallocating money presently spent for marijuana control.

5. There is a significant need to change marijuana laws in this country.

6. Legalization of marijuana will be beneficial.

7. One-fourth of all marijuana users are under the age of seventeen.

8. Marijuana sale and consumption will be regulated by the Food and Drug Administration.

9. Harmful substances such as paraquat will be eliminated, protecting consumers.

10. The possession, sale, and use of marijuana will be legalized.

11. Experts estimate that marijuana regulation will prevent a significant percentage of the 10 million underage smokers from trying marijuana.

12. These problems are caused by present marijuana laws that are vaguely worded and inconsistently enforced.

13. Monitoring and regulating the sale of marijuana is the only way to decrease youth consumption.

14. Some of the illegally sold marijuana contains paraquat, which causes physiological damage.

15. Young people will no longer be affected by marijuana and its harmful side effects.

16. The following plan of action should be adopted.

17. Decreasing usage has significant beneficial effects.

NOTES

1. A valuable resource for reading and reviewing contemporary topics that are used in competitive academic debate can be found at *Debatepedia* at http://idebate.org. This conversation was adapted from *Debatepedia* contributors, and can be found online at http://idebate.org/debatabase/debates/health/house-would-legalize-sale-human-organs (accessed June 21, 2012).

2. Peggy Saari, "Medicine and Disease: When Did the First Heart Transplant Take Place?" *History Fact Finder*, Julie L. Carnagie, ed. UXL-GALE, 2001, eNotes.com., 2006,http://www.enotes.com/history-fact-finder/medicine-disease/when-did-first-heart-transplant-take-place (accessed May 29, 2008); and American Heart Association, "Organ Donation," http://www.americanheart.org/presenter.jhtml?identifier=4697 (accessed May 29, 2008).

3. Jo Revill, "The Right Patients for a Face Transplant is Out There Today," guardian.co.uc, October 29, 2006, at http://www.guardian.co.uk/science/2006/oct/29/medicineandhealth.theobserver (accessed June 7, 2012).

4. "Understanding Donation Statistics," *Website of Donate America*, at http://donatelife.net/understanding-donation/statistics/ (accessed June 21, 2012).

5. "Living Donors, the Gift of Life," *Website of Johns Hopkins Comprehensive Transplant Center*, at http://www.hopkinsmedicine.org/transplant/living_donors/index.html (accessed June 21, 2012).

6. "Living Donors, the Gift of Life."

7. United Network for Organ Sharing, at http://www.unos.org/ (accessed June 21, 2012).

8. "Understanding Donation Statistics."

9. Mayo Clinic, "Organ donation: Don't let these 10 myths confuse you," at http://www.mayoclinic.com/health/organ-donation/FL00077 (accessed June 4, 2012).

10. http://www.economist.com/node/12380981

11. Alex Tabarrok, "Meat Market," *The Wall Street Journal*, January 8, 2010, at http://online.wsj.com/article/SB10001424052748703481004574646233272990474.html#MARK (accessed June 21, 2012); see also Steve Hensley, "Iran Sets Innovative Example For Organ Donation," *NPR*, January 11, 2010, at http://www.npr.org/blogs/health/2010/01/iran_leads_in_innovation_on_or.html?ft=1&f=103537970 (accessed June 21, 2012).

12. Denis Campbell and Nicola Davison, "Illegal Kidney Trade Booms as New Organ is 'Sold Every Hour'," *The Guardian*, May 27, 2012, at http://www.guardian.co.uk/world/2012/may/27/kidney-trade-illegal-operations-who (accessed June 21, 2012).

13. Campbell and Davison.

14. Campbell and Davison.

15. Brian Handwerk, "Organ Shortage Fuels Illicit Trade in Human Parts," *National Geographic*, May 29, 2008, http://news.nationalgeographic.com/news/2004/01/0116_040116_EXPLorgantraffic.html (accessed June 7, 2012).

16. Kaitlin Warner, "Philosophy Professor Makes the Case for Mandatory Organ Procurement," *Vox Magazine*, March 11, 2010, http://www.voxmagazine.com/stories/2010/03/11/organ-donation/ (accessed June 21, 2012).

17. The stock issues suggested here are taken from Paul W. Taylor, *Normative Discourse* (Englewood Cliffs: Prentice-Hall, 1961), 14–103. An earlier version of this explanation appeared in Barbara Warnick, "Arguing Value Propositions," *Journal of the American Forensic Association* 18 (1981): 109–119.

18. Richard W. Paul and Gerald M. Nosich, "A Model for the National Assessment of Higher Order Thinking," in A. J. A. Binker, ed., *Critical Thinking; What Every Person Needs to Survive in a Rapidly Changing World* (Santa Rosa, Calif.: Foundation for Critical Thinking, 1992), 101.

19. http://www.merriam-webster.com/dictionary/desirable (accessed June 12, 2012).

20. http://www.merriam-webster.com/dictionary/desirable (accessed June 12, 2012).

21. Jerome R. Corsi, "The Continuing Evolution of Policy System Debate: An Assessment and Look Ahead," *Journal of the American Forensic Association* 22 (1986): 158.

22. Loyd F. Bitzer, "The Rhetorical Situation," *Philosophy and Rhetoric* 1 (1968): 4

23. William L. Benoit, Steve R. Wilson, and Vincent F. Follert, "Decision Rules for the Policy Metaphor," *Journal of the American Forensic Association* 22 (1986): 141.

24. Austin J. Freeley, *Argumentation and Debate: Critical Thinking for Reasoned Decision Making*, 8th ed. (Belmont, Calif.: Wadsworth, 1993), 196–199.

25. Richard Kluger, *Simple Justice: The History of* Brown v. Board of Education *and Black America's Struggle for Equality* (New York: Vintage Books, 1975), 781–782.

26. *Brown, et al. v. Board of Education* 347 U.S. 483 (1954).

27. Many authorities have examined the nature of policy benefits and advantages. For more information, see Russel R. Windes and Arthur Hastings, *Argumentation and Advocacy* (New York: Random House, 1965), 229.

28. Freeley, 215.

29. http://donatelife.net/number-of-registered-organ-eye-tissue-donors-continues-to-rise/

30. W. Scott Nobles, "Analyzing the Proposition," in *Decision by Debate*, 2nd ed. Douglas Ehninger and Wayne Brockriede, eds. (New York: Harper and Row, 1978), 169.

CHAPTER NINE

REFUTATION

CHAPTER OUTLINE

SKILLS AND TECHNIQUES
Approaches
Techniques
   Exploratory Refutation
   Expose Contradictions and Inconsistencies
   Apply Tests of Evidence
   Apply Tests of Reasoning
   Develop Counterarguments
Listening
Four-Step Refutation
STRATEGIES
Fact-Based Cases

Value-Based Cases
Policy-Based Cases
   Defense of the Status Quo
   Defense of the Status Quo with Minor
     Repairs
   Counterproposals
   Disadvantages
   Critiques
SUMMARY
EXERCISES

KEY CONCEPTS

Active listening (p. 263)
Bargaining refutation (p. 260)
Burden of rejoinder (p. 258)
Case-level refutation (p. 259)
Competitive listening (p. 263)
Constructive refutation (p. 259)
Counter advocacy (p. 260)
Counterproposal (p. 273)
Critique (p. 274)

Defense of the present
  system (p. 271)
Direct refutation (p. 259)
Disadvantage (p. 273)
Exploratory refutation (p. 260)
Four-step refutation (p. 264)
Minor repairs (p. 272)
Passive listening (p. 264)
Refutation (p. 257)

When advocates interact with recipients and present arguments designed to change beliefs, attitudes, and behaviors, they also face counterarguments from those who support alternative views. This makes sense, of course, because propositions represent challenge and change as we discussed in Chapter 4. An extended case supporting a proposition, then, challenges the comfort and predictability of the *status quo*. The result is that those who support the present system will tend to develop arguments against the extended case for the proposition.

And, even those who think change should happen may offer arguments for an alternative direction. These are the roles of refutation. *Refutation is the process of responding to someone's argument by revealing weaknesses in it or by presenting counterarguments.*

In contexts in which extended cases are presented such as courts of law, legislative hearings, and political debates, responding to arguments is appropriate and necessary. In Box 9.1, "The Case Against Human Organ Sales," Laura and Phil came up with objections

---

BOX 9.1

THE CASE AGAINST HUMAN ORGAN SALES

In Chapter 8, we explored the arguments in support of selling human organs on the open market. Box 8.1 outlined many of the issues related to this controversy. The conversation highlighted several issues including the need for more donors and a thriving illicit market in human organs. While there is strong evidence pointing to the need for more human organs, there remain many questions about whether a policy allowing them to be sold on the open market would solve the shortage of organs in the status quo, what the costs and disadvantages associated with such a proposal would be, and even what value assumptions underpin the discussion of such a policy. In the discussion below, Laura and Phil discuss some of the issue.

Laura: I realize that we have a shortage of organs, and that this means many people die waiting for organs, but we need to consider the implications for the poor. They can be easily exploited for the sale of their organs, which would be an abuse of their basic human dignity. I think there's a really good chance that allowing the sale of human organs would end up creating a market that benefits only the wealthy and the powerful. And what about families who might be pressured to stop medical treatment of loved ones so that organs can be harvested?

Phil: It does seem like allowing organs to be sold on the open market privileges the rich over the poor, unless there were some very strict controls over it. But what really bothers me is that this assumes that people can claim ownership over body parts of the deceased. This objectification of the human body has serious implications for society.

Laura: I've heard some compare selling organs to selling blood plasma or sperm, but I think there are more ethical and safety issues to be considered with organ selling. For one thing, transplants are much riskier than donating blood plasma or donating sperm. The safety factors and risks of the surgery make the market for organs more dangerous. And the scarcity of organs in comparison to sperm or blood means that the costs would be much higher.

Phil: We certainly should try to find a way to increase the number of donors in the United States, but we have to think about the ethical implications of selling organs. The issue is much larger than getting paid to save a life. It's not the right way to solve the problem.

Laura: I agree, it seems like a better policy might be to crack down on the illicit market while finding nonmonetary ways to compensate those willing to donate, such as health care credits, or help with funeral expenses for families who donate the organs of deceased loved ones.

(continued)

BOX 9.1   CONTINUED

Laura and Phil have raised some serious objections to the arguments in favor of allowing human organs to be sold on the open market. Consider the following questions:

1. What questions of fact and value are suggested by the discussion?
2. What arguments do you think would be most effective in refuting the idea of allowing human organs to be sold on the open market?
3. Can you think of any other objections, issues, or questions you could raise to oppose the sale of human organs?
4. If you were going to do a presentation on this topic, how would you organize it?
5. What alternatives to allowing the sale of human organs are suggested by the discussion? Can you think of any others?

---

to the policy proposal of allowing the sale of human organs. However, they needed to carefully consider variables such as the situation and audience before they will be ready to present their responses in an extended, opposing case.

Too often we attempt to respond to arguments without having undertaken the necessary preparation. The skilled critical thinker, as we have been discussing, will begin by carefully considering the argument situation, the needs of the recipients, and the goals of the argumentation process. Recall that the issues map, introduced in Chapter 7, is a neutral exploration of the issues that exist within the propositional arena. A thorough issues map will assist the arguer in considering the values, attitudes, and beliefs of the recipients of argument. It will also guide the arguer toward an understanding of the argument potential—what outcomes are possible, and what resources or information the audience will need to achieve the best outcomes.

In Chapter 8, we developed the issues brief as a way of looking at how extended cases can be built around core, stock issues and we offered some strategies for designing arguments favoring the proposition. As part of our discussion we showed how opponents might respond to extended cases. This chapter explores the refutation process and will pick up on those themes and consider how arguers can make strategic and persuasive choices to respond to cases. Only when the advocates have an in-depth understanding of the issues in the propositional arena should they begin to choose a refutation strategy. We begin, though, with a discussion of the principal skills and techniques advocates can use to refute extended cases.

SKILLS AND TECHNIQUES

Advocates for change have the burden of proof. Arguers fulfill their burden of proof through the creation of extended cases that are *prima facie*—arguments that present good and sufficient reasons to accept a proposition. We discussed these requirements in Chapter 8. Just as advocates favoring a proposition have certain responsibilities, so do opponents. Opponents have a burden of rejoinder. *The burden of rejoinder is the requirement that those who oppose a proposal respond reasonably to the issues presented by the original advocate.* For example, in a murder case, the prosecution has the burden to prove beyond a reasonable doubt that the defendant committed the crime. The defense has a burden of rejoinder to refute the arguments presented by the prosecution. And, the defendant has the presumption of innocence until the burden of proof has been met by the state. Meeting the burden of rejoinder means that the arguer must engage systematically in refutation of an opponent's case.

Approaches

Advocates have several broad approaches available to them for refuting cases. Generally, though, these can be classified into four groups: direct refutation, constructive, case-level, and bargaining. These are detailed in Box 9.2, "Refutation Approaches." Each approach is designed to achieve a different outcome. The simplest, direct refutation, seeks to respond directly to the arguments developed in the extended case. *Direct refutation is an approach that is designed to argue and disprove at least one of the stock issues in the proposal.* With direct refutation, opponents focus on disproving one or more of the stock issues. If opponents successfully argue against any of the stock issues, the case can be rejected because it is no longer *prima facie. Constructive refutation also focuses on specific arguments but suggests that while the argument in the case may be true, comparatively there are better ways of looking at the issue.*

Case-level refutation is more complex. It *focuses on the case as a whole and considers the overall implications of the proposition.* Case-level refutation can be designed in three ways: direct refutation, counter advocacy, or a combination of the two. Direct refutation systematically addresses an extended case by refuting the claims as well as subclaims. When using direct refutation, advocates refute the claim and then synthesize these individual responses into

■ ■ ■ ■ ■

BOX 9.2
REFUTATION APPROACHES

APPROACH	GOAL	EXAMPLE
Direct	Oppose particular arguments to diminish the case and, ideally, disprove at least one of the stock issues	The arguments about organ shortages are vastly overstated
Constructive	Offers comparative arguments demonstrating the proposition is not the best alternative	This case focuses on a narrow set of issues and when we look at organ donation overall we find that on balance the current system is superior
Case-Level	Oppose the entire extended case holistically	Allowing the sale of organs is immoral and should never be considered
Bargaining	Seeks a compromise or middle ground	While there are insufficient organs available currently, there are ways to modify the existing system to overcome the problems identified

a rationale for rejecting the extended argument. *Counter advocacy involves offering alternative values or policies to be weighed in comparison with the original arguments.* Counter advocacy reflects real-life decision-making in which various alternative proposals compete with one another. Refuting through counter advocacy, however, means that the arguer, like the initial advocate, assumes a burden of proof to support and defend the counterproposal.

The most commonly used method of refutation is a combination of direct refutation and counter advocacy in which the opponent responds to the arguments made by the other person while offering an alternative proposal. For instance, when an arguer supports allowing the sale of human organs, counter advocacy might focus on changing to a system of presumed consent as a better solution to the organ shortage rather than allowing the sale of human organs.

Finally, bargaining works to combine some features of the initial case with counter arguments that oppose the proposition. *With bargaining refutation, the goal is to find a "middle ground" or mutually acceptable strategy for managing the issues within the proposition.* While this approach may well make sense with a co-orientational view of argument, the argument situation determines its appropriateness. For instance, in working toward the best way for the U.S. Congress to balance a federal budget, it makes sense to compromise and work together. The decision to build or not build a nuclear reactor, however, may find compromise more difficult. The same is true of the death penalty or abortion. Certain issues such as right to life draw on deep-seated values and beliefs that make a bargaining approach unproductive and inappropriate.

Effective refutation shifts the burden of proof back to the original advocate—the idea is that whomever makes a claim has a responsibility for proving it. Refutation is not something that just one side or one person engages in. All of the parties involved in a particular argument situation can use the strategies outlined below to respond to others' arguments. This counter-refutation should also include the additional step of defending the original argument or position presented.

Techniques

Once arguers decide on a particular approach or set of approaches for refuting an extended case, they have many specific techniques available to them. Box 9.3, "Five General Refutation Techniques," includes a repertoire of techniques that can be used to address extended case arguments in a reasonable and directed approach. In extended debates, skilled arguers can use a variety of these argumentative tactics in combination to examine cases from multiple points of view and provide meaningful critiques and analysis.

Exploratory Refutation

Exploratory refutation involves asking questions or raising objections designed to cause opponents to take a stand on issues an advocate hopes to refute. Exploratory refutation is intended to expose potential areas for argument. In response to the organ argument, one might ask the following:

Who will pay donors for their organs?

How can you ensure that this will not simply allow the highest bidder to obtain available organs?

BOX 9.3

FIVE GENERAL REFUTATION STRATEGIES

STRATEGY	DEFINITION	EXAMPLE
Exploratory Refutation	Asking questions or raising objections designed to clarify an advocate's position and supporting evidence and reasoning.	Who will pay donors for their organs? Is there any evidence that suggests paying for organs will actually increase the number of donors?
Expose Contradictions and Inconsistencies	Examining arguments for incompatibilities or discrepancies that weaken or diminish the position.	You made the argument that the lack of donors is due to the beliefs and attitudes that people hold about organ donation. Yet the plan offered provides no way of changing those attitudes and beliefs.
Apply Tests of Evidence	Using the tests of evidence described in Chapter 5 to weaken or diminish the arguments.	You cited testimony from a people on the waitlist for transplants who are in favor of allowing the sale of human organs, but these people have a clear interest in opening up this market, and may be incapable of fairly considering the risks involved. They may not have the best interest of the most vulnerable in mind.
Apply Tests of Reasoning	Using the tests of reasoning developed in Chapter 6 to undermine and weaken the connections made in the argument between evidence and claim.	You argue from reciprocity that because it is morally acceptable to sell blood plasma and sperm, it should be acceptable to sell human organs. However, unlike human organs, blood and sperm can be regenerated and can be given with very little risk to the donor.
Constructive Refutation	Presenting counterevidence and counterarguments to be weighed against the arguments being refuted.	Allowing the sale of human organs is not the answer. We can diminish the shortage of organs by continuing to educate people about the importance of being registered donors, and institute programs such as those requiring students to be informed about donor programs during driver's education in order to continue to increase the number of donors.

Did you provide any evidence that allowing the sale of organs on the open market will actually lead to more people donating?

Exploratory refutation is most effective when opposing advocates take the time to pursue and examine weak arguments and responses. How much time arguers have to develop exploratory refutation depends on the field and the specific situation. Conversations with friends or classmates, legislative hearings, court cases, and many types of debates allow for at least some time to ask questions to clarify arguments. If arguers know ahead of time that there will be a question period, they should prepare questions with the following goals in mind: clarify; get advocates to commit to a particular position; expose weaknesses in arguments; and set up arguments that can be made in response.

Some questions can accomplish more than one of these goals. For example, if arguing about sale of human organs, asking how the organs will be paid for is important to clarify whether individuals, health care providers, or the government will be responsible for the costs associated with the proposal. The question of how costs will be covered will also set up future arguments about the potential negative effects of covering these costs. If the health care system is expected to pay for organs, there could be potential arguments related to the increased costs being passed on to the public. If the recipient pays, that opens the door for arguments about the potential for abuse. And if the government pays, the opponent can make arguments related to increased taxes and government spending.

Expose Contradictions and Inconsistencies

A second effective refutation process is to note contradictions or inconsistencies in the arguments. Although it is factually accurate to argue that there is a big gap between the supply and demand for organs, is it true that paying people to donate will increase the supply? The argument could be refuted if one could show that the existing attitudes and fears related to donating will not be overcome by simply offering money to potential donors. The analysis of the attitudinal blame by the advocate could then be shown to be inconsistent with their claim that selling organs on the open market will solve the shortage, since nothing new will be done to educate potential donors about the realities of donating organs.

Apply Tests of Evidence

Arguers can apply the tests of evidence described in Chapter 5 to the extended case evidence. Evidence may be biased, outdated, irrelevant, inexpert, inconsistent, unreliable, inaccurate, or inaccessible. Most often, critiquing evidence may not be as strong as countering the entire argument; it can effectively diminish the strength of an advocate's claim. For instance, one could argue that transplant recipients and those on the waiting lists for organs are incapable of providing testimony free from bias. Their inherent interest in having more organs available may make it difficult to carefully consider the potentially negative impacts on those who might be at risk of exploitation from such a policy. Another test of evidence is asking whether the source is reliable. Since virtually anyone can publish on the Internet, we should consider carefully the qualifications of the evidence presented.

Apply Tests of Reasoning

Advocates can also apply the tests of reasoning discussed in Chapter 6. Advocates should look for weak and inadequate reasoning. Refutation may focus on analogies comparing dissimilar phenomena; generalizations based on non-representative samples; or *post hoc* relationships mistaken for causal relationships. Recall from Chapter 6 that quasilogical arguments from reciprocity reasons that two things that can be put into the same category should be treated the same.

The argument that "we allow the sale of blood plasma and sperm, and even human eggs, thus we should allow the sale of organs" uses this pattern of reasoning. Yet there are a couple of big differences between human organs given from live donors and blood, sperm, and human eggs. First, the body regenerates blood and sperm; once they are given the body can make more. Human eggs do not regenerate, but women are born with many millions of them, and if they are not used the body discards them. Second, the risks associated with donating blood and sperm are extremely low, and even donating eggs is low risk compared to giving up a major organ. Thus, one could argue that the two are not symmetrical enough to be treated the same, and that different standards are appropriate.

Develop Counterarguments

With counterarguments, advocates present counterevidence and counterclaims to be weighed against the arguments being refuted. Opponents of allowing the sale of human organs might argue that this policy will have serious negative consequences such as the exploitation of the most vulnerable in society, the costs associated with paying all donors, and the potential loss in altruism related to requiring payment for the act of donating. A strong argument to go along with those arguments would be to support current efforts at education, and point out that these efforts have produced a great increase in the number of donors over the last several years. Some have called for increased education efforts, such as requiring mandatory discussion of organ donation during driver's training. Since most donor registries are tied to drivers' licenses, some have argued that informing about this requirement during driver's education will increase the number of registered donors.

The experience of preparing refutations of others' arguments and of anticipating others' refutations of arguments can contribute substantially to the development of critical-thinking abilities. Often, arguments seem quite strong and airtight until skeptics oppose them. By carefully considering objections that might be raised against arguments, advocates can improve their reasoning and become more discriminating in their use of evidence.

Listening

One of the most important skills arguers must master is the art of listening carefully to what others say—both in preparation and in presentation of arguments. Arguers should listen actively before developing and presenting a response. *Active listening means to hear for meaning.* Arguers should listen to *how* something is said as much as to *what* is said. They should endeavor to understand the meaning of the message as the speaker intended it.[1] Active listening is different from other types of listening.[2] It is not an easy skill to master and involves careful concentration and reflective questions, but it is important.

Active listening is preferred because it helps advocates understanding the context for argument beyond what is said. There are two other types of listening that can impede a recipient's ability to truly understand the meaning of a message. *Competitive listening is characterized by advocates who are more interested in winning an argument or a particular position rather than understanding other viewpoints.* Academic debate, legislative assemblies, and political debates are all contexts in which competitive listening can dominate. Competitive listeners focus on coming up with responses, often at the expense of reaching a thorough understanding of the others' argument. *Passive listening involves hearing other points of view but does not verify or affirm understanding.* This means that arguers and recipients hear arguments and then respond to what they heard, assuming that they correctly understood the intentions and meaning behind what was said. Active listening focuses on hearing *and* verifying the meaning so that there is a common understanding of the argument.

Active and accurate listening to arguments is essential—but it is not easy. Active listening requires the hearer to engage, focus, and attend the messages. The tone, strength, and emotions behind arguments can reveal agendas, needs, or fears. Constructive argument moves speakers beyond exclusive reliance on understanding logical arguments and toward adaptive and flexible understandings that allow arguers to be sensitive to the issues of culture, ethics, occasion, and situation. Constructive argumentation assumes that the feelings and contexts behind arguments can be as important as the arguments themselves. Box 9.4, "Apply the Theory," is designed to help sharpen the skill of active and engaged listening.

Four-Step Refutation

Once and arguer has listened carefully to an extended case, has asked questions as appropriate of the advocate, and decided how to approach the proposition, the arguer begins a process of refutation. The goal with this process is to provide the hearers with a clearly developed response to the argument they have heard and construct a path that supports an opposing narrative. This process is called four-step refutation. *Four-step refutation is named for its form that unfolds in four steps from address to effect.* Figure 9.1, "Four-Step Refutation," illustrates this process.

Four-step refutation begins with an address. What is the specific claim made in the extended case that is being refuted? For instance, if an extended case develops claims about banning nuclear energy, an address might be, "I would like to talk about the claim that says nuclear energy is the most dangerous form of energy known to humankind." The goal is to help recipients clearly understand what issues and arguments are being discussed—much like a physical address, this type of address points hearers to a part of the extended case.

FIGURE 9.1   Four-Step Refutation

BOX 9.4

APPLY THE THEORY: SHARPENING ACTIVE LISTING SKILLS

There are many books and journal articles that focus on developing active listening skills.[3] The Department of State, for instance, identified four specific rules for active listening:

1. Seek to understand before you can be understood.
2. Do not make judgments about what you are hearing until you have heard it.
3. Give your undivided attention to the arguer.
4. Use silence effectively to process ideas and understand the situation.

Generally, the research on active listening recommends the following:

1. *Reduce distractions.* This may sound obvious, but busy rooms, background noise, or even environmental distractions such as wind or rain can interfere with our ability to accurately hear or remain focused on what the speaker is saying.
2. *Be present to the speaker.* This means that hearers should face the speaker, maintain eye contact, and focus on the speaker as well as the message. Being focused on writing text messages or scanning written materials are all ways in which we disengage from a speaker.
3. *Respond appropriately.* Even though hearers are listening and not speaking, it is important that they communicate their interest and engagement to the speaker. Nodding and leaning a little forward are ways to express interest and engagement.
4. *Focus on the message.* Remember that the message is more than simply the words. It is reflected on how the speaker looks, interacts with their hearers, and the words they choose. Hearers should avoid thinking of their own arguments, rather work to understand all of the message.
5. *Wait to respond.* Hearers sometimes want to respond to an argument immediately and as soon as it is said. They may interrupt the speaker or become fixated on a particular point while losing the rest of the meaning and message. Wait for the speaker to finish making their argument before responding.
6. *Avoid overlaying.* Sometimes, as a speaker is trying to make a point, it is tempting to interject how we might have handled a similar experience by overlaying our own examples, background, and history. When we do that, we make an assumption that the speaker's point, background, and ideas are the same as ours. This gets in the way of our understanding a speaker's message.
7. *Ask constructive questions.* Active listening is more than simply being polite. It is intended to help you fully understand the arguments presented. It is important, therefore, to be able to ask questions that help you fully understand the messages. For instance, you might ask:
   a. What did you do to accomplish….?
   b. How did you prepare for….?
   c. What happened next?
   d. Was anyone else involved?
   e. What were your main goals?
   f. What do you think will happen next?

Using these principles, select a case study from one of the chapters in the text. Have a partner read the study, listen actively, and then ask questions that will help you better understand the deeper meanings and ideas in the text. Then, reverse roles and read a case study to your partner.

Second, an advocate should provide a clear counterclaim such as, "My research demonstrates clearly that nuclear energy is safer than oil and coal based energy production." Here, the goal is to provide contrast for the recipients—one point of view compared with another. Third, the counterclaim needs to be supported with evidence as with any other type of claim. And, finally, the arguer needs to discuss the effect. The effect is essentially the "impact" of the counterargument. How does this compare to what the extended case says? It might be as simple as saying, "Therefore, as you can see from the evidence provided, nuclear energy—even if not perfectly safe—is considerably safer than the alternatives." Essentially, this step is a reasoning step that brings the parts of the counterargument together. Box 9.5, "Apply the Theory," offers an opportunity to work through the four-step process.

BOX 9.5
APPLY THE THEORY: FOUR-STEP REFUTATION

If you have the opportunity to engage in refutation, you will want to ensure that you deliver your arguments in a way that is easy for your recipients to follow. Four-step refutation is a systematic way to ensure that you clearly and thoroughly develop and articulate your arguments.

Step 1: Address.   Make sure that you are clear about what claim in the extended case you are refuting. Four-step refutation begins when you clearly identify the point that you are about to refute. This is a way of sign-posting for your audience what argument you are about to address. *Example: My opponent claims that cats make better pets than dogs.*

Step 2: Response.   State your own claim that refutes the argument you identified in Step 1. *Example: I would argue that dogs are actually the best pets, much better than cats.*

Step 3: Support.   Develop your argument using evidence or analysis. Explain what reasoning or information provides support for the claim stated in Step 2. *Example: Dogs will protect their owners and their owner's property, they can be easily trained, and they like to be around their owners. Cats are aloof, will not alert you to danger, and are difficult to train.*

Step 4: Effect.   In this final step, tell the audience and your opponent what your refutation means. Depending on context, this may simply be providing a summary of your refutation. This could also involve explaining how this particular argument affects the overall case being discussed or debated. *Example: Therefore, it is clear to see that it is untrue that cats make better pets than dogs.*

With a partner, take turns making simple claims for the other person to refute using four-step refutation. You can begin with the claims below:

Star Wars: Episode IV is the best science fiction movie ever made.

Grades for courses should be abolished.

The United States should eliminate the penny.

Vegetarianism is the best choice of a diet.

There should be a special tax on foods high in sugar and fat.

STRATEGIES

In Chapter 8, we described how extended cases could be built based on an issues map and the stock issues inherent to the proposition. And, just as there are broad, strategic approaches for designing cases supporting each proposition type, there are broad strategic approaches for opposing them. This section describes the kinds of strategic choices an advocate might make. It is important to remember that the techniques described in the previous section work well with all of these strategies.

Fact-Based Cases

Though it is often assumed that facts and statistics are simply true, there are many facts about which people disagree. Is nuclear power a safe source of energy? Will allowing unfettered access to sex selection technologies lead to a gender imbalance? Would allowing the sale of human organs result in an end to the shortage of organs? The answers to these fact-based questions vary depending on the way the issues are defined and interpreted. When an advocate creates extended cases for fact propositions, there are three stock issues that must be addressed: definition, threshold, and application.

A starting point for refuting any extended case is to examine the arguments presented by the advocate to support each stock issue to decide which makes the most sense to refute. Opponents can begin by considering the strength of presumption—how much do the recipients believe the central question of the extended case? In other words, what existing attitudes and beliefs does the audience have about the issue, and how can those be used to persuade them to oppose the proposition?

If the fact advocate has created a *prima facie* case, then the facts will have been defined and the threshold for the definitions articulated. If the opponent agrees with the definitions, there is no need to refute this stock issue. If, however, the definitions seem unreasonable, they should be challenged. Since fact propositions should be about proving statements of historic fact, causal relationships, and predictive facts, the definition used should be provable. Consider a fact-based proposition that "Allowing for organ compensation will put an end to the shortage of most organs." This proposition is a predictive fact claim, and to prove that it is true there must be some discussion about what "an end to the shortage of most organs" means. If the advocate's definition only includes ending the need for kidneys, the opponent might object such a limited threshold by pointing out the fact that there are many people on the transplant wait list for organs other than kidneys.

The third stock issue for fact-based cases is application. With the application the advocate will try to prove that the example or phenomenon under investigation meets the definition and threshold. While the opponent might agree that the definition and threshold provided by the advocate are acceptable, whether the case under consideration actually meets the definition is a matter of interpretation of the empirical facts. Opponents can argue that the fact definition and threshold are not supported by the application. For example, in the organ donation case the advocate provided evidence that Iran had eliminated its wait list for kidneys by allowing the sale of organs on the open market. Opponents should point out that this example does not prove that the need for all other organs has been met or dramatically decreased. Recall that the fact claim says that allowing compensation would "result in an elimination of the need for most organs." The Iran example does not prove the statement true.

Finally, opponents can introduce additional facts that could shed a new or different light on the situation and call for a new interpretation of the evidence, and ultimately disprove the fact claim. For example, the opponent might provide evidence that reveals many people have strong attitudes that preclude them from becoming voluntary donors and argue that the advocate has provided no information indicating that compensation would change those attitudes. Thus, a policy of compensation would not eliminate the need for most organs since it does nothing to address existing attitudes.

Value-Based Cases

The stock issues for extended value cases include value, criteria, and application. When refuting a value proposition, a good starting point is assessing the beliefs and attitudes of the audience. Opponents of value propositions should seek a good understanding of how the audience presently views the value object and whether the advocate has characterized the value hierarchy appropriately. In Chapter 8 we explored principles for constructing value-based cases. Recall that terminal values should be viewed as more significant than instrumental values, that the needs of the particular situation should be primary, and that value hierarchies exist which can be used to support value preferences. These principles apply to refutation of value cases, as well.

The first stock issue of value involves defining the value object and setting up the value hierarchy. In Box 8.5, we developed a case in support of the proposition "Allowing compensation for human organ donation is desirable." In that argument, the value object was compensation for organ donation. Opponents may choose to accept or to challenge the definition of the value object. If the terms are defined fairly and accurately, then there is no need for refutation. If not, opponents should challenge the definition of the value object and provide justification for why the audience should accept the alternative definitions.

The second component of the stock issue of value is value hierarchy, or the ranking of values favored by the advocate. There are two strategies for challenging value hierarchies, which can be used independently or together. The first option is to challenge the hierarchy by arguing it has not been adequately justified by the advocate—selecting the appropriate value hierarchy requires a clear argument. The second option is to present an alternative hierarchy with reasons it is more appropriate than the one that has already been presented. To challenge the hierarchy presented, arguers must show that the claims and evidence used to support it were questionable.

For example, if supporters of allowing compensation for organ donation argued that Americans place a high value on autonomy and the free market, their opponents could respond appealing to popular opinion does not demonstrate for this particular case that the argument is reasonable. Just because many people believe something does not make it correct. In Chapter 11 we will talk about errors in argument and inappropriate claims as fallacies when we discuss issues of responsibility. This type of argument is an example of a fallacy. For instance, many Americans favored school segregation at one time, but it was not morally "right." Perhaps the values currently ranked highly by most Americans reflect excessive self-interest and ought not to be the ones most valued. And while many would agree that the power of the free market is a fundamental part of America, not all would agree that it is the most important value in all situations.

If opponents choose to present their own value hierarchies, their goal, as with the other advocates, is to persuade the recipients that the alternative hierarchy is more desirable and appropriate in the given situation. In Chapter 8 we outlined some particular hierarchies that seem to be widely accepted in Western society, including the hierarchies of quantity, quality, the existent, essence, and the person. These five hierarchies can be used to strengthen the audience's adherence to the core values at the top of their hierarchy.

Opponents should carefully consider the criteria presented by the advocate. Criteria are standards that help illuminate whether the value object fulfills the particular values set up in the value hierarchy. Criteria are the measures or rules that will be used to judge whatever is being evaluated. Opponents have two options when addressing the criteria. First, they may choose to present arguments that show the value object does not meet or measure up to the criteria. Opponents may also choose to argue that the criteria are inappropriate measures for the particular situation, in which case they might choose to present alternative criteria. For example, there might be sphere- or field-specific standards that are more appropriate than those offered by the advocate. If so, what are they and why are they more appropriate?

For example, in the debate about compensating organ donors, opponents could argue that social ethics should be the field for evaluation rather than a measure that only considers what is desirable for the individual. On a societal level, alternative standards might come into play, and the opponent might argue that the poor, the weak, and the old should be protected, that life (the highest value) should be preserved, and conclude that only the lives of those with the means to buy what they need are valued if we endorse compensating organ donors.

An example of appropriate alternative criteria for the organ donation debate was developed by a professor of philosophy, Debra Satz, in her book *Why Some Things Should not be for Sale: The Moral Limits of Markets*.[4] The book outlined criteria for evaluating the ethical limits of the free market, including the trade of human organs. Applying these criteria, one could argue that although the market might be efficient (meaning there would indeed be people willing to buy and sell organs, and we might even eliminate the waiting list for kidneys), that does not mean it is desirable. Instead, we should prioritize political and ethical considerations, or what Satz calls the "noxious" levels of the market. This can be measured, according to Satz, by examining whether those affected might be without access to adequate information, might be vulnerable to exploitation by the market, and whether there are negative outcomes for society or individuals. Selecting criteria from field experts strengthens the arguments and provides opponents with a legitimate argument as to why an alternative is better.

The final stock issue is the application of the application. Recall that with the issue of criteria, advocates will have argued that the value object meets the standards for fulfilling the values in question. This is where factual information and experience can be used for evidence. Supporters for allowing financial incentives for organ donation should be able to show that these types of incentives encourage giving and thus save lives, or meet the criteria for being "desirable." The extent to which the criteria apply and the number of people affected by the criteria are both significant here. How many patients are in need of organ transplants? What proportion of these patients is likely to actually get the needed organs if we allow financial incentives for donation? If the proportion is small or there is likely to few people donating organs, the advocates' argument may lack significance. Opponents can use factual information to disprove the significance of the proposition. For example, if opponents can provide credible evidence that there will be very few lives saved, while at the same time there is potential for many to be exploited, then opponents will have proven that the advocate has not met their own criteria, and thus the proposition must be judged negatively.

Policy-Based Cases

There are many approaches that can be used to support policy proposals, as we discussed in Chapter 8; there are also many options for opposing them. When faced with a policy proposal, one strategy is the use of direct refutation discussed earlier. In using a direct refutation approach to a proposal, opponents argue against one of the stock issues of ill, blame, cure, and cost-benefits. Direct refutation does not require opponents to support any current or proposed policy system, only to argue against the one presented. Essentially, with direct refutation, the advocate takes the position, "I am not going to defend any policy system, but I will challenge everything my opponent has said and show the case to be insufficiently proven by undermining at least one stock issue."

Fundamentally, arguers using this strategy take advantage of the issue of presumption. Because audiences are naturally predisposed to favor the current, known policy system, arguers using direct refutation simply must show that the policy proponents have failed to fulfill their burden of proof on one or more stock issues to show that the proposed plan should not be adopted.

Arguers using the strategy of direct refutation generally parallel the case they oppose in organization and argumentation. If the case presents significant ills, the advocate claims that these ills are caused by certain attitudes or structures, that a certain plan will correct the ills, and that it will produce certain benefits; then the person using direct refutation would attempt to show that the ills do not exist or are insignificant, that the causes for them have been misidentified, that the proposed plan is flawed and unworkable, that it will not correct the ill, and that the claimed benefits will not be produced. Since opponents only need to prove that one of the stock issues has not been adequately addressed to show that the case is not *prima facie*, every stock issue does not need to be refuted with this strategy.

Direct refutation presents a clear counterargument for each of the significant arguments developed by advocates for the proposition. Minimally, the responders need to disprove any one of the stock issues because, in doing so, one of the elements of a *prima facie* case is disproved. Notice too that beyond simply answering the case argument, an opponent would also describe the costs associated with a system change. Since it is difficult to deny that there are many more people waiting for organs than there are donors, opponents may not want to spend time refuting the ills of the case. However, opponents could find considerable evidence supporting the claim that proposed plan to allow the sale of human organs would not solve the problem (refuting solvency) and that such a policy would have negative consequences much larger than any benefit (costs). An additional example of a case using direct refutation can be seen in Box 8.11, which outlines arguments against the comparative advantage case, "The United States should increase its commitment to nuclear power."

Beyond direct refutation, opponents may employ broad strategies that respond to the case and proposition as a whole. These strategies include defense of present policy system, minor repairs, counterproposals, disadvantages, and critiques. The remainder of this section will describe each of these options and illustrate how each can be used to oppose policy cases. Though we will describe these strategies individually, they are not mutually exclusive, and often when combined they create the strongest overall strategy for refutation of a policy case.

Defense of the *Status Quo*

When advocates elect to defend the present policy system; they commit themselves to the argument that the present system has greater systemic benefits than the proposal. *Defense of the present policy system rests on a comparison of the proposal and the present system, and argues that the present system is superior.* Opponents of a proposal who use this strategy take the position that "compared with the proposed alternative, the present system is more beneficial." Arguers using this approach focus primarily on the issues of ill and blame, and they argue that present structures and attitudes are sufficient to cure the ill identified in the proposal.

Defense of present policies can be very effective. As with the strategy of direct refutation, it parallels the organization of the extended case and seeks to disprove at least one of the stock issues. The difference between this approach and direct refutation is that the utility and benefits of the current system become arguments against the proposal. In a sense, what is good about the present system is a reason not to replace it.

Respondents defending the current policy system should be able to argue that the present system is adequate and that any deficiencies have been erroneously identified or exaggerated by those advocating change. After all, any change involves risk and may result in disadvantages that outweigh the supposed benefits of correcting an ill or problem. As with those who use direct refutation, advocates of present policies take advantage of the presumption in their favor. It is advisable to assume that most audiences would prefer to stay with known policies than to assume the risk of adopting an untested policy, unless the present policy is proven to be inadequate or problematic.

The case for banning sex selection technologies is a good example of a case in which not everyone would agree that there is an existing ill. In defending the current system, an opponent of the ban might argue that there is no gender imbalance in the United States, and that there is even evidence which indicates that when sex selection is used, it is split evenly between males and females. Thus, opponents might argue that the current system, which allows parents to use existing technologies to select the sex of the babies, is not flawed, and is more desirable than the alternative ban. However, defense of the present policy system is not always a suitable counterargument. For example, since it would be difficult to support the current system's inability to meet demand for organ transplants, this would probably not be a good case for using the strategy of defense of the present system.

Defending current policies requires arguers to support structures as they exist and currently function. When arguers choose to defend current policies, a commitment is made to adopt a consistent and systemic view of the argument. With direct refutation, any responsive argument could be made; with support of present policies, the answers should not contradict present policies. This approach should be used when the systemic benefits of the present system are greater than the benefits of the proposed system.

Defense of the *Status Quo* with Minor Repairs

Occasionally, people opposing policy proposals may recognize that the current policy, if left unaltered, cannot correct the ill or solve the problem. They believe, however, that if minor flaws such as inadequate funding, lack of information, or improper administration are corrected, the present policy could be made adequate. The premise of this strategy is that "the present system is basically fine, but it could be streamlined and improved with minor additions or changes that don't involve wholesale systemic changes." *The defense of present policies with minor repairs strategy offers small changes to existing policies to improve their effectiveness and efficiency in meeting the needs.*

Minor repairs are by definition minor. As such, they should not involve significant structural or attitudinal changes to the policies or their administration. To do so involves a fundamental change in the nature of the policy system and means that the arguer is no longer defending the present system, but is proposing a new and different system. Advocates using this strategy should defend the integrity of the present system. Offering minor repairs means that the essential characteristics of the present policy must remain intact.

The strategy of defending present policies with minor repairs focuses on the blame issue. If the respondent can prove that minor system changes can accomplish the same objective as the proposed case, there is no reason to act. The present system cannot be held accountable for shortcomings if it has the capacity to adapt to new challenges and ills. The minor-repairs approach argues for a flexible system. Often, what is needed is increased enforcement or funding of an existing policy, rather than structural change. There are also cases in which attitudes are to blame for existence of the ills, and increased education can solve the ills without major policy change. For example, when a group of college students advocated for a ban of smoking on their campus, opponents of the ban supported a minor repair of the existing policy. Advocates argued that exposure to second-hand smoke made their campus environment dangerous and unhealthy, and that the current policy, which banned smoking within 20 feet of buildings and on major walkways, was regularly violated. Opponents of the ban argued that with education and enforcement, the current policy was enough to ensure zero exposure to secondhand smoke. Since the policy in place already prohibited smoking in most areas, opponents were able to successfully argue that enforcement and education of current policies would eliminate the ills. Another way to argue using minor repairs might be to support reprioritizing funding so that the current structures are allowed to work. The system is not changed with a minor repair, just its implementation.

Defense of present policies with minor repairs is advisable when arguers believe the blame has been exaggerated and that the change proposed by the opponents is greater than what is needed to correct the ill. Making minor modifications in an existing policy, it can be argued, is less risky than implementing an entirely new policy system.

Counterproposals

The strategy of counterproposal argues that the alternative presented should supersede the proposed policy. Consequently, arguers presenting counterproposals develop extended cases independent of the original case argued. Opponents of allowing the sale of human organs, for example, might argue that changing to a system of presumed consent, a system in which people have to opt out of being donors upon their death, is a better way of achieving the same benefits of increasing the number of available organs. The counterproposal does not disagree with the needs or blame analysis presented in the original extended case. Instead, the argument centers only on the relative ability of the two systems to achieve the benefits. The argument becomes a comparison of two systems. If the counterproposal is better able to cure the ill and overcome the blame than the original proposal, then it should be accepted instead.

When should a counterproposal be used? A counterproposal does not enjoy the same presumption of strategies using present policies to ground them because counterproposals offer new plans of action. As with any new plan of action, there is risk involved with change. When advocates put forward a counterproposal, they assume the burden of proof to demonstrate that the proposed alternative policy system can cure the ill and blame better than the originally proposed system. Therefore, a counterproposal probably should be used only when there is consensus that something must be done about a problem, but there is disagreement about the nature or scope of the policy that will be necessary to correct it. It can be particularly effective when offered in conjunction with arguments about the significant costs and disadvantages of the initial proposal.

Disadvantages

In Chapter 8 we discussed the systems perspective as it applies to policy propositions, in which we recognize that when we change one part of a system, there can be widespread, sometimes unintended, consequences to other parts of the system. We referred to these as the costs or disadvantages associated with change. The disadvantage argument uses causal reasoning and the systems perspective to argue that there will be negative consequences to adopting the new proposal. *Disadvantages are the unintended negative consequences that could occur if the plan were put into effect.* Disadvantages can be articulated as part of the refutation of the stock issue of cost-benefits, or they can stand as their own argument independent from the advocate's case structure. The job of the opponent when arguing disadvantages is to show that any advantages or benefits which result from the successful implementation of the plan are outweighed by the disadvantages it causes, which are far worse than the present policy system.

The first step in arguing a disadvantage is to show a connection between the specific actions of the proposal and the disadvantage. Next, opponents argue that the negative consequences are uniquely caused by the plan offered by the advocate. In other words, opponents argue that with the proposal, serious consequences will occur. Finally, advocates should show what the specific impact of the disadvantage would be. This last step is similar to arguing significance for ills. How widespread will the disadvantage be? Who will be affected, and in what ways?

Students arguing against the smoking ban on their college campus employed the strategy of arguing disadvantages in addition to advocating minor repairs of the status quo policy. They pointed out that students, staff, and faculty who smoke will need to seek alternative places to smoke, since the average smoker will not be inclined to go the entire day without a cigarette. This particular college had a river running adjacent to its campus, and opponents argued that there would be a high likelihood smokers would end up smoking near it due to its proximity to campus.

Opponents argued there would be three negative impacts related to people smoking by the river. First, cigarette butts would be left on the ground and in the river, which would threaten the ecosystem and wildlife of the river. Second, since the river area has thick brush which is extremely dry for much of the year, these cigarette butts would be a fire hazard. Finally, opponents argued that smoking by the river would be a safety risk, particularly for women taking night classes, since there had been past cases of rape and robbery near river trails. Risks of ecosystem and wildlife damage, fires, and even rape, the students argued, were much worse than the *status quo*, in which a few students failed to adhere to smoking policies.

The arguments about the ecosystem and wildlife as well as the fire risk were shown to be particularly significant since they potentially affected the entire community, not just a few students. Coupling these disadvantages with the minor repair argument was a particularly strong strategy, since it offered those who believed there was an ill related to secondhand smoke on campus another way to deal with that problem without creating a risky situation for the entire community. Box 9.6, "Direct Refutation, Minor Repairs, and Disadvantage Arguments," provides an outline of what these strategies look like against the proposition "The university should ban smoking on campus."

Critiques

Part of the critical thinking cycle, which we described in Chapter 1, is the exploration of assumptions, biases, and the multiple points of view that affect how we understand and approach issues and ideas. Assumptions are the presuppositions and viewpoints that we take for granted. These assumptions are often so ingrained in our way of thinking that they frequently remain unknown or unexplored. However, as we discussed in the first chapter, if these assumptions are flawed, then the reasoning that stems from them can also be flawed. And, if we act on these assumptions as we often do when making policy decisions, there can be negative implications associated with extending those flawed assumptions. Testing and challenging assumptions are important ways to understand our thinking and help us to make clearer, better choices. Arguing critiques is a part of this process. A *critique is an objection to the philosophical assumptions that underpin the proposition or the specific plan being proposed.*

Sometimes when people object to policies, it is not that they disagree that there is an ill, or even that the proposal might solve those ills. Rather, an opponent may argue that the underlying assumptions of the proposition are flawed which, in turn, means that any proposal stemming from those assumption is also flawed and needs to be re-examined. Critiques are value arguments, though they can include discussions about the implications of adopting

■ ■ ■ ■ ■

BOX 9.6

DIRECT REFUTATION, MINOR REPAIR, AND DISADVANTAGE ARGUMENTS

Proposition: The University should ban smoking on campus.

I. Secondhand smoke exposure causes cancer and other illnesses.
   A. Exposure to secondhand smoke causes an estimated 49,000 deaths a year in America.[5]
   B. There are cigarette butts littered all over the campus.
II. The current policy forbids smoking on major walkways and within 20 feet of building entrances.
   A. This policy is regularly violated and there is no enforcement.
III. Banning smoking on campus would solve these problems.
   A. This university should ban smoking on campus.
      1. There should be no smoking areas.
      2. There will be a fine for violations.
      3. The policy will be enforced by campus police.
   B. Bans are less ambiguous and easier to enforce.
   C. Banning smoking on campus would eliminate the risk of exposure to secondhand smoke and cigarette butt litter.
IV. There will be the additional advantages.
   A. Smoking bans encourage smokers to quit.
   B. A smoking ban will discourage students from starting smoking.
   C. A smoke-free campus will encourage healthy lifestyles.

I. There is very little exposure to secondhand smoke when it is outside.
   A. Most studies on deaths from secondhand smoke were conducted on indoor air.
II. The current policy only needs minor repairs to solve the ills.
   A. The current policy should be enforced.
   B. Citations should be issued with enforcement.
   C. Fines would fund the increased personnel needed for enforcement and would discourage people from breaking the rules.
   D. There should be increased education about where smoking is allowed.
      1. Cigarette butt receptacles will be placed in these areas to discourage litter.
III. The disadvantages that will be worse than the potential advantages.
   A. Smokers will have to smoke off campus.
   B. Many will smoke near the river, since it is adjacent to campus.
   C. Since there are no cigarette receptacles, butts will be littered on the river bank.
   D. Litter on the river will get into waterways and potentially harm wildlife and the precious river ecosystem.
   E. There is a high risk of fire when the brush by the river is dry.
   F. Smoking off campus presents other risks.
      1. Areas such as those near the river are sparsely populated at night.
      2. There are cases of rape and robbery near the river.

policies that are grounded on the wrong assumptions. They are similar to the disadvantage arguments in that critiques can present negative consequences to adopting a particular proposal. But with critiques, the assumptions and not the specific plan action are what opponents argue about. For example, much of the debate about health care reform in the United States is at the value level and carries assumptions—about the question of whether health care is a basic human right that should be protected and guaranteed by the U.S. federal government. Assumptions about this question drive the way policies are designed, which, in turn, means the assumptions should be exposed and evaluated.

Some who oppose the sale of human organs do so based on the value assumptions underpinning policy proposals. When some people hear the idea, their first reaction is often revulsion at the notion of selling human body parts, whether from a living or deceased person. Usually, this reaction is not because people don't think organ donation is a good idea, or because they don't think that there is a great need of more donors. Instead, it's the underlying assumption that body parts can and should be considered objects which can be bought and sold on the open market that some people find reprehensible. As with the disadvantage argument, arguers must clearly articulate the impacts of the critique and not assume that what they find to be a faulty assumption will be seen as a flawed by the audience. Why is objectifying the human body bad? What are the negative impacts of allowing a policy with this underlying assumption to move forward?

One could also offer a critique of free market capitalism in general when opposing the sale of human organs, and argue that our assumption that markets can be used for things such as health care and education, and human body parts, leads to inequities, exploitation, and ultimately the devaluing of human life. During the global recession of 2008, a movement of people began to organize in protest of the policies that were implemented to help with the economic recovery. The Occupy Movement, as they were called, was essentially critiquing the assumptions that underpinned many economic policies. These policies, they claimed, prioritized large corporations and the wealthy while the many people worldwide were struggling to survive the high rates of unemployment and home foreclosures. Essentially, the Occupy Movement argued a critique that unless we stop making policies using flawed assumptions about capitalism, the United States and other countries will see even greater divisions between the rich and the poor, with more and more people living in poverty.

With both critiques and disadvantages, it is important to consider how the argument fits into the overall refutation strategy. Advocates must ensure that arguments do not contain contradictions or inconsistencies. If they argue a critique of the free market system, for example, it would be inconsistent and potentially even hypocritical to then offer a counterproposal that relies on free markets to achieve benefits.

The argument strategies for refutation presented in this section are not mutually exclusive. Nor do any of these broad strategic approaches preclude using direct refutation. Depending on the respondent's analysis of the proposal, it may be appropriate to use two or more of the strategies in combination. Each offers different options for the arguer, and each addresses different issues. The objective of the respondent is to provide an argument against adoption of the proposed policy system. As long as using multiple strategies do not lead the arguer to contradict his or her own arguments, a combination of approaches is useful.

SUMMARY

Once advocates have fulfilled the burden of proof and presented a satisfactory case for change, their opponents have the burden of rejoinder to respond reasonably to the issues raised in the case. In responding, opponents engage in refutation. Refutation is the process of discrediting someone's argument by revealing weaknesses in it or by presenting a counter-argument. Refutation can be divided into case-level (aimed at an opponent's case as a whole) or specific (aimed at individual arguments).

Arguers have several approaches available to them for designing their refutation strategy. For instance, arguers can use direct refutation in which they work to disprove at least one of the stock issues presented. Similarly, constructive refutation focuses on specific arguments but adds alternative ways of thinking about them. Case-level refutation, though, examines the extended argument as a whole and demonstrates that the case or the proposition, on balance, is insufficient. Finally, bargaining seeks a middle ground and works for common acceptable solutions. Arguers can choose among these approaches to find the best "fit" for the given argument situation.

There are five specific refutation techniques which are directed at individual arguments that can be used singly or in combination. First, arguers can use exploratory refutation; they can raise questions and objections to draw out their opponents and make them take positions on issues on which their opponents might be vulnerable. Second, they can note contradictions and inconsistencies in their opponents' case. Third, they can indict their opponents' evidence, showing it to be biased, outdated, irrelevant, inexpert, or unreliable. Fourth, refuters can attack reasoning by revealing fallacies and mistakes in their opponents' inferences. Fifth, advocates can produce arguments and evidence of their own that can be weighed against the arguments their opponents have made. Knowing these techniques of refutation and anticipated objections and criticism of one's own arguments can contribute substantially to critical-thinking ability and to the skills of advocacy.

The success of any of these approaches and techniques is contingent on effective listening and understanding of the arguments. Active listening means that the arguer is engaged in the conversation and strives to hear for meaning. This is opposed to competitive or passive listening, which can interfere with comprehension. Active listing is not easy; however, without it, important features of the arguments and the argument situation can be lost.

When arguers begin the process of refutation, they should engage in four-step refutation. This technique focuses on addressing the argument to the specific claims being refuted, presenting a clear counterclaim, proving the counterclaim, and presenting the effect or "impact" of the argument. Four-step refutation is an essential technique for keeping debates organized and focused.

Opponents of fact propositions should challenge one or more of the stock issue of definition, threshold, and application. They have the option of direct refutation of the issues alone or combined with offering counter definitions and thresholds. Opponents can question whether the phenomenon under consideration meets the definition and threshold and offer additional empirical evidence disproving the fact claim in the application portion of the case.

When opposing a value proposition, any of the stock issues of value, criteria, or application can be challenged. Opponents may challenge the value hierarchy offered and may offer their own, alternate hierarchy. The criteria can be challenged by showing that the value object does not meet the standards presented by the advocate, or on the grounds that a different sphere or field offers a more appropriate criteria. When challenging the application, opponents can argue the advocate's criteria do not apply, or refer to alternative criteria they have proposed and argue that applying those criteria better fulfills certain values.

This chapter also discussed strategies that can be used to oppose extended policy arguments: direct refutation of the stock issues, defense of present policies, defense of present policies with minor repairs, disadvantages, critiques, and counterproposals. The strategy should be aligned with the nature of the topic, the characteristics of the case to be opposed, and the beliefs and attitudes of the audience. The first strategy, direct refutation, does not involve defending any particular positions, but instead tests each of the significant arguments presented in the opponent's case. Defense of present policies, however, defends existing structures and proves that such structures are of greater utility and benefits than the plan of action proposed in the case. When existing policies have minor flaws that prevent them from functioning correctly, a respondent may offer a defense of present policies with minor repairs. The minor repairs are intended as modifications designed to overcome minor problems in existing policies. Disadvantages are the systemic consequences that would result if the proposal goes into effect. They are the costs associated with the proposal that are actually worse than the benefits associated with solving the problems identified by the advocate. Critiques present arguments that challenge the assumptions that ground the proposition or the proposal. They argue the assumptions are flawed and should thus be rejected. Finally, advocates may use counterproposals. Counterproposals are an effective strategy if the opponent's case fails to understand the nature of the problem or if the respondent has a better proposal for curing the problem. These strategies are not mutually exclusive, and an arguer may draw from multiple strategies to refute a policy case.

Taken as a whole, policy arguments are an important element in our daily lives. We decide whether or not to take action based on individual assessment of the cost and benefits derived from different extended policy arguments. This chapter was intended to help describe and systematize a process familiar to all of us and fundamental to the process of our decision making about facts, values, and policies.

EXERCISES

Exercise 1: Refutation. This chapter discussed different ways of refuting extended cases. First, we discussed strategies for refutation. These included the following:

- Case-level refutation, which is aimed at the entire case
- Specific refutation, which is aimed at individual arguments within the case

Second, we talked about styles of refutation, which included:

- Destructive refutation, which is aimed at tearing down the opponent's arguments
- Constructive refutation, which is aimed at offering alternatives through counterarguments
- Bargaining refutation, which attempts to provide a negotiated or compromise argument

Consider the following outlines, the first for a fact-based case argument and the second for a value-based case argument. Develop a refutation strategy for these cases:

CASE 1

Proposition: **Banning handguns saves lives**

CASE ARGUMENTS	REFUTATION

  I. Definitions
  A. Handguns are personal weapons.
  B. A ban would prohibit private ownership.

 II. Threshold
  A. We are talking about private guns, not guns owned by military or police.
  B. Handguns include any weapon that can be reasonably concealed on a person.

III. Application
  A. Thousands die each year from the intentional discharge of private concealed weapons.
  B. Countries that have banned handguns have been successful at saving lives.

---

*CASE 2

Proposition: **Euthanasia is desirable**

CASE ARGUMENTS	REFUTATION

  I. Value.

 II. A. Definition: Euthanasia can be defined as passive-withholding or removing life-support
     systems from moribund patients.
     1. "Life-support systems" include equipment that provides basic life functions—respiration,
        heartbeat, etc.—through artificial means.
     2. "Moribund" patients are people with no possibility of recovery who will die in the
        normal course of events.
     3. This definition is supported by etymology and the opinion of experts.

III. Hierarchy: Euthanasia preserves and promotes personal freedom, comfort, and self-respect.
     1. Freedom, comfort, and self-respect are three of the eight top-ranked values in Rokeach's
        value survey.
     2. Freedom of choice and dignity are the essence of what it means to be human.

IV. Criteria: To be beneficial, euthanasia should meet certain standards.
     A. Euthanasia should allow free choice concerning the manner and timing of a person's death.
     B. Euthanasia should pr edless suffering and futile prolongation of life.
     C. Euthanasia should prevent hardship for the families of terminally ill patients.

 V. Application: Euthanasia is beneficial and desirable.
     A. It preserves freedom and dignity of the individual.
     B. It ends patients' suffering.
     C. It gives families a say in patients' treatment decisions.
     D. Society's attitudes toward the preservation of life will be negatively affected.

Exercise 2: Following are two sets of scrambled claims for cases opposing legalization of marijuana. The first is a direct refutation opposing the needs-analysis case included in Exercise 3 from Chapter 8. The second set of statements develops a counterproposal. Unscramble the claims in each case, and construct an outline from them.

Direct Refutation

1. The plan to legalize marijuana won't work.
2. Two-thirds of high school seniors oppose marijuana use.
3. Reallocating present enforcement funds will not provide sufficient revenue to support the plan.
4. There is no need to change marijuana laws.
5. Young people who wish to experiment with marijuana will still be able to obtain it after it has been legalized.
6. Use among young people is decreasing.
7. Because marijuana is not physically or psychologically harmful or addictive, regulating its use will provide no benefits.
8. Funds spent on marijuana enforcement are insignificant; only 4 percent of drug arrests are for marijuana violations.
9. No benefits will result from the plan.
10. Paraquat is no longer used to destroy marijuana plants.
11. Personnel and funding to regulate and control marijuana distribution are unavailable.

Counterproposal

1. The counterproposal is a better proposal than legalization of marijuana.
2. It is true that there is a significant need to change marijuana laws.
3. Revenue collected from these fines will be given to law enforcement agencies for control of hard drugs.
4. Under decriminalization, we no longer need to use resources and time prosecuting people for a minor, victimless offense.
5. People found to possess marijuana in small amounts for personal use will be subject to minimal fines.
6. Decriminalization allows redirection of funds to areas in which enforcement is most needed.
7. Decriminalizing marijuana continues to indicate society's disapproval of substance abuse.
8. Instead of legalizing marijuana, we should decriminalize its use through following proposal.

Exercise 3: Opposing Cases. Consider two cases you constructed in Chpater 8. For each of them, construct an opposing case. Use a different opposing strategy for each of the propositions: direct refutation, defense of present policies, defense of present policies with minor repairs, counterproposal, disadvantage, and critique. After you have completed your outlines, explain how each differs from the others. What are the advantages of each, and in what type of situation would each be most appropriate?

NOTES

1. There are several good resources to help build listening skills. For instance, consider Paul J. Donoghue and Mary E. Siegel, *Are You Really Listening? Keys to Successful Communication* (Notre Dame, Ind.: Sorein Books, 2005); or Madelyn Burley-Allen, *Listening: The Forgotten Skill*, 2nd ed. (New York: John Wiley & Sons, 1995).

2. A discussion of listening types can be found at Larry Alan Nadig, "Tips on Effective Listening," http://www.drnadig.com/listening.htm (accessed May 27, 2008).

3. Some good examples and resources include: US Department of State, "Dipolomacy in Action: Active Listening," http://www.state.gov/m/a/os/65759.htm (accessed October 24, 2012); Susie Michelle Cortright, "10 Tips to Effective & Active Listening Skills," http://powertochange.com/students/people/listen/ (accessed October 1, 2012); London Deanery, "Skillful Questioning and Active Listening," http://www.faculty.londondeanery.ac.uk/e-learning/appraisal/skilful-questioning-and-active-listening (accessed October 20, 2012); and Wendy Connick, "What is Active Listening?" http://sales.about.com/od/glossaryofsalesterms/g/What-Is-Active-Listening.htm (accessed on October 24, 2012).

4. Debra Satz, *Why Some Things Should Not be for Sale: The Moral Limits of the Market* (New York: Oxford University Press, 2010).

5. "Tobacco Use: Targeting the Nation's Leading Killer," *Center for Disease Control*, 2011, http://www.cdc.gov/chronicdisease/resources/publications/aag/osh.htm (accessed June 25, 2012).

SECTION **IV**

COMMUNICATING ARGUMENTS

CHAPTER TEN

PERSUASION

CHAPTER OUTLINE

ARGUER AND RECIPIENT
Role of Recipients
Recipients and Situations
Adversarial Recipients
Co-Orientational Recipients

ADAPTING ARGUMENTS
Narrative Paradigm
Universal Audience
Spherical Audience

PERSUASION PRINCIPLES
Compliance
Identification
Internalization

Expertise and Trustworthiness
Enhancing Credibility
Goals
Strategies

DEVELOPING PERSUASIVE ARGUMENTS
Supporting Reasoning
Supporting Evidence
Authoritative Evidence
Perceptions of Bias
Novel Evidence

SUMMARY

EXERCISES

KEY CONCEPTS

The last section of this text is devoted to how advocates work to persuade their audiences with extended argument cases—a task that is not always as easy as it may seem. Box 10.1, "Nuclear Energy," provides a good illustration of the challenges speakers face when presenting arguments. In this case, Liam and Camille did many things correctly, especially when compared to opponents who did not present the same quality or depth of background and research. They conducted extensive research to become well informed on their topic, they

---

BOX 10.1
NUCLEAR ENERGY

Nuclear power has been a controversial source of energy since the first reactor, the Soviet Union's Obninsk Nuclear Power Plant, went online on June 27, 1954. It produced just 5 megawatts of electricity. By 2012 there were 430 reactors operating worldwide, supplying 13.5 percent of the world's energy.[1] Proponents touted it as a clean, inexpensive source of power, while those opposed warned of the potential catastrophic effects of a nuclear meltdown. Still, the industry grew steadily during the 1960s and 1970s. Then, in 1979, the Three Mile Island Nuclear Generating Station in Pennsylvania experienced a partial meltdown, releasing small amounts of radiation into the atmosphere. The accident confirmed opponents' worst fears; even the safest reactors could suffer significant failures. Although the official federal investigation into the event found no deaths or major injuries associated with the incident, the potential risk seemed too significant to ignore.[2]

Seven years later an explosion and fire at the Chernobyl nuclear power plant in Ukraine sent radioactive contamination over much of the Soviet Union and parts of Europe. That blast and ensuing meltdown released 400 times more radiation into the environment than the atomic bomb dropped on Hiroshima, Japan. Within three months of the meltdown, thirty-one people were dead with a projected loss of life from cancers related to the meltdown at 4,000 people.[3] These two accidents marked a shift in the global development of nuclear power.[4] Few reactors have been built since and, for the United States, the period has become known as the "nuclear brown out."[5]

The cost of energy, increased global competition for petroleum products, concerns about global climate change, and unstable politics that threatened supply shortages prompted a "nuclear renaissance" in the United States after 2000.[6] By 2007 there were plans for the construction of up to six new plants to come online by 2020.[7]

Then, in March 2011, northern Japan was struck by a massive earthquake and tsunami. The Fukushima Daiichi nuclear power plant and its presumed fail-safe systems failed. The resulting chain of events led to the first triple meltdown of a nuclear power plant.[8] The world first watched the tragic natural disaster, which claimed an estimated 19,000 lives, and then the worst nuclear accident in history.[9]

Following the accident, public support for nuclear energy in the United States declined and only 14% of Americans said their views on nuclear power had not been adversely affected by the disaster.[10] The same study found support for new nuclear reactors dropped from 62 percent in March of 2010 to 44 percent after the Fukushima meltdown.[11] Though plans were underway in the United States for four plants before the disaster, only one had begun construction a year after the accident.

College students Liam and Camille were participating in a public debate on their campus about the nuclear power controversy. Their assignment was to argue in support of the increased

(continued)

BOX 10.1   CONTINUED

use of nuclear power. In preparation for the debate they did extensive research about the safety, costs, and benefits of nuclear energy. They interviewed their university's top nuclear physicists and consulted field specific journal articles. Well equipped with strong evidence, Liam and Camille carefully designed their arguments and organized their presentation. They practiced multiple times, and when the day of the debate finally arrived, they were confident in their level of preparation. In a technical but succinct analysis, Liam and Camille argued that with growing energy demands and increasing geopolitical uncertainties, the United States should increase its use of nuclear power to achieve energy independence.[12] They carefully described the various systems in place that virtually guarantee plants will be safe and how loan guarantees can ensure that companies are able to provide consumers with inexpensive electricity.

Their opponents in the debate, Cara and Tiffani, did not present the same depth of evidence. Instead, their reasoning focused on the human toll of nuclear accidents and the risks associated with nuclear power. They included vivid descriptions of past disasters, and reminded the audience that what happened in these accidents could easily happen anywhere, including in their own community.

When the debate ended, Liam and Camille were certain they had impressed the audience by virtue of their strong research, clear technical analysis, complete information, and carefully constructed arguments. They had presented clear evidence, logical arguments, and well worded claims.

Yet, when the audience members were polled about who did the better job, Liam and Camille were surprised to find that the audience reacted negatively to their arguments, and were bored and confused by their presentation. Audience members reported that they were largely against the use of nuclear power because of what they had recently seen happen in Japan. Much to Liam and Camille's dismay, the audience responded much more favorably to Cara and Tiffani's logically weaker but more emotionally connected arguments.

Whereas the audience members commended Cara and Tiffani for being clear and connecting their arguments to the stories the audience had recently heard about the risks of nuclear power, they said that Liam and Camille had failed to make their arguments clear and did not address the fears and attitudes of the majority of the people in the room who believed that nuclear energy is inherently risky and would not want a new nuclear power plant near their homes. Audience members complained that Liam and Camille used overly complex evidence, filled with technical jargon and complex descriptions of the way that federal loan guarantees work. The audience also commented that Liam and Camille used too much evidence from nuclear power industry, which they perceived as biased because it stood to gain from the increased use of nuclear energy.

Liam and Camille left the debate discouraged. They didn't understand what went wrong with such a carefully crafted and researched presentation.

1. How is it possible that well-crafted and thoroughly researched arguments fail when presented to an audience?
2. Beyond the evidence claims and reasoning, what other factors determine whether recipients accept or reject arguments?
3. Under what conditions do technically weaker arguments such as those presented by Cara and Tiffani become more persuasive for audiences?
4. In Chapter 2 we explored how an arguer's relationship with the audience is important. What role did that relationship play here?
5. What could or should Liam and Camille have done differently?

organized their speeches carefully, and they used sound reasoning to support their claims. But, they failed to consider fundamental questions about the recipients and their attitudes that were vital toward getting their message accepted. These included the following: How much does this audience already know about the topic? What are the audience's present values and beliefs about nuclear power? What sources are likely seen as credible? How should the presentation be organized so that the arguments will have the greatest effect? How many arguments can be developed in the time available? What are the recipients' attitudes toward the arguers? What can the arguers do to appear credible, especially about a topic that most of the audience may have strong opinions about?

While Liam and Camille did many things well, they failed to ask key questions during the preparation process. In short, they forgot about one of the most important considerations when crafting arguments: the recipient. They focused on technical aspects of nuclear energy, and on complex policy issues related to loan guarantees. The audience was put off by Liam and Camille's technical explanation of the safety features of nuclear power, and their statistics-heavy presentation of facts about the growing need for energy security. The audience of primarily college students was not prepared to evaluate arguments from the technical sphere—it was a public audience in a public debate. Because Liam and Camille focused on the technical aspects of nuclear reactor safety, they failed to address the most recent stories and fears the audience members had heard about the nuclear disaster in Japan.

In this chapter, we will examine how arguers can develop and enhance strong relationships and messages for their listeners. First, we will examine the relationships between arguers and recipients, then we will consider issues related to audiences and how they come to believe or reject arguments. Next, we will focus on issues related to arguers and how they can develop arguments in a way that will build relationships and interact with their recipients. And, finally, we will consider strategies for how arguers can work to enhance their relationship with the audience and become more persuasive while speaking.

ARGUER AND RECIPIENT

Advocates attempt to influence recipients by selecting and making the best arguments possible for the situation and recipients. Their goal is to communicate effectively in a way that persuades the hearers. The concept of argument spheres and fields developed in Chapter 1 is important here because, by focusing their arguments in the wrong sphere, Liam and Camille had little hope of successfully convincing their audience that nuclear power is the best way to achieve energy independence. In other words, Liam and Camille had presented good arguments that were lost on the audience because the presentation was not appropriately designed or presented for a public sphere discussion.

In Chapter 2, we developed a co-orientational approach for understanding how arguments function in the relationship between arguer and recipient. We made the point that argument recipients play a significant role in argument situations. They do not function as blank slates or logic machines responding only to the truth and validity of an arguer's reasoning or evidence. Recipients are influenced by the relationships they have with one another and with the advocates, by the subject matter, and their own knowledge, experience, and attitudes (among many other variables). The best evidence, strongest arguments, and most clearly designed presentations will not be successful if recipients reject or fail to understand them.

The primary role of an advocate is to ethically and persuasively communicate arguments that recipients can understand and choose to accept or not. The concept of ethics is important and we will address it in Chapter 11. *Ethics is the study of what is morally right or just.* Sometimes it is tempting to do whatever is necessary to convince recipients of our arguments but it is important to remember that argumentation should empower all participants in a dispute.

Co-orientation assumes that arguers and recipients work together in a relationship to share argument content and achieve mutually beneficial outcomes. Argumentation theorists Chaim Perelman and Lucie Olbrechts-Tyteca suggested that advocates consider argumentation as a collaborative process toward problem solution.[13] We should attend to multiple points of view and seek solutions that embrace alternatives.

Role of Recipients

Two of the questions an advocate needs to ask first are, "Who am I addressing and what do they need?" Although these questions are relatively simple, finding and developing the answers can be a challenge. Typically, audiences are made of many people and, consequently, they are complex and varied. They have different needs, interests, backgrounds, and enthusiasm, depending on the topic. Additionally, their roles as recipients change depending on the situation.

Often, people assume that the argumentation process places two speakers in opposition over an issue. Recipients listen to arguments and then decide which were best. But this is only one type of audience that judges arguments in a competitive style, which was introduced in Chapter 2, using the logical perspective that was introduced in Chapter 1. In fact, much argumentation theory and practice is based on this competitive and adversarial style of argumentation that assumes the proper role of the recipient is that of objective decision-makers, much like a judge or jury. This model has been the traditional one for teaching argument and debate for decades.[14]

Recipients and Situations

Chapter 2 explored how argument situations are shaped by several factors. For every argument and persuasive case presented, arguers work to adapt their style and approach to the recipients and the situation. Some situations call for a facilitative or collaborative style, whereas others require competing, negotiating, or any of the other styles discussed in Chapter 2. There are four types of argument relationships that are defined by situation. These, for the most part, parallel the discussion we had of argument spheres in Chapter 2 and include personal decision-makers, technical decision-makers, public decision-makers, and extra-systemic decision-makers.

These audience types are shown in Figure 10.1, "Continuum of Audience Relationships." It is important to note in this model that "decision-maker" defines the audience relationships. This is because these relationships define how arguments will be understood, defined, and evaluated. Also, note that at each step from private to extra-systemic relationships, argumentation strategies become increasingly adversarial and less collaborative as they affect more and more people.

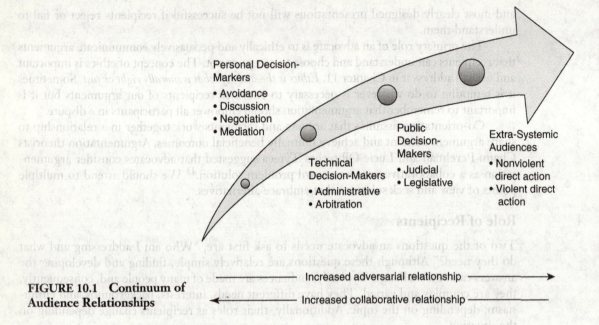

Personal Decision-Markers
- Avoidance
- Discussion
- Negotiation
- Mediation

Technical Decision-Makers
- Administrative
- Arbitration

Public Decision-Makers
- Judicial
- Legislative

Extra-Systemic Audiences
- Nonviolent direct action
- Violent direct action

⟶ Increased adversarial relationship ⟶
⟵ Increased collaborative relationship ⟵

FIGURE 10.1   Continuum of Audience Relationships

Because the recipients, their expectations, and the situations vary at each argumentation level, arguers necessarily employ different strategies of persuasion, ranging from avoidance and discussion through legislative action. Each persuasive choice should be made with an understanding of the role the recipient plays in the argument situation.

The construction of a new nuclear power plant in Georgia provides a good example of the connection between recipient and situation. In 2012 permits were granted for the first time since 1978 to begin the construction of a new nuclear power plant in the United States.[15] However, one of the five members of the Nuclear Regulatory Commission (NRC) voted against granting the license because of concerns that the new reactors had not been adequately modified to meet safety recommendations that followed the meltdown at the Fukushima Daiichi nuclear power plant in Japan.[16] Following the decision to grant the license, ten antinuclear groups said they would file a suit against the NRC based on the grounds that they broke the law by allowing construction of new plants without instituting safety modifications deemed necessary following the disaster in Japan.[17]

When arguers and recipients work together to develop issues and reach decisions, they are engaged in personal decision-making. *Personal decision-makers argue in the personal sphere and use rules and conventions that are decided among the participants.* This is represented in Figure 10.1 as a relatively small circle because it influences the fewest people. The advocates at this level function as arguer, recipient, and evaluator because all sides work to find agreement. Personal decision-making arguments tend to be more facilitative, collaborative, and informal than other types.

Families who lived near the proposed nuclear power site likely engaged in discussions about the safety, costs, and potential risks of living near a nuclear power plant. Some might have decided to sell their homes and move. In this case, they would be arguing for their own benefit to decide whether they would accept the risks of living near the plant. People would explore the issues and make decisions based on their own, personal criteria. Because they would use their own rules and norms and then make their own decisions about which issues were most important, they would be functioning as personal decision-makers.

Technical decision-makers are private third-party recipients who act as an external audience. Arguments aimed at third-party recipients tend to be technical-sphere arguments for specialized audiences. The decision-makers are no longer the arguers themselves but are instead a third party. The conventions and issues for argument come from within the technical sphere and are decided by those who understand the rules and norms of a particular field. Third-party audiences remove the power of decision-making from the individual advocates. Competition and negotiation are dominant styles in this type of discussion. Lawyers win or lose and may negotiate settlements. Power plants are permitted or not.

In this case, decisions about whether to issue permits for new nuclear plants are up to scientists, regulators, or other technical recipients. Unlike arguments in the personal sphere, the arguers here provide information, contexts, and claims but do not decide. The members of the NRC, though, had sufficient technical expertise to properly evaluate the arguments about the safety of the proposed construction and make a decision. And, if anti-nuclear groups chose to oppose a decision to build, they would engage the technical decision-makers of the legal system by filing suit.

Public decision-makers are third-party audiences that largely apply the norms and conventions of the public sphere. Arguers speak to these audiences in the larger context of public debate and use public rules and expectations to govern arguments and decisions. Such arguments rely on the public audience, rather than the arguers, to make the decision. Public audiences tend to use many styles to argue and evaluate. They may compete, negotiate, withdraw, avoid, or facilitate.

This was the primary audience Liam and Camille addressed in the debate discussed in Box 10.1. Instead of focusing on the technical issues related to nuclear energy and loan guarantees, they would have been more successful in developing a common understanding of the issues and arguments if they had adapted to the expectations of the public sphere and the public audience. When the NRC granted the permits to build the new plant in Georgia, the debate again moved back into the public sphere because of media reports about the anti-nuclear group's plans to challenge that decision.

Extra-systemic decision-makers operate outside the normal and regular realm of advocacy. In some ways, they seek recourse to grievances that, they perceive, have not been adequately addressed by the normal decision-making processes we have discussed. *Extra-systemic audiences are groups that use nonviolence, direct action, or violence to influence or overturn decision processes.* Nonviolent protest may include sit-ins, boycotts, picketing, or other means to disrupt social control. Direct action might include other extralegal means, such as computer hacking or verbal protest.

An incident at the University of California, Davis, on November 17, 2011, provides us with a powerful example of extra-systemic decision-making. In this case, students protested a proposed increase in tuition by setting up tents and camping in the university's quad on November 16, 2011. The next day, as students linked arms and blocked some of the side-walks, university police in riot gear ordered them to disband and clear the paths. When a 3 P.M. deadline for the students to leave passed, the campus police again ordered them to leave and when that failed, police officers used pepper spray to disband the protesters.[18]

Video of the incident went viral quickly and what had begun as a small, local protest became the subject of international criticism and condemnation.

The UC Davis pepper spray incident, along with many other nonviolent protests from the Occupy Wall Street movement to anti-war protests, do not craft arguments in the sense we have been discussing. Rather, they challenge the assumptions of the system that has failed to address issues and concerns through normal, rhetorical, and argumentative processes.

Extra-systemic protest is not truly a form of argument because violating the law and becoming violent are not rhetorical strategies. They use force as opposed to argument to compel a decision. However, when advocates become frustrated with their lack of success in the public sphere, they sometimes decide to take extra-systemic action. For example, if those fighting against the construction of the nuclear power plants did not feel satisfied with the outcome in the courts, they might stage protests or demonstrations to bring more public attention to the issue.

It is important to note from Figure 10.1, however, that as we move from private, facilitative argument toward external, third-party decision-makers, we have a tendency to assume that argument becomes a win-lose situation among opposing groups. Generally, co-orientational argument is most successful when the people engaged in the discussion are the ones who will ultimately decide the outcome. Box 10.2, "Audience and Strategy," considers some of the choices advocates have for presenting arguments in each sphere.

BOX 10.2
AUDIENCE AND STRATEGY

AUDIENCE TYPE	STRATEGY	DEFINITION
Personal Decision-Maker	Avoidance	Ignore the argument
	Informal Discussion	Talk about the issues
	Negotiation	Advocate for a position
	Mediation	Find someone to help facilitate the discussion
Technical Decision-Maker	Administrative Decision	Appeal to a superior or expert to make the decision
	Arbitration	Have a person consider the arguments and make a judgment
Public Decision-Maker	Judicial decision	Allow the court or similar system to decide
	Legislative decision	Ask government to address the issues
Extra-Systemic Audience	Nonviolent direct action	Protest and make public systemic inadequacies
	Violent direct action	Use force to highlight systemic problems

Adversarial Recipients

Adversarial argumentation focuses on a clash between two points of view and is competitive. With this style, advocates develop persuasive presentations and refute the opposing points of view. It is a fight that is often characterized by warlike metaphors: "I beat their arguments," "My case won," "I tore down my opposition," or "I crushed my opponent." In most formal and institutional argument forums, such as law, politics, or opinion journalism, advocates argue only one side.

Politicians are often referred to as "flip-floppers" if they try to adapt and evolve their positions as new information and ideas develop. The same is true in other situations as well. In academic debate, students argue for or against a particular position. In courts of law, attorneys prosecute or defend the guilt or innocence of a person. And, in legislative assemblies, two sides will debate for or against a particular bill or amendment. In these cases, we proceed from the assumption that there are two sides, and one will win while the other will lose.

When we focus on argument as an adversarial exchange between two combatants holding two opposite points of view, we tend to rely on external audiences to decide which side is right. For example, when a prosecutor argues to convict an accused criminal, the lawyer is seeking to persuade a jury, not the defense counsel. The jury is supposed to be an unbiased, external entity. When legislators debate over the merits of a bill, the bill's author is usually not the audience. Rather, the legislators who will vote on the bill are the audience. Adversarial argumentation assumes there will be a winner and a loser and that the arguers' role is to persuade an external audience of the merits of the case. Adversarial argumentation is appropriate and effective in the proper situation, but it is not the only style and is not always appropriate.

Co-Orientational Recipients

The perception that argumentation and debate are simply a clash between two sides is limited, and many theorists have been critical of teaching methods that focus on argumentation as a competitive process in which one side wins while the other loses.[19] Rather, in some situations, argument and debate are a partnership or collaboration among the participants, and multiple sides are expressed and developed. We have previously referred to this relationship as co-orientational—arguer and recipient participate together to create arguments. A facilitative argumentation style allows for the participants to achieve common goals, enhance their relationships, and create common solutions to significant issues. Generally, this style is regarded as a preferred approach for managing disputes because it allows for more points of view and fosters a collaborative decision-making environment.[20]

Once disputes rise to a level that involves third parties in the technical or public spheres, collaborative problem solving is more difficult to achieve because those arguments tend to result in a winner and a loser. Court cases, contract disputes, and formal grievances are all examples of this type of argumentation. However, in the personal sphere, partnership and collaboration can guide arguers.[21] The nuclear power controversy provides a good example of how overlapping audiences can result from overlapping spheres.

The arguments discussed above about nuclear power function at different levels for different recipients, and different strategies are necessary within each level of dispute. Figure 10.2, "Spheres and Recipients," illustrates how overlapping spheres and audiences affected the debate

Private Third-Party Decision-Making
Decision to use the legal system.
Filing legal briefs and arguments
to prevent the plant licenses.

Technical
Sphere

Public
Sphere

Private
Sphere

Public Third-Party Decision-Making
Public debate about impact of new
nuclear plants on the community.
Media outlets cover issues providing
the public with information from technical
sphere and stories from personal sphere.

Private Decision-Making by Parties
Family discussions about whether to
live near new nuclear plant sites.
Private arguments and decision making.

Where the spheres overlap, personal,
technical, and public arguments converge.
People come forward to discuss what might
happen to them. Lawyers consider
lawsuits and legal strategies. The public
listens to individual stories and evaluates
private and technical arguments.

FIGURE 10.2   Spheres and Recipients

developed in Box 10.1. Understanding the argument situation, who the decision-makers are, and the kind of decision the arguer wants is central to adapting and developing persuasive presentations.

ADAPTING ARGUMENTS

To be successful in presenting arguments, arguers need to understand their recipients and adapt arguments to address the audience's needs and knowledge. This involves making a decision about where to place the level of dispute. In Chapter 2 we noted that, to function as evidence in an argument, a statement must fall below the level of dispute—that is, audience members must believe the statement is true or can be verified. If a statement is uncontroversial and accepted by the people to whom the argument is made, then the arguers can begin building an argument chain. Otherwise, the arguers will run into trouble if they incorrectly ground arguments. This is why having a clear understanding of audience type and context for argument is particularly important.

Arguers must have some knowledge of the recipients' values and attitudes to be assured that evidence will be accepted and not challenged or rejected. What are the recipients' needs and interests? What are their priorities? In the topic area in which the argument is made, what do they value? Finding out the answers to such questions will ensure that the process of making the argument goes smoothly.

As the example of Liam and Camille's debate on nuclear power demonstrates, in selecting starting points, it is also important to consider the sphere of argument and the type of audience with which you are engaging in argumentation. The sphere of argumentation—private, public, or technical—will help determine the choice of starting points. Moreover, the type of audience—personal decision-makers, technical decision-makers, public decision-makers, or extra-systemic audiences—will also affect the starting points for argument.

Consider the following example:

Car Salesperson: This is a wonderful example of a 1965 Triumph TR4A. You will never see such a good example of British engineering. In fact, this one happens to have the dual Stromberg setup and the all-synchro 4-speed with the 3.91 differential. Tough to find that in this kind of vehicle. That, with the 87-mm sleeves, makes this quite a collectible classic.

Buyer: What is a Stromberg, and why is that important? How many miles are on this car?

To help the buyer understand the product, the salesperson needed to explain how the car met the buyer's needs and expectations, and the arguments needed to be adapted to the buyer's level of understanding. As presented, the salesperson relied too much on technical argument for a buyer making a personal decision. The same thing happened with Liam and Camille. They focused their presentation within the technical sphere. It did not meet the recipients' needs or expectations.

Although crafting arguments for the correct sphere is important, it is also critical to think about the members of your specific audience. Regardless of the quality of the organization, reasoning, and presentation of arguments, if speakers do not begin by considering what the audience knows, believes, and values, the recipients may reject what is said—even if logically true and valid. Arguers should strive to create connections with audiences by adapting arguments to the backgrounds, situations, needs, and values of the particular audience. In Chapter 2, we described the rhetorical perspective for viewing arguments, which is concerned with the arguer's relationship to the audience and how messages can be persuasive. In the following sections we will explore some rhetorical perspectives on argument that will help you to design effective arguments that resonate and connect with your recipients.

Narrative Paradigm

The rhetorical perspective of argument focuses on the goal of selecting arguments that are relevant and persuasive to an audience. Working from this perspective, rhetorician Walter Fisher developed what he called a "Narrative Paradigm." The term *paradigm* is important because Fisher viewed narration not as an "element in rhetorical discourse," but instead as a "conception of reality."[22] In other words, he argued that all human communication could be viewed as stories.[23] The narrative paradigm, from an arguer's point of view, helps us see the argument situation as an opportunity to create a connection among recipient, arguer, and situation—to develop a coherent and consistent explanation of events, issues, and ideas. Fisher's *Narrative paradigm proposes that we experience life as a series of narrative events, which shape our understanding of our world, our beliefs, and even our values*. We are constantly exposed to stories that help to shape our beliefs and values.

For example, U.S. students are taught about American history through stories, such as those about the bravery of George Washington, the ingenuity of Benjamin Franklin, and the vision and intellect of Thomas Jefferson. These stories not only tell of the origins of the United States and the events of that time, but they also describe and highlight the culture and central values of the United States. These are the creation narratives of America. These types of narratives are important even if they are partly constructed of myths and exaggeration. They highlight what a given culture perceives are the most important themes.

The Cold War that dominated much of the second half of the twentieth century has many such examples. Many of its narratives continue today. For instance, some Americans continue to be fearful of communism. Others are concerned with the amount of international trade with former Cold War adversaries. And, in North Korea, junior high school students are required to read *The Diary of Anne Frank*, the story of a young Jewish girl during World War II who hid with her family from the Nazis but was discovered, sent to a concentration camp, and died before the end of the war. North Korean students read her diary and learn that from a particular perspective the United States is an evil imperialist nation and a threat to the sovereignty of North Korea.[24] Though the book is not about Americans or North Koreans, the story is used to teach the students that Americans are like the Nazis in the book, and are a people who love war. Students learn to equate the American president with Hitler.

This narrative supports the North Korean need to maintain a strong military; even at the expense of other needs the nation might have, because it must be vigilant and prepare for war with America.[25] These differences illustrate the way stories can be used to shape our perceptions of our world, our values, and ourselves.

The view of human communication as storytelling does not presume that advocates should make up tall tales to share experiences (though even fiction often aims to teach us values). Instead, the narrative paradigm holds that our experiences are shared and understood in narrative form. From this perspective arguments can be viewed as narratives. Imagine a student who misses an important paper deadline and tries to persuade the teacher to accept the late assignment. The student's explanation for why the deadline was missed would likely be in the form of a story, such as in the following example:

Student: I was unable to turn in my paper by the deadline and was hoping you would accept it now.

Teacher: My policy clearly states that I do not accept late papers.

Student: I know, but I had the terrible luck of having my car towed yesterday. I didn't have the money to get it out of impound. My backpack was in the car, and my paper was in my backpack. I didn't even have an electronic copy of my paper, because my computer was in my backpack, too. I finally was able to borrow the money to get my car this morning. So, will you make an exception and let me turn in my paper in?

Whether or not you have ever asked for an extension on an assignment, most people have told a story to try to persuade someone to accept their point of view. And, most people have been recipients of such stories.

The narrative paradigm offers an explanation for why someone might or might not be persuaded by a particular theme or storyline. If advocates make arguments that seem to "fit" an audience's dominant narrative, the recipients are more likely to believe the argument than one that does not "fit." This is common in courtrooms in which attorneys attempt to explain the facts as clearly as possible by telling the story of the crime and the story of the defense to a jury. A dominant narrative is a story that aligns with the existing values, beliefs and experiences of the recipients. It is more powerful because it contains information or values that recipients already accept and best fits their assumptions and worldview.

Understanding that arguments are viewed and assessed as stories by recipients is important for advocates to keep in mind as they construct arguments. Fisher made the point that because we are constantly exposed to stories, regardless of training in argumentation, all people have the capacity to evaluate the arguments contained in stories. Fisher argued that we naturally reason through narrative structures to decide whether we will be persuaded by the stories we hear.[26] There are two tests, Fisher says, recipients use to assess the strength, truth, and validity of narratives.

The test of narrative probability asks whether a story is coherent. When we assess a story's probability, we ask ourselves if the story makes sense by examining the way the characters behave, whether the timeline makes sense, and whether it contains contradictions. We can think of this test the way we think about the plot of a film. If there are unexplained or out of sequence events in a film, or if a character acts in an unexplained way, we might say that there were holes in the plot. In *The Sixth Sense*, audiences were shocked during the final minutes when the film revealed that the main character, played by Bruce Willis, was actually a ghost who could be seen only by a young boy. Many people watched the film multiple times looking for holes in the plot. But, upon close examination it turned out that Willis' character didn't directly interact with any of the other characters in the film. The strength or coherence of the plot was one reason the film was such a success.

The nuclear power plant example at the beginning of the chapter and the debate presented by Liam and Camille offers another example. Their audience was familiar with the narratives surrounding Fukushima, Chernobyl, and Three Mile Island. They were aware of the failure of primary and failsafe systems in each of these plants that experts had assured communities and lawmakers were safe. When Camille and Liam turned to the technical sphere to find expert evidence supporting new permits and touting nuclear energy safety, they ran into a problem with narrative probability. The opposing narrative that included the history of nuclear disasters was more compelling than the narrative of experts who had been wrong. Cara and Tiffani were able to use the dominant narrative of nuclear experience to reinforce their recipient's existing mind-set—even if their individual arguments were not as deeply researched or logically strong.

The second way that audiences assess stories is through the test of narrative fidelity. *Narrative fidelity is the test in which we decide whether the story matches up with our values, our life experiences, or with our social reality.* With this test, recipients ask whether the story's facts can be confirmed as true and reliable, and whether the story is consistent with other stories we have heard before we accept it as true. Fidelity is strongly linked with our values. Recipients ask for more than the reasoning internal to the narrative. They look for whether the reasoning resonates with their own experiences, value systems, and beliefs. This is why, even if arguments are true and valid, recipients may reject them if they fail to "ring true" with their experiences.

As long as the teacher in the earlier example believes that making exceptions for some students and not others is unfair, it will not matter how compelling the student's story is; the reasons contained in the student's story will not persuade the teacher to change her mind because they do not represent *good reasons* according to her values and beliefs. Similarly, Liam and Camille's recipients knew about the stories of nuclear disasters. They were aware of families that had been displaced and people who had been killed or became ill. And, they were familiar with the stories of environmental devastation following Chernobyl and Fukushima that would take generations to address. These stories were repeated in the media and became part of the nuclear energy opposition narrative in the United States.

Liam and Camille faced a narrative fidelity challenge in overcoming what their recipients already believed to be true based on recent history and events. Part of their task as nuclear energy advocates was to provide an alternative narrative that would have told a more compelling story. They were not able to do that. For their recipients, even though the arguments were not as logically strong, the narrative offered by Cara and Tiffani was a better fit to what they had read and heard. Box 10.3, "Apply the Theory," works through the development of a nuclear narrative.

Fisher argued that people like to have their values affirmed, and we are more likely to reject stories that do not align with our values and experiences. Audiences more easily accept stories that affirm their values and beliefs, while stories that do not are easier for an audience to reject. So, in addition to ensuring that arguments are coherent, advocates need to frame their stories in ways that appeal to the values and the life experiences of their recipients.

■ ■ ■ ■ ■

BOX 10.3
APPLY THE THEORY: NUCLEAR NARRATIVE

The opening case contained in Box 10.1 provided background and information about nuclear energy, accidents, and public sentiment. If you were working with Liam and Camille with their public debate presentation, what would you have advised them to do? What narrative should they have offered? Specifically,

1. What is the current, dominant narrative held by public sphere audiences? Is this different than technical or personal sphere audiences?
2. What is the current narrative probability? Are there any weaknesses?
3. What is the current narrative fidelity? Are there any gaps?
4. What alternative narrative could they have constructed? For instance, is there a strong narrative to be found in the number of safely operating plants in the world or the effects of eliminating nuclear energy?
5. How should they address issues of probability and fidelity?

Narratives should take into account the experiences of the recipients, what they know and believe, and appeal to their values.

We are constantly exposed to stories that vie for our attention, many of which contain arguments. Viewing arguments as narratives and considering how recipients will assess them helps us choose which arguments to highlight and what values to focus on in an effort to more effectively persuade. The point, as discussed in Chapter 2, is that as useful as formal logic is as a critical tool, understanding how audiences naturally evaluate arguments using narratives provides us with a way to more successfully connect with recipients.

Universal Audience

When arguers approach a topic, their background, experiences, and values guide their choices about what the best arguments on the given topic are. At the same time, recipients have their own unique backgrounds, experiences, and needs. It is important for an advocate to understand both their own and their recipients' dominant narratives. The advocate's task, then, is to choose which arguments are most appropriate for the given situation and audience.

Because recipients are varied and come from many different backgrounds, cultures, and experiences, it can be difficult to figure out where to locate the level of dispute and select which arguments to highlight when we prepare narratives. Much depends on the argument context in which the argument is presented. Fisher, Perelman, and Olbrechts-Tyteca argued that sole reliance on formal logic to study practical arguments was inadvisable. *Practical arguments are arguments in process within a particular context and situation.* In Chapter 2 we defined formal logic as the study of how conclusions are reached using structured statements. Formal logic reduces arguments to their most basic elements and expresses them in standardized, almost mathematical forms, such as the syllogism. The co-orientational approach, by contrast, considers the evolutionary nature of arguments—the idea that arguments are in process with situations and relationships that influence arguers and recipients.

When we refer to practical arguments we assume the co-orientational approach, in which arguments are seen as fluid, changing and evolving with the particular situation. This was the perspective of Perelman and Olbrechts-Tyteca when they posited that we evaluate arguments not based on rules of formal logic or patterns of reasoning alone, but by comparing the arguments we are presented with to something else we already know or believe, such as a fact, value, law, or tradition. Based on that comparison recipients decide which viewpoint to prefer. This is why people may be persuaded by many kinds of arguments and sometimes by their own personal backgrounds and experiences, even if those are not part of the discussion. So how do we choose which arguments to highlight and what values to focus on?

Audiences may be made up of people of similar age, education level, or with some common interest. People who share demographic characteristics such as age, sex, ethnic background, culture, religion, social and other group affiliations, and even geographic information are likely to have shared experiences, beliefs, and values.

For example, if trying to find values shared by the students in an argumentation class, one might be correct in assuming that many would value education since they are all college students. They would be less likely to uniformly agree that environmental protection is an important value. The case in Box 10.1 makes this point. Liam and Camille did not consider the values held by their audience. Since they were debating in the public sphere, they could have consulted public opinion surveys to find out what general public attitudes toward nuclear power generally were at the time. They might have considered their particular community—was there currently, or might there be in the future, a nuclear plant nearby? Or was their audience mostly made up of people who lived far enough away from the nearest nuclear power plant to put them out of immediate danger in the event of a meltdown?

Understanding the demographic characteristics of an audience can be a useful first step and advocates can make some broad assumptions about issues that are likely to be important. If we think that our audience may have limited knowledge about our topic area, we might lower our assessment of where the level of dispute should be placed and highlight what we think will be persuasive to them. However, shared demographic characteristics do not necessarily mean shared values. To learn about those, it is important for advocates to study the situation and culture they are addressing.

In the example of the debate about nuclear power, Cara and Tiffani focused primarily on connecting their arguments with the emotional experiences of the recipients because they thought that would be the best way for their hearers to understand the larger issues. There is an important note to be made here. While advocates should connect their arguments to their recipients, they should not do so at the expense of sound reasoning and clear evidence. Adapting to an audience does not mean tricking them or obscuring truth. Rather, adapting to an audience means that we seek ways to make arguments relevant to the experiences and background of the people we address. Box 10.4, "Apply the Theory," gives you an opportunity to assess the values of the audience and link those values to arguments.

Figuring out how to position arguments within a context is a challenge. Perelman and Olbrechts-Tyteca's theory of the universal audience offers a starting point for understanding how to resolve that tension. *The universal audience is a construct in the imagination of the arguer, and includes all people who are rational and competent with respect to the issues being debated.*[27] In a way, the arguer mentally constructs an audience that is composed of the most qualified experts for the subject under discussion.

■ ■ ■ ■ ■

BOX 10. 4

APPLY THE THEORY: ANALYZE YOUR AUDIENCE

Consider the nuclear power controversy, outlined in Box 10.1. Imagine you will be giving a presentation either in support of or against the construction of a new nuclear power plant in your community. For each of the following audiences, make a list of the values you think would be shared by many of the recipients. Why do you think the people in the group share those values? Make a list of arguments that would be most persuasive given the values you identified.

1. A local environmental club.
2. A mother's club.
3. A group of college students.
4. A professional organization for real estate agents.

The arguer uses this conceptual audience to assess which arguments are most likely to gain adherence by actual hearers. Perelman and Olbrechts-Tyteca's theory guides arguers in their selection of which arguments are best to stand up to the scrutiny of the experts in a way that, presumably, will be persuasive to other recipients. This approach recognizes the importance of the technical sphere and requires that arguers adapt those arguments to the particular context.

Spherical Audience

However, the idea of the universal audience can be a bit abstract, and could lead advocates to choose arguments that, despite their strength and logic, might be inappropriate for the hearers—we could place the level of dispute too far up for a specific audience. This is what happened in the debate about nuclear energy at the beginning of the chapter. Liam and Camille made arguments that probably would have stood up to the scrutiny of nuclear engineers and energy policy experts, but they failed to persuade those who are rational but not expert—those who were in their actual audience. Liam and Camille, as well-researched advocates, would not want to abandon strong arguments simply because they were arguing in the public sphere, but even the best arguments are not relevant if the recipients cannot comprehend them. We can use the concept of argument spheres as a more concrete guide for choosing the best and most appropriate arguments for the particular situation and context in which we are arguing.

In Chapter 1 we described the idea that argument spheres guide how arguments are produced and evaluated. When we are deciding which arguments to highlight, we must also consider the notion of the rhetorical situation, which we defined in Chapter 2 as the context of people, events, objects, and relationships in which we make arguments. Figure 1.3 illustrated that there is an area of overlap among the personal, technical, and public spheres. Each informs the situation and arguments of the other. And, of spheres, the technical is the most powerful because it is where field expertise resides and where the most rigorous tests of knowledge exist. This is why, in public sphere debate, we look to expertise from the technical sphere, and why, even in personal arguments, we may rely on external, technical knowledge to inform our decisions.

The nuclear energy debate we discussed is a good example. There is a personal sphere argument that happens when families decide whether they want to live next to a nuclear power station. But, technical experts influence personal discussions when they assign risk variables, discuss ground water pollution, and examine the possible consequences of a catastrophic failure. In the public sphere, media and officials interviewed and questioned technical experts to understand the possible long-range implications of building more reactors. The distinction of audiences here, though, is important and ultimately the question is simply: "Who is empowered to decide?" In technical contexts, that answer is based on field-dependent standards designed by members of the sphere. In personal discussions, the participants decide and irrespective of the field producing the evidence, decisions are made individually using standards designed by the members of the relationship. In the public sphere, opinion matters as do beliefs, values, and background.

This is why we can think of our recipients as universal in one sense but also in terms of specific contexts. While the concept of the universal audience is important, the contextual and situational elements of the spheres create a spherical audience. *The spherical audience is made up of the range of possible audience members that exist in a given rhetorical situation.* The challenge for the arguer, then, is to identify arguments that are appropriate for that overlap for their particular rhetorical situation.

What technical arguments would also be necessary and appropriate in the personal and public spheres? In what situations might arguments from the personal sphere be relevant to the technical or public sphere? Arguments should be shaped to fit within the range of expertise and experiences of the audience members. Rather than an abstract notion of an expert or reasonable audience, the spherical audience is one which the speaker identifies the most expert and informed audience within a particular sphere.

Consider Liam and Camille's spherical audience. They were engaged in public debate at their university in front of a group of students who were nonexperts—a public sphere debate. However, the advocates needed to select some arguments from the technical sphere since much of the information on nuclear power is produced in that sphere. They should have been more sensitive to the public audiences and avoided technical language or jargon when sharing evidence from experts. In other words, while the evidence was sound and grounded in the technical sphere, the arguments needed design and reason using public sphere standards. Since audience members bring their own experiences, values and attitudes to their evaluation of the arguments, Liam and Camille must also consider those arguments that exist in the personal sphere as well. That would mean they needed to consider the stories that audience members might have recently heard, and consider which arguments would be likely to have probability and fidelity.

Aspects of the nuclear energy issue that might not be prominent in the technical sphere, but are very important to address in the public and private sphere would be important to consider, such as the fears of those living near the plants, and the negative attitudes many had about nuclear power following the disaster in Japan. By considering the audience in this way, the arguer will have made an effort to engage their actual audience with the strongest and most persuasive arguments. This helps to achieve our goal of creating a close connection with our audience.

PERSUASION PRINCIPLES

Social psychologists have studied persuasion strategies and ways in which advocates can convince recipients to comply or agree with their requests or claims: compliance, identification, and internalization.[28] The first two forms depend heavily on nonlogical responses to messages and are independent of many of the reasoning processes described in this book. The third, however, is closely related to the quality of argument in a message and will be carefully considered later in this section.

Compliance

Compliance is the use of rewards and punishments by a powerful source to get recipients to believe or act in a certain manner. A familiar example is demonstrated by the way students undertake an academic assignment. They recognize that the teacher possesses the means to reward them in the form of a favorable grade, so they carefully structure their work to conform to the teacher's expectations. For a person to gain acceptance of a position through rewards and punishments, other people must believe that person has the resources to reward or punish them and cares whether or not they comply.[29] Argumentation, however, is not a necessary condition for compliance. A teacher may attempt to justify an assignment; a supervisor may explain a work order. But such actions are not required to produce the outcome they desire. The power they possess causes others to do as they say. This form of influence is, therefore, relatively unimportant for our purposes because it is independent of argumentation.

Identification

Identification is influence that occurs because people find a source attractive and wish to enhance their own self-concept by establishing a relationship with the source. People identify with other people whom they like and admire. People often want to be like someone who possesses traits similar or complementary to their own. Advertising often uses this principle. Because we want to be attractive and sexy like the models in the ads, we buy *New Religion* or *Diesel* jeans even if they cost more than others. Because we admire the athletic prowess of LeBron James or Tom Brady, we are persuaded to buy the athletic shoes and products they endorse. In one of the largest athletic endorsement deals in history, soccer star David Beckham was signed to a $160.8 million deal with *Addidas* to endorse their products.

R. Glen Hass has observed that attitudes changed through identification "are not incorporated into the individual's system of beliefs and values; nor are they maintained independent of the message source."[30] In other words, people's acceptance of an argument because of identification is not related to message content but rather to the identity of its source. If the source loses his or her attractiveness or changes the claim in the message, then the recipients will change their own positions as well. For instance, when golfer Tiger Woods was mired in controversy related to his marital infidelity, many of his sponsors such as *Gatorade, Tag Heuer*, and *Gillette* distanced themselves from him and his tainted image.

Researchers demonstrated this principle in an interesting and revealing experiment that showed the influence of attractiveness. Experimenters designed a questionnaire, and a female confederate volunteered to assist by contributing to the group discussions led by the experimenters. She responded the same way in both discussions, and the same people participated in both groups. For one discussion, she looked very attractive, with a stylish haircut, chic clothing, and becoming makeup. In the other, she appeared unattractive, with ugly clothing, messy hair, and a trace of a mustache on her upper lip. The results showed that as an attractive woman, she was much more effective in influencing the group.[31] The group's reactions were based on her attractiveness and not on cognitive processes. They had not thought about her message or about its quality.

Internalization

Unlike compliance and identification, internalization is based on the thought that recipients give to the content of a message. *Internalization is a process in which people accept an argument by thinking about it and by integrating it into their cognitive systems.* Whereas attitudes and beliefs acquired because of compliance or identification usually fade or disappear when the message source loses power or attractiveness, attitudes and beliefs that are internalized often persist and are maintained.

Before continuing our discussion of internalization and the form of source credibility connected with it, we should pause to stress that, like all category schemes, this three-part division of source influence by means of compliance, identification, and internalization is somewhat oversimplified. Power, attractiveness, and content-related credibility often are closely related in any given argumentative situation. If a confident, attractive, highly respected supervisor explains a new marketing plan to subordinates and details a strategy for implementing the plan, that supervisor has clearly influenced the subordinates in all three ways simultaneously. Furthermore, one study of attractiveness revealed that attractive persuaders also tended to be perceived as better communicators, more highly educated, and better informed.[32] In many situations, it would be difficult, if not impossible, to separate any one of these three forms from the other two.

Nevertheless, researchers have linked internalization most closely to what is actually said in the message. People who believe an argument because of its content are most affected by two aspects of the arguer's credibility: expertise and trustworthiness. *Expertise is the possession of a background of knowledge and information relevant to the argument.* It depends on whether people believe an arguer knows the correct position on a topic. *Trustworthiness depends on whether people believe the arguer is motivated to tell them the truth.*[33] Although expertise and trustworthiness are often established partly by initial credibility (the arguer's reputation for being knowledgeable, sincere, and honest), what the arguer actually says and does while presenting the argument is even more vital.

Expertise and Trustworthiness

There are five situational factors that determine the importance of expertise and trustworthiness in judging an arguer's credibility. First, expertise and trustworthiness are especially influential when the question being discussed appears to have a right or wrong answer. For example, if the question is whether violence on television causes violent behavior in children, we are more likely to accept the claims of a media scholar who has studied the relationship over the claims of the "average" parent. However, if the question relates to values and preferences, such as what television programs are most enjoyable and entertaining, we may be heavily influenced by persons we find attractive.[34] The issue of argument spheres and fields applies here. If the question being discussed emerges from the technical sphere, then arguers should provide claims from experts from the relevant fields.

Second, the less involved people are in a message and the less knowledge they have of the topic, the more influenced they will be by the credibility of the source. Presumably, people with low levels of knowledge and interest are unprepared or disinclined to think about the content of arguments or to weigh the merit of claims and evidence advanced in their support. Arguers with low credibility who must address uninformed and disinterested recipients face a greater challenge than that encountered by arguers with high credibility.

Third, people who hear and read arguments from arguers with varying degrees of credibility will tend to forget who made the argument and remember only its content. So people who are initially influenced by an arguer's credibility may later forget the source and remember only the arguments. Researchers call this the "sleeper effect." Although research experiments showing this phenomenon have been somewhat inconsistent, they do indicate that people often forget the identity of a message's source and remember only what was said.[35]

Fourth, expertise seems particularly important when recipients disagree strongly with the position an arguer favors. In a situation in which the position advanced is extremely controversial and in basic disagreement with the recipients' position, a highly credible source will be more persuasive than one who has less expertise. In an experiment reported by Richard E. Petty and John T. Cacioppo, the argument concerned how many hours of sleep were necessary per night. It was attributed to either a Nobel Prize–winning physiologist or a YMCA director. The highly knowledgeable source influenced recipients even when advocating extreme positions (such as two or three hours of sleep per night). When the less expert source advocated the same extreme position, however, recipients were much less likely to believe it.[36] The researchers concluded that the more extreme the discrepancy between an arguer and the audience, the more pronounced will be the influence of credibility in producing attitude change.

Fifth, it is vital that recipients perceive a source as being free of bias and vested interest and concerned primarily with their welfare. Researchers have found that subjects were more influenced by a message when they thought arguers were unaware they were being overheard and thus did not intend to persuade them.[37] Research has also shown that when arguers are expected to have a personal interest in one side of an issue but in fact favor the other side, they have high credibility. For example, a union officer who opposes a strike is more likely to be believed than one who advocates a strike simply because he would be expected to do so. These results and others indicate that recipients' perception of arguers' objectivity, fairness, sincerity, and disinterestedness all contribute to both their trustworthiness and their credibility.

Enhancing Credibility

In the 1968 presidential campaign, opponents of Richard Nixon mass-produced a button portraying a picture of a shifty-eyed Nixon above the question, "Would you buy a used car from this man?" The button's producers were attempting to impugn Nixon's source credibility. *Source credibility refers to an arguer's ability to be believed and trusted by recipients.* The buttons functioned as an argument with an implied claim: "If you wouldn't trust this man enough to buy a used car from him, you should not elect him president." The button makers counted on the public's recollection of charges that Nixon had illegally used campaign funds in 1952, that he had used questionable campaign tactics in the past, and that he had been an ill-humored bad sport after losing a campaign for governor of California in 1962. The button was intended to make voters once again question Nixon's trustworthiness and integrity. Factors such as expertise, trustworthiness, and integrity cause people to accept claims because they have confidence in the character of the person making them. Such factors also contribute to an arguer's source credibility.

The importance of credibility as a factor in persuasion has been recognized at least since the time of Aristotle's *Rhetoric*, written more than 2000 years ago. Aristotle identified the personal character of the speaker as one of the three modes of persuasion and called it *ethos* (the other two modes are *pathos*, the way the audience's emotions put them in a certain frame of mind, and *logos*, the rational proof offered within the message). Of *ethos*, Aristotle said:

> Persuasion is achieved by the speaker's personal character where the speech is so spoken as to make us think him credible. We believe good men more fully and more readily than others: this is true generally whatever the question is, and absolutely true where exact certainty is impossible and opinions are divided. This kind of persuasion, like the others, should be achieved by what the speaker says, not by what people think of his character before he begins to speak.[38]

Aristotle's statements about credibility bring out four points that should be kept in mind when we consider its relationship to argumentation. First, credibility is not a characteristic that the arguer possesses, but one that is attributed to the arguer by the recipients. When Aristotle said that the "speech is spoken so as to make us think [the speaker is] credible," he emphasized the fact that how the speaker appears and what he or she does lead recipients to form certain impressions and beliefs, both about the speaker and about the claims being made. These impressions and beliefs then influence the recipients and cause them to accept or reject the speaker's message.

A second and related point is that credibility is a field- and situation-dependent phenomenon. If credibility results from what recipients perceive about the arguer rather than from intrinsic characteristics of the arguer, then it will vary from one time and situation to another, depending on what an arguer does or says. For example, once elected, Nixon found his credibility rising after foreign policy successes—people responded positively to his trips to China and Russia and the settlement of the Vietnam War. However, once revelations about his involvement in the Watergate scandal become public, his credibility dropped quickly and sharply.[39] Even as arguments are made and refuted, the credibility of advocates may increase or decrease depending on how recipients perceive and react to their points.[40]

The third point Aristotle made is that we value credibility most "where certainty is impossible and opinions are divided." If we cannot verify facts to learn whether a claim is true, or if the claim is value-based rather than fact-based, we will rely heavily upon credibility as a source of our belief. Four decades of research in social psychology and communication have confirmed the importance of credibility.[41] Having reviewed this research, R. Glen Hass concluded, "Few areas of research have produced results as consistent as the findings that sources high in expertise and/or trustworthiness are more persuasive than those low in these qualities."[42] The implications for argument, of course, are that advocates should design arguments to enhance their audience's perceptions of expertise and trustworthiness.

The fourth point Aristotle made is to distinguish between credibility "achieved by what the speaker says" and that attributed to the speaker based on prior reputation. The latter form is called initial credibility. *Initial credibility is based on an arguer's credentials, status, and reputation as known to recipients before they hear or read the message.* Although initial credibility is an important factor in persuasion, its role is based largely on the extent to which a speaker's audience finds the speaker to be attractive or influential. *Derived credibility results from what is said in the message—the quality of the claims and evidence used and the ways arguers employ their own expertise to get their claims accepted.* Compared with initial credibility, derived credibility depends much more on what the audience thinks about the arguer's claims, the extent to which they produce counterarguments, and their assessment of the quality of an arguer's evidence.

Arguers with low credibility, such as students or entry-level workers, face a challenge every time they produce a persuasive message. That challenge is to enhance credibility through and by means of the message itself. This sort of derived credibility comes from features of the message and depends on the arguer's ability to incite listeners to believe that the arguer has their best interests at heart.

Goals

Generally, arguers have three goals toward establishing credibility: (1) to focus the attention of the audience on the content of the message; (2) to make an initial favorable impression on the audience; and (3) to cause the audience to form a favorable impression of their expertise and trustworthiness. The first two are preliminary but necessary conditions for the development of the third. Initial impressions are based on advocates' attractiveness and self-presentation. Although those impressions may seem superficial, they are important. Arguers who cause negative perceptions because of careless appearance or an offhand or grating manner create a deficit against which they must work to get their message fairly considered. If arguments are presented orally and in person, such matters as appearance, delivery, and vocal mannerisms will be significant. If arguments are in written form, poor style, misspellings, and other visual cues will adversely affect the reader.

Once arguers have made a favorable personal impression; they must win a favorable consideration of their claims and evidence by holding the audience's attention and keeping them engaged in the argument. This task is essential to the process of internalization discussed previously by which listeners integrate new beliefs and attitudes into their cognitive systems through an active consideration of claims. As discussed in the previous section, a useful mindset is to think of an extended argumentative case as a narrative. Engaging narratives use examples close to the recipients' experiences, concrete information, good style, personal stories, new and unknown facts, and other materials to contribute to the immediacy of the message. Recipients with low involvement with and little prior knowledge of the advocate's topic will attend more to the credibility of the source than to the content of the message. The arguer with low to moderate credibility, therefore, should expend effort in getting recipients to actively listen to and consider the message.

Strategies

The next item an arguer should have on the agenda is to enhance recipients' perceptions of his or her expertise and trustworthiness. Showing that the position advocated is well supported and thus "correct" enhances expertise. Trustworthiness is developed when arguers show that they have no biases or vested interests they are trying to hide from their recipients. Below are seven specific strategies for enhancing credibility. The first four relate to expertise and the last three to trustworthiness.

1. *Show that the arguer or evidence sources have experience with the topic.* Before seriously considering an arguers' positions, audiences must be reassured that the advocates have studied the matter. Therefore, when arguers present an argument, it is important not only to reference the appropriate sources but to provide their source qualifications as well. If advocates are the authorities on a subject, it is equally important to establish their qualifications or experience with the argument.

2. *Use as many qualified sources as possible.* Qualified and respected sources have a halo effect. They endow those who cite them with their own credibility. If a well-intentioned and earnest, but inexperienced and unqualified, arguer assures us of something, we may be equally as likely to believe her as not to believe her. But if the same speaker cites several respected authorities in support of her claim, the claim gains cogency.

3. *Use sources the recipients are likely to respect.* Sources that one audience might perceive as highly respectable may not be respected by another audience. For example, a labor union officer might be highly credible with union members but have very low credibility with management on the subject of working conditions and employee benefits.

4. *Use sound reasoning.* Recipients of an arguer's message who are being persuaded through the process of internalization will often detect weaknesses in the inferences an advocate makes, and they will think of counterarguments. Well-educated or intelligent recipients often have native reasoning skills and can criticize the arguments of others. A weak and easily rejected argument will often do more harm to one's case than no argument at all because it will raise doubts in recipients' minds about the arguer's credibility on all the other issues in the message.

5. *Demonstrate fairness.* Recall that audiences often become suspicious when they believe an arguer is presenting a one-sided or biased treatment of an issue. Directing attacks at opponents and not their arguments, ignoring or superficially citing their points of view, twisting or misconstruing their position, or engaging in similar practices are not only unethical but also have a boomerang effect, causing audiences to suspect an arguer of unfairness and to distrust his or her overall trustworthiness.

6. *Use reluctant testimony. Reluctant testimony is testimony made by sources that speak against their own vested interest.* Anyone who furnishes evidence against his or her own interests or prejudices is likely to be highly credible to most audiences. The student who argues that tuition should be increased to maintain quality in education, the teacher who maintains that competency tests for teachers are necessary, and the lawyer who supports no-fault divorce laws are all likely to be believed. That is because they are advocating positions opposite to ones they would be expected to advocate.

7. *Avoid inconsistency.* People who take a strong position on an issue and then reverse it lose considerable credibility in the eyes of the public. Such sudden reversals give people the impression that the arguer has not thought through his or her position and lacks a sense of principle.

DEVELOPING PERSUASIVE ARGUMENTS

Finally, advocates may work hard to convince recipients of their credibility and motivate them to accept new claims and causes. However, it is also important for arguers to strengthen the structure of their arguments as well. This process means reviewing the material from Chapters 4, 5, and 6 to consider ways to enhancing the persuasive message within individual arguments.

Supporting Reasoning

In Chapter 1, we noted that an argument's reasoning constructs a link between its evidence, or starting point, and the claim that the arguer wants the audience to accept. Selecting reasoning recognizable to the audience is just as important as selecting a starting point acceptable to them. Arguers should use reasoning acceptable to the recipients. If arguers use an analogy to make a comparison, for example, the audience should view the two things that are compared as similar. If a speaker makes a causal connection (e.g., between nuclear power and energy security), then the audience should clearly understand the reasoning being used.

Consider the following argument made by a defense attorney attempting to persuade a jury not to convict a defendant based on circumstantial evidence:

> DEFENSE ATTORNEY: Just because the defendant was seen leaving the victim's home the evening of the murder, owned a .22-caliber gun of the type used in the crime, and had recently quarreled with the victim, we cannot conclude he is guilty. His guilt must be proven beyond a reasonable doubt.

The attorney's *claim* is, "You should not vote for a conviction." His *evidence* is that the defendant was *only* seen leaving the home, owned a .22-caliber gun, and had quarreled with the victim. His *reasoning* is unstated but is probably that the signs shown in the evidence are circumstantial and insufficient to support a conviction. Why? Because in our judicial system an accused person is assumed innocent until proven guilty beyond a reasonable doubt. If challenged, the defense attorney would further support his reasoning by stating this principle, which he knows is recognized and accepted by the members of the jury.

As a second example, consider a student making a classroom speech opposing capital punishment. Here she attempts to refute an argument often put forward by supporters of capital punishment:

> Some people have argued that capital punishment saves taxpayers money because it costs society $35,000 per year to keep an inmate in prison. Over a lifetime, that amounts to hundreds of thousands of dollars. I would argue that this expense does not mean we should put a person to death. How can we put a monetary value on human life, particularly when there is a chance that the accused may be proven innocent?

Here, the arguer's *evidence* consists of her opponent's cost argument; her *claim* is that cost is an insufficient reason for putting a person to death; and her *reasoning* comes from the prioritization of human life in our culture. Her reasoning, then, is based culturally in the sanctity of human life—a value not all cultures share. Her argument is likely to succeed in a Western culture that orders values in the same way as she does because she has adapted her reasoning to the reasoning habits of her audience.

Knowledge about the audience, therefore, can provide materials useful for supporting reasoning. Principles, conventions, rules, laws, value hierarchies, and other cultural artifacts act as resources arguers can call on in constructing arguments. These resources can be related to the argument field and sphere as well as to the audience type. Certain conventions and rules that guide the use of supporting reasoning in the legal system may hold true in the private sphere as well. For example, argumentation in the private sphere with a private audience may rely upon relational hierarchies and cultural beliefs that may influence the choice of supporting reasoning. Arguers preparing their arguments should ask questions about their audiences, such as, What principles and laws are recognized by my audience? How do audience members order their values and priorities? What rules or conventions do they accept and follow? By determining the answers to such questions, an arguer can locate a foundation for the reasoning and inferences drawn in the argument as a whole.

Supporting Evidence

An arguer who knows how audiences are likely to respond to evidence will generally be more effective than one who does not. A good deal of experimental research has been undertaken on the use and effectiveness of evidence in speeches and arguments. The results of this research have at least three implications for the planning and presentation of arguments.

Authoritative Evidence

Arguments are more effective if advocates use authoritative evidence. Researchers who study the persuasive effects of messages have found that arguers who use evidence are more influential with their audiences.[43] Unless advocates are widely recognized experts on a topic, they should use evidence from authorities accepted by their audiences. No matter how thoroughly arguers may have prepared or how much they may know about a proposition, audiences are unlikely to take their word alone as sufficient support for their claims.

Arguers should identify authorities of their particular topic that the audience is likely to perceive as credible and unbiased. Calling upon the statements and observations of individuals perceived as credible enhances an arguer's credibility. For example, Martin Luther King, Jr. is widely recognized as a civil rights leader who modeled the principles of nonviolent resistance. Bill Gates of *Microsoft* and Phil Knight of *Nike* are both good examples of business leaders who serve as role models of the values and ideals in their respective fields. For this reason, they are considered credible when the state of American business and economics are discussed, especially as related to their respective industries. In addition, although both of these authorities have an interest in the success of their businesses, their agendas are clear and not hidden.

Perceptions of Bias

Advocates should also be aware of the audience's perceptions of bias in authoritative statements. A biased source is one who has personal, political, or economic reasons for supporting a particular point of view. A biased source has a "hidden agenda"—a vested interest in the outcome of the matter being discussed. Audiences are suspicious of biased sources and are likely to reject arguments based on their opinions.[44] Before citing the American Tobacco Institute's claims that there is no causal link between smoking and cancer, or the National Rifle Association's arguments against gun control, the arguer should consider the effect of these authorities on the audience. Even if the facts or opinions of such authorities are well founded, an audience, because of suspicion, may reject their content over their motives.

Novel Evidence

Arguers should introduce facts and information that are "news" to the audience rather than relying on information already well known. When people initially encounter evidence that shocks or disturbs them, they make an effort to reconcile or cope with it. Once the evidence has entered their cognitive systems and they have dealt with it, they are much less impressed or disturbed by it when they encounter it again. Research about the effects of evidence shows that people are more influenced by novel information than by information they have heard before.[45] Therefore, before preparing an argument, arguers should have some idea of their audience's prior exposure to the subject. Facts already known to the audience will not be as effective as new information gleaned from current in-depth research, which was discussed in Chapter 5. New information contained in stories that dramatize the nature and extent of a problem or value discrepancy will be more likely to change or influence the attitudes and values of the audience.

Persuasion research supports that advocates should use and cite external evidence, draw from authorities the audience views as credible, and use novel information and statistics. Evidence is one of the most important factors in an argument. If advocates have done their task, they will be more likely to produce an effective and persuasive argument.

SUMMARY

This chapter emphasized the persuasive use of argument and how advocates could develop a strong relationship with recipients to strengthen their message. It considered how arguments are designed and constructed to be suited to particular argument situations.

The primary role of arguers is to persuasively communicate arguments to recipients in ways that are clear and easily understood. Therefore, arguers must have some knowledge of the recipients and the argument situation. In particular, advocates should strive for a co-orientational view of the relationship with the audience as opposed to using adversarial strategies. We noted the importance of understanding, clearly, the characteristics of the argument situation. Specifically, we looked at the roles of recipients in a variety of situations including private decision-making, private third-party decision-making, public third-party audiences, and extralegal actors.

Arguers should select starting points appropriate to the situation and the recipients' knowledge. We introduced the theory of the narrative paradigm as a way to understand the values, attitudes, and beliefs of our recipients. The narrative paradigm stresses that all humans reason through narrative structures. When recipients hear a new story, they evaluate its probability and fidelity to decide whether it is believable and whether the values it contains resonate with their own values and beliefs. Considering the sphere of argument can help us to choose which arguments will be appropriate for the needs and expectations of the audience.

Social psychologists have identified three major ways arguers can influence recipients. Compliance uses rewards or punishments. Identification is based on the recipients' desire to be more like or close to the arguer. And internalization is the integration of new information and ideas into recipients' cognitive systems.

Internalization occurs when a source is perceived to possess expertise and trustworthiness. Expertise depends on whether an arguer is viewed as knowing the correct position on a topic. Trustworthiness is the extent to which recipients believe the arguer is willing to communicate that position for their benefit. Other research findings indicate that over time people tend to remember the content of a message more than the source from which it came. Also, people who are disinterested and uninformed about a topic will rely more on whether its source appears credible than on what they think of the message content. The two most important aspects of an arguer's credibility are expertise and trustworthiness.

It is important that arguers work to enhance their credibility to provide a stronger connection with the audience. We explored several strategies for enhancing credibility. Additionally, selecting acceptable reasoning is vital if arguers and recipients are to effectively connect evidence through claims. We should use evidence that is appropriate for the situation and acceptable for the audience.

EXERCISES

Exercise 1: Adapting Arguments. Select a situation in which you have recently made or will soon make an argument to a particular recipient or group of recipients.

1. Think of at least three strategies you could use to find out information about your audience's values and attitudes.

2. How could you incorporate the information you would gather into the planning of your message? Specifically, what changes or adjustments could you make in your argument to design it for this particular audience?

3. What strategies could you use to appear credible to this audience? How could you enhance the credibility of your arguments so they would be accepted?

Exercise 2: Strategies. This chapter provided a number of strategies arguers could use to relate their arguments to the orientations of their audiences and to enhance their own credibility. These included the following:

A. Use premises the audience accepts.
B. Use audience values and principles for supporting your reasoning.
C. Cite authorities the audience is likely to respect.
D. Use novel evidence.
E. Keep the audience interested and involved in the argument.
F. Focus on issues the audience is likely to be concerned about.
G. Be aware of possible audience objections and reservations.
H. Appear attractive, and emphasize similarities you share with the audience.
I. Emphasize your own and your source's experience with the topic.
J. Use unbiased and reluctant testimony.
K. Avoid inconsistency.
L. Craft your narrative so that it has probability and fidelity for your audience.

Examine each of the arguments below in which the speaker or writer adheres to or violates one or more of these strategies. Decide whether the audience would respond more or less favorably to the argument because of what is said. Also, decide which of the strategies the arguer uses or violates. Some information about the audience is provided.

*1. Consider the following presentation by a female CEO of a Fortune 500 company:

> And yet women are still in just a fraction of important business leadership positions. One of the biggest barriers to women serving in these leadership positions is the lack of women currently in those roles. Mentorship programs are a vital way we can increase the number of women in the highest positions of power. WalMart has already created such programs to great success. And perhaps CEOs such as Meg Whitman of HP, Virginia Rometty of IBM, Marissa Mayer of Yahoo, Rosalind Brewer of Sams Club, Indra Nooyi

of PepsiCo and other powerful women will show young women and girls that leadership positions are indeed attainable.

2. Senator John McCain, *Congressional Record* (April 8, 2004): S3996–S3999. This speech was delivered to the U.S. Senate:

The sport of baseball is America's pastime and an institution inextricably interwoven into the fabric of our culture. If Major League Baseball and its players fail to act to preserve and protect the sport by adopting a drug-testing policy that effectively deters the players from using anabolic steroids or any other similar performance-enhancing substances, this important part of our culture will remain tarnished. The resolution we are introducing today would call on Major League Baseball and its players to restore legitimacy to professional baseball and make the welfare of the sport more important than the self-serving interests that have a chokehold on America's game.

3. Representative Bart Stupak, *Congressional Record* (November 18, 2004): H9992. This speech was delivered to the U.S. House of Representatives:

I come tonight to put people first, to put our children first as I continue to speak out against the acne drug Accutane. As a legislator, I have called for more restrictions on the distribution and use of this drug, which is known to cause severe birth defects and a form of impulsive behavior and depression in young people taking this drug. This drug has devastated my family with the loss of our son BJ and more than 250 other families who have lost their young son or daughter across this nation while they were taking Accutane.

As we were flying back from Little Rock, Arkansas, CBS news ran a story tonight, and I quote an FDA safety reviewer, Dr. David Graham, when he spoke to the Senate Finance Committee. Dr. Graham said, "I would argue that the FDA as currently configured is incapable of protecting America against another Vioxx." He told the Senate Finance Committee that "there are at least five other drugs on the market today that should be looked at seriously to see whether they should remain on the market." He cited the acne drug Accutane.

*4. From Glenna M. Crooks, director of the policy division of the American Pharmaceutical Association, "How to Make a Difference: Shaping Public Policy," a speech delivered to the First Annual National Conference on Women's Health, Washington, D.C., June 18, 1986. Reprinted in *Vital Speeches of the Day* 52 (1986): 756.

When I first began to work on this topic I was a government official assigned to attend an international meeting of policymakers, theologians, philosophers and scientists to discuss the ways in which the religious values and cultural ethics of a nation affected the ways in which health policy was made…

They assigned me a title, "Policymaking in America," and I set out to explore how I made my living in the public policy arena. My social science perspective shifted into high gear. I read the Declaration of Independence and the Constitution and observed the actions of my contemporaries in government, associations and as individuals in a new light. My observations impressed and awed me. I saw a process that I have come to passionately believe in and promote; one that in my opinion truly capitalizes on the great strengths of the nation.

Some of my friends and colleagues here today know that I have just returned from the Soviet Union where I led a group of health professionals in an international professional exchange. As a result of that experience and my observations of such an oppressive society, my views about the strengths and value of our consensus-building passions as Americans are even stronger. It is one of our greatest national treasures.

5. Former president William J. Clinton, remarks delivered at the Democratic National Convention, September 5, 2012. Transcript reprinted by National Public Radio, http://www.npr.org/2012/09/05/160643183/transcript-bill-clintons-convention-speech (accessed May 16, 2013).

And I have been honored to work with both Presidents Bush on natural disasters in the aftermath of the South Asian tsunami, Hurricane Katrina, the horrible earthquake in Haiti. Through my foundation, both in America and around the world, I'm working all the time with Democrats, Republicans and independents. Sometimes I couldn't tell you for the life who I'm working with because we focus on solving problems and seizing opportunities and not fighting all the time.

6. The following is a student speech presented in a debate for the presidency of the student body at a U.S. university:

We are all here for the same reason—to earn a degree. Yet earning that degree is becoming increasingly difficult. Since I started school here three years ago, fees have increased 15 percent and classes have gotten harder to get into. Like many of you, I spent the first two weeks of the semester begging professors to let me into classes that were already over capacity. If elected your president, I will use my experience not just as a member of your student government, but as a fellow student, to ensure we get what we came for—our degrees!

7. "President's Response to the Tower Commission Report: Iranian Affair, March 4, 1987," *The Public Papers of President Ronald W. Reagan.* Ronald Reagan Presidential Library. http://www.reagan.utexas.edu/archives/speeches/1987/030487h.htm (accessed May 9, 2013).

Let's start with the part that is most controversial. A few months ago I told the American people I did not trade arms for hostages. My heart and my best intentions still tell me that is true, but the facts and evidence tell me it is not.

As the Tower board reported, what began as a strategic opening to Iran deteriorated in its implementation into trading arms for hostages. This runs counter to my own beliefs, to Administration policy, and to the original strategy we had in mind. There are reasons why it happened but no excuses. It was a mistake.

8. "Remarks by the president at the Martin Luther King, Jr. Memorial Dedication," October 16, 2011, http://www.whitehouse.gov/the-press-office/2011/10/16/remarks-president-martin-luther-king-jr-memorial-dedication (accessed May 9, 2013).

And then when, even after the Civil Rights Act and the Voting Rights Act passed, African Americans still found themselves trapped in pockets of poverty across the country, Dr. King didn't say those laws were a failure; he didn't say this is too hard; he didn't say, let's settle for what we got and go home. Instead he said, let's take those victories and broaden our mission to achieve not just civil and political equality but also economic justice; let's fight for a living wage and better schools and jobs for all who are willing to work. In other words, when met with hardship, when confronting disappointment, Dr. King refused to accept what he called the "isness" of today. He kept pushing towards the "oughtness" of tomorrow.

And so, as we think about all the work that we must do—rebuilding an economy that can compete on a global stage, and fixing our schools so that every child—not just some, but every child—gets a world-class education, and making sure that our health care system is affordable and accessible to all, and that our economic system is one in which everybody gets a fair shake and everybody does their fair share, let us not be trapped by what is.

We can't be discouraged by what is. We've got to keep pushing for what ought to be, the America we ought to leave to our children, mindful that the hardships we face are nothing compared to those Dr. King and his fellow marchers faced fifty years ago, and that if we maintain our faith, in ourselves and in the possibilities of this nation, there is no challenge we cannot surmount.

NOTES

1. World Nuclear Association, "Nuclear Power in the World Today," http://www.world-nuclear.org/info/inf01.html (accessed May 31, 2012).

2. "Background on the Three Mile Island Accident," *Website of the US Nuclear Regulatory Commission*, http://www.nrc.gov/reading-rm/doc-collections/fact-sheets/3mile-isle.html (accessed March 11, 2012).

3. "Quick Study: The Facts on Nuclear Power," *Reader's Digest*, nd, http://www.rd.com/home/nuclear-energy-facts/?v=print (accessed May 31, 2012); "Chernobyl's Legacy: Health, Environmental and Socio-Economic Impacts and Recommendations to the Governments of Belarus, the Russian Federation and Ukraine," *Report by the Chernobyl Forum, 2003-2005*, http://www.iaea.org/Publications/Booklets/Chernobyl/chernobyl.pdf (accessed May 31, 2012); and Fred Mettler, "Chernobyl's living legacy," *International Atomic Energy Agency Bulletin* 47, 2006, http://www.iaea.org/Publications/Magazines/Bulletin/Bull472/htmls/chernobyls_legacy2.html (accessed May 31, 2012).

4. Website of the International Atomic Energy Agency, "50 Years of Nuclear Energy," at http://www.iaea.org/About/Policy/GC/GC48/Documents/gc48inf-4_ftn3.pdf (accessed March 8, 2012).

5. Website of the World Nuclear Association, "Outline History of Nuclear Energy," at http://www.world-nuclear.org/info/inf54.html (accessed March 8, 2012).

6. "Outline History of Nuclear Energy."

7. World Nuclear Association, "Nuclear Power in the USA," May 8, 2012, at http://www.world-nuclear.org/info/inf41.html (accessed June 2, 1012).

8. Jake Adelstein and David McNeill, "Meltdown: What Really Happened at Fukushima?" *The Atlantic Wire*, July 2, 2011, at http://www.theatlanticwire.com/global/2011/07/meltdown-what-really-happened-fukushima/39541/ (accessed June 2, 1012).

9. Adelstein and McNeill.

10. Survey conducted by the Civil Society Institute, "After Fukushima: American Attitudes About Nuclear Power Policy Questions," March 22, 2011, at http://www.civilsocietyinstitute.org/media/pdfs/032111%20ORC%20International%20Japan%20Nuclear%20Reactor%20survey%20report%20FINAL1.pdf (accessed June 2, 2012).

11. Civil Society Institute.

12. James M. Action, "Nuclear Power is Worth the Risk," *Foreign Policy*, March 14, 2011, at http://www.foreignpolicy.com/articles/2011/03/14/nuclear_power_is_worth_the_risk (accessed June 2, 2012).

13. Chaim Perelman and Lucie Olbrechts-Tyteca, *The New Rhetoric: A Treatise on Argumentation*, J. Wilkinson and P. Weaver, trans. (Notre Dame, Ind.: University of Notre Dame Press, 1969).

14. Irwin Mallin and Karrin Vasby Anderson, "Inviting Constructive Argument," *Argumentation & Advocacy* 36 (Winter 2000): 120–134.

15. Several news sources reported on the licensing, including Steven Mufson, "NRC Approves Construction of New Nuclear Power Plants in Georgia," *The Washington Post*, February 9 2012, http://www.washingtonpost.com/business/economy/nrc-approves-construction-of-new-nuclear-power-reactors-in-georgia/2012/02/09/gIQA36wv1Q_story.html (accessed June 21, 2012); Steve Hargreaves, "First New Nuclear Power Reactors Ok'd in Over 30 Years," *CNN Money*, February 9, 2012, http://money.cnn.com/2012/02/09/news/economy/nuclear_reactors/index.htm (accessed June 21, 2012); and Ralph Vartabedian and Ian Duncan, "First New U.S. Nuclear Reactors in Decades Approved," *Los Angeles Times*, February 9, 2012, http://articles.latimes.com/2012/feb/09/nation/la-na-nuclear-20120210 (accessed June 21, 2012).

16. Mufson; Hargreaves; Vartabedian and Duncan.

17. Mufson; Hargreaves; Vartabedian and Duncan.

18. Sam Stanton, "Report: UC Davis Pepper Spray Incident Should and Could Have Been Prevented," *Sacramento Bee*, April 11, 2012, http://blogs.sacbee.com/crime/archives/2012/04/report-uc-davis-pepper-spray-incident-should-and-could-have-been-prevented.html (accessed on June 26, 2012).

19. Mallin and Anderson, 120; Gordon R. Mitchell, "Simulated Public Argument as a Pedagogical Play on Worlds," *Argumentation & Advocacy* 36 (Winter 2000): 134–151; David E. Williams and Brian R. McGee, "Negotiating a Change in the Argumentation Course: Teaching Cooperative Argument," *Argumentation & Advocacy* 36 (Winter 2000): 105–130.

20. There are several good resources that discuss the advantages of collaborative argument. These include J. M. Makau, *Reasoning and Communication: Thinking Critically about Arguments* (Belmont, Calif.: Wadsworth, 1990); Williams and McGee, 105–119; Carol K. Winkler and David M. Cheshier, "Revisioning Argumentation Education for the New Century: Millennial Challenges," *Argumentation & Advocacy* 36 (2000): 101–104.

21. Mallin and Anderson, 120–134.

22. Walter R. Fisher, *Human Communication as Narration: Toward a Philosophy of Reason, Value, and Action* (Columbia: University of South Carolina Press, 1987): 58–59.

23. Fisher laid out his Narrative Paradigm in a series of articles including, "Toward a Logic of Good Reasons," *The Quarterly Journal of Speech* 64 (1978); "Narration as a Human Communication Paradigm: The Case of Public Moral Argument," *Communication Monographs* 51 (1984); "The Narrative Paradigm: An Elaboration," *Communication Monographs* 52 (1985); "Clarifying the Narrative Paradigm," *Communication Monographs* 56 (1989). Fisher's theory is not without its critics. For criticism see Robert C. Rowland, "Mode of Discourse, or Paradigm?" *Communication Monographs* 54 (1987); and Barbara Warnick, "The Narrative Paradigm: Another Story," *Quarterly Journal of Speech* 73 (1987).

24. Fisher (1985): 347.

25. Rebecca Leung, "If Anne Frank Only Knew," *CBS News 60 Minutes*, 5 December 2007, http://www.cbsnews.com/2100-18560_162-602415.html (accessed June 2, 2012); See also Damien McElroy, "North Korea Twists Diary of Anne Frank to Attack US as Nazis," *The Telegraph*, 7 March, 2004, http://www.telegraph.co.uk/news/worldnews/asia/northkorea/1456269/N-Korea-twists-Diary-of-Anne-Frank-to-attack-US-as-Nazis.html (accessed June 2, 2012).

26. Fisher (1989): 64–65.

27. Perelman and Olbrechts-Tyteca, 48.

28. R. Glen Hass, "Effects of Source Characteristics on Cognitive Responses and Persuasion," in *Cognitive Responses in Persuasion*, Richard E. Petty, Thomas M. Ostrom, and Timothy C. Brock, eds. (Hillsdale, N.J.: Lawrence Erlbaum Associates, 1981), 142–151. Hass's account is based on H. Kelman, "Compliance, Identification, and Internalization: Three Processes of Attitude Change," *Journal of Conflict Resolution* 2 (1958): 51–60.

29. Hass, 149.

30. Hass, 144.

31. J. Mills and E. Aronson, "Opinion Change as a Function of the Communicator's Attractiveness and Desire to Influence," *Journal of Personality and Social Psychology* 1 (1965): 173–177.

32. S. Chaiken, "Communicator Physical Attractiveness and Persuasion," *Journal of Personality and Social Psychology* 37 (1979): 1387–1397.

33. Hass, 143.

34. Hass, 153.

35. Richard E. Petty and John T. Cacioppo, *Attitudes and Persuasion: Classic and Contemporary Approaches* (Dubuque, Iowa: William C. Brown, 1981), 89–94.

36. Petty and Cacioppo, 64, report a study by S. Bochner and C. A. Insko, "Communicator Discrepancy, Source Credibility, and Opinion Change," *Journal of Personality and Social Psychology* 4 (1966): 614–621.

37. Hass, 159.

38. Aristotle, *Rhetoric*, 1356a.

39. B. E. Bradley, *Fundamentals of Speech Communication*, 4th ed. (Dubuque, Iowa: William C. Brown, 1984), 66.

40. R. Brooks and T. Scheidel, "Speech as Process: A Case Study," *Speech Monographs* 35 (1968): 1–7.

41. See, for example, Hass, 141–172; R. N. Bostrom, *Persuasion* (Englewood Cliffs, N.J.: Prentice-Hall, 1983), 63–87; Gary Cronkhite and Jo Liska, "A Critique of Factor Analytic Approaches to the Study of Credibility," *Communication Monographs* 43 (1976): 91–107; Jesse G. Delia, "A Constructivist Analysis of the Concept of Credibility," *Quarterly Journal of Speech* 62 (1976): 361–375; and James C. McCroskey and Thomas J. Young, "Ethos and Credibility: The Construct and Its Measurement after Three Decades," *Central States Speech Journal* 32 (1981): 24–34.

42. Hass, 154.

43. These studies are summarized in James C. McCroskey, "A Summary of Experimental Research on the Effects of Evidence in Persuasive Communication," *Quarterly Journal of Speech* 55 (1969): 169–170.

44. McCroskey, 172.

45. McCroskey, 174–175.

RESPONSIBILITY

CHAPTER OUTLINE

KEY CONCEPTS

The focus of this chapter is responsibility. And, when we talk about responsibility, we are talking about the obligations arguers accept whenever they try to change the behavior, beliefs, or values of their audiences. Recipients are entitled to well-developed, coherent, and honest discourse because they are being asked to change—that is the point of having a proposition or proving a claim as we discussed in Chapter 4. At the same time, though, recipients have a responsibility to critically understand, evaluate, and research arguments that may change their way of thinking or behaviors. Responsibility for arguments, decisions, and actions rests with all the participants engaged in any argument situation.

This is the point made in Box 11.1, "First Sale." Who is right? There is a legal answer to this question—what does the law say and how does this case fit the law? That is for the

BOX 11.1
FIRST SALE

In 1997, Thai student Supap Kirtsaeng came to the United States to study mathematics at Cornell University in Ithaca, New York. Following Cornell, he continued his studies as a doctoral student at the University of Southern California, Los Angeles. It is unlikely that Kirtsaeng imagined he would become the focus of a U.S. Supreme Court case, but he did. In fact, the lawsuit involving him, *Kirtsaeng v. John Wiley & Sons*, has significant implications for commerce and the success of large and small organizations such as Amazon, Costco, eBay, Craigslist, among many others including used bookstores, used car dealers, libraries, and even garage sales—in essence, his case could determine the success or failure of anyone who engages in the trade of products manufactured or purchased outside the United States.[1]

When Kirtsaeng first arrived in the United States and despite having some financial support, he quickly discovered that the cost of living at Cornell was considerably higher than in Thailand. To pay for books, tuition, and living expenses, he looked for ways to make money and he came across a creative solution. Kirtsaeng knew that textbooks published abroad often have a much lower retail price than the same book published for U.S. sale. This is because publishers price according to their market—a textbook that might sell for $100 in the United States would not achieve many sales at that price in Africa or Asia. Consequently, prices for identical textbooks can vary significantly.

At Cornell, Kirtsaeng found eight widely used textbooks that had English equivalents sold in Thailand for much less money. These books were published by John Wiley & Sons and were sold globally in Europe, Latin America, Africa, and Asia—all at much lower retail prices. Kirtsaeng asked family members to buy copies of these texts in Thailand and send them to the United States where he resold them on eBay using the handle BlueChristine99.

His business was lucrative. While it is unclear exactly how much profit he made, court papers indicate he had gross revenues of more than $1.2 million. For Wiley, this represented a significant loss of profit leading the publisher to sue him in 2008 for copywriter infringement and loss. The New Jersey publisher argued that its disclaimer found on every foreign edition should have been sufficient notice to Kirtsaeng that he was engaging in illegal activities. The disclaimer on foreign editions read, "This book is authorized for sale in Europe, Asia, Africa, and the Middle East only and may not be exported. Exportation or importation of this book to another region without the publisher's authorization is illegal." The lower courts sided with

(continued)

BOX 11.1   CONTINUED

the publisher finding that Kirtsaeng's illegal conduct was willful and he was ordered to pay $600,000 in damages.

While this decision might appear to be fairly straightforward, there is an important legal issue at stake—the idea that "you bought it, you own it." The U.S. Supreme Court held in 1908 that once a copyright owner legally sells a product initially, the ownership claim is then exhausted and gives the buyer the power to keep, share, resell, destroy, or donate the item. This is referred to as the "First Sale Doctrine" that, in essence, allows someone to purchase an item such as a book, artwork, music, or any other consumer good and then resell it without paying fees to the original owner. Once a person buys a product, it is theirs to do with as they please. This is how used bookstores, eBay, Craigslist, or any other of a number of resellers are able to make a profit. Without this doctrine, every transaction of property would require a fee paid to the original copyright or license holder.

Although the "First Sale Doctrine" allows for sale of used goods manufactured and sold within the United States, it is less clear if the same principle exists for property acquired in a foreign country. If the law does not apply to foreign goods, then someone selling a used foreign car, book, artwork, DVD, or music that was imported to the United States needs to pay a royalty for the transaction. This has the potential to drive resellers, libraries, and many other merchants out of business.

The courts, siding with Wiley, accepted the argument that the "First Sale Doctrine" applied only in the United States and that the disclaimer about resale outside of defined territories were sufficient evidence of illegal behavior. Kirtsaeng countered that if this ruling were allowed to stand, there were clear financial incentives for all U.S. manufacturers to shut down domestic manufacturing and move to other countries ensuring that they would be paid twice for every product sold. Libraries would have to pay royalties for every foreign-printed work such as magazines and journals. Art galleries would need to pay additional royalties for works of art purchased abroad. Charitable donations would be subject to proof of origin and subsequently potential fees resulting in declining donations. And, technology becomes an issue when the origin of cloud-based applications may or may not subject purchasers to additional fees and royalties. In March of 2013, the Supreme Court of the United States issued its ruling and on a 6–3 vote found in favor of Kirtsaeng.[2]

This case is interesting on many levels. Consider the following questions

1. Is it possible that both sides of the question are correct? Can Wiley claim ownership of materials even after first sale? Is their disclaimer enough? Could you, or anyone, put a similar disclaimer on a computer, book, or car that commits future owners to paying you a royalty?
2. Is it possible that Kirtsaeng is correct? Do you think that once purchased, any property is his to do what he chooses?
3. Should the courts consider the possible outcomes of their decisions? If siding with Wiley means that eBay, libraries, and used bookstores are damaged, should that shape the final outcome?
4. Putting the legal issue aside for a moment, did Kirtsaeng act immorally? Did he do anything intrinsically wrong?
5. Which way would you have decided the case? Do you think Kirtsaeng should be held accountable for $600,000 in potential lost revenue and fines? Is Wiley in the wrong for challenging the application of "First Sale Doctrine"? What arguments are most likely to sway your decision about this case?

courts to decide as a question of fact. We explored the development of extended fact-based cases in Chapter 7. But there are deeper and more central issues to the questions raised in the case study discussed in Box 11.1—Which side is morally correct? How clearly defined is the idea of "First Sale Doctrine?" Which side made the most ethical arguments? Or, are some of the arguments designed to manipulate or trick an audience? The answers to these depend on values, cultures, spheres, fields and an individual sense of right and wrong.

The idea of ethics was introduced in Chapter 1 as one of the defining characteristics of argument fields. *Ethics is the study of what is morally right or just.* And, *ethical codes are sets of interrelated ethical principles that guide our thoughts, values, and behaviors.*

Too often, poor-quality arguments are unrecognized by recipients, and decisions made using them have the potential to adversely affect recipients and others. As both producers and consumers of argument, our responsibility is to be aware of the quality of our arguments and knowledgeable about standards that will enable us to distinguish arguments that are ethically or morally right from those that are wrong.

Much of this book, leading to this point, has looked at how to make responsible and well-designed arguments. Chapter 2, for instance, focused on developing an honest relationship with recipients. Chapter 3 examined cultural differences that may lead to misunderstandings about intention, right, and wrong including issues related to plagiarism, which was discussed in Chapter 5. Chapters 4, 5, and 6 all considered mistakes and tests of evidence, claims, and reasons to help recipients "test" argument structures. This chapter will focus on how arguments can go wrong and then discuss developing an ethical framework for understanding argument.

The remainder of this chapter, therefore, considers the questions, "How can advocates craft quality arguments?" "What is an ethical argument?" and "How can I avoid unethical argument practice?" First, we will consider the important role played by language and language choices made by advocates. Then, we will examine mistakes made by arguers known as "fallacies" and finally turn our attention to the important role of ethics in argument.

LANGUAGE

From the first chapter, we have stressed the importance of developing credible, collaborative relationships with recipients that can facilitate mutually agreeable outcomes. Part of this process involves selecting appropriate language to communicate effectively and provide the appropriate strength and credibility in an argument situation. This was part of the theme introduced in Chapter 10. This section examines the nature and functions of language in general and then makes specific recommendations regarding its use in argument.

Language can be tricky. The case developed in Box 11.1 hinges on what a particular phrase in the law means. The phrase "lawfully made under this title" could apply to property purchased abroad and imported as Kirtsaeng did or the term *this title* could mean only things made within the United States are covered.[3] How words are used, what they mean, and how they are interpreted shape the outcome of arguments. Perhaps one of the most famous passages in U.S. history that illustrates the importance of language choice comes from a speech delivered by President Abraham Lincoln in his Gettysburg Address on November 19, 1863. It began:

> Four score and seven years ago our fathers brought forth on this continent a new nation, conceived in liberty, and dedicated to the proposition that all men are created equal.[4]

Is there any significance to Lincoln's words? The speech itself certainly carried with it an importance and elegance suitable not only for 1863 but for the twenty-first century as well. But do the actual words used to convey the message carry with them any particular significance? Lincoln's opening could just as easily have begun:

> Eighty-seven years ago those who came before us established in this country a new system of government created in freedom and based on the idea that all people are created equal.

Is there a difference? The content remains the same, but the words are now simpler and perhaps more contemporary. But the change in language seems to change more than just the words; some of the force and spirit of the original version are gone.

The language Lincoln used to express his message was not chosen randomly—nor is the language used to express everyday arguments. Even if we are not aware of our language choices, we adhere to the rules of grammar and vocabulary inherent in our language. The stronger our command of language, the better able we are to select which words to use. As you will see later in this chapter, the eloquent language Lincoln used contributed not only to the beauty of his address, but also to its persuasiveness. Harold Zyskind, in his study of Lincoln's address, noted that, although the occasion was ceremonial (dedication of the cemetery at Gettysburg), the address itself was argumentative and was designed by Lincoln to persuade members of his audience to rededicate themselves to the reunification and continuance of the federal government after the Civil War.[5] Gilbert Highet, writing of Lincoln's address, observed:

> No one thinks that when he was drafting the Gettysburg Address, Lincoln deliberately looked up these quotations and consciously chose these particular patterns of thought. No, he chose the theme. From its development and from the emotional tone of the entire occasion, all the rest followed, or grew—by the marvelous process of choice and rejection, which is essential to artistic creation.[6]

In the course of devising and framing arguments, we select the words by which our arguments are expressed. These words have a profound impact on the use and interpretation of arguments because their significance lies not in the words themselves, but in what they come to mean for the people who use them. The effects of language depend upon the degree of concreteness and emotive significance of the words themselves.

George Orwell once lamented about the decline of the English language. He argued that when people use language inaccurately or sloppily, they cloud the ability of others to think clearly. They make the language unclear such that their thinking becomes unclear. His argument is that when we allow language to be used poorly, we create a self-fulfilling prophecy that will result in our own thoughts becoming muddled and sloppy. He said, "[Language] becomes ugly and inaccurate not because our thoughts are foolish, but the slovenliness of our language makes it easier for us to have foolish thoughts."[7] His point was that we can reverse this process IF we choose to use language carefully and with clear meaning.

As we discussed in Chapter 1, the ability to think critically about arguments is important for both arguers and analysts. When language is used inaccurately and sloppily, it becomes a barrier to our ability to think critically and argue intelligently. Howard Kahane highlighted the importance of understanding how language is used and misused when he commented, "It is quite useful for students to gain insight into how language, the medium through which they obtain information from others, can be and often is used to obfuscate and otherwise deceive the unwary."[8]

Orwell's argument is important. If we communicate our ideas clearly, we are able to engage our audiences' minds in more complex and accurate ways. If we are not clear, then our ideas may become lost in our audiences' confusion. We need to be careful with our language choices, and we need to avoid patterns of confusing language choices. In other words, advocates have a responsibility to develop habits that allow them to think clearly and focus on positive approaches for engaging and energizing civic engagement. Orwell's point was that this is a first and necessary step toward "political regeneration."[9]

Meaning

Words by themselves have no intrinsic meaning. They acquire meaning only insofar as people use them to describe their world. This is the point made by C. K. Ogden and I. A. Richards in their book *The Meaning of Meaning*.[10] Their argument was that humans are symbol users who develop symbols to stand for thoughts and ideas in their minds. The mental image, also known as a representation, is the result of direct experience or imagination. For example, if John Smith sees a green pine tree, he develops a representation of the tree through direct experience. John is also able to imagine a green pine tree that he has never seen—based on his past experience with pine trees.

Communication involves the process of transforming such representations into symbols. Therefore, the user's mental image of a tree is translated into the word *tree*, and the language provides the tool for sharing representations, or meanings, with other language users. Ogden and Richard's model is illustrated in Figure 11.1, Symbol, Reference, and Referent.

FIGURE 11.1 Symbol, Reference, and Referent   (Symbol) The word *tree*   (Referent)

The referent is the actual material object referred to in language. The symbol is the word used to refer to the referent. The reference is the association the language user makes between the symbol *tree* and the material object that the user has experienced.

The major point this model makes is that the symbol is connected with the referent only by way of an association made by the language user. In other words, the meaning of the word rests in the people using the word. Therefore, the connection is indirect and represented by a broken line. What is the implication of this for communication? Because there is no direct relation between symbol and referent, there is room for misunderstanding. Two language users could make the connection differently and therefore have two diverse understandings of what is meant by *pine tree*. Language user 1 may think of a giant evergreen tree, while language user 2 may think of a dwarf pine. It is not difficult to imagine the misunderstandings in language use that arise when symbols are ambiguous or when language users have widely discrepant experiences with some set of referents. Because of this, the level of abstraction and concreteness of words and symbols in the language system affects the precision and accuracy of communication.

Abstraction

Because the relationship between the symbol and the referent is subject to variation; communication is not 100 percent efficient. Variations occur for many reasons, and thus complex meanings can become lost or changed. This can occur because members of different cultures have different meanings for symbols, or when people within the same culture do not share the same frame of reference.

For communication to be entirely efficient, the representation in the recipient's mind should be identical to the representation in the speaker's mind. In other words, if Sue says, "There is a tree outside my window," a hearer would have to be able to know exactly to which tree Sue is referring. This is not possible, because the symbol used is not the referent. It is only indirectly related to the referent through the user's mind.

Language serves as a vehicle for conveying meaning between a source and a receiver. When we speak, we not only select words and gestures we think will effectively communicate our thoughts and intentions, but we also select those we think will have some meaning for the recipient. The difference in each case is the knowledge and experience the recipient is able to use in understanding the language. If the recipient has a great deal of knowledge about the subject, advocates would not need to dwell on aspects of definition or concrete examples. Instead, they could develop more abstract and theoretical discussions, and the language used could be more complex.

The complexity of the connection between the referent and the symbol is measured by the relative abstractness of the symbol. *Abstraction refers to the degree to which relevant characteristics are omitted in language.* As a recipient's knowledge of a subject increases, the language used to convey the subject can be more abstract. Consider the following:

Melissa: Would you go to my car and get my book?

Mark: Sure, but what book in what car?

Melissa: My car is the white Nissan Altima license plate MELISSA-1. I need my argumentation textbook.

Mark: Sure, no problem.

In the first part of the conversation, Melissa assumed that Mark knew which car was hers and what book she wanted. Her language choices were relatively vague and abstract because she assumed Mark had a level of knowledge that would supply the missing details. After it became apparent that Mark was unsure about which car and book, Melissa added more information to help make the request clearer and less ambiguous.

When we argue, we use language that we assume the recipients can understand. We develop examples and speak with a level of abstraction and ambiguity appropriate for the given audience. It is important, however, to recognize that not all recipients have the necessary background and experience to understand abstract language. Based on the advocate's understanding of the particular recipients being addressed, relatively more or less ambiguous language and examples may be used to convey the argument.

S. I. Hayakawa was noted for his work in the area of language abstractness and the development of the abstraction ladder.[11] He argued that when we use language, we choose to make it more or less abstract as the situation warrants. His abstraction ladder looks much like the one in Figure 11.2, Language Abstraction Ladder.

The bottom of the ladder represents the most concrete—and least abstract—form of language. It uses symbols that represent the referent as specifically as possible. The top of the ladder, however, is the least specific. A manufactured item can be almost any human-made product. A listener hearing more specific language would be better able to develop a mental representation of the referent than a listener hearing the more abstract language.

Abstract language is, by its nature, ambiguous. Arguers selecting ambiguous language run the risk of being misunderstood. Why, then, would a speaker choose to use abstract language? The answer can be found in the nature of the audience. For instance, most people have never seen John's car. If he refers to it and wants to persuade his listeners to buy it, they would be unable to create an accurate mental image if the language he uses is too specific for them to understand. Therefore, as a speaker, he needs to orient the recipients with language they can understand by using more abstract, commonly understood language. He might say:

Come buy my truck. It is a Toyota Tacoma built in one of the Toyota plants in San Antonio, Texas.

By blending the concrete with the abstract, arguers can orient their recipients to the reference and then move to more concrete symbols. We do this often because it is important that recipients understand the context, or orientation, of the argument. Even the process of giving directions involves a careful blend of the concrete with the abstract. If a speaker invites someone to her home and says, "I live at 4111 North 37th Street," she assumes that the recipient understands what city and how to get there. The address alone is very concrete. But if the recipient was from another city or country, the speaker would need to be more concrete until the recipient was oriented. For instance she might have to say:

I live in the United States.

I live in Sacramento, California.

Go east on Highway 50, take Exit 8A.

In this case, the speaker begins by providing directions with a common frame of reference, which may be relatively abstract, and then provides greater focus and concreteness as the discussion moves forward. The significance of appropriately placing words on the ladder of

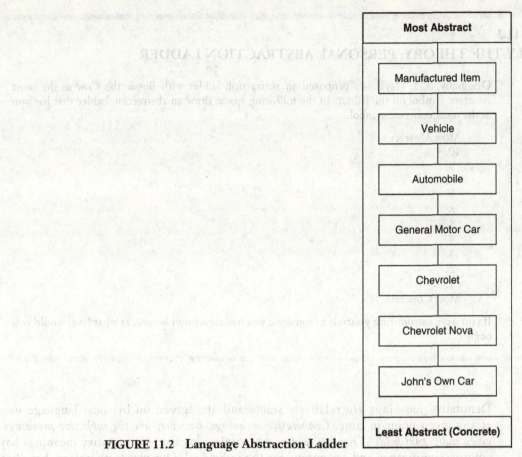

FIGURE 11.2 Language Abstraction Ladder

abstraction when making arguments will be explored further in the last section of this chapter. In Box 11.2, "Apply the Theory," you can use the abstraction ladder to describe yourself.

Connotations and Denotations

The triangle of meaning and abstraction have several important implications for arguers. If one recognizes that people may interpret words differently depending on the degree of abstraction, then an arguer should be able to consciously select words that affect people in the way the arguer intends.

The process to be used in selecting words can best be understood by considering the two poles of meaning in language use. Each word when used has a denotative meaning and also a connotative meaning. *The denotative meaning is the objective meaning held by language users in general.* A word's denotative meaning can be found in a dictionary. Dictionaries record the meanings of words established in the culture as a whole.

■ ■ ■ ■ ■

BOX 11.2

APPLY THE THEORY: PERSONAL ABSTRACTION LADDER

Originally, S. I. Hayakawa proposed an abstraction ladder with Bessie the Cow as the most concrete symbol on the ladder. In the following space, draw an abstraction ladder that has you as the most concrete symbol.

Most Abstract
10.
  9.
  8.
  7.
  6.
  5.
  4.
  3.
  2.
  1.
Most Concrete

If you were introducing yourself to someone you had never met before, at what level would you begin?

Denotative meanings are relatively stable and are agreed on by most language users at any given point in time. *Connotative meanings, however, are the subjective meanings a given individual holds of symbols used in a particular situation.* Connotative meanings have emotive significance and are unique for the individual. Our words, therefore, have both denotative and connotative significance.

For example, consider the word *fag. Webster's New Collegiate Dictionary* defines *fag* as "toil or drudgery."[12] Yet, if you were to call someone a "fag," referring to the nature of that person's work, odds are that person would respond impolitely. This is because most people have a negative connotation of the word—many find it to be derogatory, despite the definition in the dictionary. The meaning of the word *fag* is found not in the word itself, but in the person to whom the word is addressed. Similarly, in the seventeenth century, the word *good-bye* was seen as blasphemous because it contracted the Lord's name. The correct phrase to use when parting was "God be with you," and the shortened form, "God b'ye," was seen as inappropriate and disrespectful. Over time, the meanings of words change and adapt as the culture changes and as words become used and acquire new or different meanings. (Box 11.3, "Lost Symbols," for example, lists some rather obscure words that are so dated or infrequently used that they may disappear from the English language entirely.)

Our language is full of words that have been replaced by other words carrying less negative or more positive connotations. This is the function of euphemisms. *Euphemism is a linguistic device for replacing words and phrases that carry a negative connotation with those that*

■ ■ ■ ■ ■

BOX 11.3
LOST SYMBOLS

Symbols are important to our thinking and communicating processes. Without them, the communication becomes nearly impossible, and the ability to share complex thoughts is remote at best. Language symbolizes the importance of things by naming them or giving them a symbol. People, for example, are important because we have names. Some symbols, however, are almost lost in the huge collection of English symbols. For example:

Aglet—the covering on the end of a shoelace.

Duff—the decaying organic matter found on a forest floor.

Harp—the small metal hoop that supports a lampshade.

Phosphenes—the lights you see when you close your eyes hard.

Piggin—a small wooden pail with one long stave used as a handle.

Quarrel—a small, diamond-shaped pane of glass, like that used in lattice glass.

Solidus—the oblique stroke (/) used between words or in fractions such as 7/8.

Zarf—a holder for a handleless coffee cup.

carry a positive connotation. (Of course a speaker intending to convey a negative feeling might also substitute negative words for positive words.) For example:

POSITIVE TERM	NEGATIVE TERM
collateral damage	unavoidable innocent deaths
daytime drama	soap opera
indiscretion	moral wrong
inappropriate	illegal
air support	bombing
terminated	fired
destabilize	overthrow
intelligence gathering	spying
sanitation engineer	garbage collector
correctional facility	prison
low-income	poor
freedom fighters	revolutionary guerrillas
passed away	died
differently abled	disabled

There are many other possible examples, but in each case words with the same denotative meaning may be substituted for one another with the objective of changing the connotative meanings.

This section has illustrated three characteristics of language. First, the meaning of language depends on language users because symbols by themselves have no intrinsic meaning.

Second, language can be abstract or concrete, and arguers must decide what degree of abstraction is appropriate for a given situation and audience. And third, because language allows room for different interpretations of the meanings of symbols by both the speaker and the listener, meanings of symbols may vary. Whereas denotative meanings are the objective meanings of words agreed on by the language users, connotative meanings are the subjective interpretations of words that depend on the individual symbol user. Arguers should be sensitive to the fact that the words they use have both denotative and connotative meanings when they are interpreted. The list of words in Box 11.4, "Apply the Theory," provides many examples of words and phrases that have meanings specific to time and person. Sometimes these words become overused to the point where their original meanings become lost.

Using Language

Understanding the nature of language can help you better construct effective arguments. Because language is used referentially, artistically, and persuasively in arguments, to be effective it must be understood, adhered to, and remembered. Certain strategies for the choice of language and phrasing in your arguments will make them clearer, more vivid, and more persuasive. In his essay "Politics and the English Language," George Orwell warned that if we allow our language to become imprecise and ambiguous, each of us contributes to the decline of our society. To avoid such decline, he offered the following six guidelines that communicators should use in the presentation of ideas—written or oral:

1. Avoid the use of clichés. These are figures of speech such as analogies or examples that advocates and recipients are used to seeing or hearing. Arguers should seek new and interesting ways of developing their points.

BOX 11.4
APPLY THE THEORY: BANISHED WORDS

Below is the "Lake Superior State University 2012 List of Banished Words." Each year, people nominate words for the list based on "their misuse and overuse by the general public."[13]

Amazing
Baby bump
Shared sacrifice
New normal
Occupy
Man cave
Blowback
Thank you in advance
Pet parent
Ginormous
Trickeration

Choose a word or phrase from this list or your own vocabulary and see if you can go a day without saying it. Make a list of words or phrases that you would nominate for this year's list.

2. Use clear and plain language. Avoid using a long or complex word when simple and clear language will suffice.

3. Seek clarity through brevity. Orwell recommended that if a speaker could cut a word or sentence, then cut it.

4. Work to use an active voice over passive. This is a way to help keep recipients engaged in the message.

5. Avoid the use of jargon, technical terms, or foreign phrases where possible. Unless recipients clearly understand these terms, Orwell recommended the use of everyday language.

6. Finally, Orwell noted that sometimes these rules should be broken if necessary, but those occasions should be rare.[14]

Orwell's point was that we need to be vigilant when it comes to our communication skills and language use. Our ideas and arguments should be clear. We should work to minimize confusion and maximize common understandings and shared meanings. What follows are general guidelines and principles for language use, not hard-and-fast rules. As you recall from previous sections, the use of language in argument depends as much on the situation and the listeners as it does on the argument itself; however, these guidelines will help to ensure that you make the best possible use of the resources language has to offer. Box 11.4.1, "Apply the Theory," will guide you through a way of designing e-mail messages using Orwell's principles. Then, see how your e-mails work with the following criteria.

1. *Use clear language.* Clarity is composed of two factors: selecting language at the appropriate level of abstraction for the recipient, and avoiding convoluted or ambiguous language. Matching the concreteness of the word choice to the experience of the recipient and expressing oneself simply and directly ensure that the argument will be understood as the arguer intended.

As we noted earlier in the chapter, the appropriate use of abstraction/concreteness depends on the relationship between the arguer and recipient. If the recipient does not know of or understand very concrete references made by the arguer, the language is too concrete. Likewise, if the arguer and recipient understand each other's personal references or the background to the argument, then more concrete terms can be used.

The second requirement of clarity is simplicity. Often people use convoluted and ambiguous language to convey their argument when simpler language might be just as effective. But such practices as circumlocution (using an unnecessarily large number of words to express an idea) and obfuscation (using words confusingly) are not always intentional. Their unintentional use often muddles arguments and interferes with their effectiveness.

Because the objective of the arguer is to get the audience to understand the argument, the language should be as simple and concise as possible. Consider the following:

> In my well-considered interpretation of the events preceding this encounter and considering what others have said to me as well as my own background, I think we should increase the expenditures for the bus fare by 10 cents.

A simpler way of conveying the same message is:

> I think we should raise the bus fare by 10 cents.

■ ■ ■ ■ ■

BOX 11.4.1

APPLY THE THEORY: USING ORWELL

A recent article by Stephanie Vozza in *Entrepreneur* challenged e-mail writers in professional settings to attempt to constrain the length of e-mail messages to five sentences.[15] The goal, as with Orwell's instructions, is to write clearly, concisely, and effectively. The challenge, she noted, is that people try to explain too much and go on for too long with the result that meanings get lost or confused.

Her recommendation is that professional e-mails be limited to answering the following five questions:

1. Who is sending the e-mail? In other words, the author should introduce himself or herself to the recipient.
2. What do you want of the recipient? What, specifically, is the author asking of the recipient?
3. Why are you asking the recipient? Presumably, an e-mail could have gone to any number of other people. Why this person? What is it about their position or their abilities that led you to write to them?
4. Why should be recipient "do" the request? There should be some reason for a person to take time and expend energy to perform the requested action.
5. What next? A well-written e-mail should offer the next steps once the request is accomplished. This provides the recipient with a sense of how the response will be used and how it "fits" into a larger picture.

Take a look at your last e-mail to a professor or business colleague and analyze it using these criteria (and Orwell's six rules for using language). How does it fare? Redraft it using these principles. Does it seem clearer? Can you make it clearer and more concise? Try using these principles for one week and check with the recipients if they liked or did not like this approach compared with previous e-mails.

If the argument is not understood or if there is confusion about what the arguer's claim is, the argument will not be effective.

2. *Define terms when necessary.* If an argument hinges on a particular term, and if there's a chance that the audience might not understand the term in the way the arguer intended, then the term should be defined. By providing clear definitions, the arguer can help reduce unwanted connotations or ambiguities that might otherwise develop. For example:

> I think that regardless of the politics in any given country, we should provide the people with support—by support I don't mean military aid; I do mean economic and food assistance.

By defining "support," the arguer avoided possible pitfalls from a misinterpretation of what "support" is used to mean. The definition helps shed the connotation of military assistance and makes the claim more concrete.

3. *Express arguments vividly.* An important dimension of an argument's persuasiveness is the vividness with which it is expressed. We can select words and modes of expression that depersonalize what we say and make it seem distant and remote from the audience. Using the passive voice, the antecedentless "it," and complex formal language makes what we say less vivid. Compare the following two arguments (which say essentially the same thing):

> Sometimes the debate over abortion asks the wrong question. What is truly at issue is not a balancing of the rights of one person against the rights of another. Rights are not zero sum, and they do not shrink when they are extended to someone else.[16]
>
>   Sometimes the abortion controversy is directed at incorrect issues. It is believed that one person's prerogatives are counterbalanced against another's. Individuals' rights are not differentially assigned so that rights accorded to some individuals are removed from others.

The second passage uses the passive voice and such formal words as:

prerogatives
counterbalanced
differentially assigned
accorded

The original version uses active voice and everyday language. In addition, it employs colorful terms and metaphor to engage readers and enliven their interest, such as:

asks the wrong question
truly at issue
balancing...against
zero sum
shrink

When we make a problem or a description comes alive for the audience, we endow it with what Perleman and Olbrechts-Tyteca call "presence."[17] *Presence is a quality of argument that moves things near to us in space and time so they act directly on our sensibility*. This quality is best demonstrated by the following story:

> A king sees an ox on its way to sacrifice. He is moved to pity for it and orders that a sheep be used in its place. He confesses that he did so because he could see the ox, but not the sheep.[18]

We care much more about what is immediate to us than about what is distant. Vivid language increases the immediacy of the arguer's subject and point of view.[19] By engaging his or her audience's care and concern, the arguer can use vividness to make arguments more effective.

4. *Avoid sexist and racist language.* Our earlier discussion of George Orwell and language use made the point that language can limit and shape the way its users think and act. It is important to be aware that there are words and phrases that negatively label and disparages or devalues women, minorities, and other economically and culturally oppressed groups. Many people are unaware of how their conscious forms of expression reflect unconscious assumptions about groups that may be a part of their audience. When those assumptions are negative and are reflected in the claims an arguer makes, the argument's effectiveness is undermined.

Sexist use of language occurs in many of our habits. When we are referring to a group of mixed gender, we often use the masculine pronoun. The structure of our language typically gives men first priority.

The men and women in this room…
The men and women of this university…
Mr. and Mrs. Smith

It is traditionally women who abandon part of their identity or definition upon marriage by giving up their "maiden" names. Furthermore, women are often equated with children. The expression "women and children first" testifies to the linguistic equality women share with children. There are many terms used to define women as children or subhuman people. For instance, a woman may be called a "babe," "chick," "doll," or "fox."[20] Likewise, women are referred to as girls—even when they are twenty, thirty, forty, fifty, and even sixty years old ("The office girls got this for you").

Sexism can creep into our language in subtle ways. Consider the following paragraph:

> The standards of achievement in this profession are set by the men who have been most productive. The exceptional manager should recognize that his productivity depends upon his sales team and the women in his office staff.

Several sexist uses of language are embedded in this passage. In the first sentence, *men* is used to refer generically to all practitioners of the profession (and they are productive). Again, in the second sentence, the manager is referred to by the masculine possessive pronoun *his*. Furthermore, supervisors are characterized as male, while clericals ("the office staff") are assumed to be female. Similarly, it has become common to begin using the male term "guy" to refer to both women and men. Consider the sentence to a classroom of both women and men: "Good morning. I hope you guys have all finished the reading for today because there will be a pop quiz at the end of class." The term "guy," as with its predecessor "man," is a sexist term that has become part of common language use. The assumptions made by using such language should be avoided.[21] Although nonsexist language rarely, if ever, alienates recipients, sexist language is almost certain to do so.

Unconscious racism in language use is also highly problematic. In the century following the Civil War, America became increasingly committed to equality among races and ethnic origins. In such Supreme Court cases as *Brown v. Board of Education* in 1954, in the Civil Rights Act of 1964, and in affirmative action measures, efforts have been systematically made to eliminate discrimination against minority groups.

These measures were important, but failed to provide for equality because, at least in part, they did nothing to override the attitudes of the people opposed to racial and ethnic equality. The laws changed, but the language did not, and because language helps to shape a culture's reality, the language fostered the attitudes.

Civil rights leader Stokely Carmichael recognized the power of language as a barrier to racial equality when he spoke in 1967. His point was that to be truly free, a people needed to exercise their ability to define themselves and use language to empower and not oppress:

> …for white people to be allowed to define us by calling us Negroes, which means apathetic, lazy, stupid, and all those other things, is for us to accept those definitions. We must define what we are and move from our definitions and tell them to recognize what we are.[22]

African Americans and other minorities have objected to labels and terms of reference having negative connotations. The key terms to keep in mind when discussing minorities and minority, issues are "respect" and "equality." Minorities should not be set apart unless there is good reason to do so and if they are, they should be referred to in non-oppressive ways. At one school, a discussion was held concerning salary differentials related to people's ethnic origin. Caucasians discussing the issue continually referred to themselves as "majority faculty." This self-reference reasserted their status within the system. When reminded that a term such as "nonminority faculty" might be more neutral, one officer responded that he was not about to make that concession. Evidently, he was well aware of the role language plays in reasserting power relations between Caucasians and minority groups in this country.

In framing arguments in language, arguers should make every possible effort to engage, befriend, and appeal to the audience through the medium of their expression. Conversely, they should systematically avoid sexist and racist language along with obscenity or other inappropriate word choices. Nothing is to be gained by insulting or alienating recipients. It is in the arguer's best interest to word arguments with care, taste, and sensitivity for those to whom the argument is directed.

FALLACIES

When you examine the arguments you produce or try and understand those made by other advocates, you may discover that some of the relationships among the argument parts do not seem to work—they may be disjointed, confused, or simply incorrect. If this happens, you have probably found a fallacy in the argument. *A fallacy is an argument that is flawed by irrelevant or inadequate evidence, erroneous reasoning, or improper expression.* Fallacies can be persuasive because they are false arguments that may seem reasonable and acceptable but are based on erroneous assumptions or invalid reasoning. If recipients are not critically wary, they can be easily swayed by these arguments—they can sound appealing and, on the surface, make sense.

The ability to think and act critically depends in many ways on our ability to understand how arguments work as well as the ability to identify flaws that may appear. This means that identifying fallacies is an important skill for arguers to develop because it helps them understand when an argument is flawed even when it is persuasive. Precisely because the purpose of argument is to persuade recipients to accept sound, well-supported claims, advocates should avoid practices that lead them to decisions based on erroneous inferences and assumptions.

The case developed in Box 11.1 helps illustrate these points. Kirtsaeng argued that if the courts hold that "First Sale Doctrine" does not include foreign goods, U.S. manufacturers would have a financial incentive to move manufacturing abroad. The clear implication is that the United States will lose its factories, jobs, and other revenues. Does this argument make sense? Is it valid? These are the questions recipients should ask when faced with potentially persuasive viewpoints. Box 11.5, "Apply the Theory," will provide you with a guided discussion of this argument.

Although fallacies represent a misuse of argument, someone who commits a fallacy is not necessarily unethical. Arguers may commit fallacies unintentionally as well as intentionally. Unintentional fallacies occur when an arguer is unaware of proper argument

BOX 11.5

APPLY THE THEORY: WHICH FALLACY?

Kirtsaeng made an argument suggesting that a court decision against him has the potential to create a financial incentive for U.S. manufacturers to move their factories to foreign countries. The possibility, he suggested, is that manufacturing could be destroyed in the United States and consumers would end up paying higher prices.

In the following sections, we will explore types of fallacies. These are identified in Box 11.7. As you read, try and identify the following fallacies by considering the following questions:

1. Are there any audience-based fallacies in this argument?
2. Any language-based fallacies?
3. Any grounding fallacies?
4. Reasoning fallacies?

If you found any of these fallacies, how might you "fix" his argument to strengthen it legitimately?

---

construction or use and commits a fallacy without realizing it. In this sense, fallacies are not only deceptive to audiences, but to speakers and writers as well.

Some arguers, however, may intentionally commit a fallacy so as to persuade a listener rather than search out appropriate support for argument positions. Intentional fallacies represent a deliberate attempt to mislead an audience into taking some action based on false information. For example, an arguer might use a biased source, omit part of a quotation and thereby misrepresent what a source said, or attribute a statement to an opponent that was never made. Such intentional fallacies carry important ethical implications.

Consider the argument developed in Box 11.6, The Case of Lawrence West. It illustrates how fallacies find their way into arguments and how we can justify contradictory premises.

West's argument that building weapons of mass destruction saves lives is interesting because it juxtaposes two seemingly irreconcilable premises. On the one hand, a recipient is faced with the premise that nuclear weapons can destroy the world and, on the other hand, with West's conclusion that such weapons made by the United States are not weapons of death but are instead weapons of salvation. The argument is almost Orwellian in the sense that "War is peace" and "Weapons of mass destruction save lives."[23]

This is an example of a flawed argument because the arguer uses the way it is expressed to convince the audience to simultaneously hold two mutually exclusive beliefs. Although its surface meaning may seem apparent, closer examination of the argument reveals a flaw. The way it is expressed may seem reasonable, but its development is not.

For example, West says that bad weapons are weapons of death, which can result in world destruction. However, the weapons he helps build are weapons of life, weapon-killers, anti-weapons, which preserve world peace. The problem with the argument is that it assumes the positive attributes through assertion without any justification for or evidence supporting his claims. Instead, West uses strong and emotion-laden language to focus attention away from his lack of evidence and support. The resulting argument is fallacious.

■ ■ ■ ■ ■

BOX 11.6
THE CASE OF LAWRENCE WEST

Lawrence West's career had focused on developing nuclear weapons at the Lawrence Livermore National Laboratory. When he began, he expressed reservations about working on weapons of mass destruction and his role in their manufacture. Over time, however, he was able to dismiss his concerns and argued:

> Nowadays I would be quite willing to go and do full-time weapons work because I see the vast possibilities.... A tremendous amount of creativity is needed, and there are very few scientists willing to do it. Nuclear weapons can devastate the world. I recognize that. But we are making anti-weapons. My primary interest is not trying to find better ways to kill people, but better ways to kill arms.... I don't think I fall in that category of working on weapons of death. We're working on weapons of life, ones that will save people from the weapons of death.[24]

Theorists who study argument agree almost unanimously that fallacies are deceptive and consequently dangerous.[25] Aristotle observed that honest speakers needed to prepare for spurious arguments and arguments that look genuine but are no more than shams.[26] All recipients of argument, therefore, need to develop a critical capacity to understand and assess the arguments directed at them.

Although many theorists have identified countless types and variations of fallacies, our focus here is to examine how fallacies can infiltrate arguments and unsuspecting audiences and deceive them. Box 11.7, Types of Fallacies, describes a classification system that illustrates how fallacies function in the argument situation and the specific parts of the argument. Before we proceed, we have a final word of caution. Just because an argument is fallacious does not necessarily mean that the claim is incorrect. The claim may, in fact, be reasonable and valid, but not for the reasons and evidence expressed in the argument.

The fallacies in this section are divided into four groups: (1) fallacies related to audience that focus the recipient's attention away from the relevant issues; (2) fallacies of language use that occur when words and grammar used by an arguer mislead or confuse the recipients; (3) fallacies of grounding that stem from a lack, poor quality, or incorrect use of evidence; and (4) fallacies of faulty reasoning that provide erroneous or insufficient connections between the evidence and the claim.

Audience-Based

When arguers present arguments to direct a recipient's attention away from the central argument and to some other irrelevant argument, then the advocate has committed a fallacy to misdirect the audience's attention. Most often, fallacies of this type are called *ad* fallacies, *Ad* is Latin for "to," and fallacies of misdirection are often called *ad* fallacies because they appeal to the audience and not to the arguments. When an arguer shifts attention away from the argument and to the audience or something else, then the arguer has committed this fallacy.[27]

■ ■ ■ ■ ■

BOX 11.7

TYPES OF FALLACIES

AUDIENCE-BASED FALLACIES

- *Ad Hominem* — *Ad hominem* fallacies launch an irrelevant attack on the person or source originating an argument instead of responding to substantial issues raised in the argument.

- *Ad Populum* — *Ad populum* fallacies occur when the substance of an argument is avoided and the advocate appeals instead to popular opinion as a justification for the claim.

- Appeal to Tradition — Appeal to tradition fallacies occur when someone claims that we should continue to do things the way we have always done them simply because we have always done them that way.

- Straw Arguments — The straw argument fallacy attacks a weakened form of an opponent's argument or an argument the opponent did not advance as a way to obscure the important issues.

LANGUAGE USE FALLACIES

- Equivocation — The fallacy of equivocation exploits the multiple meanings most words have by using secondary meanings to lead to a false conclusion.

- Amphiboly — The fallacy of amphiboly exploits ambiguity in grammatical structure to lead to a false or questionable conclusion.

- Emotive Language — The fallacy of emotive language manipulates the connotative meaning of words to establish a claim without proof.

GROUNDING FALLACIES

- Begging the Question — The fallacy of begging the question assumes as a premise or as evidence for an argument the very claim or point that is in question.

- *Non Sequitur* — The *non sequitur* fallacy contains a claim that is irrelevant to or unsupported by the evidence or premises purportedly supporting it.

REASONING FALLACIES

- False Analogy — A false analogy compares two things that are not alike in significant respects or have critical points of difference.

- Hasty Generalization — A hasty generalization draws a conclusion about a class based on too few or atypical examples.

- False Cause — False-cause fallacies occur when the arguer offers a cause for a consequence that is not directly related to the consequence.

- *Post Hoc* — *Post hoc* fallacies mistake temporal succession for causal sequence.

- Single Cause — Single-cause fallacies occur when an advocate attributes only one cause to a complex problem.

- Slippery Slope — The slippery-slope fallacy assumes, without evidence, that a given event is the first in a series of states that will lead inevitably to some outcome.

Such arguers may appeal to our stereotypes or prejudices about people, our tendency to go along with the crowd, our admiration for celebrities and famous people, or our respect for past practices. By appealing to such prejudices, which are often irrelevant to the claim, arguments circumvent the substantive issues that should be considered in reaching a decision. Various forms of this category of fallacies include personal attacks on the arguer, appealing to audience emotions, and taking advantage of the audience's ignorance and gullibility to get a claim accepted.[28] In this section, we will discuss four of the most common fallacies in this category—*argumentum ad hominem, argumentum ad populum,* appeal to tradition, and straw arguments.

Ad Hominem

The issues arguers raise and the reasonability of the arguer's claim are usually separate from the personal character, behavior, or characteristics of the arguer, yet the *ad hominem fallacy* diverts attention from the issue at hand and focuses instead on the personal character of the argument source. Translated literally as "to the person," *the ad hominem fallacy launches an irrelevant attack on the person or source originating an argument instead of responding to substantial issues raised in the argument.* For such an argument to qualify as a fallacy, the accusation must be irrelevant to the claim at issue and must be an effort to divert attention from it.

To illustrate this fallacy consider the following example:

Parent: I am really concerned about your grades this past semester. You were always such a good student in high school and now you have slipped to straight Cs. I think you need to study more and forget about seeing so much of your friends.

Student: Why are you always on my back for not studying? *Your* grades in college were nothing to write home about!

In raising the issue of the student's grades, the parent makes three points—that the student had done well in the past, that his grades had slipped, and that he needed to cut back on his social life and study more. The student does not acknowledge or respond to any of these points, but instead accuses the parent of being a slovenly student so as to put the parent on the defensive.

One way to detect *ad hominem* responses such as these is to be alert to instances in which an indictment of an argument seems intended to divert the discussion away from the central issues it raises so as not to respond to them. There are, however, many occasions in which the arguer's character is and should be a central issue. Assessment of the integrity of political candidates in election years may be an important part of determining whether they are fit to hold office. Questioning the qualifications of a source is also legitimate when one is responding to argument from authority in which the evidence offered is the statement of a source other than the arguer. An argument is *ad hominem* and fallacious only when it is used to circumvent and avoid a legitimate issue by arbitrarily attacking the person who raised it.

Ad Populum

Literally, *ad populum* means "to the people." *An ad populum fallacy occurs when the substance of an argument is avoided and the advocate appeals instead to popular opinion as a justification for the claim.* Consequently, the argument's claim is predicated on popular beliefs and opinions rather than on reason and evidence. Consider the following three examples:

The president's approval rating has dropped to less than 35 percent. This is the first time during his term that his rating has dropped this low and proves, I think, that he is doing a very poor job.

Most new parents buy Dr. Spock's *Baby and Child Care* book to learn about the care and feeding of newborn infants. So, it seems obvious that Dr. Spock has the best book available.

Eighty-five percent of those polled believe immunizations could be a cause of autism. Therefore, parents should be allowed to opt out of having their children immunized.

Each example presumes that if enough people believe something, it must be true. In fact, popular belief may even run counter to objective reality. As you can see in these three examples, just because many people agree about something does not necessarily mean it is true. The president's popular approval rating, taken alone, is not an absolutely reliable indicator of the quality of his work. Some decisions or actions in the short term may be very unpopular but in the longer term may prove the president acted appropriately. Dr. Spock's book may contain no useful advice and still be a best seller. And, the medical community, based on extensive research, reports that immunizations do not cause autism—at least no compelling evidence has been found to support the claim.

The point is that public opinion cannot control the factual nature of the world; public opinion only reflects the opinions and attitudes of a large group of people. If the claim of the argument does not involve the attitudes and opinions of people, then arguments appealing to opinions commit *ad populum* fallacies. Appealing to popular beliefs, however, hides the reality of the argument and substitutes an extraneous issue.

We can think of many more examples to illustrate this point, and some have important social and economic consequences. Consider what happens when financial analysts and forecasters warn of a potential stock market collapse. When this happens, investors may fear that market instability or collapse will wipe out their wealth and they sell. When people begin selling stocks, other investors interpret this action as a sign of market instability and begin to sell their stocks as well. The result is that the market collapses because of popular opinion.

We are not suggesting here that arguments based on popular opinions are fallacious *per se*. Sometimes arguments focus on opinion. For instance:

The Nielsen Ratings showed that *Seinfeld* was the most popular television show in history.

Overwhelming popular support elected the president to office.

Ford is the most popular automobile manufacturer of all time.

In these cases, appeals to popular opinion are warranted because the crux of the argument is what the public thinks. The *ad populum* fallacy occurs only when the issues involved are not related to public opinion. Skillful argument critics should be able to discern the difference between arguments that depend on popular opinion and those that use popular opinion to avoid discussion of issues. Argument recipients who detect *ad populum* fallacies should attempt to redirect the arguments back to the issues developed in the propositional arena and not those that are extraneous.

Appeal to Tradition

Recall from Chapter 4 that presumption is an assumption in favor of existing beliefs and states of affairs when proposals for change are made. Presumption exists as a convention of argument that reflects people's tendency to favor what is presently in practice until a good reason for changing it is offered.

Appeal to tradition attempts to convert that convention or practice into a reason for not making a change even when a good reason for doing so is offered—in other words, people might counter that "We have always done it this way so we should continue to do it this way regardless of your arguments." *The fallacy of appeal to tradition occurs when someone claims that we should continue to do things the way we have always done them simply because we have always done them that way.* Appeal to tradition takes advantage of people's reverence for past practice and attempts to avoid dealing with meritorious reasons for changing it.

Appeals to tradition are based on the often mistaken assumptions that what has worked in the past will work well in the future, that conditions have not changed, and that there is no better way of doing things. Consider the following true examples (from a college curriculum committee meeting):

Professor Smith: We should change the college grading scale to include plus and minus grading distinctions. A recent study by this committee indicates that there is a big difference between a B+ (94 out of 100 on most exam scales) and a B– (82 out of 100). Further defining the range of grades gives more precise information about a student's performance in the course.

Professor Jones: Why should we change? We've had simple letter grades without plus or minus distinctions in this college for over ten years and it's worked fine.

Professor Smith presented a good reason for changing the grading system—that the change will provide more precise information about student performance. Instead of responding to Smith's substantive argument, Jones merely appealed to tradition, saying that the way things have been done in the past should continue. When a cogent and meritorious argument for making a change occurs, then the fallacy of appeal to tradition ignores the rationale given for change and assumes that traditional practice is the best way of doing things.

Straw Arguments

Straw arguments are often called straw person or straw man arguments. They frequently occur in debates, discussions, and other situations where there is interactive argument. *The straw argument fallacy attacks a weakened form of an opponent's argument or an argument the opponent did not advance.* In committing this fallacy, arguers use as evidence an argument not advanced by their opponents but nonetheless an argument that bolsters their own position. The result is that the opponent's position may be misrepresented because of the way it was paraphrased, how misleading words were chosen and used, or how the argument was restated or overextended to look absurd.[29] The result is that by restating an opponent's argument in an extreme or trivial way, the arguer sets up a weakened argument for response and fails to address the core issues in dispute.

As we noted earlier, when we discuss the analysis and criticism of arguments, arguers should begin by grounding their arguments and criticisms on fair and reasonable representations of an opponent's argument. To do anything less is unethical. Consider the following examples of the straw-argument fallacy:

Mary: I think it's time for this university to move most of its courses online. Just think, we could work on classes on our own time, courses would be much more interesting and interactive with online discussion groups. Plus, we wouldn't have to get up and go to a boring classroom and listen to a boring lecture—we could fast-forward. Online education has been available for a long time now, other universities have put all of their programs in the cloud and it is time for us to move that way too—it is the next generation of education. Professors can better integrate audio and visual aids; there are more opportunities for informal discussions and seminars. Our school is too stuck in the past.

Derrick: Yeah, but that idea will never work. I agree that the school is stuck in the past, but that means it would take forever to teach the professors how to use the software or migrate courses to an online environment. We will end up wasting more time than we save. People will get frustrated and then they will stop using it.

Derrick took one aspect of Mary's proposal—that the school is stuck in the past—and discussed obvious problems with it. He did not, however, respond to the central issue she raised—whether moving to online education is a good idea and the future of the university. By ignoring the major thrust of her argument, he created a straw argument.

Language-Based

As we discussed in the last section, language plays an important role in the way arguments are perceived and interpreted. Most fallacies of language use occur when arguers are careless about how they speak and when they equivocate, use amphiboly, or use emotive language to get their claims accepted by deliberately trying to evade issues and avoid presenting solid evidence and reasoning in favor of what they advocate.

Equivocation

Many words have more than one meaning, and occasionally arguers may exploit the ambiguity in language to make a fallacious claim. One way to do this is through equivocation. *The fallacy of equivocation exploits the fact that a word has more than one meaning so as to lead to a false conclusion.* For example, someone might say, "You shouldn't take that course in reasoning that is supposed to improve your ability to argue; you argue too much with your friends now!" Here the meaning of the term "argue" has shifted from "reasoning and correctly supporting claims" to "engaging in interpersonal squabbles." The arguer has made a false causal connection between the two based on the ambiguity of the meaning of the term *argue*.

Equivocation is often used in deceptive advertising. For example, an advertisement that appeared in several national publications proclaimed that "Parents can receive a FREE college education" for their children. On its face, the bold letters across the top of the ad made a fairly spectacular promise that the average person might have a difficult time ignoring. For most people, the word *free* means without charge, cost, or obligation. But the word *free* means something very different to the producers of the ad. To them, *free* meant that parents needed to invest a substantial sum of money in their "tax-free open-end mutual funds and unit trusts" and pay for a variety of administrative "charges and expenses." The point was that if enough money was invested, then the interest produced should be sufficient to send a child to college. But placing money into a long-term investment is not "free" because there is an opportunity cost to having the money committed, and there are administrative and other charges that are not free. Words mean different things to different people, and when word choice misdirects the audience's understanding of the argument, then an equivocation has taken place.

The question the recipient needs to ask is whether the argument contains any language that might be misconstrued by the arguer. If the answer is yes, then the recipient should ascertain what the words are intended to mean so that both recipient and arguer share a common understanding of the argument.

Amphiboly

Equivocation exploits ambiguities in word meanings, but *amphiboly exploits ambiguity in grammatical structure to lead to a false or questionable conclusion.* Just as there are many types of grammatical structures, there are many forms of amphiboly. For example, an advertisement might claim:

New, improved product X is unquestionably more effective.

Our product is new and improved.

More effective than what? New and improved compared to what? Here we have comparative adjectives used but no object provided for comparison. Perhaps product X is being compared with the original product, or perhaps with other brands of the product. We don't know.

Here is another example. An arguer claims, "When we compare the danger of spreading AIDS with the incursion of privacy involved in widespread AIDS testing, we must conclude that it is a risk we have to take." Is the antecedent of "it" the spread of AIDS or the incursion of privacy? Until we know what the arguer is referring to, the meaning of the claim is unclear.

An excellent example of the exploitation of amphiboly appeared in an article on the writing of recommendation letters. The article was in response to a number of defamation suits that had been filed against people who wrote unfavorable letters of recommendation. Faced with the problem of writing an honest letter without subjecting themselves to lawsuits, many letter-writers are puzzled about what to do. Robert J. Thornton, in his *Lexicon of Inconspicuously Ambiguous Recommendations* (LIAR, for short), recommends the circumspect use of amphiboly. Some examples of using his approach include:

I wholeheartedly recommend this candidate with no qualifications whatsoever.

I truly believe that absolutely no one would be better for this job.

You would be truly fortunate to get this person to work for you.[30]

Because of the ambiguity in the way the sentences are constructed, the reader of the first sentence assumes that the recommendation is unqualified (when it is actually the *candidate* who is unqualified). The reader of the second sentence may interpret it to mean that the candidate is the best alternative (when in fact hiring *no one* would be the best alternative). And, the third sentence might lead the reader to assume the person is a good hire when in fact the candidate is unlikely to do any work. Such examples remind us to be on the lookout for intentional and manipulative ambiguity. If we are confused about what the arguer meant by the wording of a claim, there may be a good reason.

Emotive Language

The language used to express thoughts and ideas often is a potent force in influencing our opinions and actions. As one philosopher of argument observed, "An emotional appeal to us for some specific action may be so powerful as to inhibit our capacity to exercise critical judgment on the reasons offered in favor of the action urged."[31] *The fallacy of emotive language manipulates the connotative meaning of words to establish a claim without proof.* It attempts to persuade an audience by getting them to respond emotionally to images and associations evoked by the language used rather than by judging the quality of the arguer's evidence and reasoning.

Politicians, advertisers, and propagandists often use emotive language to gain acceptance for ideas that cannot be effectively supported through reasoning and evidence. The idea behind the fallacy of emotive language is to set up associations in the audience's mind with either pleasant or favorable values and attitudes (in order to win acceptance for an idea) or with unpleasant experiences or disfavored values (to get an idea rejected). Language is therefore used suggestively and can have an unconscious influence.

President Harry Truman can serve as an interesting example. In 1962, historian Herbert Feis contacted Truman with several questions about Truman's decision to use the atomic bomb on Hiroshima and Nagasaki during World War II. Truman had been the subject of much criticism on his decision, and he responded with an emotionally laden letter that he never sent:

> My dear Mr. Feis:
>
> You write just like the usual egghead. The facts are before you but you'd like to garble them. The instruction of July 25th, 1945 was final. It was made by the Commander in Chief after Japan refused to surrender.
>
> Churchill, Stimson, Patterson, Eisenhower and all the rest agreed that it had to be done. It was. It ended the...War. That was the objective. Now if you can think of any other "if, as, and when" egghead contemplations, bring them out....
>
> It is a great thing that you or any other contemplator "after the fact" didn't have to make the decision. Our boys would all be dead.[32]

Although Truman's response may be understandable, it does not address the criticisms posed by others, nor did it address Feis's request for information about the decision on whether to use the bomb to end the war. Instead, Truman used several emotionally charged words to place the researcher on the defensive. Terms such as "egghead," "contemplator 'after the fact,' " and "dead" all help charge the letter.

Advertisements for many "self-improvement" cosmetics and health products often use emotive language to appeal to the prospective buyer's desire for a sudden and dramatic improvement in personal appearance. An advertisement for tan accelerator claims that:

> Once in a generation there's a breakthrough so revolutionary it can change forever the way people tan.

Terms such as *breakthrough* and *revolutionary* are intended to convince consumers that the product's effects must be singular and a striking advance over other tanning methods. Or, consider this claim from a weight-loss ad:

> After years of research and testing, a scientist from Princeton University has finally developed a miracle weight loss formula that has clearly proven to be the strongest fat-burning compound in the entire world! [This product] is so radically powerful that it can actually make the slim and shapely figure of your dreams a reality.

The emotive language in this advertisement may persuade readers who are seeking a "radically powerful" "miracle" formula to make them "slim and shapely." But the "Princeton scientist" is not identified, nor is the method used in the supposed study explained. Educated recipients of arguments should be skeptical of product claims that promise "revolutionary breakthroughs" and "miraculous results." Such language is often substituted for hard evidence and valid reasoning in order to make arguments and claims persuasive.

Grounding Fallacies

Fallacies that relate to evidence occur when arguments are poorly grounded. This happens when arguers use evidence that is of poor quality or, in some cases, nonexistent. Poorly grounded arguments tend to confuse reasoning or claims with evidence. In Chapter 5, we explored how evidence is used well, how it can be tested, and how it can strengthen arguments. Grounding fallacies occur when arguers misuse their evidence.

When arguers commit it this type of fallacy, they are asking recipients to draw conclusions from premises that are either missing or inappropriate to the claim. As you may recall from our earlier discussion of evidence, there are many tests of evidence that help critics determine whether evidence is relevant, reliable, and valid. When arguers ground their arguments in evidence that fails these tests, then a fallacy of evidence occurs. Although many such fallacies are possible, the following are significant and prevalent forms of problems with evidence or lack of evidence.

Begging the Question

The fallacy of begging the question assumes as a premise or as evidence for an argument the very claim or point that is in question. Often, when arguers beg the question they are accused of circular reasoning because they use the argument's premises as their claims and reason that one supports the other when, in fact, there is little or no difference. Arguers who beg the question fail to seek external support for their claims so that they assume the point they are expected to prove. Consequently, the evidence for such claims is not externally valid and, in fact, cannot be validated through external sources.

You may recall that when we discussed the level of dispute in Chapter 1, we pointed out that in an argument, one begins with evidence (statements that the audience accepts) and moves to prove a conclusion that is not yet accepted. Begging the question fallacies, however, are circular because they depend upon premises whose truth is assumed rather than established.

There are many ways to beg the question. Two of them are illustrated in the following examples.

The soul is immortal because it lives forever.

In this example, the arguer has simply stated the claim in two different ways. "Living forever" may be a definition of "immortal," but stipulating a definition does not constitute proof of immortality's existence. Put simply, the evidence in the argument cannot possibly be verified.

> We must accept the traditions of men of old time who affirm themselves to be the offspring of the gods—that is what they say—and they must surely have known their own ancestors. How can we doubt the word of the children of the gods?[33]

The issue here is whether the ancestors' word can be trusted. To address the issue, the author commits an *ad verecundiam (appeal to authority) fallacy to claim that we should trust their authority because their word on the matter is authoritative!* This is a very clear example of the kind of circular reasoning often found in fallacies that beg the question.

When we suspect that a question-begging fallacy has been committed, we should determine whether premises independent of the claim have been offered to support it and, if they have, whether these premises are any more certain or acceptable than the claim itself. If the arguer has not offered established or accepted evidence to support the claim, then he or she has begged the question.

Non Sequitur

This Latin phrase, literally translated, means "it does not follow." *The non sequitur fallacy contains a claim that is irrelevant to or unsupported by the evidence or premises purportedly supporting it.* In other words, the arguer grounds the argument in evidence that fails to support the claim advanced.

This fallacy, also known as "irrelevant reason," occurs very frequently. We are likely to be misled by it because the reasons or premises offered to support a conclusion somehow resemble the type of evidence that would be necessary to support it. People often present standards that *look* like evidence and connect them with claims in the same topic area, but actually the statements have no logical relation to each other. Consider the following two examples of *non sequitur* arguments:

> Plea bargaining affects many people. In 2012 in Sacramento County, there were 3,115 burglaries, 85 robberies, 109 rapes, and 31 murders.

In this argument, the first sentence is intended to be the claim and the second the evidence for it. But they are unrelated. The evidence does not tell us how many perpetrators of the listed crimes were arrested or charged, nor does it contain any information as to whether the charges were plea-bargained. The only claim the evidence proves is there were crimes in Sacramento County in 2012. The argument is clearly a *non sequitur*. The next one is subtler.

> The United States is the only industrialized country in the world where teenage pregnancy is increasing. The Guttmachur study found that the U.S. pregnancy rate is twice that of Canada, England, or France, and seven times that of the Netherlands.

The first sentence is intended to be the claim, and the second serves as evidence. Someone attending to this argument that is not aware of *non sequitur* fallacies might easily be fooled. But notice that the evidence does not say that the pregnancy rate is *increasing*, only that it is higher than that in other countries. To prove there's an increase, we would need comparable rates for different time periods showing that rates have increased in the recent past.

Non sequitur fallacies are often subtle and yet seem obvious when they are pointed out. To detect them, we need constantly to ask, "What kind of evidence would be needed to support this claim?" and "Does this evidence qualify?"

Reasoning-Based

As we have noted elsewhere, there are many ways that arguments can go wrong and thus deceive an audience. Flawed arguments can grow out of inadequate evidence, emotive language, appeals to ignorance or prejudice, or inadequate reasoning. In this section, we will discuss fallacies of the last kind, those that result when an arguer uses an inference that fails to meet the tests of quality reasoning developed in Chapter 6. In particular, we will discuss standard types of fallacies in arguments from analogy, generalization, and cause.[34] These three types of fallacies occur very often in practical arguments.

False Analogy

A false analogy compares two things that are not alike in significant respects or have critical points of difference. You may recall from Chapter 6 that one of the criteria for judging the adequacy of an analogy is whether it meets the test of quality, that is, whether it compares two things in the same class that share significant similarities relevant to the conclusion drawn by the arguer. Furthermore, it needs to meet the test of quantity, which requires that there be a significant number of similarities between the two things being compared. A false analogy does not meet these tests. Consider the following two examples:

We should not teach socialism in the university any more than we should teach arson.

The success of the forty-hour workweek in making corporate America efficient and productive suggests that we should use it on farms as well.

In the first example, the arguer is comparing two things that share very few similarities. Socialism is a school of thought and political philosophy, a theory only potentially applicable to practice, whereas arson is an illegal activity. Indeed, the only way to see any similarity between the two would be to begin by assuming that socialism is patently illegal or aberrant, and there is no support for this assumption.

The second example does compare situations that are, in a sense, similar. Both corporate business and farming are lines of work that generate income and are productive for society. The question in this case is whether there are *enough* similarities to support the claim that a forty-hour workweek would be equally efficient and productive on farms.

Farming is seasonal, depends on temporary labor, and requires certain labor-intensive actions at particular times. Someone seeking to refute this analogy might emphasize how vital the pattern and cycle of work in the two environments is to the viability of the comparison itself.

False analogies also result when someone attempts to use a figurative analogy to prove a point. Figurative analogies, which we discussed in Chapter 6, do not meet the test of opposition because they compare things in different classes. Their function in an argument is more illustrative and metaphorical than probative. Such comparisons enliven arguments and bring their points home. The state has been compared to an organism, the kingdom of God to a mustard seed, and life to a theatrical play. When figurative analogies are used as if they were literal comparisons, however, and are the only form of support offered for a claim, they may be fallacious.

Hasty Generalization

The adequacy of a generalization, which reasons from some to all members of a class, depends on whether enough members of the class have been observed and whether those members possess the same characteristics as other members of that class. The argument based on too few examples fails the test of quantity for a generalization, and the argument based on an atypical example fails the test of quality. *A hasty generalization draws a conclusion about a class based on too few or atypical examples.*

Drawing general conclusions from too few examples is a common error of reasoning. For example, someone might say:

> I owned two European cars—an Audi and a Land Rover—and they gave me nothing but trouble. The electrical system was unreliable on the Audi and I had lots of transmission problems with the Land Rover. They were always in the shop. European cares are poorly constructed, and I think they should be avoided.

This generalization is unwarranted. The arguer's experience may have resulted from the way the two cars were driven and the care they received. Maybe the arguer failed to perform regular maintenance or maybe these two cars were anomalies. We could only place confidence in the conclusion if we had performance and maintenance records for thousands of other European cars and could compare them with other classes of cars comparable to Audis and Land Rovers. Unwarranted generalizations of this type when applied to people are called "stereotypes." Someone who believes that all Southerners are slow or that all Californians are easygoing based on an acquaintance with just a few members of either class is committing this fallacy.

Likewise, hasty generalizations can be based on observed samples that are not typical of the class about which the arguer's observation is made. Consider the following example:

> The growth and success of cottage industries in the Appalachian Mountains suggest that other impoverished areas can build small industries to raise their people out of debt.

This generalization is hasty because businesses in areas other than Appalachia are not like businesses there. The Appalachian Mountains are rural and remote, travel in portions of that area is difficult, and settled areas are widely dispersed and located some distance from shopping malls and convenience stores. These characteristics make patronage of cottage industries more likely. In other geographical areas, however, people might prefer accessible, inexpensive, mass-produced goods, and cottage industries, which normally have a small profit margin, would fail.

Anyone to whom generalizations are addressed should ask the question, Are there other equally common examples that deny the conclusion? The key to discovering hasty generalizations is in finding exceptions to the claim made. Stereotypes, for example, can always be undermined if one can cite instances of people who belong to the class in question but do not possess the characteristics attributed to the class.

False Cause

People who make causal connections between one condition or event and another are prone to two types of error—*post hoc* and single-cause fallacies. The first misidentifies a cause, and the second fails the test of quantity by assuming that only one cause led to an effect when many causes, working together, might be necessary.

Post hoc comes from the Latin *post hoc ergo propter hoc*, which, literally translated, means "after this therefore because of this." *A* post hoc *fallacy mistakes temporal succession for causal sequence.* That is, one assumes that because two events are associated in time, one event must have caused the other. Consider three separate examples of *post hoc* reasoning:

> Serial killer Ted Bundy was found guilty of murder and executed in Florida. Before his sentence was carried out, he told an interviewer that he blamed pornography for causing his crime spree. Had it not been for pornography, he claimed, he would not have committed the crimes.

> John Hinckley shot President Reagan after seeing violent acts on TV. Therefore, violence on TV must have influenced his behavior.

> All people who have cancer drink milk. Therefore, drinking milk must cause cancer.

The arguer in each of these passages bases the claim on the assumption that some antecedent condition (pornography, TV violence, or milk) resulted in some consequent condition (murder, assassination attempt, or cancer). The connection between the antecedent and consequent, however, is temporal. In other words, the only apparent connection in each argument is that one condition followed the other, but in no argument does the advocate prove that there is a causal relationship that connects the antecedent with the consequent.

The sense in which antecedent and subsequent events in these examples are not causally connected can be clarified if one remembers the role of necessary and sufficient conditions we discussed in Chapter 6. If a subsequent event can and often does occur without the so-called cause preceding it, then the two events are not necessarily causally related. They may be, but the information provided in the argument does not provide sufficient warrant for the claim. Do all people who see pornography act violently? Do people who do not watch violent television programming commit violent acts? Do people who never drink milk have cancer? If so, then the antecedent conditions cited are neither necessary nor sufficient for the effects claimed. Just because two events occur one after another in a sequence does not mean that they are causally related; they might be, but then again they might not.

Recipients of these arguments would need to seek out additional support to confirm or deny the reasoning. For instance, does TV violence cause violence, or are violent people predisposed toward violent programming? In other words, is TV violence simply a symptom and not a cause of violence in society? Do all people who drink milk get cancer? Why are there exceptions? What the argument critic needs to look for is the regularity with which the time sequence of events holds true for the argument. If there are exceptions or other unexplained conditions that might account for the conclusion, then a fallacy has probably been committed.

The second causation fallacy is single cause. *Single-cause fallacies occur when an advocate attributes a complex problem to only one cause.* There is almost never a single cause or explanation for any problem we face. Rather, most events in our complex society arise from myriad conditions and events. Yet advocates, hoping to simplify their arguments, attribute complex social problems to a single cause. This is misleading because it does not account for other, possibly important variables worth considering. Consider the following two examples:

Low interest rates are the reason for increased housing purchases.

Poor communication is the reason for the high American divorce rate.

In both cases only one cause is listed, but for an advocate to argue that there is only one cause for either housing purchases or the high divorce rate is naive at best. Increased housing purchases might be the result of a glut of houses on the market and higher individual incomes produced by a stronger economy. Financial problems and career choices may be alternative reasons for the high divorce rate. For any complex social, political, or economic problem we can think of, there is more than one cause, and an arguer should take care not to oversimplify.

Slippery Slope

A frequent argument made against those who argue for change or propose a new policy is slippery slope. *The slippery-slope fallacy assumes, without evidence, that a given event is the first in a series of steps that will lead inevitably to some outcome.* This sort of erroneous reasoning assumes a "domino effect"—that once one event occurs, a whole series of subsequent events or developments will occur in an uncontrollable sequence. Slippery slope is thus a fallacy of evidence use because no support is given that the subsequent events will occur. In this sense, a slippery slope argument pretends to use causal reasoning whereby an event will lead to a series of outcomes that cannot be avoided once the first step is taken. Fundamentally, though, as theorist Edward Damer noted, while this is an easy argument to make, it misrepresents how causal reasoning works. Because the first step down the slope may lead to a particular outcome, there should no presumption that once the outcome occurs that it will necessarily cause another. Every step of causal reasoning requires a separate and complete argument.[35]

In other words, to conclude that event A leads to event B, we must have substantial evidence that one cannot occur without the other and that event B will always be produced by event A. This is what constitutes a sufficient condition and thus a causal claim. In most instances of the slippery slope, however, the relationship and predicted outcome are much less certain. Consider the following example of a conversation between James and his father, Jason:

James: I was really struggling with Biology 101 and I needed to drop it. I'm sorry because I know college is expensive, but I just wasn't getting it and I was concerned about my grade point average. I went in and I spoke to the prof. She seemed to think that dropping it was a good idea because I am so far behind.

Jason: I don't care about the money as much as I care that you have dropped a class in your very first semester in college. It seems to me that once the going gets rough you're just going to quit. Is this going to be a pattern with you? Next time, will you drop the first class that is tough? I'm afraid that you might, and if you keep this up you may never finish your degree.

Jason is concerned about his son's welfare. He wants him to succeed in college and he wants him to finish his degree. However, Jason commits a slippery-slope fallacy. The implication here is that James will drop future classes if he is afraid of failure and that this one instance serves as a sign of a larger pattern of behavior. But Jason offers no proof for this claim. Instead, he discusses a particular event and reasons without evidence that it proves a larger pattern. Any evidence that the predicted series of events will in fact occur rarely accompanies the slippery slope.

Argument theorists agree that fallacies have a significant potential to be deceptive and consequently dangerous because they may lead to poor decision-making.[36] Recipients may make emotional decisions as opposed to reasoned ones. Arguers who intentionally use fallacies to trick an audience are behaving unethically. Arguers should strive to construct the strongest arguments possible based on their evidence and reason. At the same time, recipients need to understand which appeals are justified and reasonable and which are not. Aristotle once warned that honest speakers need to prepare for spurious arguments and arguments that look genuine but are simply shams.[37] Both arguer and recipient need to be able to tell the two apart.

It is important to recognize, however, that not all fallacies are the same. Just as arguments can be stronger or weaker, fallacies can be strong and weak as well. Identifying an argument as fallacious does not necessarily mean that the argument should be rejected. It might simply mean that the argument is weak. Many times, fallacious arguments can be made into strong arguments with further and better evidence or reasoning. For example, consider the following:

> The prohibition of smoking in public places in California has been a remarkable success. Physicians there have reported that respiratory illness among restaurant workers has decreased as a direct result of this ban. Since it has been so successful in California, we should support a smoking ban in New York.

A critical recipient might correctly point out that this arguer has potentially committed a fallacy of false analogy because there is not clear evidence that California and New York are substantially the same. And, for people who live in those two states, a better argument could probably be made that they are substantially dissimilar. However, if the advocate were able to produce evidence and supporting arguments to demonstrate that California and New York are substantially similar in enough respects that are related to smoking and health, the argument would become stronger.

Finally, context can determine whether an argument that appears fallacious is truly fallacious. There are times when speakers use arguments that might appear fallacious to motivate and inspire an audience. Consider, for example, a speaker at a political rally. When speaking to a group of recipients who are supportive of the political cause, a speaker might use emotive language to help the audience visualize the issues and ideas—to inspire, not to evade. Using rhetorical flourishes, emotive language, and other methods for delivering a powerful speech can be appropriate and persuasive, as long as the speaker focuses on the central issues of the argument and inspires people to act critically and through knowledge. When speakers act to reduce an audience's understanding of the central issues and dissuade them from critically evaluating the arguments, then fallacies are probably present.

Ultimately, fallacies depend on the relationship between an arguer and audience, whether they are intentionally or unintentionally deceptive, and the extent to which they weaken or divert attention away from an argument. Ethical arguers should strive to construct arguments that are not deceptive, that are as strong as possible, and that move the audience. Thinking critically about your own and others' arguments includes evaluating potential fallacies.

ETHICS

Our understanding of what is right or wrong stems from our cultural and personal background, our fields, faith, and personal value sets. Shared value systems help inform us of right and wrong, good and bad behavior within different spheres and argument contexts. How we approach values of life, freedom, or respect for others all shape our behavior and serve as a basis for living and working together. They serve as the primary underpinnings of our conduct. A strong value hierarchy that prized education, support of family, and entrepreneurship led Kirtsaeng in Box 11.1 to seek ways to support himself. The range of acceptable options was based on his values and cultural background—concepts introduced in Chapter 3.

Because of their potential to affect people's lives for both good and bad, arguers and recipients have a responsibility to be vigilant about the quality and integrity of arguments they present and receive. In other words, all people involved in arguing share an ethical responsibility. In Chapter 1, we introduced the concept of argument spheres. Each sphere—personal, technical, and public—prescribes its own set of standards.

Ethics in the personal sphere grow from our own personal background, values, and beliefs. Each of us develops our own, personal ethical code that informs how we interact with others from family, to work, to our communities. We carry our personal code into our argument contexts and spheres. For instance, in the public sphere, we know we should not deceive people. But there are times when things said publicly can cause harm. This was an issue that came up when CIA agent Valarie Plame's identity as a spy was revealed publicly. The public sphere adds elements to our ethical codes that place public interests in balance with personal needs. Similarly, in the technical sphere, field guidelines develop ethical codes which tend to be more formalized.

For instance, medical doctors swear to abide by the Hippocratic Oath (see Box 11.8, "The Hippocratic Oath") or other medical ethic. Public relations professionals use the "Code of Professional Standards for the Practice of Public Relations" generated by the Public Relations Society of America.[38] These are only two among many such ethical codes. Most professional organizations have some code of ethics intended to guide their members toward moral and just actions. In fact, almost any field one can identify has an ethical code associated with it.

When we abide by the prescriptions of our personal and professional ethical codes—for example, when we do not lie, deceive, or attempt to injure others—our arguments are considered ethical. However, when we use the power inherent in arguments to persuade people based on deception or argumentative trickery, then our arguments are considered unethical. Evasion, deception, and misrepresentation cause public distrust, poor decision-making, and, occasionally, outright harm and injury to individuals.

BOX 11.8
THE HIPPOCRATIC OATH

There are several codes of ethics governing medical doctors, and which code applies to which doctors is often dependent on professional association or membership. For example, a physician practicing in the United States will probably be governed by the "American Medical Association Principles of Medical Ethics." Members of the World Medical Association practice the "Physician's Oath." However, the most widely known of all the ethical codes governing the practice of medicine is the Hippocratic Oath. Hippocrates was a Greek physician who practiced medicine in the fifth century B.C. and worked diligently to end the plague in Athens as well as teach young doctors the practice and art of medicine.

I SWEAR by Apollo the physician and Æsculapius, and Hygiea, and Panacea, and all the gods and goddesses, that, according to my ability and judgment, I will keep this Oath and this stipulation— to reckon him who taught me this Art equally dear to me as my parents, to share my substance with him, and relieve his necessities if required; to look upon his offspring in the same footing as my own brothers, and to teach them this Art, if they shall wish to learn it, without fee or stipulation; and that by precept, lecture, and every other mode of instruction, I will impart a knowledge of the Art to my own sons, and those of my teachers, and to disciples bound by a stipulation and oath according to the law of medicine, but to none others. I will follow that system of regimen which, according to my ability and judgment, I consider for the benefit of my patients, and abstain from whatever is deleterious and mischievous. I will give no deadly medicine to any one if asked, nor suggest any such counsel; and in like manner I will not give to a woman a pessary to produce abortion. With purity and with holiness I will pass my life and practice my Art. I will not cut persons laboring under the stone, but will leave this to be done by men who are practitioners of this work. Into whatever houses I enter, I will go into them for the benefit of the sick, and will abstain from every voluntary act of mischief and corruption; and, further, from the seduction of females or males, of freemen and slaves. Whatever, in connection with my professional service, or not in connection with it, I see or hear, in the life of men, which ought not to be spoken of abroad, I will not divulge, as reckoning that all such should be kept secret. While I continue to keep this Oath unviolated, may it be granted to me to enjoy life and the practice of the Art, respected by all men, in all times. But should I trespass and violate this Oath, may the reverse be my lot.[39]

Each day we are presented with opportunities to make ethical decisions. For example, what would you do if you found a $100 bill on a sidewalk outside a store? If there is no identification on the money, do you keep it? Do you give it to the clerk in the store? Do you take it to a police station? This can be a difficult choice, and your decision will depend on what you believe to be the correct or just choice. Was it appropriate for Kirtsaeng to resell textbook even with the disclaimer inside? Consider the ethical issue raised by the *Mason Country Journal*, a newspaper in Shelton, Washington, that routinely published the names of rape suspects and victims alike (including juvenile rape victims). The newspaper's argument was that its job is to publicize the full record of Shelton, and rapes are a part of that record. However, releasing the names has disrupted the lives of many women and girls. Is that ethical? The answers are not always clear.

Political ads often strain what is ethically reasonable by making claims far beyond what the evidence supports or by omitting details to obscure evidence or reasons. In either case, the goal is to diminish the recipient's ability to make reasonable and informed choices. This is one reason that organizations such as POLITICO.com and FactCheck.org have become popular checks on political excess. There are many similar websites that have the goal of identifying unethical or questionable arguments so that recipients have a way to make better decisions.[40]

The question, then, is how do we know what is the moral or just action? Ethicists have long considered the nature of ethical conduct and how different ethical requirements and rules emerge from a variety of contexts.[41] Although understanding how ethics function in any given context can be difficult, generally arguments are considered ethical and just when they enhance the individual or strengthen the community. Arguers who act to undermine their audiences or weaken community bonds and structures are generally considered unethical.

Strengthening the Individual

Arguments strengthen the individual either when they provide recipients with opportunities to make free, informed, and critical choices, or when they help recipients become better people in their community. Individuals, explained ethicist Thomas Nilsen, should have a right of free choice and free decision making.[42] When arguers educate, offer alternative perspectives, or provide new information, they offer their audiences greater opportunities for free and better decision-making. Similarly, when arguers help audiences self-actualize by moving them toward certain culturally based ideals such as honesty, courage, compassion, generosity, fidelity, integrity, and fairness, among others, they are acting ethically. Arguments should work to create opportunities for their recipients and not limit them. The recipient's right to make free choices should be respected. Arguers should recognize that people are not objects for manipulation, but are equal participants in argumentative interactions.

Whenever a person engages in arguments with another, a relationship is created, and that relationship is an important part of the process of argumentation. Wayne Brockriede explained this fact when he wrote an article titled "Arguers as Lovers."[43] Brockriede noted that beyond the content of argument transactions and the content within those exchanges, there is also a relationship among the arguers that can provide argument analysts with a way of classifying the transactions.[44]

Brockriede takes the position that arguers, as the title of his article suggests, in their attempt to influence and relate to their recipients, should act as lovers toward their audiences; they need to respect and understand the needs of their recipients. The goal or ethically correct choice for the arguer is to approach the audience as a partner rather than to coerce them.

Brockriede wrote that the relationship between arguers and their audiences could be classified as one of three different types: rapist, seducer, and lover. When arguers rape, they view their relationship with the audience as a unilateral one. The arguer will tend to objectify the audience and seek to manipulate the recipients. "The rapist wants to gain or to maintain a position of superiority," Brockriede wrote. Argument rapists do this by creating a strong "intellectual front" and on "the interpersonal front of putting the other person down."[45]

Whether or not we like to admit it, argument rape is a common practice, and many people engage in it without even thinking. But we live in an adversarial society in which one person's success often means another's failure and where success at whatever cost is prized over failure. It can be easy for arguers—who may not even be aware of their actions—to "rape" their recipients. Even our language describing arguments suggests this. We often say:

I beat their arguments.

I destroyed their position.

I demolished the competition.

Yet, each of these examples points to our tendency to objectify and treat people who oppose us as less than human.

A second type of relationship between the arguer and recipient is that of the seducer who seeks to win covertly through charm or deceit—intentional use of fallacious arguments is an example of this. Seducers, Brockriede noted, are similar to argument rapists in many respects. Like the rapist, they see the relationship between arguer and recipient as unilateral—arguer to recipient. While the seducer may not "force" arguments on their audience, they are "indifferent to the identity and integrity of the other person. Whereas the intent of the rapist is to force assent, the seducer tries to charm or trick his victim into assent."[46]

There are many ways for arguers to trick their recipients. Different types of fallacies make faulty arguments appear reasonable and believable. When employed by a crafty arguer, fallacies may cause audiences to believe in faulty arguments. Similarly, withholding information, telling half-truths, taking evidence out of context, fabricating evidence, among other deceptions, all provide arguers with the means of fooling audiences.

The third type of relationship between arguer and recipient is that of lover. The arguer as lover seeks to empower the recipient through argument and to expand and enlighten the recipient. The lover, according to Brockriede, wants "power parity" in which arguer and recipient share equally in the exchange of arguments. Arguer rapists and seducers, as we noted, focus on one-way relationships with audiences that seek to overpower or manipulate. Arguer lovers, according to Brockriede, engage recipients as peers and are willing to compromise, negotiate, collaborate, and risk in an "attempt to establish a bilateral relationship."[47]

The arguer-as-lover relationship views the process of giving reasons in argument as a person-centered enterprise. Its central tenet was summarized by Thomas Nilsen when he concluded that "whatever develops, enlarges, enhances human personalities is good; whatever restricts, degrades, or injures human personalities is bad."[48] For Nilsen, this meant that arguers should always give their recipients a *"significant choice," which means that arguers should provide their audiences with enough information to draw their own conclusions.*

Strengthening the Community

Arguers who work to strengthen the community look for opportunities to help groups of people live and work together more effectively. They seek ways of equitably sharing resources and look to provide a means for audiences to make difficult decisions.

In the nineteenth century, two British ethicists, Jeremy Bentham and his student John Stuart Mill, developed a standard that was intended as a guide for legislators to determine which laws were morally best.[49] Their criterion, utilitarianism, holds that the greatest balance of good over evil for a given community is ethical in comparison with other actions. Arguers, then, consider various courses of action and then argue for the approach that derives the greatest benefits and causes the least harm. Ethical arguments are those that balance outcomes and promote the decisions that achieve the greatest good for the greatest number.

However, not all decisions or actions can be reduced into such a simple assessment of good and evil. There is also a question of what is just or fair in the decision-making process. Aristotle took the position that arguers should also consider the issues of what is fair and just for the members of a community.[50] He advocated that the basic moral question an arguer should ask is, "Does the decision treat everyone the same way, or does it show favoritism and discrimination?" Ethical decisions are generally fair, whereas unethical decisions are based on inequality and preferential treatment.

Ultimately, if arguers seek to enhance the integrity of the community, they should balance the needs of the majority with principles of fairness and justice that protect the interests of the minority. This means that advocates appealing to community needs engage in an assessment of the "common good" for a given group of people.

The concept of the common good is grounded in the writings of Plato, Aristotle, and Cicero, among other ancient theorists. More recently, ethicist John Rawls defined the common good as "certain general conditions that are...equally to everyone's advantage."[51] Using the common good as an ethical standard, arguers focus on ensuring that social policies, social systems, institutions, and environments on which we depend are equally beneficial to all. Examples of policies and decisions that are based in the common good might include affordable health care, effective public safety, peace among nations, a just legal system, and an unpolluted environment.

Arguers who appeal to the common good urge recipients to view themselves as members of the same community reflecting on broad questions concerning the kind of society we want to become and how we want to achieve that society. While respecting and valuing the freedom of individuals to pursue their own goals within a community, advocates challenge their audience to recognize and further the goals shared in common by all the members of a given community.

As is probably apparent, there is the potential for an inherent tension between individual and community interests. In Box 11.9, "Apply the Theory," you will have an opportunity to work through the tension that can exist between individual and community values.

Developing an Ethical Code

The inherent power of arguments requires each of us to take responsibility in argumentative encounters to ensure the quality and integrity of the arguments presented. This is why arguers should have a clear understanding of arguments, their construction, and their ethical uses. Recipients should have a clear understanding of how arguments can be critically evaluated. Because argumentation involves both arguer and recipient, both share in the ethical responsibility for decision-making and the consequences of their actions. Therefore, both arguer and recipient should have a clear sense of their own ethic of argument.[52] This section considers the process involved in creating individual codes of ethics.

■ ■ ■ ■ ■

BOX 11.9

APPLY THE THEORY: INDIVIDUAL AND COMMUNITY INTERESTS

There are times when the interests of the individual and community diverge and making a decision about the best ethical path forward can be difficult. Consider the case developed in Box 11.1 and develop arguments around the following ideas:

1. What are the three best arguments that support the individual in this case?
2. What are the three best arguments that undermine his position?
3. Do you think Wiley's prosecution of Kirtsaeng supported the community or individual good? Develop three arguments that support this position.
4. How would you decide the case using the points of view discussed here?

Ethics for Arguers

1. *Arguers should be accountable and responsible for their arguments.* As the producer of argument, the arguer is responsible for developing quality, ethical arguments. If the arguer misleads the recipient or, through poorly constructed arguments, motivates an audience to take wrong actions, then the arguer is ethically accountable. Sometimes arguers may take the position that the responsibility for action rests entirely with the audience, suggesting that the ultimate choice to act or not rests with the recipient. While true, this position ignores the role argument plays in the interaction—it has the potential to function as a catalyst. Without the argument, the recipients may not have acted. Hence, arguers are ethically liable for their arguments. The example in Box 11.10, Tom Metzger: Neo-Nazi Messages, makes this point clearly. Speakers such as Metzger have a responsibility to their audience for the arguments they make. And, although we have a right to free speech, that right comes with a responsibility to use it well.

2. *Arguers should promote significant choice.* That is, arguments should provide their recipients with the ability to make voluntary decisions that are free from physical or mental coercion. Arguers should furnish the best available information for their hearers so that they may make well-informed and reasoned decisions. This means that arguers should ensure that audiences are aware of the sources of information, the possible alternatives, and the potential consequences of their decisions. Further, recipients should be aware of the motivations and qualifications of those who seek to influence them, the values they hold, and the goals they seek. If evidence is falsified or misrepresented, if arguers deliberately employ fallacies, or if any action is taken or argument is made that interferes with the ability of others to make a reasonable decision, the arguer is acting unethically.

3. *Arguers should promote positive relationships with their audiences.* A positive relationship is predicated on the view by the arguer that recipients of argument are partners in the decision-making process. As such, the arguer's job is not to force ideas on the recipients, but rather to provide audience members with the information necessary to produce their own decisions.

■ ■ ■ ■ ■

BOX 11.10

TOM METZGER: NEO-NAZI MESSAGES[53]

In 1988, Mulugeta Seraw, an Ethiopian man who worked as an Avis airport shuttle-bus driver, was murdered in Portland, Oregon. He was attacked while returning from a party close to his home by a man named David Mazzella. Mazzella, vice president of the White Aryan Resistance (WAR), struck the Ethiopian man repeatedly with a baseball bat until Seraw was dead. Mazzella, along with a group of local racists, had been out during the evening looking for black and Hispanic people to attack.

During the following investigation and subsequent trial in which Mazzella was convicted for the murder, evidence was uncovered to suggest that he acted on behalf of Tom Metzger and WAR. In fact, letters produced in court made it appear as though Metzger had ordered Mazzella to go to Portland and show the local skinheads "how we operate." Subsequently, attorney Morris Dees, director of the Southern Poverty Law Center in Montgomery, Alabama, filed a civil lawsuit against Metzger and WAR under the common law principle of "vicarious liability," which is most frequently used against employers for employee negligence. Dees claimed that WAR and Metzger were civilly responsible for the murder because they had incited Mazzella to act as their agent in Portland. Therefore, Metzger and WAR, through their messages, were responsible for the death.

In the civil trial that followed, Dees characterized Metzger as a "racial separatist" who motivated others to act on his behalf. Because Metzger, WAR, Mazzella, and the Oregon Skinheads formed a "civil conspiracy" to murder, Metzger acted recklessly and negligently in his message. Metzger, acting as his own attorney in his trial, argued that he was simply a populist who shared his ideas with others. He murdered no one and did not ask anyone to murder for him. He was not the cause of violence. He only provided the message; what others chose to do with that message was their own business. The people acting violently were the cause of the murder.

The court ruled against Metzger and found him liable for the consequences of his messages. It emphasized the power of the spoken word and the responsibilities for its judicious use. Metzger and WAR were ordered to pay $12.5 million in damages.

Ethics for Recipients

Just as arguers have an ethical responsibility for constructing quality arguments, recipients must also be critically aware and vigilant of the arguments they find compelling. Therefore, recipients have the following responsibilities in an argumentative encounter.

1. *Recipients should be aware of attempts to influence them.* Each of us is subjected to attempted influences every day. From advertisements to public speeches, arguers attempt to tell us how to vote, spend our money, or design our relationships. If we accept their messages without any clear consideration or understanding of the consequences and implications, we are acting irresponsibly. Argument consumers should constantly ask, "How am I being affected by this message?" They should understand that arguers have biases and viewpoints that are reflected in their arguments. This means, then, that we need to consider the validity and worth of arguments beyond their surface and seek to understand the biases and opinions that motivate the claims. We may then choose to accept the claims or not, but the choice will be a considered one.

2. *Receivers should be informed.* Although it is impossible to know everything, recipients of argument need to be informed about important topics. If we as audience members rely exclusively on the advocate to provide the necessary information for making the decisions facing us, we are acting naively on the assumption that arguers will always be motivated by our best interests. Although it is much easier to rely on the word of the arguer than to take time to investigate the strength of the message, it is time well spent. We need to ask ourselves, "Is there another answer that makes equal or better sense?" Or, "Are there other possibilities that remain unexplored?" Responsible receivers look for alternatives and are curious about other ways of approaching issues and problems. It is easy for arguers to persuade an uninformed audience; the recipient's best defense against unethical attempts at influence is knowledge.

3. *Recipients should be aware of their own biases.* Each of us has messages we want to hear, and there are messages we choose to avoid. We like hearing messages that support our positions and affirm our decisions. We tend to avoid those arguments that seem to attack us and fail to affirm our understanding of either our own worldviews or ourselves. We tend to avoid messages that are inconsistent with our own positions, and information that we find unpleasant. Responsible receivers should seek out and be open to many different viewpoints.

4. *Recipients should understand how fallacies persuade.* Fallacies, as we discussed, have tremendous appeal and capacity to persuade audience members to act erroneously. We should be aware of how arguers employ argumentative devices and fallacies to shape and direct our decisions by constraining or confusing our understanding of issues.

SUMMARY

This chapter talked about responsibility. Specifically, we discussed the responsibilities shared by all the members of an argument situation. Arguers are responsible for developing arguments and using language in ways that promote significant choice and support recipients' abilities to make decisions. Recipients are responsible for understanding what persuades them and understand when arguments are flawed or unethical.

We began with a consideration of how language shapes arguments. Language should be used deliberately and not accidentally. Speakers should adapt language to their audiences. Arguers, in particular, can enhance their effectiveness through their use of language. Words used to refer to objects or experiences have certain characteristics that influence their use in language. They are abstract (having general reference to broad classes of objects) or concrete (referring to specific or particular objects or experiences). They are also used denotatively as symbols with objective, generally agreed-upon meanings, or connotatively as symbols with subjective or emotive meaning for each individual. People manipulate words by replacing negative connotations with positive ones. These result in euphemisms such as "daytime drama" for soap operas, "projects" for slums, and "correctional facility" for prison.

Understanding how language functions can assist arguers in getting their arguments understood, remembered, and adhered to by recipients. Four guidelines for using language can assist in this process. First, arguers should be clear. They should employ language that is sufficiently concrete to keep their messages interesting. They should also speak or write simply, avoiding convoluted or ambiguous language. Second, arguers should define any terms that their recipients might misunderstand. This is particularly true when the terms have an important role in the argument, and the arguers' usage of the terms departs from ordinary usage. Third, arguers should express their arguments vividly. Using active rather than passive voice, personalized constructions, and informal language along with colorful terms and metaphors will engage recipients and cause them to be more likely to accept an arguer's claim. Fourth, arguers should avoid sexist or racist language. Although few arguers intentionally try to offend recipients, many do so inadvertently by expressing their ideas in ways that set women and minorities apart as having less status in society than men and European Americans. Concerted efforts to eliminate discriminatory forms of reference and ways of speaking will ensure that no recipients are inadvertently alienated by the way an argument is expressed.

The second part of the chapter explored how fallacies function. Fallacies are arguments that are flawed by irrelevant or inadequate evidence, erroneous reasoning, or improper expression. We discussed the nature of fallacies and their types. We identified four: audience based, language use, grounding, and reasoning. Each of these has several subtypes.

Audience-based fallacies divert the recipient's attention away from the main issues. These include *ad hominem, ad populum,* appeal to tradition, and straw arguments. Language-based fallacies occur when arguers use language to mislead audiences. These include equivocation, amphiboly, and emotive language. Grounding fallacies are the result of arguments that use either no evidence or poor evidence. These include begging the question and *non sequitur.* Finally, fallacies of faulty reasoning occur when arguers make errors in their inferences. These include false analogy, hasty generalization, false cause, *post hoc,* single-cause, and slippery slope.

Although many theorists have identified countless types and variations of fallacies, our focus here is to make you aware of how fallacies can infiltrate arguments and deceive unsuspecting audiences. One word of caution: Just because an argument is fallacious does not necessarily mean that the claim is incorrect. The claim may, in fact, be reasonable and valid, but not for the reasons and evidence expressed in the argument.

The final part of the chapter examined ethics and argumentation. Misleading or deceptive uses of argument can greatly harm society and individuals, and therefore argument practices should be governed by sound ethical principles. Ethics is defined as the study of what is morally right or just, but sometimes this is not easy to determine. This is because the question of what ethical standards should be applied to an argument may depend on the culture or situation in which the argument occurs.

Ethical argument practices are related to both the content of the argument and the relationship between the arguer and his or her audience. Ethicists who have written on argument content believe that content that is ethically sound is content that furthers open inquiry, quotes evidence in context, and makes use of sound reasoning. On the relational level, arguers can attempt to manipulate and objectify their audiences, or charm and trick them, or empower and enlighten them. Only the third of these three approaches further opens inquiry and choice among recipients.

Arguers should keep in mind that in any argument situation, there are many opportunities for arguments to be poorly crafted or unethically delivered. This is why we work to understand the argument situation, adhere to an ethical code, and try to understand the different value and cultural systems that affect others' arguments. To this end, we offered some general guidelines to ensure that arguers do not hide their agendas, are collaborative with their listeners, and empower their audiences.

EXERCISES

Exercise 1: Connotations and Denotations. Each of the following words has a denotative and connotative meaning. Next to each word write the first definition that comes to mind, and then look up the word in the dictionary. Is there a large difference? Why? Do you think your peers' answers would be closer to the connotative definitions you generated or the denotative definitions you looked up? Test it on five friends. What did your test show?

Connotative	Denotative
Schoolteacher	
Pontiac	
Boss	
Turkey	
Sex	
Trip	
Work	
Career	
Education	
Car	
Love	

Exercise 2: Finding Fallacies. Read an editorial from the local newspaper and identify fallacies. Then, answer the following questions about each fallacy:

1. Why might this fallacy be persuasive to an audience?
2. What additional support or reasoning, if any, would you need to make the argument less fallacious?
3. Is it possible to make the argument less fallacious?
4. How would you change this argument to make it less fallacious?

Exercise 3: Identifying Fallacies. Read the following arguments and identify the fallacies.

   *1. In a debate about the benefits of a policy to reduce military spending, an arguer retorts, "You can't listen to him because he is an atheist."

   2. The new Lady Gaga album is number one on the charts, so I think you should buy it.

   3. We should not allow homosexual marriages because traditionally marriage is defined as being between a man and a woman.

4. The polls say that the president has a high popularity level, so I am going to vote for her.

5. Teachers and students are concerned with the quality of education. They should be trained more rigorously.

6. Dogs provide companionship to lonely individuals. All people living alone should have a cat.

7. California and Mississippi are both U.S. states that rely on farming, so the economies of these states must be the same.

*8. I know about twenty-five students at the university who like The Shins. Therefore, The Shins must be popular among college students.

9. The cause of global climate change is human-caused carbon emissions.

10. Ellie is a college student who will graduate in four years; therefore all college students should graduate in four years.

*11. I did well on that test because I was wearing my lucky shirt that day.

12. The reason there are so many teenage pregnancies is that kids don't get enough information at school about sex.

13. One student says, "I think that our professor is going to be a good teacher." The other replied, "Oh, I don't think so. Did you hear that he dodged the draft during the Vietnam War?"

14. A syllogism is a form of formal logic because it uses formal structures of logic.

15. It started raining right before I got into the car, so I think my accident resulted from the slippery and wet roads.

Exercise 4: Official Language. The question of whether English should be the "official" language of the United States has been the subject of much debate. Read the following case study and consider the following questions:

- What functions of language are apparent in this argument?
- Based on what you know about how language affects our thoughts and perceptions, what would be the effects of making English our "official" language?
- Do you think that Bill Emerson used language effectively in his argument?
- Should the United States have an official language?

English is our common thread

Mr. Speaker, many times before I have taken to the floor to speak about the importance of the English language. For decades, English has been the de facto language of the United States. In recent years, 19 States have designated English as their official language. Support for these efforts has been overwhelming. I strongly believe that English should be the official language of the United States Government. I have been a persistent sponsor of such legislation, and I will again today introduce the Language of Government Act.

At the same time, however, I want to recognize the important contributions of other languages through a sense-of-the-Congress resolution. In an increasingly global world, foreign languages are key to international communication. I strongly encourage those who already speak English to learn foreign languages.

As a nation of immigrants, America is comprised of people of all races, nationalities and languages. These differences make our Nation the wonderful place it is. While being different, all of these people can find a common means of communication in the English language. English is the common thread that connects every citizen in our great Nation.

Hon. Bill Emerson, House of Representatives, *Congressional Record* (January 4, 1995): E13.

English language tax credit

Mr. Speaker, I rise today to introduce an important piece of legislation that I believe to be an integral part of the official English movement. As you may know, I am the author of H.R. 123, the Language of Government Act which seeks to make English the official language of the United States Government. This legislation is the perfect complement to the Language of Government Act. It recognizes the need for a highly skilled labor force and provides a tax credit to employers for the cost of providing English language instruction to their limited-English-proficient employees.

Many Americans lack the language skills and literacy necessary to take full advantage of roles as responsible citizens and productive workers. While many employers acknowledge the need to educate their workers and have demonstrated an interest in establishing on-site training programs for their employees, the high cost of doing so often prevents them from taking any concrete action. This legislation will provide them with an incentive to offer this crucial instruction to their employees and make the workplace a friendlier, and less daunting environment for non-English-proficient employees.

Hon. Bill Emerson, House of Representatives, *Congressional Record* (January 4, 1995): E24.

The language of government

Mr. Speaker, today I am pleased to introduce once again the Language of Government Act. America is a nation of immigrants. As President Franklin Delano Roosevelt once said, "All of our people all over this country—except the pure-blooded Indians—are immigrants or descendants of immigrants, including those who came over here on the Mayflower."

Indeed, we are a diverse lot. We are a country of many peoples, each with an individual *cultural* heritage and tradition. It is not often that people of so many varying cultures and backgrounds can live together in harmony, for human nature often leads us to resist and fear those who are different from us. Yet despite our differences, we do have a common bond. We have a common tongue, the English language, that connects us to one another and creates our national identity. It is this unity in diversity that defines us as uniquely American.

The time is right for passage of this important, unifying legislation. H.R. 123 offers a balanced, sensible approach to the common language issue. This legislation states that the government has an affirmative obligation to promote the English language, elevating that goal to official capacity. At the same time, the bill seeks to set some common sense parameters on the number and type of government services that will be offered in a language other than English. We do not need nor should we want a full-scale multilingual government. But, if we do not address this issue in a forward-thinking, proactive manner, that is just what we would allow to develop.

I want to stress that the Language of Government Act is not "English only." It simply states that English is the language in which all official United States Government business will be conducted. We have an obligation to ensure that non-English-speaking citizens get the chance to learn English so they can prosper—and fully partake of all the economic, social, and political opportunities that exist in this great country of ours.

The late Senator Hayakawa, founder of this movement, was a profile writer, and I offer you one of my favorite quotes of his:

> America is an open society—more open than any other in the world. People of every race, of every color, of every culture are welcomed here to create a new life for themselves and their families. And what do these people who enter into the American mainstream have in common? English our shared, common language....

As Americans, we should not remain strangers to each other, but must use our common language to develop a fundamental and open means of communication and to break down artificial language barriers. By preserving the bond of a unifying language in government, this nation of immigrants can become a stronger and more unified country.

Hon. Bill Emerson, House of Representatives, *Congressional Record* (January 4, 1995): E35.

Exercise 5: *Decision-Making.* Almost daily we are faced with decisions that have a moral or ethical character. Consider the following example and decide what the most ethical course of action is.

> What should we do when bad money supports good causes? If, for instance, organized crime offered the Scouts a million dollars, should the Scouts take the money? Should they publicize it or keep it secret? This scenario may seem far-fetched, but it really isn't. Although tobacco companies are not the same as organized crime, their products contribute to more than 440,000 deaths a year, to say nothing of the suffering inflicted on surviving family members. Yet, tobacco companies support good causes. Consider:
>
> ■ Many sporting events are sponsored by tobacco companies and some would argue that women's tennis would never have become a high-profile, high-paying sport were it not for the support of companies such as Virginia Slims.
> ■ Tobacco companies support political candidates and give Democrats and Republicans alike large amounts of money for their campaigns.
> ■ The Partnership for a Drug-Free America receives large financial support from the tobacco industry, enabling it to get its message and programs across.
> ■ Tobacco money also supports the American Civil Liberties Union, the NAACP, the Urban League, the National Women's Political Caucus, and the Poetry Society of America. Beyond that, tobacco money supports many different children's charities, environmental groups, and even some health organizations.
>
> There are many more examples. The problem is that money is tight and budgets are being cut and when the tobacco industry offers to help, then good programs survive and flourish. But is there a larger issue at stake? For instance, the Coalition for the Homeless no longer takes money from the tobacco industry because of its source. Amnesty International USA no longer takes money from the industry. Yet, the ACLU has no difficulty taking money from the industry because it allows the organization to survive and do good work to help people.
>
> And the tobacco industry is only one example. There are many other instances of foreign industries and organizations supporting specific candidates for office in the United States. Is there a problem when bad money allows good organizations to be effective?
>
> Consider the following issues:
>
> 1. What are the ethical considerations inherent in bad money supporting good causes?
> 2. Formulate an argument on both sides of the issue. Why is it all right to take the money, and why should we reject the money?
> 3. Considering all the information you have been presented, should "good causes" take the money?
> 4. Do cultural considerations play a role in the decision to take the money or not?
> 5. In general, are there some basic ethical guidelines that might help us decide when to accept money and when not to? What might these criteria be?

Exercise 6: *Identities.* In 1996, *Playboy Magazine* published an article titled *"Playboy's* College Sex Survey." In the article, the magazine reported the sex habits of college students based on a survey that had been given to college students across the United States. *Playboy* distributed the survey to university professors who then distributed them in class. The students were not aware of the source of the survey—they did not know that it came from *Playboy*.

When the article was published, none of the students were named. However, the article did identify student gender, age, and university. Several of the students were upset and believed that it was possible to identify them based on the information in the article. They said they wished they had known who it was for and how the data was going to be used. Many had assumed it was only for a class project and had no idea it would ever be published. *Playboy* countered that it wanted to have as objective a survey as possible and therefore had chosen to keep its name secret as the source of the survey. Besides, none of the students were identified.

Who is ethically right? Who is wrong? Explain.

Exercise 7: Assignment too far? In 1998, a journal titled *Lingua Franca* published an article written by Ruth Shalit. The article, titled "The Man Who Knew Too Much," outlined how a successful professor at a small university was terminated from his employment over a controversial assignment that was held to be "inappropriate" by the university administration.

Adam Weisberger was a professor at Maine's Colby College. He was well regarded as a successful teacher who was engaging with his students. His student evaluations were consistently very strong. In his Sociology 215 class, in an effort to make some of the critical theories more interesting, he developed an assignment to have students analyze their families using the material discussed in class. His syllabus read as follows:

> What I am aiming for in the assignment is for you to reflect on the class readings and discussion by means of analyzing an important part of your lives—namely, your family. I am willing to entertain other ideas as written work, but you must make a persuasive case. You may be as personal or impersonal as you wish.... The outward form of the papers is less important than your using ideas to investigate the relationships of your family.

Some students became upset by the assignment, criticizing that it asked them to reveal too much about their personal lives. After considerable pressure applied to the administration by some students, Weisberger's employment was terminated.

Do you think this assignment is ethically justifiable? How far can a professor probe into a student's life? Is it ever ethically permissible to ask students about their personal lives?

Exercise 8: Making Choices. Consider the following two scenarios. How would you act given the ethical considerations of the chapter?

SITUATION 1

You are an employee for ChemCon, a corporation that makes various chemical products. You have recently been asked to appear on a local news program to discuss the economic growth stimulated by your company's presence in that area. You are to make a two-minute presentation about the company. This will be followed by a question-and-answer session.

Two hours before you are to be interviewed on television, one of ChemCon's tanker trucks overturns and spills hundreds of gallons of toxins into a rural riverbed. You are told about the spill by an executive officer of the company who asks you to refrain from discussing the issue and indicates that the situation is under control—there is no need to cause a scare. You recognize the spilled chemical as one of the deadliest made by your company. You know that the chemical does not break down quickly or easily (so it will dissipate or dissolve), and you know that it is virtually impossible to "clean up" because it spreads rapidly in water flow. You also know that farmers graze cattle and grow crops using that river as a primary water source.

It is time to give your speech. What does your ethical code compel you to say?

SITUATION 2

You are an employee for PlayCorp, a corporation that makes various sporting goods. Your job includes many aspects of marketing, management, and production. However, you have been primarily responsible for tracking information regarding overseas production. Informally, you happen to know that the executives of PlayCorp have motivated others to generate a high return on their overseas investments (those who significantly improve the company's profit margin receive a substantial annual bonus). You also know that many approaches were used to generate that profit, including cutting necessary overhead costs.

Your company has been discussed and challenged in the press lately. The main focus of the media is PlayCorp's overseas practices. The media has discussed everything from poor wages to toxic working conditions to the economic support for dictatorships. Simultaneously to the media coverage, the Multi-National Corporation Investigation Team (MNCIT) has made formal allegations that PlayCorp is engaged in illegal practices overseas. The allegations have led to a formal congressional hearing. Depending on the committee's finding, a formal hearing may follow.

As the individual responsible for tracking information regarding overseas production, you have been called to speak before the congressional hearing. The first question you are asked is open-ended: "Please tell us, what do you know about your company's overseas operations?"

What does your ethical code compel you to say?

NOTES

1. Much has been written about this case and its potential to shape commerce. For more information, please see Bill Mears, "Supreme Court to Hear Arguments in Case of Student Who Resold Books," *CNN Justice*, http://www.cnn.com/2012/10/26/justice/court-student-copyright/index.html (accessed on November 4, 2012); Jennifer Howard, "Supreme Court Appears Divided on Copyright Case Affecting Libraries and Publisher," *The Chronicle of Higher Education*, October 29, 2012, at http://chronicle.com/article/Supreme-Court-Appears-Divided/135478/ (accessed on October 29, 2012); and Adam Liptak, "Justices Weigh Case on Imported Textbooks," *New York Times*, at http://www.nytimes.com/2012/10/30/business/supreme-court-hears-copyright-case-on-imported-textbooks.html?ref=textbooks (accessed on October 29, 2012).

2. Eriq Gardner, "Supreme Court Rules Against Entertainment Industry in Landmark Copyright Case," *Hollywood Reporter*, March 19, 2003, at http://m.hollywoodreporter.com/thr-esq/supreme-court-rules-entertainment-industry-429695 (accessed on May 17, 2013).

3. Jennifer Howard, "Supreme Court Appears Divided on Copyright Case Affecting Libraries and Publishers," *The Chronicle of Higher Education*, October 29, 2012, at http://chronicle.com/article/Supreme-Court-Appears-Divided/135478/ (accessed on October 31, 2012).

4. Abraham Lincoln, "Gettysburg Address," as cited in Philip B. Kunhardt Jr., *A New Birth of Freedom* (Boston, Mass: Little, Brown, and Co., 1983), 240.

5. Harold Zyskind, "A Rhetorical Analysis of the Gettysburg Address," *Journal of General Education* 4 (1950):

202–212. For other analyses of the rhetorical effects of this speech, see Ronald F. Reid, "Newspaper Response to the Gettysburg Address," *Quarterly Journal of Speech* 53 (1967): 50–60; and Barbara Warnick, "A Ricoeurian Approach to Rhetorical Criticism," *Western Journal of Speech Communication* 51 (1987): 227–244.

6. Gilbert Highet, "The Gettysburg Address," in *Readings in Speech*, 2nd ed., Haig A. Bosmajian, ed. (New York: Harper, 1971), 227.

7. George Orwell, "Politics and the English Language," in *Collected Essays* (London: Mercury Books, 1961), 357.

8. Howard Kahane, *Logic and Contemporary Rhetoric: The Use of Reason in Everyday Life*, 4th ed. (Belmont, Calif.: Wadsworth, 1984), 158.

9. Orwell (1961), 357.

10. C. K. Ogden and I. A. Richards, *The Meaning of Meaning* (London: Kegan, Paul Trench, Trubner, 1923).

11. S. I. Hayakawa, *Language in Thought and Action* (New York: Harcourt, Brace, 1964), 180.

12. *Merriam-Webster's Collegiate Dictionary*, http://www.merriam-webster.com/dictionary/fag (accessed on July 20, 2013), s.v. "fag."

13. "Lake Superior State University 2012 List of Banished Words," at http://www.lssu.edu/banished/current.php (accessed June 21, 2012).

14. Orwell (1961), 366–367.

15. Adapted from Stephanie Vozza, "Productivity Lifesaver: The 5-Sentence Email," *Entrepreneur*, May 8, 2013, http://www.entrepreneur.com/article/226581?hoot

PostID=0e787a63ceddadf04cd51de82180a75d (accessed May 19, 2013).

16. Jack Kemp, "Why Abortion Is a Human Rights Issue," *Conservative Digest* (August 1986): 40.

17. Chaim Perelman and Lucie Olbrechts-Tyteca, *The New Rhetoric: A Treatise on Argumentation*, trans. J. Wilkinson and P. Weaver (Notre Dame, Ind.: University of Notre Dame Press, 1969), 116.

18. Vilfredo Pareto, *The Mind and Society*, vol. II, sec. 1135 (New York: Harcourt, Brace, 1935), p. 671, as cited in Perelman and Olbrechts-Tyteca, 116.

19. A wonderful little guide to making one's style more vivid is W. Strunk and E. B. White, *The Elements of Style*, 3rd ed. (New York: Macmillan, 1979).

20. Haig A. Bosmajian, *The Language of Oppression* (Lanham, Md.: University Press of America, 1983), 118.

21. An excellent guide to how to avoid sexist and racist language is the *Publication Manual of the American Psychological Association*, 4th ed. (Washington, D.C.: American Psychological Association, 1994), 50–60.

22. Stokely Carmichael, "Address to Students at Morgan State College," January 16, 1967; cited in Bosmajian, 45.

23. George Orwell, *1984* (New York: Signet Classic, 1977).

24. Fallacies of this type were identified as a group by C. C. Hamblin, *Fallacies* (London: Methuen, 1970): 135–176. He traced the origin of this group of arguments to Francis Bacon's *Advancement of Learning* in the early 1600s. Bacon identified four types of "idols," or prejudicial habits of thought, that affect reasoning. Hamblin (p. 146) noted that after Bacon the study of fallacies included the study of the influence of psychological factors on human reasoning.

25. C. L. Hamblin, *Fallacies* (London: Methuen, 1970), p. 41; lists the Latin names for the first type of these as *Ad Hominem* and *Ad Passiones*. Hamblin noted that there are many varieties of "argument ad" and concluded that "We feel like adding: *Ad Nauseam*—but even that has been suggested before."

26. T. Edward Damer, *Attacking Faulty Reasoning*, 2nd ed. (Belmont, Calif.: Wadsworth, 1987): 128–129.

27. Hamblin, 40–41.

28. Hamblin, 41.

29. Damer, 128–129.

30. Robert J. Thornton, *L.I.A.R. the Lexicon of Intentionally Ambiguous Recommendations* (New York: Barnes & Noble Books, 2005).

31. Irving Copi, *Informal Logic* (New York: Macmillan, 1986), 114.

32. Monte M. Poen, ed., *Strictly Personal and Confidential: The Letters Harry Truman Never Mailed* (Boston, Mass.: Little, Brown, and Co., 1982), 34.

33. From Plato, *Timaeus*, cited in Irving Copi, *Informal Logic* (New York: Macmillan, 1986), 111.

34. The reasoning fallacies discussed here are included in many standard lists of fallacies. For discussions of fallacies, see Hamblin, 135–176; Howard Kahane, *Logic and Contemporary Rhetoric*, 4th ed. (Belmont, Calif.: Wadsworth, 1984).

35. Damer, 94.

36. Copi, 69–97.

37. Copi, 114.

38. The Gersten Institute, "The Oath of Hippocrates," at http://www.imagerynet.com/hippo.orig.html (accessed February 1, 2001).

39. Public Relations Society of America, *Code of Professional Standards for the Practice of Public Relations*, April 4, 2000, at http://www.prsa.org/profstd.html (accessed February 1, 2001). Additionally, there are many different codes of ethics from many varied organizations. Some of the more interesting include *American Medical Association Principles of Medical Ethics*, http://www.ama-assn.org/ama/pub/category/2512.html (accessed February 1, 2001). *American Psychological Association Ethical Principles of Psychologists and Code of Conduct*, http://www.apa.org/ethics/code.html (accessed February 1, 2001).

40. There are many good sources for political fact-checking, these are two of the most popular.

41. Manuel Velasquez, Clare Andre, Thomas Shanks, S. J., and Michael J. Meyer, "Thinking Ethically: A Framework for Moral Decision Making," *Issues in Ethics* 7 (1996): 1–3; see also Robert B. Ashmore, *Building a Moral System* (Englewood Cliffs, N.J.: Prentice-Hall 1987); William K. Frankena, *Ethics* 2nd ed. (Englewood Cliffs: Prentice Hall, 1978); and Tom Regan, ed., *Matters of Life and Death: New Introductory Essays in Moral Philosophy* (New York: Random House, 1980).

42. Thomas R. Nilsen, *Ethics of Speech Communication*, 2nd ed. (Indianapolis, Ind.: Bobbs-Merrill Publishing Co., 1974), 45.

43. Wayne Brockriede, "Arguers as Lovers," *Philosophy and Rhetoric* 5 (1972): 1–11.

44. Brockriede, 2.

45. Brockriede, 3.

46. Brockriede, 4.

47. Brockriede, 5.

48. Nilsen.

49. Velasquez et al., 1.

50. Velasquez et al., 1.

51. Velasquez et al., 2.

52. Sarah Trenholm, *Persuasion and Social Influence* (Englewood Cliffs, N.J.: Prentice Hall, 1987), 18–20.

53. Adapted from Morris Dees, "Hate Crimes: Our Nation Is Greater Because of Our Diversity," *Vital Speeches of the Day* 66 (2000): 247–253; and J. Willwerth, "Making War on WAR," *Time* 136 (1990): 60–62.

ANSWERS TO SELECTED EXERCISES

CHAPTER 1

Exercise 1

1. This is an argument. The first sentence, that "there is a plethora of credible scenarios for achieving human-level intelligence in a machine," is the claim. The rest of the paragraph provides examples of this to prove that the claim is true.

5. This is an argument. Eakin makes the claim that our ability to think has become impaired. It is backed with evidence from a linguistics professor who supports that formal English is on the decline and then reasons from this that it will begin to undermine our cognitive abilities.

10. This is an argument. Chevelle offers evidence to support a claim that the system puts too much pressure on students. Amy counters with a claim that says "That's the deal" and then provides evidence in support of the argument.

Exercise 3

- *What kinds of grounds do medical doctors use…?*
  The medical profession in general and doctors specifically ground their arguments in many different ways. These include patient case studies, patient charts, and laboratory experiments. Generally, the medical profession uses evidence that is verifiable and observable and tends to generalize from specific cases or experiments to understand how different diseases or injuries affect people.

- *What constitutes acceptable evidence for medical arguments?*
  Medical evidence needs to be verifiable. In other words, if one doctor conducts a study and finds evidence of a cure for AIDS, other professionals will attempt to verify those results through replications. Much medical research makes use of "double-blind" studies, in which a large number of people receive a medicine or a placebo and then their subsequent condition is studied. Also, long-term studies of particular populations reveal whether a given treatment has been effective.

- *In what spheres do medical doctors operate?*
  Doctors operate in all three of the spheres discussed in the text. When medical professionals brainstorm ideas about treatment or discuss in relatively informal settings how their cases have gone, they are arguing in the personal sphere. When they discuss

experimental evidence or debate the merits of various treatments, they are making arguments in the technical sphere. And when they talk with a patient's family members about the costs and benefits of a particular treatment, they adapt their arguments to a public sphere so they can be better understood.

- *What are audience expectations of this field?*
  Patients want doctors to be correct. Because much of the medical profession is mysterious and frightening to patients, doctors need to be reassuring and speak from experience and knowledge. Patients, then, want their doctors to know what the appropriate answer is.

- *What are some conventions or rules followed by doctors?*
  There are many. Typically, doctors advise their patients to get second opinions. They look for strong empirical support for conclusions. They consult with the family members and patient about the proper methods of treatment. And they live by the Hippocratic Oath, which governs the medical profession's ethics.

CHAPTER 2

Exercise 2

Note: There is often more than one correct way to diagram an argument using either model. Since there may be individual variations in the way various analysts number and connect statements and supply principles as warrants in the Toulmin model, there are often two or three correct ways to diagram an argument. There are, however, incorrect diagrams. The claim should not be mistaken for data, for example. The following diagrams are therefore suggestive. Further refinements should be made through class discussion and consultation with your instructor.

1. ① It is the chemical firms that release the most troubling types of molecules into the environment. ② In Baton Rouge, according to company data, an Exxon chemical plant was leaking 560,000 pounds of benzene yearly, while just south of there, ③ according to a survey by the Sierra Club, eighteen plants in and around St. Gabriel and Geismar dumped about 400 billion pounds of toxic chemicals into the air during the first nine months of 1986.

Co-Orientational Model

Toulmin Model

DATA

– Exxon chemical plant leaked 560,000 pounds.

– Eighteen plants dumped 400 billion pounds.

CLAIM

It is the chemical firms that release the most troubling molecules.

WARRANT

These examples represent the problem.

Criticism

The argument seems too ready to indict chemical plants as the main source of the problem. The evidence focuses on only two examples, and one of those is water and the other air pollution. What other sources of pollution (such as nonpoint pollution) might there be? Have the impacts of the various possible sources been compared?

CHAPTER 3

Exercise 1

1. This is an inductive pattern. The point made in the argument is that American education has reached a crisis point. To prove this, the arguer provided evidence from *Academically Adrift* as well as reports about student debt. The evidence supports that higher education has lowered its standards, costs more, and students are worse prepared than a generation ago.

4. This is a narrative pattern. The arguer's point is that power and privilege shape so many lives. The illustrations from the students serve to ground the argument in the narrative of the region's history.

Exercise 2

Values affirmed by Brennan: freedom of expression, inclusiveness of all ideas. Values opposed to Brennan's position: loyalty to the country first and foremost, patriotism Criteria for evaluation:

- To respect legal principles for treatment of the flag
- To avoid offense to others
- To protect any behavior construed as "communication"
- To preserve the principles on which the nation was founded
- To preserve free expression
- To allow various views to be heard
- To preserve the dignity of the flag

CHAPTER 4

Exercise 1

1. Noncontroversial. This is a factually true statement.

5. Double-barreled. Whether a practice is "desirable" and whether it is "necessary" are two different issues. Here they have been combined in one claim.

14. May or may not challenge the present system. Whether or not this claim is well formulated will depend on the jurisdiction in which it is made. If there are legal limitations on abortion availability—parental consent or limitation on trimester, for example—the claim would challenge the present system. But if abortion is generally available, then it would not challenge the system.

Exercise 2

1. Past fact

CHAPTER 5

Exercise 1

1. *Expertise:* Is Kause an expert? What are his credentials? Neither his title nor his position is cited.

   Statistical method: No information is given about the size or representativeness of the sample or the method used.

5. *Relevance and Accuracy of Citation:* Is Kennedy's quotation relevant to the military draft? In what context was it made? The crucial part of this argument—that the country is in a military force crisis—is not supported by any evidence.

   Relevance: Kennedy's claim (in his inaugural address) was made in relation to volunteer service. Since he was not calling for mandatory service (which is just the opposite of his point), the claim here is unsupported by the quote cited because the quote is irrelevant to it.

10. *Expertise:* Who is Dr. Harvey Brenner? His credentials are not given.
    Recency: This study was conducted in 1975. It is questionable whether it applies to current conditions.

    Relevance: The argument assumes a causal connection between unemployment and death, but the evidence does not state a causal relation, only a correlation.

CHAPTER 6

1. *Analogy*

   Evidence: A painter paints his painting so that light shines on all parts of the work.

   Claim: The listener should…be shown the conclusion contained in the principle.

   Inference: (implied) [The speaker's task is like the painter's.]

   Questions: Is writing a composition or giving a speech like painting a picture in this sense? How is aesthetics like composition?

5. *Analogy*

   Evidence: North America did not remain empty of cities; the continent is not a poorer place now than 20,000 years ago.

   Claim: We have more practical reasons for not burning Amazon forests than to stave off natural catastrophe.

Inference: (implied) [The forests of the Amazon are like the natural state of the North American continent 20,000 years ago.]

Questions: Were the original North American forests as essential to environmental preservation as Amazon forests? Have conditions changed in 20,000 years such that destruction of Amazon forests would have more impact now?

11. *Dissociation*

Evidence: We could act through bitterness and hatred; we could allow our protest to degenerate into violence.

Claim: We must struggle on the high plane of dignity and discipline; we must meet physical force with soul force.

Inference: (implied) [Effective response to oppression need not be violent; it can be dignified yet forceful.]

Questions: Should not oppression, which is a form of violence itself, be responded to by violence? Are not bitterness, hatred, and violence justified in such circumstances?

20. *Generalization*

Evidence: Asian Americans denied entrance; impossible job market in academia; people seek treatment as disadvantaged minorities; Chicago firm fined; white teacher fired.

Claim: Affirmative action for qualified minorities has turned into affirmative discrimination....

Inference: (implied) [The instances cited are representative of a general pattern of reverse discrimination.]

Questions: What about the issue of underrepresentation in certain schools and occupations; how is this to be corrected? Are the instances cited atypical?

CHAPTER 7

Exercise 1

2. Marijuana should be legalized

Fact issues:
How expensive is prosecuting marijuana cases?
Does it cause jail overcrowding?
Is marijuana a "gateway" drug to harder narcotics?
Has the war on drugs reduced the use of marijuana in the United States?
Will legalization increase marijuana consumption?
How much revenue could taxing marijuana sales generate?

Value issues:
Is marijuana better than "legal" drugs such as alcohol?
Is marijuana consumption really a "victimless" crime?
Is government regulation overly intrusive into people's privacy?
Shouldn't protecting privacy be the highest value?

3. The death penalty should be abolished.

Fact Issues:

1. Does the death penalty deter crime?
2. Does the death penalty cost more to administer than life in prison?
3. Have innocent people been executed?
4. Are minorities more likely to receive the death penalty than Caucasians?

Value Issues:

1. Is the death penalty administered fairly?
2. Is the death penalty an inhumane form of punishment?
3. What are the moral and ethical implications of having a death penalty?

Exercise 2

ISSUES MAP: THE DEATH PENALTY SHOULD BE ABOLISHED.

PROPOSITION	
Proposition	The death penalty should be abolished.
Definitions	The death penalty: the punishment of execution, which is administered when someone is convicted of committing a capital crime.

DESCRIPTION	
Situation	The death penalty has been used in the United States since it was reinstated by the Supreme Court in 1976. In addition to being legal at the federal level, the death penalty is legal in thirty-three states. In many states where it is legal, executions can take years to carry out due to lengthy appeals processes. Those calling for an end to its use cite financial and humanitarian concerns and raise questions about whether it serves as a deterrent and is administered fairly.
Context	The debate about the death penalty takes place primarily in the public and technical spheres. In the legal field, challenges are often brought against the death penalty, and high profile cases often cross over into the public sphere when they are covered by the media.
Parties	States and the federal government would be primary parties with a stake in the debate, since they currently allow its use. There are many public groups that are organized in opposition to the death penalty. Family members of the death row inmates as well as the victims of capital crimes would also have an interest in the issue.

ISSUES	
Fact issues	Does the death penalty deter crime?
	Does the death penalty cost more to administer than life in prison?
	Have innocent people been executed?
	Are minorities more likely to receive the death penalty than Caucasians?
Value issues	Is the death penalty administered fairly?
	Is the death penalty an inhumane form of punishment?
	What are the moral and ethical implications of having a death penalty?
Policy issues	Should the federal government abolish the death penalty?
	Should states abolish the death penalty?

ARGUMENT
POTENTIAL

Goals   The goal for opponents of the death penalty is to have its use abolished, while advocates of its use want the status quo to remain intact.

Parties   Since the two sides of the issue have opposing goals, both cannot have these goals achieved. However, if deficiencies in the death penalty are identified, then a discussion of how to fix those deficiencies while preserving the right to use execution as a punishment would be a way to try to alleviate the ills while keeping the policy.

Resources   All parties involved will need access to the facts about whether the death penalty is costlier than life in prison and whether it is administered fairly. Current studies on the deterrent effect would also be necessary to reach a conclusion about the efficacy of the death penalty.

Alternatives   Alternatives to abolishing the death penalty would include seeking ways to make it less costly and to ensure that it is administered fairly. A moratorium on its use is while studies are conducted has been seen as a compromise in the past.

CHAPTER 8

Exercise 1

1. Third-party candidates cause diversity in the political process.
  I. Definitions
    A. Third parties are parties that field presidential candidates for the presidential election.
    B. Third parties are not Democrats or Republicans.
    C. Diversity means multiple points of view.
    D. Diversity means focus on many issues.
  II. Threshold
    A. At a minimum, the third parties must be beyond the existing two parties.
    B. At a minimum, the issues must be outside the mainstream issues of the two parties.
  III. Application
    A. The Green Party is outside the Republican and Democratic sphere.
    B. The Green Party contributes many unique issues related to environmentalism.
3. Leif Eriksson discovered America.
  I. Definitions
    A. Definitions of *discovery*
      1. He must have landed on North American soil.
      2. He must have been the first nonnative to land.
      3. He must have recorded the incident.
    B. Definitions of *America*
      1. This refers to the North American continent.
      2. This refers to the mainland only.

    II. Threshold
      A. The minimal requirement is to have landed somewhere in North America.
      B. The minimal requirement is to have provided some lasting record of the discovery.
    III. Application
      A. Leif Eriksson landed in what is now Maine in North America.
      B. Leif Eriksson recorded the discovery in his ship's logs.

9. The United States should ban the sale of all tobacco products.
    I. Thousands of people are dying every day. (ill)
      A. Cancer and heart disease are on the rise.
      B. Nonsmokers are being severely harmed.
    II. Current efforts are not adequate to solve the problem. (blame)
      A. People want to smoke and circumvent the laws. (attitudinal)
      B. Individual state efforts are fragmented and inadequate to reduce the consumption of tobacco. (structural)
      C. Current federal and state laws are inadequate to stop tobacco consumption. (structural)
    III. A ban on the sale and consumption of tobacco products will eliminate the problem.
      A. The federal government should render all tobacco products illegal. (plan of action)
      B. A ban will prevent the consumption of tobacco products and eliminate the harms. (effects)
    IV. The benefits to this action are tremendous. (benefits)
      A. Because of reduced medical expenditures related to smoking, the health care system will be saved.
      B. We have the potential to save thousands of lives each year.
        1. Nonsmokers will be saved.
        2. Smokers will be saved.

Exercise 2

4. *Proposition:* I should attend a different school.

NEEDS CASE

    I. My personal situation is such that I should transfer to another college.
      A. Northeast Exclusive College no longer meets my needs.
        1. It does not offer a program in my chosen major.
        2. The high tuition is causing me to go into debt.
      B. The prospects of getting the education I want here are dim.
        1. No curriculum changes in my interest area are planned.
        2. The high tuition will force me to drop out of school.
    II. Transferring to another college seems the best plan.
      A. My parents and I will discuss my options during spring break.
      B. Next fall I will probably transfer to State University.
      C. This action will allow me to stay in school in my chosen major.

III. A transfer to another college will be beneficial.
    A. It will save thousands of dollars in tuition.
    B. It will broaden my educational experience.
    C. It will allow me to enroll in a major department that is highly ranked nationally.

COMPARATIVE-ADVANTAGES CASE

I. Transferring to another college next year is my plan.
    A. I will consult my parents about the decision.
    B. I will transfer to State University next year.
II. The transfer will be economically beneficial.
    A. I will save $4,000 in tuition next year alone.
    B. Neither my parents nor I will have to go into debt to finance my last two years of college.
    C. $4,000 is a significant proportion of my family's annual income.
    D. Only a transfer will avoid indebtedness since I do not qualify for financial aid or scholarships.
III. The transfer will be educationally beneficial.
    A. State University offers the major program I've selected.
    B. This major is exciting to me and offers excellent career opportunities.
    C. Northeast Exclusive College does not offer this major and has no plans to do so.

Exercise 3

NEEDS CASE

I. (5)
    A. (2)
    B. (7)
    C. (14)
    D. (12)

II. (16)
    A. (10)
    B. (4)
    C. (8)

III. (6)
    A. (1)
    B. (3)
    C. (9)

COMPARATIVE-ADVANTAGES CASE

I. (16)
    A. (4)
    B. (8)
    C. (10)

II. (6)
  A. (3)
  B. (9)
III. (1)
  A. (11)
  B. (13)
  C. (15)
  D. (17)

CHAPTER 9

Exercise 1, Case 2

Proposition: Euthanasia is desirable.

I. Value.
  A. Definition: Euthanasia will be defined as passive withholding or removing life-support systems from moribund patients.
    1. "Life-support systems" include equipment that provides basic life functions—respiration, heartbeat, etc.—through artificial means.
    2. "Moribund" patients are people with no possibility of recovery who will die in the normal course of events.
    3. This definition is supported by etymology and the opinion of experts.
II. A. Hierarchy: Euthanasia preserves and promotes personal freedom, comfort, and self-respect.
    1. Freedom, comfort, and self-respect are three of the eight top-ranked values in Rokeach's value survey.
    2. Freedom of choice and dignity are the essence of what it means to be human.

This definition is overly restrictive and should include active euthanasia.

1. Active euthanasia has traditionally been included in the term.
2. Some "moribund" and comatose patients have, in fact, recovered consciousness.
3. *Merriam-Webster's Collegiate Dictionary* includes the act or practice of killing hopelessly sick or injured individuals in its definition of *euthanasia*.[1]

Euthanasia undermines our respect for life, which should be the highest value.

1. If life is not preserved and protected, all other values are moot.
2. Our Christian belief tells us that life is a gift, not ours to do with as we please.
3. A human life is unique and irreplaceable.
4. A society that does not value life becomes degraded and immoral.

Other standards are more important.

A. Treatment of the terminally ill should protect and preserve life.

(continued)

Criteria:

To be beneficial, euthanasia should meet certain standards.

   A. Euthanasia should allow free choice concerning the manner and timing of a person's death.

   B. Euthanasia should prevent needless suffering and futile prolongation of life.

   C. Euthanasia should prevent hardship for the families of terminally ill patients.

III. Application: Euthanasia is beneficial and desirable.

   A. It preserves freedom and dignity of the individual.

   B. It ends patients' suffering.

   C. It gives families a say in patients' treatment decisions.

   D. Society's attitudes toward the preservation of life will be negatively affected.

   B. Treatment of the terminally ill should enhance the will to survive.

   C. Treatment should not undermine the general respect for life in our society.

Euthanasia is harmful to society.

   A. It puts pressure on terminally ill patients and undermines the will to survive.

   B. In the absence of active euthanasia, patients will continue to suffer anyway.

   C. Families can be distressed and torn apart by the responsibility to make these.

---

[1]Merriam-Webster's Collegiate Dictionary, s.v., "Euthanasia," *Merriam-Webster Online*, 2001, www.m-w.com (accessed February 9, 2001).

Exercise 2

DIRECT REFUTATION

    I. (4)
       A. (8)
       B. (6)
       C. (10)
       D. (2)
    II. (1)
       A. (3)
       B. (11)
    III. (9)
       A. (5)
       B. (7)

COUNTERPROPOSAL

    I. (2)

   II. (8)
       A. (5)
       B. (3)

  III. (1)
       A. (4)
       B. (6)
       C. (7)

CHAPTER 10

Exercise 2

1. Lamkin cites the author Rosabeth Moss Kanter to give credibility to her own claim that women must work to gain organizational power. By focusing on the specific sources and methods of gaining power, Lamkin keeps her audience interested in her topic. She emphasizes a feminist perspective by citing a female authority when addressing an all-female audience.

Because of her lively content, similarity in attitudes with the audience, and focus on a topic the audience is probably interested in, Lamkin will probably be able to hold audience attention and win acceptance for her ideas.

4. First and foremost, Ms. Crooks stresses her long and intensive experience with the topic. She stresses the American value of consensus-building through open exchange—a value her audience shares.

One problem with this treatment is that the author's purpose is vague. Her audience may wonder what her point is and lose interest in what she has to say.

CHAPTER 11

Exercise 3

1. *Ad Hominem*
8. Hasty Generalization
11. *Post Hoc*

GLOSSARY

Abductive argument (p. 83)   are those wherein speakers work collectively to reach a common conclusion.

Abstraction (p. 321)   refers to the degree to which relevant characteristics are omitted in language.

Access (p. 147)   depends on whether someone offering an opinion is or has been in a position to observe firsthand the matter being disputed.

Accommodating style (p. 68)   is used when the importance of the relationship is much greater than the importance of the content.

Active listening (p. 263)   means to hear for meaning.

Ad hominem **fallacy (p. 335)**   launches an irrelevant attack on the person or source originating an argument instead of responding to substantial issues raised in the argument.

Ad populum **fallacy (p. 335)**   occurs when the substance of an argument is avoided and the advocate appeals instead to popular opinion as a justification for the claim.

Ad verecundiam **(p. 342)**   is an example of circular reasoning used to validate argument based on the perceived authority of the arguer or source.

Amphiboly (p. 339)   exploits ambiguity in grammatical structure to lead to a false or questionable conclusion.

Analogy (p. 170)   reasons that because two objects resemble each other in certain known respects, they will also resemble each other in respects that are unknown.

Appeal to tradition (p. 337)   occurs when someone claims that we should continue to do things the way we have always done them simply because we have always done them that way.

Application (p. 230)   is the illustration that the case examined is sufficient proof to verify the definition and its threshold.

Argument (p. 13)   a set of statements in which a claim is made, support is offered for it, and there is an attempt to influence someone in a context of disagreement.

Argument chain (p. 62)   uses a proved argument as evidence for an unproved claim.

Argument contexts (p. 20)   grow out of the confluence of arguer, question or need, and audience.

Argument fields (p. 20)   are sociological contexts for arguments and are marked by patterns of communication that participants in argumentative dispute can recognize.

Argument from authority (p. 181)   reasons that statements by someone presumed knowledgeable about a particular issue can be taken as evidence sufficient to justify a claim.

Argument from cause (p. 177)   claims that one condition or event contributes to or brings about another condition or event.

Argument from coexistence (p. 180)   reasons from something that can be observed (a sign) to a condition or feature that cannot be observed.

Argument from example (p. 175)   seeks acceptance for some general rule or principle by offering a concrete, particular case.

Argument potential (p. 210)   refers to the opportunity to influence the propositional arena through argument.

Argument relationships (p. 66)   are the interdependent connections that exist between arguers and recipients.

Argument situation (p. 64)   refers to the rhetorical situation of the argument.

Argument spheres (p. 23)   are social constructs that guide how arguments are produced and evaluated.

Argument style (p. 66)   is the orientation arguers choose to use to balance content and relationship needs in an argument situation.

Argumentation (p. 11)   is the process of making arguments intended to justify beliefs, attitudes, and values so as to influence others.

Artifacts (p. 141)   are physical evidence that helps to prove an argument. An artifact is simply a physical object that a speaker might use to prove a point.

Associative scheme (p. 166)   brings together elements and evaluates or organizes them in terms of one another.

Assumptions (p. 7)   are the presuppositions and viewpoints we take for granted.

Attitudinal blame (p. 242)   arises from people's beliefs and values, rather than from a law or some other structure of the present system.

Backing (p. 53)   consists of further facts or reasoning used to support or legitimate the principle contained in the warrant.

Balance (p. 117)   is the requirement that the issues for and against a proposition be included equally in the propositional field.

Bargaining refutation (p. 260)   works to combine some features of the initial case with counter arguments in search of a mutually acceptable strategy for managing the issues within the proposition.

Begging the question (p. 341)   assumes as a premise or as evidence for an argument the very claim or point that is in question.

Benefits (p. 244)   are the positive consequences of policy action.

Bias (p. 144)   is an unreasoned distortion of judgment or a prejudice on a topic.

Blame (p. 242)   is the attribution of an ill to causes within the present policy system.

Burden of proof (p. 118)   obligates arguers to provide good and sufficient reasons for changing what is already accepted.

Burden of rejoinder (p. 258)   is the requirement that those who oppose a proposal respond reasonably to the issues presented by the original advocate.

Case (p. 196)   is an extended argument supporting or opposing a proposition.

Case-level refutation (p. 259)   focuses on the case as a whole and considers the overall implications of the proposition.

Categorical syllogism (p. 48)   is a logical argument that draws a necessary conclusion from two premises stated as simple propositions containing categorical terms that designate classes.

Challenge (p. 117)   means that an arguer's claim confronts recipients' existing values, beliefs, or behaviors.

Claim (p. 14) is an expressed opinion or a conclusion that the arguer wants accepted.

Claim of historical fact (p. 121) rests on the strength of probable evidence to which we have access.

Clarity (p. 114) refers to how well a claim focuses arguments on a particular set of issues.

Collectivist cultures (p. 80) focuses on the success of group affiliations over individual achievement.

Comparative advantages (p. 249) is a strategy that develops the position that in comparison with the current system, the proposed system has more benefits.

Competitive listening (p. 263) is characterized by advocates who are more interested in winning an argument or a particular position rather than understanding other viewpoints.

Competing style (p. 67) prizes the content far more than the relationship, and it seeks to demonstrate that a particular set of arguments is superior to alternatives.

Compliance (p. 300) is the use of rewards and punishments by a powerful source to get recipients to believe or act in a certain manner.

Concepts (p. 7) are the theories, definitions, rules, and laws that govern how we think and act.

Connotative meaning (p. 324) is the subjective meaning a given individual holds of symbols used in a particular situation.

Constructive refutation (p. 259) focuses on specific arguments but suggests that while the argument in the case may be true, comparatively there are better ways of looking at the issue.

Controversiality (p. 113) means that a claim or proposition states a position that is not currently accepted or adhered to by the audience.

Co-orientational approach (p. 40) presumes that the relationship between arguer and recipient is as important as the content of the argument.

Correlation (p. 179) claims that two events or phenomena vary together; an increase or decrease in one is accompanied by an increase or decrease in the other.

Cost (p. 244) is the problems or disadvantages associated with taking a policy action.

Counter advocacy (p. 260) involves offering alternative values or policies to be weighed in comparison with the original argument.

Counterproposal (p. 273) argues that the alternative presented should supersede the proposed policy.

Criteria (p. 233) are field- or sphere-dependent standards to be used to decide whether the value object fulfills certain values. Criteria are the measures, norms, or rules used to judge whatever is being evaluated.

Critical thinking (p. 4) is an investigation whose purpose is to explore a situation, phenomenon, question, or problem to arrive at a hypothesis or conclusion about it that integrates all available information and that therefore can be convincingly justified.

Critique (p. 274) is an objection to the philosophical assumptions that underpin the proposition or the specific plan being proposed.

Cultures (p. 78) are systems of shared meanings that are expressed through different symbolic forms such as rituals, stories, symbols, and myths that hold a group of people together.

Cure (p. 243) demonstrates that some course of action can work to solve the ill.

Data (p. 52) are facts or conditions that are objectively observable beliefs or premises accepted as true by the audience, or conclusions previously established.

Deductive approach (p. 83) makes claims directly and at the beginning of an argument.

Deductive reasoning (p. 45) is the process of moving from general statements to specific conclusions.

Defense of the present system (p. 271) rests on a comparison of the proposal and the present system, and argues that the present system is superior.

Denotative meaning (p. 323) is the objective meaning held by language users in general.

Derived credibility (p. 304) results from what is said in the message—the quality of the claims and evidence used and the ways arguers employ their own expertise to get their claims accepted.

Dialectical perspective (p. 42) focuses on and enhances a candid, critical, and comprehensive examination of all positions relevant to the topic.

Direct refutation (p. 259) is an approach used by policy opponents that is designed to argue and disprove at least one of the stock issues in the proposal.

Disadvantages (p. 271) are the unintended negative consequences that could occur if the plan were put into effect.

Disjunctive syllogism (p. 49) sets forth two alternatives in the major premise, denies one of them in the minor premise, and affirms the other in the conclusion.

Dissociation (p. 183) disengages one idea from another and seeks a new evaluation of both ideas.

Dissociative scheme (p. 166) aims to disengage or disunite elements originally considered as a unity.

Double-barreled claims (p. 115) advance two or more claims simultaneously and, as with ambiguous terms, often lead arguers in separate directions because the relevant issues for each part of the claim are different.

Emergent claims (p. 127) are claims and propositions that develop within an exchange among advocates; they are not agreed to in advance.

Emotive language (p. 340) manipulates the connotative meaning of words to establish a claim without proof.

Enthymeme (p. 50) is a rhetorical syllogism that calls upon the audience's existing beliefs for one or both of its premises.

Equivocation (p. 338) exploits the fact that a word has more than one meaning so as to lead to a false conclusion.

Escapist style (p. 67) is used when neither the content nor the relationship is considered very important because it means that issues needing resolution are ignored or abandoned.

Ethical code (p. 318) is a set of interrelated principles that guide thoughts, values, and behaviors.

Ethics (p. 287) is the study of what is morally right or just.

Euphemism (p. 324) is a linguistic device for replacing words and phrases that carry a negative connotation with those that carry a positive connotation.

Evidence (p. 15) consists of facts or conditions that are objectively observable, beliefs or statements generally accepted as true by the recipients, or conclusions previously established.

Exigence (p. 64) is an imperfection marked by urgency; it is a defect, an obstacle, something waiting to be done, a thing that is other than it should be. It is also a contemporary problem or issue that needs to be addressed.

Expertise (p. 143) is the possession of a background of knowledge and information relevant to the argument being made and/or the subject matter under discussion.

Explicit claims (p. 125) are stated clearly and publicly such that both the arguer and the recipient are equally aware of their meaning.

Exploratory refutation (p. 260) involves asking questions or raising objections designed to cause opponents to take a stand on issues an advocate hopes to refute.

External consistency (p. 145) is the agreement of evidence with sources of information other than the source being used.

Extra-systemic audiences (p. 289) are groups that use nonviolence, direct action or violence to influence or overturn decision processes.

Facilitative style (p. 67) seeks to find ways in which all participants succeed mutually.

Fact definition (p. 228) statements are those of historical fact, causal relationships, and predictive facts.

Factual claims (p. 120) make inferences about past, present, or future conditions or relationships.

Fallacy (p. 331) is an argument that is flawed by irrelevant or inadequate evidence, erroneous reasoning, or improper expression.

False analogy (p. 343) compares two things that are not alike in significant respects or have critical points of difference.

Field-dependent standards (p. 23) are the rules, norms, and prescriptions guiding the production of arguments in a particular field.

Field-invariant standards (p. 23) apply generally, regardless of the field of argument.

Figurative analogy (p. 172) is a comparison between two objects of different classes in which a relation or quality within one is said to be similar to a relation or quality within the other.

Formal logic (p. 45) is the study of how conclusions are reached using structured statements.

Four-step refutation (p. 264) is the systematic articulation of an argument, beginning with (1) identification of the claim being refuted, (2) stating the refutation, (3) supporting and (4) resolving the refutation.

Generalization (p. 173) is reasoning that what is true of certain members of a class will also be true of other members of the same class or of the class as a whole.

Hasty generalization (p. 344) draws a conclusion about a class based on too few or atypical examples.

Hierarchy of essence (p. 201) values what is at the core of a group or class rather than what is on the fringes.

Hierarchy of the existent (p. 201) values the concrete over the possible.

Hierarchy of quality (p. 201) values what is unique, irreplaceable, or original.

Hierarchy of quantity (p. 201) that which produces the greatest good for the largest number of people at the least cost.

Hierarchy of the person (p. 201) values the dignity and autonomy of the person over all competing values

High-context situations (p. 81) omit large parts of argument meaning and advocates depend on the recipients' ability to interpret meaning from the situation.

Homeostasis (p. 204) means to find an internal stability or balance.

Hypothetical syllogism (p. 50) is an argument that does not involve a direct comparison, rather it contains a conditional major premise that is either affirmed or denied in the minor premise.

Identification (p. 301)   is the influence that occurs because people find a source attractive and wish to enhance their own self-concept by establishing a relationship with the source.

Ill (p. 240)   is a current wrong or harm the advocate is trying to resolve.

Implicit claims (p. 125)   are not stated publicly and are understood by the participants engaged in the argument.

Incompatibilities (p. 167)   are similar to disjunctive syllogisms in that they imply two alternatives between which a choice must be made; that is, one must choose one or the other, not both.

Individualistic cultures (p. 79)   focus on individual achievement and regard each person as distinct.

Inductive arguments (p. 83)   are those wherein claims are stated at the end of the argument.

Inductive reasoning (p. 46)   is a process of moving from particular examples, observations, or instances to general conclusions.

Inference (p. 164)   states the step one has made in linking the evidence to the claim.

Initial credibility (p. 304)   is based on an arguer's credentials, status, and reputation as known to recipients before they hear or read the message.

Instrumental values (p. 88)   concern modes of conduct or the means for fulfilling other values.

Intercultural competence (p. 87)   is the ability of an arguer to function in a manner that is perceived to be relatively consistent with the needs, capacities, goals, and expectations of individuals from one cultural environment while satisfying one's own needs, capacities, goals, and expectations.

Internal consistency (p. 145)   is the absence of self-contradiction within the information provided by a source.

Internalization (p. 301)   is a process in which people accept an argument by thinking about it and by integrating it into their cognitive systems.

Issues (p. 108)   are the various points of potential disagreement related to a proposition.

Issues brief (p. 225)   is a synthesis of opposing views on the stock issues of a proposition.

Issues map (p. 207)   is a synthesis of the context, situation, participants, and issues associated with a proposition.

Level of dispute (p. 60)   is the level of agreement or imaginary line that separates what is accepted by the audience from what is not accepted.

Literal analogy (p. 170)   compares two objects of the same class that share many characteristics and concludes that a known characteristic that one possesses is shared by the other.

Logical perspective (p. 41)   emphasizes the accuracy of the premises and the correctness of the inferences linking premises and evidence to the claims they support.

Low-context situations (p. 80)   refer to situations which arguers have the majority of contextual information available to them within the arguments themselves.

Minor repairs (p. 272)   offer small changes to existing policies to improve their effectiveness and efficiency in meeting the needs.

Narrative argument (p. 84)   rely on stories and reports to express views.

Narrative fidelity (p. 295)   is the test in which we decide whether the story matches up with our values, our life experiences, or with our social reality.

Narrative paradigm (p. 294)   proposes that we experience life as a series of narrative events which shape our understanding of our world, our beliefs and even our values.

Narrative probability (p. 295)   tests whether a story is coherent.

Necessary condition (p. 177)   is one that must be present for the effect to occur.

Needs-analysis case (p. 245)   claims that the ill existing in the current system cannot be corrected within the present system, but can be cured by the advocate's policy proposal.

Negotiating style (p. 67)   is used when content goals and relationship goals are both moderately important.

Non sequitur **(p. 342)**   contains a claim that is irrelevant to or unsupported by the evidence or premises purportedly supporting it.

Objectivity (p. 144)   refers to a source's tendency to hold a fair and undistorted view on a question or an issue.

Parameter (p. 109)   is the boundary that defines the propositional area and determines which issues are inside the arena and which are outside.

Passive listening (p. 264)   involves hearing other points of view but does not verify or affirm understanding.

Person/act argument (p. 181)   reasons from a person's actions to his or her character or essence.

Personal decision-maker (p. 288)   argues in the personal sphere and uses rules and conventions that are decided among the participants.

Personal sphere (p. 25)   contains the relatively informal arguments among people in typically casual settings.

Plagiarism (p. 153)   is the use of another person's ideas or words without proper attribution.

Plan (p. 243)   is the specific program advocated in support of the proposition.

Policy claims (p. 123)   call for a specific course of action and focus on whether a change in policy or behavior should take place.

Post hoc ergo propter hoc **(p. 345)**   mistakes temporal succession for causal sequence.

Practical arguments (p. 297)   are arguments in process within a particular context and situation.

Predetermined claims (p. 126)   are claims that precede and guide an extended argument.

Predictive claim (p. 121)   is based on the assumption that past relationships and conditions will be repeated in the future.

Presence (p. 329)   is a quality of argument that moves things near to us in space and time so they act directly on our sensibility.

Presumption (p. 118)   is the assumption in favor of existing beliefs and states of affairs when proposals for change are made.

Prima facie **case (p. 213)**   presents good and sufficient arguments for adopting the viewpoint or action proposed by an advocate.

Primary source (p. 152)   is the original source of the evidence. The primary source is the source in which the evidence first appeared.

Propositional arena (p. 108)   is the ground for dispute and includes all the issues for controversy within a given proposition.

Propositions (p. 108)   are overarching or main claims that serve as the principal claim of an extended argument.

Public decision-makers (p. 289) *are* third-party audiences that largely apply the norms and conventions of the public sphere.

Public sphere (p. 25) contains arguments that are intended for public or general audiences.

Qualifier (p. 53) is a colloquial adverb or adverbial phrase that modifies the claim and indicates the rational strength the arguer attributes to it.

Qualitative significance (p. 240) is related to the intensity of the effect; we assess something as significant to the extent that it strengthens or diminishes life.

Quantitative significance (p. 241) is related to the scope of the effects claimed; it asks how many people will be affected and how frequently.

Quasilogical argument (p. 166) places two or three elements in a relation to one another so as to make the connections between them similar to the connections in formal logic.

Reasoning (p. 16) constructs a rational link between the evidence and the claim and authorizes the step we make when we draw a conclusion.

Reciprocal relationships (p.168) are reflected in the "if-then" nature of the argument.

Refutation (p. 257) is the process of responding to someone's argument by revealing weaknesses in it or by presenting a counterargument.

Relational claim (p. 120) attempts to establish a causal relation between one condition or event and another.

Relevance (p. 146) refers to whether the evidence as stated is topically and sufficiently related to the claim as made.

Reliable source (p. 143) is one that has proven to be correct many times in the past.

Reluctant testimony (p. 306) is evidence provided by sources against their own vested interest, thus increasing its perceived credibility.

Reports and descriptions (p. 140) are nonnumerical or narrative accounts of some object or occurrence.

Representative sample (p. 150) is one that possesses all the characteristics of the larger group from which it is drawn.

Reservation (p. 53) states the circumstances or conditions that undermine the argument.

Rhetorical perspective (p. 42) holds that arguments are viewed as appeals to an audience, and we must take account of the circumstances in which the argument was made and the strategies used to influence its audience.

Rhetorical situation (p. 64) is a natural context of persons, events, objects, relations, and an exigence that strongly invites arguments.

Sample (p. 150) is a population or group of people or objects that researchers survey when a study is conducted.

Secondary sources (p. 152) are those that compile, analyze, or summarize primary sources.

Significant choice (p. 351) refers to the responsibility of the arguer to provide audiences with enough information to draw their own conclusions.

Single-cause (p. 345) fallacies occur upon the attribution of a complex problem to only one cause.

Slippery slope (p. 346) assumes, without evidence, that a given event is the first in a series of steps that will lead inevitably to some outcome.

Solvency (p. 243) is the argument that the plan of action can solve or cure the ill.

Source credibility (p. 303)   is an arguer's ability to be believed and trusted by recipients.

Spherical audience (p. 299)   is made up of the range of possible audience members that exist in a given rhetorical situation

Statistics (p. 140)   are facts and figures that have been systematically collected and ordered so as to convey information.

Stock issues (p. 213)   depend on the type of proposition and are the issues that recipients expect to see addressed in order for the arguer to meet the burden of proof.

Straw-argument (p. 337)   attacks a weakened form of an opponent's argument or an argument the opponent did not advance.

Structural blame (p. 242)   is the result of a defect that is an integral part of the nature of the current policy system.

Structures (p. 242)   are fixed elements or features of a policy system.

Sufficient condition (p. 177)   is a circumstance in whose presence the event or effect must occur.

Syllogism (p. 46)   is made up of three statements, includes three terms associated in pairs with each other throughout the statements, and draws a conclusion from a major and a minor premise.

Systems perspective (p. 204)   recognizes that the world is a complex and interconnected set of relationships between and among component parts that compose a whole, and that one change in any part of the system changes the other elements of the system.

Technical decision-makers (p. 287)   are private third-party recipients who act as an external audience.

Technical sphere (p. 24)   contains arguments that adhere to rules that are more formalized and rigorous and tend to be generated by particular groups of people, such as doctors or lawyers.

Terminal values (p. 88)   concern desirable end states of existence.

Threshold (p. 229)   establishes the acceptable limits of definitions.

Transitivity arguments (p.185)   have three terms that are associated with one another through a process of classification, but the relationships among the terms are probable and not certain, as in the syllogism.

Trustworthiness (p. 302)   depends on whether people believe the arguer is motivated to tell them the truth.

Truth (p. 47)   represents the degree to which the premises for an argument align with verifiable facts and reality.

Universal audience (p. 298)   is a construct in the imagination of the arguer, and includes all people who are rational and competent with respect to the issues being debated.

Validity (p. 47)   is the degree to which the evidence supports the claim.

Value claims (p. 122)   assess the worth or merit of an idea, object, or practice according to standards or criteria supplied by the arguer.

Value consensus (p. 92)   is the degree of concurrence among members of a society concerning their values.

Value content (p. 89)   refers to the motivational goals expressed in the value.

Value deemphasis (p. 93)   occurs when values move downward in a value hierarchy.

Value emphasis (p. 93)   occurs when values move upward in a value hierarchy.

Value hierarchy (p. 90) is the ordering of values so that some are ranked more highly than others.

Value object (p. 232) is an idea, practice, event, policy, or state of affairs that is to be judged by means of evaluation.

Value redistribution (p. 93) is a process in which a value becomes more and more widely diffused throughout a society until virtually all its members adhere to it.

Value restandardization (p. 93) is a process in which standards used to measure whether a value is being met increase or decrease.

Values (p. 88) are the desirable, transituational goals, varying in importance, that serve as guiding principles in people's lives.

Value structure (p. 90) refers to the dynamic relations among the values in our individual value system.

Value system (p. 90) is an enduring organization of beliefs concerning preferred modes of conduct or end states of existence according to their relative importance.

Warrant (p. 52) expresses the reasoning used to link the data to the claim.

INDEX